PENGUIN

THE ESSENTI

JOHN MAYNARD KEYNES (1883–1946) is widely considered to have been the most influential economist of the twentieth century. His key books include *The Economic Consequences of the Peace* (1919); *A Treatise on Probability* (1921); *A Tract on Monetary Reform* (1923); *A Treatise on Money* (1930); and his *magnum opus*, *The General Theory of Employment, Interest and Money* (1936).

ROBERT SKIDELSKY is Emeritus Professor of Political Economy at Warwick. His three-volume biography of Keynes received numerous awards, including the Lionel Gelber Prize and the Council on Foreign Relations Prize.

JOHN MAYNARD KEYNES

The Essential Keynes

Edited and with an Introduction by
ROBERT SKIDELSKY

PENGUIN BOOKS

PENGUIN CLASSICS

UK | USA | Canada | Ireland | Australia
India | New Zealand | South Africa

Penguin Books is part of the Penguin Random House group of companies
whose addresses can be found at global.penguinrandomhouse.com.

This edition first published in Penguin Classics 2015
017

Introduction and Notes copyright © Robert Skidelsky, 2015
All rights reserved

The moral right of the author of the editorial material has been asserted

Set in 10.25/12.25 pt Adobe Sabon
Typeset by Jouve (UK), Milton Keynes
Printed in Great Britain by Clays Ltd, Elcograf S.p.A.

ISBN: 978-1-846-14813-2

www.greenpenguin.co.uk

Penguin Random House is committed to a
sustainable future for our business, our readers
and our planet. This book is made from Forest
Stewardship Council® certified paper.

Contents

Preface   xi
List of Abbreviations   xiii
Introduction   xv
Bibliography   xxxiii
Keynes's World, Main Characters   xxxv

THE ESSENTIAL KEYNES

ONE
The Philosopher

1. 'Ethics in Relation to Conduct' (1904)   3
2. 'The Political Doctrines of Edmund Burke' (1904)   5
3. The Adding-Up Problem (1904)   7
4. 'The Principles of Probability' (1908)   8
5. CW 8, *A Treatise on Probability* (1921)   9
6. CW 10, 'My Early Beliefs' (1938)   13

TWO
The Social Philosopher

7. CW 2, *The Economic Consequences of the Peace*
    (1919)   28
8. CW 4, *A Tract on Monetary Reform* (1923)   35
9. CW 9, 'The End of *Laissez-faire*' (1926)   39

10. CW 9, 'Am I a Liberal?' (1925)   61

11. CW 9, 'A Short View of Russia' (1925)   65

12. CW 9, 'Economic Possibilities for Our
    Grandchildren' (1930)   75

13. CW 21, 'National Self-Sufficiency' (1933)   86

14. CW 28, 'The Arts Council of Great Britain:
    Its Policy and Hopes' (1945)   91

THREE
The Economist

15. CW 2, *The Economic Consequences of the Peace*
    (1919)   99

16. CW 4, *A Tract on Monetary Reform* (1923)   102

17. CW 5 and 6, *A Treatise on Money* (1930)   107

18. The Great Depression   142

    CW 6, *A Treatise on Money* (1930)   144

    CW 9, ' "The Great Slump" of 1930' (1930)   152

    CW 13, 'An Economic Analysis
    of Unemployment' (1931)   158

    CW 9, 'The Consequences to the Banks
    of the Collapse of Money Values' (1932)   166

19. CW 13, 'A Monetary Theory of Production'
    (1933)   174

20. CW 7, *The General Theory of Employment,
    Interest and Money* (1936)   176

21. CW 14, 'The General Theory of Employment'
    (1937)   262

22. CW 14, 'Alternative Theories of the Rate of
    Interest' (1937)   274

23. CW 14, Methodological Issues: Tinbergen, Harrod
    (1938)   275

FOUR
The Policy-maker

24. CW 2, *The Economic Consequences of the Peace*
    (1919)   286

25. CW 17, 'A Plan for a Russian Settlement' (1922)   287

26. CW 4, *A Tract on Monetary Reform* (1923)   290

27. CW 9, 'The Economic Consequences of
    Mr Churchill' (1925)   299

28. CW 9, 'Can Lloyd George Do It?' (1929)   318

29. Policies for the Slump   338

    CW 9, 'Proposals for a Revenue Tariff' (1931)   339

    CW 9, 'The Economy Report' (1931)   345

    CW 9, 'On the Eve of Gold Suspension' (1931)   349

    CW 9, 'The Economy Bill' (1931)   353

    CW 9, 'The End of the Gold Standard' (1931)   355

30. CW 9, 'The Means to Prosperity' (1933)   359

31. The New Deal   372

    CW 21, 'Dear Mr President' (1933)   372

    CW 21, 'Agenda for the President' (1934)   380

    CW 21, 'Can America Spend Its
    Way into Recovery?' (1934)   385

    CW 21, 'Letter to the President' (1938)   389

32. CW 28, 'British Foreign Policy' (1937)   394

33. CW 21, 'How to Avoid a Slump' (1937)   398

34. CW 22, 'Paying for the War' (1939)   407

35. Full Employment Policy   417

    CW 27, Keynes to Sir Richard Hopkins (1942)   417

    CW 27, Keynes to J. E. Meade (1943)   419

CW 27, The Long-Term Problem
of Full Employment (1943)   421

CW 27, Letter to T. S. Eliot (1945)   425

36. CW 25, 'The Clearing Union' (1941)   426

37. CW 24, 'Overseas Financial Policy in Stage III'
(1945)   444

38. CW 27, 'The Balance of Payments of the
United States' (1946)   459

FIVE
The Essayist

39. CW 10, 'The Council of Four, Paris' (1919), 'Lloyd
George: A Fragment' (1933)   461

40. CW 10, 'Dr Melchior: A Defeated Enemy'
(1920)   479

41. CW 10, 'Alfred Marshall' (1924)   483

42. CW 10, 'Thomas Robert Malthus' (1933)   489

43. CW 10, 'Newton the Man' (1946)   503

Quotable Quotes   513
Notes   525

To Warwick University,
which gave me the time to study economics

'Economics is a very dangerous science'

John Maynard Keynes,
'Thomas Robert Malthus'

Preface

I have arranged the selected material in such a way as to help the reader rather than for strict consistency. Almost all the excerpts are taken from *The Collected Writings of John Maynard Keynes*, published in thirty volumes between 1971 and 1989. They are numbered sequentially and are identified by the volume number (CW, 10), title and date of original publication. The page numbers of the volumes of the *Collected Writings* from which they are taken are included in square brackets, marking the end of the page they refer to. I have grouped together some excerpts under the following topics: The Great Depression, Policies for the Slump, The New Deal and Full Employment Policy. Those readers who want a quick education in Keynes as an analyst of, and policy-maker for, slumps should turn to excerpts 18, 28–31 and 33.

This collection would not have been possible but for the magnificent *Collected Writings*. Elizabeth Johnson was the first editor; she was succeeded by Donald Moggridge. I would like to thank the Royal Economic Society for permission to publish excerpts from these volumes; King's College, Cambridge for permission to publish excerpts 1, 2, and 3 from the unpublished papers of J. M. Keynes; Paul Davidson, Meghnad Desai, Geoff Harcourt, Pete Mills and Rod O'Donnell, for their comments on sections of the draft; King's College archivist Patricia McGuire in helping me locate some handwritten notes in the Keynes Papers; and my impeccable copy editor, David Watson. My research assistant Pete Mills was invaluable in downloading the material I selected from the electronic edition of the *Collected Writings*.

List of Abbreviations

CW *The Collected Writings of John Maynard Keynes*
EB *Essays in Biography*
ECC 'The Economic Consequences of Mr Churchill'
ECP *The Economic Consequences of the Peace*
EP *Essays in Persuasion*
EPG 'Economic Possibilities for our Grandchildren'
GT *The General Theory of Employment, Interest and Money*
JMK John Maynard Keynes
KP Keynes Papers, King's College, Cambridge
ICU International Clearing Union
QTM Quantity Theory of Money
RT *A Revision of the Treaty*
TMR *A Tract on Monetary Reform*
TM *A Treatise on Money*
TP *A Treatise on Probability*

Introduction

'Keynes's ideas will live so long as the world has need of them'
Robert Skidelsky

I

There are hardly any single-volume selections of Keynes writings, and no comprehensive ones.[1] This selection aims to make them much more accessible to both students of economics and the general reader perplexed and confused by the war of economists which broke out afresh with the economic collapse of 2008. By this time Keynes's star had long been in eclipse. A new orthodoxy had arisen which cut economics off from the rest of life, claimed that market economies were naturally stable, and that the only macro-economic task of government was to maintain sound money. Robert Lucas, the high priest of the new classical economics, is said to have told his students at Chicago University, 'We need spend only ten minutes on Keynes; we know it doesn't work.' The things which worked were unimpeded markets.

Keynes had set out to destroy the argument of 'classical' economics that a competitive market economy would always ensure full use of potential resources. He invented almost single-handedly a new branch of economics, macro-economics, to show why this was not true, and to justify active fiscal and monetary policy. The task of overturning orthodox theory seemed all the more urgent in the wake of the Great Depression of 1929–33. The result was *The General Theory of Employment, Interest and Money*, whose publication in 1936 is conventionally taken to be the start of the Keynesian Revolution. Its main policy fruit was the commitment, till the mid-1970s, by most Western governments, to maintain high and stable levels of employment.

The charge that Keynes failed to provide secure micro-foundations for his macro-theory, as well as the contentious implications of that theory for the role of state, led to the view that Keynesian theory was flawed and Keynesian policy led to inflation.

So when the world economy collapsed in 2008–9 the only thing most younger economists, policy-makers and businessmen knew about Keynes was that one did not need to know anything about him. He had largely vanished from their textbooks, briefings and indeed from their consciousness. This left them unprepared for the catastrophic nature of the economic collapse. Today macro-economics is disabled. We are still struggling experimentally with the aftermath of the banking collapse. People talk of the need for a new Keynes. But the old Keynes still has superlative wisdom to offer for a new age.

Students and others are hungry for clues to the riddle of economic life. There have been many books about Keynes, including a rather massive one of my own. But Keynes's own writings are largely unavailable. The purpose of this single-volume Keynes reader – I have called it *The Essential Keynes* – is to give the reader a flavour of the quality of Keynes's mind, style and range, and his approach to ethical, theoretical and practical problems which, so far from having vanished, clamour for a contemporary answer. Keynes is known, if at all, only as the creator of a short-run theory of fiscal stabilization. This was the fiscal tool which emerged from the ferment of ideas in his day. But it was in his explorations of the problem of capitalist instability, and his futurist vision of a world without work, that many today will find their inspiration. My hope is that the selections I have chosen, which include some writings never before published, will provide both meat for the student and food for a wider public. Above all, this book provides readers with the opportunity to acquaint themselves with one of the most remarkable thinkers and characters of the twentieth century.

II

John Maynard Keynes was born at 6 Harvey Road, Cambridge, England on 5 June 1883 into an academic family. He was the eldest son of John Neville Keynes, a logician and economist, and Florence Ada Brown, the daughter of a Congregational divine. He had an outstandingly successful school career at Eton College, which was followed by an equally glittering under-graduate one at King's College, Cambridge, where he gained a first-class honours degree in Mathematics, wrote papers on the medieval theologian Peter Abelard and the Conservative polit-ical philosopher Edmund Burke and became president of the Cambridge Union and the University Liberal Club. Of crucial importance to his intellectual and moral formation was his election, in 1902, to the Cambridge Apostles, an exclusive 'con-versation' society, where he fell under the influence of the philosopher G. E. Moore, and which brought him the friend-ship of the subversive biographer Lytton Strachey. Moore's *Principia Ethica* remained his 'religion under the surface' for the rest of his life. It taught that the highest forms of civilized life were friendship, aesthetic enjoyments and the pursuit of truth. His economic activities were always in the service of these eth-ical goals. That is why he wanted the economic machine to work full blast till the material conditions for the 'good life' were achieved, at which point economists might retire in favour of philosophers.

In 1906 Keynes was placed second in the Civil Service Exam-ination, his worst marks being in economics, which he had studied briefly under Alfred Marshall, professor of economics at Cambridge University. (He never got a degree in economics.) After two years in the India Office, in which he wrote a thesis on probability in his spare time, he started lecturing on monetary economics at Cambridge; in 1909 his thesis won him a fellow-ship at King's College, which remained his academic home for the rest of his life. His membership of the Bloomsbury group, a commune of Cambridge-connected writers and painters who lived in the Bloomsbury district of London, dates from the start of his friendship with the painter Duncan Grant, Lytton Strachey's cousin, in 1908. In 1913 he published his first book, *Indian Currency and Finance*, and served on the Royal Commission on Indian Finance and Currency. Cambridge and Bloomsbury formed the two fortresses of his spiritual life, from which radiated out his friendships, interests and activities in the great world of affairs.

Keynes's advice to the UK Treasury helped to avert the collapse of the gold standard in the banking crisis of August 1914 which accompanied the outbreak of the First World War. From January 1915 to June 1919 he was a temporary civil servant at the Treasury, showing a notable ability to apply economic theory to the practical problems of war finance. He was against military conscription and would have been a conscientious objector had his Treasury work not exempted him from military service. When Lloyd George succeeded Asquith as prime minister in December 1916, Keynes, then aged thirty-four, became head of the Treasury's new 'A' Division, set up to manage Britain's external finance. He helped build up the whole system of inter-Allied purchases, while chafing at Britain's growing dependence on American loans and the failure to arrange a compromise peace.

Keynes was chief Treasury representative at the Paris Peace Conference in 1919, where he tried unavailingly to limit Germany's bill for reparations, and to promote an American loan for the reconstruction of Europe. His resignation from the Treasury on 5 June 1919 was followed by the publication, in December, of *The Economic Consequences of the Peace*, the book which first brought him international fame. A bitter polemic, informed by both economic argument and moral passion, against Lloyd George's policy of trying to make Germany pay for the war 'till the pips squeak', it reflected his fears for the future of European civilization. Unless the Versailles Treaty were drastically revised, vengeance, he predicted, would follow.

In 1925 he took the lease of Tilton, a farmhouse in East Sussex, next door to Charleston, where Duncan Grant lived with the painter Vanessa Bell. This move coincided with his marriage to the Russian ballerina Lydia Lopokova, for whom his love and fascination never waned, who softened the edges of his astringency and who gave his life the emotional stability and regular routine for sustained intellectual effort. Thereafter, his life was divided between Cambridge, London, and East Sussex.

He was a spectacularly successful investment bursar of his college, King's College, and despite some major reverses, made a small fortune for himself. He was worth £400,000 (£14 million, or $22 million in today's values) when he died. In London, where he rented a house at 46 Gordon Square, he was, at various times, on the boards of five investment and insurance companies, the chief one being the National Mutual Life Assurance Company, which he chaired from 1921 to 1937. Between 1923 and 1931 he was chief proprietor and chairman of the board of the weekly journal the *Nation and Athenaeum*, contributing regular articles on financial and economic topics. He remained chairman of the board of the *New Statesman and Nation* when the two journals merged in 1931. Between 1911 and 1945 he edited the *Economic Journal*. In the 1920s his ideas on economic policy permeated Whitehall through monthly meetings of the Tuesday Club, a dining club started by his friend and stockbroker, Oswald Falk. In the 1930s, he sought to influence policy through his membership of the prime minister's Economic Advisory Council.

In the 1920s the post-war European inflations, succeeded in Britain by heavy unemployment, formed the background to his two theoretical books *A Tract on Monetary Reform* (1923) and *A Treatise on Money* (1930), which dealt with the causes and consequences of monetary instability, and their remedies. These theoretical books chronicle Keynes's 'struggle to escape from the stranglehold of the Quantity Theory [of Money] . . .'[2] They were punctuated by two notable polemical pamphlets, 'The Economic Consequences of Mr Churchill' (1925) and 'Can Lloyd George Do It?' (1929), the latter co-authored with Hubert Henderson. The first attacked Churchill's decision, as chancellor of the exchequer, to put the pound back on the gold standard at an overvalued exchange rate against the dollar; the second was a plea for a large programme of public investment.

Reconciled to Lloyd George in 1926, Keynes attempted to provide the Liberal Party with a social philosophy of the 'middle
way' between individualism and state socialism, suitable for an
inflexible industrial structure. Regulation of demand, he would
later write, was the only way to maintain capitalism in conditions of freedom.

By this time Keynes was the most famous economist in the
world, made so by his superb style and the audacity of his ideas.
But he had not 'revolutionized' economics, and he himself felt
that his theoretical work was incomplete. The Great Depression
of 1929–32, together with technical flaws in *A Treatise on
Money*, took Keynes back to the theoretical drawing board.
What now seemed to be needed was not an explanation of Britain's 'special problem' of heavy unemployment, or even of the
business cycle, but an explanation of how plant and labour
could remain unused for long periods in a world in which wants
were far from being satisfied. He felt this to be both economically and morally inefficient. He drew inspiration from the 'first
Cambridge economist', Thomas Robert Malthus, from whom
he got the phrase, and possibly the idea of, 'effective demand'.
From the autumn of 1931 to the summer of 1935, Keynes
worked on a new book of theory, initially entitled 'The Monetary Theory of Production'. He was helped not just by older
economists like Ralph Hawtrey and Dennis Robertson, but
by Roy Harrod and a 'Cambridge Circus' of young disciples
headed by Richard Kahn, his 'favourite pupil'. There was just
one major pamphlet in these years, 'The Means to Prosperity',
written in June in 1933. On a trip to the United States in 1934 to
study the New Deal first-hand, he wrote: 'Here, not in Moscow,
is the economic laboratory of the world.'

In February 1936, Keynes published *The General Theory of
Employment, Interest and Money*, in which he felt had finally
cracked the riddle of unused resources. In this book, he sought
to demonstrate both that 'under-employment equilibrium' is logically possible and how cheap money combined with an extensive
'socialisation of investment' could maintain full employment.
These propositions divided the economics profession, since
the core of the *General Theory* was Keynes's rejection of the

'classical' thesis of an optimally self-adjusting economy. The publication of the *General Theory* marked the birth of a 'Keynesian school' of economics led by Richard Kahn and Joan Robinson at Cambridge, Roy Harrod and James Meade at Oxford, and Nicholas Kaldor and Abba Lerner at the London School of Economics. In the United States, the book supplied the younger generation of (mainly Harvard-trained) economists with a practical rationale for the New Deal. Keynes himself joined in the fierce controversies which his *General Theory* generated, even though he was severely incapacitated, from May 1937 to March 1939, with heart disease. As another European war, and with it the return to full employment, became increasingly likely, Keynes sought to win acceptance for his revolution by showing how the management of aggregate demand to avert depression could just as easily be used to control inflation in a war economy.

The upshot was his pamphlet *How to Pay for the War* (1940), which won the approval of his arch-critic Friedrich Hayek, and whose logic influenced Chancellor of the Exchequer Kingsley Wood's war budget of 1941. Restored to a semblance of health by his doctor, Janos Plesch, Keynes himself returned to the Treasury in August 1940 as unpaid adviser to the chancellor of the exchequer and remained its dominating force for the rest of his life. Elevated to the House of Lords in 1942 as Baron Keynes of Tilton, his influence was felt in the Employment White Paper of 1944, which pledged the UK government to maintain a 'high and stable level of employment' after the war. In 1942, Keynes became chairman of the Council for the Encouragement of Music and the Arts (CEMA), a wartime innovation which, transformed into the Arts Council of Great Britain shortly before he died, inaugurated permanent state patronage of the arts.

The US demand that, in return for Lend-Lease, Britain scrap its imperial preference system after the war inspired Keynes to his last great constructive effort, his plan for an International Clearing Union (1941). This was designed to shift balance-of-payments adjustment from debtor to creditor countries, so as to avoid the externally generated deflationary shocks which had spread depression under the gold standard. The Bretton Woods Agreement of 1944, which set up a system of fixed, but adjustable, exchange rates and two new institutions, the International Monetary Fund and the International Bank for Reconstruction and Development, fell short of his hopes. The abrupt US cancellation of Lend-Lease in August 1945 led him to undertake the fifth of his six Treasury missions to the United States to secure an American grant or interest-free loan of $5 billion. Forced to accept a semi-commercial loan for an amount far less than he had requested, Keynes gave an eloquent defence of his policy in his last speech to the House of Lords on 7 December 1945.

On 21 April 1946, worn out by his labours, he suffered a fatal heart attack at Tilton, a little short of his sixty-third birthday. Lionel Robbins wrote to his widow that 'he has given his life for his country, as surely as if he had fallen on the field of battle'. To his greatest intellectual opponent, Friedrich Hayek, 'he was the one really great man I ever knew'. In an imposing memorial service at Westminster Abbey, Britain's prime minister, Clement Attlee, headed a list of mourners drawn from all walks of Keynes's life.

III

Any account of Keynes's contributions to economics must start with his distinctive theory of probability.

In his *Treatise on Probability* (1921), he sought to rescue the ordinary language (or ordinal) use of probability from the statistical (or cardinal) theory of probability. He put forward a logical theory of probability, of which the then dominant frequency theory was a special case. In ordinary life, we will often have enough evidence to say that something is more likely to happen than not, without having enough evidence to say it is three times as likely. Furthermore, Keynes distinguished between probability and uncertainty – situations in which people don't have enough evidence to form any probabilities at all. Applied to economics, this was the distinction between risk and uncertainty. He accused the classical economic theories of his day of reducing ordinal to cardinal risk, and of excluding uncertainty as a factor in economic life. This led to the fallacy of misplaced precision: we assume we know the odds in many situations in which we have no odds at all. This was particularly applicable to financial markets. Keynes identified as a tacit axiom of the classical theory of the self-regulating economy that 'at any given time facts and expectations were ... given in a definite and calculable form'.[3] This myopia prevented precautions being taken against catastrophe.

Keynes's contributions to economic theory are contained in three books, *A Tract on Monetary Reform* (1923) (hereafter TMR), *A Treatise on Money* (1930) (heareafter TM) and *The General Theory of Employment, Interest and Money* (1936) (hereafter GT).

The first two are concerned with the causes of business fluctuations. In TMR business fluctuations are said to be *mainly* caused by changes in the price level. TM is the theory of a credit cycle, in which the cycle results from shifts in investment sentiment. GT is not concerned with fluctuations or cycles (though it has one chapter, chapter 22, called 'Notes on the Trade Cycle'), but aims to show that a deficiency of aggregate demand can produce quasi-permanent stagnation. The duty of the monetary authority/government is different in the three cases. In the first it is to stabilize the price level; in the second it is to maintain equilibrium between saving and investment; in the third, it is to maintain full employment. There are theoretical shifts and technical improvements between the first and third books, but their preoccupations are the same: to find policy capable of maintaining continuous prosperity.

For Keynesians, GT is the important book, because it broke so radically from the mainstream assertion that a market economy had an automatic tendency towards full employment. Non-Keynesians prefer TMR. This is because they regard the 'Keynesian' innovations of GT as wrong.[4] GT is also Keynes's *magnum opus* in that in it he came nearest to fitting his intuitive understanding of things into a formal framework suitable for economists. TM has its defenders, though, notably Roy

Harrod, John Hicks, Axel Leijonhufvud and Tim Congdon, who praise the subtlety of its monetary discussions.[5] In some respects, its theory of deep cycles and sluggish recoveries is more 'general' than the *General Theory*.

Even non-Keynesians would admit that Keynes's influence on the discipline was profound. But whereas Keynesians see it as inspirational, for non-Keynesians like Hayek it was 'tragic',[6] pointing economics the wrong way. All agree that Keynes was a wonderful thinker and character; they disagree about the theoretical value of his work. Keynes's 'favourite pupil', Richard Kahn, notes that 'Keynes was far happier writing for a non-academic audience – whether members of the intelligent public, politicians or bankers. His popular and other non-academic writings were unlaboured, in contrast to the elements of strain and torture that entered into his academic writing. To secure conviction he relied on sincerity and commonsense.'[7] The non-Keynesian Schumpeter sees him as 'a man who would have conquered a place in history even if he had never done a stroke of specifically scientific work'.[8]

In GT Keynes sought to demonstrate that a market economy can oscillate indefinitely round a sub-normal level of activity. The concept of 'under-employment equilibrium' may be read as a stylized picture of the global economy in the 1930s. Much more radically, GT implied that this was not just a possible condition, but a normal condition. Economists before Keynes had been prepared to accept the possibility of 'lapses from full employment', due to this, that, or the other disturbance to 'normal' conditions. No one had hitherto asserted that market economies lapsed *into* full employment only in 'moments of excitement'.

GT was by far the most influential of Keynes's books. It led directly to the development of National Income and Expenditure Accounts, to enable governments to estimate the size of the 'output' gap – the gap between what the economy was producing and what it could produce at full employment (or, in a later refinement, what it could produce when it was growing to trend). Keynes also insisted that the aggregate demand and supply framework of GT could be used to work out how much spending needed to be *withdrawn* from an economy to prevent inflation if aggregate demand exceeded aggregate supply. *How to Pay for the War* (1940) was an explicit application of GT to an inflationary full employment economy. Governments used the aggregate supply and demand apparatus as the main framework for policy for thirty years during and after the war, and, in modified form, it is still the basis of contemporary macro-economic policy.

In principle, stabilization policy can be either monetary or fiscal, or some combination of both. In the 1920s, Keynes believed that monetary policy could and should be used to iron out fairly modest fluctuations in prices and output. In TM he advocated the offset of 'open-market operations *à outrance*' (a massive central bank injection of money) for an economy sliding down into a deep recession. In GT Keynes downplayed the role of monetary management. He did not deny the efficacy of cheap money in stimulating a depressed economy but warned that 'if ... we are tempted to assert that money is the drink which stimulates the system to activity, we must remind ourselves that there may be several slips between the cup and the lip'.[9] He thought that interest rate changes were too uncertain in their effect on investment and worried that if interest rates were raised to check a boom it would be difficult to bring them down to check a slump, since investors would keep resources liquid in expectation of a rise. So he advocated a policy of permanently cheap money. This left fiscal policy as the main instrument for preventing both slumps and inflationary booms.

Keynes's fiscal philosophy must be distinguished from Keynesian fiscal policy as understood and practised after his death. It was based on a sharp distinction between the government's 'ordinary' or current-account budget and what he called the 'capital' budget. The government's ordinary budget should be balanced, with a surplus earmarked for debt repayment in 'normal' times (the Victorian 'golden rule'). It was the task of the capital budget to balance the 'national accounts'. Keynes believed that a great deal of investment was already 'socialised', that is, subject to public policy even if it was technically private. As he put it in 1943: 'If two-thirds or three-quarters of total investment is carried out or can be influenced by public or semi-public bodies, a long-term programme of a stable character should be capable of reducing the range of fluctuation to much narrower limits than formerly ... If this is successful it should not be too difficult to offset small fluctuations by expediting or retarding some items in this long-term programme.'[10]

Finally, Keynes attached only minor importance to exchange-rate adjustments. His Clearing Union plan (1941) provided for fixed, but adjustable, rates, and this was a feature of the Bretton Woods Agreement (1944). Keynes's attitude – like that of most economists of his day – was governed by price-elasticity pessimism. He preferred countries to use, if necessary, capital controls to protect their balance of payments in the framework of a monetary regime of fixed exchange rates, low tariffs and automatic creditor lending through international institutions.

IV

Keynes was not an ivory-tower theorist. His theorizing was controlled by real-world events. His own investment experience enabled him to identify the 'speculative' motive for holding money; his sense of political fragility led him to concentrate on the economics of stabilization; his civil service experience enabled him to turn theories into workable plans. His economic theorizing was less directly, but still importantly, controlled by his ethical beliefs, particularly his conception of the good life and the conditions of just exchange.

There is much more to Keynes than his economic theory and policy. He reflected and wrote on the art of statesmanship ('politicians have ears but no eyes'), on the 'agenda' of government in a modern society, and on the relationship between the state and the arts. He had an acute sense of character and place, and wrote some outstanding short biographies and essays. He loved literature, acquired an exceptional collection of paintings, sponsored English art and ballet and built the Cambridge Arts Theatre in 1936, in homage to both Cambridge and the dramatic arts. He was chairman-designate of the Arts Council of Great Britain when he died. He had an ethically based vision of the future in which 'love of money' would cease to be a driving force in human affairs, and thought that this condition might come about in a fairly short space of time.

Keynes wrote:

> the master-economist must possess a rare *combination* of gifts. He must reach a high standard in several different directions and must combine talents not often found together. He must be mathematician, historian, statesman, philosopher – in some degree. He must understand symbols and speak in words. He must contemplate the particular in terms of the general, and touch abstract and concrete in the same flight of thought. He must study the present in the light of the past for the purposes of the future. No part of man's nature or his institutions must be entirely outside his regard. He must be purposeful and disinterested in a simultaneous mood; as aloof and incorruptible as an artist, yet sometimes as near to earth as a politician.[11]

This is Keynes on his teacher Alfred Marshall. It has little to do with Marshall, but tells us a lot about how Keynes saw himself. In truth his 'mixed training and divided nature' gave him a much more vivid many-sidedness than that possessed by his teacher. In GT, he paid tribute to 'the brave army of heretics . . . who, following their intuitions, have preferred to see the truth obscurely and imperfectly rather than to maintain error, reached indeed with clearness and consistency and by easy logic but on hypotheses inappropriate to the facts'.[12] Keynes's genius lay in his ability to convert heretical intuitions into a logic which satisfied, at least for a time, the formal requirements of economics. He brought the worlds of art and science together. No one else in economics has been able to do this. That is what enabled him to leave such a large mark on modern civilization and makes him today as fresh as he ever was.

There were gaps in Keynes's equipment as an economist, unsurprising in someone who had only studied the subject for a couple of terms before he started teaching it. He relied heavily on students like Richard Kahn and Joan Robinson to fill these gaps. The marginalist revolution, which was the main innovation in economics in the late nineteenth century, never really got under his skin. He was not especially learned in economic history or the history of his own discipline, telling a student in the 1920s that '[w]hen he was old and no longer alert enough for difficult and exact analysis, he . . . would like to give his time, as a refuge and diversion . . . to . . . economic history and the history of economic thought'.[13] He would revise his views in the 1930s, when he became keen to establish a lineage for his own economic heresy. He preferred the eighteenth century to the nineteenth and always treated 'Victorian values' ironically. By the late 1920s even his mathematics was rusty, and he had to get Kahn to check his equations.

After Keynes's death, the economics profession discarded his intuitions and kept those pieces of his theory which could be justified in terms of its own formalism. Keynesians are now confined to fringes of economics departments or in adjacent fields of study. But it is from the heresies that post-crash economics will come, if it comes at all.

Readers are invited to read this selection to catch the flavour of Keynes's intuitions about the matters in which he was involved and find out to what extent they correspond to their own.

V

The selections I have chosen represent a compromise between the claims of economics and the claims of understanding. Keynes wrote as well in economics as that subject allows, and even better. He found it hard to disguise the elevation and subtlety of his mind, the vivacity and wit of his prose. But economics is difficult and has to be done in a way which non-economists often find both repellent and inaccessible. So the selections present Keynes in two guises: that of the economist and that of the public intellectual who wrote and thought about the great issues of his day and about the meaning of life.

Any selector has to make judgements of relevance. I have chosen those writings of Keynes which, in my view, can stimulate thought in our world, as well as giving pleasure. Some things he wrote are simply dead and have not been included. Separate chapters treat Keynes as philosopher, social philosopher, economist, policy-maker and essayist. Strictly speaking, one cannot separate the elements of his thought in this way, and my method sometimes suffers from the practical disadvantage of placing different sections of his main books in chapters. *The Economic Consequences of the Peace* and *A Tract on Monetary Reform* suffer particularly from being spliced up in this way. The advantage, though, is that it enables the reader to identify the separate building blocks of Keynes's thinking and appreciate the force of his wife's observation that he was 'more than an economist'. Most of chapter 3, 'The Economist', will be fully accessible only to the specialist, but even here, the non-specialist can catch glimpses of the 'more'.

What gives his work its special flavour is not only its breadth but its style. Only Keynes's stylistic panache could have invested concepts like 'fallacy of composition' and the 'paradox of thrift' with the force of common sense. The popular reception of the Keynesian Revolution was promoted by Keynes's journalism. Much of this was published in the *Nation and Athenaeum* and then the *New Statesman*. Keynes also wrote for the 'quality' press, especially *The Times*, and popular newspapers like the *Daily Mail*, the *Evening Standard* and the *Sunday Express*, which would be highly unlikely to accept such contributions today. A favourite American outlet was the *New Republic*, and his articles were syndicated worldwide. His most quotable quotes are given at the end of the book.

Keynes's greatness is to be seen not just in his 'divided nature', but in the quality of the practical judgement which resulted from it. In 1915–16 he argued for a compromise peace in the First World War. In 1919 he wanted a cancellation of inter-Allied debts and the drastic scaling-down of German reparations. In 1922 he proposed the cancellation of Tsarist debts and a loan to Russia to revive exports, so as to offer an alternative to Bolshevik economics. In 1923 he advocated the managed floating of the two main currencies, the dollar and the pound, and two years later he opposed Britain's return to the gold standard at the pre-war sterling–dollar parity. He would have fought the Great Depression with a mixture of monetary expansion and public works. In 1939–40 he urged a method of financing the Second World War to avoid the hyper-inflation and collapse which followed the first; and in 1941 he proposed an International Clearing Union which could impose penalties on persistent current account surpluses.

A consistent thread runs through his attitude to statecraft which my hope is that the reader will be able to follow. One may call it prudence, or common sense. It consisted of trying to wrest the best results from the world as it is, and not sacrificing overmuch for a necessarily uncertain future. How much better we would have been if some of his suggestions had been adopted in his lifetime. The First World War would have had less destructive consequences; there would probably have been no Great Depression, no Hitler dictatorship, no Second World War. Bolshevism might have been nipped in the bud. Hundreds of millions fewer would have suffered and died. The developed capitalist world, reconstructed on a Keynesian basis after the second war, enjoyed twenty-five years of unparalleled growth, prosperity and stability. But he was no longer alive to plan for their continuation and amendment.

NOTES

1   Excluding *Essays in Persuasion* (1931) and *Essays in Biography* (1933), which Keynes himself selected for publication. In 1944 there appeared in Zagreb J. M. Keynes, *Problemi novca izmedu dva rata* – an odd place to be published and an even odder time. Fifty years later, in 1994, an updated version appeared: J. M. Keynes, *Izabrana djela*, with a slightly different selection, and including an essay by J. K. Galbraith. Donald Moggridge has edited a collection of Keynes's broadcasts, *Keynes on the Wireless* (2010); Giorgio La Malfa has edited a selection of Keynes's writings: J. M. Keynes, *Sono un liberale?* (2010), which includes essays taken from *Essays in Persuasion* (CW 9) and *Essays in*

> *Biography* (CW 10), and J. M. Keynes, *Le mie prime convinzi-oni* (2012), reproduces, in an Italian translation, *Two Memoirs* by J. M. Keynes, edited by D. Garnett (collected in CW 10), with a foreword by Giorgio La Malfa.

2   R. F. Kahn, *The Making of Keynes's General Theory* (1984), pp. 50–51.

3   CW 14, p. 112.

4   For example, Milton Friedman, *The Economist*, 4 June 1983.

5   Roy Harrod, *The Life of John Maynard Keynes* (1951), pp. 403–4; John Hicks, 'A Note on the *Treatise*', in *Critical Essays in Monetary Theory* (1967), pp. 189–91; Axel Leijonhufvud, *On Keynesian Economics and the Economics of Keynes* (1968), pp. 16–26; Tim Congdon, *Keynes, the Keynesians and Monetarism* (2007), pp. 50–53.

6   F. A. Hayek, *New Studies in Philosophy, Politics, Economics and the History of Ideas* (1978), pp. 283, 7.

7   Kahn, *Making of Keynes's General Theory*, p. 77.

8   Joseph Schumpeter, *History of Economic Analysis* (1954), p. 1170.

9   CW 7, p. 173.

10   CW 27, p. 322.

11   CW 10, pp. 173–4.

12   CW 7, p. 371.

13   H. M. Robertson, 'J. M. Keynes and Cambridge in the 1920s', *South African Journal of Economics*, vol. 51, issue 3 (1983); quoted in Robert Skidelsky, *John Maynard Keynes*, vol. 2 (1992), p. 676, fn. 18.

Bibliography

The Collected Writings of John Maynard Keynes, cited here as CW 1, 2, etc., is published in hard copy in thirty volumes, including bibliography and index, by Macmillan/Cambridge University Press for the Royal Economic Society, 1971–89. Volumes 15 to 18 were edited by Elizabeth Johnson, the remainder by Donald Moggridge. An electronic version is available at: http://universitypublishingonline.org/royaleconomicsociety/series_landing.jsf?seriesCode=CJMK&seriesTitle=The+Collected+Writings+of+John+Maynard+Keynes&productCode=&publisherCode=RES&sort=print_date_range>. The following are the volumes from which excerpts or quotations have been made:

Vol. 2: *The Economic Consequences of the Peace*, 1971
Vol. 3: *A Revision of the Treaty*, 1971
Vol. 4: *A Tract on Monetary Reform*, 1971
Vol. 5: *A Treatise on Money: The Pure Theory of Money*, 1971
Vol. 6: *A Treatise on Money: The Applied Theory of Money*, 1971
Vol. 7: *The General Theory of Employment, Interest and Money*, 1973
Vol. 8: *A Treatise on Probability*, 1973
Vol. 9: *Essays in Persuasion*, 1972. Full text with additions
Vol. 10: *Essays in Biography*, 1972. Full text with additions
Vol. 13: *The General Theory and After: Part 1: Preparation*, 1973
Vol. 14: *The General Theory and After: Part 2: Defence and Development*, 1973
Vol. 17: *Activities 1920–1922: Treaty Revision and Reconstruction*, 1977
Vol. 21: *Activities 1931–1939: World Crises and Policies in Britain and America*, 1982

Vol. 22: *Activities 1939–1945: Internal War Finance*, 1978

Vol. 24: *Activities 1944–1946: The Transition to Peace*, 1979

Vol. 25: *Activities 1940–1944: Shaping the Post-War World: The Clearing Union*, 1980

Vol. 26: *Activities 1941–1946: Shaping the Post-War World: Bretton Woods and Reparations*, 1980

Vol. 27: *Activities 1940–1946: Shaping the Post-War World: Employment and Commodities*, 1980

Vol. 28: *Social, Political and Literary Writings*, 1982

The other main source drawn upon is Keynes Papers, King's College Cambridge.

OTHER WORKS

For fuller Keynes bibliographies see Robert Skidelsky, *John Maynard Keynes*, 3 vols. (1983, 1992, 2000), and his abridged *John Maynard Keynes 1883–1946, Economist, Philosopher, Statesman* (2003); and D. E. Moggridge, *Maynard Keynes: An Economist's Biography* (1992). The 2008 crisis has produced a spate of Keynes books, including Paul Davidson, *The Keynes Solution* (2009); Robert Skidelsky, *Keynes: The Return of the Master* (2010 edition); Robert and Edward Skidelsky, *How Much Is Enough?* (2012); and Peter Temin and David Vines, *Keynes: Useful Economics for the World Economy* (2014); as well as books critical of today's mainstream economics and economic policies, not necessarily from a Keynesian standpoint. A small sample of works: John Cassidy, *How Markets Fail: The Logic of Economic Calamities* (2009); Roman Frydman and Michael D. Goldberg, *Beyond Mechanical Markets: Asset Price Swings, Risk, and the Role of the State* (2011); Felix Martin, *Money: The Unauthorised Biography* (2013); Philip Roscoe, *I Spend Therefore I Am: The True Cost of Economics* (2014); Tomas Sedlacek, *Economics of Good and Evil* (2011); George Akerlof and Robert Shiller, *Animal Spirits: How Human Psychology Drives the Economy and Why It Matters for Global Capitalism* (2009); Adair Turner, *Economics After the Crisis* (2012).

Keynes's World,
Main Characters

Below are short CVs of the main people cited in the texts. For fuller dramatis personae, see Robert Skidelsky, *John Maynard Keynes*, 3 vols. (1983, 1992, 2000), and his abridged *John Maynard Keynes 1883–1946, Economist, Philosopher, Statesman* (2003); and D. E. Moggridge, *Maynard Keynes: An Economist's Biography* (1992).

Charles Addis (1861–1945), English banker, member of the Tuesday Club. Jousted with JMK over the return to the gold standard, but sympathized with his argument for delay.

Frederick Ashton (1904–1988), choreographer and ballet dancer, friend of Lydia Lopokova and JMK.

Herbert Henry Asquith (1852–1928), English Liberal politician, prime minister 1908–16. JMK got to know him well in the First World War. His break with Asquith in 1926 was the most important political rupture of his life.

Stanley Baldwin (1867–1947), English Conservative politician, prime minister 1923, 1924–9, 1935–7. JMK looked to him to bring about a modified socialism in line with English traditions.

Lord Beaverbrook, Maxwell Aitken (1879–1964), Canadian-born newspaper proprietor. His newspapers the *Daily Express* and the *Evening Standard* gave JMK a platform, especially in the campaign against the gold standard.

Clive Bell (1881–1964), art critic, member of the Bloomsbury group and friend of JMK.

Vanessa Bell, *née* **Stephen** (1879–1961), English painter, member of the Bloomsbury group and friend of JMK. He used to stay at Charleston, her rented farmhouse in Sussex.

William Beveridge (1879–1963), English statistician and administrator, author of the Beveridge Report, 1942, which established Britain's welfare state. He and JMK were part of the Liberal mandarin circle, though they were not friends.

Ernest Bevin (1881–1951), English trade union leader and Labour politician. JMK educated him in economics on the Macmillan Committee in 1930–31 but failed to win his support for deferred pay in 1940.

John Bradbury (1872–1950), English civil servant, joint permanent secretary at the Treasury 1913–19. Treasury notes issued in the First World War were called 'Bradburies'. JMK clashed with him about the gold standard and on the Macmillan Committee.

Robert Henry Brand (1878–1963), English banker and public servant. The meeting point between Keynes's economics and City orthodoxy.

Edwin Cannan (1861–1935), English economist, professor of political economy 1907–26. An old-fashioned QTM man.

Neville Chamberlain (1869–1940), English Conservative politician, chancellor of the exchequer 1932–7, prime minister 1937–40. His policy of balanced budgets in the 1930s enraged JMK. JMK shared his unwillingness to fight Hitler, but not his eagerness to reach an agreement with him.

Georgi Vasilevich Chicherin (1872–1936), Soviet diplomat, whom JMK met at the Genoa Conference in 1922. His old-world courtesy gave spurious respectability to Soviet aims.

Winston Spencer Churchill (1874–1965), English politician and author, chancellor of the exchequer 1924–9, prime minister 1940–45, 1951–5. JMK attacked Churchill's decision to put Britain back on the gold standard in 1925, but Churchill proposed his election to the Other Club in 1927, and there was respect, and even affection, between the two men.

Colin Clark (1905–89), Australian statistician. His pioneering work on national income statistics underpinned JMK's *How to Pay for the War* (1940). Keynes thought he was the 'only economic statistician I have met who seems to me to be quite first-rate'.

Georges Clemenceau (1841–1929), French politician, prime minister of France 1917–19. JMK encountered him at the Paris Peace Conference in 1919.

J. R. Commons (1862–1945), American institutionalist economist, professor of economics, Wisconsin University, 1904–34. He influenced JMK (see excerpt 10).

Leo Crowley (1889–1972), American businessman of Irish descent, head of the Foreign Economic Administration 1943–45. Frequent butt of JMK's derision. His face reminded JMK of 'the buttocks of a baboon'. This inspired the 'BABOON' codename for British telegrams from the Treasury during the Washington loan negotiations of 1945 (see Robert Skidelsky, *John Maynard Keynes*, vol. 3 (2000), p. 410).

Charles Gates Dawes (1865–1951), American businessman and banker. Author of the Dawes Plan (1924) for settling German reparations.

Geoffrey Dawson (1874–1944), English journalist, editor of *The Times* 1923–44. *The Times* gave JMK a platform for several columns in the 1930s, including 'Paying for the War' in November 1939.

Major Clifford Hugh Douglas (1879–1952), engineer turned economist. The most famous 'crank' of the interwar years, his A + B theorem inspired a passionate political following in the farming communities of Canada, Australia and New Zealand by promising a cure for the deflation of credit.

John Thomas Dunlop (1914–2003), American economist. His article 'The Movement of Real and Money Wage Rates', *Economic Journal*, September 1938, attracted a reply from JMK.

Wilfrid Eady (1890–1962), British Treasury official 1942–52, opposed JMK's negotiating strategy for the American loan of 1945.

Marriner Eccles (1890–1977), American banker from Utah.

Albert Einstein (1879–1955), German-born physicist, Nobel laureate, a great cultural influence on JMK's generation. The title of GT was consciously modelled on Einstein's distinction between the 'special' (Newtonian) and the 'general' theory of relativity.

T. S. Eliot (1888–1965), American-born poet and High Anglican. Partly under Eliot's influence, JMK came to see his employment theory as a secular application of Christian social doctrine.

Irving Fisher (1867–1947), American economist, professor of political and social science at Yale 1898–1935. Founder of the modern quantity theory of money, advocate of the compensated dollar.

Sigmund Freud (1856–1939), Austrian-born founder of psychoanalysis. JMK was influenced by his psychological theory of 'love of money'.

Milton Friedman (1912–2006), American economist. He 'restated' the QTM and started the anti-Keynesian movement known as 'monetarism'.

David ('Bunny') Garnett (1892–1981), English writer, friend of JMK, member of the Bloomsbury group.

Silvio Gesell (1862–1930), German-French merchant and monetary heretic, who lived in Argentina and Switzerland. His proposal for stamped money (endorsed by Irving Fisher) provided for banknotes to retain their value only if they were stamped each month, with the stamp being bought at the post office. It was intended as a disincentive to hoarding and in concept is similar to JMK's proposal, in his Clearing Union plan, to tax persistent surpluses on current accounts.

Duncan Grant (1885–1978), English painter, member of the Bloomsbury group, friend and sometime lover of JMK.

Alvin Hansen (1887–1975), American economist. An early convert to JMK's GT, he tirelessly promoted Keynesian economics in the USA, especially in the form of 'secular stagnation'.

Roy Forbes Harrod (1900–1978), English economist, student (i.e. fellow) of Christ Church, Oxford 1924–67. Wrote the authorized biography of JMK, *The Life of John Maynard Keynes*, 1951. Chiefly known for the Harrod–Domar model of economic development.

Friedrich A. Hayek (1899–1992), Austrian-born economist and philosopher, JMK's most formidable critic. See Bruce Caldwell, *Hayek's Challenge: An Intellectual Biography of F. A. Hayek* (2004).

Hubert Henderson (1890–1952), British economist and long-term collaborator of JMK. They fell out over policies for dealing with the Great Depression, and Henderson never accepted JMK's GT.

John Atkinson Hobson (1858–1940), British economist and journalist, best known for his critique of imperialism, which influenced Lenin, and for his doctrine of under-consumption. He failed to get a university job, remarking in his *Confessions of an Economic Heretic*, 'I hardly realized that in appearing to question the virtue of unlimited thrift I had committed the unpardonable sin.'

Richard Hopkins (1880–1955), leading Treasury official in JMK's time, who brought JMK into the Treasury in 1940. JMK had great respect and affection for 'Hoppy', who in turn was shifted from his pre-war monetary and fiscal orthodoxies.

Richard Ferdinand Kahn (1905–89), British economist. His multiplier theory was published as 'The Relation of Home Investment to Unemployment' in the *Economic Journal*, June 1931.

Florence Ada Keynes (1861–1958) and John Neville Keynes (1852–1949), JMK's parents. Geoffrey Keynes (1887–1982), a surgeon, was his younger brother, and Margaret Hill (1885–1970), his younger sister.

D. H. Lawrence (1885–1930), English writer. Lawrence's attack on Bloomsbury prompted JMK's 'My Early Beliefs' (see excerpt 6).

Abba Lerner (1903–82), Russian-born American economist, author of the theory of 'functional finance'.

David Lloyd George (1863–1945), British Liberal politician, prime minister 1916–22. JMK quarrelled with him over the Treaty of Versailles, but they were reconciled in the late 1920s (see excerpt 28).

Lydia Lopokova (1892–1981), Russian ballerina, married Keynes 1925.

James Ramsay MacDonald (1866–1937), British Labour politician, prime minister 1924, 1929–35. Used JMK as an adviser after 1929, but was too pessimistic to take his advice.

Reginald McKenna (1863–1943), British Liberal politician and banker. Chancellor of the exchequer 1915–16. JMK served under him at the Treasury, and they remained friends and political allies.

Alfred Marshall (1842–1924), English economist, professor of political economy, Cambridge University, 1883–1907. JMK's economics teacher and foremost economist of his age. His hugely influential *Principles of Political Economy* was published in 1890. Sceptics of JMK's claim to originality would say 'It's all in Marshall.'

James E. Meade (1907–95), English economist, friend and admirer of JMK. Served in the Economic Section of the War Cabinet.

Carl Melchior (1871–1933), German banker, friend of JMK. Excerpt 40 is from JMK's memoir of him.

G. E. Moore (1873–1958), fellow of Trinity College, Cambridge 1894–1904, professor of philosophy, Cambridge 1925–39. Author of *Principia Ethica*, 1903.

Ottoline Morrell (1873–1938), pre-1914 Bloomsbury hostess. Her country house in Garsington, Oxfordshire, provided a refuge for pacifists in the war.

Arthur Cecil Pigou (1877–1959), British economist, colleague of JMK at King's College, Cambridge, professor of political economy at Cambridge 1908–48. One of the founders of welfare economics.

Frank Ramsey (1903–30), English mathematician and philosopher, fellow of King's College, Cambridge 1924–30. Friend of JMK, but critical of his theory of probability.

Lionel Robbins (1898–1984), British economist. Defended free trade and the policy of cutting spending in a slump against JMK. But he was a staunch ally of JMK in pushing through the Bretton Woods agreement and the American loan. In his autobiography, *Autobiography of an Economist* (1971), he partly retracted his opposition to JMK but nevertheless considered that economics as a study of 'remoter effects' was still a better guide to policy than the 'gay reminder' that 'in the long run we are all dead'.

Dennis Holme Robertson (1890–1963), English economist. JMK's main intellectual stimulus in the 1920s, but rejected JMK's 'revolution' in the 1930s, with bad effects on their personal relations.

Edward Austin Robinson (1897–1993), British Cambridge economist.

Joan Robinson (1903–83), British Cambridge economist, wife of Austin Robinson, author of *The Economics of Imperfect Competition* (1933) and one of the most able expositors (and simplifiers) of JMK's ideas. She said: 'As I never learnt mathematics, I have had to think.'

Franklin Delano Roosevelt (1882–1945), American politician, president of the USA 1933–45. JMK put his hopes in FDR for a democratic escape from the Depression, and later to help Britain generously in the Second World War. He had four meetings with him and was, as most were, charmed by him.

Bertrand Russell (1872–1970), English philosopher. His *Principles of Mathematics* (1903) influenced JMK's theory of probability.

Joseph Alois Schumpeter (1883–1950), Austrian-born American economist, professor of economics at Harvard 1932–50, theorist of 'creative destruction'.

Henry Sidgwick (1838–1900), Cambridge philosopher, friend of the Keynes family in Cambridge, Knightbridge professor of moral philosophy, Cambridge University, 1883–1900.

Philip Snowden (1864–1937), English Labour politician. Chancellor of the exchequer 1929–31.

Arthur Spiethoff (1873–1957), German institutional and business-cycle economist. In 1933 JMK contributed an important article, 'A Monetary Theory of Production', to his Festschrift (excerpt 19).

Oliver Sprague (1873–1953), American-born economist, economic adviser to the Bank of England 1930–33.

Piero Sraffa (1898–1983), Italian-born economist, Cambridge University lecturer in economics 1927–31. So great was his horror of teaching that Keynes had to invent for him the job of editing Ricardo's papers to keep him in Cambridge.

Lytton Strachey (1880–1932), English biographer and literary critic, member of the Bloomsbury group, a close friend of JMK and a mentor in matters of taste.

Jan Tinbergen (1903–94), Dutch statistician, 'father of econometrics'.

Knut Wicksell (1851–1926), Swedish economist, founder of the Stockholm school and a key figure in modern economics. Wicksell led the break from the quantity theory of money, which JMK followed. In TM, JMK adopted his 'natural rate of interest' theory but later discarded it as it suggested a unique position of equilibrium.

Ludwig Wittgenstein (1889–1951), Austrian-born philosopher, fellow of Trinity College, Cambridge 1930–36, professor of philosophy, Cambridge University 1939–47. 'God has arrived. I met him on the 5.15 train,' JMK wrote to his wife when Wittgenstein came to stay with him in Cambridge in 1929.

Virginia Woolf (1882–1941), English writer, member of the Bloomsbury group, friend of JMK. With her husband, Leonard Woolf (1880–1963), she started the Hogarth Press, which published Keynes's essays and pamphlets in the 1920s and 1930s.

THE ESSENTIAL KEYNES

ONE

The Philosopher

'Philosophy provided the foundation of Keynes's life. It came before economics; and the philosophy of ends came before the philosophy of means.'

Robert Skidelsky, *John Maynard Keynes*, vol. 1 (1983), p. 133

Five elements of Keynes's philosophy, acquired early in life, had a profound influence on his economics: his intuitionism; the primacy of ethics; the relationship between ethics and morals; the doctrine of organic unity; and the logical theory of probability. Keynes owed the first four directly to the Cambridge philosopher G. E. Moore; his probability theory developed from a disagreement with Moore.

I

'Ethics in Relation to Conduct' (1904)

[In October 1902, the nineteen-year-old Keynes entered King's College, Cambridge to study mathematics. In February 1903 he was elected to the Cambridge Conversazione Society, or Apostles, an exclusive student club which met on Saturday evenings to discuss papers written by members or former members. Its intellectual atmosphere when Keynes joined was dominated by the views and character of G. E. Moore. In October 1903 came the publication of Moore's Principia Ethica. *Its influence on the young Keynes was instant, profound and permanent.*

At the heart of Principia *was the notion of the indefinability of good, and the distinction between 'ethics' and 'morals'. We knew what was good through moral intuition. The primary ethical question is 'What sort of things ought to exist for their own sake?' The moral questions, 'What ought I to do?', 'How ought I to behave?', must be answered by reference to the primary question, taking into account the probable consequences of action. Moore's doctrine is both startling and austere:*

> *By far the most valuable things, which we know or can imagine, are certain states of consciousness, which may be roughly described as the pleasures of human intercourse and the enjoyment of beautiful objects ... it is only for the sake of these things – in order that as much of them as possible may at some time exist – that any one can be justified in performing any public or private duty ... it is they ... that form the rational ultimate end of human action and the sole criterion of social progress.[1]*

Keynes cut his philosophic teeth on Moore in a paper on 'Ethics in Relation to Conduct', read to the Apostles on 23 January 1904. It survives only in manuscript form, without page numbers. It is filed in KP: UA/19/2. For its dating, see Robert Skidelsky, John Maynard Keynes, *vol. 2 (1992), p. 655, fn. 7. In this paper, he criticizes Moore's theory of probability.*

Keynes interprets Moore as arguing that probability is frequency: the ratio of times something happens to times it might happen. Since we lacked frequencies – and therefore probabilities – of the effects of our actions over time, we should, Moore argues, follow the generally accepted rules of conduct, what is now called 'rule utilitarianism'. Keynes agreed with Moore that we lacked frequencies over time, but argued against him that our actions should aim to produce the greatest good in the circumstances of the case – what is now called 'act utilitarianism'. To support his position Keynes advanced a modified form of the 'principle of indifference'. This held that alternatives are equally probable if, given our evidence, there is no reason to choose between them. Its main purpose was to neutralize the effect of the unknown. Keynes's subsequent book, A Treatise on Probability, *was an attack on the frequency theory of probability. His rejection of the*

*identification of probability with frequency determined his views
on the limits of mathematical forecasting in economics.*]
On the interpretation of probability which I have supported in
this paper, even if we have no knowledge whatever as to the
result of our actions . . . after a lapse of (say) 100 years, it is still
possible for us to make such a statement as 'x is probably right'
without falsehood.

For suppose that we have evidence to show that an action will
produce more good than not in the next year and *have no reason
for supposing either that it will produce more good than evil or
the reverse after the end of that period* [*my italics*] if, in fact, we
are in complete ignorance as to all events subsequent to the end
of the year, – in that case we have, in my opinion, more evidence
to support the view that x is right than to support the contrary
and hence we are justified in saying 'x is probably right'.

2

'The Political Doctrines of Edmund Burke' (1904)

[*This eighty-six-page unpublished typed essay is filed at KP:
UA/20/315. Dated November 1904, it was written the same
year as 'Ethics in Relation to Conduct' above and won the University Members Prize for English Essay. In it, Keynes invokes
the principle of indifference to support the political doctrine of
prudence. Burke's doctrine of prudence had a profound effect
on Keynes's theory of economic policy and, more generally, his
theory of statesmanship. It is reflected in his most celebrated
remark: 'In the long run we are all dead.'*]
In regard to the remaining point – [Burke's] timidity in
introducing present evil for the sake of future benefits – he is
emphasising a principle that is often in need of such emphasis.
Our power of prediction is so slight, our knowledge of remote
consequences so uncertain, that it is seldom wise to sacrifice a
present benefit for a doubtful advantage in the future. Burke ever
held, and held rightly, that it can seldom be right to sacrifice

[14] the well-being of a nation for a generation, to plunge whole communities in distress, or to destroy a beneficent institution for the sake of a supposed millennium in the comparatively remote future. We can never know enough to make the chance worth taking, and the fact that cataclysms in the past have sometimes inaugurated lasting benefits is no argument for cataclysms in general. These fellows, says Burke, have 'glorified in making a Revolution, as if revolutions were good things in themselves'.

He is continually insisting that it is the paramount duty of governments and of politicians to secure the well-being of the community under their care in the present, and not to run risks overmuch for the future; it is not their function, because they are not competent to perform it. 'In their political arrangements, men have no right to put the well-being of the present generation wholly out of the question. Perhaps the only moral trust with any certainty in our hands is the care of our own time . . . If ever we ought to be economists even to parsimony it is in the voluntary production of evil.'

In addition to the risk involved in any violent method of progress, there is this further consideration that is often in need of emphasis:– it is not sufficient that the state of affairs which we seek to promote should be better than the state which preceded it; it must be sufficiently better to make up for the evils of the transition. Burke . . . presses this doctrine further than it will bear, but there is no small element of truth in it and no [15] small tendency in revolutionary reformers to overlook it.
. . .
It is on this principle that Burke's attitude towards war is mainly based; there are occasions, he maintains, when it is necessary as a means, and never can such occasions altogether cease, but it is a means that brings innumerable evils in its train. It is not sufficient that a nation's legal claim should have been infringed. Only great causes justify it; with much prudence, [16] reverence, and calculation must it be approached.

3
The Adding-Up Problem (1904)

[*Keynes subscribed to Moore's doctrine of organic unity, a surviving vestige of Hegelianism in his thinking. This is the view that a whole consists of interdependent parts, so that its value – as in a work of art – can be greater or smaller than the sum of those parts. Keynes uses this is as an argument against trying to sum goodness by adding up individual goods. This is in line with his rejection of methodological individualism as a generally valid method of analysis in economics. The macro-economy is not equal to the sum of individual choices. Key ideas in Keynes's economics like the 'fallacy of composition' and the 'paradox of thrift' originate in the doctrine of organic unity. Individual decisions, rational in isolation, can have effects greater or lesser than intended because of their reactions on others.[2] This imparts inescapable uncertainty to many outcomes of interest to the individual decision-maker.*

In 'Ethics in Relation to Conduct' he writes:]
. . . the unpopularity of the principle of organic unities shows very clearly how great is the danger of the assumption of unproved additive formulas.

The fallacy, of which ignorance of organic unity is a particular instance, may perhaps be mathematically represented thus:

suppose $f(x)$ is the goodness of x and $f(y)$ is the goodness of y. It is then assumed that the goodness of x and y together is $f(x) + f(y)$

when it is clearly $f(x + y)$

and only in special cases will it be true that $f(x + y) = f(x) + f(y)$.

4

'The Principles of Probability' (1908)

[*This excerpt is from the (unpublished) dissertation Keynes submitted for a prize fellowship at King's College, Cambridge, in 1908. It is filed under KP: 20D. He was unsuccessful that year but was elected to a prize fellowship a year later. In this thesis, Keynes sought to extend the field of logical argument to include those cases in which the conclusion is partly, but not wholly, entailed by the premiss. This allows for the play of logical intuitionism: we intuit that the conclusion follows from the premiss, even though it lacks the formal quality of the syllogism. His aim in this was to align probability to ordinary discourse, 'through which practical conclusions of action are most often reached'. This view would lead Keynes to attack the exaggerated use of mathematical formalism in economics. The following extract is taken from the first chapter of his dissertation.*]*

In the ordinary course of thought and argument we are constantly asserting that the truth of one statement, while not *proving* another, is nevertheless some *ground* for believing the second. We assert that with the evidence at our command, we *ought* to hold such and such a belief. We expressly say we have *rational* grounds for assertions which are, in the usual logical sense, unproved. We allow, in fact, that statements may be unproved, without for that reason being unfounded. Nor does reflection show that it is information of purely psychological import which we wish to convey when we use such expressions as these . . . We are in fact claiming to cognize correctly a logical connexion between one set of propositions which we call our evidence and which we take to be true, and another set which we call our conclusions and to which we attach more or less weight according to the grounds supplied by the first. We recognize that *objectively* evidence can be *real* evidence and yet not *conclusive* evidence . . . I do not think I am straining the use of words in speaking of this as the probability relation or the

[3]   relation of probability. The idea of a premiss's having some

weight to establish a conclusion, of its lying somewhere between cogency and irrelevancy is altogether foreign to a logic in which the premiss must either prove or not prove the alleged conclusion. This opinion is, from the nature of the case, incapable of positive proof. The notion presents itself to the mind, I feel, as something independent and unique.

. . .

Yet that 'probability' is, in the strict sense, indefinable, need not trouble us much; it is a characteristic which it shares with many of our most necessary and fundamental ideas.   [8]

5

CW 8, *A Treatise on Probability* (1921)

[*The* Treatise *was finished in* 1914, *following the addition of a section on 'The Foundations of Statistical Inference', but the war delayed its publication. In the following excerpt, from chapter 1, Keynes states the logical concept of probability.*]

The terms *certain* and *probable* describe the various degrees of rational belief about a proposition which different amounts of knowledge authorise us to entertain. All propositions are true or false, but the knowledge we have of them depends on our circumstances; and while it is often convenient to speak of propositions as certain or probable, this expresses strictly a [3] relationship in which they stand to a *corpus* of knowledge, actual or hypothetical, and not a characteristic of the propositions in themselves. A proposition is capable at the same time of varying degrees of this relationship, depending upon the knowledge to which it is related, so that it is without significance to call a proposition probable unless we specify the knowledge to which we are relating it.

To this extent, therefore, probability may be called subjective. But in the sense important to logic, probability is not subjective. It is not, that is to say, subject to human caprice. A proposition is not probable because we think it so. When once the facts are given which determine our knowledge, what is probable or improbable in these circumstances has been fixed objectively, and is independent of our opinion. The theory of probability is logical, therefore, because it is concerned with the degree of belief which it is *rational* to entertain in given conditions, and not merely with the actual beliefs of particular individuals, which may or may not be rational.

Given the body of direct knowledge which constitutes our ultimate premisses, this theory tells us what further rational beliefs, certain or probable, can be derived by valid argument from our direct knowledge. This involves purely logical relations between the propositions which embody our direct knowledge and the propositions about which we seek indirect knowledge. What particular propositions we select as the premisses of *our* argument naturally depends on subjective factors peculiar to ourselves; but the relations, in which other propositions stand to these, and which entitle us to probable beliefs are objective and logical.

Let our premisses consist of any set of propositions *h*, and our conclusion consist of any set of propositions *a*, then, if a knowledge of *h* justifies a rational belief in *a* of degree α, we can say

[4] that there is a *probability-relation* of degree α between *a* and *h*.*
[*The most striking feature of Keynes's theory was the large class of non-numerical probabilities it contained. Keynes's universe of probability contained three types of probability: numerical (where the probability lies on a line between 0 and 1); non-numerical (where x is more/less likely to happen than y); and unknown (due to lack of logical insight or in presence of non-comparable arguments). The first two divisions correspond to cardinal and ordinal rankings. Keynes attacked the tendency to convert non-numerical probabilities into numerical ones. This would later become standard in both probability and economic theory through the application of Bayes' Theorem, by which subjective bets are converted into objective frequencies through repeated instances. Agents in contemporary economics are modelled as having 'mathematical expectations', that is,*

---

* This will be written $a/h = α$.

as being able to calculate possible benefits multiplied by the probability of attaining them into an infinite future.

The question of which parts of unknown probabilities are unknown because of the complexity of the interacting parts of the social system, which defies our present power of computation, or are ontologically unknowable, because 'we create our own future', is currently debated in the behavioural sciences. The doctrine of organic unity would have inclined Keynes to the latter view. In this extract, it is only possible to give a flavour of his style and method of argument.]

There seems to me to be extremely strong reasons for [doubting] whether any two probabilities are in every case theoretically capable of comparison in terms of number. Let us examine a few more cases.

. . .

[We] may sometimes have some reason for supposing that one object belongs to a certain category if it has points of similarity to other known members of the category (e.g. if we are considering whether a certain picture should be ascribed to a certain painter), and the greater the similarity the greater the probability of our conclusion. But we cannot in these cases *measure* the increase; we can say that the presence of certain peculiar marks in a picture increases the probability that the artist of whom these marks are known to be characteristic painted it, but we cannot say that the presence of these marks makes it two or three or any other number of times more probable than it would have been without them. We can say that one thing is more like a second object than it is like a third; but there will very seldom be any meaning in saying that it is twice as like. Probability is, so far as measurement is concerned, closely analogous to similarity.   [30]

. . .

[*Keynes gives an example where it may not be possible even to rank probabilities.*]

This leads up to a contention, which I have heard supported, that, although not all measurements and not all comparisons of probability are within our power, yet we can say in the case of every argument whether it is *more* or *less* likely than not. Is our expectation of rain, when we start out for a walk, always *more* likely than not, or *less* likely than not, or *as* likely as not? I am prepared to argue that on some occasions *none* of these alternatives hold, and that it be an arbitrary matter to decide for or against the umbrella. If the barometer is high, but the clouds are black, it is not always rational that one should prevail over the other in our minds, or even that we should balance them, – though it will be rational to allow caprice to determine us and [32] waste no time on the debate.

. . .

I maintain, then, in what follows, that there are some pairs of probabilities between the members of which *no* comparison of magnitude is possible; that we can say, nevertheless, of some pairs of relations of probability that one is greater and the other less, although it is not possible to measure the difference between them; and that in a very special type of case . . . a meaning can [36– be given to a *numerical* comparison of magnitude. [*The first* 7] *case becomes the 'radical uncertainty' of GT.*]

[*In chapter 6, Keynes introduces the notion of 'weight' of evidence as determining not the magnitude of the probability but the amount of confidence it is rational to have in making a judgement of probability; and in chapter 26, 'The Application of Probability to Conduct', the notion of 'moral risk': the idea that a smaller good more certain of attainment is better than a greater good whose attainment is less certain. Both principles are independent of probability, but necessary for a rational judgement on conduct. 'At any rate,' Keynes writes on p. 347, 'there seems . . . a good deal to be said for the conclusion that, other things being equal, that course of action is preferable, which involves least risk and about the results of which we have the most complete knowledge'. He doubted (p. 83) that the theory of 'evidential weight' had 'much practical significance'; but he takes it up in his discussion of investment behaviour in chapter 12 of GT (see below, p. 204).*][3]

6

CW 10, 'My Early Beliefs' (1938)

[*'My Early Beliefs' was a paper Keynes read, at the age of fifty-five, to the Memoir Club, a group of friends consisting of older and younger members of the Bloomsbury group, at his country house, Tilton, on 9 September 1938. It was published posthumously in* Two Memoirs, *with an introduction by David Garnett, in 1949. (For the second of the two memoirs, see excerpt 40.)*

Keynes set out to defend himself – and his Bloomsbury friends – from D. H. Lawrence's charge that they were frivolous. He aimed to show that his 'early beliefs' may have been utopian, but they were not lightly held. They were 'still my religion under the surface'.]

I went up to Cambridge at Michaelmas 1902, and Moore's *Principia Ethica* came out at the end of my first year. I have never heard of the present generation having read it. But, of course, its effect on *us*, and the talk which preceded and followed it, dominated, and perhaps still dominate, everything else. We were at an age when our beliefs influenced our behaviour, a characteristic of the young which it is easy for the middle-aged to forget, and the habits of feeling formed then still persist in a recognisable degree. It is those habits of feeling, influencing the majority of us, which make this Club a collectivity and separate us from the rest.   [435]

. . .

Now what we got from Moore was by no means entirely what he offered us. He had one foot on the threshold of the new heaven, but the other foot in Sidgwick and the Benthamite calculus and the general rules of correct behaviour. There was one chapter in the *Principia* of which we took not the slightest notice. We accepted Moore's religion, so to speak, and discarded his morals. Indeed, in our opinion, one of the greatest advantages of his religion, was that it made morals unnecessary – meaning by 'religion' one's attitude towards oneself and the ultimate and by 'morals' one's attitude towards the outside world and the intermediate. To the consequences of having a religion and no morals I return later.

Even if the new members of the Club know what the religion was (do they?), it will not do any of us any harm to try and recall the crude outlines. Nothing mattered except states of mind, our own and other people's of course, but chiefly our own. These states of mind were not associated with action or achievement or with consequences. They consisted in timeless, passionate states of contemplation and communion, largely unattached to 'before' and 'after'. Their value depended, in accordance with the principle of organic unity, on the state of affairs as a whole which could not be usefully analysed into parts. For example, the value of the state of mind of being in love did not depend merely on the nature of one's own emotions, but also on the worth of their object and on the reciprocity and nature of the object's emotions; but it did not depend, if I remember rightly, or did not depend much, on what happened, or how one felt about it, a year later, though I myself was always an advocate of a principle of organic unity through time, which still seems to me only sensible. The appropriate subjects of passionate contemplation and communion were a beloved person, [436] beauty and truth, and one's prime objects in life were love, the creation and enjoyment of aesthetic experience and the pursuit of knowledge. Of these love came a long way first. But in the early days under Moore's influence the public treatment of this and its associated acts was, on the whole, austere and platonic. Some of us might argue that physical enjoyment could spoil and detract from the state of mind as a whole. I do not remember at what date Strachey issued his edict that certain Latin technical terms of sex were the correct words to use, that to avoid them was a grave error, and, even in mixed company, a weakness, and the use of other synonyms a vulgarity. But I should certainly say that this was later. In 1903 those words were not even esoteric terms of common discourse.

Our religion closely followed the English puritan tradition of being chiefly concerned with the salvation of our own souls. The divine resided within a closed circle. There was not a very intimate connection between 'being good' and 'doing good'; and we had a feeling that there was some risk that in practice the latter might interfere with the former. But religions proper, as distinct from modern 'social service' pseudo-religions, have always been of that character; and perhaps it was a sufficient offset that our religion was altogether unworldly – with wealth, power, popularity or success it had no concern whatever, they were thoroughly despised.

How did we know what states of mind were good? This was a matter of direct inspection, of direct unanalysable intuition about which it was useless and impossible to argue. In that case who was right when there was a difference of opinion? There were two possible explanations. It might be that the two parties were not really talking about the same thing, that they were not bringing their intuitions to bear on precisely the same object, and, by virtue of the principle of organic unity, a very small difference in the object might make a very big difference in the result. Or it might be that some people had an acuter sense of judgment, just as some people can judge a vintage port and others cannot. On the whole, so far as I remember, this explanation prevailed. In practice, victory was with those who could [437] speak with the greatest appearance of clear, undoubting conviction and could best use the accents of infallibility. Moore at this time was a master of this method – greeting one's remarks with a gasp of incredulity – *Do* you *really* think *that*, an expression of face as if to hear such a thing said reduced him to a state of wonder verging on imbecility, with his mouth wide open and wagging his head in the negative so violently that his hair shook. *Oh!* he would say, goggling at you as if either you or he must be mad; and no reply was possible.

. . .

I have called this faith a religion, and some sort of relation of neo-Platonism it surely was. But we should have been very angry at the time with such a suggestion. We regarded all this as entirely rational and scientific in character. Like any other branch of science, it was nothing more than the application of logic and rational analysis to the material presented as sense-data. Our apprehension of good was exactly the same as our apprehension of green, and we purported to handle it with the same logical and analytical technique which was appropriate to the latter. Indeed we combined a dogmatic treatment as to the nature of experience with a method of handling it which was extravagantly scholastic. Russell's *Principles of Mathematics* came out in the same year as *Principia Ethica;* and the [438] former, in spirit, furnished a method for handling the material provided by the latter. Let me give you a few examples of the sort of things we used to discuss.

If A was in love with B and believed that B reciprocated his feelings, whereas in fact B did not, but was in love with C, the state of affairs was certainly not so good as it would have been if A had been right, but was it worse or better than it would become if A discovered his mistake? If A was in love with B under a misapprehension as to B's qualities, was this better or worse than A's not being in love at all? If A was in love with B because A's spectacles were not strong enough to see B's complexion, did this altogether, or partly, destroy the value of A's state of mind? Suppose we were to live our lives backwards, having our experiences in the reverse order, would this affect the value of successive states of mind? If the states of mind enjoyed by each of us were pooled and then redistributed, would this affect their value? How did one compare the value of a good state of mind which had bad consequences with a bad state of mind which had good consequences? In valuing the consequences did one assess them at their actual value as it turned out eventually to be, or their probable value at the time? If at their probable value, how much evidence as to possible consequences was it one's duty to collect before applying the calculus? Was there a separate objective standard of beauty? Was a beautiful thing, that is to say, by definition that which it was good to contemplate? Or was there an actual objective quality 'beauty', just like 'green' and 'good'? And knowledge, too, presented a problem. Were all truths equally good to pursue and contemplate? – as for example the number of grains in a given tract of sea-sand. We were disposed to repudiate very strongly the idea that useful knowledge could be preferable to

useless knowledge. But we flirted with the idea that there might
be some intrinsic quality – though not, perhaps, quite on a par
with 'green' and 'good' and 'beautiful' – which one could
call 'interesting', and we were prepared to think it just possible
that 'interesting' knowledge might be better to pursue than
'uninteresting' knowledge. Another competing adjective was [439]
'important', provided it was quite clear that 'important' did
not mean 'useful'. Or to return again to our favourite subject,
was a violent love affair which lasted a short time better than a
more tepid one which endured longer? We were inclined to
think it was. But I have said enough by now to make it clear
that the problems of mensuration, in which we had involved
ourselves, were somewhat formidable.

It was all under the influence of Moore's method, according
to which you could hope to make essentially vague notions clear
by using precise language about them and asking exact questions. It was a method of discovery by the instrument of
impeccable grammar and an unambiguous dictionary. 'What
exactly do you mean?' was the phrase most frequently on our
lips. If it appeared under cross-examination that you did not
mean *exactly* anything, you lay under a strong suspicion of
meaning nothing whatever. It was a stringent education in dia-
lectic; but in practice it was a kind of combat in which strength
of character was really much more valuable than subtlety of
mind. In the preface to his great work, bespattered with the
numerous italics through which the reader who knew him could
actually hear, as with Queen Victoria, the vehemence of his utterance, Moore begins by saying that error is chiefly 'the attempt to
answer questions, without first discovering precisely *what* question it is which you desire to answer . . . Once we recognise the
exact meaning of the two questions, I think it also becomes plain
exactly what kind of reasons are relevant as arguments for or
against any particular answer to them.' So we spent our time
trying to discover *precisely what* questions we were asking, confident in the faith that, if only we could ask precise questions,
everyone would know the answer. Indeed Moore expressly
claimed as much. In his famous chapter on 'The Ideal' he wrote:

Indeed, once the meaning of the question is clearly understood, the answer to it, in its main outlines, appears to be so obvious, that it runs the risk of seeming to be a platitude. By far the most valuable things, which we know or can imagine, are certain states [440] of consciousness, which may be roughly described as the pleasures of human intercourse and the enjoyment of beautiful objects. No one, probably, who has asked himself the question, has ever doubted that personal affection and the appreciation of what is beautiful in Art or Nature, are good in themselves; nor if we consider strictly what things are worth having *purely for their own sakes*, does it appear probable that any one will think that anything else has *nearly* so great a value as the things which are included under these two heads.

And then there was the question of pleasure. As time wore on towards the nineteen-tens, I fancy we weakened a bit about pleasure. But, in our prime, pleasure was nowhere. I would faintly urge that if two states of mind were similar in all other respects except that one was pleasurable and the other was painful there *might* be a little to be said for the former, but the principle of organic unities was against me. It was the general view (though not quite borne out by the *Principia*) that pleasure had nothing to do with the case and, on the whole, a pleasant state of mind lay under grave suspicion of lacking intensity and passion.

. . .

Socrates had persuaded Protarchus that pure hedonism was [441] absurd. Moore himself was only prepared to accept pleasure as enhancement of a state of affairs otherwise good. But Moore hated evil and he found a place in his religion for vindictive punishment. 'Not only is the pleasantness of a state *not* in proportion to its intrinsic worth; it may even add positively to its vileness . . . The infliction of pain on a person whose state of mind is bad may, if the pain be not too intense, create a state of things that is better *on the whole* than if the evil state of mind had existed unpunished. Whether such a state of affairs can ever constitute a *positive* good is another question.' I call attention to the qualification 'if the pain be not too intense'. Our Ideal was a merciful God.

Thus we were brought up – with Plato's absorption in the good in itself, with a scholasticism which outdid St Thomas, in Calvinistic withdrawal from the pleasures and successes of Vanity Fair, and oppressed with all the sorrows of Werther. It did not prevent us from laughing most of the time and we enjoyed supreme self-confidence, superiority and contempt towards all the rest of the unconverted world. But it was hardly a state of mind which a grown-up person in his senses could sustain literally.

. . .

It seems to me looking back, that this religion of ours was a very good one to grow up under. It remains nearer the truth than any other that I know, with less irrelevant extraneous matter and nothing to be ashamed of; though it is a comfort today to be able to discard with a good conscience the calculus and the mensuration and the duty to know *exactly* what one means and feels. It was a purer, sweeter air by far than Freud cum Marx. It is still my religion under the surface.   [442]

. . .

The New Testament is a handbook for politicians compared with the unworldliness of Moore's chapter on 'The Ideal'. I know no equal to it in literature since Plato. And it is better than Plato because it is quite free from *fancy*. It conveys the beauty of the literalness of Moore's mind, the pure and passionate intensity of his vision, *un*fanciful and *un*dressed-up. Moore had a nightmare once in which he could not distinguish propositions from tables. But even when he was awake, he could not distinguish love and beauty and truth from the furniture. They took on the same definition of outline, the same stable, solid, objective qualities and common-sense reality.

I see no reason to shift from the fundamental intuitions of *Principia Ethica*; though they are much too few and too narrow to fit actual experience which provides a richer and more various content. That they furnish a justification of experience wholly independent of outside events had become an added comfort, even though one cannot live today secure in the undisturbed individualism which was the extraordinary achievement of the early Edwardian days, not for our little lot only, but for everyone else, too.

I am still a long way off from D. H. Lawrence and what he might have been justified in meaning when he said that we were 'done for'. And even now I am not quite ready to approach that theme. First of all I must explain the other facet of our faith. So [444] far it has been a question of our attitude to ourselves and one another. What was our understanding of the outside world and our relation to it?

It was an important object of Moore's book to distinguish between goodness as an attribute of states of mind and rightness as an attribute of actions. He also has a section on the justification of general rules of conduct. The large part played by considerations of probability in his theory of right conduct was, indeed, an important contributory cause to my spending all the leisure of many years on the study of that subject: I was writing under the joint influence of Moore's *Principia Ethica* and Russell's *Principia Mathematica*. But for the most part, as I have said, we did not pay attention to this aspect of the book or bother much about it. We were living in the specious present, nor had begun to play the game of consequences. We existed in the world of Plato's *Dialogues*; we had not reached the *Republic*, let alone the *Laws*.

This brought us one big advantage. As we had thrown hedonism out of the window and, discarding Moore's so highly problematical calculus, lived entirely in present experience, since social action as an end in itself and not merely as a lugubrious duty had dropped out of our Ideal, and not only social action, but the life of action generally, power, politics, success, wealth, ambition, with the economic motive and the economic criterion less prominent in our philosophy than with St Francis of Assisi, who at least made collections for the birds, it follows that we were amongst the first of our generation, perhaps alone amongst our generation, to escape from the Benthamite tradition. In practice, of course, at least so far as I was concerned, the outside world was not forgotten or forsworn. But I am recalling what our Ideal was in those early days when the life of passionate contemplation and communion was supposed to

oust all other purposes whatever. It can be no part of this memoir for me to try to explain why it was such a big advantage for
us to have escaped from the Benthamite tradition. But I do now
regard that as the worm which has been gnawing at the insides
of modern civilisation and is responsible for its present moral
decay. We used to regard the Christians as the enemy, because [445]
they appeared as the representatives of tradition, convention
and hocus-pocus. In truth it was the Benthamite calculus, based
on an over-valuation of the economic criterion, which was
destroying the quality of the popular Ideal.

Moreover, it was this escape from Bentham, joined with the
unsurpassable individualism of our philosophy, which has
served to protect the whole lot of us from the final *reductio ad
absurdum* of Benthamism known as Marxism. We have completely failed, indeed, to provide a substitute for these economic
bogus-faiths capable of protecting or satisfying our successors.
But we ourselves have remained – am I not right in saying *all* of
us? – altogether immune from the virus, as safe in the citadel of
our ultimate faith as the Pope of Rome in his.

This is what we gained. But we set on one side, not only that
part of Moore's fifth chapter on 'Ethics in relation to Conduct'
which dealt with the obligation so to act as to produce by
causal connection the most probable maximum of eventual
good through the whole procession of future ages (a discussion
which was indeed riddled with fallacies), but also the part
which discussed the duty of the individual to obey general
rules. We entirely repudiated a personal liability on us to obey
general rules. We claimed the right to judge every individual
case on its merits, and the wisdom, experience and self-control
to do so successfully. This was a very important part of our
faith, violently and aggressively held, and for the outer world it
was our most obvious and dangerous characteristic. We repudiated entirely customary morals, conventions and traditional
wisdom. We were, that is to say, in the strict sense of the term,
immoralists. The consequences of being found out had, of
course, to be considered for what they were worth. But we
recognised no moral obligation on us, no inner sanction, to
conform or to obey. Before heaven we claimed to be our own

judge in our own case. I have come to think that this is, perhaps, rather a Russian characteristic. It is certainly not an English one. It resulted in a general, widespread, though partly covert, suspicion affecting ourselves, our motives and our [446] behaviour. This suspicion still persists to a certain extent, and it always will. It has deeply coloured the course of our lives in relation to the outside world. It is, I now think, a justifiable suspicion. Yet so far as I am concerned, it is too late to change. I remain, and always will remain, an immoralist.

I am not now concerned, however, with the fact that this aspect of our code was shocking. It would have been not less so, even if we had been perfectly right. What matters a great deal more is the fact that it was flimsily based, as I now think, on an *a priori* view of what human nature is like, both other people's and our own, which was disastrously mistaken.

I have said that we were amongst the first to escape from Benthamism. But of another eighteenth-century heresy we were the unrepentant heirs and last upholders. We were among the last of the Utopians, or meliorists as they are sometimes called, who believe in a continuing moral progress by virtue of which the human race already consists of reliable, rational, decent people, influenced by truth and objective standards, who can be safely released from the outward restraints of convention and traditional standards and inflexible rules of conduct, and left, from now onwards, to their own sensible devices, pure motives and reliable intuitions of the good. The view that human nature is reasonable had in 1903 quite a long history behind it. It underlay the ethics of self-interest – rational self-interest as it was called – just as much as the universal ethics of Kant or Bentham which aimed at the general good; and it was because self-interest was *rational* that the egoistic and altruistic systems were supposed to work out in practice to the same conclusions.

In short, we repudiated all versions of the doctrine of original sin, of there being insane and irrational springs of wickedness in most men. We were not aware that civilisation was a thin and precarious crust erected by the personality and the will of a very few, and only maintained by rules and conventions skilfully put across and guilefully preserved. We had no respect for traditional wisdom or the restraints of custom. We lacked reverence, as Lawrence observed and as Ludwig [Wittgenstein] [447] with justice also used to say – for everything and everyone. It did not occur to us to respect the extraordinary accomplishment of our predecessors in the ordering of life (as it now seems to me to have been) or the elaborate framework which they had devised to protect this order. Plato said in his *Laws* that one of the best of a set of good laws would be a law forbidding any young man to enquire which of them are right or wrong, though an old man remarking any defect in the laws might communicate this observation to a ruler or to an equal in years when no young man was present. That was a *dictum* in which we should have been unable to discover any point or significance whatever. As cause and consequence of our general state of mind we completely misunderstood human nature, including our own. The rationality which we attributed to it led to a superficiality, not only of judgment, but also of feeling. It was not only that intellectually we were pre-Freudian, but we had lost something which our predecessors had without replacing it. I still suffer incurably from attributing an unreal rationality to other people's feelings and behaviour (and doubtless to my own, too). There is one small but extraordinarily silly manifestation of this absurd idea of what is 'normal', namely the impulse to *protest* – to write a letter to *The Times*, call a meeting in the Guildhall, subscribe to some fund when my presuppositions as to what is 'normal' are not fulfilled. I behave as if there really existed some authority or standard to which I can successfully appeal if I shout loud enough – perhaps it is some hereditary vestige of a belief in the efficacy of prayer.

I have said that this pseudo-rational view of human nature led to a thinness, a superficiality, not only of judgment, but also of feeling. It seems to me that Moore's chapter on 'The Ideal' left out altogether some whole categories of valuable emotion. The attribution of rationality to human nature, instead of enriching it, now seems to me to have impoverished it. It ignored certain powerful and valuable springs of feeling. Some of the spontaneous, irrational outbursts of human nature can have a sort of value from which our schematism was cut off. [448]

Even some of the feelings associated with wickedness can have value. And in addition to the values arising out of spontaneous, volcanic and even wicked impulses, there are many objects of valuable contemplation and communion beyond those we knew of – those concerned with the order and pattern of life amongst communities and the emotions which they can inspire. Though one must ever remember Paley's *dictum* that 'although we speak of communities as of sentient beings and ascribe to them happiness and misery, desires, interests and passions, nothing really exists or feels but *individuals*', yet we carried the individualism of our individuals too far.

And as the years wore on towards 1914, the thinness and superficiality, as well as the falsity, of our view of man's heart became, as it now seems to me, more obvious; and there was, too, some falling away from the purity of the original doctrine. Concentration on moments of communion between a pair of lovers got thoroughly mixed up with the, once rejected, pleasure. The pattern of life would sometimes become no better than a succession of permutations of short sharp superficial 'intrigues', as we called them. Our comments on life and affairs were bright and amusing, but brittle – as I said of the conversation of Russell and myself with Lawrence – because there was no solid diagnosis of human nature underlying them. Bertie [Russell] in particular sustained simultaneously a pair of opinions ludicrously incompatible. He held that in fact human affairs were carried on after a most irrational fashion, but that the remedy was quite simple and easy, since all we had to do was to carry them on rationally. A discussion of practical affairs on these lines was really very boring. And a discussion of the human heart which ignored so many of its deeper and blinder passions, both good and bad, was scarcely more interesting. Indeed it is only states of mind that matter, provided we agree to take account of the pattern of life through time and give up regarding it as a series of independent, instantaneous flashes, [449] but the ways in which states of mind can be valuable, and the objects of them, are more various, and also much richer, than we allowed for. I fancy we used in old days to get round the rich variety of experience by expanding illegitimately the field of aesthetic appreciation (we would deal, for example, with all branches of the tragic emotion under this head), classifying as aesthetic experience what is really human experience and somehow sterilising it by this mis-classification.

If, therefore, I altogether ignore our merits – our charm, our intelligence, our unworldliness, our affection – I can see us as water-spiders, gracefully skimming, as light and reasonable as air, the surface of the stream without any contact at all with the eddies and currents underneath. And if I imagine us as coming under the observation of Lawrence's ignorant, jealous, irritable, hostile eyes, what a combination of qualities we offered to arouse his passionate distaste; this thin rationalism skipping on the crust of the lava, ignoring both the reality and the value of the vulgar passions, joined to libertinism and comprehensive irreverence, too clever by half for such an earthy character as Bunny [David Garnett], seducing with its intellectual *chic* such a portent as Ottoline, a regular skin-poison. All this was very unfair to poor, silly, well-meaning us. But that is why I say that there may have been just a grain of truth when Lawrence said in 1914 that we were 'done for'. [450]

TWO

The Social Philosopher

For Keynes economics was a means to social goals; his 'short-run' economic plans are set in a long-run perspective of economic progress which ends with the disappearance of capitalism.

The excerpts in this chapter show his concern with the unstable psychology of capitalist society, the social precariousness of the capitalist system and his hopes for a civilized future. They form the indispensable background of his commitment to stabilization, whether of the price level in the 1920s or employment in the 1930s.

Excerpts 7 and 8 emphasize what he calls the 'unstable and peculiar' conditions of pre-war Europe, and its new vulnerability to fluctuations in the value of money.

Excerpts 9–12, dating from 1924–30, touch on the moral inadequacy of capitalist civilization, and particularly on the contrast between its economic efficiency and its moral deficiencies, this latter reflection initiated by Keynes's visit to Soviet Russia in 1925. The contradiction arises from capitalism's most important motive, which Keynes calls 'love of money'.

Excerpt 12, 'Economic Possibilities for Our Grandchildren' (1930) ingeniously resolved the issue between capitalism and communism in favour of capitalism: capitalism is a felix culpa, 'extremely objectionable' in itself, but necessary as a means to produce the wealth which will enable people to live 'wisely and agreeably and well'.

Civilizational reflections are less frequent in the 1930s, when Keynes was mainly working on GT. But excerpt 13, 'National Self-Sufficiency' (1933), argues a principled case against international laissez-faire. *In excerpt 14, dating from 1945, Keynes commends a new institution, the Arts Council of Great Britain, as a modest preparation for the good life to come.*

7

CW 2, *The Economic Consequences of the Peace* (1919)

[*This was Keynes's attack on the economic clauses of the Treaty of Versailles, which formally ended the First World War. It was the book that first brought him world fame. His technical criticism of the Article on Reparations is considered in excerpt 15 in chapter 3 below, his policy proposals in excerpt 24 in chapter 4, and the famous portraits of the leading participants are given in excerpt 39 in chapter 5. The nub of his attack on the Treaty was moral and political: it involved a breach of faith, it did nothing to reconstruct Europe after the devastation of the war and it threatened dire political and social consequences, of which the Bolshevik Revolution in Russia was a grim portent. The first excerpt recalls the vanished world of pre-war Europe, the second the additional instability which the war created.*]

[*From chapter 2, 'Europe before 1914'.*]

After 1870 . . . the economic condition of Europe became during the next fifty years unstable and peculiar. The pressure of population on food, which had already been balanced by the accessibility of supplies from America, became for the first time in recorded history definitely reversed . . . Up to about 1900 a unit of labour applied to industry yielded year by year a purchasing power over an increasing quantity of food. As numbers increased, food was actually easier to secure. Larger proportional returns from an increasing scale of production became true of agriculture as well as industry. With the growth of the European population there were more emigrants on the one hand to till the soil of the new countries and, on the other, more

workmen were available in Europe to prepare the industrial products and capital goods which were to maintain the emigrant populations in their new homes, and to build the railways and ships which were to make accessible to Europe food and raw products from distant sources. It is possible that about the year 1900 this process began to be reversed, and a diminishing yield of nature to man's effort was beginning to assert itself. But the tendency of cereals to rise in real cost was balanced by other improvements; and – one of many novelties – the resources of tropical Africa then for the first time came into large employ. [5]
. . .

In this economic Eldorado, in this economic Utopia, as the earlier economists would have deemed it, most of us were brought up.

That happy age lost sight of a view of the world which filled with deep-seated melancholy the founders of our political economy. Before the eighteenth century mankind entertained no false hopes. To lay the illusions which grew popular at that age's latter end, Malthus disclosed a devil. For half a century all serious economical writings held that devil in clear prospect. For the next half century he was chained up and out of sight. Now perhaps we have loosed him again.

What an extraordinary episode in the economic progress of man that age was which came to an end in August 1914! The greater part of the population, it is true, worked hard and lived at a low standard of comfort, yet were, to all appearances, reasonably contented with this lot. But escape was possible, for any man of capacity or character at all exceeding the average, into the middle and upper classes, for whom life offered, at a low cost and with the least trouble, conveniences, comforts, and amenities beyond the compass of the richest and most powerful monarchs of other ages. The inhabitant of London could order by telephone, sipping his morning tea in bed, the various products of the whole earth, in such quantity as he might see fit, and reasonably expect their early delivery upon his doorstep; he could at the same moment and by the same means adventure his wealth in the natural resources and new enterprises of any quarter of the world, and share, without exertion or even trouble, in their prospective fruits and advantages; or he could decide to couple the security of his fortunes with the good faith of the townspeople of any substantial municipality in any continent that fancy or information might recommend. He could secure forthwith, if he wished it, cheap and comfortable means of transit to any country or climate without passport or other formality, could despatch his servant to the neighbouring office [6] of a bank for such supply of the precious metals as might seem convenient, and could then proceed abroad to foreign quarters, without knowledge of their religion, language, or customs, bearing coined wealth upon his person, and would consider himself greatly aggrieved and much surprised at the least interference. But, most important of all, he regarded this state of affairs as normal, certain, and permanent, except in the direction of further improvement, and any deviation from it as aberrant, scandalous, and avoidable. The projects and politics of militarism and imperialism, of racial and cultural rivalries, of monopolies, restrictions, and exclusion, which were to play the serpent to this paradise, were little more than the amusements of his daily newspaper, and appeared to exercise almost no influence at all on the ordinary course of social and economic life, the internationalisation of which was nearly complete in [7] practice.

. . .

The Psychology of Society

Europe was so organised socially and economically as to secure the maximum accumulation of capital. While there was some continuous improvement in the daily conditions of life of the mass of the population, society was so framed as to throw a great part of the increased income into the control of the class least likely to consume it. The new rich of the nineteenth century were not brought up to large expenditures, and preferred the power which investment gave them to the pleasures of immediate consumption. In fact, it was precisely the inequality of the distribution of wealth which made possible those vast accumulations of fixed wealth and of capital improvements which distinguished that age from all others. Herein lay, in fact, the main justification of the capitalist system. If the rich had spent their new wealth on their own enjoyments, the world would long ago have found such a regime intolerable. But like bees they saved and accumulated, not less to the advantage of the whole community because they themselves held narrower ends in prospect.

The immense accumulations of fixed capital which, to the great benefit of mankind, were built up during the half century before the war, could never have come about in a society where wealth was divided equitably. The railways of the world, which that age built as a monument to posterity, were, not less than the pyramids of Egypt, the work of labour which was not free to consume in immediate enjoyment the full equivalent of its efforts.

Thus this remarkable system depended for its growth on a double bluff or deception. On the one hand the labouring classes accepted from ignorance or powerlessness, or were compelled, [11] persuaded, or cajoled by custom, convention, authority, and the well-established order of society into accepting, a situation in which they could call their own very little of the cake that they and nature and the capitalists were co-operating to produce. And on the other hand the capitalist classes were allowed to call the best part of the cake theirs and were theoretically free to consume it, on the tacit underlying condition that they consumed very little of it in practice. The duty of 'saving' became nine-tenths of virtue and the growth of the cake the object of true religion. There grew round the non-consumption of the cake all those instincts of puritanism which in other ages has withdrawn itself from the world and has neglected the arts of production as well as those of enjoyment. And so the cake increased; but to what end was not clearly contemplated. Individuals would be exhorted not so much to abstain as to defer, and to cultivate the pleasures of security and anticipation. Saving was for old age or for your children; but this was only in theory – the virtue of the cake was that it was never to be consumed, neither by you nor by your children after you.

In writing thus I do not necessarily disparage the practices of that generation. In the unconscious recesses of its being society knew what it was about. The cake was really very small in proportion to the appetites of consumption, and no one, if it were shared all round, would be much the better off by the cutting of it. Society was working not for the small pleasures of today but for the future security and improvement of the race – in fact for 'progress'. If only the cake were not cut but was allowed to grow in the geometrical proportion predicted by Malthus of population, but not less true of compound interest, perhaps a day might come when there would at last be enough to go round, and when posterity could enter into the enjoyment of our labours. In that day overwork, overcrowding, and underfeeding would come to an end, and men, secure of the comforts and necessities of the body, could proceed to the nobler exercises

[12] of their faculties. One geometrical ratio might cancel another, and the nineteenth century was able to forget the fertility of the species in a contemplation of the dizzy virtues of compound interest.

There were two pitfalls in this prospect: lest, population still outstripping accumulation, our self-denials promote not happiness but numbers; and lest the cake be after all consumed, prematurely, in war, the consumer of all such hopes.

But these thoughts lead too far from my present purpose. I seek only to point out that the principle of accumulation based on inequality was a vital part of the pre-war order of society and of progress as we then understood it, and to emphasise that this principle depended on unstable psychological conditions, which it may be impossible to re-create. It was not natural for a population, of whom so few enjoyed the comforts of life, to accumulate so hugely. The war has disclosed the possibility of consumption to all and the vanity of abstinence to many. Thus the bluff is discovered; the labouring classes may be no longer willing to forgo so largely, and the capitalist classes, no longer confident of the future, may seek to enjoy more fully their liberties of consumption so long as they last, and thus precipitate the

[13] hour of their confiscation.

. . .

[*From chapter 6, 'Europe after the Treaty'.*]
Lenin is said to have declared that the best way to destroy the capitalist system was to debauch the currency. By a continuing

process of inflation, governments can confiscate, secretly and
unobserved, an important part of the wealth of their citizens. [148]
By this method they not only confiscate, but they confiscate
arbitrarily; and, while the process impoverishes many, it actually enriches some. The sight of this arbitrary rearrangement of
riches strikes not only at security, but at confidence in the
equity of the existing distribution of wealth. Those to whom
the system brings windfalls, beyond their deserts and even
beyond their expectations or desires, become 'profiteers', who
are the object of the hatred of the bourgeoisie, whom the infla-
tionism has impoverished, not less than of the proletariat. As
the inflation proceeds and the real value of the currency fluctuates wildly from month to month, all permanent relations
between debtors and creditors, which form the ultimate foundation of capitalism, become so utterly disordered as to be
almost meaningless; and the process of wealth-getting degener-
ates into a gamble and a lottery.

Lenin was certainly right. There is no subtler, no surer means
of overturning the existing basis of society than to debauch the
currency. The process engages all the hidden forces of economic
law on the side of destruction, and does it in a manner which
not one man in a million is able to diagnose.

In the latter stages of the war all the belligerent governments
practised, from necessity or incompetence, what a Bolshevist
might have done from design. Even now, when the war is over,
most of them continue out of weakness the same malpractices.
But further, the governments of Europe, being many of them at
this moment reckless in their methods as well as weak, seek to
direct on to a class known as 'profiteers' the popular indignation against the more obvious consequences of their vicious
methods. These 'profiteers' are, broadly speaking, the entrepreneur class of capitalists, that is to say, the active and constructive
element in the whole capitalist society, who in a period of rapidly rising prices cannot but get rich quick whether they wish it
or desire it or not. If prices are continually rising, every trader
who has purchased for stock or owns property and plant inevitably makes profits. By directing hatred against this class,
therefore, the European governments are carrying a step further

[149] the fatal process which the subtle mind of Lenin had consciously conceived. The profiteers are a consequence and not a cause of rising prices. By combining a popular hatred of the class of entrepreneurs with the blow already given to social security by the violent and arbitrary disturbance of contract and of the established equilibrium of wealth which is the inevitable result of inflation, these governments are fast rendering impossible a continuance of the social and economic order of the nineteenth century. But they have no plan for replacing it.

We are thus faced in Europe with the spectacle of an extraordinary weakness on the part of the great capitalist class, which has emerged from the industrial triumphs of the nineteenth century, and seemed a very few years ago our all-powerful master. The terror and personal timidity of the individuals of this class is now so great, their confidence in their place in society and in their necessity to the social organism so diminished, that they are the easy victims of intimidation. This was not so in England twenty-five years ago, any more than it is now in the United States. Then the capitalists believed in themselves, in their value to society, in the propriety of their continued existence in the full enjoyment of their riches and the unlimited exercise of their power. Now they tremble before every insult – call them pro-Germans, international financiers, or profiteers, and they will give you any ransom you choose to ask not to speak of them so harshly. They allow themselves to be ruined and altogether undone by their own instruments, governments of their own making, and a Press of which they are the proprietors. Perhaps it is historically true that no order of society ever perishes save by its own hand. In the complexer world of Western Europe the Immanent Will may achieve its ends more subtly and bring in the revolution no less inevitably through a Klotz [French finance minister] or a [Lloyd] George than by the intellectualisms, too ruthless and self-conscious for us, of the

[150] bloodthirsty philosophers of Russia.

8

CW 4, *A Tract on Monetary Reform* (1923)

[In TMR, Keynes continues the discussion of ECP on the effect of changes in prices on the distribution of wealth and the prestige of the capitalist class. Deflation, though, has replaced inflation as the evil of the day, and this leads Keynes to emphasize the importance of price stability. Chapter 1, 'The Consequences to Society of Changes in the Value of Money', analyses the effects of changing prices on class shares of the national income. Chapter 2, 'Public Finance and Changes in the Value of Money', describes why and how a government debauches the currency.]

[From chapter 1, 'The Consequences to Society of Changes in the Value of Money'. After analysing the differential effects of inflation and deflation, Keynes concludes:]

Each process, inflation and deflation alike, has inflicted great injuries. Each has an effect in altering the *distribution* of wealth between different classes, inflation in this respect being the worse of the two. Each has also an effect in overstimulating or retarding the *production* of wealth, though here deflation is the more injurious.   [3]

. . .

We see, therefore, that rising prices and falling prices each have their characteristic disadvantage. The inflation which causes the former means injustice to individuals and to classes, particularly to investors; and is therefore unfavourable to saving. The deflation which causes falling prices means impoverishment to labour and to enterprise by leading entrepreneurs to restrict production, in their endeavour to avoid loss to themselves; and is therefore disastrous to employment.   [35]

. . .

Thus inflation is unjust and deflation is inexpedient. Of the two perhaps deflation is, if we rule out exaggerated inflations such as that of Germany, the worse; because it is worse, in an impoverished world, to provoke unemployment than to disappoint the *rentier*. But it is not necessary that we should weigh one evil against the other. It is easier to agree that both are evils to be shunned. The individualistic capitalism of today, precisely because it entrusts saving to the individual investor and production to the individual employer, *presumes* a stable measuring-rod of value, and cannot be efficient – perhaps cannot survive – without one.

For these grave causes we must free ourselves from the deep distrust which exists against allowing the regulation of the standard of value to be the subject of *deliberate decision*. We can no longer afford to leave it in the category of which the distinguishing characteristics are possessed in different degrees by the weather, the birth rate, and the Constitution – matters which are settled by natural causes, or are the resultant of the separate action of many individuals acting independently, or

[36] require a revolution to change them.

. . .

[*From chapter 2, 'Public Finance and Changes in the Value of Money'*]

Inflation as a Method of Taxation

A government can live for a long time, even the German government or the Russian government, by printing paper money. That is to say, it can by this means secure the command over real resources, resources just as real as those obtained by taxation. The method is condemned, but its efficacy, up to a point, must be admitted. A government can live by this means when it can live by no other. It is the form of taxation which the public find hardest to evade and even the weakest government can enforce, when it can enforce nothing else. Of this character have been the progressive and catastrophic inflations practised in Central and Eastern Europe, as distinguished from the limited and oscillatory inflations, experienced for example in Great Britain and the United States,

[37] which have been examined in the preceding chapter.

. . .

Like other forms of taxation, these exactions, if overdone and out of proportion to the wealth of the community, must diminish its prosperity and lower its standards, so that at the lower standard of life the aggregate value of the currency may fall and still be enough to go round.   [39–40]

. . .

But sooner or later the second phase sets in. The public discover that it is the holders of notes who suffer taxation and defray the expenses of government, and they begin to change their habits and to economise in their holding of notes. They can do this in various ways: (1) instead of keeping some part of their ultimate reserves in money they can spend this money on durable objects, jewellery or household goods, and keep their reserves in this form instead; (2) they can reduce the amount of till money and pocket money that they keep and the average length of time for which they keep it, even at the cost of great personal inconvenience; and (3) they can employ foreign money in many transactions where it would have been more natural and convenient to use their own.   [41]

. . .

Nevertheless, it is evident that so long as the public use money at all, the government can continue to raise resources by inflation. Moreover, the conveniences of using money in daily life are so great that the public are prepared, rather than forgo them, to pay the inflationary tax, provided it is not raised to a prohibitive level. Like other conveniences of life the use of money is taxable, and, although for various reasons this particular form of taxation is highly inexpedient, a government can get resources by a *continuous* practice of inflation, even when this is foreseen by the public generally, unless the sums they seek to raise in this way are very grossly excessive. Just as a toll can be levied on the use of roads or a turnover tax on business transactions, so also on the use of money. The higher the toll and the tax, the less traffic on the roads, and the less business transacted, so also the less money carried. But some traffic is so indispensable, some business so profitable, some money payments so convenient, that only a very high levy will stop completely all traffic, all business, all payments. A government has to remember, however, that even if a tax is not prohibitive it may be unprofitable, and that a medium, rather

[43] than an extreme, imposition will yield the greatest gain ... In the last phase, when the use of the legal-tender money has been discarded for all purposes except trifling out-of-pocket expenditure, inflationary taxation has at last defeated itself. For in that case the total value of the note issue, which is sufficient to meet the public's minimum requirements, amounts to a figure relatively so trifling that the amount of resources which the government can hope to raise by yet further inflation – without pushing it to a point at which the money will be discarded even for out-of-pocket trifles – is correspondingly small. Thus at [44] last, unless it is employed with some measure of moderation, this potent instrument of governmental exaction breaks in the hands of those that use it, and leaves them at the same time with the rest of their fiscal system in total ruins – out of which, in the ebb and flow of the economic life of nations, may emerge once more a reformed and admirable system. The chervonetz of Moscow and the krone of Vienna are already stabler units [45] than the franc or the lira.

. . .

Currency Depreciation versus Capital Levy

[*After having discussed the rival claims of devaluation and capital levy as methods of reducing the national debt inherited from the war, Keynes continues.*]

There is a respectable and influential body of opinion which, repudiating with vehemence the adoption of either expedient, fulminates against devaluations and levies, on the ground that they infringe the untouchable sacredness of contract ... Yet such persons, by overlooking one of the greatest of all social principles, namely the fundamental distinction between the right of the individual to repudiate contract and the right of the State to control vested interest, are the worst enemies of what they seek to preserve. For nothing can preserve the integrity of contract between individuals, except a discretionary authority in the State to revise what has become intolerable. The powers of uninterrupted usury are too great. If the accretions of vested interest were to grow without mitigation for many generations, half the population would be no better than slaves to the other half. Nor can the fact that in time of war it is easier for the State to borrow than to tax, be allowed permanently to enslave the taxpayer to the bondholder. Those who insist that in these matters the State is in exactly the same position as the individual will, if they have their way, render impossible the continuance of an individualist society, which depends for its existence on moderation.

These conclusions might be deemed obvious if experience did not show that many conservative bankers regard it as more consonant with their cloth, and also as economising thought, to shift public discussion of financial topics off the logical onto an alleged 'moral' plane, which means a realm of thought where vested interest can be triumphant over the common good without further debate. But it makes them untrustworthy guides in a perilous era of transition. The State must never neglect the importance of so acting in ordinary matters as to promote certainty and security in business. But when great decisions are to be made, the State is a sovereign body of which the purpose is to promote the greatest good of the whole. When, therefore, we enter the realm of State action, *everything* [56] is to be considered and weighed on its merits. Changes in death duties, income tax, feudal rights, slavery, and so on throughout the ages, have received the same denunciations from the absolutists of contract, who are the real parents of revolution.   [57]

9

CW 9, 'The End of *Laissez-faire*' (1926)

[*This essay, first published separately by the Hogarth Press, was based on the Sidney Ball Lecture given by Keynes at Oxford in November 1924 and revised for a lecture he gave at the University of Berlin in June 1926. A truncated version appeared in* Essays in Persuasion. *It is Keynes's most learned essay in political economy, and I have retained his footnotes to illustrate his range of references.*]

I

The disposition towards public affairs, which we conveniently sum up as individualism and *laissez-faire*, drew its sustenance from many different rivulets of thought and springs of feeling. For more than a hundred years our philosophers ruled us because, by a miracle, they nearly all agreed or seemed to agree on this one thing. We do not dance even yet to a new tune. But a change is in the air. We hear but indistinctly what were once the clearest and most distinguishable voices which have ever instructed political mankind. The orchestra of diverse instruments, the chorus of articulate sound, is receding at last into the distance.

At the end of the seventeenth century the divine right of monarchs gave place to natural liberty and to the compact, and the divine right of the church to the principle of toleration, and to the view that a church is 'a voluntary society of men', coming together, in a way which is 'absolutely free and spontaneous'.* Fifty years later the divine origin and absolute voice of duty gave place to the calculations of utility. In the hands of Locke and Hume these doctrines founded Individualism. The compact presumed rights in the individual; the new ethics, being no more than a scientific study of the consequences of rational self-love, placed the individual at the centre. 'The sole trouble Virtue demands', said Hume, 'is that of just Calculation, and a steady preference of the greater Happiness.'†
[272] These ideas accorded with the practical notions of conservatives and of lawyers. They furnished a satisfactory intellectual foundation to the rights of property and to the liberty of the individual in possession to do what he liked with himself and with his own. This was one of the contributions of the eighteenth century to the air we still breathe.

The purpose of promoting the individual was to depose the monarch and the church; the effect – through the new ethical significance attributed to contract – was to buttress property and prescription. But it was not long before the claims of

---

* Locke, *A Letter Concerning Toleration*.
† *An Enquiry Concerning the Principles of Morals*, section LX.

society raised themselves anew against the individual. Paley
and Bentham accepted utilitarian hedonism* from the hands of
Hume and his predecessors, but enlarged it into social utility.
Rousseau took the Social Contract from Locke and drew out of
it the General Will. In each case the transition was made by
virtue of the new emphasis laid on equality. 'Locke applies his
Social Contract to modify the natural equality of mankind, so
far as that phrase implies equality of property or even of priv-
ilege, in consideration of general security. In Rousseau's version
equality is not only the starting-point but the goal.'†

Paley and Bentham reached the same destination, but by
different routes. Paley avoided an egoistic conclusion to his
hedonism by a God from the machine. 'Virtue', he says, 'is the
doing good to mankind, in obedience to the will of God, and for
the sake of everlasting happiness' – in this way bringing back *I*
and *others* to a parity. Bentham reached the same result by pure
reason. There is no rational ground, he argued, for preferring
the happiness of one individual, even oneself, to that of any
other. Hence the greatest happiness of the greatest number is
the sole rational object of conduct – taking utility from Hume, [273]
but forgetting that sage man's cynical corollary: ''Tis not contrary to reason to prefer the destruction of the whole world to
the scratching of my finger. 'Tis not contrary to reason for me to
choose my total ruin to prevent the least uneasiness of an Indian,
or person totally unknown to me . . . Reason is and ought only
to be the slave of the passions, and can never pretend to any
other office than to serve and obey them.'

Rousseau derived equality from the state of nature, Paley
from the will of God, Bentham from a mathematical law of
indifference. Equality and altruism had thus entered political

---

* 'I omit', says Archdeacon Paley, 'much usual declamation upon the dignity
and capacity of our nature, the superiority of the soul to the body, of the
rational to the animal part of our constitution; upon the worthiness, refinement, and delicacy of some satisfactions, and the meanness, grossness, and
sensuality of others: because I hold that pleasures differ in nothing but in continuance and intensity' (*Principles of Moral and Political Philosophy*, Bk
I, chap. 6).
† Leslie Stephen, *English Thought in the Eighteenth Century*, II, 192.

philosophy, and from Rousseau and Bentham in conjunction sprang both democracy and utilitarian socialism.

This is the second current – sprang from long-dead controversies, and carried on its way by long-exploded sophistries – which still permeates our atmosphere of thought. But it did not drive out the former current. It mixed with it. The early nineteenth century performed the miraculous union. It harmonised the conservative individualism of Locke, Hume, Johnson, and Burke with the socialism and democratic egalitarianism of Rousseau, Paley, Bentham, and Godwin.*

Nevertheless, that age would have been hard put to it to achieve this harmony of opposites if it had not been for the *economists*, who sprang into prominence just at the right moment. The idea of a divine harmony between private advantage and the public good is already apparent in Paley. But it was the economists who gave the notion a good scientific basis. Suppose that by the working of natural laws individuals pursuing their own interests with enlightenment in conditions of freedom always tend to promote the general interest at the same time! Our philosophical difficulties are resolved – at least [274] for the practical man, who can then concentrate his efforts on securing the necessary conditions of freedom. To the philosophical doctrine that government has no right to interfere, and the divine that it has no need to interfere, there is added a scientific proof that its interference is inexpedient. This is the third current of thought, just discoverable in Adam Smith, who was ready in the main to allow the public good to rest on 'the natural effort of every individual to better his own condition', but not fully and self-consciously developed until the nineteenth century begins. The principle of *laissez-faire* had arrived to harmonise individualism and socialism, and to make at one Hume's egoism with the greatest good of the greatest number.

* Godwin carried *laissez-faire* so far that he thought all government an evil, in which Bentham almost agreed with him. The doctrine of equality becomes with him one of extreme individualism, verging on anarchy. 'The universal exercise of private judgement', he says, 'is a doctrine so unspeakably beautiful that the true politician will certainly feel infinite reluctance in admitting the idea of interfering with it' (see Leslie Stephen, op. cit. II, 477).

The political philosopher could retire in favour of the business man – for the latter could attain the philosopher's *summum bonum* by just pursuing his own private profit.

Yet some other ingredients were needed to complete the pudding. First the corruption and incompetence of eighteenth-century government, many legacies of which survived into the nineteenth. The individualism of the political philosophers pointed to *laissez-faire*. The divine or scientific harmony (as the case might be) between private interest and public advantage pointed to *laissez-faire*. But above all, the ineptitude of public administrators strongly prejudiced the practical man in favour of *laissez-faire* – a sentiment which has by no means disappeared. Almost everything which the State did in the eighteenth century in excess of its minimum functions was, or seemed, injurious or unsuccessful.

On the other hand, material progress between 1750 and 1850 came from individual initiative, and owed almost nothing to the directive influence of organised society as a whole. Thus practical experience reinforced *a priori* reasonings. The philosophers and the economists told us that for sundry deep reasons unfettered private enterprise would promote the greatest good of the whole. What could suit the business man better? And could a practical observer, looking about him, deny that the blessings of improvement which distinguished the age [275] he lived in were traceable to the activities of individuals 'on the make'? Thus the ground was fertile for a doctrine that, whether on divine, natural, or scientific grounds, state action should be narrowly confined and economic life left, unregulated so far as may be, to the skill and good sense of individual citizens actuated by the admirable motive of trying to get on in the world.

By the time that the influence of Paley and his like was waning, the innovations of Darwin were shaking the foundations of belief. Nothing could seem more opposed than the old doctrine and the new – the doctrine which looked on the world as the work of the divine watchmaker and the doctrine which seemed to draw all things out of Chance, Chaos, and Old Time. But at this one point the new ideas bolstered up the old. The economists were teaching that wealth, commerce, and machinery were the children of free competition – that free competition built London. But the Darwinians could go one better than that – free competition had built man. The human eye was no longer the demonstration of design, miraculously contriving all things for the best; it was the supreme achievement of chance, operating under conditions of free competition and *laissez-faire*. The principle of the survival of the fittest could be regarded as a vast generalisation of the Ricardian economics. Socialistic interferences became, in the light of this grander synthesis, not merely inexpedient, but impious, as calculated to retard the onward movement of the mighty process by which we ourselves had risen like Aphrodite out of the primeval slime of ocean.

Therefore I trace the peculiar unity of the everyday political philosophy of the nineteenth century to the success with which it harmonised diversified and warring schools and united all good things to a single end. Hume and Paley, Burke and Rousseau, Godwin and Malthus, Cobbett and Huskisson, Bentham and Coleridge, Darwin and the Bishop of Oxford, were all, it [276] was discovered, preaching practically the same thing – individualism and *laissez-faire*. This was the Church of England and those her apostles, whilst the company of the economists were there to prove that the least deviation into impiety involved financial ruin.

These reasons and this atmosphere are the explanations, whether we know it or not – and most of us in these degenerate days are largely ignorant in the matter – why we feel such a strong bias in favour of *laissez-faire*, and why state action to regulate the value of money, or the course of investment, or the population, provokes such passionate suspicions in many upright breasts. We have not read these authors; we should consider their arguments preposterous if they were to fall into our hands. Nevertheless we should not, I fancy, think as we do, if Hobbes, Locke, Hume, Rousseau, Paley, Adam Smith, Bentham, and Miss Martineau had not thought and written as they did. A study of the history of opinion is a necessary preliminary to the emancipation of the mind. I do not know which makes a man more conservative – to know nothing but the present, or nothing but the past.

II

I have said that it was the economists who furnished the scientific pretext by which the practical man could solve the contradiction between egoism and socialism which emerged out of the philosophising of the eighteenth century and the decay of revealed religion. But having said this for shortness' sake, I hasten to qualify it. This is what the economists are *supposed* to have said. No such doctrine is really to be found in the writings of the greatest authorities. It is what the popularisers and the vulgarisers said. It is what the Utilitarians, who admitted Hume's egoism and Bentham's egalitarianism at the same time, were *driven* to believe in, if they were to effect a synthesis.* The language of the economists lent itself to the *laissez-faire* inter- [277] pretation. But the popularity of the doctrine must be laid at the door of the political philosophers of the day, whom it happened to suit, rather than of the political economists.

The maxim *laissez-nous faire* is traditionally attributed to the merchant Legendre addressing Colbert some time towards the end of the seventeenth century.† But there is no doubt that the first writer to use the phrase, and to use it in clear association with the doctrine, is the Marquis d'Argenson about 1751.‡ The Marquis was the first man to wax passionate on the economic advantages of governments leaving trade alone.

* One can sympathise with the view of Coleridge, as summarised by Leslie Stephen, that 'the Utilitarians destroyed every element of cohesion, made Society a struggle of selfish interests, and struck at the very roots of all order, patriotism, poetry, and religion'.

† 'Que faut-il faire pour vous aider?' asked Colbert. 'Nous laisser faire', answered Legendre.

‡ For the history of the phrase, see Oncken, 'Die Maxime Laissez faire et laissez passer', from whom most of the following quotations are taken. The claims of the Marquis d'Argenson were overlooked until Oncken put them forward, partly because the relevant passages published during his lifetime were anonymous (*Journal Œconomique*, 1751), and partly because his works were not published in full (though probably passed privately from hand to hand during his lifetime) until 1858 (*Mémoires et Journal inédit du Marquis d'Argenson*).

To govern better, he said, one must govern less.* The true cause of the decline of our manufactures, he declared, is the protection we have given to them.† 'Laissez faire, telle devrait être la devise de toute puissance publique, depuis que le monde est civilisé.' 'Detestable principe que celui de ne vouloir grandeur que par l'abaissement de nos voisins! Il n'y a que la méchanceté et la malignité du cœur de satisfaites dans ce principe, et l'intérêt y est opposé. Laissez faire, morbleu! Laissez faire!!'

Here we have the economic doctrine of *laissez-faire*, with its most fervent expression in free trade, fully clothed. The phrases and the idea must have passed current in Paris from that time on. But they were slow to establish themselves in literature; and the tradition associating with them the physiocrats, and particularly de Gournay and Quesnay, finds little support in the writings of this school, though they were, of course, proponents of the [278] essential harmony of social and individual interests. The phrase *laissez-faire* is not to be found in the works of Adam Smith, of Ricardo, or of Malthus. Even the idea is not present in a dogmatic form in any of these authors. Adam Smith, of course, was a Free Trader and an opponent of many eighteenth-century restrictions on trade. But his attitude towards the Navigation Acts and the usury laws shows that he was not dogmatic. Even his famous passage about 'the invisible hand' reflects the philosophy which we associate with Paley rather than the economic dogma of *laissez-faire*. As Sidgwick and Cliff Leslie have pointed out, Adam Smith's advocacy of the 'obvious and simple system of natural liberty' is derived from his theistic and optimistic view of the order of the world, as set forth in his *Theory of Moral Sentiments*, rather than from any proposition of political economy proper.‡ The phrase *laissez-faire* was, I think, first brought into popular usage in England by a well-known passage of Dr Franklin's.§ It is not, indeed, until we come to the later works

---

* 'Pour gouverner mieux, il faudrait gouverner moins.'
† 'On ne peut dire autant de nos fabriques: la vraie cause de leur declin, c'est la protection outrée qu'on leur accorde.'
‡ Sidgwick, *Principles of Political Economy*, p. 20.
§ Bentham uses the expression '*laissez-nous faire*' (*Works*, p. 440).

of Bentham – who was not an economist at all – that we discover
the rule of *laissez-faire*, in the shape in which our grandfathers
knew it, adopted into the service of the Utilitarian philosophy.
For example, in *A Manual of Political Economy*,* he writes:
'The general rule is that nothing ought to be done or attempted
by government; the motto or watchword of government, on
these occasions, ought to be – *Be quiet* ... The request which
agriculture, manufacturers, and commerce present to governments is as modest and reasonable as that which Diogenes made
to Alexander: Stand out of my sunshine.'

From this time on it was the political campaign for free
trade, the influence of the so-called Manchester School and of
the Benthamite Utilitarians, the utterances of secondary economic authorities, and the education stories of Miss Martineau
and Mrs Marcet, that fixed *laissez-faire* in the popular mind as
the practical conclusion of orthodox political economy – with [279]
this great difference, that the Malthusian view of population
having been accepted in the meantime by this same school of
thought, the optimistic *laissez-faire* of the last half of the eighteenth century gives place to the pessimistic *laissez-faire* of the
first half of the nineteenth century.†

In Mrs Marcet's *Conversations on Political Economy* (1817)
Caroline stands out as long as she can in favour of controlling
the expenditure of the rich. But by page 418 she has to admit
defeat:

CAROLINE. The more I learn upon this subject, the more I feel
convinced that the interests of nations, as well as those of individuals, so far from being opposed to each other, are in the most
perfect unison.

* Written in 1793, a chapter published in the Bibliothèque Britannique in
1798, and the whole first printed in Bowring's edition of his *Works* (1843).
† Cf. Sidgwick, op. cit. p. 22: 'Even those economists, who adhered in the
main to Adam Smith's limitations of the sphere of government, enforced these
limitations sadly rather than triumphantly; not as admirers of the social order
at present resulting from "natural liberty", but as convinced that it is at least
preferable to any artificial order that government might be able to substitute
for it.'

MRS B. Liberal and enlarged views will always lead to similar conclusions, and teach us to cherish sentiments of universal benevolence towards each other; hence the superiority of science over mere practical knowledge.

By 1850 the *Easy Lessons for the Use of Young People*, by Archbishop Whately, which the Society for Promoting Christian Knowledge was distributing wholesale, do not admit even of those doubts which Mrs B. allowed Caroline occasionally to entertain. 'More harm than good is likely to be done', the little book concludes, 'by almost any interference of Government with men's money transactions, whether letting and leasing, or buying and selling of any kind.' *True* liberty is 'that every man should be left free to dispose of his own property, his own time, and strength, and skill, in whatever way he himself may think fit, provided he does no wrong to his neighbours'.

In short, the dogma had got hold of the educational machine; it had become a copybook maxim. The political philosophy, which the seventeenth and eighteenth centuries had forged in order to throw down kings and prelates, had been made milk [280] for babes, and had literally entered the nursery.

Finally, in the works of Bastiat we reach the most extravagant and rhapsodical expression of the political economist's religion. In his *Harmonies Economiques*,

> I undertake [he says] to demonstrate the Harmony of those laws of Providence which govern human society. What makes these laws harmonious and not discordant is, that all principles, all motives, all springs of action, all interests, co-operate towards a grand final result ... And that result is, the indefinite approximation of all classes towards a level, which is always rising; in other words, the *equalisation* of individuals in the general *amelioration*.

And when, like other priests, he drafts his Credo, it runs as follows:

> I believe that He who has arranged the material universe has not withheld His regard from the arrangements of the social world. I

believe that He has combined and caused to move in harmony
free agents as well as inert molecules ... I believe that the invin-
cible social tendency is a constant approximation of men towards
a common moral, intellectual, and physical level, with, at the
same time, a progressive and indefinite elevation of that level. I
believe that all that is necessary to the gradual and peaceful development of humanity is that its tendencies should not be disturbed,
nor have the liberty of their movements destroyed.

From the time of John Stuart Mill, economists of authority
have been in strong reaction against all such ideas. 'Scarcely a
single English economist of repute', as Professor Cannan has
expressed it, 'will join in a frontal attack upon Socialism in
general,' though, as he also adds, 'nearly every economist,
whether of repute or not, is always ready to pick holes in most
socialistic proposals'.* Economists no longer have any link
with the theological or political philosophies out of which the
dogma of social harmony was born, and their scientific analysis
leads them to no such conclusions.

   Cairnes, in the introductory lecture on 'Political Economy
and *Laissez-faire*' which he delivered at University College,
London, in 1870, was perhaps the first orthodox economist to   [281]
deliver a frontal attack upon *laissez-faire* in general. 'The
maxim of *laissez-faire*', he declared, 'has no scientific basis
whatever, but is at best a mere handy rule of practice.'† This,
for fifty years past, has been the view of all leading economists.
Some of the most important work of Alfred Marshall – to take

* *Theories of Production and Distribution*, p. 494.
† Cairnes well described the 'prevailing notion' in the following passage from
the same lecture: 'The prevailing notion is that P.E. undertakes to show that
wealth may be most rapidly accumulated and most fairly distributed; that is to
say, that human well-being may be most effectually promoted, by the simple
process of leaving people to themselves; leaving individuals, that is to say, to
follow the promptings of self-interest, unrestrained either by State or by the
public opinion, so long as they abstain from force and fraud. This is the doctrine commonly known as *laissez-faire*; and accordingly political economy is,
I think, very generally regarded as a sort of scientific rendering of this maxim –
a vindication of freedom of individual enterprise and of contract as the one
and sufficient solution of all industrial problems.'

one instance – was directed to the elucidation of the leading cases in which private interest and social interest are *not* harmonious. Nevertheless, the guarded and undogmatic attitude of the best economists has not prevailed against the general opinion that an individualistic *laissez-faire* is both what they ought to teach and what in fact they do teach.

III

Economists, like other scientists, have chosen the hypothesis from which they set out, and which they offer to beginners, because it is the simplest, and not because it is the nearest to the facts. Partly for this reason, but partly, I admit, because they have been biased by the traditions of the subject, they have begun by assuming a state of affairs where the ideal distribution of productive resources can be brought about through individuals acting independently by the method of trial and error in such a way that those individuals who move in the right direction will destroy by competition those who move in the wrong direction. This implies that there must be no mercy or protection for those who embark their capital or their labour in the wrong direction. It is a method of bringing the most successful profit-makers to the top by a ruthless struggle for survival, [282] which selects the most efficient by the bankruptcy of the less efficient. It does not count the cost of the struggle, but looks only to the benefits of the final result which are assumed to be permanent. The object of life being to crop the leaves off the branches up to the greatest possible height, the likeliest way of achieving this end is to leave the giraffes with the longest necks to starve out those whose necks are shorter.

Corresponding to this method of attaining the ideal distribution of the instruments of production between different purposes, there is a similar assumption as to how to attain the ideal distribution of what is available for consumption. In the first place, each individual will discover what amongst the possible objects of consumption *he* wants most by the method of trial and error 'at the margin', and in this way not only will each consumer come to distribute his consumption most advantageously, but each object of consumption will find its way into the mouth of the consumer whose relish for it is greatest compared with that of the others, because that consumer will outbid the rest. Thus, if only we leave the giraffes to themselves, (1) the maximum quantity of leaves will be cropped because the giraffes with the longest necks will, by dint of starving out the others, get nearest to the trees; (2) each giraffe will make for the leaves which he finds most succulent amongst those in reach; and (3) the giraffes whose relish for a given leaf is greatest will crane most to reach it. In this way more and juicier leaves will be swallowed, and each individual leaf will reach the throat which thinks it deserves most effort.

This assumption, however, of conditions where unhindered natural selection leads to progress, is only one of the two provisional assumptions which, taken as literal truth, have become the twin buttresses of *laissez-faire*. The other one is the efficacy, and indeed the necessity, of the opportunity for unlimited private money-making as an incentive to maximum effort. Profit accrues, under *laissez-faire*, to the individual who, whether by skill or good fortune, is found with his productive resources in [283] the right place at the right time. A system which allows the skilful or fortunate individual to reap the whole fruits of this conjuncture evidently offers an immense incentive to the practice of the art of being in the right place at the right time. Thus one of the most powerful of human motives, namely, the love of money, is harnessed to the task of distributing economic resources in the way best calculated to increase wealth.

The parallelism between economic *laissez-faire* and Darwinianism, already briefly noted, is now seen, as Herbert Spencer was foremost to recognise, to be very close indeed. Just as Darwin invoked sexual love, acting through sexual selection, as an adjutant to natural selection by competition, to direct evolution along lines which should be desirable as well as effective, so the individualist invokes the love of money, acting through the pursuit of profit, as an adjutant to natural selection, to bring about the production on the greatest possible scale of what is most strongly desired as measured by exchange value.

The beauty and the simplicity of such a theory are so great that it is easy to forget that it follows not from the actual facts, but from an incomplete hypothesis introduced for the sake of simplicity. Apart from other objections to be mentioned later, the conclusion that individuals acting independently for their own advantage will produce the greatest aggregate of wealth, depends on a variety of unreal assumptions to the effect that the processes of production and consumption are in no way organic, that there exists a sufficient foreknowledge of conditions and requirements, and that there are adequate opportunities of obtaining this foreknowledge. For economists generally reserve for a later stage of their argument the complications which arise – (1) when the efficient units of production are large relatively to the units of consumption, (2) when overhead costs or joint costs are present, (3) when internal economies tend to the aggregation of production, (4) when the time required for adjustments is long, (5) when ignorance prevails over knowledge, and (6) when monopolies and combinations interfere with equality in bargaining – they reserve, that is to say, for a later stage their analysis of the actual facts. Moreover, many of those who recognise that the simplified hypothesis does not accurately correspond to fact conclude nevertheless that it does represent what is 'natural' and therefore ideal. They regard the simplified hypothesis as health, and the further complications as disease.

[284]

Yet besides this question of fact there are other considerations, familiar enough, which rightly bring into the calculation the cost and character of the competitive struggle itself, and the tendency for wealth to be distributed where it is not appreciated most. If we have the welfare of the giraffes at heart, we must not overlook the sufferings of the shorter necks who are starved out, or the sweet leaves which fall to the ground and are trampled underfoot in the struggle, or the overfeeding of the long-necked ones, or the evil look of anxiety or struggling greediness which overcasts the mild faces of the herd.

But the principles of *laissez-faire* have had other allies besides economic textbooks. It must be admitted that they have been confirmed in the minds of sound thinkers and the reasonable public by the poor quality of the opponent proposals – protectionism on one hand, and Marxian socialism on the other.

Yet these doctrines are both characterised, not only or chiefly by their infringing the general presumption in favour of *laissez-faire*, but by mere logical fallacy. Both are examples of poor thinking, of inability to analyse a process and follow it out to its conclusion. The arguments against them, though reinforced by the principle of *laissez-faire*, do not strictly require it. Of the two, protectionism is at least plausible, and the forces making for its popularity are nothing to wonder at. But Marxian socialism must always remain a portent to the historians of opinion – how a doctrine so illogical and so dull can have exercised so powerful and enduring an influence over the minds of men and, through them, the events of history. At any rate, the obvious [285] scientific deficiencies of these two schools greatly contributed to the prestige and authority of nineteenth-century *laissez-faire*.

Nor has the most notable divergence into centralised social action on a great scale – the conduct of the late war – encouraged reformers or dispelled old-fashioned prejudices. There is much to be said, it is true, on both sides. War experience in the organisation of socialised production has left some near observers optimistically anxious to repeat it in peace conditions. War socialism unquestionably achieved a production of wealth on a scale far greater than we ever knew in peace, for though the goods and services delivered were destined for immediate and fruitless extinction, none the less they were wealth. Nevertheless, the dissipation of effort was also prodigious, and the atmosphere of waste and not counting the cost was disgusting to any thrifty or provident spirit.

Finally, individualism and *laissez-faire* could not, in spite of their deep roots in the political and moral philosophies of the late eighteenth and early nineteenth centuries, have secured their lasting hold over the conduct of public affairs, if it had not been for their conformity with the needs and wishes of the business world of the day. They gave full scope to our erstwhile heroes, the great business men. 'At least one-half of the best ability in the Western world', Marshall used to say, 'is engaged in business.' A great part of 'the higher imagination' of the age was thus employed. It was on the activities of these men that our hopes of progress were centred.

Men of this class [Marshall wrote]* live in constantly shifting
visions, fashioned in their own brains, of various routes to their
desired end; of the difficulties which Nature will oppose to them
on each route, and of the contrivances by which they hope to get
the better of her opposition. This imagination gains little credit
with the people, because it is not allowed to run riot; its strength
is disciplined by a stronger will; and its highest glory is to have
attained great ends by means so simple that no one will know,
and none but experts will even guess, how a dozen other expedi-
[286]   ents, each suggesting as much brilliancy to the hasty observer,
were set aside in favour of it. The imagination of such a man is
employed, like that of the master chess-player, in forecasting the
obstacles which may be opposed to the successful issue of his
far-reaching projects, and constantly rejecting brilliant suggestions because he has pictured to himself the counter-strokes to
them. His strong nervous force is at the opposite extreme of
human nature from that nervous irresponsibility which conceives hasty Utopian schemes, and which is rather to be compared to the bold facility of a weak player, who will speedily
solve the most difficult chess problem by taking on himself to
move the black men as well as the white.

This is a fine picture of the great captain of industry, the
master-individualist, who serves us in serving himself, just as
any other artist does. Yet this one, in his turn, is becoming a
tarnished idol. We grow more doubtful whether it is he who
will lead us into paradise by the hand.

These many elements have contributed to the current intellectual bias, the mental make-up, the orthodoxy of the day. The
compelling force of many of the original reasons has disappeared but, as usual, the vitality of the conclusions outlasts
them. To suggest social action for the public good to the City
of London is like discussing the *Origin of Species* with a bishop
sixty years ago. The first reaction is not intellectual, but moral.
An orthodoxy is in question, and the more persuasive the arguments the graver the offence. Nevertheless, venturing into the

* 'The Social Possibilities of Economic Chivalry', *Economic Journal*, XVII
(1907), 9.

den of the lethargic monster, at any rate I have traced his claims and pedigree so as to show that he has ruled over us rather by hereditary right than by personal merit.

IV

Let us clear from the ground the metaphysical or general principles upon which, from time to time, *laissez-faire* has been founded. It is *not* true that individuals possess a prescriptive 'natural liberty' in their economic activities. There is no 'compact' conferring perpetual rights on those who Have or on those who Acquire. The world is *not* so governed from above [287] that private and social interest always coincide. It is *not* so managed here below that in practice they coincide. It is *not* a correct deduction from the principles of economics that enlightened self-interest always operates in the public interest. Nor is it true that self-interest generally *is* enlightened; more often individuals acting separately to promote their own ends are too ignorant or too weak to attain even these. Experience does *not* show that individuals, when they make up a social unit, are always less clear-sighted than when they act separately.

We cannot therefore settle on abstract grounds, but must handle on its merits in detail what Burke termed 'one of the finest problems in legislation, namely, to determine what the State ought to take upon itself to direct by the public wisdom, and what it ought to leave, with as little interference as possible, to individual exertion'.* We have to discriminate between what Bentham, in his forgotten but useful nomenclature, used to term *Agenda* and *Non-Agenda*, and to do this without Bentham's prior presumption that interference is, at the same time, 'generally needless' and 'generally pernicious'.† Perhaps the chief task of economists at this hour is to distinguish afresh the *Agenda* of government from the *Non-Agenda*; and the companion task of politics is to devise forms of government within a democracy which shall be capable of accomplishing

* Quoted by McCulloch in his *Principles of Political Economy*.
† Bentham's *Manual of Political Economy*, published posthumously, in Bowring's edition (1843).

the *Agenda*. I will illustrate what I have in mind by two examples.

(1) I believe that in many cases the ideal size for the unit of control and organisation lies somewhere between the individual and the modern State. I suggest, therefore, that progress lies in the growth and the recognition of semi-autonomous bodies within the State – bodies whose criterion of action within their own field is solely the public good as they understand it, and from whose deliberations motives of private advantage are excluded, though some place it may still be necessary to leave, [288] until the ambit of men's altruism grows wider, to the separate advantage of particular groups, classes, or faculties – bodies which in the ordinary course of affairs are mainly autonomous within their prescribed limitations, but are subject in the last resort to the sovereignty of the democracy expressed through Parliament.

I propose a return, it may be said, towards medieval conceptions of separate autonomies. But, in England at any rate, corporations are a mode of government which has never ceased to be important and is sympathetic to our institutions. It is easy to give examples, from what already exists, of separate autonomies which have attained or are approaching the mode I designate – the universities, the Bank of England, the Port of London Authority, even perhaps the railway companies. In Germany there are doubtless analogous instances.

But more interesting than these is the trend of joint stock institutions, when they have reached a certain age and size, to approximate to the status of public corporations rather than that of individualistic private enterprise. One of the most interesting and unnoticed developments of recent decades has been the tendency of big enterprise to socialise itself. A point arrives in the growth of a big institution – particularly a big railway or big public utility enterprise, but also a big bank or a big insurance company – at which the owners of the capital, i.e. the shareholders, are almost entirely dissociated from the management, with the result that the direct personal interest of the latter in the making of great profit becomes quite secondary. When this stage is reached, the general stability and reputation of the institution are the more considered by the management than the maximum of profit for the shareholders. The shareholders must be satisfied by conventionally adequate dividends; but once this is secured, the direct interest of the management often consists in avoiding criticism from the public and from the customers of the concern. This is particularly the case if their great size or semi-monopolistic position renders them conspicuous in the public eye and vulnerable to public attack. The extreme instance, perhaps, of this tendency in the case of an [289] institution, theoretically the unrestricted property of private persons, is the Bank of England. It is almost true to say that there is no class of persons in the kingdom of whom the Governor of the Bank of England thinks less when he decides on his policy than of his shareholders. Their rights, in excess of their conventional dividend, have already sunk to the neighbourhood of zero. But the same thing is partly true of many other big institutions. They are, as time goes on, socialising themselves.

Not that this is unmixed gain. The same causes promote conservatism and a waning of enterprise. In fact, we already have in these cases many of the faults as well as the advantages of State Socialism. Nevertheless, we see here, I think, a natural line of evolution. The battle of Socialism against unlimited private profit is being won in detail hour by hour. In these particular fields – it remains acute elsewhere – this is no longer the pressing problem. There is, for instance, no so-called important political question so really unimportant, so irrelevant to the reorganisation of the economic life of Great Britain, as the nationalisation of the railways.

It is true that many big undertakings, particularly public utility enterprises and other business requiring a large fixed capital, still need to be semi-socialised. But we must keep our minds flexible regarding the forms of this semi-socialism. We must take full advantage of the natural tendencies of the day, and we must probably prefer semi-autonomous corporations to organs of the central government for which ministers of State are directly responsible.

I criticise doctrinaire State Socialism, not because it seeks to engage men's altruistic impulses in the service of society, or because it departs from *laissez-faire*, or because it takes away from man's natural liberty to make a million, or because it has courage for bold experiments. All these things I applaud. I criticise it because it misses the significance of what is actually happening; because it is, in fact, little better than a dusty survival of a plan to meet the problems of fifty years ago, based on a misunderstanding of what someone said a hundred years ago. Nineteenth-century State Socialism sprang from Bentham, free competition, etc., and is in some respects a clearer, in some respects a more muddled version of just the same philosophy as underlies nineteenth-century individualism. Both equally laid all their stress on freedom, the one negatively to avoid limitations on existing freedom, the other positively to destroy natural or acquired monopolies. They are different reactions to the same intellectual atmosphere.

[290]

(2) I come next to a criterion of *Agenda* which is particularly relevant to what it is urgent and desirable to do in the near future. We must aim at separating those services which are *technically social* from those which are *technically individual*. The most important *Agenda* of the State relate not to those activities which private individuals are already fulfilling, but to those functions which fall outside the sphere of the individual, to those decisions which are made by *no one* if the State does not make them. The important thing for government is not to do things which individuals are doing already, and to do them a little better or a little worse; but to do those things which at present are not done at all.

It is not within the scope of my purpose on this occasion to develop practical policies. I limit myself, therefore, to naming some instances of what I mean from amongst those problems about which I happen to have thought most.

Many of the greatest economic evils of our time are the fruits of risk, uncertainty, and ignorance. It is because particular individuals, fortunate in situation or in abilities, are able to take advantage of uncertainty and ignorance, and also because for the same reason big business is often a lottery, that great inequalities of wealth come about; and these same factors are also the cause of the unemployment of labour, or the disappointment of reasonable business expectations, and of the impairment of efficiency and production. Yet the cure lies outside the operations of individuals; it may even be to the interest [291] of individuals to aggravate the disease. I believe that the cure for these things is partly to be sought in the deliberate control of the currency and of credit by a central institution, and partly in the collection and dissemination on a great scale of data relating to the business situation, including the full publicity, by law if necessary, of all business facts which it is useful to know. These measures would involve society in exercising directive intelligence through some appropriate organ of action over many of the inner intricacies of private business, yet it would leave private initiative and enterprise unhindered. Even if these measures prove insufficient, nevertheless, they will furnish us with better knowledge than we have now for taking the next step.

My second example relates to savings and investment. I believe that some coordinated act of intelligent judgement is required as to the scale on which it is desirable that the community as a whole should save, the scale on which these savings should go abroad in the form of foreign investments, and whether the present organisation of the investment market distributes savings along the most nationally productive channels. I do not think that these matters should be left entirely to the chances of private judgement and private profits, as they are at present.

My third example concerns population. The time has already come when each country needs a considered national policy about what size of population, whether larger or smaller than at present or the same, is most expedient. And having settled this policy, we must take steps to carry it into operation. The time may arrive a little later when the community as a whole must pay attention to the innate quality as well as to the mere numbers of its future members.

V

These reflections have been directed towards possible improvements in the technique of modern capitalism by the agency of [292] collective action. There is nothing in them which is seriously incompatible with what seems to me to be the essential characteristic of capitalism, namely the dependence upon an intense appeal to the money-making and money-loving instincts of individuals as the main motive force of the economic machine. Nor must I, so near to my end, stray towards other fields. Nevertheless, I may do well to remind you, in conclusion, that the fiercest contests and the most deeply felt divisions of opinion are likely to be waged in the coming years not round technical questions, where the arguments on either side are mainly economic, but round those which, for want of better words, may be called psychological or, perhaps, moral.

In Europe, or at least in some parts of Europe – but not, I think, in the United States of America – there is a latent reaction, somewhat widespread, against basing society to the extent that we do upon fostering, encouraging, and protecting the money-motives of individuals. A preference for arranging our affairs in such a way as to appeal to the money-motive as little as possible, rather than as much as possible, need not be entirely *a priori*, but may be based on the comparison of experiences. Different persons, according to their choice of profession, find the money-motive playing a large or a small part in their daily lives, and historians can tell us about other phases of social organisation in which this motive has played a much smaller part than it does now. Most religions and most philosophies deprecate, to say the least of it, a way of life mainly influenced by considerations of personal money profit. On the other hand, most men today reject ascetic notions and do not doubt the real advantages of wealth. Moreover, it seems obvious to them that one cannot do without the money-motive, and that, apart from certain admitted abuses, it does its job well. In the result the average man averts his attention from the problem, and has no clear idea what he really thinks and feels about the whole confounded matter.

[293]   Confusion of thought and feeling leads to confusion of speech. Many people, who are really objecting to capitalism as a way of life, argue as though they were objecting to it on the ground of its inefficiency in attaining its own objects. Contrariwise, devotees of capitalism are often unduly conservative, and reject reforms in its technique, which might really strengthen and

preserve it, for fear that they may prove to be first steps away from capitalism itself. Nevertheless, a time may be coming when we shall get clearer than at present as to when we are talking about capitalism as an efficient or inefficient technique, and when we are talking about it as desirable or objectionable in itself. For my part I think that capitalism, wisely managed, can probably be made more efficient for attaining economic ends than any alternative system yet in sight, but that in itself it is in many ways extremely objectionable. Our problem is to work out a social organisation which shall be as efficient as possible without offending our notions of a satisfactory way of life.

The next step forward must come, not from political agitation or premature experiments, but from thought. We need by an effort of the mind to elucidate our own feelings. At present our sympathy and our judgement are liable to be on different sides, which is a painful and paralysing state of mind. In the field of action reformers will not be successful until they can steadily pursue a clear and definite object with their intellects and their feelings in tune. There is no party in the world at present which appears to me to be pursuing right aims by right methods. Material poverty provides the incentive to change precisely in situations where there is very little margin for experiments. Material prosperity removes the incentive just when it might be safe to take a chance. Europe lacks the means, America the will, to make a move. We need a new set of convictions which spring naturally from a candid examination of our own inner feelings in relation to the outside facts.   [294]

10

CW 9, 'Am I a Liberal?' (1925)

[*First given as a lecture to the Liberal Summer School, in August 1925, then published as two articles in the* Nation and Athenaeum, *8 and 15 August 1925, then reproduced in* Essays in Persuasion. *In the first part of the lecture Keynes discusses whether he should join the Conservative, Liberal or Labour Party. He can't be a Conservative – 'they offer me neither food or drink – neither intellectual . . . nor spiritual nourishment'; the Labour Party repels by being a class party, 'and the class is not my class. I can be influenced by what seems to me to be justice and good sense; but the class war will find me on the side of the educated bourgeoisie.' That leaves the Liberal Party 'as the best instrument of future progress – if only it has strong leadership and the right programme' (pp. 296–7). As to the latter, he divided the 'questions of today' under five headings: (1) peace questions; (2) questions of government; (3) sex questions; (4) drug questions; (5) economic questions (p. 301). The excerpt starts with his discussion of (3).]*

The questions which I group together as sex questions have not been party questions in the past. But that was because they were never, or seldom, the subject of public discussion. All this is changed now. There are no subjects about which the big general public is more interested; few which are the subject of wider discussion. They are of the utmost social importance; they cannot help but provoke real and sincere differences of opinion. Some of them are deeply involved in the solution of certain economic questions. I cannot doubt that sex questions are about to enter the political arena. The very crude beginnings represented by the suffrage movement were only symptoms of deeper and more important issues below the surface.

Birth control and the use of contraceptives, marriage laws, the treatment of sexual offences and abnormalities, the economic position of women, the economic position of the family – in all these matters the existing state of the law and of orthodoxy is still medieval – altogether out of touch with civilised opinion and civilised practice and with what individuals, educated and uneducated alike, say to one another in private. Let no one deceive himself with the idea that the change of opinion on these matters is one which only affects a small educated class on the crust of the human boiling. Let no one suppose that it is the working women who are going to be shocked by ideas of birth control or of divorce reform. For them these things suggest new liberty, emancipation from the most intolerable of tyrannies. A party which would discuss these things openly and wisely at its meetings would discover a new and living interest [302] in the electorate – because politics would be dealing once more with matters about which everyone wants to know and which deeply affect everyone's own life.

These questions also interlock with economic issues which cannot be evaded. Birth control touches on one side the liberties of women, and on the other side the duty of the State to concern itself with the size of the population just as much as with the size of the army or the amount of the budget. The position of wage-earning women and the project of the family wage affect not only the status of women, the first in the performance of paid work, and the second in the performance of unpaid work, but also raise the whole question whether wages should be fixed by the forces of supply and demand in accordance with the orthodox theories of *laissez-faire*, or whether we should begin to limit the freedom of those forces by reference to what is 'fair' and 'reasonable' having regard to all the circumstances.

Drug questions in this country are practically limited to the drink question; though I should like to include gambling under this head. I expect that the prohibition of alcoholic spirits and of bookmakers would do good. But this would not settle the matter. How far is bored and suffering humanity to be allowed, from time to time, an escape, an excitement, a stimulus, a possibility of change? – that is the important problem. Is it possible to allow reasonable licence, permitted saturnalia, sanctified carnival, in conditions which need ruin neither the health nor the pockets of the roisterers, and will shelter from irresistible temptation the unhappy class who, in America, are called addicts?

I must not stay for an answer, but must hasten to the largest of all political questions, which are also those on which I am most qualified to speak – the economic questions.

An eminent American economist, Professor Commons, who has been one of the first to recognise the nature of the economic transition amidst the early stages of which we are now living, [303] distinguishes three epochs, three economic orders, upon the third of which we are entering.

The first is the era of scarcity 'whether due to inefficiency or to violence, war, custom, or superstition'. In such a period 'there is the minimum of individual liberty and the maximum of communistic, feudalistic or governmental control through physical coercion'. This was, with brief intervals in exceptional cases, the normal economic state of the world up to (say) the fifteenth or sixteenth century.

Next comes the era of abundance. 'In a period of extreme abundance there is the maximum of individual liberty, the minimum of coercive control through government, and individual bargaining takes the place of rationing.' During the seventeenth and eighteenth centuries we fought our way out of the bondage of scarcity into the free air of abundance, and in the nineteenth century this epoch culminated gloriously in the victories of *laissez-faire* and historic Liberalism. It is not surprising or discreditable that the veterans of the party cast backward glances on that easier age.

But we are now entering on a third era, which Professor Commons calls the period of stabilisation, and truly characterises as 'the actual alternative to Marx's communism'. In this period, he says, 'there is a diminution of individual liberty, enforced in part by governmental sanctions, but mainly by economic sanctions through concerted action, whether secret, semi-open, open, or arbitrational, of associations, corporations, unions, and other collective movements of manufacturers, merchants, labourers, farmers, and bankers'.

The abuses of this epoch in the realms of government are Fascism on the one side and Bolshevism on the other. Socialism offers no middle course, because it also is sprung from the presuppositions of the era of abundance, just as much as *laissez-faire* individualism and the free play of economic forces, before which latter, almost alone amongst men, the City editors, all [304] bloody and blindfolded, still piteously bow down.

The transition from economic anarchy to a regime which deliberately aims at controlling and directing economic forces in the interests of social justice and social stability, will present enormous difficulties both technical and political. I suggest, nevertheless, that the true destiny of New Liberalism is to seek [305] their solution.

II

CW 9, 'A Short View of Russia' (1925)

[*Keynes and his wife, Lydia Lopokova, visited Russia in September 1925 soon after their marriage, he as official representative of Cambridge University at the bicentennial celebrations of the Russian Academy of Sciences. Following the visit, he wrote the three articles which were later published as 'A Short View of Russia'. The articles first appeared in the* Nation and Athenaeum, *10, 17 and 25 October 1925, and were reprinted by the Hogarth Press as one of the series of Hogarth Essays in December of the same year. A shortened version appeared in* Essays in Persuasion. *Keynes's visit to Russia was a defining moment for him, setting him off on a track of thinking centring on the conflict between 'economic efficiency and moral efficiency'. Keynes started to use the phrase 'love of money' to describe the psychology of capitalist civilization. This essay was penned before the Stalin dictatorship had taken hold. It characterizes Soviet Communism as both a religion and an economic system.*]

What Is the Communist Faith?

It is extraordinarily difficult to be fair-minded about Russia. And even with fair-mindedness, how is a true impression to be conveyed of something so unfamiliar, shifting, and contradictory, of which no one in England has a background of knowledge or experience? No English newspaper has a regular correspondent resident in Russia. We rightly attach small credence to what the Soviet authorities say about themselves. Most of our news is from prejudiced labour deputations or from prejudiced émigrés. Thus a belt of fog separates us from what goes on in the other world where the Union of Soviet Socialist Republics rules and experiments and evolves a kind of order. Russia is suffering the penalty of years of 'propaganda' which, by taking away credence from words, almost destroys, in the end, the means of communication at a distance.

Leninism is a combination of two things which Europeans have kept for some centuries in different compartments of the soul – religion and business. We are shocked because the religion is new, and contemptuous because the business, being subordinated to the religion instead of the other way round, is highly inefficient.

Like other new religions, Leninism derives its power not from the multitude but from a small minority of enthusiastic converts, whose zeal and intolerance make each one the equal in strength of a hundred indifferentists. Like other new religions, it is led by those who can combine the new spirit, perhaps sincerely, with seeing a good deal more than their followers, politicians with at least an average dose of political cynicism, who can smile as well as frown, volatile experimentalists, released by religion from truth and mercy but not blinded to facts and expediency, and open therefore to the charge (superficial and useless though it is where politicians, lay or ecclesiastical, are concerned) of hypocrisy. Like other new religions, it seems to [256] take the colour and gaiety and freedom out of everyday life and to offer a drab substitute in the square wooden faces of its devotees. Like other new religions, it persecutes without justice or pity those who actively resist it. Like other new religions, it is filled with missionary ardour and œcumenical ambitions. But to say that Leninism is the faith of a persecuting and propagating minority of fanatics led by hypocrites is, after all, to say no more nor less than that it is a religion and not merely a party, and Lenin a Mahomet, not a Bismarck. If we want to frighten ourselves in our capitalist easy-chairs, we can picture the Communists of Russia as though the early Christians led by Attila were using the equipment of the Holy Inquisition and the Jesuit missions to enforce the literal economics of the New Testament; but when we want to comfort ourselves in the same chairs, can we hopefully repeat that these economics are fortunately so contrary to human nature that they cannot finance either missionaries or armies and will surely end in defeat?

There are three questions to answer. Is the new religion partly true, or sympathetic to the souls of modern men? Is it on the material side so inefficient as to render it incapable to survive? Will it, in the course of time, with sufficient dilution and added impurity, catch the multitude?

As for the first question, those who are completely satisfied by Christian capitalism or by egotistic capitalism untempered by subterfuge will not hesitate how to answer it; for they either have a religion or need none. But many, in this age without religion, are bound to feel a strong emotional curiosity towards any religion which is really new and not merely a recrudescence of old ones and has proved its motive force; and all the more when the new thing comes out of Russia, the beautiful and foolish youngest son of the European family, with hair on his head, nearer both to the earth and to heaven than his bald brothers in the West – who, having been born two centuries later, has been able to pick up the middle-aged disillusionment of the rest of the family before he has lost the genius of youth or become addicted to comfort and to habits. I sympathise with [257] those who seek for something good in Soviet Russia.

But when we come to the actual thing, what is one to say? For me, brought up in a free air undarkened by the horrors of religion, with nothing to be afraid of, Red Russia holds too much which is detestable. Comfort and habits let us be ready to forgo, but I am not ready for a creed which does not care how much it destroys the liberty and security of daily life, which uses deliberately the weapons of persecution, destruction, and international strife. How can I admire a policy which finds a characteristic expression in spending millions to suborn spies in every family and group at home, and to stir up trouble abroad? Perhaps this is no worse and has more purpose than the greedy, warlike, and imperialist propensities of other governments; but it must be far better than these to shift me out of my rut. How can I accept a doctrine which sets up as its bible, above and beyond criticism, an obsolete economic textbook which I know to be not only scientifically erroneous but without interest or application for the modern world? How can I adopt a creed which, preferring the mud to the fish, exalts the boorish proletariat above the bourgeois and the intelligentsia who, with whatever faults, are the quality in life and surely carry the seeds of all human advancement? Even if we need a religion, how can we find it in the turbid rubbish of the Red bookshops? It is hard for an educated, decent, intelligent son of western Europe to find his ideals here, unless he has first suffered some strange and horrid process of conversion which has changed all his values.

Yet we shall miss the essence of the new religion if we stop at this point. The Communist may justly reply that all these things belong not to his ultimate faith but to the tactics of revolution. For he believes in two things: the introduction of a new order upon earth, and the *method* of the revolution as the *only* means thereto. The new order must not be judged either by the horrors of the revolution or by the privations of the transitionary period. The revolution is to be a supreme example of the means justified by the end. The soldier of the revolution must crucify his own human nature, becoming unscrupulous and ruthless, and suffering himself a life without security or joy – but as the means to his purpose and not its end.

[258]

What, then, is the essence of the new religion as a new order upon earth? Looking from outside, I do not clearly know. Sometimes its mouthpieces speak as though it was purely materialistic and technical in just the same sense that modern capitalism is – as though, that is to say, Communism merely claimed to be in the long run a superior technical instrument for obtaining the same materialistic economic benefits as capitalism offers, that in time it will cause the fields to yield more and the forces of nature to be more straitly harnessed. In this case there is no religion after all, nothing but a bluff to facilitate a change to what may or may not be a better economic technique. But I suspect that, in fact, such talk is largely a reaction against the charges of economic inefficiency which we on our side launch, and that at the heart of Russian Communism there is something else of more concern to mankind.

In one respect Communism but follows other famous religions. It exalts the common man and makes him everything. Here there is nothing new. But there is another factor in it which also is not new but which may, nevertheless, in a changed form and a new setting, contribute something to the true religion of the future, if there be any true religion. *Leninism is*

*absolutely, defiantly non-supernatural, and its emotional and
ethical essence centres about the individual's and the community's attitude towards the love of money.*

I do not mean that Russian Communism alters, or even
seeks to alter, human nature, that it makes Jews less avaricious
or Russians less extravagant than they were before. I do not
merely mean that it sets up a new ideal. I mean that it tries to
construct a framework of society in which pecuniary motives
as influencing action shall have a changed relative importance, [259]
in which social approbations shall be differently distributed,
and where behaviour, which previously was normal and
respectable, ceases to be either the one or the other.

In England today a talented and virtuous youth, about to
enter the world, will balance the advantages of entering the
civil service and of seeking a fortune in business; and public
opinion will esteem him not less if he prefers the second.
Money-making, as such, on as large a scale as possible, is not
less respectable socially, perhaps more so, than a life devoted to
the service of the State or of religion, education, learning, or
art. But in the Russia of the future it is intended that the career
of money-making, as such, will simply not occur to a respectable young man as a possible opening, any more than the career
of a gentleman burglar or acquiring skill in forgery and embezzlement. Even the most admirable aspects of the love of money
in our existing society, such as thrift and saving, and the attainment of financial security and independence for one's self and
one's family, whilst not deemed morally wrong, will be rendered so difficult and impracticable as to be not worth while.
Everyone should work for the community – the new creed
runs – and, if he does his duty, the community will uphold him.

This system does not mean a complete levelling down of
incomes – at least at the present stage. A clever and successful
person in Soviet Russia has a bigger income and a better time
than other people. The commissar with £5 a week (*plus* sundry
free services, a motor-car, a flat, a box at the ballet, etc.) lives
well enough, but not *in the least* like a rich man in London. The
successful professor or civil servant with £6 or £7 a week
(*minus* sundry impositions), has, perhaps, a real income three

times those of the proletarian workers and six times those of the poorer peasants. Some peasants are three or four times richer than others. A man who is out of work receives part pay, [260] not full pay. But no one can afford on these incomes, with high Russian prices and stiff progressive taxes, to save anything worth saving; it is hard enough to live day by day. The progressive taxation and the mode of assessing rents and other charges are such that it is actually disadvantageous to have an acknowledged income exceeding £8 to £10 a week. Nor is there any possibility of large gains except by taking the same sort of risks as attach to bribery and embezzlement elsewhere – not that bribery and embezzlement have disappeared in Russia or are even rare, but anyone whose extravagance or whose instincts drive him to such courses runs serious risk of detection and penalties which include death.

Nor, at the present stage, does the system involve the actual prohibition of buying and selling at a profit. The policy is not to forbid these professions, but to render them precarious and disgraceful. The private trader is a sort of permitted outlaw, without privileges or protection, like the Jew in the Middle Ages – an outlet for those who have overwhelming instincts in this direction, but not a natural or agreeable job for the normal man.

The effect of these social changes has been, I think, to make a real change in the predominant attitude towards money, and will probably make a far greater change when a new generation has grown up which has known nothing else. People in Russia, if only because of their poverty, are very greedy for money – at least as greedy as elsewhere. But money-making and money accumulating cannot enter into the life-calculations of a rational man who accepts the Soviet rule in the way in which they enter into ours. A society of which this is even partially true is a tremendous innovation.

Now all this may prove Utopian, or destructive of true welfare, though, perhaps, not so Utopian, pursued in an intense religious spirit, as it would be if it were pursued in a matter-of-fact way. But is it appropriate to assume, as most of us have [261] assumed hitherto, that it is insincere or wicked?

The Economics of Soviet Russia

We shall not understand Leninism unless we view it as being at the same time a persecuting and missionary religion and an experimental economic technique. What of the second aspect – Is the economic technique so inefficient that it courts disaster?

The economic system of Soviet Russia has undergone and is undergoing such rapid changes that it is impossible to obtain a precise and accurate account of it. The method of trial-and-error is unreservedly employed. No one has ever been more frankly experimentalist than Lenin was in everything which did not touch the central truths of his faith. At first there was much confusion as to what was essential and what not. For example, the doctrine held at the outset that money must be abolished for most purposes is now seen to be erroneous, there being nothing inconsistent with the essence of Communism in continuing to use money as an instrument of distribution and calculation. The government has also come round to the view that it is wiser to combine a policy of limited toleration with intermittent teasing and harrying towards (for example) the old intelligentsia who have stuck to their country, towards private traders, and even towards foreign capitalists, rather than to attempt to crush out these elements altogether – trusting on the one hand to the complete control of the educational machine and the upbringing of the young, and on the other hand to the gradual improvement of the technique of state trading and to the growth of state capital, to dispense with these pagan auxiliaries in course of time. Thus almost all the members of the non-Communist intelligentsia with pre-war educations are now in the service of the government, often in important and responsible posts with relatively high salaries; private trade is again lawful, though precarious and difficult; and foreign capitalists, who grant short-period trade credits against government imports into Russia, can reckon for the present with some certainty, in my opinion, that they will see their money back in due course. The fluctuating pursuits of [262] these expediencies make it difficult to generalise about anything in Soviet Russia. Almost everything one can say about the country is true and false at the same time – which is the reason why friendly and hostile critics can each in good faith produce totally different pictures of the same thing.

A further difficulty in estimating the efficiency of the economic system is caused by the hard material conditions attending its earlier years, which would have tried severely any economic system. The material losses and disorganisation of the Great War were followed by those of a succession of civil wars, by outlawry from the rest of the world, and by several bad harvests. The bad harvests were partly due to bad management as well as to bad luck. Nevertheless the Soviet experimentalists can fairly claim, I think, that at least five years of peace and fair weather must elapse before they can be judged merely by results.

If one is to make any generalisation in present conditions, it must be this – that at a low level of efficiency the system does function and possesses elements of permanence. I estimate the truth about the economic condition of Russia in its present phase to be roughly as follows.

. . .

[*Keynes explains how Russia's urban population is supported by exploiting the peasantry through price policy (pp. 263–6). This was before the forced collectivization of the farms by Stalin, which started in 1930. The essay then continues.*]

Communism's Power to Survive

My third question is not yet answered. Can Communism in the course of time, with sufficient dilution and added impurity, catch the multitude?

I cannot answer what only time will show. But I feel confident of one conclusion – that if Communism achieves a certain success, it will achieve it, not as an improved economic technique, but as a religion. The tendency of our conventional criticisms is to make two opposed mistakes. We hate Communism so much, regarded as a religion, that we exaggerate its economic inefficiency; and we are so much impressed by its economic inefficiency that we under-estimate it as a religion.

On the economic side I cannot perceive that Russian Communism has made any contribution to our economic problems of intellectual interest or scientific value. I do not think that it

[266]

contains, or is likely to contain, any piece of useful economic technique which we could not apply, if we chose, with equal or greater success in a society which retained all the marks, I will not say of nineteenth-century individualistic capitalism, but of British bourgeois ideals. Theoretically at least, I do not believe that there is any economic improvement for which revolution is a necessary instrument. On the other hand, we have everything to lose by the methods of violent change. In Western industrial conditions the tactics of Red revolution would throw the whole population into a pit of poverty and death.

But as a religion what are its forces? Perhaps they are considerable. The exaltation of the common man is a dogma which has caught the multitude before now. Any religion and the bond which unites co-religionists have power against the egotistic atomism of the irreligious.

For modern capitalism is absolutely irreligious, without internal union, without much public spirit, often, though not always, a mere congeries of possessors and pursuers. Such a system has to be immensely, not merely moderately, successful to survive. In the nineteenth century it was in a certain sense idealistic; at any rate it was a united and self-confident system. It was not only immensely successful, but held out hopes of a continuing crescendo of prospective successes. Today it is only moderately successful. If irreligious capitalism is ultimately to defeat religious Communism it is not enough that it should be economically [267] more efficient – it must be many times as efficient.

We used to believe that modern capitalism was capable, not merely of maintaining the existing standards of life, but of leading us gradually into an economic paradise where we should be comparatively free from economic cares. Now we doubt whether the business man is leading us to a destination far better than our present place. Regarded as a means he is tolerable; regarded as an end he is not so satisfactory. One begins to wonder whether the material advantages of keeping business and religion in different compartments are sufficient to balance the moral disadvantages. The Protestant and Puritan could separate them comfortably because the first activity pertained to earth and the second to heaven, which was elsewhere. The believer in progress could separate them comfortably because he regarded the first as the means to the establishment of heaven upon earth hereafter. But there is a third state of mind, in which we do not fully believe either in a heaven which is elsewhere or in progress as a sure means towards a heaven upon earth hereafter; and if heaven is not elsewhere and not hereafter, it must be here and now or not at all. If there is no moral objective in economic progress, then it follows that we must not sacrifice, even for a day, moral to material advantage – in other words, that we may no longer keep business and religion in separate compartments of the soul. In so far as a man's thoughts are capable of straying along these paths, he will be ready to search with curiosity for something at the heart of Communism quite different from the picture of its outward parts which our press paints.

At any rate to me it seems clearer every day that the moral problem of our age is concerned with the love of money, with the habitual appeal to the money motive in nine-tenths of the activities of life, with the universal striving after individual economic security as the prime object of endeavour, with the social [268] approbation of money as the measure of constructive success, and with the social appeal to the hoarding instinct as the foundation of the necessary provision for the family and for the future. The decaying religions around us, which have less and less interest for most people unless it be as an agreeable form of magical ceremonial or of social observance, have lost their moral significance just because – unlike some of their earlier versions – they do not touch in the least degree on these essential matters. A revolution in our ways of thinking and feeling about money may become the growing purpose of contemporary embodiments of the ideal. Perhaps, therefore, Russian Communism does represent the first confused stirrings of a [269] great religion.

. . .

For how much rather, even after allowing for everything, if I were a Russian, would I contribute my quota of activity to Soviet Russia than to Tsarist Russia! I could not subscribe to the new official faith any more than to the old. I should detest the actions of the new tyrants not less than those of the old. But I should feel that my eyes were turned towards, and no longer away from, the possibilities of things; that out of the cruelty and stupidity of Old Russia nothing could ever emerge, but that beneath the cruelty and stupidity of New Russia some speck of the ideal may lie hid.   [271]

12

CW 9, 'Economic Possibilities for Our Grandchildren' (1930)

[*On 6 November 1925, Keynes wrote to his wife: 'This morning I felt a little inspiration and wrote some philosophical pages about Love of Money.' These include the following, dated 23 December 1925 (KP: TM2/7, TM/2/241-6).*]

The . . . test of money measurement constantly tends to minimise the area where we weigh concrete goods against abstract money. Our imaginations are too weak for the choice, abstract money overweighs them. The sanctification of saving tends dangerously on the side of abstract money. The growth of individual wealth does the same.

It would not be good for us to know the consequences of all our actions in terms of money. We should be transmuting real values into money values without enough knowledge or strength of imagination to translate them back again; so that we should be making unreal decisions all the time; e.g. suppose we were to know beforehand with certainty the different incomes which would ensue from different ways of [life?]

It is not right to sacrifice the present to the future unless we can conceive of the future in sufficiently concrete terms, in terms approximately as concrete as the present sacrifice, to be sure that the exchange was worth while.

We ought more often to be in the state of mind, as it were, of not counting the money cost at all.

. . .

We want to diminish, rather than to increase, the area of monetary comparisons.

[*When he wrote these pages, Keynes was in the throes of his 'Babylonian madness' – he had embarked on a book on ancient currencies (never completed), and the following may come from a fragment of that work.*]
The fluctuations of history [are] due to the fact that the social system which is economically efficient is morally inefficient. The Babylonian economy raises states to great affluence and comfort and this leads to their collapse for moral reasons.

The fundamental problem of the human race [is] to find a social system which is efficient economically and morally.

[*From EP (CW 9, p. xviii) comes the following, dated 8 November 1931.*]
Thus the author of these essays . . . still hopes and believes that the day is not far off when the economic problem will take the back seat where it belongs, and that the arena of the heart and the head will be occupied, or reoccupied, by our real problems, the problems of life and of human relations, of creation and behaviour and religion. And it happens that there is a subtle reason drawn from economic analysis why, in this case, faith may work. For if we consistently act on the optimistic hypothesis, this hypothesis will tend to be realised; whilst by acting on the pessimistic hypothesis we can keep ourselves for ever in the pit of want.

[*The 'subtle reason' was given in Keynes's 'futuristic' essay 'Economic Possibilities for our Grandchildren', first read as a talk in 1928 and published in* Essays in Persuasion *three years later.*][1]

I

We are suffering just now from a bad attack of economic pessimism. It is common to hear people say that the epoch of enormous economic progress which characterised the nineteenth century is over; that the rapid improvement in the standard of life is now going to slow down – at any rate in Great Britain; that a decline in prosperity is more likely than an improvement in the decade which lies ahead of us.

I believe that this is a wildly mistaken interpretation of what is happening to us. We are suffering, not from the rheumatics of old age, but from the growing-pains of over-rapid changes, from the painfulness of readjustment between one economic period and another. The increase of technical efficiency has been taking place faster than we can deal with the problem of labour absorption; the improvement in the standard of life has been a little too quick; the banking and monetary system of the world has been preventing the rate of interest from falling as fast as equilibrium requires. And even so, the waste and confusion which ensue relate to no more than 7½ per cent of the national income.   [321]

. . .

The prevailing world depression, the enormous anomaly of unemployment in a world full of wants, the disastrous mistakes we have made, blind us to what is going on under the surface – to the true interpretation of the trend of things. For I predict that both of the two opposed errors of pessimism which now make so much noise in the world will be proved wrong in our own time – the pessimism of the revolutionaries who think that things are so bad that nothing can save us but violent change, and the pessimism of the reactionaries who consider the balance of our economic and social life so precarious that we must risk no experiments.

My purpose in this essay, however, is not to examine the present or the near future, but to disembarrass myself of short views and take wings into the future. What can we reasonably expect the level of our economic life to be a hundred years hence? What are the economic possibilities for our grandchildren?

From the earliest times of which we have record – back, say to two thousand years before Christ – down to the beginning of the eighteenth century, there was no very great change in the standard of life of the average man living in the civilised centres of the earth. Ups and downs certainly. Visitations of plague, famine, and war. Golden intervals. But no progressive, violent

change. Some periods perhaps 50 per cent better than others –
at the utmost 100 per cent better – in the four thousand years
[322] which ended (say) in A.D. 1700. This slow rate of progress, or
lack of progress, was due to two reasons – to the remarkable
absence of important technical improvements and to the failure
of capital to accumulate.

The absence of important technical inventions between the
prehistoric age and comparatively modern times is truly remarkable. Almost everything which really matters and which the
world possessed at the commencement of the modern age was
already known to man at the dawn of history. Language, fire, the
same domestic animals which we have today, wheat, barley, the
vine and the olive, the plough, the wheel, the oar, the sail, leather,
linen and cloth, bricks and pots, gold and silver, copper, tin,
and lead – and iron was added to the list before 1000 B.C. –
banking, statecraft, mathematics, astronomy, and religion. There
is no record of when we first possessed these things.

At some epoch before the dawn of history – perhaps even in
one of the comfortable intervals before the last ice age – there
must have been an era of progress and invention comparable to
that in which we live today. But through the greater part of
recorded history there was nothing of the kind.

The modern age opened, I think, with the accumulation of
capital which began in the sixteenth century. I believe – for reasons with which I must not encumber the present argument – that
this was initially due to the rise of prices, and the profits to
which that led, which resulted from the treasure of gold and
silver which Spain brought from the New World into the Old.
From that time until today the power of accumulation by compound interest, which seems to have been sleeping for many
generations, was reborn and renewed its strength. And the
power of compound interest over two hundred years is such as
to stagger the imagination.

Let me give in illustration of this a sum which I have worked
out. The value of Great Britain's foreign investments today is
estimated at about £4,000 million. This yields us an income at
[323] the rate of about 6½ per cent. Half of this we bring home and
enjoy; the other half, namely, 3¼ per cent, we leave to accumulate

abroad at compound interest. Something of this sort has now been going on for about 250 years.

For I trace the beginnings of British foreign investment to the treasure which Drake stole from Spain in 1580. In that year he returned to England bringing with him the prodigious spoils of the *Golden Hind*. Queen Elizabeth was a considerable share-holder in the syndicate which had financed the expedition. Out of her share she paid off the whole of England's foreign debt, balanced her budget, and found herself with about £40,000 in hand. This she invested in the Levant Company – which prospered. Out of the profits of the Levant Company, the East India Company was founded; and the profits of this great enterprise were the foundation of England's subsequent foreign investment. Now it happens that £40,000 accumulating at 3¼ per cent compound interest approximately corresponds to the actual volume of England's foreign investments at various dates, and would actually amount today to the total of £4,000 million which I have already quoted as being what our foreign investments now are. Thus, every £1 which Drake brought home in 1580 has now become £100,000. Such is the power of compound interest![2]

From the sixteenth century, with a cumulative crescendo after the eighteenth, the great age of science and technical inventions began, which since the beginning of the nineteenth century has been in full flood – coal, steam, electricity, petrol, steel, rubber, cotton, the chemical industries, automatic machinery and the methods of mass production, wireless, printing, Newton, Darwin, and Einstein, and thousands of other things and men too famous and familiar to catalogue.

What is the result? In spite of an enormous growth in the population of the world, which it has been necessary to equip with houses and machines, the average standard of life in Europe and the United States has been raised, I think, about fourfold. The growth of capital has been on a scale which is far [324] beyond a hundred-fold of what any previous age had known. And from now on we need not expect so great an increase of population.

If capital increases, say, 2 per cent per annum, the capital equipment of the world will have increased by a half in twenty years, and seven and a half times in a hundred years. Think of this in terms of material things – houses, transport, and the like.

At the same time technical improvements in manufacture and transport have been proceeding at a greater rate in the last ten years than ever before in history. In the United States factory output per head was 40 per cent greater in 1925 than in 1919. In Europe we are held back by temporary obstacles, but even so it is safe to say that technical efficiency is increasing by more than 1 per cent per annum compound. There is evidence that the revolutionary technical changes, which have so far chiefly affected industry, may soon be attacking agriculture. We may be on the eve of improvements in the efficiency of food production as great as those which have already taken place in mining, manufacture, and transport. In quite a few years – in our own lifetimes I mean – we may be able to perform all the operations of agriculture, mining, and manufacture with a quarter of the human effort to which we have been accustomed.

For the moment the very rapidity of these changes is hurting us and bringing difficult problems to solve. Those countries are suffering relatively which are not in the vanguard of progress. We are being afflicted with a new disease of which some readers may not yet have heard the name, but of which they will hear a great deal in the years to come – namely, *technological unemployment*. This means unemployment due to our discovery of means of economising the use of labour outrunning the pace at which we can find new uses for labour. But this is only a temporary phase of maladjustment. All this means in the long run *that mankind is solving its economic problem*. I would predict that the standard of life in progressive countries one hundred years hence will be between four and eight times as high as it is today. There would be nothing surprising in this even in the light of our present knowledge. It would not be foolish to contemplate the possibility of a far greater progress still.

[325]

II

Let us, for the sake of argument, suppose that a hundred years hence we are all of us, on the average, eight times better off in the economic sense than we are today. Assuredly there need be nothing here to surprise us.

Now it is true that the needs of human beings may seem to be insatiable. But they fall into two classes – those needs which are absolute in the sense that we feel them whatever the situation of our fellow human beings may be, and those which are relative in the sense that we feel them only if their satisfaction lifts us above, makes us feel superior to, our fellows. Needs of the second class, those which satisfy the desire for superiority, may indeed be insatiable; for the higher the general level, the higher still are they. But this is not so true of the absolute needs – a point may soon be reached, much sooner perhaps than we all of us are aware of, when these needs are satisfied in the sense that we prefer to devote our further energies to non-economic purposes.

Now for my conclusion, which you will find, I think, to become more and more startling to the imagination the longer you think about it.

I draw the conclusion that, assuming no important wars and no important increase in population, the *economic problem* may be solved, or be at least within sight of solution, within a hundred years. This means that the economic problem is not – if we look into the future – *the permanent problem of the human race.*

Why, you may ask, is this so startling? It is startling because – if, instead of looking into the future, we look into the past – we find that the economic problem, the struggle for subsistence, [326] always has been hitherto the primary, most pressing problem of the human race – not only of the human race, but of the whole of the biological kingdom from the beginnings of life in its most primitive forms.

Thus we have been expressly evolved by nature – with all our impulses and deepest instincts – for the purpose of solving the economic problem. If the economic problem is solved, mankind will be deprived of its traditional purpose.

Will this be a benefit? If one believes at all in the real values of life, the prospect at least opens up the possibility of benefit. Yet I think with dread of the readjustment of the habits and instincts of the ordinary man, bred into him for countless generations, which he may be asked to discard within a few decades.

To use the language of today – must we not expect a general 'nervous breakdown'? We already have a little experience of what I mean – a nervous breakdown of the sort which is already common enough in England and the United States amongst the wives of the well-to-do classes, unfortunate women, many of them, who have been deprived by their wealth of their traditional tasks and occupations – who cannot find it sufficiently amusing, when deprived of the spur of economic necessity, to cook and clean and mend, yet are quite unable to find anything more amusing.

To those who sweat for their daily bread leisure is a longed-for sweet – until they get it.

There is the traditional epitaph written for herself by the old charwoman:

> Don't mourn for me, friends, don't weep for me never,
> For I'm going to do nothing for ever and ever.

This was her heaven. Like others who look forward to leisure, she conceived how nice it would be to spend her time listening-in – for there was another couplet which occurred in her poem:

> With psalms and sweet music the heavens'll be ringing,
[327]   But I shall have nothing to do with the singing.

Yet it will only be for those who have to do with the singing that life will be tolerable – and how few of us can sing!

Thus for the first time since his creation man will be faced with his real, his permanent problem – how to use his freedom from pressing economic cares, how to occupy the leisure, which science and compound interest will have won for him, to live wisely and agreeably and well.

The strenuous purposeful money-makers may carry all of us along with them into the lap of economic abundance. But it will be those peoples, who can keep alive, and cultivate into a fuller perfection, the art of life itself and do not sell themselves for the means of life, who will be able to enjoy the abundance when it comes.

Yet there is no country and no people, I think, who can look forward to the age of leisure and of abundance without a dread. For we have been trained too long to strive and not to enjoy. It is a fearful problem for the ordinary person, with no special talents, to occupy himself, especially if he no longer has roots in the soil or in custom or in the beloved conventions of a traditional society. To judge from the behaviour and the achievements of the wealthy classes today in any quarter of the world, the outlook is very depressing! For these are, so to speak, our advance guard – those who are spying out the promised land for the rest of us and pitching their camp there. For they have most of them failed disastrously, so it seems to me – those who have an independent income but no associations or duties or ties – to solve the problem which has been set them.

I feel sure that with a little more experience we shall use the new-found bounty of nature quite differently from the way in which the rich use it today, and will map out for ourselves a plan of life quite otherwise than theirs.

For many ages to come the old Adam will be so strong in us that everybody will need to do *some* work if he is to be contented. We shall do more things for ourselves than is usual with the rich today, only too glad to have small duties and tasks and [328] routines. But beyond this, we shall endeavour to spread the bread thin on the butter – to make what work there is still to be done to be as widely shared as possible. Three-hour shifts or a fifteen-hour week may put off the problem for a great while. For three hours a day is quite enough to satisfy the old Adam in most of us!

There are changes in other spheres too which we must expect to come. When the accumulation of wealth is no longer of high social importance, there will be great changes in the code of morals. We shall be able to rid ourselves of many of the pseudo-moral principles which have hag-ridden us for two hundred years, by which we have exalted some of the most distasteful of human qualities into the position of the highest virtues.

We shall be able to afford to dare to assess the money motive at its true value. The love of money as a possession – as distinguished from the love of money as a means to the enjoyments and realities of life – will be recognised for what it is, a somewhat disgusting morbidity, one of those semi-criminal, semi-pathological propensities which one hands over with a shudder to the specialists in mental disease. All kinds of social customs and economic practices, affecting the distribution of wealth and of economic rewards and penalties, which we now maintain at all costs, however distasteful and unjust they may be in themselves, because they are tremendously useful in promoting the accumulation of capital, we shall then be free, at last, to discard.

Of course there will still be many people with intense, unsatisfied purposiveness who will blindly pursue wealth – unless they can find some plausible substitute. But the rest of us will no longer be under any obligation to applaud and encourage them. For we shall inquire more curiously than is safe today into the true character of this 'purposiveness' with which in varying degrees Nature has endowed almost all of us. For pur-posiveness means that we are more concerned with the remote [329] future results of our actions than with their own quality or their immediate effects on our own environment. The 'purposive' man is always trying to secure a spurious and delusive immortality for his acts by pushing his interest in them forward into time. He does not love his cat, but his cat's kittens; nor, in truth, the kittens, but only the kittens' kittens, and so on forward for ever to the end of catdom. For him jam is not jam unless it is a case of jam tomorrow and never jam today. Thus by pushing his jam always forward into the future, he strives to secure for his act of boiling it an immortality.

. . .

Perhaps it is not an accident that the race which did most to bring the promise of immortality into the heart and essence of our religions has also done most for the principle of compound interest and particularly loves this most purposive of human institutions.

I see us free, therefore, to return to some of the most sure [330] and certain principles of religion and traditional virtue – that avarice is a vice, that the exaction of usury is a misdemeanour, and the love of money is detestable, that those walk most truly in the paths of virtue and sane wisdom who take least thought for the morrow. We shall once more value ends above means and prefer the good to the useful. We shall honour those who can teach us how to pluck the hour and the day virtuously and well, the delightful people who are capable of taking direct enjoyment in things, the lilies of the field who toil not, neither do they spin.

But beware! The time for all this is not yet. For at least another hundred years we must pretend to ourselves and to everyone that fair is foul and foul is fair; for foul is useful and fair is not. Avarice and usury and precaution must be our gods for a little longer still. For only they can lead us out of the tunnel of economic necessity into daylight.

I look forward, therefore, in days not so very remote, to the greatest change which has ever occurred in the material environment of life for human beings in the aggregate. But, of course, it will all happen gradually, not as a catastrophe. Indeed, it has already begun. The course of affairs will simply be that there will be ever larger and larger classes and groups of people from whom problems of economic necessity have been practically removed. The critical difference will be realised when this condition has become so general that the nature of one's duty to one's neighbour is changed. For it will remain reasonable to be economically purposive for others after it has ceased to be reasonable for oneself.

The *pace* at which we can reach our destination of economic bliss will be governed by four things – our power to control population, our determination to avoid wars and civil dissensions, our willingness to entrust to science the direction of those matters which are properly the concern of science, and the rate of accumulation as fixed by the margin between our production and our consumption; of which the last will easily look after itself, given the first three.   [331]

Meanwhile, there will be no harm in making mild preparations for our destiny, in encouraging, and experimenting in, the arts of life as well as the activities of purpose.

But, chiefly, do not let us overestimate the importance of the economic problem, or sacrifice to its supposed necessities other

matters of greater and more permanent significance. It should
be a matter for specialists – like dentistry. If economists could
manage to get themselves thought of as humble, competent
[332] people, on a level with dentists, that would be splendid!

13

CW 21, 'National Self-Sufficiency' (1933)

[*'National Self-Sufficiency' was first given as the Finlay Lecture
in Dublin on 19 April 1933. It was published, without the Irish
sections, in the* New Statesman *on 8 and 15 July 1933. It
can be read partly as a reaction to the failure of international
coordination – notably at the World Economic Conference
then taking place in London – to counter the slump, particularly in its rejection of British proposals, partly inspired by
Keynes, for a reformed world monetary system (see excerpt
30 below). But it also shows the strength of his reaction, following the Great Depression, against the 'decadent' financial
capitalism of his own day.*[3] *His first argument was that it was
not obvious that the competitive scramble for markets was the
best guarantee of international peace (p. 235).*]

I sympathise, therefore, with those who would minimise, rather
than with those who would maximise, economic entanglement
between nations. Ideas, knowledge, art, hospitality, travel –
these are the things which should of their nature be international.
But let goods be homespun whenever it is reasonably and conveniently possible; and, above all, let finance be primarily
national. Yet, at the same time, those who seek to disembarrass
a country of its entanglements should be very slow and wary. It
should not be a matter of tearing up roots but of slowly train-
[236] ing a plant to grow in a different direction.

. . .

[*Secondly*] I am not persuaded that the economic advantages of
the international division of labour today are at all comparable
with what they were . . . over an increasingly wide range of

industrial products, and perhaps of agriculture also, I become doubtful whether the economic cost of national self-sufficiency is great enough to outweigh the other advantages of gradually bringing the producer and the consumer within the ambit of the same national, economic, and financial organization. Experience accumulates to prove that most modern mass-production processes can be performed in most countries and climates with almost equal efficiency. Moreover, as wealth increases, both primary and manufactured products play a smaller relative part in the national economy compared with houses, personal services and local amenities which are not the subject of international exchange. National self-sufficiency, in short, though it costs something, may be becoming a luxury which we can afford if we happen to want it.   [238]

. . .

The decadent international but individualistic capitalism, in the hands of which we found ourselves after the War, is not a success. It is not intelligent, it is not beautiful, it is not just, it is not virtuous – and it doesn't deliver the goods. In short, we dislike it and we are beginning to despise it. But when we wonder what to put in its place, we are extremely perplexed.

Each year it becomes more obvious that the world is embarking on a variety of politico-economic experiments, and that different types of experiment appeal to different national temperaments and historical environments. The nineteenth century free trader's economic internationalism assumed that the whole world was, or would be, organised on a basis of private competitive capitalism and of the freedom of private contract inviolably protected by the sanctions of law – in various phases, of course, of complexity and development, but conforming to a uniform type which it would be the general object to perfect and certainly not to destroy. Nineteenth-century protectionism was a blot upon the efficiency and good sense of this scheme of things, but it did not modify the general presumption as to the fundamental characteristics of economic society.

But today one country after another abandons these presumptions. Russia is still alone in her particular experiment, but no longer alone in her abandonment of the old presumptions.

Italy, Ireland, Germany have cast their eyes, or are casting them, towards new modes of political economy. Many more countries after them will soon be seeking, one by one, after new economic gods. Even countries such as Great Britain and the United States, though conforming in the main to the old model, are striving, under the surface, after a new economic plan. We do not know what will be the outcome. We are – all of us, I expect – about to make many mistakes. No one can tell which of the new systems will prove itself best.

[239]   But the point for my present discussion is this. We each have our own fancy. Not believing that we are saved already, we each would like to have a try at working out our own salvation. We do not wish, therefore, to be at the mercy of world forces working out, or trying to work out, some uniform equilibrium according to the ideal principles, if they can be called such, of *laissez-faire* capitalism. There are still those who cling to the old ideas, but in no country of the world today can they be reckoned as a serious force. We wish – for the time at least and so long as the present transitional, experimental phase endures – to be our own masters, and to be as free as we can make ourselves from the interferences of the outside world.

Thus, regarded from this point of view, the policy of an increased national self-sufficiency is to be considered not as an ideal in itself but as directed to the creation of an environment in which other ideals can be safely and conveniently pursued.

Let me give as dry an illustration of this as I can devise, chosen because it is connected with ideas with which recently my own mind has been largely preoccupied. In matters of economic detail, as distinct from the central controls, I am in favour of retaining as much private judgement and initiative and enterprise as possible. But I have become convinced that the retention of the structure of private enterprise is incompatible with that degree of material well-being to which our technical advancement entitles us, unless the rate of interest falls to a much lower figure than is likely to come about by natural forces operating on the old lines. Indeed the transformation of society, which I preferably envisage, may require a reduction in the rate of interest towards vanishing point within the next thirty years. But under a system by which the rate of interest finds, under the operation of normal financial forces, a uniform level throughout the world, after allowing for risk and the like, this is most unlikely to occur. Thus for a complexity of reasons, which I cannot elaborate in this place, economic internationalism embracing the free movement of capital and of loanable funds as well as of traded goods may condemn this country for a generation to come to a much [240] lower degree of material prosperity than could be attained under a different system.

But this is merely an illustration. The point is that there is no prospect for the next generation of a uniformity of economic systems throughout the world, such as existed, broadly speaking, during the nineteenth century; that we all need to be as free as possible of interference from economic changes elsewhere, in order to make our own favourite experiments towards the ideal social republic of the future; and that a deliberate movement towards greater national self-sufficiency and economic isolation will make our task easier, in so far as it can be accomplished without excessive economic cost.

There is one more explanation, I think, of the reorientation of our minds. The nineteenth century carried to extravagant lengths the criterion of what one can call for short the financial results, as a test of the advisability of any course of action sponsored by private or by collective action. The whole conduct of life was made into a sort of parody of an accountant's nightmare. Instead of using their vastly increased material and technical resources to build a wonder-city, they built slums; and they thought it right and advisable to build slums because slums, on the test of private enterprise, 'paid', whereas the wonder-city would, they thought, have been an act of foolish extravagance, which would, in the imbecile idiom of the financial fashion, have 'mortgaged the future'; though how the construction today of great and glorious works can impoverish the future no man can see until his mind is beset by false analogies from an irrelevant accountancy. Even today we spend our time – half vainly, but also, I must admit, half successfully – in trying to persuade our countrymen that the nation as a whole will assuredly be richer if unemployed men and machines are used to build much needed

[241] houses than if they are supported in idleness. For the minds of this generation are still so beclouded by bogus calculations that they distrust conclusions which should be obvious, out of a reliance on a system of financial accounting which casts doubt on whether such an operation will 'pay'. We have to remain poor because it does not 'pay' to be rich. We have to live in hovels, not because we cannot build palaces, but because we cannot 'afford' them.

The same rule of self-destructive financial calculation governs every walk of life. We destroy the beauty of the countryside because the unappropriated splendours of nature have no economic value. We are capable of shutting off the sun and the stars because they do not pay a dividend. London is one of the richest cities in the history of civilisation, but it cannot 'afford' the highest standards of achievement of which its own living citizens are capable, because they do not 'pay'.

If I had the power today I should surely set out to endow our capital cities with all the appurtenances of art and civilisation on the highest standards of which the citizens of each were individually capable, convinced that what I could create, I could afford – and believing that money thus spent would not only be better than any dole, but would make unnecessary any dole. For with what we have spent on the dole in England since the War we could have made our cities the greatest works of man in the world.

Or again, we have until recently conceived it a moral duty to ruin the tillers of the soil and destroy the age-long human traditions attendant on husbandry if we could get a loaf of bread thereby a tenth of a penny cheaper. There was nothing which it was not our duty to sacrifice to this Moloch and Mammon in one; for we faithfully believed that the worship of these monsters would overcome the evil of poverty and lead the next generation safely and comfortably, on the back of compound interest, into economic peace.

Today we suffer disillusion, not because we are poorer than we were – on the contrary even today we enjoy, in Great
[242] Britain at least, a higher standard of life than at any previous

period – but because other values seem to have been sacrificed and because, moreover, they seem to have been sacrificed unnecessarily. For our economic system is not, in fact, enabling us to exploit to the utmost the possibilities for economic wealth afforded by the progress of our technique, but falls far short of this, leading us to feel that we might as well have used up the margin in more satisfying ways.

But once we allow ourselves to be disobedient to the test of an accountant's profit, we have begun to change our civilisation. And we need to do so very warily, cautiously and self-consciously. For there is a wide field of human activity where we shall be wise to retain the usual pecuniary tests. It is the state, rather than the individual, which needs to change its criterion. It is the conception of the Chancellor of the Exchequer as the chairman of a sort of joint-stock company which has to be discarded. Now if the functions and purposes of the state are to be thus enlarged, the decision as to what, broadly speaking, shall be produced within the nation and what shall be exchanged with abroad, must stand high amongst the objects of policy. [243]
[*The essay ends (pp. 243–6) with Keynes warning against the risks of Silliness, Haste and Intolerance, exhibited in varying measure by Communism and Fascism.*]

14

CW 28, 'The Arts Council of Great Britain: Its Policy and Hopes' (1945)

[*In EPG, Keynes had talked of making 'mild preparations for our destiny, in encouraging, and experimenting in, the arts of life . . .' (CW 9, p. 332). During the Second World War the government had set up a 'Council for the Encouragement of Music and the Arts' (CEMA), jointly financed by the Pilgrim Trust and the Treasury, under Keynes's chairmanship. The Arts Council of Great Britain, of which Keynes was chairman-designate when he died, was its successor. This talk, which was broadcast on the BBC, was published in the* Listener *on 12 July 1945. The original recording is in the BBC archives.*]

At last the public exchequer has recognised the support and encouragement of the civilising arts of life as part of their duty. But we do not intend to socialise this side of social endeavour. Whatever views may be held by the lately warring parties, whom you have been hearing every evening at this hour, about socialising industry, everyone, I fancy, recognises that the work of the artist in all its aspects is, of its nature, individual and free, undisciplined, unregimented, uncontrolled. The artist walks where the breath of the spirit blows him. He cannot be told his direction; he does not know it himself. But he leads the rest of us into fresh pastures and teaches us to love and to enjoy what we often begin by rejecting, enlarging our sensibility and purifying our instincts. The task of an official body is not to teach or to censor, but to give courage, confidence and opportunity. Artists depend on the world they live in and the spirit of the age. There is no reason to suppose that less native genius is born into the world in the ages empty of achievement than in those [368] brief periods when nearly all we most value has been brought to birth. New work will spring up more abundantly in unexpected quarters and in unforeseen shapes when there is a universal opportunity for contact with traditional and contemporary arts in their noblest forms.

But do not think of the Arts Council as a schoolmaster. Your enjoyment will be our first aim. We have but little money to spill, and it will be you yourselves who will by your patronage decide in the long run what you get. In so far as we instruct, it is a new game we are teaching you to play – and to watch. Our wartime experience has led us already to one clear discovery: the unsatisfied demand and the enormous public for serious and fine entertainment. This certainly did not exist a few years ago. I do not believe that it is merely a war-time phenomenon. I fancy that the B.B.C. has played a big part, the predominant part, in creating this public demand, by bringing to everybody in the country the possibility of learning these new games which only the few used to play, and by forming new tastes and habits and thus enlarging the desires of the listener and his capacity for enjoyment. I am told that today when a good symphony concert is broadcast as many as five million people may listen to it. Their ears become trained. With what anticipation many of them look forward if a chance comes their way to hear a living orchestra and to experience the enhanced excitement and concentration of attention and emotion, which flows from being one of a great audience all moved together by the surge and glory of an orchestra in being, beating in on the sensibilities of every organ of the body and of the apprehension. The result is that half the world is being taught to approach with a livelier appetite the living performer and the work of the artist as it comes from his own hand and body, with the added subtlety of actual flesh and blood.

I believe that the work of the B.B.C. and the Arts Council can react backwards and forwards on one another to the great advantage of both. It is the purpose of the Arts Council to feed these newly-aroused and widely-diffused desires. But for success we shall have to solve what will be our biggest problem, [369] the shortage – in most parts of Britain the complete absence – of adequate and suitable buildings. There never were many theatres in this country or any concert-halls or galleries worth counting. Of the few we once had, first the cinema took a heavy toll and then the blitz; and anyway the really suitable building for a largish audience which the modern engineer can construct had never been there. The greater number even of large towns, let alone the smaller centres, are absolutely bare of the necessary bricks and mortar. And our national situation today is very unfavourable for a quick solution. Houses for householders have to come first.

And so they should. Yet I plead for a certain moderation from our controllers and a few crumbs of mortar. The re-building of the community and of our common life must proceed in due proportion between one thing and another. We must not limit our provision too exclusively to shelter and comfort to cover us when we are asleep and allow us no convenient place of congregation and enjoyment when we are awake. I hope that a reasonable allotment of resources will be set aside each year for the repair and erection of the buildings we shall need. I hear that in Russia theatres and concert-halls are given a very high priority for building.

And let such buildings be widely spread throughout the country. We of the Arts Council are greatly concerned to decentralise and disperse the dramatic and musical and artistic life of the country, to build up provincial centres and to promote corporate life in these matters in every town and country. It is not our intention to act on our own where we can avoid it. We want to collaborate with local authorities and to encourage local institutions and societies and local enterprise to take the lead. We already have regional offices in Birmingham, Cambridge, Manchester, Nottingham, Bristol, Leeds, Newcastle-on-Tyne, Cardiff and Edinburgh. For Scotland and for Wales special committees have been established. In Glasgow, in particular, the work of the Citizens Theatre is a perfect model of what we should like to see established everywhere, with their own playwrights, their own company and an ever-growing and more appreciative local public. We have great hopes of our new Welsh Committee and of the stimulus it will give to the special genius of the Welsh people. Certainly in every blitzed town in this country one hopes that the local authority will make provision for a central group of buildings for drama and music and art. There could be no better memorial of a war to save the freedom of the spirit of the individual. We look forward to the time when the theatre and the concert-hall and the gallery will be a living element in everyone's upbringing, and regular attendance at the theatre and at concerts a part of organised education. The return of the B.B.C. to regional programmes may play a great part in reawakening local life and interest in all these matters. How satisfactory it would be if different parts of this country would again walk their several ways as they once did and learn to develop something different from their neighbours and characteristic of themselves. Nothing can be more damaging than the excessive prestige of metropolitan standards and fashions. Let every part of Merry England be merry in its own way. Death to Hollywood.

But it is also our business to make London a great artistic

metropolis, a place to visit and to wonder at. For this purpose London today is half in ruin. With the loss of the Queen's Hall there is no proper place for concerts. The Royal Opera House at Covent Garden has been diverted to other purposes throughout the war. The Crystal Palace has been burnt to the ground. We hope that Covent Garden will be re-opened early next year as the home of opera and ballet. The London County Council has already allotted a site for a National Theatre. The Arts Council has joined with the Trustees of the Crystal Palace in the preparation of plans to make that once again a great People's Palace. No one can yet say where the tides of the times will carry our new-found ship. The purpose of the Arts Council [371] of Great Britain is to create an environment to breed a spirit, to cultivate an opinion, to offer a stimulus to such purpose that the artist and the public can each sustain and live on the other in that union which has occasionally existed in the past at the great ages of a communal civilised life.   [372]

THREE

The Economist

This chapter assembles the main elements of Keynes's economic thinking, reserving for the next chapter, 'The Policy-maker', the proposals to which his theories (as well as events) gave rise. The aim is to give the reader a sense of Keynes as an economic theorist. In making the selections, I faced the problem of either cutting too much to make Keynes's ideas understandable, or cutting too little to make this volume manageable. So I have compromised, with texts supplemented by ample summaries, and pointers to fuller treatments of the key topics.

For Keynes economics was one of the two branches of practical ethics – the other being politics. He called it a 'moral science'. It demanded a specialized technique, but it was infused with judgements of value, and the kind of economics he did reflected the kind of society he wanted. Thus unemployment was a moral problem, but its solution was a technical matter, and one that could be tackled with good or bad technique. Keynes always tried to apply economic theory to problems which gave rise to serious moral and political consequences; and turned to inventing economic theory when the older theories seemed unable to explain or prescribe for those problems.

The analytical story in this chapter can be told as a shift from the quantity theory of money to a monetary theory of production. This was a matter of context as well as of theoretical logic. It is thus a mistake to think of Keynes as ascending, up a ladder as it were, from the simplistic formulations and 'errors' of his earlier works to the heights of GT.[1] His theories always had something of the character of 'horses for courses'. They may, though, be seen as part of a single endeavour in two *ways: as a sequence of attempts 'first unsuccessful, then increasingly successful, at implementing [a] particular vision of the economic process of our time'[2] and as an expression of a generalizing tendency.[3]*

The chief problem which set Keynes on his theoretical journey was the disorganization of money and prices which followed the First World War. In the 1930s the problem was persisting mass unemployment. The two diseases seemed to call for different analytical treatment and different prescriptions. In particular, there was no clear sense, till the Great Depression struck and lingered on, that monetary disturbances were anything but short-run interruptions to the 'normal' state of full employment, which could be prevented by the right monetary policy. By the 1930s Keynes was persuaded that deep disturbances, originating on the side of investment, could change the level of the 'normal' itself. Keynes's response was his 'theory of monetary production'. 'A monetary economy, we shall find, is essentially one in which changing views about the future are capable of influencing the quantity of employment and not merely its direction' (CW 7, p. xxii). The issue which is still debated is whether Keynes was inventing a theory for a 'once in a lifetime' event or for the general case of a capitalist credit-money economy. If the former, he was wrong to call his theory 'general'.

In his economic writings Keynes used the probabilistic logic he had developed in his youth, appealing to his reader's intuitions and common sense. His style of economic exposition was one of rigorous informality, suitable to intellectual persuasion, and laced with passages of vivid imagery, irony and occasionally passion to lodge a point unforgettably in the mind.

It is important to remember that Keynes started his professional career as a monetary economist. The theory of money was cut off from the theory of value. Its focus was on the movement of aggregates, not on the logic of individual choice, on changes in quantities, not in relative prices.[4] Macro-economics, with its emphasis on quantity adjustments and uncertainty, was always more likely to emerge from the theory of money than from the theory of value.

15

CW 2, *The Economic Consequences of the Peace* (1919)

[*Following the First World War, Keynes shared the general view that the resumption of normal business life required the restoration of global monetary order. Two strands stand out in Keynes's polemics of the subject: cancelling or writing down war debts – the subject of ECP, 1919 – and freeing the monetary system from the incubus of the gold standard, the topic of TMR, 1923.*

Although ECP was a work of political economy – and as such is considered in chapter 2 – it has a theoretical core, given by the discussion of Germany's capacity to pay reparations. This illustrates Keynes's use of his theory of probability, exhibiting both the strength and weakness of his method, since, though it secured him against accepting 'nonsense' figures concerning Germany's ability to pay reparations, it led him to underestimate the recuperative powers of both Germany and her customers.

Article 231 of the Treaty of Versailles required that Germany compensate the victorious allies for all the damage it had done to their 'civilian population and . . . property'. The French finance minister, Louis-Lucien Klotz, wanted to invoice Germany for £15 billion, which could be paid in thirty-four annual instalments of £1 billion a year.[5] Keynes responded by saying 'the fact that all things are possible *is no excuse for talking foolishly'.*]

We shall lose ourselves in mere hypothesis unless we return in some degree to first principles and, whenever we can, to such statistics as there are. It is certain that an annual payment can only be made by Germany over a series of years by diminishing her imports and increasing her exports, thus enlarging the balance in her favour which is available for effecting payments abroad. Germany can pay in the long run in goods, and in goods only, whether these goods are furnished direct to the Allies, or whether they are sold to neutrals and the neutral credits so arising are then made over to the Allies. The most solid basis for estimating the extent to which this process can be carried is to be found, therefore, in an analysis of her trade returns before the war. Only on the basis of such an analysis, supplemented by some general data as to the aggregate wealth-[118] producing capacity of the country, can a rational guess be made as to the maximum degree to which the exports of Germany could be brought to exceed her imports.

In the year 1913 Germany's imports amounted to £538 million and her exports to £505 million, exclusive of transit trade and bullion. That is to say, imports exceeded exports by about £33 million. On the average of the five years ending 1913, however, her imports exceeded her exports by a substantially larger amount, namely, £74 million. It follows, therefore, that more than the whole of Germany's pre-war balance for new foreign investment was derived from the interest on her existing foreign securities, and from the profits of her shipping, foreign banking, etc. As her foreign properties and her mercantile marine are now to be taken from her, and as her foreign banking and other miscellaneous sources of revenue from abroad have been largely destroyed, it appears that, on the pre-war basis of exports and imports, Germany, so far from having a surplus wherewith to make a foreign payment, would be not nearly self-supporting. Her first task, therefore, must be to effect a readjustment of consumption and production to cover this deficit. Any further economy she can effect in the use of imported commodities, and any further stimu-[119] lation of exports will then be available for reparation.

[*There then follow data showing the surplus of Germany's pre-war imports over exports; and the extent to which exports might be increased and imports diminished. Typically ironic is Keynes's remark (p. 123): 'If it were possible to enforce a regime in which for the future no German drank beer or coffee, or smoked any tobacco, a substantial saving [on imports] could be effected.'*]

. . .

Let us put our guess as high as we can without being foolish, and suppose that after a time Germany will be able, in spite of the reduction of her resources, her facilities, her markets, and her productive power, to increase her exports and diminish her imports so as to improve her trade balance altogether by £100 million annually, measured in pre-war prices. This adjustment is first required to liquidate the adverse trade balance, which in the five years before the war averaged £74 million; but we will assume that after allowing for this, she is left with a favourable trade balance of £50 million a year. Doubling this to allow for the rise in pre-war prices, we have a figure of £100 million. Having regard to the political, social, and human factors, as well as to the purely economic, I doubt if Germany could be made to pay this sum annually over a period of 30 years; but it would not be foolish to assert or to hope that she could.

Such a figure, allowing 5% for interest, and 1% for repayment of capital, represents a capital sum having a present value of about £1,700 million.

I reach, therefore, the final conclusion that, including all methods of payment – immediately transferable wealth, ceded property, and an annual tribute – £2,000 million is a safe maximum figure of Germany's capacity to pay. In all the actual circumstances, I do not believe that she can pay as much.   . [127]
[*This calculation was subject to three provisos: no loans, in money or kind; no 'revolutionary changes' in the price of gold; no positive productivity shocks.*

Keynes's discussion of Germany's 'capacity' to pay started a debate on the 'transfer problem' which rumbled on for many years, and is by no means dead.[6]

His attitude is summed up in the following quotation from the Economic Journal *of March 1929, reproduced in CW XI, pp. 457–8:*

My own view is that at a given time the economic structure of a country, in relation to the economic structures of its neighbours, permits of a certain 'natural' level of exports, and arbitrarily to effect a material alteration of this level by deliberate devices is extremely difficult ... Those who see no difficulty in this – like those who saw no difficulty in Great Britain's return to the gold standard – are applying the theory of liquids to what is, if not a solid, at least a sticky mass with strong internal resistances.

For Keynes's policy proposals to deal with war debts see excerpt 24 in chapter 4 below.]

16

CW 4, *A Tract on Monetary Reform* (1923)

[*Keynes started lecturing on 'Money, Credit, and Prices' at Cambridge in* 1909. *For most of his professional career, he subscribed to some version of the quantity theory of money – the theory that the price level varies proportionately with the quantity of money, with the causation running from money to prices. In the simplest version, Santa Claus doubles the amount of money in the possession of each individual. All recipients spend the extra money; this causes prices to double. In TMR, Keynes, like Irving Fisher and all sensible proponents of the QTM,[7] conceded that this proportionality held only in the long run; in the short run, changes in monetary conditions could cause changes in distribution and production (excerpts 7 and 8 above).*

In section 1 *of chapter* 3, '*The Quantity Theory of Money*', *Keynes defines the sense in which he is a quantity theorist and also why he is a quantity theorist. The excerpt below explicitly identifies money with cash – that is, with notes and coin issued by the central bank; it contains Keynes's most famous phrase:* '*In the long run we are all dead.*'[8]]

1 *The Quantity Theory of Money*

The [quantity theory of money] is fundamental. Its correspondence with fact is not open to question. Nevertheless it is often misstated and misrepresented. Goschen's saying of sixty years ago, that 'there are many persons who cannot hear the relation of the level of prices to the volume of currency affirmed without a feeling akin to irritation', still holds good.

The theory flows from the fact that money as such has no utility except what is derived from its exchange value, that is to say from the utility of the things which it can buy. Valuable articles other than money have a utility in themselves. Provided that they are divisible and transferable, the total amount of this utility increases with their quantity – it will not increase in full

proportion to the quantity, but, up to the point of satiety, it does increase.[9]   [61]
. . .

Consequently what the public want is not so many ounces [of gold] or . . . or even so many £ sterling of currency notes, but a quantity sufficient to cover a week's wages, or to pay their bills, or to meet their probable outgoings on a journey or a day's shopping. When people find themselves with more cash than they require for such purposes, they get rid of the surplus by buying goods or investments, or by leaving it for a bank to employ, or, possibly, by increasing their hoarded reserves. Thus the *number* of notes which the public ordinarily have on hand is determined by the amount of *purchasing power* which it suits them to hold or to carry about, and by nothing else. The amount of this purchasing power depends partly on their wealth, partly on their habits. The wealth of the public in the aggregate will only change gradually. Their habits in the use of money – whether their income is paid them weekly or monthly or quarterly, whether they pay cash at shops or run accounts, whether they deposit with banks, whether they cash small cheques at short intervals or larger cheques at longer intervals, whether they keep a reserve or hoard of money about the house – are more easily altered. But if their wealth and their habits in the above respects are unchanged, then the amount of purchasing power which they hold in the form of money is definitely fixed. We can measure this definite amount of purchasing power in terms of a unit made up of a collection of specified quantities of their standard articles of consumption or other objects of expenditure; for example, the kinds and quantities of articles which are combined for the purpose of a cost-of-living index number. Let us call such a unit a 'consumption unit' and assume that the pub-   [62] lic require to hold an amount of money having a purchasing power over k consumption units. Let there be n currency notes or other forms of cash in circulation with the public, and let p be the price of each consumption unit (i.e. p is the index number of the cost of living), then it follows from the above that $n = pk$. This is the famous quantity theory of money. So long as k remains unchanged, n and p rise and fall together; that is to say,

the greater or the fewer the number of currency notes, the higher
or the lower is the price level in the same proportion.

So far we have assumed that the whole of the public requirement for purchasing power is satisfied by cash, and on the other
hand that this requirement is the only source of demand for
cash; neglecting the fact that the public, including the business
world, employ for the same purpose bank deposits and overdraft
facilities, whilst the banks must for the same reason maintain a
reserve of cash. The theory is easily extended, however, to cover
this case. Let us assume that the public, including the business
world, find it convenient to keep the equivalent of k consumption in cash and of a further k' available at their banks against
cheques, and that the banks keep in cash a proportion r of their
potential liabilities (k') to the public. Our equation then becomes

$$n = p(k + rk').$$

So long as k, k', and r remain unchanged, we have the same result
as before, namely, that n and p rise and fall together. The proportion between k and k' depends on the banking arrangements of
the public; the absolute value of these on their habits generally;
and the value of r on the reserve practices of the banks. Thus, so
long as these are unaltered, we still have a direct relation between
[63]   the *quantity* of cash (n) and the level of prices (p).

We have seen that the amount of k and k' depends partly on
the wealth of the community, partly on its habits. Its habits are
fixed by its estimation of the extra convenience of having more
cash in hand as compared with the advantages to be got from
spending the cash or investing it. The point of equilibrium is
reached where the estimated advantages of keeping more cash
in hand compared with those of spending or investing it about
balance.

. . .

So far there should be no room for difference of opinion. The
[64]   error often made by careless adherents of the quantity theory,
which may partly explain why it is not universally accepted, is
as follows.

Every one admits that the habits of the public in the use of money and of banking facilities and the practices of the banks in respect of their reserves change from time to time as the result of obvious developments. These habits and practices are a reflection of changes in economic and social organisation. But the theory has often been expounded on the further assumption that a *mere* change in the quantity of the currency cannot affect k, r, and k' – that is to say, in mathematical parlance, that n is an *independent variable* in relation to these quantities. It would follow from this that an arbitrary doubling of n, since this in itself is assumed not to affect k, r, and k', must have the effect of raising p to double what it would have been otherwise. The quantity theory is often stated in this, or a similar, form.

Now 'in the long run' this is probably true. If, after the American Civil War, the American dollar had been stabilised and defined by law at 10 per cent below its present value, it would be safe to assume that n and p would now be just 10 per cent greater than they actually are and that the present values of k, r, and k' would be entirely unaffected. But this *long run* is a misleading guide to current affairs. *In the long run* we are all dead. Economists set themselves too easy, too useless a task if in tempestuous seasons they can only tell us that when the storm is long past the ocean is flat again.

In actual experience, a change of n is liable to have a reaction both on k and k' and on r. It will be enough to give a few typical instances.   [65]
. . .

[*The chief instances Keynes gave were the tendency of central banks to increase their reserves* (r) *when increased supplies of gold came their way, and for peasants in agricultural countries to 'hoard' increased receipts for their products in the early stages of an inflation.*]

The terms *inflation* and *deflation* are used by different writers in varying senses. It would be convenient to speak of an increase or decrease in n as an inflation or deflation of *cash*; and of a decrease or increase in r as an inflation or deflation of *credit*. The characteristic of the 'credit cycle' (as the alternation of boom and depression is now described) consists in a tendency of k and k' to diminish during the boom and increase during the depression, irrespective of changes in n and r, these movements representing respectively a diminution and an increase of 'real' balances (i.e. balances, in hand or at the bank, measured in terms of purchasing power); so that we might call this phenomenon deflation and [67] inflation of real balances . . . The moral of this discussion . . . is that the price level is not mysterious, but is governed by a few, definite, analysable influences. Two of these, n and r, are under the direct control (or ought to be) of the central banking authorities. The third, namely k and k', is not directly controllable, and depends on the mood of the public and the business world. The business of stabilising the price level, not merely over long periods but so as also to avoid cyclical fluctuations, consists partly in exercising a stabilising influence over k and k', and, in so far as this fails or is impracticable, in deliberately varying n and r so as to *counterbalance* the movement of k and k'.

The usual method of exercising a stabilising influence over k and k', especially over k', is that of bank rate. A tendency of k' to increase may be somewhat counteracted by lowering the bank rate, because easy lending diminishes the advantage of keeping a margin for contingencies in cash. Cheap money also operates to *counterbalance* an increase of k', because, by encouraging borrowing from the banks, it prevents r from increasing or causes r to diminish. But it is doubtful whether bank rate by itself is always a powerful enough instrument, and, if we are to achieve [68] stability, we must be prepared to vary n and r on occasion.

Our analysis suggests that the first duty of the central banking and currency authorities is to make sure that they have n and r thoroughly under control. For example, so long as inflationary taxation is in question n will be influenced by other than currency objects and cannot, therefore, be fully under control; moreover, at the other extreme, under a gold standard n is not always under control, because it depends on the unregulated forces which determine the demand and supply of gold throughout the world. Again, without a central banking system r will not be under proper control because it will be determined by the unco-ordinated decisions of numerous different banks.

At the present time in Great Britain r is very completely controlled, and n also, so long as we refrain from inflationary finance on the one hand and from a return to an unregulated gold standard on the other. The second duty of the authorities is therefore worth discussing, namely, the *use* of their control over *n* and *r* to counterbalance changes in *k* and *k'*. Even if *k* and *k'* were entirely outside the influence of deliberate policy, which is not in fact the case, nevertheless *p* could be kept reasonably steady by suitable modifications of the values of *n* and *r*.

Old-fashioned advocates of sound money have laid too much emphasis on the need of keeping *n* and *r* steady, and have argued as if this policy by itself would produce the right results. So far from this being so, steadiness of *n* and *r*, when *k* and *k'* are not steady, is bound to lead to unsteadiness of the price level. Cyclical fluctuations are characterised, not primarily by changes in *n* or *r*, but by changes in *k* and *k'*. It follows that they can only be cured if we are ready deliberately to increase and decrease *n* and *r*, when symptoms of movement are showing in the values of *k* and *k'*.   [69]

[*The rather lame discussion of the theory of money above fails to bring out that Keynes perfectly well understood that banks create deposits as well as receive them. Thus prices were to be controlled not by regulating the number of notes but the terms on which credit could be obtained – that is, the rate of interest.*[10]

Omitted is section 2 of chapter 3, 'The Theory of Purchasing Power Parity' (pp. 70–87), which gives a sparkling account of forward markets as hedges against currency risk.]

17

CW 5 and 6, *A Treatise on Money* (1930)

[*TM shows Keynes still beholden in his theorizing to QTM and, more generally, to the Walrasian system of general equilibrium. Essentially what he does is set up a model of an ideal equilibrium – the Fundamental Equations – and then spend most of the book explaining why the conditions for the attainment of the ideal position are rarely realized in practice.*[11] *TM thus develops into an exploration of the forces generating disequilibrium, notably the 'credit cycle', and a specification of the monetary policy needed to achieve the 'stability of purchasing power'.*

Unfortunately, this method involved Keynes in trying to explain output changes in terms of a model – QTM – which ruled out such changes by assumption.[12] Keynes (and other monetary reformers) remained attached to QTM, not because they believed prices changed proportionately to money, certainly not in the short term, but because they wanted to retain for M[oney] a 'role in economic therapy'. As Schumpeter pointed out, 'Whoever treats M as an independent variable inevitably pays some tribute to [the QTM]'.[13]

The chief strengths of TM are exactly what one would expect of Keynes. First is his detailed understanding of the financial system, its psychology and its institutions. Second, it is Keynes's most extensive discussion of the possibilities and limitations of monetary policy, including what is now called 'quantitative easing'. Third, in contrast to the later GT, TM was a theory of an 'open economy' – one with a trade sector. It can thus be read as a stylized account of Britain's 'special problem' of maintaining full employment in the 1920s. A country in which interest rates were forced upwards by the need to defend an over-valued currency and in which wages could not be forced downwards to restore exports and profits was quite likely to find itself in a low-employment trap (CW 5, p. 153). This remains relevant for policy in any trading country with a fixed exchange rate. In such circumstances, fiscal policy comes into its own (CW 6, p. 338).

Chapter 2 sets out the 'credit' theory of money: money comes into existence not by the central bank minting coins or printing notes, but by the banks actively creating deposits, that is, making loans. A 'closed' banking system, in which actively created deposits in bank A produce passively created deposits in bank B, would have an 'inherent instability'; for 'any event which tended to influence the behaviour of the majority of the banks, would meet with no resistance and would be capable of setting up a violent movement of the whole system' (p. 23). It is the task of the central bank to lean against any such cumulative tendency: 'it is the conductor of the orchestra and sets the tempo' (p. 26).

The main story of TM then follows by way of a 'very long argument as to the manner in which the creation of bank deposits by the banking system is related to the price level' (p. 43).

Starting from a position in which employment and business profits are 'normal' and saving equals investment, the economy expands when profits (actual or anticipated) rise, and shrinks when they fall. (These shifts in actual or anticipated profits are typically triggered off by actual or anticipated movements of asset prices.) A rise in the anticipated profitability of new investment triggers a rise in the price of capital goods ('capital inflation'), followed by increased employment and a rise in the consumer price index ('commodity inflation'); the reverse is precipitated by a decline in profit expectations, which leads to capital and then commodity 'deflation', the whole constituting the 'credit cycle'. The central bank's task is to maintain equilibrium by ensuring that business remains normally profitable. Using the language of Knut Wicksell, TM sets the monetary authority the task of keeping the market rate of interest equal to the 'natural rate' – the rate at which it pays employers to provide a 'normal' or 'equilibrium' amount of employment.

The Fundamental Equations are presented with a great fanfare on p. 121 of CW 5. He will start, Keynes says, not from the stock of money (as in the traditional QTM) but from the flow of earnings (income) directed to buying consumption goods and investment goods. These flows result in two price levels – of consumption goods and investment goods. It is then true by definition that the stability of the consumer price level depends on the ratio of saving out of income being equal to the amount of investment, any inequality between the two causing that price level to go up or down. Because profit/loss has been defined as net of income, inequality between saving and investment is the same as profit and loss.[14]

This is the 'model' of TM, but like in many badly constructed operas, the action takes place off-stage, for, as Keynes remarks, 'the price level of investment depends on a different set of considerations, which we shall come to later' (CW 5, p. 121). It is from this point that we take up the 'credit cycle' story.]

[CW 5]

Chapter 10

The Fundamental Equations of Value

III *The Price Level of New Investment Goods*[15]

When a man is deciding what proportion of his money income to save, he is choosing between present consumption and the ownership of wealth. In so far as he decides in favour of consumption, he must necessarily purchase goods – for he cannot consume money. But in so far as he decides in favour of saving, there still remains a further decision for him to make. For he can own wealth by holding it either in the form of money (or the liquid equivalent of money) or in other forms of loan or real capital. The second decision might be conveniently described as the choice between 'hoarding' and 'investing', or, alternatively, as the choice between 'bank deposits' and 'securities'.

There is also a further significant difference between the two types of decision. The decision as to the volume of saving, and also the decision relating to the volume of new investment, relate wholly to current activities. But the decision as to holding bank deposits or securities relates, not only to the current increment to the wealth of individuals, but also to the whole block of their existing capital. Indeed, since the current increment is but a trifling proportion of the block of existing wealth, it is a minor element in the matter.

Now when an individual is more disposed than before to hold his wealth in the form of savings deposits and less disposed to hold it in other forms, this does not mean that he is determined to hold it in the form of savings deposits *at all costs*. It means that he favours savings deposits (for whatever reason) more than before at the existing price level of other securities. But his distaste for other securities is not absolute and depends on his expectations of the future return to be obtained from sav-
[127] ings deposits and from other securities respectively, which is obviously affected by the price of the latter – and also by the rate of interest allowed on the former. If, therefore, the price level of other securities falls sufficiently, he can be tempted back

into them. If, however, the banking system operates in the opposite direction to that of the public and meets the preference of the latter for savings deposits by buying the securities which the public is *less* anxious to hold and creating against them the additional savings deposits which the public is *more* anxious to hold, then there is no need for the price of investments to fall at all. Thus the change in the relative attractions of savings deposits and securities respectively has to be met either by a fall in the price of securities or by an increase in the supply of savings deposits, or partly by the one and partly by the other. A fall in the price of securities is therefore an indication that the 'bearishness' of the public – as we can conveniently designate, in anticipation of late discussions, an increased preference for savings deposits as against other forms of wealth and a decreased preference for carrying securities with money borrowed from the banks – has been insufficiently offset by the creation of savings deposits by the banking system – or that the 'bullishness' of the public has been more than offset by the contraction of savings deposits by the banking system.

It follows that the actual price of investments is the resultant of the sentiment of the public and the behaviour of the banking system.   [128]

. . .

The price level of investments as a whole, and hence of new investments, is that price level at which the desire of the public to hold savings deposits is equal to the amount of savings deposits which the banking system is willing and able to create.   [129]

Chapter 11
The Conditions of Equilibrium

11 *The Rate of Interest or Bank Rate*

The attractiveness of investment depends on the prospective income which the entrepreneur anticipates from current investment relatively to the rate of interest which he has to pay [138] in order to finance its production; or, putting it the other way round, the value of capital goods depends on the rate of

interest at which the prospective income from them is capitalised. That is to say the higher . . . the rate of interest, the lower,
other things being equal, will be the value of capital goods . . .
The rate of saving, on the other hand, is stimulated by a high
rate of interest and discouraged by a low rate. It follows that an
increase in the rate of interest tends – other things being equal –
to make the rate of investment (whether measured by its value
or by its cost) decline relatively to the rate of saving . . . so that
the price level tends to fall.

Following Wicksell, it will be convenient to call the rate of
interest which would cause the [difference between saving and
investment] to be zero the *natural rate* of interest, and the rate
[139] which actually prevails the *market rate* of interest.

. . .

If, therefore, the banking system can regulate the amount which
it lends in such a way that the market rate of interest is equal to
the natural rate, then the value of investment will be equal to
the volume of saving, total profits will be zero, [and] the price
[142] of output, as a whole, will be at an equilibrium level . . .

v *The Behaviour of Entrepreneurs*

In so far . . . as production takes time . . . and in so far as entrepreneurs are able at the beginning of a production period to
forecast the . . . demand for their product at the end of this
production period, it is obviously the anticipated profit or loss
on new business, rather than the actual profit or loss on business just concluded, which influences them in deciding the scale
on which to produce and the offers which it is worthwhile to
make to the factors of production. Strictly, therefore, we should
say that it is the *anticipated* profit or loss which is the main-
spring of change, and that it is by causing anticipations of the
appropriate kind that the banking system is able to influence
the price level. Indeed it is well known that one reason for the
rapid efficacy of changes in bank rate . . . is the anticipations to
which they give rise. Thus entrepreneurs will sometimes begin
to act before the price changes which are the justification of
[143] their action have actually occurred.

. . .

VII *Changes in Price Levels due to 'Spontaneous' Changes in Earnings*

[I]f – which is the case usually assumed by monetary reformers – we have at least a partial control of the currency system but not of the earnings system, so that we have some power of deciding what the equilibrium price level and rate of earnings is to be, but no power of bringing about this equilibrium except by setting into operation the mechanism of induced changes [in wage rates], then we may do well in choosing our standard to consider what will fit in best with whatever may be the natural tendencies of spontaneous change which characterise the earnings system as it actually is.

. . .   [152]

For my own part I am somewhat inclined to think, without having reached a final conclusion, that it is more important to have a system which avoids, so far as possible, the necessity for induced changes . . . For the worst of all conceivable systems (apart from the abuses of a *fiat* money which has lost all its anchors) is one in which the banking system fails to correct periodic divergences . . . between investment and saving, and where, besides, spontaneous changes in earnings tend upwards, but monetary changes, due to the relative shortage of gold, tend downwards, so that, even apart from fluctuations from the side of investment and superimposed on them, we have a chronic necessity for induced changes sufficient not only to counteract the spontaneous changes but reverse them. Yet it is possible that this is the sort of system which we have today.   [153]

Chapter 12
A Further Elucidation of the Distinction between Savings and Investment

II *An Illustration*

A parable or illustration may possibly make the conclusion clearer – or at least more vivid. Let us suppose a community owning banana plantations and labouring to cultivate and collect bananas and nothing else; and consuming bananas and nothing else. Let us suppose, further, that there has been an equilibrium between saving and investment in the sense that the money income of the community, not spent on the consumption of bananas but saved, is equal to the cost of production of new investment in the further development of plantations; and that the selling price of bananas is equal to their cost of production (including in this the normal remuneration of entrepreneurs). Finally, let us suppose, what is plausible, that ripe bananas will not keep for more than a week or two.

Into this Eden there enters a thrift campaign, urging the members of the public to abate their improvident practices of devoting nearly all their current incomes to buying bananas for daily food. But at the same time there is no corresponding increase in the development of new plantations – for one or other of many reasons: it may be that counsels of prudence are influencing entrepreneurs as well as savers, fears of future [158] over-production of bananas and a falling price level deterring them from new development; or technical reasons may exist which prevent new development at more than a certain pace; or the labour required for such development may be highly specialised and not capable of being drawn from labour ordinarily occupied in harvesting bananas; or there may be a considerable time-lag between the initial preparations required for development and the date of the bulk of the expenditure eventually required by it. What, in such a case, will happen?

The same quantity of bananas as before will continue to be marketed, whilst the amount of current income devoted to their purchase will, by reason of the thrift campaign, be diminished. Since bananas will not keep, their price must fall; and it will fall proportionately to the amount by which saving exceeds investment. Thus, as before, the public will consume the whole crop of bananas, but at a reduced price level. This is splendid, or seems so. The thrift campaign will not only have increased saving; it will have reduced the cost of living. The public will have saved money, without denying themselves anything. They will be consuming just as much as before, and virtue will be sumptuously rewarded.

But the end is not yet reached. Since wages are still unchanged, only the selling price of bananas will have fallen and not their cost of production; so that the entrepreneurs will suffer an abnormal loss. Thus the increased saving has not increased in the least the aggregate wealth of the community; it has simply caused a transfer of wealth from the pockets of the entrepreneurs into the pockets of the general public. The savings of the consumers will be required, either directly or through the intermediary of the banking system, to make good the losses of the entrepreneurs. The continuance of this will cause entrepreneurs to seek to protect themselves by throwing their employees out of work or reducing their wages. But even this will not improve [159] their position, since the spending power of the public will be reduced by just as much as the aggregate costs of production. By however much entrepreneurs reduce wages and however many of their employees they throw out of work, they will continue to make losses so long as the community continues to save in excess of new investment. Thus there will be no position of equilibrium until either (a) all production ceases and the entire population starves to death; or (b) the thrift campaign is called off or peters out as a result of the growing poverty; or (c) investment is stimulated by some means or another so that its cost no longer lags behind the rate of saving.   [160]

[The banana parable sits awkwardly with the story of TM, which is cyclical. It also fails as an anticipation of GT, since the fall in income fails to restore the equilibrium between saving and investment. Rather, it should be read as a flawed attempt to illustrate Britain's 'special problem' of the 1920s, in which an overvalued pound prevents the fall in interest rates which would have cured the unemployment problem. (See CW 20, pp. 78–9, where Keynes says this explicitly.)]

. . .

Chapter 13
The 'Modus Operandi' of Bank Rate

1 *The Traditional Doctrine*

[Bank rate] . . . . is the instrument by which a disturbance is set up or equilibrium restored between the rates of saving and of investment; for to raise it stimulates the one and retards the
[166] other, and conversely if it is reduced.

. . .

The simplest way of putting the point, as I conceive it, is to say that to raise the bank rate discourages investment relatively to saving, and therefore lowers prices, which, by causing the receipts of entrepreneurs to fall below the normal, influences them to offer less employment all round; and this, sooner or later, brings down the rate of earnings in the same proportions as that in which prices have fallen; at which point a new position of equilibrium can be established. Now no writer, so far as I know, has clearly distinguished these two stages, i.e. the fall of prices and the fall of the costs of production, the initial fall of
[171] prices having been treated as if it were the end of the story.

. . .

Chapter 15
The Industrial Circulation and the
Financial Circulation

[*The purpose of the discussion below is to show that a change in the quantity of money need not occur as a result of a definite act of inflation or deflation by the central bank, but may be the result of the movement of money between bank deposits and securities.*]

1 *Industry and Finance Distinguished and Defined*

[It] is necessary to make a further classification cutting, to a certain extent, across our division of the total quantity of money (in chapter 3) into the income deposits, the business deposits and the savings deposits – namely a division between the deposits used for the purposes of industry, which we shall call the *industrial circulation*, and those used for the purposes of finance, which we shall call the *financial circulation*.

By *industry* we mean the business of maintaining the normal process of current output, distribution and exchange and paying the factors of production their incomes for the various duties they perform . . . By *finance*, on the other hand, we mean the business of holding and exchanging existing titles to wealth . . . including stock exchange and money market transactions, speculation and the process of conveying current savings and profits into the hands of entrepreneurs.

Each of these two branches of business utilises a certain part of the total stock of money. Broadly speaking, industry requires the use of the income deposits and of a part of the business deposits, which we shall call business deposits A; whilst finance [217] requires the use of the savings deposits and the remainder of the business deposits, which we shall call business deposits B. Thus the sum of the two former is the industrial circulation and of the two latter the financial circulation. [218]

[*Sections II and III, pp. 218–27: the industrial circulation (income deposits plus business deposits A) will vary with incomes, so it is changes in the financial circulation which are causative. The variability of business deposits B is small, so the variability in the demand for money for financial purposes arises from changes in the volume of savings deposits (p. 223). Savings deposits are made up of deposits A and B. Savings deposits A are held by owners of wealth who 'permanently prefer to hold savings deposits in preference to securities' (p. 223), so changes in volume of savings deposits arise from changes in savings deposits B, whose owners, in the later language of GT, hold money for 'speculative' purposes, but are here described as 'bears' on securities. They are those who have sold securities short, and 'also those who would normally be holders of securities but prefer for the time to hold liquid claims on cash' (p. 224). When bullish sentiment is high, savings deposits B fall towards zero, as savers use cash to buy securities; when bear sentiment is in the ascendant they sell securities for cash. This is equivalent to saying that when business confidence is high, as in a 'bull' market, money flows from hoards to investments; when it is low, as in a 'bear' market, it flows from investments into hoards. But in the later stages of a boom money is diverted from the industrial to the financial circulation as speculation runs ahead of new investment. Keynes believed this happened in the run-up to the Wall Street crash of 1929 (CW 6, p. 341). These shifts in flows of money are the financial expression of 'investment running ahead of saving' (boom) and 'saving running ahead of investment' (slump). The economy is in equilibrium when there is a division of opinion between 'bulls' and 'bears' such that there is no cumulative movement towards either securities or cash; but this state of affairs is accidental.]*

. . .

We conclude, therefore, that changes in the financial situation are capable of causing changes in the value of money in two ways. They have the effect of altering the quantity of money available for the industrial circulation; and they may have the effect of altering the attractiveness of investment. Thus, unless the first effect is balanced by a change in the total quantity of money and the latter by a change in the terms of lending, an instability in the price level of current output will result.

. . .

The dilemma [*for monetary policy*] . . . is as follows. If the bank increases the volume of bank money so as to avoid any risk of the financial circulation stealing resources from the industrial circulation, it will encourage the 'bull' market to continue, with every probability of . . . over-investment later on; whereas if it refuses to increase the volume of bank money, it may so diminish the amount of money available for industry, or so enhance the rate of interest at which it is available, as to have an immediately deflationary tendency.

The solution lies – so far as the stability of purchasing power is concerned – in letting both finance and industry have all the money they want, but at a rate of interest which in its effect on the rate of *new* investment (relatively to saving) exactly balances the effect of bullish sentiment. To diagnose the position precisely at every stage and to achieve this exact balance may sometimes be, however, beyond the wits of man. Moreover it may happen in practice that a rate of interest high enough to avoid future over-investment has the result of reducing present [227] output below the optimum – though I think this can only occur through inaccurate forecasting,[16] or from the difficulties of changing over from one type of output to another. In this event some disturbance to stability may be inevitable. For there is then no way out except what has sometimes been attempted both in Great Britain and in the United States, though with dubious success, namely to discriminate in the terms of lending (either in the rate charged or by rationing the amount lent) between financial and industrial borrowers. If the terms of lending to both categories of borrowers have to be nearly identical, then, given inaccurate forecasting by certain purchasers of securities, it may be that a rate of interest high enough to avoid prospective over-investment is calculated to produce present unemployment.

We are left, therefore, with the broad conclusion that the stability of purchasing power and of output requires that the total deposits should be allowed to rise and fall *pari passu* with any changes in the volume of the savings deposits; but that the terms of lending should be adjusted – to the extent that this is practically possible – so as to balance the effect of bullish or bearish sentiment in the financial markets on the rate of new investment . . .

In the long run the value of securities is entirely derivative from the value of consumption goods . . . But in the very short run, it depends on opinion largely uncontrolled by any present [228] monetary factors. A higher value for securities is not immediately checked by monetary factors in the same way that a similar enhancement of the prices of currently consumed goods would be checked by lack of sufficient income to purchase them . . .

Accordingly *opinion* has a dominating influence on the position to a degree which does not apply in the case of the quantity of money required to look after a given wages bill. If everyone agrees that the securities are worth more, and if everyone is a 'bull' in the sense of preferring securities at a rising price to increasing his savings deposit, there is no limit to the rise in prices of securities and no effective check arises from a shortage of money.

Nevertheless, as soon as the price of securities has risen high

enough, relatively to the short-term rate of interest, to occasion a difference of opinion as to prospects, a 'bear' position will develop, and some people will begin to increase their savings deposits either out of their current savings or out of their current profits or by selling securities previously held. Thus in proportion as the prevailing opinion comes to seem unreasonable to more cautious people, the 'other' view will tend to develop, with the result of an increase in the 'bear' position – which does bring into existence a monetary factor, though one [229] which is corrective only in a 'bull' market.
. . .

I should say, therefore, that a currency authority has no *direct* concern with the level of value of existing securities, as determined by opinion, but that it has an important indirect concern if the level of value of existing securities is calculated to stimulate new investment to outrun saving, or contrariwise. For example, a boom in land values or a revaluation of the equities of monopolies, entirely dissociated from any excessive stimulus to new investment, should not divert a currency authority from keeping the terms of lending and the total supply of money at such a level as to leave over, after satisfying the financial circulation, the optimum amount for the industrial circulation (so far as this is compatible with the preservation of external equilibrium where our system is not a closed one). The main criterion for interference with a 'bull' or a 'bear' financial market should be, that is to say, the probable reactions of this financial situation on the [230] prospective equilibrium between savings and *new* investment.
. . .

Chapter 19
Some Special Aspects of the Credit Cycle

III *The Normal Course of the Credit Cycle*

Having emphasised sufficiently the endless variety of the paths which a credit cycle can follow, we may allow ourselves, by way of simplification, to pick out one path in particular which seems to us to be sufficiently frequented to deserve, perhaps, to be called the usual or normal course.

Something happens – of a non-monetary character – to increase the attractions of investment. It may be a new invention, or the development of a new country, or a war, or a return of 'business confidence' as the result of many small influences tending the same way. Or the thing may start – which is more likely if it is a monetary cause which is playing the chief part – with a stock exchange boom, beginning with speculation in natural resources or *de facto* monopolies, but eventually affecting by sympathy the price of new capital goods.

The rise in the natural rate of interest, corresponding to the increased attractions of investment, is not held back by increased saving; and the expanding volume of investment is not restrained by an adequate rise in the market rate of interest.

This acquiescence of the banking system in the increased volume of investment may involve it in allowing some increase in the total quantity of money; but at first the necessary increase is not likely to be great and may be taken up, almost unnoticed, out of the general slack of the system, or may be supplied by a falling off in the requirements of the financial circulation without any change in the total volume of money.

At this stage the output and price of capital goods begin to rise. Employment improves and the wholesale index rises. The increased expenditure of the newly employed then raises the [271] price of consumption goods and allows the producers of such goods to reap a windfall profit. By this time practically all categories of goods will have risen in price and all classes of entrepreneurs will be enjoying a profit.

At first the volume of employment of the factors of production will increase without much change in their rate of remuneration. But after a large proportion of the unemployed factors have been absorbed into employment, the entrepreneurs bidding against one another under the stimulus of high profits will begin to offer higher rates of remuneration.

All the while, therefore, the requirements of the industrial circulation will be increasing – first of all to look after the increased volume of employment and subsequently to look after, in addition, the increased rates of remuneration. A point will come, therefore, when the banking system is no longer able to supply the necessary volume of money consistently with its principles and traditions.

It is astonishing, however – what with changes in the financial circulation, in the velocities of circulation, and in the reserve proportions of the central bank – how large a change in the earnings bill can be looked after by the banking system without an apparent breach in its principles and traditions.

It may be, therefore, that the turning-point will come, not from the reluctance or the inability of the banking system to finance the increased earnings bill, but from one or more of three other causes. The turn may come from a faltering of financial sentiment, due to some financiers, from prescience or from their experience of previous crises, seeing a little further ahead than the business world or the banking world. If so, the growth of 'bear' sentiment will, as we have seen, increase the requirements of the financial circulation. It may be, therefore, the tendency of the financial circulation to increase, on the top of the increase in the industrial circulation, which will break the back of the banking system and cause it at long last to [272] impose a rate of interest, which is not only fully equal to the natural rate but, very likely in the changed circumstances, well above it.

Or it may be that the attractions of new investment will wear themselves out with time or with the increased supply of certain kinds of capital goods.

Or, finally – failing a turnabout from any of the above causes – there is likely to be a sympathetic reaction, not much more than one production period after the secondary phase of the boom (the increased activity in the production of consumption goods) has properly set in, owing to the inevitable collapse in the prices of consumption goods below their higher level.

Thus the collapse will come in the end as the result of the piling up of several weighty causes – the evaporation of the attractions of new investment, the faltering of financial sentiment, the reaction in the price level of consumption goods, and the growing inability of the banking system to keep pace with the increasing requirements, first of the industrial circulation and later of the financial circulation also.

The order of events is, therefore, as follows. First, a capital inflation leading to an increase of investment, leading to commodity inflation; second, still more capital inflation and commodity inflation for approximately one production period of consumption goods; third, a reaction in the degree of the commodity and capital inflations at the end of this period; fourth, a collapse of the capital inflation; and finally, a decrease of investment below normal, leading to a commodity deflation.   [273]

[CW 6]

Chapter 30
Historical Illustrations

[*In Books V and VI of CW 6, the expert will find impressive statistical material on fluctuations in the different types of bank deposits. Then Keynes turns to argue that it is 'enterprise not thrift' which builds civilizations. Enterprise, in the pre-modern world, had often taken the form of piracy.*][17]

It has been usual to think of the accumulated wealth of the world as having been painfully built up out of that voluntary abstinence of individuals from the immediate enjoyment of consumption which we call thrift. But it should be obvious that mere abstinence is not enough by itself to build cities or drain fens. The abstinence of individuals need not increase accumulated wealth; it may serve instead to increase the current consumption of other individuals. Thus the thrift of a man may lead either to an increase of capital wealth or to consumers getting better value for their money. There is no telling which, until we have examined another economic factor.

Namely, enterprise. It is enterprise which builds and improves the world's possessions. Now, just as the fruits of thrift may go to provide either capital accumulation or an enhanced value of money income for the consumer, so the outgoings of enterprise may be found either out of thrift or at the expense of the consumption of the average consumer. Worse still, not only may thrift exist without enterprise, but as soon as thrift gets ahead of enterprise, it positively discourages the recovery of enterprise and sets up a vicious circle by its adverse effect on profits.

If enterprise is afoot, wealth accumulates whatever may be happening to thrift; and if enterprise is asleep, wealth decays whatever thrift may be doing.

Thus, thrift may be the handmaid and nurse of enterprise. But [132] equally she may not. And, perhaps, even usually she is not. For enterprise is connected with thrift not directly but at one remove; and the link which should join them is frequently missing. For the engine which drives enterprise is not thrift, but profit.

Now, for enterprise to be active, two conditions must be fulfilled. There must be an expectation of profit; and it must be possible for enterprisers to obtain command of sufficient resources to put their projects into execution. Their expectations partly depend on non-monetary influences – on peace and war, inventions, laws, race, education, population and so forth. But the argument of our first volume has gone to show that their power to put their projects into execution on terms which they deem attractive, almost entirely depends on the behaviour of the banking and monetary system.

Thus the rate at which the world's wealth has accumulated [133] has been far more variable than habits of thrift have been.
. . .

Chapter 31
The Problem of the Management of Money

1 *The Control of Prices Through the Rate of Investment*

The banking system has no direct control over the prices of individual commodities or over the rates of money earnings of the factors of production. Nor has it, in reality, any *direct* control over the quantity of money; for it is characteristic of monetary systems that the central bank is ready to buy for money at a stipulated rate of discount any quantity of securities of certain approved types.

Thus – in spite of the qualifications which we shall have to introduce later in respect of the so-called 'open market' operations of the central banks – it is broadly true to say that the governor of the whole system is the rate of discount. For this is the only factor which is directly subject to the will and *fiat* of the central authority . . .

This means . . . that the control of prices is exercised in the contemporary world *through control of the rate of investment.* There is nothing that the central authority can do . . . except to influence the rate of investment . . .

Thus the art of the management of money consists partly in [189] devising technical methods . . . to exercise control over the rate of investment . . . and partly in possessing enough knowledge and prognosticating power to enable the technical methods to be applied at the right time and in the right degree . . .   [190]

. . .

Chapter 32
Methods of National Management
I *The Control of the Member Banks*

[T]he central bank will be able to control the volume of cash and of bank money in circulation, if it can control the volume of its own total assets; . . . and if the central bank can control the latter, it will control, indirectly, the total of cash and bank money . . . [201] What are these assets? A triple classification of a central bank's variable assets . . . [is]: (1) gold, (2) investments and (3) advances.

. . .

The amount of the central bank's investments . . . is entirely within its own control . . . Action directed towards varying the amount of these is now usually called 'open-market policy'. The amount of advances is generally supposed at least partially . . . within its control by means of variations in bank rate, i.e. by raising or lowering the terms on which it will make advances . . . [202]

. . .

III *The British System*

The new post-war element of 'management' consists in the habitual employment of an 'open-market' policy by which the Bank of England buys and sells investments with a view to keeping the reserve resources of the member banks at the level which it desires. This method . . . seems to be the ideal

[206] one ... [I]t enables the Bank of England to maintain an absolute control over the creation of credit by the member banks ... It is not an exaggeration to say that the individual member banks have virtually no power to influence the aggregate volume of bank money – unless they depart from their reserve-ratio
[207] conventions.

...

VI *Methods of Varying Member Bank Reserve Ratios*

The possibility of an inadequacy of ammunition interfering in exceptional circumstances with the efficacy of open-market operations makes it worth while to mention a further expedient which has never yet been put into practice, namely, a
[232] discretion to the central bank to vary with due notice and by small degrees the proportion of legal reserves which the member banks are required to hold.

...

Though it may seem revolutionary now, nevertheless some such provision, duly safeguarded, should, I think, be added to the powers of the ideal central bank of the future. It goes straight to the root of the matter, instead of relying on the indirect and roundabout influences which our empirical systems of monetary management have evolved for themselves. If member banks are lending too much and increasing cash balances without due regard to the requirements of their customers ... or if, on the other hand, they are lending too little, the variation in their reserve proportions puts on them the directest possible pressure
[233] to move in the desired direction.

...

Chapter 35
[*'Auri Sacra Fames' was an interlude disquisition, decked out in typical Keynes imagery, on the fading role of gold.*]

I *Auri Sacra Fames*

Dr Freud relates that there are peculiar reasons deep in our subconsciousness why gold in particular should satisfy strong

instincts and serve as a symbol. The magical properties, with [258]
which Egyptian priestcraft anciently imbued the yellow metal,
it has never altogether lost. Yet, whilst gold as a store of value
has always had devoted patrons, it is, as the sole standard of
purchasing power, almost a parvenu. In 1914 gold had held
this position in Great Britain *de jure* over less than a hundred
years (though *de facto* for more than two hundred), and in most
other countries over less than sixty. For except during rather
brief intervals gold has been too scarce to serve the needs of the
world's principal medium of currency. Gold is, and always has
been, an extraordinarily scarce commodity. A modern liner
could convey across the Atlantic in a single voyage all the gold
which has been dredged or mined in seven thousand years. At
intervals of five hundred or a thousand years a new source of
supply has been discovered – the latter half of the nineteenth
century was one of these epochs – and a temporary abundance
has ensued. But as a rule, generally speaking, there has been not
enough.

Of late years the *auri sacra fames* has sought to envelop
itself in a garment of respectability as densely respectable as
was ever met with, even in the realms of sex or religion. Whether
this was first put on as a necessary armour to win the hard-won
fight against bimetallism and is still worn, as the gold advocates allege, because gold is the sole prophylactic against the
plague of fiat moneys, or whether it is a furtive Freudian cloak,
we need not be curious to enquire. But before we proceed with a
scientific and would-be unbiased examination of its claims, we
had better remind the reader of what he well knows – namely,
that gold has become part of the apparatus of conservatism
and is one of the matters which we cannot expect to see handled without prejudice.

One great change, nevertheless – probably, in the end, a
fatal change – has been effected by our generation. During the [259]
war individuals threw their little stocks into the national melt-
ing pots. Wars have sometimes served to disperse gold, as when
Alexander scattered the temple hoards of Persia or Pizarro
those of the Incas. But on this occasion war concentrated gold
in the vaults of the central banks; and these banks have not

released it. Thus, almost throughout the world, gold has been withdrawn from circulation. It no longer passes from hand to hand, and the touch of the metal has been taken away from men's greedy palms. The little household gods, who dwelt in purses and stockings and tin boxes, have been swallowed by a single golden image in each country, which lives underground and is not seen. Gold is out of sight – gone back again into the soil. But when gods are no longer seen in a yellow panoply walking the earth, we begin to rationalise them; and it is not long before there is nothing left.

Thus the long age of commodity money has at last passed finally away before the age of representative money. Gold has ceased to be a coin, a hoard, a tangible claim to wealth, of which the value cannot slip away so long as the hand of the individual clutches the material stuff. It has become a much more abstract thing – just a standard of value; and it only keeps this nominal status by being handed round from time to time in quite small quantities amongst a group of central banks, on the occasions when one of them has been inflating or deflating its managed representative money in a different degree from what is appropriate to the behaviour of its neighbours. Even the handing [260] round is becoming a little old-fashioned, being the occasion of unnecessary travelling expenses, and the most modern way, called 'earmarking', is to change the ownership without shifting the location. It is not a far step from this to the beginning of arrangements between central banks by which, without ever formally renouncing the rule of gold, the quantity of metal actually buried in their vaults may come to stand, by a modern alchemy, for what they please, and its value for what they choose. Thus gold, originally stationed in heaven with his consort silver, as Sun and Moon, having first doffed his sacred attributes and come to earth as an autocrat, may next descend to the sober status of a constitutional king with a cabinet of banks; and it may never be necessary to proclaim a republic. But this is not yet – the evolution may be quite otherwise. The friends of gold will have to be extremely wise and moderate if [261] they are to avoid a revolution.

. . .

Chapter 36
Problems of International Management –
The Problem of National Autonomy

I *The Dilemma of an International System*

... [C]ircumstances may exist in which, if a country's rate of
interest is fixed for it by outside circumstances, it is impracticable for it to reach investment equilibrium at home. This will
happen, if its foreign balance is inelastic, and if, at the same
time, it is unable to absorb the whole of its savings in new
investment at the world rate of interest. It will also tend to
happen ... if its money costs of production are sticky.   [271]
...

This, then, is the dilemma of an international monetary system –
to preserve the advantages of the stability of the local currencies
of the various members of the system in terms of the international standard, and to preserve at the same time an adequate
local autonomy for each member over its domestic rate of
interest and its volume of foreign lending.   [272]
...

IV *Should Standards of Value Be International?*

What, then, should be our final conclusion in the choice
between an international and a national standard of value?

Let us first make sure that the claims of the international
standard – namely, the conveniences and facilities secured to foreign trade and foreign lending – do not receive *more* than justice. [297]
So far as foreign trade is concerned ... it is ... little more than a
convenience ... [the advantages of which] can be satisfactorily
secured ... by a free and reliable market in forward exchange.
...

When we come to foreign lending ... the advantages of a fixed
exchange must ... be estimated much higher. In this case the
contracts between borrower and lender may cover a far longer
period than would be contemplated by any practicable dealings
in forward exchange. This uncertainty as to the future rate of
foreign exchange would inevitably introduce an element of

doubt into the transaction which would certainly have some
[298] deterrent effect on the international mobility of loan capital.
. . .

If we deliberately desire that there should be a high degree of
mobility for international lending, both for long and for short
periods, then this is, admittedly, a strong argument for a fixed
rate of exchange and a rigid international standard.

What, then, is the reason for hesitating before we commit ourselves to such a system? Primarily a doubt whether it is wise to
have a currency system with a much wider ambit than our banking system, our tariff system and our wage system. Can we afford
to allow a disproportionate degree of mobility to a single element
in an economic system which we leave extremely rigid in several
other respects? . . . [To] introduce a mobile element, highly sensitive to outside influences, as a connected part of a machine of
which the other parts are much more rigid, may invite breakages.

Therefore this is not a question to be answered lightly. The
belief in an extreme mobility of international lending and a policy of unmitigated *laissez-faire* towards foreign loans, on which
most Englishmen have been brought up, has been based . . .
on too simple a view of the causal relations between foreign
lending and foreign investment. Because – apart from gold
movements – *net* foreign lending and *net* foreign investment
[299] must always exactly balance, it has been assumed that no
serious problem presents itself. Since lending and investment
must be equal, an increase of lending must cause an increase in
investment – so the argument runs – and decrease of lending
must cause a decrease of investment; in short, the prosperity of
our export industries is bound up with the volume of our
foreign lending . . . All this, however, neglects the painful, and
perhaps violent, reactions of the mechanism which has to be
brought into play in order to force *net* foreign lending and *net*
foreign investment into equality.[18]

I do not know why this should not be considered obvious. If
English investors, not liking the outlook at home . . . begin to
buy more American securities than before, why should it be supposed that this will be naturally balanced by increased British
exports? For, of course, it will not. It will, in the first instance, set

up a serious instability of the domestic credit system – the ultimate working out of which it is difficult or impossible to predict.

    ... If it were as easy to put wages up and down as it is to put
bank rate up and down, well and good. But this is not the actual
situation. A change in international financial conditions or in
the wind and weather of speculative sentiment may alter the
volume of foreign lending, if nothing is done to counteract it, by
tens of millions in a few weeks. Yet there is no possibility of
altering the balance of imports and exports to correspond.   [300]
...

Assuming, however, that these practical and probably temporary, even if prolonged, difficulties are out of the way, there still
remains an objection to an international standard, in that it
commits the world to one particular type of standard of value
as governing the long-period norm.

    For our long-period standard of value we have to choose,
broadly speaking, between three general types. The first of these
is the purchasing power of money or consumption standard, or
something of that type. The second is the earnings standard, the
ratio of which to the consumption standard rises in proportion
to any increase in the efficiency of the factors of production. The
third is some version of the international standard, i.e. a standard based on the prices of the principal commodities which enter
into international trade weighted in proportion to their importance in world commerce, which in practice might not be very
different from a wholesale standard of raw materials.   [301]

[*After briefly considering the advantages of the first two,
Keynes concludes:*]

Today the reasons seem stronger ... to accept, substantially, the
fait accompli of an international standard; and to hope for progress from that starting point towards a scientific management of
the central controls – for that is what our monetary system surely
is – of our economic life. For to seek the ultimate good *via* an
autonomous national system would mean not only a frontal
attack on the forces of conservatism, entrenched with all the
advantages of possession, but it would divide the forces of intelligence and goodwill and separate the interests of nations.   [302]
...

Chapter 37
Methods of National Management – III The Control
of the Rate of Investment

I *Can the Banking System Control*
the Price Level?

Those who attribute sovereign power to the monetary authority on the governance of prices do not, of course, claim that the
terms on which money is supplied is the *only* influence affecting the price level. To maintain that supplies in a reservoir can
be maintained at any required level by pouring enough water
into it is not inconsistent with admitting that the level of the
reservoir depends on many other factors besides how much
water is poured in – for example, natural rainfall, evaporation,
leakage and the habits of the users of the system. Such a claim
would only be unjustified if the amount of evaporation or leakage or other source of loss, or the consumption of those using
[304] the system, were a direct function of the amount of water
poured in, of such a character that the more poured in the
greater for that reason the consumption or the diminution in
the natural rainfall or other occasion of loss, so that no amount
of inflow would raise the supplies in the reservoir above a certain level. Which of these alternatives is the true analogy for the
effect on the price level of the creation of additional supplies of
[305] money by the banking system?
       . . .

II *Short-Term Rates of Interest and*
Long-Term Rates

[*The main discussion in TM of the psychology of investment.
It anticipates chapter 13 of GT; see below p. 218.*]
The main, direct influence of the banking system is over the
short-term rate of interest. But when it is a question of controlling the rate of investments, not in working capital but in fixed
capital, it is the long-term rate of interest which chiefly matters.
How can we be sure that the long-term rate of interest will
respond to the wishes of a currency authority which will be

exerting its direct influence, as it must, mainly on the short-term rate? . . . It may . . . seem illogical that the rate of interest fixed [315] for a period three months should have any noticeable effect on the terms needed for loans of twenty years or more.

In fact, however, experience shows that, as a rule, the influence of the short-term rate of interest on the long-term rate [*the bond rate*] is much greater than anyone who argued on the above lines would have expected. We shall find, moreover, that there are some sound reasons, based on the technical character of the market, why it is not unnatural that this should be so.   [316] . . .

(a) If the running yield on bonds is greater than the rate payable on short-term loans, a profit is obtained by borrowing short in order to carry long-term securities so long as the latter [319] do not actually fall in value during the currency of the loan. . . .

It is rarely the case that bond yields will fail to rise (or fall) if the short-term rate remains at an absolutely higher (or lower) level than the bond yield even for a few weeks.

(b) . . . Where short-term yields are high, the safety and liquidity of short-term securities appear extremely attractive. But when short-term yields are very low, not only does this attraction disappear, but another motive enters in, namely a fear lest the institution [*banks, insurance companies, unit trusts, etc.*] may be unable to maintain its established level of income . . . A point comes, therefore, when they hasten to move into long-dated securities; the movement itself sends up the prices of the latter; and this movement seems to confirm the wisdom of those who were recommending the policy of the changeover.   [320] . . .

(c) How far the motives which I have been attributing above to the market are strictly rational, I leave it to others to judge. They are best regarded, I think, as an example of how sensitive – over-sensitive if you like – to the near future, about which we may think that we know a little, even the best-informed must be, because, in truth, we know almost nothing about the more remote future. And the exaggerations of this same tendency, to which we now come, also play a part.

For part of the explanation which we are seeking is to be found in [a] psychological phenomenon which appears even more strikingly in the current market valuation of ordinary shares. The value of a company's shares, and even of its bonds, will be found to be sensitive to a degree, which a rational observer from outside might consider quite absurd, to short-period fluctuations in its known or anticipated profits. The shares of a railway company will be highly sensitive to its weekly traffic returns, even if it be well known that these are influenced by necessarily transient factors, such as an exceptionally good or bad harvest in the country concerned, or a strike in the district served by the railway, or even an international exhibition. Such events will often cause the capital value of the shares to fluctuate by an amount which far exceeds any possible change in its [322] profits due to the event in question. These are extreme cases, perhaps; but it must be well known to anyone who follows the prices of ordinary shares that their market valuation shows a strong bias towards the assumption that whatever conditions and results have been characteristic of the present and the recent past, and even more those which are expected to be characteristic of the near future, will be lasting and permanent. And the bond market is not exempt from the same weakness.

Nor need we be surprised. The ignorance of even the best-informed investor about the more remote future is much greater than his knowledge, and he cannot but be influenced to a degree which would seem wildly disproportionate to anyone who really knew the future, by the little which he knows for certain, or almost for certain, about the recent past and the near future, and be forced to seek a clue mainly here to trends further ahead.

But if this is true of the best-informed, the vast majority of those who are concerned with the buying and selling of securities know almost nothing whatever about what they are doing. They do not possess even the rudiments of what is required for a valid judgment, and are the prey of hopes and fears easily aroused by transient events and as easily dispelled. This is one of the odd characteristics of the capitalist system under which we live, which, when we are dealing with the real world, is not to be overlooked.

But there is also a further reason why it may often profit the wisest to anticipate mob psychology rather than the real trend of events, and to ape unreason proleptically. For the value of a security is determined, not by the terms on which one could expect to purchase the whole block of the outstanding interest, but by the small fringe which is the subject of actual dealing; just as current new investment is only a small fringe on the edge of the totality of existing investments. Now this fringe is largely dealt in by professional financiers – speculators you may call them – who have no intention of holding the securities long enough for the influence of distant events to have its effect; their object is to re-sell to the mob after a few weeks or at most a few months. It is natural, therefore, that they should [323] be influenced by the cost of borrowing, and still more by their expectations on the basis of past experience of the trend of mob psychology. Thus, so long as the crowd can be relied on to act in a certain way, even if it be misguided, it will be to the advantage of the better-informed professional to act in the same way – a short period ahead. Apart, moreover, from calculations of greater or less ignorance, most people are too timid and too greedy, too impatient and too nervous about their investments, the fluctuations in the paper value of which can so easily obliterate the results of so much honest effort, to take long views or to place even as much reliance as they reasonably might on the dubieties of the long period; the apparent certainties of the short period, however deceptive we may suspect them to be, are much more attractive.

Nor is it so precarious as might be supposed to depend upon these psychological characteristics of the market. It is a case, indeed, of a homoeopathic cure. For it is just these half-unreasonable characteristics of the market which are the source of many of the troubles which it is the object of management to remedy. If investors were capable of taking longer views, the fluctuations in the natural rate of interest would not be so great as they are. The real prospects do not suffer such large and quick changes as does the spirit of enterprise. The willingness to invest is stimulated and depressed by the immediate prospects. It is not unreasonable, therefore, to depend on short-period influences for counteracting a violent, and perhaps unreasoning, change in sentiment.

We may carry away, therefore, to the next section of our argument the conclusion that short-term rates influence long-term rates more than the reader might expect, and that it is not dif-
[324] ficult to find sufficient explanations for this observed fact.

III *Can the Banking System Control the Rate of Investment?*

[T]here is no reason to doubt the ability of a central bank to make its short-term rate of interest effective in the market. These changes in themselves must have *some* effect in the desired
[325] direction; for they at least determine the interest cost of the revolving fund of working capital and of carrying liquid stocks.

. . .

(b) *The fringe of unsatisfied borrowers*

The relaxation or contraction of credit . . . does not operate, however, merely through a change in the rate charged to bor-
[326] rowers; it also functions through a change in the abundance of credit. If the supply of credit was distributed in an absolutely free competitive market, these two conditions – quantity and price – would be uniquely correlated . . . and we should not need to consider them separately. But in practice . . . the conditions of a free competitive market for bank loans are imperfectly fulfilled. For it is not the case . . . that anyone offering security can borrow as much as he likes from the British banking system . . . There is, that is to say, in Great Britain an habitual system of rationing in the attitude of banks to borrowers . . . Thus there is normally a fringe of unsatisfied borrowers who are not considered to have the first claim on a bank's favours, but to whom the bank would be quite ready to lend if it were to find itself in a position to lend more.

The existence of this unsatisfied fringe . . . allows the banking system a means of influencing the rate of investment supple-
[327] mentary to mere changes in the short-term rate of interest.

. . .

(d) *Open-market operations to the point of saturation*

So far we have been dealing with the normal and orthodox

methods by which a central bank can use its powers for easing (or stiffening) the credit situation to stimulate (or retard) the rate of new investment. If these measures are applied in the right degree and *at the right time*, I doubt whether it would often be necessary to go beyond them or to apply the extraordinary methods next to be considered. It is only, that is to say, if the milder remedies have not been applied in time, so that conditions of acute slump or boom have been allowed to develop, that more extreme measures will have to be invoked and that doubts may be reasonably entertained whether even these more extreme measures will be wholly efficacious.

These extraordinary methods are, in fact, no more than an intensification of the normal procedure of open-market operations. I do not know of any case in which the method of open-market operations has been carried out *à outrance*. Central banks have always been too nervous hitherto – partly, perhaps, under the influence of crude versions of the quantity theory – of taking measures which would have the effect of causing the total volume of bank money to depart widely from its normal volume, [331] whether in excess or in defect. But this attitude of mind neglects, I think, the part which the 'bullishness' or 'bearishness' of the public plays in the demand for bank money; it forgets the financial circulation in its concern for the industrial circulation, and overlooks the statistical fact that the former may be quite as large as the latter and much more capable of sharp variation.

I suggest, therefore, that bolder measures are sometimes advisable, and that they are quite free from serious danger whenever there has developed on the part of the capitalist public an obstinate 'bullishness' or 'bearishness' towards securities. On such occasions the central bank should carry its open-market operations to the point of satisfying to saturation the desire of the public to hold savings deposits, or of exhausting the supply of such deposits in the contrary case.

The risk of bringing to bear too rapidly and severely on the industrial circulation, when it is the financial circulation which is being aimed at, is greater I think in the case of a contraction of credit than in the case of an expansion. But, on the other hand, it is less likely to be necessary to resort to extreme

measures to check a boom than to check a slump. Booms, I suspect, are almost always due to tardy or inadequate action by
the banking system such as should be avoidable; there is much
more foundation for the view that it is slumps which may
sometimes get out of hand and defy all normal methods of
control. It will be, therefore, on the problem of checking a slump
that we shall now concentrate our attention.

My remedy in the event of the obstinate persistence of a
slump would consist, therefore, in the purchase of securities by
the central bank until the long-term market rate of interest has
been brought down to the limiting point, which we shall have to
admit a few paragraphs further on. It should not be beyond the
power of a central bank (international complications apart) to
bring down the long-term market rate of interest to any figure
at which it is itself prepared to buy long-term securities. For the
[332]   bearishness of the capitalist public is never *very* obstinate, and
when the rate of interest on savings deposits is next door to
nothing the saturation point can fairly soon be reached. If the
central bank supplies the member banks with more funds than
they can lend at short term, in the first place the short-term rate
of interest will decline towards zero, and in the second place the
member banks will soon begin, if only to maintain their profits,
to second the efforts of the central bank by themselves buying
securities. This means that the price of bonds will rise unless
there are many persons to be found who, as they see the prices
of long-term bonds rising, prefer to sell them and hold the proceeds liquid at a very low rate of interest. If (e.g.) the long-term
rate is 3 per cent per annum above the short-term rate, this
means that the mathematical expectation for bond prices in the
minds of such persons is for a fall of 3 per cent per annum; and
at a time when bond prices are in fact rising and the central
bank is accentuating the cheapness of money, there is not likely
to be a large volume of such selling – unless the price of bonds
has been driven to a level which is generally believed to be quite
excessive from the long-period point of view, a contingency and
a limiting factor to the consideration of which we will return
shortly. If the effect of such measures is to raise the price of
'equities' (e.g. ordinary shares) more than the price of bonds, no

harm *in a time of slump* will result from this; for investment can be stimulated by its being unusually easy to raise resources by the sale of ordinary shares as well as by high bond prices. Moreover, a very excessive price for equities is not likely to occur at a time of depression and business losses.

Thus I see small reason to doubt that the central bank can produce a large effect on the cost of raising new resources for long-term investment, if it is prepared to persist with its open-market policy far enough. What, however, are in practice the factors limiting the degree in which it can push such a policy home?

There is, first of all, the question of the sufficiency of its 'ammunition', i.e. of its power to go on buying or selling in adequate quantity securities of a suitable kind. The lack of suitable ammunition is more likely to hamper a central bank when it is seeking to contract the volume of bank money than when it is seeking to expand it, since its stock of securities at the commencement of its contraction policy is necessarily limited. But it also operates, in a sense, against an expansionist policy, since a central bank is generally limited in the type of securities which it purchases, so that, if it continues such purchases beyond a certain point, it may create an entirely artificial position in them relatively to other securities. It is to provide against the contingency of insufficient ammunition for the carrying on of open-market operations *à outrance*, that I have suggested ... that the central bank should have power to vary within limits the reserve requirements of its member banks. [333]

In the second place, circumstances can arise when, for a time, the natural rate of interest [*the expected rate of profit on investment*] falls so low that there is a very wide and quite unusual gap between the ideas of borrowers and of lenders in the market on long-term. When prices are falling, profits low, the future uncertain and financial sentiment depressed and alarmed, the natural rate of interest may fall, for a short period, almost to nothing. But it is precisely at such a time as this that lenders are most exigent and least inclined to embark their resources on long term unless it be on the most unexceptionable security; so that the bond rate, far from falling towards nothing, may be expected – apart from the operations of the central bank – to be higher than normal. How is it possible in such circumstances, we may reasonably ask, to keep the market rate and the natural rate of long-term interest at an equality with one another, *unless we impose on the central bank the duty of purchasing bonds up to a price far beyond what it considers to be the long-period norm*. Yet, if its instincts as to the long-period norm are correct, this will mean that these purchases, when in due course they have to be reversed by sales at a later date, may show a serious financial loss [*that is, involve* [334] *taxpayer liabilities*]. This contingency – the reader should notice – can only arise as the result of inaccurate forecasting by the capitalist public and of a difference of opinion between the central bank and long-term borrowers as to the prospective rate of returns.

We might perhaps expect the central bank, as representing the public interest, to be ready to run the risks of future prospects when private interests reckon these risks to be unusually high. But the choice may conceivably lie between assuming the burden of a prospective loss, allowing the slump to continue, and socialistic action by which some official body steps into the shoes which the feet of the entrepreneurs are too cold to occupy.

I would repeat, however, that these extreme situations are not likely to arise except as the result of some previous mistake which has prevented the slumping tendency from being remedied at an earlier stage before so complete a lack of confidence had sapped the spirits and the energies of enterprise.

. . .

The third limiting factor arises out of the presence of international complications which we have been excluding so far from our purview but to which we must now attend.

We come finally to what is in the world of today the insuperable limitation on the power of skilled monetary management to avoid booms and depressions – a limitation which it would be foolish to overlook or to minimise. No national central bank which is a member of an international system, not even the Federal Reserve System of the United States, can expect to preserve the stability of its price level, if it is acting in isolation and is not assisted by corresponding action on the part of the other central banks. Moreover, whilst the broad interests of the various central banks are likely to be concordant, we cannot rely on their being so in detail and at all times. For the reasons which we have explained above in dealing with the problem whether the standard of value should be international in character, the [335] immediate interests of different countries may be divergent, and action calculated to preserve the stability of employment in one of them may not necessarily have the same result in another.

Against the international complications which at present prevent any successful attempt at managing our standard of value scientifically and preserving investment equilibrium throughout the world, the only adequate remedy could be found in a system of supernational management such as we shall outline very briefly in the next chapter. [336]

. . .

Finally, there remains in reserve a weapon by which a country can partially rescue itself when its international disequilibrium is involving it in severe unemployment. In such an event open-market operations by the central bank intended to bring down the market rate of interest and stimulate investment may, by misadventure, stimulate foreign lending instead and so provoke an outward flow of gold on a larger scale than it can afford. In such a case it is not sufficient for the central authority to stand ready to lend – for the money may flow into the wrong hands – it must also stand ready to borrow. In other words, the Government must itself promote a programme of domestic investment. It may be a choice between employing labour to create capital wealth, which will yield less than the market rate of interest, or not employing it at all. If this is the position, the national interest, both immediate and prospective, will be promoted by choosing the first alternative. But if foreign borrowers are ready and eager, it will be impossible in a competitive open market to bring the rate down to the level appropriate to domestic investment. Thus the desired result can only be obtained through some method by which, in effect, the Government subsidises approved types of domestic investment or itself directs domestic schemes of capital development.

About the application of this method to the position of
[337] Great Britain in 1929–30 I have written much elsewhere, and
need not enlarge on it here. Assuming that it was not practicable, at least for a time, to bring costs down relatively to costs
abroad sufficiently to increase the foreign balance by a large
amount, then a policy of subsidising home investment by promoting (say) 3 per cent schemes of national development was a
valid means of increasing both employment today and the
national wealth hereafter. The only alternative remedy of
immediate applicability, in such circumstances, was to subsidise foreign investment by the exclusion of foreign imports, so
that the failure of increased exports to raise the foreign balance
to the equilibrium level might be made good by diminishing the
[338] volume of imports.

[*For Keynes's proposal for 'supernational management', see
chapter 4, pp. 437–43 below.*]

18

The Great Depression

[*Keynes offered several analyses of the causes of the Great
Depression, and slowness of recovery, which point to both differences from and similarities to the economic contraction of
2008. The main differences are as follows.*

*(1) The decade of the 2000s was a decade of ultra-cheap
money and a low rate of real capital accumulation, whereas
the leading characteristic of the 1920s was 'an extraordinary
willingness to borrow money for the purposes of new real
investment at very high rates of interest'.[19] However, speculative excitement – housing in the late 2000s, stock exchange
securities in 1928–9 – emerged before both collapses.*

*(2) Banking collapse was a much more important causal fac-
tor in 2008–9 than in 1929–31. The US economy was about
twice as heavily leveraged in the 2000s as in the 1920s, with
the banks spreading mortgage risk through securitization.*

Because the economy in the 1920s was much less dependent on bank loans, the effect on the banking system of the collapse in asset values was delayed. In 2008, the collapse of the banks caused the depression; in 1929–31 the banks collapsed because of the depression. The major banking collapse came almost two years after the start of the Great Depression. Describing the situation in autumn 1929, Kindleberger wrote: 'Deflation, then, moved from the decline in stock markets to production cuts and inventory runoffs in one sequence, and from stock prices to commodity prices to the reduced value of imports in another. Both were fast.'[20]

(3) The collapse in commodity prices in 1929 was a triggering cause of the Great Depression rather than an induced effect of the economic downturn, because commodities constituted a much greater share of world output, in both developed and developing countries, than they do today. Hence debt deflation – the rise in the real burden of debt owing to the fall in prices – played a bigger part in the unfolding of the Great Depression than it did in the contraction of 2008–9, and explains Keynes's insistence on the importance of engineering a rise in the price level.

(4) In the 1920s there was no deposit insurance, and no bank bail-outs. Thousands of small banks (in the United States) failed, and depositors lost their money.

(5) Policy made a big difference. The decline in output and prices continued for thirteen quarters after the crash of 1929, but only for four after the crash of 2008. This was because the major countries used monetary and fiscal policy to offset the collapse of 2008 but failed to do so in the earlier episode. As a result falling prices were a much bigger feature of post-1929 than post-2008. In 1929–31 countries were constrained in the use of monetary and fiscal instruments by being on the gold standard, but the main resistance to their use was ideological, since in the USA, with its large current account surplus, the Fed could have used open-market operations 'à outrance' without fear of being driven off gold. This would have eased monetary conditions elsewhere.[21] The stimulus measures in 2009 stopped a repeat of the Great Depression, but at the cost of a huge

*increase in public indebtedness which terminated the fiscal
stimulus prematurely, leaving economies in what Keynes in
1931 described as 'long, dragging conditions of semi-slump, or
at least subnormal prosperity' (CW 13, p. 344) – which, despite some recovery, is roughly where much of the world is at
the time of writing (April 2014).*

*The following four excerpts give the flavour of Keynes's 'real
time' analysis of the Great Depression. The first comes from
chapter 37 of TM, as above.]*

CW 6, A Treatise on Money (1930)

IV *The Slump of* 1930

I am writing these concluding lines in the midst of the worldwide
slump of 1930. The wholesale indexes have fallen by 20 per cent
in a year. The prices of a large group of the world's most important staple commodities – wheat, oats, barley, sugar, coffee; cotton,
wool, jute, silk; copper, tin, spelter; rubber – stood a year ago
50 per cent higher in price than they do now. The American index
of production has receded by more than 20 per cent. In Great Britain, Germany and the United States at least 10 million workers
stand unemployed. One cannot but be moved by a feeling of the
importance of diagnosing correctly the scientific causes of these
misfortunes. Was the catastrophe avoidable? Can it be remedied?

Thus I am lured on to the rash course of giving an opinion
on contemporary events which are too near to be visible
distinctly; namely, my view of the root causes of what has happened, which is as follows.

The most striking change in the investment factors of the
post-war world compared with the pre-war world is to be
found in the high level of the market rate of interest. As a rough
[338] generalisation one may say that the long-term rate of interest is
nearly 50 per cent higher today than twenty years ago. Yet the
population of the industrial countries is not increasing as fast
as formerly, and is a good deal better equipped per head than it
was with housing, transport and machines. On the other hand,

the volume of lending to the less advanced parts of the world is not markedly large – indeed the contrary, since Russia, China and India, which include within their borders a substantial proportion of the population of the world, are able, for one reason or another, to borrow next to nothing on the international markets; whilst the United States has converted itself from a borrowing to a lending country. Why, then, should the rate of interest be so high?

The answer is, I suggest, that for some years after the war sundry causes, to be enumerated, interposed to maintain the natural rate of interest at a high level; that these, more recently, have ceased to operate; that sundry other causes have nevertheless maintained the market rate of interest; and that, consequently, there has now developed, somewhat suddenly, an unusually wide gap between the ideas of borrowers and those of lenders, that is, between the natural rate of interest and the market rate.

For a few years after the war there were obvious reasons why the natural rate of interest should stand for a time above its long-period norm. In particular, a large volume of investment was required to restore the revolving fund of working capital for peacetime production. Then there was war damage to be made good, arrears of housing, etc., to be made up. Perhaps this phase was coming to an end in 1924–5. Meanwhile, certain new industries were leading to large-scale investment, especially in the United States – public utilities based on the use of electricity (and also natural gas), the motor industry and roads to serve motorists, the cinema and radio industries. These operated to maintain the natural rate of interest to some extent. But, looking back, I am inclined to think that the seeds of the [339] recent collapse were already being sown so long ago as 1925. By that date the natural rate of interest, outside the United States, was probably due for a fall. But round about that date – some of them beginning rather earlier, others rather later – there supervened two sets of events, not wholly disconnected, which served to maintain the market rate of interest somewhat regardless of the underlying realities of the natural rate – namely, the general return to the gold standard, and the settlement of reparations and the war debts.

For these events, though they had no bearing whatever on the real yield of new investment, were a powerful influence on the market rate of interest. Those central banks which had entered upon the new responsibility of maintaining gold parity, were naturally nervous and disposed to take no risks – some of them because they had but just emerged from currency catastrophes attended by a total loss of credit, others (especially Great Britain) because they had returned to the gold standard at a dangerously high parity probably inconsistent with their existing domestic equilibrium. This nervousness inevitably tended in the direction of credit restriction, which was not in the least called for by the real underlying economic facts, throughout Europe and, sympathetically, in many other quarters. Great Britain played a leading part in tightening the hold on credit and in urging a hurried all-round return back to gold. The inadequacy of free gold supplies (i.e. gold in the hands of ready sellers of the metal) much aggravated the position. At this stage, indeed, only the United States was entirely exempt from some measure of credit restriction.

Whilst this tendency towards restriction was tightening the terms of lending and stiffening the attitude of the purchasers of securities, another aspect of the same set of events was providing a supply of borrowers who were prepared to pay terms which were not based on any calculation of the probable yield of actual new investment. These borrowers were of two types. [340] The first were the 'distress' borrowers – as they are conveniently called – chiefly governments, who were borrowing, not for investment in productive enterprise, but to meet their urgent liabilities, to satisfy their creditors, and to comply with their treaty obligations. The terms which such borrowers will pay have but little to do with the prospective returns of current investment and are dictated by the lenders. The second class were the 'banking' borrowers – sometimes governments and sometimes banks – who were borrowing, again not for investment in productive enterprise, but to build up liquid reserves, partly gold and partly foreign balances, with which to protect their newly restored currencies. We had the extraordinary situation in 1927–8 of the United States lending on long term at high rates of interest, largely to Europe, amounts several times greater than her favourable balance, and being able to do so because these borrowers at once re-deposited with her on short term the major part of what they had just borrowed on long term at rates nearly double, perhaps, those which they could obtain on short term for their re-deposits. In two or three years some £500 million was thus borrowed on long term and re-deposited on short term – which naturally had a tendency to upset the normal relation between short-term and long-term rates of interest, such as these would be, if they were mainly determined, as in the long run they must be, by the ideas of those who are borrowing for actual investment.

Finally, in 1928–9 these 'artificial' borrowers on long term – if we may so designate borrowers who are not influenced by the return on actual current investment – were reinforced by a third class of 'artificial' borrowers, this time on short term, namely, the 'speculative' borrowers, who, once more, were borrowing not for investment in new productive enterprise, but in order to participate in the feverish 'bull' movement in 'equities' (mostly of a semi-monopolistic character which could not easily be duplicated), which was occurring most sensationally in the United States but also in varying degrees on most of the stock exchanges of the world. Moreover, the anxiety of conservative [341] banking opinion to bring this speculative fever somehow to an end provided a new motive for credit restriction by the central banks.

By the middle of 1929 'genuine' borrowers – if we may so designate borrowers for purposes of actual new investment which they deem profitable on the terms offering – whose activities were already, in my judgment, below par in most countries other than the United States, were becoming squeezed out. The more urgent needs of post-war reconstruction and of the new types of industry having been satisfied, it simply was not worth their while to borrow on a scale equal to the volume of savings at the high market rate of interest, which was being maintained partly by the 'artificial' borrowers and partly by the credit policy of the central banks.

The divergence thus arising between the market rate of

interest and the natural rate was, therefore, the primary cause of the sagging price level. But once this had proceeded far enough to generate 'slump' psychology in the minds of entrepreneurs, it was of course reinforced, as usual, by other and perhaps quantitatively greater influences.

For I should not suppose that – taking the world as a whole – the deficiency of current investment relatively to saving, which initially engendered the slump, would be responsible by itself for a fall in the price level of much more than 5 per cent. But as soon as the losses thus caused have become sufficiently patent to entrepreneurs to lead them to curtail output, there is at once developed a far greater deficiency in net investment, due to the reduction in the volume of working capital corresponding to the lower level of production. Thus each curtailment of production by further reducing net investment causes a further fall of prices, which increases the losses of those entrepreneurs who are still carrying on and thus tends to reproduce itself in the [342] shape of a still further curtailment . . .

During the earliest phase of the slump th[e] reduction in working capital was probably partly offset by an increase in liquid capital as a result of the accumulation in stocks. In the second phase, stocks usually begin to fall, and this prolongs the period during which the aggregate deficiency of net investment exceeds the deficiency of fixed investment. But in the end a point comes – because firms cannot keep together their organisation and their connections if they cut output any further, even though they are making a loss, or because the expectations of the business world change, or because stocks are at a minimum, or, if for no other reason prior in time, because the general impoverishment of the community reduces saving – when neither working capital nor liquid capital are falling any further; and when this point is reached the slump touches bottom.

For the disinvestment in working capital, which so greatly aggravates the deficiency of investment in fixed capital, only proceeds so long as production is in the act of slumping. When production has got down to a low level and remains there, the reduction of working capital ceases; for the latter is a function, not of a low level of output, but of a declining level of output.

Thus, as soon as the index of production ceases to fall further, the deficiency of net investment is immediately decreased, which by itself tends in the direction of raising prices and diminishing losses; for the low level reached by prices is one which is only possible so long as output is declining, and when output ceases to decline prices must necessarily take a kick upwards again. Not only so – as soon as the index of production is rising again, increased investment in working capital will be necessary to balance the previous disinvestment. During the time that this is going on, the reinvestment in working capital may balance, partly or wholly, the deficiency of investment in fixed capital, and the natural rate of interest will temporarily catch up the market rate. But as soon as the index of production ceases to rise, then, if the excess of the long-term market rate of interest over the long-term natural rate has not been remedied by a decrease of the former or an increase of the lat- [343] ter, again a kickback of prices will be started. In this way, as a result of these self-generating secondary oscillations, an intermediate revival of quite impressive dimensions might be staged in spite of the basic conditions being unfavourable to a lasting recovery.

A partial recovery, therefore, is to be anticipated merely through the elapse of time and without the application of purposeful remedies. But if my diagnosis is correct, we cannot hope for a complete or lasting recovery until there has been a very great fall in the long-term market rate of interest throughout the world towards something nearer pre-war levels. Failing this, there will be a steady pressure towards profit deflation and a sagging price level. Yet the fall in the rate of interest is likely to be a long and a tedious process, unless it is accelerated by deliberate policy. For the slump itself produces a new queue of 'distress' borrowers who have to raise money on the best terms available to meet their losses, particularly governments of countries whose international equilibrium has been upset by the fall in the price of their exports – Australia and Brazil being notable examples. The thing will never cure itself by the lack of borrowers forcing down the rate; *for it absorbs just as much savings to finance losses as to finance investment.* In the second place, lenders have now been long accustomed to high rates of interest. The war, the post-war reconstruction, the epoch of 'artificial' borrowing have kept rates up for fifteen years to a level which would have seemed a generation ago quite beyond reasonable probability. Consequently a first-class bond yielding 4½ to 5 per cent, at a time when the short-term rate is not much above 2 per cent, does not strike the modern financier as the outstanding bargain that it would have seemed to his father. For there are very few people whose test of the normal and the permanent is not mainly fixed by the actual experience of the last fifteen years.

[344] Yet who can reasonably doubt the ultimate outcome – unless the obstinate maintenance of misguided monetary policies is going to continue to sap the foundations of capitalist society? In the leading financial countries savings are high enough, when they are being embodied in investment and are not being spilt in the financing of losses, to cause capital to increase five times faster than population. Unless we spill our savings, how are we to go on year after year finding an outlet for them in projects which will yield anything approaching the present long-term rate of interest? I am bold to predict, therefore, that to the economic historians of the future the slump of 1930 may present itself as the death struggle of the war-rates of interest and the re-emergence of the pre-war rates.

Now, at long last, this will doubtless come by itself. In Great Britain, perhaps £1,000 million, and in the United States, perhaps £4,000 million of investment resources, not required as cash, are being held on short term. Until quite lately these funds have earned a handsome rate of interest. In these difficult and dangerous days their holders may be slow and reluctant to move them. But in time they will. It will bore them in time to be earning 2 per cent or 1 per cent or nothing, when they might be earning 6 per cent or 5 per cent or 4 per cent. In time the multitude will move; and then it will suddenly be found that the supply of bonds at the present rate of interest is very strictly limited.

If, then, these are the causes, was the slump avoidable? And is it remediable? The causes to which we have assigned it were the outcome of policy; and in a sense, therefore, it was avoidable.

Yet it is evident that the policy could not have been radically different, unless the mentality and ideas of our rulers had also been greatly changed. That is to say, what has occurred is not exactly an accident; it has been deeply rooted in our general way of doing things.

But, granted that the past belongs to the past, need we be fatalistic about the future also? If we leave matters to cure themselves, the results may be disastrous. Prices may continue below the cost of production for a sufficiently long time for [345] entrepreneurs to feel that they have no recourse except an assault on the money incomes of the factors of production. This is a dangerous enterprise in a society which is both capitalist and democratic. It would be foolish of us to come to grief at a time when the pace of technical improvements is so great that we might, if we choose, be raising our standard of life by a measurable percentage every year. It has been my role for the last eleven years to play the part of Cassandra, first on the economic consequences of the peace and next on those of the return to gold; I hope that it may not be so on this occasion.

The level at which prices will ultimately settle down will depend on whether a fall in the rate of interest or a successful assault on the earnings of the factors of production comes first; for, in so far as the latter comes first and an income deflation is accomplished, the equilibrium price level, after profit deflation has come to an end, will be correspondingly lower. The risk ahead of us is, as I have suggested in chapter 30 (VIII), lest we are to experience the operation of the 'Gibson paradox', that is to say, of a market rate of interest which is falling but never fast enough to catch up the natural rate of interest, so that there is a recurrent profit deflation leading to a recurrent income deflation and a sagging price level. If this occurs, our present regime of capitalistic individualism will assuredly be replaced by a far-reaching socialism.

The remedy should come, I suggest, from a general recognition that the rate of investment need not be beyond our control, if we are prepared to use our banking systems to effect a proper adjustment of the market rate of interest. It might be sufficient merely to produce a general belief in the long continuance of a very low rate of short-term interest. The change, once it has begun, will feed on itself.

Of specific remedies the argument of this chapter suggests two as appropriate to the occasion. The Bank of England and the Federal Reserve Board might put pressure on their member [346] banks to do what would be to the private advantage of these banks if they were all to act together, namely, to reduce the rate of interest which they allow to depositors to a very low figure, say ½ per cent. At the same time these two central institutions should pursue bank-rate policy and open-market operations *à outrance*, having first agreed amongst themselves that they will take steps to prevent difficulties due to international gold movements from interfering with this. That is to say, they should combine to maintain a very low level of the short-term rate of interest, and buy long-dated securities either against an expansion of central bank money or against the sale of short-dated securities until the short-term market is saturated. It happens that this is an occasion when, if I am right, one of the conditions limiting open-market operations *à outrance* does not exist; for it is not an occasion – at least not yet – when bonds are standing at a price above reasonable expectations as to their long-term normal, so that they can still be purchased without the prospect of a loss.

Not until deliberate and vigorous action has been taken along such lines as these and has failed, need we, in the light of the argument of this treatise, admit that the banking system can *not*, on this occasion, control the rate of investment and, [347] therefore, the level of prices.

CW 9, ' "The Great Slump" of 1930' (1930)

[*The second of the depression excerpts, ' "The Great Slump" of 1930', originally appeared in the* Nation and Athenaeum, *20 and 27 December 1930. It was published in EP.*]

The world has been slow to realise that we are living this year in the shadow of one of the greatest economic catastrophes of modern history. But now that the man in the street has become aware of what is happening, he, not knowing the why and wherefore, is as full today of what may prove excessive fears as, previously, when the trouble was first coming on, he was lacking in what would have been a reasonable anxiety. He begins to doubt the future. Is he now awakening from a pleasant dream to face the darkness of facts? Or dropping off into a nightmare which will pass away?

He need not be doubtful. The other was *not* a dream. This *is* a nightmare, which will pass away with the morning. For the resources of nature and men's devices are just as fertile and productive as they were. The rate of our progress towards solving the material problems of life is not less rapid. We are as capable as before of affording for every one a high standard of life – high, I mean, compared with, say, twenty years ago – and will soon learn to afford a standard higher still. We were not previously deceived. But today we have involved ourselves in a colossal muddle, having blundered in the control of a delicate machine, the working of which we do not understand. The result is that our possibilities of wealth may run to waste for a time – perhaps for a long time.

I doubt whether I can hope to bring what is in my mind into fully effective touch with the mind of the reader. I shall be saying too much for the layman, too little for the expert. For – though no one will believe it – economics is a technical and [126] difficult subject. It is even becoming a science. However, I will do my best – at the cost of leaving out, because it is too complicated, much that is necessary to a complete understanding of contemporary events.

First of all, the extreme violence of the slump is to be noticed. In the three leading industrial countries of the world – the United States, Great Britain, and Germany – 10 million workers stand idle. There is scarcely an important industry anywhere earning enough profit to make it expand – which is the test of progress. At the same time, in the countries of primary production the output of mining and of agriculture is selling, in the case of almost every important commodity, at a price which for many or for the majority of producers, does not cover its cost. In 1921, when prices fell as heavily, the fall was from a boom level at which producers were making abnormal profits; and there is no example in modern history of so great and rapid a fall of prices from a normal figure as has occurred in the past year. Hence the magnitude of the catastrophe.

The time which elapses before production ceases and unemployment reaches its maximum is, for several reasons, much longer in the case of the primary products than in the case of manufacture. In most cases the productive units are smaller and less well organised amongst themselves for enforcing a process of orderly contraction; the length of the production period, especially in agriculture, is longer; the costs of a temporary shut-down are greater; men are more often their own employers and so submit more readily to a contraction of the income for which they are willing to work; the social problems of throwing men out of employment are greater in more primitive communities; and the financial problems of a cessation of production of primary output are more serious in countries where such primary output is almost the whole sustenance of the people. Nevertheless we are fast approaching the phase in which the output of primary producers will be restricted almost [127] as much as that of manufacturers; and this will have a further adverse reaction on manufacturers, since the primary producers will have no purchasing power wherewith to buy manufactured goods; and so on, in a vicious circle.

In this quandary individual producers base illusory hopes on courses of action which would benefit an individual producer or class of producers so long as they were alone in pursuing them, but which benefit no one if every one pursues them. For example, to restrict the output of a particular primary commodity raises its price, so long as the output of the industries which use this commodity is unrestricted; but if output is restricted all round, then the demand for the primary commodity falls off by just as much as the supply, and no one is further forward. Or again, if a particular producer or a particular country cuts wages, then, so long as others do not follow suit, that producer or that country is able to get more of what trade is going. But if wages are cut all round, the purchasing power of the community as a whole is reduced by the same amount as the reduction of costs; and, again, no one is further forward. [*A good example of Keynes's use of the 'fallacy of composition'.*]

Thus neither the restriction of output nor the reduction of wages serves in itself to restore equilibrium.

Moreover, even if we were to succeed eventually in re-establishing output at the lower level of money wages appropriate to (say) the pre-war level of prices, our troubles would not be at an end. For since 1914 an immense burden of bonded debt, both national and international, has been contracted, which is fixed in terms of money. Thus every fall of prices increases the burden of this debt, because it increases the value of the money in which it is fixed. For example, if we were to settle down to the pre-war level of prices, the British national debt would be nearly 40 per cent greater than it was in 1924 and double what it was in 1920; the Young Plan would weigh on Germany much more heavily than the Dawes Plan, which it was agreed she could not support; the indebtedness to the United States of her associates in the Great War would represent 40–50 per cent more goods and services than at the date when the settlements were made; the [128] obligations of such debtor countries as those of South America and Australia would become insupportable without a reduction of their standard of life for the benefit of their creditors; agriculturists and householders throughout the world, who have borrowed on mortgage, would find themselves the victims of their creditors. In such a situation it must be doubtful whether the necessary adjustments could be made in time to prevent a series of bankruptcies, defaults, and repudiations which would shake the capitalist order to its foundations. Here would be a fertile soil for agitation, seditions, and revolution. It is so already in many quarters of the world. Yet, all the time, the resources of nature and men's devices would be just as fertile and productive as they were. The machine would merely have been jammed as the result of a muddle. But because we have magneto trouble, we need not assume that we shall soon be back in a rumbling wagon and that motoring is over. [129]

. . .

Why is there an insufficient output of new capital goods in the world as a whole? It is due, in my opinion, to a conjunction of several causes. In the first instance, it was due to the attitude of lenders – for new capital goods are produced to a large extent with borrowed money. Now it is due to the attitude of borrowers, just as much as to that of lenders.

For several reasons lenders were, and are, asking higher terms for loans than new enterprise can afford. First, the fact that enterprise could afford high rates for some time after the war whilst war wastage was being made good, accustomed lenders to expect much higher rates than before the war. Second, the existence of political borrowers to meet treaty obligations, of banking borrowers to support newly restored gold standards, of speculative borrowers to take part in stock exchange booms and, latterly, of distress borrowers to meet the losses which they have incurred through the fall of prices, all of whom were ready if necessary to pay almost any terms, have hitherto enabled lenders to secure from these various classes of borrowers higher rates than it is possible for genuine new enterprise to support. Third, the unsettled state of the world and national investment habits have restricted the countries in which many lenders are prepared to invest on any reasonable terms at all. A large proportion of the globe is, for one reason or another, distrusted by lenders, so that they exact a premium for risk so great as to strangle new enterprise altogether. For the last two years, two out of the three principal creditor nations of the world, namely, France and the United States, have largely withdrawn their resources from the international market for long-term loans.

Meanwhile, the reluctant attitude of lenders has become matched by a hardly less reluctant attitude on the part of borrowers. For the fall of prices has been disastrous to those who have borrowed, and anyone who has postponed new enterprise has gained by his delay. Moreover, the risks that frighten lenders frighten borrowers too. Finally, in the United States, the [132] vast scale on which new capital enterprise has been undertaken in the last five years has somewhat exhausted for the time being – at any rate so long as the atmosphere of business depression continues – the profitable opportunities for yet further enterprise. By the middle of 1929 new capital undertakings were already on an inadequate scale in the world as a whole, outside the United States. The culminating blow has been the collapse of new investment inside the United States, which today is probably 20 to 30 per cent less than it was in 1928. Thus in certain countries the opportunity for new profitable investment is more limited than it was; whilst in others it is more risky.

A wide gulf, therefore, is set between the ideas of lenders and the ideas of borrowers for the purpose of genuine new capital investment; with the result that the savings of the lenders are being used up in financing business losses and distress borrowers, instead of financing new capital works.

At this moment the slump is probably a little overdone for psychological reasons. A modest upward reaction, therefore, may be due at any time. But there cannot be a real recovery, in my judgement, until the ideas of lenders and the ideas of productive borrowers are brought together again; partly by lenders becoming ready to lend on easier terms and over a wider geographical field, partly by borrowers recovering their good spirits and so becoming readier to borrow.

Seldom in modern history has the gap between the two been so wide and so difficult to bridge. Unless we bend our wills and out intelligences, energised by a conviction that this diagnosis is right, to find a solution along these lines, then, if the diagnosis is right, the slump may pass over into a depression, accompanied by a sagging price level, which might last for years, with untold damage to the material wealth and to the social stability of every country alike. Only if we seriously seek a solution, will the optimism of my opening sentences be confirmed – at least for the nearer future.

It is beyond the scope of this essay to indicate lines of future [133] policy. But no one can take the first step except the central banking authorities of the chief creditor countries; nor can any one central bank do enough acting in isolation. Resolute action by the Federal Reserve Banks of the United States, the Bank of France, and the Bank of England might do much more than most people, mistaking symptoms or aggravating circumstances for the disease itself, will readily believe. In every way the most effective remedy would be that the central banks of these three great creditor nations should join together in a bold scheme to restore confidence to the international long-term loan market; which would serve to revive enterprise and activity everywhere, and to restore prices and profits, so that in due course the wheels of the world's commerce would go round again. And even if France, hugging the supposed security of gold, prefers to stand aside from the adventure of creating new wealth, I am convinced that Great Britain and the United States, like-minded and acting together, could start the machine again within a reasonable time; if, that is to say, they were energised by a confident conviction as to what was wrong. For it is chiefly the lack of this conviction which today is paralysing the hands of authority on both sides of the Channel and of the [134] Atlantic.

CW 13, 'An Economic Analysis of Unemployment' (1931)

[*The third excerpt is a lecture 'The Road to Recovery', from a series of lectures Keynes gave in Chicago in June 1931 entitled 'An Economic Analysis of Unemployment', published in CW 13.*]
Whether or not my confidence is justified, I feel, then, no serious doubt or hesitation whatever as to the causes of the world slump. I trace it wholly to the breakdown of investment throughout the world. After being held by a variety of factors at a fairly high level during most of the post-war period, the volume of this investment has during the past two and a half years suffered an enormous decline – a decline not fully compensated as yet by diminished savings or by government deficits.

The problem of recovery is, therefore, a problem of re-establishing the volume of investment. The solution of this problem has two sides to it: on the one hand, a fall in the long-term rate of interest so as to bring a new range of propositions within the practical sphere; and, on the other hand, a return of confidence to the business world so as to incline them
[358] to borrow on the basis of normal expectations of the future. But the two aspects are by no means disconnected. For business

confidence will not revive except with the experience of improving business profits. And, if I am right, business profits will not recover except with an increase of investment. Nevertheless the mere reaction from the bottom and the feeling that it may be no longer prudent to wait for a further fall will be likely, perhaps in the near future, to bring about some modest recovery of confidence. We need, therefore, to work meanwhile for a drastic fall in the long-term rate of interest so that full advantage may be taken of any recovery of confidence.

The problem of recovery is also, in my judgment, indissolubly bound up with the restoration of prices to a higher level, although if my theory is correct this is merely another aspect of the same phenomenon. The same events which lead to a recovery in the volume of investment will inevitably tend at the same time toward a revival of the price level. But inasmuch as the raising of prices is an essential ingredient in my policy I had better pause perhaps to offer some justification of this before I proceed to consider the ways and means by which the volume of investment and at the same time the level of prices can be raised.

Unfortunately there is not complete unanimity among the economic doctors as to the desirability of raising the general price level at this phase of the cycle. Dr Sprague, for example, in an address made recently in London which attracted much attention, declared it to be preferable that 'manufactured costs and prices should come down to equilibrium level with agricultural prices rather than that we should try to get agricultural prices up to an equilibrium level with the higher prices of manufactured goods'.

For my own part, however, I dissent very strongly from this view and I should like, if I could, to provoke vehement controversy – a real discussion of the problem – in the hope that out of the clash of minds something useful might emerge. Until we have definitely decided whether or not we should wish prices to rise we are drifting without clear intentions in a [359] rudderless vessel.

Do we, then, want prices to rise back to a parity with what, a few months ago, we considered to be the established levels of our salaries, wages, and income generally? Or do we want to reduce our incomes to a parity with the existing level of the wholesale prices of raw commodities? Please notice that I emphasise the word 'want', for we shall confuse the argument unless we keep distinct what we want from what we think we can get. My own conclusion is that there are certain fundamental reasons of overwhelming force, quite distinct from the technical considerations tending in the same direction, which I have already indicated and to which I shall return later, for wishing prices to rise.

The first reason is on grounds of social stability and concord. Will not the social resistance to a drastic downward readjustment of salaries and wages be an ugly and a dangerous thing? I am told sometimes that these changes present comparatively little difficulty in a country such as the United States where economic rigidity has not yet set in. I find it difficult to believe this. But it is for you, not me, to say. I know that in my own country a really large cut of many wages, a cut at all of the same order of magnitude as the fall in wholesale prices, is simply an impossibility. To attempt it would be to shake the social order to its foundation. There is scarcely one responsible person in Great Britain prepared to recommend it openly. And if, for the world as a whole, such a thing could be accomplished, we should be no farther forward than if we had sought a return to equilibrium by the path of raising prices. If, under the pressure of compelling reason, we are to launch all our efforts on a crusade of unpopular public duty, let it be for larger results than this.

I have said that we should be no farther forward. But in fact even when we had accomplished the reduction of salaries and wages, we should be far worse off, for the second reason for wishing prices to rise is on grounds of social justice and expedi-
[360] ency which have regard to the burden of indebtedness fixed in terms of money. If we reach a new equilibrium by lowering the level of salaries and wages, we increase proportionately the burden of monetary indebtedness. In doing this we should be striking at the sanctity of contract. For the burden of monetary indebtedness in the world is already so heavy that any material addition would render it intolerable. This burden takes different forms in different countries. In my own country it is the

national debt raised for the purposes of the war which bulks largest. In Germany it is the weight of reparation payments fixed in terms of money. For creditor and debtor countries there is the risk of rendering the charges on the debtor countries so insupportable that they abandon a hopeless task and walk the pathway of general default. In the United States the main problem would be, I suppose, the mortgages of the farmer and loans on real estate generally. There is in fact what, in an instructive essay, Professor Alvin Johnson[22] has called the 'farmers' indemnity'. The notion that you solve the farmers' problem by bringing down manufacturing costs so that their own produce will exchange for the same quantity of manufactured goods as formerly is to mistake the situation altogether, for you would at the same time have greatly increased the farmers' burden of mortgages which was already too high. Or take another case – loans against buildings. If the cost of new building were to fall to a parity with the price of raw materials, what would become of the security for existing loans?

Thus national debts, war debts, obligations between the creditor and debtor nations, farm mortgages, real estate mortgages – all this financial structure would be deranged by the adoption of Dr Sprague's proposal. A widespread bankruptcy, default, and repudiation of bonds would necessarily ensue. Banks would be in jeopardy. I need not continue the catalogue. And what would be the advantage of having caused so much ruin? I do not know. Dr Sprague did not tell us that.

Moreover, over and above these compelling reasons there is also the technical reason, the validity of which is not so generally recognised, which I have endeavoured to elucidate in my [361] previous lecture. If our object is to remedy unemployment it is obvious that we must first of all make business more profitable. In other words, the problem is to cause business receipts to rise relatively to business costs. But I have already endeavoured to show that the same train of events which will lead to this desired result is also part and parcel of the causation of higher prices, and that any policy which at this stage of the credit cycle is not directed to raising prices also fails in the object of improving business profits.

The cumulative argument for wishing prices to rise appears to me, therefore, to be overwhelming, as I hope it does to you. Fortunately many if not most people agree with this view. You may feel that I have been wasting time in emphasising it. But I do not think that I have been wasting time, for while most people probably accept this view, I doubt if they feel it with sufficient intensity. I wish to take precautions beforehand against anyone asking – when I come to the second and consecutive part of my argument – whether, after all, it is so essential that prices should rise. Is it not better that liquidation should take its course? Should we not be, then, all the healthier for liquidation, which is their polite phrase for general bankruptcy, when it is complete?

Let us now return to our main theme. The cure of unemployment involves improving business profits. The improvement of business profits can come about only by an improvement in new investment relative to saving. An increase of investment relative to saving must also, as an inevitable by-product, bring about a rise of prices, thus ameliorating the burdens arising out of monetary indebtedness. The problem resolves itself, therefore, into the question as to what means we can adopt to increase the volume of investment, which you will remember [362] means in my terminology the expenditure of money on the output of new capital goods of whatever kind.

When I have said this, I have, strictly speaking, said all that an economist as such is entitled to say. What remains is essentially a technical banking problem. The practical means by which investment can be increased is, or ought to be, the bankers' business, and pre-eminently the business of the central banker. But you will not consider that I have completed my task unless I give some indication of the methods which are open to the banker.

There are, in short, three lines of approach. The first line of approach is the restoration of confidence both to the lender and to the borrower. The lender must have sufficient confidence in the credit and solvency of the borrower so as not to wish to charge him a crushing addition to the pure interest charge in order to cover risk. The borrower, on the other hand, must have sufficient confidence in the business prospects to believe that he has a reasonable prospect of earning sufficient return from a new investment proposition to recover with a margin the interest which he has to bind himself to pay to the lender. Failing the restoration of confidence, we may easily have a vicious circle set up in which the rate of interest which the lender requires to cover what he considers the risks of the situation represents a higher rate than the borrower believes that he can earn.

Nevertheless, there is perhaps not a great deal that can be done deliberately to restore confidence. The turning-point may come in part from some chance and unpredictable event. But it is capable, of course, of being greatly affected by favourable international developments, as for example, an alleviation of the war debts such as Mr Hoover has lately proposed; though if he goes no farther than he has promised to go at present, the shock to confidence, long before his year of grace is out, may come perhaps just at the moment when it will interfere most with an incipient revival. In the main, however, restoration of confidence must be based, not on the vague expectations or hopes of the [363] business world, but on a real improvement in fundamentals; in other words, on a breaking of the vicious circle. Thus if results can be achieved along the two remaining lines of approach which I have yet to mention, these favourable effects may be magnified by their reaction on the state of confidence.

The second line of approach consists in new construction programmes under the direct auspices of the government or other public authorities. Theoretically, it seems to me, there is everything to be said for action along these lines. For the government can borrow cheaply and need not be deterred by overnice calculations as to the prospective return. I have been a strong advocate of such measures in Great Britain, and I believe that they can play an extremely valuable part in breaking the vicious circle everywhere. For a government programme is calculated to improve the level of business profits and hence to increase the likelihood of private enterprise again lifting up its head. The difficulty about government programmes seems to me to be essentially a practical one. It is not easy to devise at short notice schemes which are wisely and efficiently conceived and which can be put rapidly into operation on a really large scale. Thus I applaud the idea and only hesitate to depend too much in practice on this method alone unaided by others. I am not sure that as time goes by we may not have to attempt to organise methods of direct government action along these lines more deliberately than hitherto, and that such action may play an increasingly important part in the economic life of the community.

The third line of approach consists in a reduction in the long-term rate of interest. It may be that when confidence is at its lowest ebb the rate of interest plays a comparatively small part. It may also be true that, in so far as manufacturing plants are concerned, the rate of interest is never the dominating factor. But, after all, the main volume of investment always takes the forms of housing, of public utilities and of transportation. [364] Within these spheres the rate of interest plays, I am convinced, a predominant part. I am ready to believe that a small change in the rate of interest may not be sufficient. That, indeed, is why I am pessimistic as to an early return to normal prosperity. I am ready enough to admit that it may be extremely difficult both to restore confidence adequately and to reduce interest rates adequately. There will be no need to be surprised, therefore, if a long time elapses before we have a recovery all the way back to normal.

Nevertheless, a sufficient change in the rate of interest must surely bring within the horizon all kinds of projects which are out of the question at the present rate of interest. Let me quote an example from my own country. No one believes that it will pay to electrify the railway system of Great Britain on the basis of borrowing at 5 per cent. At 4½ per cent the enthusiasts believe that it will be worth while; at 4 per cent everyone agrees it is an open question; at 3½ per cent it is impossible to dispute that it will be worth while. So it must be with endless other technical projects. Every fall in the rate of interest will bring a new range of projects within a practical sphere. Moreover, if it be true – as it probably is – that the demand for house room is elastic, every significant fall in the rate of interest, by reducing the rent which has to be charged, brings with it an additional demand for house room.

As I look at it, indeed, the task of adjusting the long-term rate of interest to the technical possibilities of our age so that the demand for new capital is as nearly as possible equal to the community's current volume of savings must be the prime object of financial statesmanship. It may not be easy and a large change may be needed, but there is no other way out.

Finally, how is the banking system to affect the long-term rate of interest? For prima facie the banking system is concerned with the short-term rate of interest rather than with the long.

In course of time I see no insuperable difficulty. There is a normal relation between the short-term rate of interest and the long-term, and in the long run the banking system can affect the long-term rate by obstinately adhering to the correct policy [365] in regard to the short-term rate. But there may also be devices for hastening the effect of the short-term rate on the long-term rate. A reduction of the long-term rate of interest amounts to the same thing as raising the price of bonds. The price of bonds amounts to the same thing as the price of non-liquid assets in terms of liquid assets. I suggest to you that there are three ways in which it is reasonable to hope to exercise an influence in this direction.

The first method is to increase the quantity of liquid assets – in other words, to increase the basis of credit by means of open-market operations, as they are usually called, on the part of the central bank. I know that this involves technical questions of some difficulty with which I must not burden this lecture. I should, however, rely confidently in due course on influencing the price of bonds by steadily supplying the market with a greater quantity of liquid assets than the market felt itself to require so that there would be a constant pressure to transform liquid assets into the more profitable non-liquid assets.

The second course is to diminish the attractions of liquid assets by lowering the rate of deposit interest. In such circumstances as the present it seems to me that the rate of interest allowed on liquid assets should be reduced as nearly as possible to the vanishing-point.

The third method is to increase the attractions of non-liquid assets, which, however, brings us back again in effect to our first remedy, namely, methods of increasing confidence.

For my own part, I should have thought it desirable to advance along all three fronts simultaneously. But the central idea that I wish to leave with you is the vital necessity for a society, living in the phase in which we are living today, to bring down the long-term rate of interest at a pace appropriate to the underlying facts. As houses and equipment of every kind increase in quantity we ought to be growing richer on the principle of compound interest. As technological changes make [366] possible a given output of goods of every description with a diminishing quantity of human effort, again we ought to be forever increasing our level of economic well-being. But the worst of these developments is that they bring us to what may be called the dilemma of a rich country, namely, that they make it more and more difficult to find an outlet for our savings. Thus we need to pay constant conscious attention to the long-term rate of interest for fear that our vast resources may be running to waste through a failure to direct our savings into constructive uses and that this running to waste may interfere with that beneficent operation of compound interest which should, if everything was proceeding smoothly in a well-governed society, lead us within a few generations to the complete [367] abolition of oppressive economic want.

CW 9, 'The Consequences to the Banks of the Collapse of Money Values' (1932)

[*The fourth excerpt is Keynes's article 'The Consequences to the Banks of the Collapse of Money Values', first published in EP in October 1931. The version below is taken from Vanity Fair, January 1932. Keynes clearly anticipated Irving Fisher's theory of debt-deflation in Fisher's* Booms and Depressions: Some First Principles *(1932) and 'The Debt-Deflation Theory of Great Depressions',* Econometrica, 1(40) (1933), pp. 337–57.]

A year ago it was the failure of agriculture, mining, manufactures, and transport to make normal profits, and the unemployment and waste of productive resources ensuing on this, which was the leading feature of the economic situation. Today, in many parts of the world, it is the serious embarrassment of the banks which is the cause of our gravest concern. The shattering German crisis of July 1931, which took the world more by surprise than it should, was in its essence a banking crisis, though precipitated, no doubt, by political events and political fears. That the top-heavy position which ultimately crumbled to the ground should have been built up at all was, in my judgement, a sin against the principles of sound banking. One watched its erection with amazement and terror. But the fact which was primarily responsible for bringing it down was a factor for which the individual bankers were not responsible and which very few people foresaw – namely, the enormous change in the value of gold money and consequently in the burden of indebtedness which debtors, in all countries adhering to the gold standard, had contracted to pay in terms of gold.

The German crisis was heralded by the Credit Anstalt trouble in Austria. It was brought to a head by the difficulties of the Darmstadter Bank in Berlin. It led to distrust of the London position on account of the heavy advances, out of relation [150] to the liquid resources held against them, which London had made to Berlin. It culminated in Great Britain's suspension of the gold standard. Its final *sequela* as I write these lines is a feverish removal of foreign balances from New York. But all this nervousness, and hysteria and panic, which is making a farce of our currency arrangements and bringing the world's financial machine to a standstill, is only superficially traceable, though it has all happened suddenly, to quite recent events. It has its roots in the slow and steady sapping of the real resources of the banks as a result of the progressive collapse of money values over the past two years. It is to this deep, underlying cause that I wish to direct attention in this article.

Let us begin at the beginning of the argument. There is a multitude of real assets in the world which constitute our capital wealth – buildings, stocks of commodities, goods in course of manufacture and of transport, and so forth. The nominal owners of these assets, however, have not infrequently borrowed *money* in order to become possessed of them. To a corresponding extent the actual owners of wealth have claims, not on real assets, but on money. A considerable part of this 'financing' takes place through the banking system, which interposes its guarantee between its depositors who lend it money, and its borrowing customers to whom it loans money wherewith to finance the purchase of real assets. The interposition of this veil of money between the real asset and the wealth owner is a specially marked characteristic of the modern world. Partly as a result of the increasing confidence felt in recent years in the leading banking systems, the practice has grown to formidable dimensions. The bank deposits of all kinds in the United States, for example, stand in round figures at $50,000 million; those of Great Britain at £2,000 million. In addition to this there is the great mass of bonded and mortgage indebtedness held by individuals.

[151]   All this is familiar enough in general terms. We are also familiar with the idea that a change in the value of money can gravely upset the relative positions of those who possess claims to money and those who owe money. For, of course, a fall in prices, which is the same thing as a rise in the value of claims on money, means that real wealth is transferred from the debtor in favour of the creditor, so that a larger proportion of the real asset is represented by the claims of the depositor, and a smaller proportion belongs to the nominal owner of the asset who has borrowed in order to buy it. This, we all know, is one of the reasons why changes in prices are upsetting.

But it is not to this familiar feature of falling prices that I wish to invite attention. It is to a further development which we can ordinarily afford to neglect but which leaps to importance when the change in the value of money is *very large* – when it exceeds a more or less determinate amount.

Modest fluctuations in the value of money, such as those which we have frequently experienced in the past, do not vitally concern the banks which have interposed their guarantee between the depositor and the debtor. For the banks allow beforehand for some measure of fluctuation in the value both of particular assets and of real assets in general, by requiring from the borrower what is conveniently called a 'margin'. That is to say, they will only lend him money up to a certain proportion of the value of the asset which is the 'security' offered by the borrower to the lender. Experience has led to the fixing of conventional percentages for the 'margin' as being reasonably safe in all ordinary circumstances. The amount will, of course, vary in different cases within wide limits. But for marketable assets a 'margin' of 20 per cent to 30 per cent is conventionally considered as adequate, and a 'margin' of as much as 50 per cent as highly conservative. Thus provided the amount of the downward change in the money value of assets is well within these conventional figures, the direct interest of the banks is not excessive – they owe money to their depositors on one side of their balance sheet and are owed it on the other, and it is no [152] vital concern of theirs just what the money is worth. But consider what happens when the downward change in the money value of assets within a brief period of time *exceeds* the amount of the conventional 'margin' over a large part of the assets against which money has been borrowed. The horrible possibilities to the banks are immediately obvious. Fortunately, this is a very rare, indeed a unique event. For it had never occurred in the modern history of the world prior to the year 1931. There have been large *upward* movements in the money value of assets in those countries where inflation has proceeded to great lengths. But this, however disastrous in other ways, did nothing to jeopardise the position of the banks; for it increased the amount of their 'margins'. There was a large downward movement in the slump of 1921, but that was from an exceptionally high level of values which had ruled for only a few months or weeks, so that only a small proportion of the banks' loans had been based on such values and these values had not lasted long enough to be trusted. *Never* before has there been such a world-wide collapse over almost the whole field of the money values of real assets as we have experienced in the last two years. And, finally, during the last few months – so recently that the bankers themselves have, as yet, scarcely appreciated it – it has come to exceed in very many cases the amount of the conventional 'margins'. In the language of the market the 'margins' have run off. The exact details of this are not likely to come to the notice of the outsider until some special event – perhaps some almost accidental event – occurs which brings the situation to a dangerous head. For, so long as a bank is in a position to wait quietly for better times and to ignore meanwhile the fact that the security against many of its loans is no longer as good as it was when the loans were first made, nothing appears on the surface and there is no cause for panic. Nevertheless, even at this stage the underlying position is likely to have a very adverse effect on new business. [153] For the banks, being aware that many of their advances are in fact 'frozen' and involve a larger latent risk than they would voluntarily carry, become particularly anxious that the remainder of their assets should be as liquid and as free from risk as it is possible to make them. This reacts in all sorts of silent and unobserved ways on new enterprise. For it means that the banks are less willing than they would normally be to finance any project which may involve a lock-up of their resources.

Now, in estimating the quantitative importance of the factor to which I am calling attention, we have to consider what has been happening to the prices of various types of property. There are, first of all, the principal raw materials and foodstuffs of international commerce. These are of great importance to the banks, because the stocks of these commodities, whether in warehouse or in transit or embodied in half-finished or unsold manufactured articles, are very largely financed through the banks. In the last eighteen months the prices of these commodities have fallen *on the average* by about 25 per cent. But this is an average, and banks cannot average the security of one customer with that of another. Many individual commodities of the greatest commercial importance have fallen in price by 40 to 50 per cent or even more.

Next come the ordinary or common shares of the great companies and corporations which are the market leaders in the stock exchanges of the world. In most countries the average fall amounts to 40 to 50 per cent; and this again is an average, which means that individual shares, even amongst those which would have been considered of good quality two years ago, have fallen enormously more. Then there are the bonds and the fixed interest securities. Those of the very highest grade have, indeed, risen slightly or, at the worst, not fallen by more than 5 per cent, which has been of material assistance in some quarters. But many other fixed interest securities which, while not of the highest grade, were and are good securities, have fallen from 10 to 15 per cent; whilst foreign government bonds have, [154] as is well known, suffered prodigious falls. These declines, even where they are more moderate, may be scarcely less serious, because such bonds (though not in Great Britain) are often owned by the banks themselves outright, so that there is no 'margin' to protect them from loss.

The declines in the prices of commodities and of securities have, broadly speaking, affected most countries alike. When we come to the next category of property – and one of great quantitative importance – namely, real estate, the facts are more various as between one country and another. A great element of stability in Great Britain and, I believe, in France also, has been the continued comparative firmness in real estate values – no slump has been experienced in this quarter, with the result that mortgage business is sound and the multitude of loans granted on the security of real estate are unimpaired. But in many other countries the slump has affected this class of property also; and particularly, perhaps, in the United States, where farm values have suffered a great decline, and also city property of modern construction, much of which would not fetch today more than 60 to 70 per cent of its original cost of construction, and not infrequently much less. This is an immense aggravation of the problem, where it has occurred, both because of the very large sums involved and because such property is ordinarily regarded as relatively free from risk. Thus a situation has been created in the United States, in which the mortgage banks and mortgage and loan associations and other real-estate financing institutions are holding a great mass of 'frozen' mortgages, the margins on which have been consumed by the fall of real estate values.

Finally, there are the loans and advances which banks have made to their customers for the purposes of their customers' business. These are, in many cases, in the worst condition of all. The security in these cases is primarily the profit, actual and prospective, of the business which is being financed; and in present circumstances for many classes of producers of raw [155] materials, of farmers and of manufacturers, there are no profits and every prospect of insolvencies, if matters do not soon take a turn for the better.

To sum up, there is scarcely any class of property, except real estate, however useful and important to the welfare of the community, the current money value of which has not suffered an enormous and scarcely precedented decline. This has happened in a community which is so organised that a veil of money is, as I have said, interposed over a wide field between the actual asset and the wealth owner. The ostensible proprietor of the actual asset has financed it by borrowing money from the actual owner of wealth. Furthermore, it is largely through the banking system that all this has been arranged. That is to say, the banks have, for a consideration, interposed their guarantee. They stand between the real borrower and the real lender. They have given their guarantee to the real lender; and this guarantee is only good if the money value of the asset belonging to the real borrower is worth the money which has been advanced on it.

It is for this reason that a decline in money values so severe as that which we are now experiencing threatens the solidarity of the whole financial structure. Banks and bankers are by nature blind. They have not seen what was coming. Some of them have even welcomed the fall of prices towards what, in their innocence, they have deemed the just and 'natural' and inevitable level of pre-war, that is to say, to the level of prices to which their minds became accustomed in their formative years. In the United States some of them employ so-called 'economists' who tell us even today that our troubles are due to the fact that the prices of some commodities and some services have not yet fallen enough, regardless of what should be the obvious fact that their cure, if it could be realised, would be a menace to the solvency of their institution. A 'sound' banker, alas! is not one who foresees danger and avoids it, but one who, when he is ruined, is ruined in a conventional and orthodox way along [156] with his fellows, so that no one can really blame him.

But today they are beginning at last to take notice. In many countries bankers are becoming unpleasantly aware of the fact that, when their customers' margins have run off, they are themselves 'on margin'. I believe that, if today a really conservative valuation were made of all doubtful assets, quite a significant proportion of the banks of the world would be found to be insolvent; and with the further progress of deflation this proportion will grow rapidly. Fortunately our own domestic British banks are probably at present – for various reasons – among the strongest. But there is a degree of deflation which no bank can stand. And over a great part of the world, and not least in the United States, the position of the banks, though partly concealed from the public eye, may be in fact the weakest element in the whole situation. It is obvious that the present trend of events cannot go much further without something breaking. If nothing is done, it will be amongst the world's banks that the really critical breakages will occur.

Modern capitalism is faced, in my belief, with the choice between finding some way to increase money values towards their former figure, or seeing widespread insolvencies and defaults and the collapse of a large part of the financial structure; after which we should all start again, not nearly so much poorer as we should expect, and much more cheerful perhaps, but having suffered a period of waste and disturbance and social injustice, and a general rearrangement of private fortunes and the ownership of wealth. Individually many of us would be 'ruined', even though collectively we were much as before. But under the pressure of hardship and excitement, we might have found out better ways of managing our affairs.

The present signs suggest that the bankers of the world are bent on suicide. At every stage they have been unwilling to [157] adopt a sufficiently drastic remedy. And by now matters have been allowed to go so far that it has become extraordinarily difficult to find any way out. In Great Britain we have gone some way towards solving our own problem by abandoning the gold standard, but unfortunately we have only made matters worse for countries still adhering to it.

It is necessarily part of the business of a banker to maintain appearances and to profess a conventional respectability which is more than human. Lifelong practices of this kind make them the most romantic and the least realistic of men. It is so much their stock-in-trade that their position should not be questioned, that they do not even question it themselves until it is too late. Like the honest citizens they are, they feel a proper indignation at the perils of the wicked world in which they live – when the perils mature; but they do not foresee them. A bankers' conspiracy! The idea is absurd! I only wish there were one! So, if they [158] are saved, it will be, I expect, in their own despite.

19

CW 13 'A Monetary Theory of Production' (1933)

[*Written as a contribution to the* Festschrift für Arthur Spiethoff, *this can be read as a prospectus for GT.*]
In my opinion the main reason why the problem of crises is unsolved . . . is to be found in the lack of what might be termed *a monetary theory of production.*

The distinction which is normally made between a barter economy and a monetary economy depends upon the employment of money as a convenient means of effecting exchanges – as an instrument of great convenience, but transitory and neutral in its effect. It is regarded as a mere link between cloth and wheat, or between a day's labour spend on building the canoe and the day's labour spend on harvesting the crop. It is not supposed to affect the essential nature of the transaction . . . between real things, or to modify the motives and decisions of the parties to it. Money, that is to say, is employed, but is treated as being in some sense *neutral.*

That, however, is not the distinction which I have in mind when I say that we lack a monetary theory of production. An economy, which uses money but uses it merely as a neutral link between transactions in real things and real assets and does not allow it to enter into motives or decisions, might be called – for want of a better name – a *real-exchange economy.* The theory which I desiderate would deal, in contradiction to this, with an economy in which money plays a part of its own and affects motives and decisions and is, in short, one of the operative factors in the situation, so that the course of events cannot be [408] predicted, either in the long period or in the short, without a knowledge of the behaviour of money between the first state and the last. And it is this which we ought to mean when we speak of a *monetary economy.*

... [409]

The divergence between the real-exchange economics and my desired monetary economics is, however, most marked and perhaps most important when we come to the discussion of the rate of interest and to the relation between the volume of employment and the amount of expenditure.

Everyone would, of course, agree that it is in a monetary economy in my sense of the term that we actually live. Professor Pigou knows as well as anyone that wages are in fact sticky in terms of money. Marshall was perfectly aware that the existence of debts gives a high degree of practical importance to changes in the value of money. Nevertheless, it is my belief that the far-reaching and in some respects fundamental differences between the conclusions of a monetary economy and those of the more simplified real-exchange economy have been greatly underestimated by the exponents of the traditional economics; with the result that the machinery of thought with which real-exchange economics has equipped the minds of practitioners in the world of affairs, and also of economists themselves, has led in practice to many erroneous conclusions and policies. The idea that it is comparatively easy to adapt the hypothetical conclusions of a real wage economics to the real world of monetary economics is a mistake. It is extraordinarily difficult to make the adaptation, and perhaps impossible without the aid of a developed theory of monetary economics.

One of the chief causes of the confusion lies in the fact that the assumptions of the real-exchange economy have been tacit, and you will search treatises on real-exchange economics in vain for any express statement of the simplifications introduced or for the relationship of its hypothetical conclusions to the facts of the real world. We are not told what conditions have to be fulfilled if money is to be neutral. Nor is it easy to supply the gap. Now the conditions required for the 'neutrality' of money, [410] in the sense in which this is assumed . . . are, I suspect, precisely the same as those which will insure that crises *do not occur*. If this is true, the real-exchange economics, on which most of us have been brought up and with the conclusions of which our minds are deeply impregnated, though a valuable abstraction in itself and perfectly valid as an intellectual conception, is a singularly blunt weapon for dealing with the problem of booms and depressions. For it has assumed away the very matter under investigation.

. . .

This is not the same thing as to say that the problem of booms and depressions is a purely monetary problem. For this statement is generally meant to imply that a complete solution is to be found in banking policy. I am saying that booms and depressions are phenomena peculiar to an economy in which – in some significant sense which I am not attempting to define precisely in this place – money is not neutral.

Accordingly I believe that the next task is to work out in some detail a monetary theory of production, to supplement the real-exchange theories which we already possess. At any rate that is the task on which I am now occupying myself, in [411] some confidence that I am not wasting my time.

20

CW 7, *The General Theory of Employment, Interest and Money* (1936)[23]

[*Keynes left the following two accounts of the genesis of GT. The first comes from its preface, the second from a letter to Roy Harrod.*]
When I began to write my *Treatise on Money* I was still moving along the traditional lines of regarding the influence of money

as something so to speak separate from the general theory of supply and demand. When I finished it, I had made some progress towards pushing monetary theory back to becoming a theory of output as a whole. But my lack of emancipation from preconceived ideas showed itself in what now seems to me to be the outstanding fault of the theoretical parts of that work (namely Books III and IV), that I failed to deal thoroughly with the effects of *changes* in the level of output. My so-called 'fundamental equations' were an instantaneous picture taken on the assumption of a given output. They attempted to show how, assuming that given output, forces could develop which involved a profit-disequilibrium, and thus required a change in the level of output. But the dynamic development, as distinct from the instantaneous picture, was left incomplete and extremely confused.

...

The composition of this book has been for the author a long struggle of escape, and so must the reading of it be for most readers if the author's assault upon them is to be successful, – a struggle of escape from habitual modes of thought and expression. The ideas which are here expressed so laboriously are extremely simple and should be obvious. The difficulty lies, not in the new ideas, but in escaping from the old ones, which ramify, for those brought up as most of us have been, into every [xxii–
corner of our minds.   xxiii]
[*JMK to Roy Harrod, 30 August 1936 (CW 14)*.]

You don't mention *effective demand*, or more precisely, the demand schedule for output as a whole ... To me the most extraordinary thing regarded historically, is the complete disappearance of the theory of the demand and supply for output as a whole, i.e. the theory of employment, *after* it had been for a quarter of a century the most discussed thing in economics. One of the most important transitions for me, after my *Treatise on Money* had been published, was suddenly realising this. It came after I had enunciated to myself the psychological law, that, when income increases, the gap between income and consumption will increase, – a conclusion of vast importance to my own thinking but not apparently, expressed just like this, to anyone else's. Then, appreciably later, came the notion of interest as being the [measure] of liquidity-preference, which became quite clear in my mind the moment I thought of it. And last [of all], after an immense lot of muddling and many drafts, the proper definition of the marginal efficiency of capital linked up [85] one thing with another.

[*The main difference between TM and GT is that Keynes drops the idea of starting from an ideal model of equilibrium and then adding imperfections which explain unemployment and cycles. The task of theory was to explain why the actual level of output and employment is what it is at any one time. He regarded this as a huge step towards making economic theory realistic. This approach entailed dropping QTM and the 'natural rate of interest' apparatus of the previous book.*

There has been continuing dispute about GT's central message. Following Alan Coddington,[24] we may call the two main schools of interpretation the 'hydraulic' and the 'fundamentalist'.

The former are Books I and III Keynesians. Their key message is that 'quantities adjust, not prices'. Output is determined by aggregate demand, or spending, made up of consumption demand and investment demand. However, all that is earned need not be spent. Investment, in particular, is volatile, so that a fall in investment spending, unmatched by an increase in consumption spending (or equivalently a fall in saving) will lead to a fall in aggregate spending and thus in the demand for labour. Say's Law, that 'supply creates its own demand', may thus be invalid. As Alvin Hansen explains: 'Current income is indeed derived from current sales proceeds. And current production is undertaken in expectation of sales proceeds adequate to cover all costs . . . But this expectation may prove false . . .'[25] In short, demand may fall below supply.

The extent of any change in output is determined by the consumption function, which specifies the proportion of their income that people spend on consumption. When investment has fallen, aggregate output (GDP) will need to fall sufficiently to reduce saving by the amount of the fall in investment. This is the point of 'under-employment equilibrium', the point at which the economy will stick in a state of suspended animation, in the absence of an external stimulus. In a 'closed' economy this stimulus will normally have to come from the government injecting extra spending power into the economy. This is the essence of hydraulic Keynesianism.

Keynes himself undoubtedly thought that the main theoretical achievement of GT was to have demonstrated the logical possibility of an equilibrium short of full employment. He had reached this conclusion by November 1932.]

Neither prices nor output will fall forever; and they will, after the introduction of some disturbing change ... come to rest again at some position from which they will have no further tendency to depart (though the position of equilibrium may not be a very stable one), so long as no new sources of disturbance intervene. But this is quite a different thing from concluding that the long-period position of equilibrium corresponding to the new situation is the same as the original position, both being positions of optimum output of the factors of production. For the decline in output may be itself one of the factors which had, by reason of its retarding effect on saving, produced the new equilibrium, so that the fact of the level of output being below the optimum may be in itself one of the conditions of the maintenance of the equilibrium.[26]

...

[*As is apparent, the working of the hydraulic machine depends on the existence of stable relations between a small number of aggregate variables: consumption, investment, interest rates, income, output, employment. A change in aggregate spending, up or down, sets in motion predictable repercussions on income, output and employment. In the short period, employment moves with output and income (GDP).*

Classical economics had supposed that in face of a shock interest rates and wage rates adjust 'automatically' to the new conditions. This was the essence of the self-adjusting market economy. The decline of investment relative to saving will lead to a fall in interest rates; the emergence of a labour surplus will lead to a fall in wages. The reduction in these prices offsets the reduced attractiveness of investment at the old set of prices, leaving the amount of output and employment unchanged. It is only if these two classical adjustment mechanisms are 'out of action'[27] that the adjustment takes place through a change in output.

But in actual life the relevant prices are 'sticky', so that output adjustment races ahead of price adjustment. Interest rates hit a 'liquidity trap' – a 'lower bound' of near zero, when the demand for money to hold becomes perfectly interest-elastic; wages are sticky for a variety of institutional reasons. So it is reasonable to rule these adjustment mechanisms 'out of action' for the relevant time period, especially when the shock to demand is large.

Hydraulic Keynesianism can thus explain how demand deficiency can arise, given a fall in the attractiveness of investment, but not why investment can suddenly become less attractive. It lacks, so to speak, an explanation of its own explanation.

The fundamentalist interpretation of Keynesianism starts at the epistemological level, emphasized by Keynes in chapters 12 and 17 of GT, and in his Quarterly Journal of Economics article 'The General Theory of Employment' of February 1937. As interpreted by the fundamentalists Keynes's central message is the existence of irreducible uncertainty. This affects two sets of decisions: those underlying private investment behaviour and those underlying the demand for liquid assets: the first affecting the expected profitability of investment at a given interest rate, the second the interest rate itself. In Coddington's words 'what Keynes is concerned to suggest is that the epistemological foundations of private sector investment are comprehensively flimsy'.[28] The consequence is that private sector investment is subject to large fluctuations, fluctuations which are independent of a change in real circumstances. Expectations concerning future yield, based on conventional valuations, collapse when confidence in the convention is undermined. Further, the development of demand deficiency following a shock to investment can be explained without any recourse to price stickiness. Fundamentalists follow Keynes in seeing interest rates as being determined in the market for money, not in the market for saving and investment. The interest-rate adjustment mechanism is not disabled by *a liquidity trap, but by the fact that a fall in the expected profitability of investment causes a growth in 'liquidity preference' and thus, with a given money supply, a rise, not fall, in interest rates.*[29] *Similarly, fully flexible money wages would not eliminate demand deficiency, since an all-round cut in money wages would depress nominal demand still further.*[30]

Fundamentalist Keynesians do not rely on determinate relationships like the consumption function or the multiplier to explain persisting mass unemployment, since to do so would be inconsistent with uncertainty. (They tend to avoid the term 'under-employment equilibrium'.) A shock to investment demand creates a pessimistic set of short-run expectations; these expectations persist into the long run in the absence of offsetting news capable of reviving the sluggish 'animal spirits' of entrepreneurs.

Fundamentalist Keynesians cling to uncertainty as Keynes's main message because they understand that without such an epistemological anchor there is no theoretical obstacle to the reinstatement of classical theory and even laissez-faire policy. And they believe this has happened via the 'neoclassical synthesis'. Joan Robinson, first leader of the fundamentalists, called the hydraulic Keynesians 'bastard Keynesians'.

The reader will see from the excerpts below that each interpretation of the central message of GT is achieved by emphasizing one aspect of Keynes's theory at the expense of the other. Perhaps the real divide is between those who have been primarily interested in using Keynes's theory for policy purposes and those who view it as a deep attack on mainstream economics. As Paul Samuelson, a tireless promoter of hydraulic Keynesianism, has remarked 'Had Keynes begun his first few chapters with the simple statement that he found it realistic to assume that modern capitalistic societies had money wage rates that were sticky and resistant to downward movements, most of his insights would have remained just as valid . . .'[31] *Crucially for the hydraulic Keynesians, the quantity-adjustment model gave policy-makers a justification and tool-kit for policies to maintain full employment (something they were passionately committed to do), without their having to dig too deep* into the theoretical foundations of their discipline. But to confine Keynes's contribution to useful tools would make him, in Leijonhufvud's words, a 'theoretical charlatan',[32] and the 'general' theory simply a 'special case' of the classical theory.

The earliest attempt to synthesize the 'hydraulic' and 'fundamentalist' interpretations of GT was J. R. Hicks's article 'Mr. Keynes and the "Classics": A Suggested Interpretation', published in Econometrica, in April 1937, which introduced the IS-LM diagram, a reliable teaching tool ever since. The GT framework, argued Hicks, was consistent with classical theory. But within the 'general theory' there is the 'economics of depression', which he called 'Mr. Keynes' special theory'. The equilibrium level of employment depends on the strength of the motive towards liquidity preference. If it is very weak, the classical theory holds, if strong, the rate of interest on long-term loans 'cannot fall very near zero'.[33]

It was 'Mr. Keynes' special theory' which made GT so plausible a narrative of the time. The reader is asked imagine that the expected returns on investment have fallen and with it the community's output (or real income) and employment. There are no 'surplus' savings waiting to be invested, because saving, being a stable proportion of income, has fallen in line with income. Real wages remain above the rate necessary for full employment, because the price level (or money demand) has fallen. The market rate of interest on loans is fixed above the MEC (marginal efficiency of capital) by liquidity preference. There is no escape from low employment via exports, because the whole world is depressed. Recovery through improvements in the 'animal spirits' of entrepreneurs is uncertain, because expectations fixed in a time of slump cast their shadow over the long period, preventing a rapid revival of activity. Only an exogenous injection of demand can get the economy moving again. This was the hydraulicist position.

But 'Mr. Keynes' special theory' goes beyond Hicks's interpretation. By the time he wrote GT, Keynes had come to believe that 'under-employment equilibrium' was not just a possible or exceptional condition, but a normal condition. He had become convinced that market economies normally operate below full *capacity, sometimes very much below it. A modern economy is, above all, an investment economy. The inducement to invest depends on expectations of profit. But these expectations are highly uncertain. Faced with irreducible uncertainty, hoarding is more rational than investing. Therefore it is only in 'moments of excitement' that the private investment machine fully utilizes available human and technical resources to bring about improvements in welfare. This was a leap of intuition that went far beyond demonstration. Economists before Keynes had been prepared to accept the possibility of 'lapses from full employment', due to this, that, or the other disturbance to 'normal' conditions. No one had hitherto asserted that market economies lapsed into full employment only in 'moments of excitement'.*

Thus the concept of 'under-employment equilibrium' was intended to make the point that the capitalist market economy rarely achieved its productive potential. Four years before GT appeared, Lionel Robbins had defined economics as the science which studies 'human behaviour as a relationship between ends and scarce means which have alternative uses'.[34] In GT, Keynes claimed that an unregulated capitalist market, because of its stagnationist tendencies, kept resources scarcer than they would otherwise be. There is thus a direct link between his preoccupation with mass unemployment between the wars and his hopes for the future as expressed in 'Economic Possibilities for Our Grandchildren' (chapter 2, excerpt 12).

Although TM uses disequilibrium, and GT equilibrium, analysis, the substantive differences between the two is less than one might think. First, no more than in TM, did Keynes envisage the economy as static. Chapter 22 of GT is about the trade cycle. There would always be a 'kick back' from the lowest point, since capital equipment wears out and will need to be replaced. As Keynes writes, 'to-day's employment can be correctly described as being governed by to-day's expectations taken in conjunction with to-day's capital equipment' (CW 7, p. 50).

Secondly, the 'under-employment equilibrium' of GT is wrongly specified as persisting mass unemployment.

'Unemployment' proper is a statistical artefact of the requirements for the receipt of unemployment benefit.[35]
'Under-employment' is the general concept of a workforce
partly employed in work below their capacity – as 'gardeners
and chauffeurs'. Thus an economy can be at full employment,
but also under-employed.[36] Keynes's idea was that as the
machinery of production shrinks the industrial system decants
workers into the bottom end of the service sector.
'Under-employment equilibrium' thus sums up better his idea
of what an inferior equilibrium would look like, combining
insights from both TM and GT.

Keynes's attack on the classical theory relies heavily on the
'fallacy of composition' – the assumption that what is true for
a part is true of the whole, notably expressed in Adam Smith's
dictum that 'What is prudence in the conduct of every private
family can scarce be folly in that of a great kingdom.' It was the
denial of this proposition that underpinned Keynes's demoli-
tion of the classical theory of wages, and his 'paradox of thrift'.
Keynes insisted on the 'two-sidedness' of all economic transactions. An increase in my saving, or a cut in my wages, means
that I have less to spend to buy your goods, and you become
that much poorer. If acts of saving or cuts in wages are not
accompanied by (because they do not necessarily induce)
increased investment, then they simply cause the economy to
run down. All this is foreshadowed in TM, but it is put more
crisply and lucidly here.[37]

GT was Keynes's one book of pure theory: unlike ECP,
TMR, TM and subsequently How to Pay for the War, it contained no specific policy proposals. For policy to fight the world
depression and maintain full employment one has to turn to
excerpts 29, 30–31 and 33, and 35 below.

Keynes's theoretical ambitions were thus larger than the
hydraulic Keynesians recognize. But he may have been wrong
to pursue them, or right to pursue them but unsuccessful in
achieving them. The following excerpts invite the reader to
judge.

Chapter 2, 'The Postulates of the Classical Economics',
makes the classical theory of employment depend on two

postulates: (1) that 'the wage is equal to the marginal product of labour'; and (2) that 'the utility of the wage when a given volume of labour is employed is equal to the marginal disutility of that amount of employment'. The second is simply a technical way of saying that someone will want to work till the extra pleasure derived from the goods he can buy with his last hour's work just equals the pleasure he derives from an extra hour of leisure. The important corollary of this is that workers choose how much they want to work; there is no 'involuntary' or 'unwanted' unemployment. Keynes accepted the first postulate but rejected the second, because it presumed labour as a whole was in a position to fix its own real wage (p. 11), whereas it is other forces which determine the general level of real wages. So flexible money wages were not the way back to full employment. GT continues:]

From the time of Say and Ricardo the classical economists have taught that supply creates its own demand – meaning by this in some significant, but not clearly defined, sense that the whole of the costs of production must necessarily be spent in the aggregate, directly or indirectly, on purchasing the product.   [18]

. . .

As a corollary of the same doctrine, it has been supposed that any individual act of abstaining from consumption necessarily leads to, and amounts to the same thing as, causing the labour and commodities thus released from supplying consumption to be invested in the production of capital wealth.

. . .

The doctrine is never stated to-day in this crude form. Nevertheless it still underlies the whole classical theory, which would collapse without it . . . The conviction, which runs, for example, through almost all Professor Pigou's work, that money makes no real difference except frictionally and that the theory of production and employment can be worked out . . . as being based   [19] on 'real' exchanges with money introduced perfunctorily in a later chapter, is the modern version of the classical tradition. Contemporary thought is still deeply steeped in the notion that if people do not spend their money in one way they will spend it in another. Post-war economists seldom, indeed, succeed in maintaining their standpoint *consistently* ... But they have not ... revised their fundamental theory.

In the first instance, these conclusions may have been applied to the kind of economy in which we actually live by false analogy from some non-exchange Robinson Crusoe economy, in which the income which individuals consume or retain as a result of their productive activity is, actually and excusively, the output *in specie* of that activity. But, apart from this, the conclusion that the *costs* of output are always covered in aggregate by the sales-proceeds resulting from demand, has great plausibility, because it is difficult to distinguish it from another, similar-looking proposition which is indubitable, namely that the income derived in the aggregate by all the elements in the community concerned in a productive activity necessarily has a value exactly equal to the *value* of the output.

[20]   Similarly, it is natural to suppose that the act of an individual, by which he enriches himself without apparently taking anything from anyone else, must also enrich the community as a whole; so that ... an act of individual saving inevitably leads to a parallel act of investment. For, once more, it is indubitable that the sum of the net increments of the wealth of individuals must be exactly equal to the aggregate net increment of the wealth of the community.

Those who think in this way are deceived, nevertheless, by an optical illusion, which makes two essentially different activities appear to be the same. They are fallaciously supposing that there is a nexus which unites decisions to abstain from present consumption with decisions to provide for future consumption; whereas the motives which determine the latter are not linked in any simple way with the motives which determine the former.

It is, then, the assumption of an equality between the demand price of output as a whole and its supply price which is to be regarded as the classical theory's 'axiom of parallels'. Granted this, all the rest follows – the social advantages of private and national thrift, the traditional attitude towards the rate of interest, the classical theory of unemployment, the quantity theory of money, the unqualified advantages of *laissez-faire* in respect of foreign trade and much else which we shall have to question. [21]

. . .

Chapter 3
The Principle of Effective Demand

[On p. 25 Keynes constructs his aggregate supply and demand functions from Marshallian micro supply and demand curves.]

I

Let Z be the aggregate supply price of the output from employing N men, the relationship between Z and N being written $Z = \phi(N)$, which can be called the *aggregate supply function*. Similarly, let D be the proceeds which enterpreneurs expect to receive from the employment of N men, the relationship between D and N being written $D = f(N)$, which can be called the *aggregate demand function*.

Now if for a given value of N the expected proceeds are greater than the aggregate supply price, i.e. if D is greater than Z, there will be an incentive to entrepreneurs to increase employment beyond N and, if necessary, to raise costs by competing with one another for the factors of production, up to the value of N for which Z has become equal to D. Thus the volume of employment is given by the point of intersection between the aggregate demand function and the aggregate supply function; for it is at this point that the entrepreneurs' expectation of profits will be maximised. The value of D at the point of the aggregate demand function, where it is intersected by the aggregate supply function, will be called the *effective demand*. Since this is the substance of the General Theory of Employment . . . the succeeding chapters will be largely occupied with examining the various factors upon which these two functions depend. [25]

. . .

II

A brief summary of the theory of employment to be worked out in the course of the following chapters may, perhaps, help the reader at this stage, even though it may not be fully intelligible. The terms involved will be more carefully defined in due course. In this summary we shall assume that the money-wage and other factor costs are constant per unit of labour employed. But this simplification, with which we shall dispense later, is introduced solely to facilitate the exposition. The essential character of the argument is precisely the same whether or not money-wages, etc., are liable to change.

The outline of our theory can be expressed as follows. When employment increases, aggregate real income is increased. The psychology of the community is such that when aggregate real income is increased aggregate consumption is increased, but not by so much as income. Hence employers would make a loss if the whole of the increased employment were to be devoted to satisfying the increased demand for immediate consumption. Thus, to justify any given amount of employment there must be an amount of current investment sufficient to absorb the excess of total output over what the community chooses to consume when employment is at the given level. For unless there is this amount of investment, the receipts of the entrepreneurs will be less than is required to induce them to offer the given amount of employment. It follows, therefore, that, given what we shall call the community's propensity to consume, the equilibrium level of employment, i.e. the level at which there is no inducement to employers as a whole either to expand or to contract employment, will depend on the amount of current investment. The amount of current investment will depend, in turn, on what we shall call the inducement to invest; and the induce- [27] ment to invest will be found to depend on the relation between the schedule of the marginal efficiency of capital and the complex of rates of interest on loans of various maturities and risks.

Thus, given the propensity to consume and the rate of new investment, there will be only one level of employment consistent with equilibrium; since any other level will lead to inequality between the aggregate supply price of output as a whole and its aggregate demand price.[38] This level cannot be *greater* than full employment, i.e. the real wage cannot be less than the marginal disutility of labour. But there is no reason in general for expecting it to be *equal* to full employment. The effective demand associated with full employment is a special case, only realised when the propensity to consume and the inducement to invest stand in a particular relationship to one another. This particular relationship, which corresponds to the assumptions of the classical theory, is in a sense an optimum relationship. But it can only exist when, by accident or design, current investment provides an amount of demand just equal to the excess of the aggregate supply price of the output resulting from full employment over what the community will choose to spend on consumption when it is fully employed.   [28]

. . .

Thus – except on the special assumptions of the classical theory . . . the economic system may find itself in stable equilibrium with N [*employment*] at a level below full employment

. . .   [30]

Moreover, the richer the community, the wider will tend to be the gap between its actual and its potential production; and therefore the more obvious and outrageous the defects of the economic system. For a poor community will be prone to consume by far the greater part of its output, so that a very modest measure of investment will be sufficient to provide full employment; whereas a wealthy community will have to discover much ampler opportunities for investment if the saving propensities of its wealthier members are to be compatible with the employment of its poorer members. If in a potentially wealthy community the inducement to invest is weak, then, in spite of its potential wealth, the working of the principle of effective demand will compel it to reduce its actual output, until, in spite of its potential wealth, it has become so poor that its surplus over its consumption is sufficiently diminished to correspond to the weakness of the inducement to invest.   [31]

III

The idea that we can safely neglect the aggregate demand function is fundamental to the Ricardian economics, which underlie what we have been taught for more than a century. Malthus, indeed, had vehemently opposed Ricardo's doctrine that it was impossible for effective demand to be deficient; but vainly. For, since Malthus was unable to explain clearly (apart from an appeal to the facts of common observation) how and why effective demand could be deficient or excessive, he failed to furnish an alternative construction; and Ricardo conquered England as completely as the Holy Inquisition conquered Spain. Not only was his theory accepted by the city, by statesmen and by the academic world. But controversy ceased; the other point of view completely disappeared; it ceased to be discussed. The great puzzle of effective demand with which Malthus had wrestled vanished from economic literature. You will not find it mentioned even once in the whole works of Marshall, Edgeworth and Professor Pigou . . . It could only live on furtively, below the surface, in the underworlds of Karl Marx, Silvio Gesell or Major Douglas.

The completeness of the Ricardian victory is something of a curiosity and a mystery. It must have been due to a complex of suitabilities in the doctrine to the environment into which it [32] was projected. That it reached conclusions quite different from what the ordinary uninstructed person would expect, added, I suppose, to its intellectual prestige. That its teaching, translated into practice, was austere and often unpalatable, lent it virtue. That it was adapted to carry a vast and consistent logical superstructure, gave it beauty. That it could explain much social injustice and apparent cruelty as an inevitable incident in the scheme of progress, and the attempt to change such things as likely on the whole to do more harm than good, commended it to authority. That it afforded a measure of justification to the free activities of the individual capitalist, attracted to it the support of the dominant social force behind authority.

But although the doctrine itself has remained unquestioned

by orthodox economists up to a late date, its signal failure for purposes of scientific prediction has greatly impaired, in the course of time, the prestige of its practitioners. For professional economists, after Malthus, were apparently unmoved by the lack of correspondence between the results of their theory and the facts of observation; a discrepancy which the ordinary man has not failed to observe, with the result of his growing unwillingness to accord to economists that measure of respect which he gives to other groups of scientists whose theoretical results are confirmed by observation when they are applied to the facts.

The celebrated *optimism* of traditional economic theory, which has led to economists being looked upon as Candides, who, having left this world for the cultivation of their gardens, teach that all is for the best in the best of all possible worlds provided we will let well alone, is also to be traced, I think, to their having neglected to take account of the drag on prosperity which can be exercised by an insufficiency of effective demand. For there would obviously be a natural tendency towards the optimum employment of resources in a society which was functioning after the [33] manner of the classical postulates. It may well be that the classical theory represents the way in which we should like our economy to behave. But to assume that it actually does so is to assume our difficulties away.   [34]

. . .

Chapter 6
The Definition of Income, Saving and Investment

Provided it is agreed that income is equal to the value of current output, that current investment is equal to that part of current output which is not consumed, and that saving is equal to the excess of income over consumption . . . the equality of saving and investment necessarily follows.   [63]

. . .

Hence, in the aggregate the excess of income over consumption, which we call saving, cannot differ from the addition to capital equipment which we call investment. And similarly with net saving and net investment. Saving, in fact, is a mere residual. The decisions to consume and the decisions to invest between them determine incomes. Assuming that the decisions to invest become effective, they must in doing so either curtail consumption or expand income. Thus the act of investment in itself cannot help causing the residual or margin, which we call saving, to increase by a corresponding amount.

. . .

[64] Clearness of mind on this matter is best reached, perhaps, by thinking in terms of decisions to consume (or refrain from consuming) rather than of decisions to save. A decision to consume or not to consume truly lies within the power of the individual; so does a decision to invest or not to invest. The amounts of aggregate income and of aggregate saving are the *results* of the free choices of individuals . . . but they are neither of them capable of assuming an independent value . . . irrespective of the decisions concerning consumption and investment. In accordance with this principle, the conception of the *propensity to consume* will, in what follows, take the place of the propensity
[65] or disposition to save.

. . .

Chapter 7
The Meaning of Saving and Investment Further Considered

The reconciliation of the identity between saving and investment with the apparent 'free-will' of the individual to save what he chooses irrespective of what he or others may be investing, essentially depends on saving being, like spending, a two-sided affair. For although the amount of his own saving is unlikely to have any significant influence on his own income, the reactions of the amount of his consumption on the incomes of others makes it impossible for all individuals simultaneously to save any given sums. Every such attempt to save more by reducing consumption will so affect incomes that the attempt necessarily defeats itself. It is, of course, just as impossible for the community as a whole to save *less* than the amount of current investment, since the attempt to do so will necessarily raise incomes to a level at which the sums which individuals choose to save add up to a figure exactly equal to the amount of investment.

The above is closely analogous with the proposition which harmonises the liberty, which every individual possesses, to change, whenever he chooses, the amount of money he holds, with the necessity for the total amount of money, which individual balances add up to, to be exactly equal to the amount of cash which the banking system has created. In this latter case the equality is brought about by the fact that the amount of money which people choose to hold is not independent of their incomes or of the prices of the things (primarily securities), the purchase of which is the natural alternative to holding money. Thus incomes and such prices necessarily change until the aggregate of the amounts of money which individuals choose to hold at the new level of incomes and prices thus brought about has come to equality with the amount of money created [84] by the banking system. This, indeed, is the fundamental proposition of monetary theory.

Both these propositions follow merely from the fact that there cannot be a buyer without a seller or a seller without a buyer. Though an individual whose transactions are small in relation to the market can safely neglect the fact that demand is not a one-sided transaction, it makes nonsense to neglect it when we come to aggregate demand. This is the vital difference between the theory of the economic behaviour of the aggregate and the theory of the behaviour of the individual unit, in which we assume that changes in the individual's own demand do not affect his income.[39] [85]

. . .

Chapter 8
The Propensity to Consume:
1 The Objective Factors

[*Chapters 8 and 9, 'The Propensity to Consume' 1 and 2, deal with the first component of aggregate demand. Keynes's consumption function – the proposition that the marginal propensity to consume is less than one – was central to GT's equilibrating mechanism. 'For if the marginal propensity to consume were equal to unity, no equilibrating mechanism would be activated by the decline in output. Specifically, as income (output) decreased, spending would decrease by exactly the same amount, so that any initial difference between aggregate demand and aggregate supply would remain unchanged. Alternatively, as income decreased, the initial excess of desired saving over investment would remain unchanged. Thus the system would be unstable.'[40]*

III

Granted, then, that the propensity to consume is a fairly stable function so that, as a rule, the amount of aggregate consumption mainly depends on the amount of aggregate income (both measured in terms of wage-units), changes in the propensity itself being treated as a secondary influence, what is the normal shape of this function?

The fundamental psychological law, upon which we are entitled to depend with great confidence both *a priori* from our knowledge of human nature and from the detailed facts of experience, is that men are disposed, as a rule and on the average, to increase their consumption as their income increases, but not by as much as the increase in their income. That is to say, if C_w is the amount of consumption and Y_w is income (both measured in wage-units) ΔC_w has the same sign as ΔY_w but is [96] smaller in amount, i.e. $\frac{dC_w}{dY_w}$ is positive and less than unity.

This is especially the case where we have short periods in view, as in the case of the so-called cyclical fluctuations of employment during which habits, as distinct from more permanent psychological propensities, are not given time enough to adapt themselves to changed objective circumstances. For a man's habitual standard of life usually has the first claim on his income, and he is apt to save the difference which discovers itself between his actual income and the expense of his habitual standard; or, if he does adjust his expenditure to changes in his income, he will over short periods do so imperfectly. Thus a rising income will often be accompanied by increased saving, and a falling income by decreased saving, on a greater scale at first than subsequently.

But, apart from short-period *changes* in the level of income, it is also obvious that a higher absolute level of income will tend, as a rule, to widen the gap between income and consumption. For the satisfaction of the immediate primary needs of a man and his family is usually a stronger motive than the motives towards accumulation, which only acquire effective sway when a margin of comfort has been attained. These reasons will lead, as a rule, to a *greater proportion* of income being saved as real income increases. But whether or not a greater proportion is saved, we take it as a fundamental psychological rule of any modern community that, when its real income is increased, it will not increase its consumption by an equal *absolute* amount, so that a greater absolute amount must be saved, unless a large and unusual change is occurring at the same time in other factors. As we shall show subsequently, the stability of the economic system essentially depends on this rule prevailing in practice. This means that, if employment and hence aggregate income increase, *not all* the additional employment will be required to satisfy the needs of additional consumption.   [97]

On the other hand, a decline in income due to a decline in the level of employment, if it goes far, may even cause consumption to exceed income not only by some individuals and institutions using up the financial reserves which they have accumulated in better times, but also by the government, which will be liable, willingly or unwillingly, to run into a budgetary deficit or will provide unemployment relief, for example, out of borrowed money. Thus, when employment falls to a low level, aggregate consumption will decline by a smaller amount than that by which real income has declined, by reason both of the habitual behaviour of individuals and also of the probable policy of governments; which is the explanation why a new position of equilibrium can usually be reached within a modest range of fluctuation. Otherwise a fall in employment and income, once started, might proceed to extreme lengths.

This simple principle leads, it will be seen, to the same conclusion as before, namely, that employment can only increase *pari passu* with an increase in investment; unless, indeed, there is a change in the propensity to consume. For since consumers will spend less than the increase in aggregate supply price when employment is increased, the increased employment will prove unprofitable unless there is an increase in investment to fill the gap.

IV

[*Keynes went on to argue (p. 98) that the larger the depreciation allowances 'the less favourable to consumption, and therefore to employment, will a given level of investment prove to be'.*]

. . .

Take a house which continues to be habitable until it is demolished or abandoned. If a certain sum is written off its value out of the annual rent paid by the tenants, which the landlord neither spends on upkeep nor regards as net income available for consumption, this provision . . . constitutes a drag on employment all through the life of the house, suddenly made good in a lump when the house has to be rebuilt.

[99]   . . .

Thus sinking funds, etc., are apt to withdraw spending power from the consumer long before the demand for expenditure on replacements (which such provisions are anticipating) comes into play; i.e. they diminish the current effective demand and only increase it in the year in which the replacement is actually made. If the effect of this is aggravated by 'financial prudence', i.e. by its being thought advisable to 'write off' the initial cost *more* rapidly than the equipment actually wears out, the cumulative result may be very serious indeed.

In the United States, for example, by 1929 the rapid capital expansion of the previous five years had led cumulatively to the setting up of sinking funds and depreciation allowances, in respect of plant which did not need replacement, on so huge a scale that an enormous volume of entirely new investment was required merely to absorb these financial provisions; and it became almost hopeless to find still more new investment on a sufficient scale to provide for such new saving as a wealthy community in full employment would be disposed to set aside. This factor alone was probably sufficient to cause a slump. And, furthermore, since 'financial prudence' of this kind continued to be exercised through the slump by those great corporations which

were still in a position to afford it, it offered a serious obstacle to
early recovery.   [100]
. . .

Chapter 9
The Propensity to Consume:
2 The Subjective Factors

We must, however, guard against a misunderstanding. The
above means that the influence of moderate changes in the rate
of interest on the *propensity* to consume is usually small. It
does not mean that changes in the rate of interest have only a
small influence on the amounts *actually* saved and consumed.
Quite the contrary. The influence of changes in the rate of interest on the amount actually saved is of paramount importance,
but is *in the opposite direction* to that usually supposed. For
even if the attraction of the larger future income to be earned
from a higher rate of interest has the effect of diminishing the
propensity to consume, nevertheless we can be certain that a
rise in the rate of interest will have the effect of reducing the
amount actually saved. For aggregate saving is governed by
aggregate investment; a rise in the rate of interest (unless it is
offset by a corresponding change in the demand-schedule for
investment) will diminish investment; hence a rise in the rate of
interest must have the effect of reducing incomes to a level at
which saving is decreased in the same measure as investment.   [110]
. . .

Thus, even if it is the case that a rise in the rate of interest would
cause the community to save more *out of a given income*, we can
be quite sure that a rise in the rate of interest (assuming no favourable change in the demand-schedule for investment) will decrease
the actual aggregate of savings . . . For incomes will have to fall
(or be redistributed) by just that amount which is required, with
the existing propensity to consume, to decrease savings by the
same amount by which the rise in the rate of interest will, with
the existing marginal efficiency of capital, decrease investment
. . .

The rise in the rate of interest might induce us to save more, *if*
our incomes were unchanged. But if the higher rate of interest

retards investment, our incomes will not, and cannot, be unchanged. They must necessarily fall, until the declining capacity to save has sufficiently offset the stimulus to save given by the higher rate of interest. The more virtuous we are, the more determinedly thrifty, the more obstinately orthodox in our national and personal finance, the more our incomes will have to fall when interest rises relatively to the marginal efficiency of capital. Obstinacy can bring only a penalty and no reward. For the result is inevitable.

Thus, after all, the actual rates of aggregate saving and spending do not depend on Precaution, Foresight, Calculation, Improvement, Independence, Enterprise, Pride or Avarice. Virtue and vice play no part.

[111]

. . .

Chapter 10
The Marginal Propensity to
Consume and the Multiplier

[Keynes underscores the logic of debt-financed public works, as given by the theory of the 'multiplier', which he describes in excerpt 30 below.]

It is curious how common sense, wriggling for an escape from absurd conclusions, has been apt to reach a preference for *wholly* 'wasteful' forms of loan expenditure rather than for *partly* wasteful forms, which, because they are not wholly wasteful, tend to be judged on strict 'business' principles. For example, unemployment relief financed by loans is more readily accepted than the financing of improvements at a charge below the current rate of interest; whilst the form of digging holes in the ground known as gold-mining, which not only adds nothing whatever to the real wealth of the world but involves the disutility of labour, is the most acceptable of all solutions.

If the Treasury were to fill old bottles with banknotes, bury them at suitable depths in disused coal-mines which are then filled up to the surface with town rubbish, and leave it to private enterprise on well-tried principles of *laissez-faire* to dig the notes up again (the right to do so being obtained, of course, by tendering for leases of the note-bearing territory), there need be no more unemployment and, with the help of the repercussions, the real income of the community, and its capital wealth also, would probably become a good deal greater than it actually is. It would, indeed, be more sensible to build houses and the like; but if there are political and practical difficulties in the way of this, the above would be better than nothing.

The analogy between this expedient and the gold-mines of [129] the real world is complete. At periods when gold is available at suitable depths experience shows that the real wealth of the world increases rapidly; and when but little of it is so available our wealth suffers stagnation or decline. Thus gold-mines are of the greatest value and importance to civilisation. Just as wars have been the only form of large-scale loan expenditure which statesmen have thought justifiable, so gold-mining is the only pretext for digging holes in the ground which has recommended itself to bankers as sound finance . . .

In addition to the probable effect of increased supplies of gold on the rate of interest, gold-mining is for two reasons a highly practical form of investment, if we are precluded from increasing employment by means which at the same time increase our stock of useful wealth. In the first place, owing to the gambling attractions which it offers it is carried on without too close a regard to the ruling rate of interest. In the second place the result, namely, the increased stock of gold, does not, as in other cases, have the effect of diminishing its marginal utility. Since the value of a house depends on its utility, every house which is built serves to diminish the prospective rents obtainable from further house-building and therefore lessens the attraction of further similar investment unless the rate of interest is falling *pari passu*. But the fruits of gold-mining do not suffer from this disadvantage, and a check can only come through a rise of the wage-unit in terms of gold, which is not likely to occur unless and until employment is substantially better.

. . .   [130]

Ancient Egypt was doubly fortunate, and doubtless owed to this its fabled wealth, in that it possessed *two* activities, namely, pyramid-building as well as the search for the precious metals, the fruits of which, since they could not serve the needs of man by being consumed, did not stale with abundance. The Middle Ages built cathedrals and sang dirges. Two pyramids, two masses for the dead, are twice as good as one; but not so two railways from London to York. Thus we are so sensible, have schooled ourselves to so close a semblance of prudent financiers, taking careful thought before we add to the 'financial' burdens of posterity by building them houses to live in, that we have no such easy escape from the sufferings of unemployment. We have to accept them as an inevitable result of applying to the conduct of the State the maxims which are best calculated to 'enrich' an individual by enabling him to pile up claims to enjoyment which he does not intend to exercise at any definite [131] time.

. . .

Chapter 11
The Marginal Efficiency of Capital

[Chapters 11 and 12, 'The Inducement to Invest', analyse the second determinant of aggregate demand.]

I

When a man buys an investment or capital-asset, he purchases the right to the series of prospective returns, which he expects to obtain from selling its output, after deducting the running expenses of obtaining that output, during the life of the asset. This series of annuities $Q_1, Q_2 \ldots Q_n$ it is convenient to call the *prospective yield* of the investment.

Over against the prospective yield of the investment we have the *supply price* of the capital-asset, meaning by this, not the market-price at which an asset of the type in question can actually be purchased in the market, but the price which would just induce a manufacturer newly to produce an additional unit of such assets, i.e. what is sometimes called its *replacement cost*. The relation between the prospective yield of a capital-asset and its supply price or replacement cost, i.e. the relation between the prospective yield of one more unit of that type of capital and the cost of producing that unit, furnishes us with the *marginal efficiency of capital* of that type. More precisely, I define the marginal efficiency of capital as being equal to that rate of discount which would make the present value of the series of annuities given by the returns expected from the capital-asset during its life just equal to its supply price. This gives us the marginal efficiencies of particular types of capital-assets. The greatest of these marginal efficiencies can then be regarded as [135] the marginal efficiency of capital in general.

The reader should note that the marginal efficiency of capital is here defined in terms of the *expectation* of yield and of the *current* supply price of the capital-asset. It depends on the rate of return expected to be obtainable on money if it were invested in a *newly* produced asset; not on the historical result of what an investment has yielded on its original cost if we look back on its record after its life is over.

If there is an increased investment in any given type of capital during any period of time, the marginal efficiency of that type of capital will diminish as the investment in it is increased, partly because the prospective yield will fall as the supply of that type of capital is increased, and partly because, as a rule, pressure on the facilities for producing that type of capital will cause its supply price to increase; the second of these factors being usually the more important in producing equilibrium in the short run, but the longer the period in view the more does the first factor take its place. Thus for each type of capital we can build up a schedule, showing by how much investment in it will have to increase within the period, in order that its marginal efficiency should fall to any given figure. We can then aggregate these schedules for all the different types of capital, so as to provide a schedule relating the rate of aggregate investment to the corresponding marginal efficiency of capital in general which that rate of investment will establish. We shall call this the investment demand-schedule; or, alternatively, the schedule of the marginal efficiency of capital.

Now it is obvious that the actual rate of current investment will be pushed to the point where there is no longer any class of capital-asset of which the marginal efficiency exceeds the current rate of interest. In other words, the rate of investment will be pushed to the point on the investment demand-schedule [136] where the marginal efficiency of capital in general is equal to the market rate of interest.

. . .

It follows that the inducement to invest depends partly on the investment demand-schedule and partly on the rate of interest. Only at the conclusion of Book IV will it be possible to take a comprehensive view of the factors determining the rate of investment in their actual complexity. I would, however, ask the reader to note at once that neither the knowledge of an asset's prospective yield nor the knowledge of the marginal efficiency of the asset enables us to deduce either the rate of interest or the present value of the asset. We must ascertain the rate of interest from some other source, and only then can we value [137] the asset by 'capitalising' its prospective yield.

. . .

III

The most important confusion concerning the meaning and significance of the marginal efficiency of capital has ensued on the failure to see that it depends on the *prospective* yield of capital, and not merely on its current yield.

This is the factor through which the expectation of changes in the value of money influences the volume of current output. The expectation of a fall in the value of money stimulates investment, and hence employment generally, because it raises [141] the schedule of the marginal efficiency of capital, i.e. the investment demand-schedule; and the expectation of a rise in the value of money is depressing, because it lowers the schedule of the marginal efficiency of capital.

[142]   . . .

It is important to understand the dependence of the marginal efficiency of a given stock of capital on changes in expectation, [143] because it is chiefly this dependence which renders the marginal efficiency of capital subject to the somewhat violent fluctuations which are the explanation of the trade cycle. In chapter 22 below we shall show that the succession of boom and slump can be described and analysed in terms of the fluctuations of the marginal efficiency of capital relatively to the rate of interest.

IV

Two types of risk affect the volume of investment which have not commonly been distinguished, but which it is important to distinguish. The first is the entrepreneur's or borrower's risk and arises out of doubts in his own mind as to the probability of his actually earning the prospective yield for which he hopes. If a man is venturing his own money, this is the only risk which is relevant.

But where a system of borrowing and lending exists, by which I mean the granting of loans with a margin of real or personal security, a second type of risk is relevant which we may call the lender's risk. This may be due either to moral hazard, i.e. voluntary default or other means of escape, possibly lawful, from the fulfilment of the obligation, or to the possible insufficiency of the margin of security, i.e. involuntary default due to the disappointment of expectation . . .

Now the first type of risk is, in a sense, a real social cost, though susceptible to diminution by averaging as well as by an increased accuracy of foresight. The second, however, is a pure addition to the cost of investment which would not exist if the borrower and lender were the same person. Moreover, it involves in part a duplication of a proportion of the entrepreneur's risk, which is added *twice* to the pure rate of interest to give the minimum prospective yield which will induce the investment. For if a venture is a risky one, the borrower will require a wider margin between his expectation of yield and the rate of interest at which he will think it worth his while to borrow; whilst the very same reason will lead the lender to require a wider margin between what he charges and the pure rate of interest in order to induce him to lend (except where the borrower is so strong and wealthy that he is in a position to offer an exceptional margin of security). The hope of a very favourable outcome, which may balance the risk in the mind of the borrower, is not available to solace the lender.

This duplication of allowance for a portion of the risk has

[144]

not hitherto been emphasised, so far as I am aware; but it may be important in certain circumstances. During a boom the popular estimation of the magnitude of both these risks, both borrower's risk and lender's risk, is apt to become unusually and imprudently low.

V

The schedule of the marginal efficiency of capital is of fundamental importance because it is mainly through this factor (much more than through the rate of interest) that the expectation of the future influences the present.

[145]

Chapter 12
The State of Long-Term Expectation

[*Chapter 12, which Keynes described as an 'epistemological digression', makes the investment demand schedule depend on uncertain expectations. It shows how investment activity governed by uncertain expectations is bound to be unstable, how the institution of the stock market exaggerates this instability, and why expectations, once disappointed, take such a long time to recover. In addition, Keynes utilizes two ideas from his earlier work on probability: the 'weight' of evidence (explicitly) and the principle of indifference (implicitly) to explain why investors, in forming their expectations, take more heed of the present than of the future. First used by the young Keynes as an argument for liberating individual judgement of probabilities from knowledge of frequencies, the principle of indifference is here utilized to explain why short-term expectations determine long-term expectations. The phrase 'animal spirits' and the analogy between investment and a beauty contest come from this chapter.*]

II

It would be foolish, in forming our expectations, to attach great weight to matters which are very uncertain. [*Keynes supplies a footnote on p. 148. 'By "very uncertain" I do not mean the same thing as "very improbable". Cf my* Treatise on Probability, *chap. 6, on "The Weight of Arguments".' For an explanation of the 'weight of arguments' see p. 12 above.*] It is reasonable, therefore, to be guided to a considerable degree by the facts about which we feel somewhat confident, even though they may be less decisively relevant to the issue than other facts about which our knowledge is vague and scanty. For this reason the facts of the existing situation enter, in a sense disproportionately, into the formation of our long-term expectations; our usual practice being to take the existing situation and to project it into the future, modified only to the extent that we have more or less definite reasons for expecting a change.

The state of long-term expectation, upon which our decisions are based, does not solely depend, therefore, on the most probable forecast we can make. It also depends on the *confidence* with which we make this forecast – on how highly we rate the likelihood of our best forecast turning out quite wrong. If we expect large changes but are very uncertain as to what precise form these changes will take, then our confidence will be weak.

The *state of confidence*, as they term it, is a matter to which practical men always pay the closest and most anxious attention. But economists have not analysed it carefully and have been content, as a rule, to discuss it in general terms. In particu- [148] lar it has not been made clear that its relevance to economic problems comes in through its important influence on the schedule of the marginal efficiency of capital. There are not two separate factors affecting the rate of investment, namely, the schedule of the marginal efficiency of capital and the state of confidence. The state of confidence is relevant because it is one of the major factors determining the former, which is the same thing as the investment demand-schedule.

There is, however, not much to be said about the state of confidence *a priori*. Our conclusions must mainly depend upon the actual observation of markets and business psychology. This is the reason why the ensuing digression is on a different level of abstraction from most of this book.

For convenience of exposition we shall assume in the following discussion of the state of confidence that there are no changes in the rate of interest; and we shall write, throughout the following sections, as if changes in the values of investments were solely due to changes in the expectation of their prospective yields and not at all to changes in the rate of interest at which these prospective yields are capitalised. The effect of changes in the rate of interest is, however, easily super-imposed on the effect of changes in the state of confidence.

III

The outstanding fact is the extreme precariousness of the basis of knowledge on which our estimates of prospective yield have to be made. Our knowledge of the factors which will govern the yield of an investment some years hence is usually very slight and often negligible. If we speak frankly, we have to admit that our basis of knowledge for estimating the yield ten years hence of a railway, a copper mine, a textile factory, the [149] goodwill of a patent medicine, an Atlantic liner, a building in the City of London amounts to little and sometimes to nothing; or even five years hence. In fact, those who seriously attempt to make any such estimate are often so much in the minority that their behaviour does not govern the market.

In former times, when enterprises were mainly owned by those who undertook them or by their friends and associates, investment depended on a sufficient supply of individuals of sanguine temperament and constructive impulses who embarked on business as a way of life, not really relying on a precise cal-culation of prospective profit. The affair was partly a lottery, though with the ultimate result largely governed by whether the abilities and character of the managers were above or below the average. Some would fail and some would succeed. But even after the event no one would know whether the average results in terms of the sums invested had exceeded, equalled, or fallen short of the prevailing rate of interest; though, if we exclude the exploitation of natural resources and monopolies, it is prob-able that the actual average results of investments, even during periods of progress and prosperity, have disappointed the hopes which prompted them. Business men play a mixed game of skill and chance, the average results of which to the players are not known by those who take a hand. If human nature felt no temptation to take a chance, no satisfaction (profit apart) in constructing a factory, a railway, a mine or a farm, there might not be much investment merely as a result of cold calculation.

Decisions to invest in private business of the old-fashioned type were, however, decisions largely irrevocable, not only for the community as a whole, but also for the individual. With the separation between ownership and management which prevails today and with the development of organised investment markets, a new factor of great importance has entered in, which sometimes facilitates investment but sometimes adds greatly to [150] the instability of the system. In the absence of security markets, there is no object in frequently attempting to revalue an investment to which we are committed. But the Stock Exchange revalues many investments every day and the revaluations give a frequent opportunity to the individual (though not to the community as a whole) to revise his commitments. It is as though a farmer, having tapped his barometer after breakfast, could decide to remove his capital from the farming business between 10 and 11 in the morning and reconsider whether he should return to it later in the week. But the daily revaluations of the Stock Exchange, though they are primarily made to facilitate transfers of old investments between one individual and another, inevitably exert a decisive influence on the rate of current investment. For there is no sense in building up a new enterprise at a cost greater than that at which a similar existing enterprise can be purchased; whilst there is an inducement to spend on a new project what may seem an extravagant sum, if it can be floated off on the Stock Exchange at an immediate profit. Thus certain classes of investment are governed by the average expectation of those who deal on the Stock Exchange as revealed in the price of shares, rather than by the genuine expectations of the professional entrepreneur. How then are these highly significant daily, even hourly, revaluations of existing investments carried out in practice? [151]

IV

In practice we have tacitly agreed, as a rule, to fall back on what is, in truth, a *convention*. The essence of this convention – though it does not, of course, work out quite so simply – lies in assuming that the existing state of affairs will continue indefinitely, except in so far as we have specific reasons to expect a change. This does not mean that we really believe that the existing state of affairs will continue indefinitely. We know from extensive experience that this is most unlikely. The actual results of an investment over a long term of years very seldom agree with the initial expectation. Nor can we rationalise our behaviour by arguing that to a man in a state of ignorance errors in either direction are equally probable, so that there remains a mean actuarial expectation based on equi-probabilities. For it can easily be shown that the assumption of arithmetically equal probabilities based on a state of ignorance leads to absurdities. We are assuming, in effect, that the existing market valuation, however arrived at, is uniquely *correct* in relation to our existing knowledge of the facts which will influence the yield of the investment, and that it will only change in proportion to changes in this knowledge; though, philosophically speaking, it cannot be uniquely correct, since our existing knowledge does not provide a sufficient basis for a calculated mathematical expectation. In point of fact, all sorts of considerations enter into the market valuation which are in no way relevant to the prospective yield.

Nevertheless the above conventional method of calculation will be compatible with a considerable measure of continuity and stability in our affairs, *so long as we can rely on the maintenance of the convention.*

For if there exist organised investment markets and if we can rely on the maintenance of the convention, an investor can legitimately encourage himself with the idea that the only risk he runs is that of a genuine change in the news *over the near future*, as to the likelihood of which he can attempt to form his own judgment, and which is unlikely to be very large. For, assuming that the convention holds good, it is only these changes which can affect the value of his investment, and he need not lose his sleep merely because he has not any notion what his investment will be worth ten years hence. Thus investment becomes reasonably 'safe' for the individual investor over short periods, and hence over a succession of short periods however many, if he

[152]

can fairly rely on there being no breakdown in the convention and on his therefore having an opportunity to revise his judgment and change his investment, before there has been time for much to happen. Investments which are 'fixed' for the community are thus made 'liquid' for the individual.

It has been, I am sure, on the basis of some such procedure as this that our leading investment markets have been developed. But it is not surprising that a convention, in an absolute view of things so arbitrary, should have its weak points. It is its precariousness which creates no small part of our contemporary problem of securing sufficient investment.

V

Some of the factors which accentuate this precariousness may be briefly mentioned.

(1) As a result of the gradual increase in the proportion of the equity in the community's aggregate capital investment which is owned by persons who do not manage and have no special knowledge of the circumstances, either actual or prospective, of the business in question, the element of real knowledge in the valuation of investments by those who own them or contemplate purchasing them has seriously declined.

(2) Day-to-day fluctuations in the profits of existing investments, which are obviously of an ephemeral and non-significant character, tend to have an altogether excessive, and even an absurd, influence on the market. It is said, for example, that the shares of American companies which manufacture ice tend to sell at a higher price in summer when their profits are seasonally high than in winter when no one wants ice. The recurrence of a bank-holiday may raise the market valuation of the British railway system by several million pounds. [153]

(3) A conventional valuation which is established as the outcome of the mass psychology of a large number of ignorant individuals is liable to change violently as the result of a sudden fluctuation of opinion due to factors which do not really make much difference to the prospective yield; since there will be no strong roots of conviction to hold it steady. In abnormal times in particular, when the hypothesis of an indefinite continuance of

the existing state of affairs is less plausible than usual even though there are no express grounds to anticipate a definite change, the market will be subject to waves of optimistic and pessimistic sentiment, which are unreasoning and yet in a sense legitimate where no solid basis exists for a reasonable calculation.

(4) But there is one feature in particular which deserves our attention. It might have been supposed that competition between expert professionals, possessing judgment and knowledge beyond that of the average private investor, would correct the vagaries of the ignorant individual left to himself. It happens, however, that the energies and skill of the professional investor and speculator are mainly occupied otherwise. For most of these persons are, in fact, largely concerned, not with making superior long-term forecasts of the probable yield of an investment over its whole life, but with foreseeing changes in the conventional basis of valuation a short time ahead of the general public. They [154] are concerned, not with what an investment is really worth to a man who buys it 'for keeps', but with what the market will value it at, under the influence of mass psychology, three months or a year hence. Moreover, this behaviour is not the outcome of a wrong-headed propensity. It is an inevitable result of an investment market organised along the lines described. For it is not sensible to pay 25 for an investment of which you believe the prospective yield to justify a value of 30, if you also believe that the market will value it at 20 three months hence.

Thus the professional investor is forced to concern himself with the anticipation of impending changes, in the news or in the atmosphere, of the kind by which experience shows that the mass psychology of the market is most influenced. This is the inevitable result of investment markets organised with a view to so-called 'liquidity'. Of the maxims of orthodox finance none, surely, is more anti-social than the fetish of liquidity, the doctrine that it is a positive virtue on the part of investment institutions to concentrate their resources upon the holding of 'liquid' securities. It forgets that there is no such thing as liquidity of investment for the community as a whole. The social object of skilled investment should be to defeat the dark forces of time and ignorance which envelop our future. The actual, private object of the most

skilled investment today is 'to beat the gun', as the Americans so
well express it, to outwit the crowd, and to pass the bad, or
depreciating, half-crown to the other fellow.

This battle of wits to anticipate the basis of conventional
valuation a few months hence, rather than the prospective yield
of an investment over a long term of years, does not even
require gulls amongst the public to feed the maws of the professional; – it can be played by professionals amongst themselves.
Nor is it necessary that anyone should keep his simple faith
in the conventional basis of valuation having any genuine
long-term validity. For it is, so to speak, a game of Snap, of Old   [155]
Maid, of Musical Chairs – a pastime in which he is victor who
says *Snap* neither too soon nor too late, who passed the Old
Maid to his neighbour before the game is over, who secures a
chair for himself when the music stops. These games can be
played with zest and enjoyment, though all the players know
that it is the Old Maid which is circulating, or that when the
music stops some of the players will find themselves unseated.

Or, to change the metaphor slightly, professional investment
may be likened to those newspaper competitions in which the
competitors have to pick out the six prettiest faces from a hundred
photographs, the prize being awarded to the competitor whose
choice most nearly corresponds to the average preferences of the
competitors as a whole; so that each competitor has to pick, not
those faces which he himself finds prettiest, but those which he
thinks likeliest to catch the fancy of the other competitors, all of
whom are looking at the problem from the same point of view. It
is not a case of choosing those which, to the best of one's judgment, are really the prettiest, nor even those which average opinion
genuinely thinks the prettiest. We have reached the third degree
where we devote our intelligences to anticipating what average
opinion expects the average opinion to be. And there are some, I
believe, who practise the fourth, fifth and higher degrees.

If the reader interjects that there must surely be large profits
to be gained from the other players in the long run by a skilled
individual who, unperturbed by the prevailing pastime, continues to purchase investments on the best genuine long-term
expectations he can frame, he must be answered, first of all,

that there are, indeed, such serious-minded individuals and that it makes a vast difference to an investment market whether or not they predominate in their influence over the game-players.
[156] But we must also add that there are several factors which jeopardise the predominance of such individuals in modern investment markets. Investment based on genuine long-term expectation is so difficult today as to be scarcely practicable. He who attempts it must surely lead much more laborious days and run greater risks than he who tries to guess better than the crowd how the crowd will behave; and, given equal intelligence, he may make more disastrous mistakes. There is no clear evidence from experience that the investment policy which is socially advantageous coincides with that which is most profitable. It needs *more* intelligence to defeat the forces of time and our ignorance of the future than to beat the gun. Moreover, life is not long enough; – human nature desires quick results, there is a peculiar zest in making money quickly, and remoter gains are discounted by the average man at a very high rate. The game of professional investment is intolerably boring and over-exacting to anyone who is entirely exempt from the gambling instinct; whilst he who has it must pay to this propensity the appropriate toll. Furthermore, an investor who proposes to ignore near-term market fluctuations needs greater resources for safety and must not operate on so large a scale, if at all, with borrowed money – a further reason for the higher return from the pastime to a given stock of intelligence and resources. Finally it is the long-term investor, he who most promotes the public interest, who will in practice come in for most criticism, wherever investment funds are managed by committees or boards or banks. For it is in the essence of his behaviour that he should be eccentric, unconventional and rash in the eyes of average opinion. If he is successful, that will only con-
[157] firm the general belief in his rashness; and if in the short run he is unsuccessful, which is very likely, he will not receive much mercy. Worldly wisdom teaches that it is better for reputation to fail conventionally than to succeed unconventionally.

(5) So far we have had chiefly in mind the state of confidence of the speculator or speculative investor himself and may have

seemed to be tacitly assuming that, if he himself is satisfied with the prospects, he has unlimited command over money at the market rate of interest. This is, of course, not the case. Thus we must also take account of the other facet of the state of confidence, namely, the confidence of the lending institutions towards those who seek to borrow from them, sometimes described as the state of credit. A collapse in the price of equities, which has had disastrous reactions on the marginal efficiency of capital, may have been due to the weakening either of speculative confidence or of the state of credit. But whereas the weakening of either is enough to cause a collapse, recovery requires the revival of *both*. For whilst the weakening of credit is sufficient to bring about a collapse, its strengthening, though a necessary condition of recovery, is not a sufficient condition.

VI

These considerations should not lie beyond the purview of the economist. But they must be relegated to their right perspective. If I may be allowed to appropriate the term *speculation* for the activity of forecasting the psychology of the market, and the term *enterprise* for the activity of forecasting the prospective yield of assets over their whole life, it is by no means always the case that speculation predominates over enterprise. As the organisation of investment markets improves, the risk of the predominance of speculation does, however, increase. In one of the greatest investment markets in the world, namely, New York, the influence of speculation (in the above sense) is [158] enormous. Even outside the field of finance, Americans are apt to be unduly interested in discovering what average opinion believes average opinion to be; and this national weakness finds its nemesis in the stock market. It is rare, one is told, for an American to invest, as many Englishmen still do, 'for income'; and he will not readily purchase an investment except in the hope of capital appreciation. This is only another way of saying that, when he purchases an investment, the American is attaching his hopes, not so much to its prospective yield, as to a favourable change in the conventional basis of valuation, i.e. that he is, in the above sense, a speculator. Speculators may do no harm as bubbles on a steady stream of enterprise. But the position is serious when enterprise becomes the bubble on a whirlpool of speculation. When the capital development of a country becomes a by-product of the activities of a casino, the job is likely to be ill-done. The measure of success attained by Wall Street, regarded as an institution of which the proper social purpose is to direct new investment into the most profitable channels in terms of future yield, cannot be claimed as one of the outstanding triumphs of *laissez-faire* capitalism – which is not surprising, if I am right in thinking that the best brains of Wall Street have been in fact directed towards a different object.

These tendencies are a scarcely avoidable outcome of our having successfully organised 'liquid' investment markets. It is usually agreed that casinos should, in the public interest, be inaccessible and expensive. And perhaps the same is true of stock exchanges. That the sins of the London Stock Exchange are less than those of Wall Street may be due, not so much to differences in national character, as to the fact that to the average Englishman Throgmorton Street is, compared with Wall Street to the average American, inaccessible and very expensive. The jobber's 'turn', the high brokerage charges and the heavy transfer tax payable to the Exchequer, which attend dealings on the London Stock Exchange, sufficiently diminish the liquidity of the market (although the practice of fortnightly accounts operates the other way) to rule out a large proportion of the transaction characteristic of Wall Street. The introduction of a substantial government transfer tax on all transactions might prove the most serviceable reform available, with a view to mitigating the predominance of speculation over enterprise in the United States.

The spectacle of modern investment markets has sometimes moved me towards the conclusion that to make the purchase of an investment permanent and indissoluble, like marriage, except by reason of death or other grave cause, might be a useful remedy for our contemporary evils. For this would force the investor to direct his mind to the long-term prospects and to those only. But a little consideration of this expedient brings us up against a dilemma, and shows us how the liquidity of

[159]

investment markets often facilitates, though it sometimes impedes, the course of new investment. For the fact that each individual investor flatters himself that his commitment is 'liquid' (though this cannot be true for all investors collectively) calms his nerves and makes him much more willing to run a risk. If individual purchases of investments were rendered illiquid, this might seriously impede new investment, so long as *alternative ways* in which to hold his savings are available to the individual. This is the dilemma. So long as it is open to the individual to employ his wealth in hoarding or lending *money*, the alternative of purchasing actual capital assets cannot be rendered sufficiently attractive (especially to the man who does [160] not manage the capital assets and knows very little about them), except by organising markets wherein these assets can be easily realised for money.

The only radical cure for the crises of confidence which afflict the economic life of the modern world would be to allow the individual no choice between consuming his income and ordering the production of the specific capital-asset which, even though it be on precarious evidence, impresses him as the most promising investment available to him. It might be that, at times when he was more than usually assailed by doubts concerning the future, he would turn in his perplexity towards more consumption and less new investment. But that would avoid the disastrous, cumulative and far-reaching repercussions of its being open to him, when thus assailed by doubts, to spend his income neither on the one nor on the other.

Those who have emphasised the social dangers of the hoarding of money have, of course, had something similar to the above in mind. But they have overlooked the possibility that the phenomenon can occur without any change, or at least any commensurate change, in the hoarding of money.

VII

Even apart from the instability due to speculation, there is the instability due to the characteristic of human nature that a large proportion of our positive activities depend on spontaneous optimism rather than on a mathematical expectation, whether moral or hedonistic or economic. Most, probably, of our decisions to do something positive, the full consequences of which will be drawn out over many days to come, can only be taken as a result of animal spirits – of a spontaneous urge to action rather than inaction, and not as the outcome of a weighted average of quantitative benefits multiplied by quanti-[161] tative probabilities. Enterprise only pretends to itself to be mainly actuated by the statements in its own prospectus, however candid and sincere. Only a little more than an expedition to the South Pole, is it based on an exact calculation of benefits to come. Thus if the animal spirits are dimmed and the spontaneous optimism falters, leaving us to depend on nothing but a mathematical expectation, enterprise will fade and die; – though fears of loss may have a basis no more reasonable than hopes of profit had before.

It is safe to say that enterprise which depends on hopes stretching into the future benefits the community as a whole. But individual initiative will only be adequate when reasonable calculation is supplemented and supported by animal spirits, so that the thought of ultimate loss which often overtakes pioneers, as experience undoubtedly tells us and them, is put aside as a healthy man puts aside the expectation of death.

This means, unfortunately, not only that slumps and depressions are exaggerated in degree, but that economic prosperity is excessively dependent on a political and social atmosphere which is congenial to the average business man. If the fear of a Labour Government or a New Deal depresses enterprise, this need not be the result either of a reasonable calculation or of a plot with political intent; – it is the mere consequence of upsetting the delicate balance of spontaneous optimism. In estimating the prospects of investment, we must have regard, therefore, to the nerves and hysteria and even the digestions and reactions to the weather of those upon whose spontaneous activity it largely depends.

We should not conclude from this that everything depends on waves of irrational psychology. On the contrary, the state of long-term expectation is often steady, and, even when it is not, the other factors exert their compensating effects. We are merely reminding ourselves that human decisions affecting the future, whether personal or political or economic, cannot [162] depend on strict mathematical expectation, since the basis for making such calculations does not exist; and that it is our innate urge to activity which makes the wheels go round, our rational selves choosing between the alternatives as best we are able, calculating where we can, but often falling back for our motive on whim or sentiment or chance.

VIII

There are, moreover, certain important factors which somewhat mitigate in practice the effects of our ignorance of the future. Owing to the operation of compound interest combined with the likelihood of obsolescence with the passage of time, there are many individual investments of which the prospective yield is legitimately dominated by the returns of the comparatively near future. In the case of the most important class of very long-term investments, namely buildings, the risk can be frequently transferred from the investor to the occupier, or at least shared between them, by means of long-term contracts, the risk being outweighed in the mind of the occupier by the advantages of continuity and security of tenure. In the case of another important class of long-term investments, namely public utilities, a substantial proportion of the prospective yield is practically guaranteed by monopoly privileges coupled with the right to charge such rates as will provide a certain stipulated margin. Finally there is a growing class of investments entered upon by, or at the risk of, public authorities, which are frankly influenced in making the investment by a general presumption of there being prospective social advantages from the invest-ment, whatever its commercial yield may prove to be within a wide range, and without seeking to be satisfied that the math-ematical expectation of the yield is at least equal to the current rate of interest, – though the rate which the public authority has [163] to pay may still play a decisive part in determining the scale of investment operations which it can afford.

Thus after giving full weight to the importance of the influ-ence of short-period changes in the state of long-term expectation as distinct from changes in the rate of interest, we are still entitled to return to the latter as exercising, at any rate, in normal circumstances, a great, though not a decisive, influence on the rate of investment. Only experience, however, can show how far management of the rate of interest is capable of continuously stimulating the appropriate volume of investment.

For my own part I am now somewhat sceptical of the success of a merely monetary policy directed towards influencing the rate of interest. I expect to see the State, which is in a position to calculate the marginal efficiency of capital-goods on long views and on the basis of the general social advantage, taking an ever greater responsibility for directly organising investment; since it seems likely that the fluctuations in the market estimation of the marginal efficiency of different types of capital, calculated on the principles I have described above, will be too great to be offset by any practicable changes in the

[164]   rate of interest.

Chapter 13
The General Theory of the Rate of Interest

[*In this 'general' theory, the classical theory of interest – that interest is the reward for saving or 'waiting' – is a special case, which applies only to a 'real exchange' economy in which no speculative demand for money exists.*]

II

The psychological time-preferences of an individual require two distinct sets of decisions to carry them out completely. The first is concerned with that aspect of time-preference which I have called the *propensity to consume*, which, operating under the influence of the various motives set forth in Book III, determines for each individual how much of his income he will consume and how much he will reserve in *some* form of command over future consumption.

But this decision having been made, there is a further decision which awaits him, namely, in *what form* he will hold the command over future consumption which he has reserved, whether out of his current income or from previous savings. Does he want to hold it in the form of immediate, liquid command (i.e. in money or its equivalent)? Or is he prepared to part with immediate command for a specified or indefinite period, leaving it to future market conditions to determine on what terms he can, if necessary, convert deferred command over specific goods into immediate command over goods in general? In other words, what is the degree of his *liquidity-preference* – where an individual's liquidity-preference is given by a schedule of the amounts of his resources, valued in terms of money or of wage-units, which he will wish to retain in the form of money in different sets of circumstances?

We shall find that the mistake in the accepted theories of the rate of interest lies in their attempting to derive the rate of interest from the first of these two constituents of psychological time-preference to the neglect of the second; and it is this neglect which we must endeavour to repair.

It should be obvious that the rate of interest cannot be a [166] return to saving or waiting as such. For if a man hoards his savings in cash, he earns no interest, though he saves just as much as before. On the contrary, the mere definition of the rate of interest tells us in so many words that the rate of interest is the reward for parting with liquidity for a specified period. For the rate of interest is, in itself, nothing more than the inverse proportion between a sum of money and what can be obtained for parting with control over the money in exchange for a debt for a stated period of time.

Thus the rate of interest at any time, being the reward for parting with liquidity, is a measure of the unwillingness of those who possess money to part with their liquid control over it. The rate of interest is not the 'price' which brings into equilibrium the demand for resources to invest with the readiness to abstain from present consumption. It is the 'price' which equilibrates the desire to hold wealth in the form of cash with the available quantity of cash; – which implies that if the rate of interest were lower, i.e. if the reward for parting with cash were diminished, the aggregate amount of cash which the public would wish to hold would exceed the available supply, and that if the rate of interest were raised, there would be a surplus of cash which no one would be willing to hold. If this explanation is correct, the quantity of money is the other factor, which, in conjunction with liquidity-preference, determines the actual rate of interest in given circumstances. Liquidity-preference is a potentiality or functional tendency, which fixes the quantity of money which the public will hold when the rate of interest is given; so that if r is the rate of interest, M the quantity of money and L the function of liquidity-preference, we have $M = L(r)$. This is where, and how, the quantity of money enters into the economic scheme.

At this point, however, let us turn back and consider why such a thing as liquidity-preference exists. In this connection we can usefully employ the ancient distinction between the use of money for the transaction of current business and its use as a store of wealth. As regards the first of these two uses, it is obvious that up to a point it is worth while to sacrifice a certain amount of interest for the convenience of liquidity. But, given that the rate of interest is never negative, why should anyone prefer to hold his wealth in a form which yields little or no interest to holding it in a form which yields interest (assuming, of course, at this stage, that the risk of default is the same in respect of a bank balance as of a bond)? A full explanation is complex and must wait for chapter 15. There is, however, a necessary condition failing which the existence of a liquidity-preference for money as a means of holding wealth could not exist.

This necessary condition is the existence of *uncertainty* as to the future of the rate of interest, i.e. as to the complex of rates of interest for varying maturities which will rule at future dates. For if the rates of interest ruling at all future times could be foreseen with certainty, all future rates of interest could be inferred from the *present* rates of interest for debts of different maturities, which would be adjusted to the knowledge of the future rates ... If the current rate of interest is positive for debts of every maturity, it must always be more advantageous to purchase a debt than to hold cash as a store of wealth.

If, on the contrary, the future rate of interest is uncertain ...

[167]

[168]

there is a risk of a loss being incurred in purchasing a long-term debt and subsequently turning it into cash, as compared with holding cash. The actuarial profit or mathematical expectation of gain calculated in accordance with the existing probabilities – if it can be so calculated, which is doubtful – must be sufficient to compensate for the risk of disappointment.

There is, moreover, a further ground for liquidity-preference which results from the existence of uncertainty as to the future of the rate of interest, provided that there is an organised market for dealing in debts. For different people will estimate the prospects differently and anyone who differs from the predominant opinion as expressed in market quotations may have a good reason for keeping liquid resources in order to profit, if he is right, from its turning out in due course that the [*debts of different maturities*] were in a mistaken relationship to one another.

This is closely analogous to what we have already discussed [169] at some length in connection with the marginal efficiency of capital. Just as we found that the marginal efficiency of capital is fixed, not by the 'best' opinion, but by the market valuation as determined by mass psychology, so also expectations as to the future of the rate of interest as fixed by mass psychology have their reactions on liquidity-preference; – but with this addition that the individual, who believes that future rates of interest will be above the rates assumed by the market, has a reason for keeping actual liquid cash, whilst the individual who differs from the market in the other direction will have a motive for borrowing money for short periods in order to purchase debts of longer term. The market price will be fixed at the point at which the sales of the 'bears' and the purchases of the 'bulls' are balanced.

The three divisions of liquidity-preference which we have distinguished above may be defined as depending on (i) the transactions-motive, i.e. the need of cash for the current transaction of personal and business exchanges; (ii) the precautionary-motive, i.e. the desire for security as to the future cash equivalent of a certain proportion of total resources; and (iii) the speculative-motive, i.e. the object of securing profit from knowing better than the market what the future will bring forth. As when we were discussing the marginal efficiency of capital, the question of the desirability of having a highly organised market for dealing with debts presents us with a dilemma. For, in the absence of an organised market, liquidity-preference due to the precautionary-motive would be greatly increased; whereas [170] the existence of an organised market gives an opportunity for wide fluctuations in liquidity-preference due to the speculative-motive.

. . .

As a rule, we can suppose that the schedule of liquidity-preference relating the quantity of money to the rate of interest is given by a smooth curve which shows the rate of interest falling as the quantity of money is increased. For there are several different [171] causes all leading towards this result.

. . .

Nevertheless, circumstances can develop in which even a large increase in the quantity of money may exert a comparatively small influence on the rate of interest. For a large increase in the quantity of money may cause so much uncertainty about the future that liquidity-preferences due to the precautionary-motive may be strengthened; whilst opinion about the future of the rate of interest may be so unanimous that a small change in present rates may cause a mass movement into cash. It is interesting that the stability of the system and its sensitiveness to changes in the quantity of money should be so dependent on the existence of a *variety* of opinion about what is uncertain. Best of all that we should know the future. But if not, then, if we are to control the activity of the economic system by changing the quantity of money, it is important that opinions should differ. Thus this method of control is more precarious in the United States, where everyone tends to hold the same opinion at the same time, than in England where differences of opinion are more [172] usual.

III

We have now introduced money into our causal nexus for the first time, and we are able to catch a first glimpse of the way in which changes in the quantity of money work their way into the economic system. If, however, we are tempted to assert that money is the drink which stimulates the system to activity, we must remind ourselves that there may be several slips between the cup and the lip. For whilst an increase in the quantity of money may be expected, *cet. par.*, to reduce the rate of interest, this will not happen if the liquidity-preferences of the public are increasing more than the quantity of money; and whilst a decline in the rate of interest may be expected, *cet. par.*, to increase the volume of investment, this will not happen if the schedule of the marginal efficiency of capital is falling more rapidly than the rate of interest; and whilst an increase in the volume of investment may be expected, *cet. par.*, to increase employment, this may not happen if the propensity to consume is falling off. Finally, if employment increases, prices will rise in a degree partly governed by the shapes of the physical supply functions, and partly by the liability of the wage-unit to rise in terms of money. And when output has increased and prices have risen, the effect of this on liquidity-preference will be to increase the quantity of money necessary to maintain a given rate of interest.[41]

[173]

. . .

Chapter 15
The Psychological and Business
Incentives to Liquidity

[*Keynes considered increased liquidity-preference to be the main obstacle to the fall in the rate of interest. However, his liquidity-preference theory of the rate of interest tended to be dropped after his death. Keynesians thought that investment was relatively insensitive to interest rates, so the question of what determined such rates was irrelevant. It was also argued that to attribute the determination of a price to the attainment of equilibrium in one market made no sense in a general equi-librium analysis. Keynes allows a choice between only two assets, cash and bonds. In TM there was a third category, 'securities'. This prefigures the modern theory of porfolio choice. Investors, it is now said, choose to store their wealth in*

*a porfolio of assets, based on a mathematical balancing of risks
and returns. The effect of this modification was to abolish
uncertainty from investors' decision making, and to reinstate
the classical connection between saving and investment. However, the 'flight into money' following the crash of 2008 and the
difficulty of open-market operations in reviving bank lending
have revived interest in Keynes's theory.*]

I

. . . [T]he *Speculative-motive* . . . needs a more detailed examination than the others because . . . it is particularly important
in transmitting the effects of a *change* in the quantity of money.

In normal circumstances the amount of money required to
satisfy the transactions-motive and the precautionary-motive is
mainly a resultant of the general activity of the economic system and of the level of money-income. But it is by playing on
the speculative-motive that monetary management (or, in the
absence of management, chance changes in the quantity of
[196] money) is brought to bear on the economic system. For the
demand for money to satisfy the former motives is generally
irresponsive to any influence except the actual occurrence of a
change in the general economic activity and the level of incomes;
whereas experience indicates that the aggregate demand for
money to satisfy the speculative-motive usually shows a continuous response to gradual changes in the rate of interest, i.e.
there is a continuous curve relating changes in the demand for
money to satisfy the speculative motive and changes in the rate
of interest as given by changes in the prices of bonds and debts
of various maturities.

Indeed, if this were not so, 'open market operations' would
be impracticable . . . [I]n normal circumstances the banking
system is in fact always able to purchase (or sell) bonds in
exchange for cash by bidding the price of bonds up (or down)
in the market by a modest amount; and the larger the quantity
of cash which they seek to create (or cancel) by purchasing (or
selling) bonds and debts, the greater must be the fall (or rise) in
[197] the rate of interest.

. . .

II

Let the amount of cash held to satisfy the transactions- and precautionary-motives be M_1, and the amount held to satisfy the speculative motive be M_2. Corresponding to these two compartments of cash, we then have two liquidity functions L_1 and L_2. L_1 mainly depends on the level of income, whilst L_2 mainly depends on the relation between the current rate of interest and the state of expectation. Thus

$$M = M_1 + M_2 = L_1(Y) + L_2(r),$$

where L_1 is the liquidity function corresponding to an income [199] Y, which determines M_1, and L_2 is the liquidity function of the rate of interest r, which determines M_2. It follows that there are three matters to investigate: (i) the relation of changes in M to Y and r, (ii) what determines the shape of L_1, (iii) what determines the shape of L_2.

...

(iii) Finally there is the question of the relation between M_2 and r. We have seen in chapter 13 that *uncertainty* as to the future course of the rate of interest is the sole intelligible explanation of the type of liquidity-preference L_2 which leads to the holding of cash M_2. It follows that a given M_2 will not have a definite quantitative relation to a given rate of interest of r; – what matters is not the *absolute* level of r but the degree of its divergence from what is considered a fairly *safe* level of r, having regard to those calculations of probability which are being relied on. Nevertheless, there are two reasons for expecting that, in any given state of expectation, a fall in r will be associ- [201] ated with an increase in M_2. In the first place, if the general view as to what is a safe level of r is unchanged, every fall in r reduces the market rate relatively to the 'safe' rate and therefore increases the risk of illiquidity; and, in the second place, every fall in r reduces the current earnings from illiquidity, which are available as a sort of insurance premium to offset the risk of loss on capital account, by an amount equal to the difference between the *squares* of the old rate of interest and the new . . . If . . . the rate of interest is already as low as 2 per cent, the running yield will only offset a rise in it of as little as 0.4 per cent per annum. This, indeed, is perhaps the chief obstacle to the fall in the rate of interest to a very low level . . . [A] long-term rate of interest of (say) 2 per cent leaves more to fear than to hope, and offers, at the same time, a running yield which is only sufficient to offset a very small measure of fear.

It is evident, then, that the rate of interest is a highly psychological phenomenon. We shall find . . . [that it cannot be] in equilibrium at a level *below* the rate which corresponds to full employment; because at such a level a state of true inflation will be produced, with the result that M_1 will absorb ever-increasing quantities of cash. But at a level *above* the rate which corresponds to full employment, the long-term market-rate of interest will depend, not only on the current policy of the monetary authority, but also on market expectations concerning its future [202] policy. The short-term rate of interest is easily controlled . . . But the long-term rate may be more recalcitrant when once it has fallen to a level which, on the basis of past experience and present expectations of *future* monetary policy, is considered 'unsafe' by representative opinion.

. . .

Thus a monetary policy which strikes public opinion as being experimental in character or easily liable to change may fail in its objective of greatly reducing the long-term rate of interest, because M_2 may tend to increase almost without limit in response to a reduction of r below a certain figure. The same policy, on the other hand, may prove easily successful if it appeals to public opinion as being reasonable and practicable and in the public interest, rooted in strong conviction, and promoted by an authority unlikely to be superseded.

It might be more accurate, perhaps, to say that the rate of interest is a highly conventional, rather than a highly psychological, phenomenon. For its actual value is largely governed by the prevailing view as to what its value is expected to be. *Any* level of interest which is accepted with sufficient convic-[203] tion as *likely* to be durable *will* be durable . . . But it may fluctuate for decades about a level which is chronically too high for full employment; – particularly if it is the prevailing opinion that the rate of interest is self-adjusting, so that the level rooted in convention is thought to be rooted in objective grounds . . .

. . .

The difficulties in the way of maintaining effective demand at a level high enough to provide full employment, which ensue from the association of a conventional and fairly stable long-term rate of interest with a fickle and highly unstable marginal efficiency of capital, should, by now, be obvious to the reader.

Such comfort as we can fairly take from more encouraging reflections must be drawn from the hope that, precisely because the convention is not rooted in secure knowledge, it will not be always resistant to a modest measure of persistence and consistency by the monetary authority.   [204]

. . .

III

Thus there are certain limitations on the ability of the monetary authority to establish any given complex of rates of interest for debts of different terms and risks, which can be summed up as follows:

(1) There are those limitations which arise out of the monetary authority's own practices in limiting its willingness to deal [in] debts of a particular type.

(2) There is the possibility, for the reasons discussed above, that, after the rate of interest has fallen to a certain level, liquidity-preference may become virtually absolute in the sense that almost everyone prefers cash to holding a debt which yields so low a rate of interest. In this event the monetary authority would have lost effective control over the rate of interest. But whilst this limiting case might become practically important in future, I know no example of it hitherto . . . Moreover, if such a situation were to arise, it would mean that the public authority itself could borrow through the banking system on an unlimited scale at a nominal rate of interest.

(3) The most striking examples of a complete breakdown in the stability of the rate of interest ... have occurred in very abnormal circumstances. In Russia and Central Europe after the war ... no one could be induced to retain holdings either of money or of debts on any terms whatever, and even a high and rising rate of interest was unable to keep pace with the marginal efficiency of capital (especially of stocks of liquid goods) under the influence of the expectation of an ever greater fall in the value of money; whilst in the United States at certain dates in 1932 there was a crisis of the opposite kind – a financial crisis [207] or a crisis of liquidation, when scarcely anyone could be induced to part with holdings of money on any reasonable terms.

(4) There is, finally, the difficulty ... [of] the intermediate costs of bringing borrower and ultimate lender together, and the allowance for risk, especially for moral risk, which the lender requires over and above the pure rate of interest ... For where the risk is due to doubt in the mind of the lender concerning the honesty of the borrower, there is nothing in the mind of a bor- rower who does not intend to be dishonest to offset the resultant [208] higher charge ...
...

Chapter 16
Sundry Observations on the Nature of Capital

[*The 'paradox of thrift'.*]

I

An act of individual saving means – so to speak – a decision not to have dinner to-day. But it does *not* necessitate a decision to have dinner or to buy a pair of boots a week hence or a year hence or to consume any specified thing at any specified date. Thus it depresses the business of preparing to-day's dinner without stimu- lating the business of making ready for some future act of consumption. It is not a substitution of future consumption-demand for present consumption-demand, – it is a net diminution of such demand. Moreover, the expectation of future consumption is so largely based on current experience of present consumption that a reduction in the latter is likely to depress the former, with the result that the act of saving will not merely depress the price of consumption-goods and leave the marginal efficiency of existing capital unaffected, but may actually tend to depress the latter also. In this event it may reduce present investment-demand as well as present consumption-demand.

If saving consisted not merely in abstaining from present consumption but in placing simultaneously a specific order for future consumption, the effect might indeed be different. For in that case the expectation of some future yield from investment would be improved, and the resources released from preparing for present consumption could be turned over to preparing for the future [210] consumption. Not that they necessarily would be, even in this case, on a scale *equal* to the amount of resources released; since the desired interval of delay might require a method of production so inconveniently 'roundabout' as to have an efficiency well below the current rate of interest, with the result that the favourable effect on employment of the forward order for consumption would eventuate not at once but at some subsequent date, so that the *immediate* effect of the saving would still be adverse to employment. In any case, however, an individual decision to save does not, in actual fact, involve the placing of any specific forward order for consumption, but merely the cancellation of a present order. Thus, since the expectation of consumption is the only *raison d'être* of employment, there should be nothing paradoxical in the conclusion that a diminished propensity to consume has *cet. par.* a depressing effect on employment.

The trouble arises, therefore, because the act of saving implies, not a substitution for present consumption of some specific additional consumption which requires for its preparation just as much immediate economic activity as would have been required by present consumption equal in value to the sum saved, but a desire for 'wealth' as such, that is for a potentiality of consuming an unspecified article at an unspecified time. The absurd, though almost universal, idea that an act of individual saving is just as good for effective demand as an act of individual consumption, has been fostered by the fallacy, much more specious than the conclusion derived from it, that an increased desire to hold wealth, being much the same thing as an increased desire to hold investments, must, by increasing the demand for investments, provide a stimulus to their production; so that current investment is promoted by individual saving to the same extent as present consumption is diminished.

[211]   It is of this fallacy that it is most difficult to disabuse men's minds. It comes from believing that the owner of wealth desires a capital-asset *as such*, whereas what he really desires is its *prospective yield*. Now, prospective yield wholly depends on the expectation of future effective demand in relation to future conditions of supply. If, therefore, an act of saving does nothing to improve prospective yield, it does nothing to stimulate investment. Moreover, in order that an individual saver may attain his desired goal of the ownership of wealth, it is not necessary that a *new* capital-asset should be produced wherewith to satisfy him. The mere act of saving by one individual, being *two-sided* as we have shown above, forces some other individual to transfer to him some article of wealth old or new. Every act of saving involves a 'forced' inevitable transfer of wealth to him who saves, though he in his turn may suffer from the saving of others. These transfers of wealth do not require the creation of new wealth – indeed, as we have seen, they may be actively inimical to it. The creation of new wealth wholly depends on the prospective yield of the new wealth reaching the standard set by the current rate of interest. The prospective yield of the marginal new investment is not increased by the fact that someone wishes to increase his wealth, since the prospective yield of the marginal new investment depends on the expectation of a demand for a specific article at a specific date.

Nor do we avoid this conclusion by arguing that what the owner of wealth desires is not a given prospective yield but the best available prospective yield, so that an increased desire to own wealth reduces the prospective yield with which the producers of new investment have to be content. For this overlooks the fact that there is always an alternative to the ownership of real capital-assets, namely the ownership of money and debts; so [212] that the prospective yield with which the producers of new investment have to be content cannot fall below the standard set by the current rate of interest. And the current rate of interest depends, as we have seen, not on the strength of the desire to hold wealth, but on the strengths of the desires to hold it in liquid and in illiquid forms respectively, coupled with the amount of the supply of wealth in the one form relatively to the supply of it in the other. If the reader still finds himself perplexed, let him ask himself why, the quantity of money being unchanged, a fresh act of saving should diminish the sum which it is desired to keep in liquid form at the existing rate of interest.   [213]

. . .

Chapter 17
The Essential Properties of Interest and Money

[*This offers a modern version of the legend of King Midas. Its central point is that the marginal utility of money, unlike that of other goods, does not fall the more abundant it is.*]

III

In attributing, therefore, a peculiar significance to the money-rate of interest, we have been tacitly assuming that the kind of money to which are accustomed has some special characteristics which lead to its own-rate of interest in terms of itself as a standard being more reluctant to fall as the stock of assets in general increases than the own-rates of interest of any other assets in terms of themselves. Is this assumption justified? Reflection shows, I think, that the following peculiarities, which commonly characterise money as we know it, are cap-   [229] able of justifying it.

. . .

(i) The first characteristic which tends towards the above conclusion is the fact that money has . . . a zero, or at any rate a very small, elasticity of production, so far as the power of private enterprise is concerned, as distinct from the monetary authority; – elasticity of production meaning, in this context, the response of the quantity of labour applied to producing it to a rise in the quantity of labour which a unit of it will command. Money, that is, cannot be readily produced; – labour cannot be turned on at will by entrepreneurs to produce money in increasing quantities as its price rises in terms of the wage unit.

. . .

Now, in the case of assets having an elasticity of production, the reason why we assumed their own-rate of interest to decline was because we assumed the stock of them to increase as the result of a higher rate of output. In the case of money, however . . . the supply is fixed. [*The manufacture of paper money involves no labour.*] Thus the characteristic that money cannot be readily produced by labour gives at once some *prima facie* presumption for the view that its own-rate of interest will be relatively reluctant to fall; whereas if money could be grown [230] like a crop or manufactured like a motor-car, depressions would be avoided or mitigated because, if the price of other assets was tending to fall in terms of money, more labour would be diverted into the production of money; – as we see to be the case in gold-mining countries, though for the world as a whole the maximum diversion in this way is almost negligible.

(ii) Obviously, however, the above condition is satisfied, not only by money, but by all pure rent-factors, the production of which is completely inelastic. A second condition, therefore, is required to distinguish money from other rent elements.

The second *differentia* of money is that it has an elasticity of substitution equal, or nearly equal, to zero; which means that as the exchange value of money rises there is no tendency to substitute some other factor for it; – except, perhaps, to some trifling extent, where the money-commodity is also used in manufacture or the arts. This follows from the peculiarity of money that its utility is solely derived from its exchange value, so that the two rise and fall *pari passu*, with the result that as the exchange value of money rises there is no motive or tendency, as in the case of rent-factors, to substitute some other factor for it.

Thus, not only is it impossible to turn more labour on to producing money . . . but money is a bottomless sink for purchasing power . . . since there is no value for it at which demand is diverted – as in the case of other rent-factors – so as to slop [231] over into a demand for other things.

. . .

[Keynes qualifies this statement in several ways, but then continues:]

... we come to what is the most fundamental consideration in this context, namely, the characteristics of money which satisfy liquidity-preference. For, in certain circumstances such as will often occur, these will cause the rate of interest to be insensitive, particularly below a certain figure, even to a substantial increase in the quantity of money in proportion to other forms of wealth. In other words, beyond a certain point money's yield from liquidity does not fall in response to an increase in its quantity to anything approaching the extent to which the yield from other types of assets falls when their quantity is comparably increased.

In this connection the low (or negligible) carrying costs of money play an essential part. For if its carrying costs were material, they would offset the effect of expectations as to the prospective value of money at future dates. The readiness of the public to increase their stock of money in response to a comparatively small stimulus is due to the advantages of liquidity (real or supposed) having no offset to contend with in the shape of carrying-costs mounting steeply with the lapse of time. In the case of a commodity other than money a modest stock of it may offer some convenience to users of the commodity. But even though a larger stock might have some attractions as representing a store of wealth of stable value, this would be offset by its carrying-costs in the shape of storage, wastage, etc. [233] Hence, after a certain point is reached, there is necessarily a loss in holding a greater stock.

In the case of money, however, this, as we have seen, is not so, – and for a variety of reasons, namely, those which constitute money as being, in the estimation of the public, *par excellence* 'liquid'. Thus those reformers, who look for a remedy by creating artificial carrying-costs for money through the device of requiring legal-tender currency to be periodically stamped at a prescribed cost in order to retain its quality as money, or in analogous ways, have been on the right track; and the practical value of their proposals deserves consideration.

The significance of the money-rate of interest arises,

therefore, out of the combination of the characteristics that, through the working of the liquidity-motive, this rate of interest may be somewhat unresponsive to a change in the proportion which the quantity of money bears to other forms of wealth measured in money, and that money has (or may have) zero (or negligible) elasticities both of production and of substitution. The first condition means that demand may be predominantly directed to money, the second that when this occurs labour cannot be employed in producing more money, and the third that there is no mitigation at any point through some other factor being capable, if it is sufficiently cheap, of doing money's duty equally well. The only relief – apart from changes in the marginal efficiency of capital – can come (so long as the propensity towards liquidity is unchanged) from an increase in the quantity of money, or – which is formally the same thing – a rise in the value of money which enables a given quantity to provide increased money-services.

[234]

Thus a rise in the money-rate of interest retards the output of all the objects of which the production is elastic without being capable of stimulating the output of money (the production of which is, by hypothesis, perfectly inelastic). The money-rate of interest, by setting the pace for all the other commodity-rates of interest, holds back investment in the production of these other commodities without being capable of stimulating investment for the production of money, which by hypothesis cannot be produced. Moreover, owing to the elasticity of demand for liquid cash in terms of debts, a small change in the conditions governing this demand may not much alter the money-rate of interest, whilst (apart from official action) it is also impracticable, owing to the inelasticity of the production of money, for natural forces to bring the money-rate of interest down by affecting the supply side. In the case of an ordinary commodity, the inelasticity of the demand for liquid stocks of it would enable small changes on the demand side to bring its rate of interest up or down with a rush, whilst the elasticity of its supply would also tend to prevent a high premium on spot over forward delivery. Thus with other commodities left to themselves, 'natural forces', i.e. the ordinary forces of the market, would tend to bring their rate of interest down until the emergence of full employment had brought about for commodities generally the inelasticity of supply which we have postulated as a normal characteristic of money. Thus in the absence of money and in the absence – we must, of course, also suppose – of any other commodity with the assumed character-istics of money, the rates of interest would only reach equilibrium when there is full employment.

Unemployment develops, that is to say, because people want the moon; – men cannot be employed when the object of desire (i.e. money) is something which cannot be produced [*by labour*] and the demand for which cannot be readily choked off. There is no remedy but to persuade the public that green cheese is practically the same thing and to have a green cheese factory (i.e. a central bank) under public control.

It is interesting to notice that the characteristic which has [235] been traditionally supposed to render gold especially suitable for use as the standard of value, namely, its inelasticity of sup-ply, turns out to be precisely the characteristic which is at the bottom of the trouble.

Our conclusion can be stated in the most general form (taking the propensity to consume as given) as follows. No further increase in the rate of investment is possible when the greatest amongst the own-rates of own-interest of all available assets is equal to the greatest amongst the marginal efficiencies of all assets, measured in terms of the asset whose own-rate of own-interest is greatest.

In a position of full employment this condition is necessarily satisfied. But it may also be satisfied before full employment is reached, if there exists some asset, having zero (or relatively small) elasticities of production and substitution, whose rate of interest declines more closely, as output increases, than the mar-ginal efficiencies of capital-assets measured in terms of it. [236]
. . .

Chapter 18
The General Theory of Employment Re-Stated

[*The 'model' of the 'General Theory'. The excerpt shows clearly that Keynes did not mean by 'under-employment equilibrium' a condition of stasis but a moderate oscillation round a 'chronic condition of sub-normal activity' which is 'neither desperate nor satisfactory'.*][42]

I

We have now reached a point where we can gather together the threads of our argument. To begin with, it may be useful to make clear which elements in the economic system we usually take as given, which are the independent variables of our system and which are the dependent variables.

We take as given the existing skill and quantity of available labour, the existing quality and quantity of available equipment, the existing technique, the degree of competition, the tastes and habits of the consumer, the disutility of different intensities of labour and of the activities of supervision and organisation, as well as the social structure including the forces, other than our variables set forth below, which determine the distribution of the national income. This does not mean that we assume these factors to be constant; but merely that, in this place and context, we are not considering or taking into account the effects and consequences of changes in them.

Our independent variables are, in the first instance, the propensity to consume, the schedule of the marginal efficiency of capital and the rate of interest, though, as we have already seen, these are capable of further analysis.

Our dependent variables are the volume of employment and [245] the national income (or national dividend) measured in wage-units.
. . .
The division of the determinants of the economic system into the two groups of given factors and independent variables is, of course, quite arbitrary from any absolute standpoint. The division must be made entirely on the basis of experience, so as to correspond on the one hand to the factors in which the changes seem to be so slow or so little relevant as to have only a small and comparatively negligible short-term influence on our *quaesitum*; and on the other hand to those factors in which the changes are found in practice to exercise a dominant influence on our *quaesitum*. Our present object is to discover what determines at any time the national income of a given economic

system and (which is almost the same thing) the amount of its employment; which means in a study so complex as economics, in which we cannot hope to make completely accurate generalisations, the factors whose changes *mainly* determine our *quaesitum*. Our final task might be to select those variables which can be deliberately controlled or managed by central authority in the kind of system in which we actually live.

II

Let us now attempt to summarise the argument of the previous chapters; taking the factors in the reverse order to that in which we have introduced them.   [247]

There will be an inducement to push the rate of new investment to the point which forces the supply price of each type of capital-asset to a figure which, taken in conjunction with its prospective yield, brings the marginal efficiency of capital in general to approximate equality with the rate of interest. That is to say, the physical conditions of supply in the capital-goods industries, the state of confidence concerning the prospective yield, the psychological attitude to liquidity and the quantity of money (preferably calculated in terms of wage-units) determine, between them, the rate of new investment.

But an increase (or decrease) in the rate of investment will have to carry with it an increase (or decrease) in the rate of consumption; because the behaviour of the public is, in general, of such a character that they are only willing to widen (or narrow) the gap between their income and their consumption if their income is being increased (or diminished). That is to say, changes in the rate of consumption are, in general, *in the same direction* (though smaller in amount) as changes in the rate of income. The relation between the increment of consumption which has to accompany a given increment of saving is given by the marginal propensity to consume. The ratio, thus determined, between an increment of investment and the corresponding increment of aggregate income, both measured in wage-units, is given by the investment multiplier.

Finally, if we assume (as a first approximation) that the employment multiplier is equal to the investment multiplier, we can, by applying the multiplier to the increment (or decrement) in the rate of investment brought about by the factors first described, infer the increment of employment.

An increment (or decrement) of employment is liable, however, to raise (or lower) the schedule of liquidity-preference; there being three ways in which it will tend to increase the [248] demand for money, inasmuch as the value of output will rise when employment increases even if the wage-unit and prices (in terms of the wage-unit) are unchanged, but, in addition, the wage-unit itself will tend to rise as employment improves, and the increase in output will be accompanied by a rise of prices (in terms of the wage-unit) owing to increasing cost in the short period.

Thus the position of equilibrium will be influenced by these repercussions; and there are other repercussions also. Moreover, there is not one of the above factors which is not liable to change without much warning, and sometimes substantially. Hence the extreme complexity of the actual course of events. Nevertheless, these seem to be the factors which it is useful and convenient to isolate. If we examine any actual problem along the lines of the above schematism, we shall find it more manageable; and our practical intuition (which can take account of a more detailed complex of facts than can be treated on general principles) will be offered a less intractable material upon which to work.

III

The above is a summary of the General Theory. But the actual phenomena of the economic system are also coloured by certain special characteristics of the propensity to consume, the schedule of the marginal efficiency of capital and the rate of interest, about which we can safely generalise from experience, but which are not logically necessary.

In particular, it is an outstanding characteristic of the economic system in which we live that, whilst it is subject to severe fluctuations in respect of output and employment, it is not violently unstable. *Indeed it seems capable of remaining in a chronic condition of sub-normal activity for a considerable*

*period without any marked tendency either towards recovery
or towards complete collapse.* [*Italics added.*] Moreover, the
evidence indicates that full, or even approximately full, employ- [249]
ment is of rare and short-lived occurrence. Fluctuations may
start briskly but seem to wear themselves out before they have
proceeded to great extremes, and an intermediate situation
which is neither desperate nor satisfactory is our normal lot. It
is upon the fact that fluctuations tend to wear themselves out
before proceeding to extremes and eventually to reverse themselves, that the theory of business *cycles* having a regular phase
has been founded. The same thing is true of prices, which, in
response to an initiating cause of disturbance, seem to be able
to find a level at which they can remain, for the time being,
moderately stable.

Now, since these facts of experience do not follow of logical
necessity, one must suppose that the environment and the psychological propensities of the modern world must be of such a
character as to produce these results. It is, therefore, useful to
consider what hypothetical psychological propensities would
lead to a stable system; and, then, whether these propensities
can be plausibly ascribed, on our general knowledge of contemporary human nature, to the world in which we live.

The conditions of stability which the foregoing analysis suggests to us as capable of explaining the observed results are the
following:

(i) The marginal propensity to consume is such that, when
the output of a given community increases (or decreases)
because more (or less) employment is being applied to its capital equipment, the multiplier relating the two is greater than
unity but not very large.

(ii) When there is a change in the prospective yield of capital
or in the rate of interest, the schedule of the marginal efficiency
of capital will be such that the change in new investment will
not be in great disproportion to the change in the former; i.e.
moderate changes in the prospective yield of capital or in the
rate of interest will not be associated with very great changes in
the rate of investment.   [250]

(iii) When there is a change in employment, money-wages

tend to change in the same direction as, but not in great disproportion to, the change in employment; i.e. moderate changes in
employment are not associated with very great changes in money-
wages. This is a condition of the stability of prices rather than
of employment.

(iv) We may add a fourth condition, which provides not so
much for the stability of the system as for the tendency of a
fluctuation in one direction to reverse itself in due course; namely,
that a rate of investment, higher (or lower) than prevailed
formerly, begins to react unfavourably (or favourably) on the
marginal efficiency of capital if it is continued for a period
[251]   which, measured in years, is not very large.

. . .

Thus our four conditions together are adequate to explain
the outstanding features of our actual experience; – namely,
that we oscillate, avoiding the gravest extremes of fluctuation
in employment and in prices in both directions, round an intermediate position appreciably below full employment and
appreciably above the minimum employment a decline below
which would endanger life.

But we must not conclude that the mean position thus determined by 'natural' tendencies, namely, by those tendencies
which are likely to persist, failing measures expressly designed
to correct them, is, therefore, established by laws of necessity.
The unimpeded rule of the above conditions is a fact of observation concerning the world as it is or has been, and not a
[254]   necessary principle which cannot be changed.

. . .

Chapter 19
Changes in Money-Wages

[*This chapter discusses the effect of cutting money wages on
output and employment. It is an attack on the simple classical
notion that an overall cut in money wages necessarily improves
employment. In refuting this proposition Keynes relies once
more on the 'fallacy of composition'. This chapter represents
Keynes's attempt to emancipate his theory from reliance on
'sticky' money wages.*]

It would have been an advantage if the effects of a change in money-wages could have been discussed in an earlier chapter. For the classical theory has been accustomed to rest the supposedly self-adjusting character of the economic system on an assumed fluidity of money-wages; and, when there is rigidity, to lay on this rigidity the blame of maladjustment.

It was not possible, however, to discuss this matter fully until our own theory had been developed. For the consequences of a change in money-wages are complicated. A reduction in money-wages is quite capable in certain circumstances of affording a stimulus to output, as the classical theory supposes. My difference from this theory is primarily a difference of analysis; so that it could not be set forth clearly until the reader was acquainted with my own method.

The generally accepted explanation is, as I understand it, quite a simple one. It does not depend on roundabout repercussions, such as we shall discuss below. The argument simply is that a reduction in money-wages will *cet. par.* stimulate demand by diminishing the price of the finished product, and will therefore increase output and employment up to the point where the reduction which labour has agreed to accept in its money-wages is just offset by the diminishing marginal efficiency of labour as output (from a given equipment) is increased.   [257]

In its crudest form, this is tantamount to assuming that the reduction in money-wages will leave demand unaffected. There may be some economists who would maintain that there is no reason why demand should be affected, arguing that aggregate demand depends on the quantity of money multiplied by the income-velocity of money and that there is no obvious reason why a reduction in money-wages would reduce either the quantity of money or its income-velocity. Or they may even argue that profits will necessarily go up because wages have gone down. But it would, I think, be more usual to agree that the reduction in money-wages may have *some* effect on aggregate demand through its reducing the purchasing power of some of the workers, but that the real demand of other factors, whose money incomes have not been reduced, will be stimulated by the fall in prices, and that the aggregate demand of the workers themselves will be very likely increased as a result of the increased volume of employment, unless the elasticity of demand for labour in response to changes in money-wages is less than unity. Thus in the new equilibrium there will be more employment than there would have been otherwise except, perhaps, in some unusual limiting case which has no reality in practice.

It is from this type of analysis that I fundamentally differ; or rather from the analysis which seems to lie behind such observations as the above. For whilst the above fairly represents, I think, the way in which many economists talk and write, the underlying analysis has seldom been written down in detail.

It appears, however, that this way of thinking is probably reached as follows. In any given industry we have a demand schedule for the product relating the quantities which can be sold to the prices asked; we have a series of supply schedules relating the prices which will be asked for the sale of different [258] quantities on various bases of cost; and these schedules between them lead up to a further schedule which, on the assumption that other costs are unchanged (except as a result of the change in output), gives us the demand schedule for labour in the industry relating the quantity of employment to different levels of wages, the shape of the curve at any point furnishing the elasticity of demand for labour. This conception is then transferred without substantial modification to industry as a whole; and it is supposed, by a parity of reasoning, that we have a demand schedule for labour in industry as a whole relating the quantity of employment to different levels of wages. It is held that it makes no material difference to this argument whether it is in terms of money-wages or of real wages. If we are thinking in terms of money-wages, we must, of course, correct for changes in the value of money; but this leaves the general tendency of the argument unchanged, since prices certainly do not change in exact proportion to changes in money-wages.

If this is the groundwork of the argument (and, if it is not, I do not know what the groundwork is), surely it is fallacious. For the demand schedules for particular industries can only be constructed on some fixed assumption as to the nature of the demand and supply schedules of other industries and as to the amount of the aggregate effective demand. It is invalid, therefore, to transfer the argument to industry as a whole unless we also transfer our assumption that the aggregate effective demand is fixed. Yet this assumption reduces the argument to an *ignoratio elenchi*. For, whilst no one would wish to deny the proposition that a reduction in money-wages *accompanied by the same aggregate effective demand as before* will be associated with an increase in employment, the precise question at issue is whether the reduction in money-wages will or will not be accompanied by the same aggregate effective demand as before measured in money, or, at any rate, by an aggregate effective demand which is not reduced in full proportion to the reduction in money-wages [259] (i.e. which is somewhat greater measured in wage-units). But if the classical theory is not allowed to extend by analogy its conclusions in respect of a particular industry to industry as a whole, it is wholly unable to answer the question what effect on employment a reduction in money-wages will have. For it has no method of analysis wherewith to tackle the problem. Professor Pigou's *Theory of Unemployment* seems to me to get out of the classical theory all that can be got out of it; with the result that the book becomes a striking demonstration that this theory has nothing to offer, when it is applied to the problem of what determines the volume of actual employment as a whole.   [260]

. . .

Chapter 21
The Theory of Prices

I

So long as economists are concerned with what is called the theory of value, they have been accustomed to teach that prices are governed by the conditions of supply and demand; and, in particular, changes in marginal cost and the elasticity of short-period supply have played a prominent part. But when they pass in volume II . . . to the theory of money and prices, we hear no more of these homely but intelligible concepts and move into a world where prices are governed by the quantity of money, by its income-velocity, by the velocity of circulation relatively to the volume of transactions, by hoarding, by forced saving, by inflation and deflation *et hoc genus omne*; and little or no attempt is made to relate these vaguer phrases to our former notions of the elasticities of supply and demand. If we reflect on what we are being taught and try to rationalise it, in the simpler discussions it seems that the elasticity of supply must have become zero and demand proportional to the quantity of money; whilst in the more sophisticated we are lost in a haze where nothing is clear and everything is possible. We have all of us become used to finding ourselves sometimes on the one side of the moon and sometimes on the other, without knowing what route or journey connects them, related, apparently, after [292] the fashion of our waking and dreaming lives.

One of the objects of the foregoing chapters has been to escape from this double life and to bring the theory of prices as a whole back to close contact with the theory of value. The division of economics between the theory of value and distribution on the one hand and the theory of money on the other hand is, I think, a false division. The right dichotomy is, I suggest, between the theory of the individual industry or firm and of the rewards and the distribution between different uses of a *given* quantity of resources on the one hand, and the theory of output and employment *as a whole* on the other . . .

Or, perhaps, we might make our line of division between the theory of stationary equilibrium and the theory of shifting equilibrium – meaning by the latter the theory of a system in which changing views about the future are capable of influencing the present situation. *For the importance of money essentially flows from its being a link between the present and the future.* We can consider what distribution of resources between different uses will be consistent with equilibrium . . . in a world in which our views concerning the future are fixed and reliable in all respects . . . Or, we can pass from this simplified propaedeutic to the problems of the real world in which our previous expecta- [293] tions are liable to disappointment and expectations concerning the future affect what we do to-day . . . But, although the theory of shifting equilibrium must necessarily be pursued in terms of a monetary economy, it remains a theory of value and distribution and not a separate 'theory of money'. [294]

. . .

III

. . . [L]et us . . . assume . . . constant returns and a rigid wage-unit, so long as there is any unemployment . . . Thus if there is a perfectly elastic supply so long as there is unemployment, and perfectly inelastic supply so soon as full employment is reached, and if effective demand changes in the same proportion as the quantity of money, the quantity theory of money [295] can be enunciated as follows: 'So long as there is unemployment, *employment* will change in the same proportion as the quantity of money; and when there is full employment, *prices* will change in the same proportion as the quantity of money'.

However, having satisfied tradition by introducing a sufficient number of simplifying assumptions to enable us to enunciate a quantity theory of money, let us consider the possible applications which will in fact influence events:

(1) Effective demand will not change in exact proportion to the quantity of money.

(2) Since resources are not interchangeable, there will be diminishing, and not constant, returns as employment gradually increases.[43]

(3) Since resources are not interchangeable, some commodities will reach a condition of inelastic supply whilst there are still unemployed resources available . . .

(4) The wage-unit will tend to rise, before full employment has been reached.

(5) The renumeration of the factors entering into marginal cost will not all change in the same proportion.

. . .

The theory of prices . . . must, therefore, direct itself to the five [296–7] complicating factors set forth above.

. . .

IV

(3) . . . It is probable that the general level of prices will not

rise very much as output increases, so long as there are available efficient unemployed resources of every type. But as soon as output has increased sufficiently to begin to reach the 'bottle-necks', there is likely to be a sharp rise in the prices of certain commodities.

[300] ...

(4) That the wage-unit may tend to rise before full employment has been reached, requires little comment or explanation. Since each group of workers will gain, *cet. par.*, by a rise in its own wages, there is naturally for all groups a pressure in this direction, which entrepreneurs will be more ready to meet when they are doing better business. For this reason a proportion of any increase in effective demand is likely to be absorbed in satisfying the upward tendency of the wage-unit.

Thus, in addition to the final critical point of full employment at which money-wages have to rise ... fully in proportion to the rise in the prices of wage-goods, we have a succession of earlier semi-critical points at which an increasing effective demand tends to raise money-wages though not fully in proportion to the rise in the price of wage-goods ... These points ... might be deemed, from a certain point of view, to be
[301] positions of semi-inflation ...

...

We have full employment when output has risen to a level at which the marginal return from a representative unit of the factors of production has fallen to the minimum figure at which a quantity of the factors sufficient to produce this output is available.

V

When a further increase in the quantity of effective demand produces no further increase in output and entirely spends itself on an increase in the cost-unit fully proportionate to the increase in effective demand, we have reached a condition which might be appropriately designed as one of true inflation. Up to this point the effect of monetary expansion is entirely a
[303] question of degree ...

...

Chapter 22
Notes on the Trade Cycle

[*Keynes contrasts his theory with other theories of the business cycle, particularly those that stress over-investment as the cause of the crisis. It may be regarded as his answer to Hayek.*]

III

The preceding analysis may appear to be in conformity with the view of those who hold that over-investment is the characteristic of the boom, that the avoidance of this over-investment is the only possible remedy for the ensuing slump, and that, whilst for the reasons given above the slump cannot be prevented by a low rate of interest, nevertheless the boom can be avoided by a high rate of interest. There is, indeed, force in the argument that a high rate of interest is much more effective against a boom than a low rate of interest against a slump.

To infer these conclusions from the above would, however, misinterpret my analysis; and would, according to my way of thinking, involve serious error. For the term over-investment is ambiguous. It may refer to investments which are destined to disappoint the expectations which prompted them or for which there is no use in conditions of severe unemployment, or it may indicate a state of affairs where every kind of capital-goods is [320] so abundant that there is no new investment which is expected, even in conditions of full employment, to earn in the course of its life more than its replacement cost. It is only the latter state of affairs which is one of over-investment, strictly speaking, in the sense that any further investment would be a sheer waste of resources. Moreover, even if over-investment in this sense was a normal characteristic of the boom, the remedy would not lie in clapping on a high rate of interest which would probably deter some useful investments and might further diminish the propensity to consume, but in taking drastic steps, by redistributing incomes or otherwise, to stimulate the propensity to consume.

According to my analysis, however, it is only in the former

sense that the boom can be said to be characterised by over-investment. The situation, which I am indicating as typical, is not one in which capital is so abundant that the community as a whole has no reasonable use for any more, but where investment is being made in conditions which are unstable and cannot endure, because it is prompted by expectations which are destined to disappointment.

It may, of course, be the case – indeed it is likely to be – that the illusions of the boom cause particular types of capital-assets to be produced in such excessive abundance that some part of the output is, on any criterion, a waste of resources; – which sometimes happens, we may add, even when there is no boom. It leads, that is to say, to *misdirected* investment. But over and above this it is an essential characteristic of the boom that investments which will in fact yield, say, 2 per cent in conditions of full employment are made in the expectation of a yield of, say, 6 per cent, and are valued accordingly. When the disillusion comes, this expectation [321] is replaced by a contrary 'error of pessimism', with the result that the investments, which would in fact yield 2 per cent in conditions of full employment, are expected to yield less than nothing; and the resulting collapse of new investment then leads to a state of unemployment in which the investments, which would have yielded 2 per cent in conditions of full employment, in fact yield less than nothing. We reach a condition where there is a shortage of houses, but where nevertheless no one can afford to live in the houses that there are.

Thus the remedy for the boom is not a higher rate of interest but a lower rate of interest! For that may enable the so-called boom to last. The right remedy for the trade cycle is not to be found in abolishing booms and thus keeping us permanently in a semi-slump; but in abolishing slumps and thus keeping us permanently in a quasi-boom.

The boom which is destined to end in a slump is caused, therefore, by the combination of a rate of interest, which in a correct state of expectation would be too high for full employment, with a misguided state of expectation which, so long as it lasts, prevents this rate of interest from being in fact deterrent. A boom is a situation in which over-optimism triumphs over a rate of interest which, in a cooler light, would be seen to be excessive.

Except during the war, I doubt if we have any recent experience of a boom so strong that it led to full employment. In the United States employment was very satisfactory in 1928–29 on normal standards; but I have seen no evidence of a shortage of labour, except, perhaps, in the case of a few groups of highly specialised workers. Some 'bottle-necks' were reached, but output as a whole was still capable of further expansion. Nor was there over-investment in the sense that the standard and equip- [322] ment of housing was so high that everyone, assuming full employment, had all he wanted at a rate which would no more than cover the replacement cost, without any allowance for interest, over the life of the house; and that transport, public services and agricultural improvement had been carried to a point where further additions could not reasonably be expected to yield even their replacement cost. Quite the contrary. It would be absurd to assert of the United States in 1929 the existence of over-investment in the strict sense. The true state of affairs was of a different character. New investment during the previous five years had been, indeed, on so enormous a scale in the aggregate that the prospective yield of further additions was, coolly considered, falling rapidly. Correct foresight would have brought down the marginal efficiency of capital to an unprecedentedly low figure; so that the 'boom' could not have continued on a sound basis except with a very low long-term rate of interest, and an avoidance of misdirected investment in the particular directions which were in danger of being over-exploited. In fact, the rate of interest was high enough to deter new investment except in those particular directions which were under the influence of speculative excitement and, therefore, in special danger of being over-exploited; and a rate of interest, high enough to overcome the speculative excitement, would have checked, at the same time, every kind of reasonable new investment. Thus an increase in the rate of interest, as a remedy for the state of affairs arising out of a prolonged period of abnormally heavy new investment, belongs to the species of remedy which cures the disease by killing the patient.

It is, indeed, very possible that the prolongation of approximately full employment over a period of years would be associated in countries so wealthy as Great Britain or the United States with a volume of new investment, assuming the existing propensity [323] to consume, so great that it would eventually lead to a state of full investment in the sense that an aggregate gross yield in excess of replacement cost could no longer be expected on a reasonable calculation from a further increment of durable goods of any type whatever. Moreover, this situation might be reached comparatively soon – say within twenty-five years or less. I must not be taken to deny this, because I assert that a state of full investment in the strict sense has never yet occurred, not even momentarily.

Furthermore, even if we were to suppose that contemporary booms are apt to be associated with a momentary condition of full investment or over-investment in the strict sense, it would still be absurd to regard a higher rate of interest as the appropriate remedy. For in this event the case of those who attribute the disease to under-consumption would be wholly established. The remedy would lie in various measures designed to increase the propensity to consume by the redistribution of incomes or otherwise; so that a given level of employment would require a smaller [324] volume of current investment to support it.

. . .

Chapter 23
Notes on Mercantilism, the Usury Laws, Stamped Money and Theories of Under-Consumption

[*In this chapter Keynes stakes out an anti-Ricardian lineage for his own ideas, finding 'fragments of practical wisdom' in the mercantilist obsession with accumulating precious metals (interpreted as an attempt to drive down the rate of interest), in the anti-usury laws of the medieval schoolmen, commending Bernard Mandeville[44] and Malthus for their praise of extravagant consumption, honouring 'the strange, unduly neglected prophet Silvio Gesell for proposing 'stamped money' ('the future will learn more from the spirit of Gesell than from that of Marx'), making handsome amends for his previous neglect of the underconsumptionist theory of J. A. Hobson, and even enrolling the founder of social credit, Major Douglas, in the 'brave army of heretics'. Roy Harrod deplored this chapter as a 'tendentious attempt to glorify imbeciles', but it was Keynes's way of honouring the 'cranks' who 'have preferred to see the truth obscurely and imperfectly rather than to maintain error, reached ... by easy logic ... on hypotheses inappropriate to the facts'. After spending several pages (pp. 335–51) on the mercantilists Keynes continues.]*

There remains an allied, but distinct ... doctrine ... which deserves rehabilitation and honour. I mean the doctrine that the rate of interest is not self-adjusting at a level best suited to social advantage but constantly tends to rise too high, so that a wise government is concerned to curb it by statute and custom and even by invoking the sanctions of the moral law.

Provisions against usury are among the most ancient economic practices of which we have record. The destruction of the inducement to invest by an excessive liquidity-preference was the outstanding evil, the prime impediment to the growth of wealth, in the ancient and medieval worlds. And naturally so, since certain of the risks and hazards of economic life diminish the marginal efficiency of capital whilst others serve to increase the preference for liquidity. In a world, therefore, which no one reckoned to be safe, it was almost inevitable that the rate of interest, unless it was curbed by every instrument at the disposal of society, would rise too high to permit of an adequate inducement to invest.

I was brought up to believe that the attitude of the Medieval Church to the rate of interest was absurd, and that the subtle discussions aimed at distinguishing the return on money-loans from the return to active investment were merely jesuitical attempts to find a practical escape from a foolish theory. But I [351] now read these discussions as an honest intellectual effort to keep separate what the classical theory has inextricably confused together, namely, the rate of interest and the marginal efficiency of capital. For it now seems clear that the disquisitions of the schoolmen were directed towards the elucidation of a formula which should allow the schedule of the marginal efficiency of capital to be high, whilst using rule and custom [352] and the moral law to keep down the rate of interest.

...

Chapter 24
Concluding Notes on the Social Philosophy Towards Which the General Theory Might Lead

[*By the time the* General Theory *was published in 1936, Keynes had abandoned his earlier view that capitalism was economically efficient, even in the long run. 'Love of money' was no longer seen as the engine of progress, but, in its form of 'hoarding', as the cause of stagnation. Hence Keynes looked forward to the 'euthanasia of the rentier'. Even in its deformed state, though, capitalism was superior to communism, but in order to realise its emancipatory promise, it had to be made economically efficient by deliberate state policy. This would hasten the day when it would be safe to get rid of it.*]

I

The outstanding faults of the economic society in which we live are its failure to provide for full employment and its arbitrary and inequitable distribution of wealth and incomes. The bearing of the foregoing theory on the first of these is obvious. But there are also two important respects in which it is relevant to the second.

Since the end of the nineteenth century significant progress towards the removal of very great disparities of wealth and income has been achieved through the instrument of direct taxation – income tax and surtax and death duties – especially in Great Britain. Many people would wish to see this process carried much further, but they are deterred by two considerations; partly by the fear of making skilful evasions too much worth while and also of diminishing unduly the motive towards risk-taking, but mainly, I think, by the belief that the growth of capital depends upon the strength of the motive towards individual saving and that for a large proportion of this growth we are dependent on the savings of the rich out of their superfluity.

Our argument does not affect the first of these considerations. But it may considerably modify our attitude towards the second. For we have seen that, up to the point where full employment prevails, the growth of capital depends not at all on a low pro- [372] pensity to consume but is, on the contrary, held back by it; and only in conditions of full employment is a low propensity to consume conducive to the growth of capital. Moreover, experience suggests that in existing conditions saving by institutions and through sinking funds is more than adequate, and that measures for the redistribution of incomes in a way likely to raise the propensity to consume may prove positively favourable to the growth of capital.

The existing confusion of the public mind on the matter is well illustrated by the very common belief that the death duties are responsible for a reduction in the capital wealth of the country. Assuming that the State applies the proceeds of these duties to its ordinary outgoings so that taxes on incomes and consumption are correspondingly reduced or avoided, it is, of course, true that a fiscal policy of heavy death duties has the effect of increasing the community's propensity to consume. But inasmuch as an increase in the habitual propensity to consume will in general (i.e. except in conditions of full employment) serve to increase at the same time the inducement to invest, the inference commonly drawn is the exact opposite of the truth.

Thus our argument leads towards the conclusion that in contemporary conditions the growth of wealth, so far from being dependent on the abstinence of the rich, as is commonly supposed, is more likely to be impeded by it. One of the chief social justifications of great inequality of wealth is, therefore, removed. I am not saying that there are no other reasons, unaffected by our theory, capable of justifying some measure of inequality in some circumstances. But it does dispose of the most important of the reasons why hitherto we have thought it prudent to move carefully. This particularly affects our attitude towards death duties: for there are certain justifications for inequality of incomes which do not apply equally to inequality [373] of inheritances.

For my own part, I believe that there is social and psychological justification for significant inequalities of incomes and wealth, but not for such large disparities as exist to-day. There are valuable human activities which require the motive of money-making and the environment of private wealth-ownership for their full fruition. Moreover, dangerous human proclivities can be canalised into comparatively harmless channels by the existence of opportunities for money-making and private wealth, which, if they cannot be satisfied in this way, may find their outlet in cruelty, the reckless pursuit of personal power and authority, and other forms of self-aggrandisement. It is better that a man should tyrannise over his bank balance than over his fellow-citizens; and whilst the former is sometimes denounced as being but a means to the latter, sometimes at least it is an alternative. But it is not necessary for the stimulation of these activities and the satisfaction of these proclivities that the game should be played for such high stakes as at present. Much lower stakes will serve the purpose equally well, as soon as the players are accustomed to them. The task of transmuting human nature must not be confused with the task of managing it. Though in the ideal commonwealth men may have been taught or inspired or bred to take no interest in the stakes, it may still be wise and prudent statesmanship to allow the game to be played, subject to rules and limitations, so long as the average man, or even a significant section of the community, is in fact strongly addicted to the money-making passion.

II

There is, however, a second, much more fundamental inference from our argument which has a bearing on the future of inequalities of wealth; namely, our theory of the rate of interest. The justification for a moderately high rate of interest has been found hitherto in the necessity of providing a sufficient inducement to save. But we have shown that the extent of effective saving is necessarily determined by the scale of investment and that the scale of investment is promoted by a *low* rate of interest, provided that we do not attempt to stimulate it in this way beyond the point which corresponds to full employment. Thus it is to our best advantage to reduce the rate of interest to that

[374]

point relatively to the schedule of the marginal efficiency of capital at which there is full employment.

There can be no doubt that this criterion will lead to a much lower rate of interest than has ruled hitherto; and, so far as one can guess at the schedules of the marginal efficiency of capital corresponding to increasing amounts of capital, the rate of interest is likely to fall steadily, if it should be practicable to maintain conditions of more or less continuous full employment – unless, indeed, there is an excessive change in the aggregate propensity to consume (including the State).

I feel sure that the demand for capital is strictly limited in the sense that it would not be difficult to increase the stock of capital up to a point where its marginal efficiency had fallen to a very low figure. This would not mean that the use of capital instruments would cost almost nothing, but only that the return from them would have to cover little more than their exhaustion by wastage and obsolescence together with some margin to cover risk and the exercise of skill and judgment. In short, the aggregate return from durable goods in the course of their life would, as in the case of short-lived goods, just cover their labour costs of production *plus* an allowance for risk and the costs of skill and supervision.

Now, though this state of affairs would be quite compatible with some measure of individualism, yet it would mean the [375] euthanasia of the rentier, and, consequently, the euthanasia of the cumulative oppressive power of the capitalist to exploit the scarcity-value of capital. Interest to-day rewards no genuine sacrifice, any more than does the rent of land. The owner of capital can obtain interest because capital is scarce, just as the owner of land can obtain rent because land is scarce. But whilst there may be intrinsic reasons for the scarcity of land, there are no intrinsic reasons for the scarcity of capital. An intrinsic reason for such scarcity, in the sense of a genuine sacrifice which could only be called forth by the offer of a reward in the shape of interest, would not exist, in the long run, except in the event of the individual propensity to consume proving to be of such a character that net saving in conditions of full employment comes to an end before capital has become sufficiently abundant. But even so, it will still be possible for communal saving through the agency of the State to be maintained at a level which will allow the growth of capital up to the point where it ceases to be scarce.

I see, therefore, the rentier aspect of capitalism as a transitional phase which will disappear when it has done its work. And with the disappearance of its rentier aspect much else in it besides will suffer a sea-change. It will be, moreover, a great advantage of the order of events which I am advocating, that the euthanasia of the rentier, of the functionless investor, will be nothing sudden, merely a gradual but prolonged continuance of what we have seen recently in Great Britain, and will need no revolution.

Thus we might aim in practice (there being nothing in this which is unattainable) at an increase in the volume of capital until it ceases to be scarce, so that the functionless investor will no longer receive a bonus; and at a scheme of direct taxation which allows the intelligence and determination and executive skill of the financier, the entrepreneur *et hoc genus omne* (who [376] are certainly so fond of their craft that their labour could be obtained much cheaper than at present), to be harnessed to the service of the community on reasonable terms of reward.

At the same time we must recognise that only experience can show how far the common will, embodied in the policy of the State, ought to be directed to increasing and supplementing the inducement to invest; and how far it is safe to stimulate the average propensity to consume, without foregoing our aim of depriving capital of its scarcity-value within one or two generations. It may turn out that the propensity to consume will be so easily strengthened by the effects of a falling rate of interest, that full employment can be reached with a rate of accumulation little greater than at present. In this event a scheme for the higher taxation of large incomes and inheritances might be open to the objection that it would lead to full employment with a rate of accumulation which was reduced considerably below the current level. I must not be supposed to deny the possibility, or even the probability, of this outcome. For in such matters it is rash to predict how the average man will react to a changed environment. If, however, it should prove easy to secure an approximation to full employment with a rate of accumulation not much greater than at present, an outstanding problem will at least have been solved. And it would remain for separate decision on what scale and by what means it is right and reasonable to call on the living generation to restrict their consumption, so as to establish in course of time, a state of full investment for their successors.[45]

III

In some other respects the foregoing theory is moderately conservative in its implications. For whilst it indicates the vital importance of establishing certain central controls in matters which are now left in the main to individual initiative, there [377] are wide fields of activity which are unaffected. The State will have to exercise a guiding influence on the propensity to consume partly through its scheme of taxation, partly by fixing the rate of interest, and partly, perhaps, in other ways. Furthermore, it seems unlikely that the influence of banking policy on the rate of interest will be sufficient by itself to determine an optimum rate of investment. I conceive, therefore, that a somewhat comprehensive socialisation of investment will prove the only means of securing an approximation to full employment; though this need not exclude all manner of compromises and of devices by which public authority will co-operate with private initiative. But beyond this no obvious case is made out for a system of State Socialism which would embrace most of the economic life of the community. It is not the ownership of the instruments of production which it is important for the State to assume. If the State is able to determine the aggregate amount of resources devoted to augmenting the instruments and the basic rate of reward to those who own them, it will have accomplished all that is necessary. Moreover, the necessary measures of socialisation can be introduced gradually and without a break in the general traditions of society.

Our criticism of the accepted classical theory of economics has consisted not so much in finding logical flaws in its analysis as in pointing out that its tacit assumptions are seldom or never

satisfied, with the result that it cannot solve the economic problems of the actual world. But if our central controls succeed in
establishing an aggregate volume of output corresponding to
full employment as nearly as is practicable, the classical theory
comes into its own again from this point onwards. If we suppose the volume of output to be given, i.e. to be determined by
forces outside the classical scheme of thought, then there is no
[378]   objection to be raised against the classical analysis of the manner
in which private self-interest will determine what in particular
is produced, in what proportions the factors of production will
be combined to produce it, and how the value of the final product will be distributed between them. Again, if we have dealt
otherwise with the problem of thrift, there is no objection to be
raised against the modern classical theory as to the degree of
consilience between private and public advantage in conditions
of perfect and imperfect competition respectively. Thus, apart
from the necessity of central controls to bring about an adjustment between the propensity to consume and the inducement to
invest, there is no more reason to socialise economic life than
there was before.

To put the point concretely, I see no reason to suppose that
the existing system seriously misemploys the factors of production which are in use. There are, of course, errors of foresight;
but these would not be avoided by centralising decisions. When
9,000,000 men are employed out of 10,000,000 willing and
able to work, there is no evidence that the labour of these
9,000,000 men is misdirected. The complaint against the present
system is not that these 9,000,000 men ought to be employed
on different tasks, but that tasks should be available for the
remaining 1,000,000 men. It is in determining the volume, not
the direction, of actual employment that the existing system has
broken down.

Thus I agree with Gesell that the result of filling in the gaps in
the classical theory is not to dispose of the 'Manchester System',
but to indicate the nature of the environment which the free play
of economic forces requires if it is to realise the full potentialities
of production. The central controls necessary to ensure full
employment will, of course, involve a large extension of the

traditional functions of government. Furthermore, the modern classical theory has itself called attention to various conditions in which the free play of economic forces may need to be curbed or [379] guided. But there will still remain a wide field for the exercise of private initiative and responsibility. Within this field the traditional advantages of individualism will still hold good.

Let us stop for a moment to remind ourselves what these advantages are. They are partly advantages of efficiency – the advantages of decentralisation and of the play of self-interest. The advantage to efficiency of the decentralisation of decisions and of individual responsibility is even greater, perhaps, than the nineteenth century supposed; and the reaction against the appeal to self-interest may have gone too far. But, above all, individualism, if it can be purged of its defects and its abuses, is the best safeguard of personal liberty in the sense that, compared with any other system, it greatly widens the field for the exercise of personal choice. It is also the best safeguard of the variety of life, which emerges precisely from this extended field of personal choice, and the loss of which is the greatest of all the losses of the homogeneous or totalitarian state. For this variety preserves the traditions which embody the most secure and successful choices of former generations; it colours the present with the diversification of its fancy; and, being the handmaid of experiment as well as of tradition and of fancy, it is the most powerful instrument to better the future.

Whilst, therefore, the enlargement of the functions of government, involved in the task of adjusting to one another the propensity to consume and the inducement to invest, would seem to a nineteenth-century publicist or to a contemporary American financier to be a terrific encroachment on individualism, I defend it, on the contrary, both as the only practicable means of avoiding the destruction of existing economic forms in their entirety and as the condition of the successful functioning of individual initiative.

For if effective demand is deficient, not only is the public scan- [380] dal of wasted resources intolerable, but the individual enterpriser who seeks to bring these resources into action is operating with the odds loaded against him. The game of hazard which he plays is furnished with many zeros, so that the players *as a whole* will lose if they have the energy and hope to deal all the cards. Hitherto the increment of the world's wealth has fallen short of the aggregate of positive individual savings; and the difference has been made up by the losses of those whose courage and initiative have not been supplemented by exceptional skill or unusual good fortune. But if effective demand is adequate, average skill and average good fortune will be enough.

The authoritarian state systems of to-day seem to solve the problem of unemployment at the expense of efficiency and of freedom. It is certain that the world will not much longer tolerate the unemployment which, apart from brief intervals of excitement, is associated – and, in my opinion, inevitably associated – with present-day capitalistic individualism. But it may be possible by a right analysis of the problem to cure the disease whilst preserving efficiency and freedom.

IV

I have mentioned in passing that the new system might be more favourable to peace than the old has been. It is worth while to repeat and emphasise that aspect.

War has several causes. Dictators and others such, to whom war offers, in expectation at least, a pleasurable excitement, find it easy to work on the natural bellicosity of their peoples. But, over and above this, facilitating their task of fanning the popular flame, are the economic causes of war, namely, the pressure of population and the competitive struggle for markets. [381] It is the second factor, which probably played a predominant part in the nineteenth century, and might again, that is germane to this discussion.

I have pointed out in the preceding chapter that, under the system of domestic *laissez-faire* and an international gold standard such as was orthodox in the latter half of the nineteenth century, there was no means open to a government whereby to mitigate economic distress at home except through the competitive struggle for markets. For all measures helpful to a state of chronic or intermittent under-employment were ruled out, except measures to improve the balance of trade on income account.

Thus, whilst economists were accustomed to applaud the prevailing international system as furnishing the fruits of the international division of labour and harmonising at the same time the interests of different nations, there lay concealed a less benign influence; and those statesmen were moved by common sense and a correct apprehension of the true course of events, who believed that if a rich, old country were to neglect the struggle for markets its prosperity would droop and fail. But if nations can learn to provide themselves with full employment by their domestic policy (and, we must add, if they can also attain equilibrium in the trend of their population), there need be no important economic forces calculated to set the interest of one country against that of its neighbours. There would still be room for the international division of labour and for international lending in appropriate conditions. But there would no longer be a pressing motive why one country need force its wares on another or repulse the offerings of its neighbour, not because this was necessary to enable it to pay for what it wished to purchase, but with the express object of upsetting the equilibrium of payments so as to develop a balance of trade in its own favour. International trade would cease to be what it is, namely, a desperate expedient to maintain employment at home by forcing sales on foreign markets and restricting purchases, which, [382] if successful, will merely shift the problem of unemployment to the neighbour which is worsted in the struggle, but a willing and unimpeded exchange of goods and services in conditions of mutual advantage.

V

Is the fulfilment of these ideas a visionary hope? Have they insufficient roots in the motives which govern the evolution of political society? Are the interests which they will thwart stronger and more obvious than those which they will serve?

I do not attempt an answer in this place. It would need a volume of a different character from this one to indicate even in outline the practical measures in which they might be gradually clothed. But if the ideas are correct – an hypothesis on which the author himself must necessarily base what he writes – it would be a mistake, I predict, to dispute their potency over a period of time. At the present moment people are unusually expectant of a more fundamental diagnosis; more particularly ready to receive it; eager to try it out, if it should be even plausible. But apart from this contemporary mood, the ideas of economists and political philosophers, both when they are right and when they are wrong, are more powerful than is commonly understood. Indeed the world is ruled by little else. Practical men, who believe themselves to be quite exempt from any intellectual influences, are usually the slaves of some defunct economist. Madmen in authority, who hear voices in the air, are distilling their frenzy from some academic scribbler of a few years back. I am sure that the power of vested interests is vastly exaggerated compared with the gradual encroachment of ideas. Not, indeed, immediately, but after a certain interval; for in the field of economic and political philosophy there are not many who [383] are influenced by new theories after they are twenty-five or thirty years of age, so that the ideas which civil servants and politicians and even agitators apply to current events are not likely to be the newest. But, soon or late, it is ideas, not vested [384] interests, which are dangerous for good or evil.

21

CW 14, 'The General Theory of Employment'
(1937)

[GT *was scarcely out before Keynes was planning to produce a simpler and more direct exposition of his theory. In August 1936, he wrote out a table of contents, in six chapters, for a book 'Footnotes to the General Theory':* 1. *The Four Parts of the Theory, a. effective demand, b. the multiplier, c. the theory of investment, d. the theory of interest.* 2. *The analysis of effective demand.* 3. *The theory of interest regarded as the marginal efficiency of money.* 4. *The analysis of liquidity preference regarded as constituting the demand for money.* 5. *The limitations on the demand for capital goods. 6. Statistical notes. This project was aborted by his heart attack in May 1937.*[46] *The direction in which his rewriting might have gone is indicated in his university lectures in the easter term of 1937 (CW 14, pp. 179–93 and the article below, which appeared in the* Quarterly Journal of Economics *in February 1937.*

*For fundamentalist Keynesians, this post-*General Theory *statement of the 'simple fundamental ideas which underlie my theory' is the authentic voice of the Master, freed from the hydraulic machinery and the encrustations of formalism.*[47] *In it, Keynes rests his theoretical structure on the existence of radical uncertainty. With whatever detours, this essay was the culmination of lines of thought which started with Keynes's first ideas about the nature of probability. People had to act on the basis of insufficient knowledge. But they needed to have confidence that their knowledge was sufficient. In this deception, economics played an inevitable and even beneficent part by constructing models which presupposed perfect information. But an economy built on a pretence to knowledge was liable to sudden collapses when reality broke through; and confidence, once deceived, could not readily be restored. That is why it was reasonable to describe periods of disenchanted expectations, as 'equilibria' – periods of sluggishness which could last a long time until 'animal spirits' revived.]*

II

It is generally recognised that the Ricardian analysis was concerned with what we now call long-period equilibrium. Marshall's contribution mainly consisted in grafting on to this the marginal principle and the principle of substitution, together with some discussion of the passage from one position of long-period equilibrium to another. But he assumed, as Ricardo did, that the amounts of the factors of production in use were given and that the problem was to determine the way in which they would be used and their relative rewards. Edgeworth and Professor Pigou and other later and contemporary writers have embroidered and improved this theory by considering how different peculiarities in the shapes of the supply functions of the factors of production would affect matters, what will happen in conditions of monopoly and imperfect competition, how far social and individual advantage coincide, what are the special problems of exchange in an open system and the like. But these more recent writers like their predecessors were still dealing with a system in which the amount of the factors employed was given and the other relevant facts were known more or less for certain. This does not mean that they were dealing with a system in which change was ruled out, or even one in which the disappointment of expectation was ruled out. But at any given time facts and expectations were assumed to be given in a definite and calculable form; and risks, of which, though admitted, not much notice was taken, were supposed to be capable of an exact actuarial computation. The calculus of probability, though mention of it was kept in the background, was supposed to be capable of reducing uncertainty to the same calculable status as that of certainty itself; just as in the Benthamite calculus of pains and pleasures or of advantage and disadvantage, by which the Benthamite philosophy assumed men to be influenced in their general ethical behaviour.

[112]

Actually, however, we have, as a rule, only the vaguest idea of any but the most direct consequences of our acts. Sometimes we are not much concerned with their remoter consequences, even though time and chance may make much of them. But sometimes we are intensely concerned with them, more so, occasionally, than with the immediate consequences. Now of all human activities which are affected by this remoter preoccupation, it happens that one of the most important is economic in character, namely, wealth. The whole object of the accumulation of wealth is to produce results, or potential results, at a comparatively distant, and sometimes at an *indefinitely* distant, date. Thus the fact that our knowledge of the future is fluctuating, vague and uncertain, renders wealth a peculiarly unsuitable subject for the methods of the classical economic theory. This theory might work very well in a world in which economic goods were necessarily consumed within a short interval of their being produced. But it requires, I suggest, considerable amendment if it is to be applied to a world in which the accumulation of wealth for an indefinitely postponed future is an important factor; and the greater the proportionate part played by such wealth accumulation the more essential does such amendment become.

By 'uncertain' knowledge, let me explain, I do not mean merely to distinguish what is known for certain from what is only probable. The game of roulette is not subject, in this sense, to uncertainty; nor is the prospect of a Victory bond being drawn. Or, again, the expectation of life is only slightly uncertain. Even the weather is only moderately uncertain. The sense in which I am using the term is that in which the prospect of a European war is uncertain, or the price of copper and the rate of interest twenty years hence, or the obsolescence of a new [113] invention, or the position of private wealth owners in the social system in 1970. About these matters there is no scientific basis on which to form any calculable probability whatever. We simply do not know. Nevertheless, the necessity for action and for decision compels us as practical men to do our best to overlook this awkward fact and to behave exactly as we should if we had behind us a good Benthamite calculation of a series of prospective advantages and disadvantages, each multiplied by its appropriate probability, waiting to be summed.

How do we manage in such circumstances to behave in a manner which saves our faces as rational, economic men? We have devised for the purpose a variety of techniques, of which much the most important are the three following:

(1) We assume that the present is a much more serviceable guide to the future than a candid examination of past experience would show it to have been hitherto. In other words we largely ignore the prospect of future changes about the actual character of which we know nothing.

(2) We assume that the *existing* state of opinion as expressed in prices and the character of existing output is based on a *correct* summing up of future prospects, so that we can accept it as such unless and until something new and relevant comes into the picture.

(3) Knowing that our own individual judgment is worthless, we endeavour to fall back on the judgment of the rest of the world which is perhaps better informed. That is, we endeavour to conform with the behaviour of the majority or the average.

The psychology of a society of individuals each of whom is endeavouring to copy the others leads to what we may strictly term a *conventional* judgment.

Now a practical theory of the future based on these three principles has certain marked characteristics. In particular, being based on so flimsy a foundation, it is subject to sudden and violent changes. The practice of calmness and immobility, of [114] certainty and security, suddenly breaks down. New fears and hopes will, without warning, take charge of human conduct. The forces of disillusion may suddenly impose a new conventional basis of valuation. All these pretty, polite techniques, made for a well-panelled board room and a nicely regulated market, are liable to collapse. At all times the vague panic fears and equally vague and unreasoned hopes are not really lulled, and lie but a little way below the surface.

Perhaps the reader feels that this general, philosophical disquisition on the behaviour of mankind is somewhat remote from the economic theory under discussion. But I think not. Though this is how we behave in the market place, the theory we devise in the study of how we behave in the market place should not itself submit to market-place idols. I accuse the classical economic theory of being itself one of these pretty, polite techniques which tries to deal with the present by abstracting from the fact that we know very little about the future.[48]

I daresay that a classical economist would readily admit this. But, even so, I think he has overlooked the precise nature of the difference which his abstraction makes between theory and practice, and the character of the fallacies into which he is likely to be led.

This is particularly the case in his treatment of money and interest. And our first step must be to elucidate more clearly the functions of money.

Money, it is well known, serves two principal purposes. By acting as a money of account it facilitates exchanges without its being necessary that it should ever itself come into the picture as a substantive object. In this respect it is a convenience which is devoid of significance or real influence. In the second place, it is a store of wealth. So we are told, without a smile on the face. But in the world of the classical economy, what an insane use to which to put it! For it is a recognised characteristic of money as a store of wealth that it is barren; whereas practically every other form of storing wealth yields some interest or profit. Why should anyone [115] outside a lunatic asylum wish to use money as a store of wealth?

Because, partly on reasonable and partly on instinctive grounds, our desire to hold money as a store of wealth is a barometer of the degree of our distrust of our own calculations and conventions concerning the future. Even though this feeling about money is itself conventional or instinctive, it operates, so to speak, at a deeper level of our motivation. It takes charge at the moments when the higher, more precarious conventions have weakened. The possession of actual money lulls our disquietude; and the premium which we require to make us part with money is the measure of the degree of our disquietude.

The significance of this characteristic of money has usually been overlooked; and in so far as it has been noticed, the essential nature of the phenomenon has been misdescribed. For what has attracted attention has been the *quantity* of money which has been hoarded; and importance has been attached to this because it has been supposed to have a direct proportionate effect on the price level through affecting the velocity of circulation. But the *quantity* of hoards can only be altered either if the total quantity of money is changed or if the quantity of current money income (I speak broadly) is changed; whereas fluctuations in the degree of confidence are capable of having quite a different effect, namely, in modifying not the amount that is actually hoarded, but the amount of the premium which has to be offered to induce people not to hoard. And changes in the propensity to hoard, or in the state of liquidity preference as I have called it, primarily affect, not prices, but the rate of interest; any effect on prices being produced by repercussion as an ultimate consequence of a change in the rate of interest.

This, expressed in a very general way, is my theory of the rate of interest. The rate of interest obviously measures – just as the books on arithmetic say it does – the premium which has to be offered to induce people to hold their wealth in some form other than hoarded money. The quantity of money and the amount of [116] it required in the active circulation for the transaction of current business (mainly depending on the level of money income) determine how much is available for inactive balances, i.e. for hoards. The rate of interest is the factor which adjusts at the margin the demand for hoards to the supply of hoards.

Now let us proceed to the next stage of the argument. The owner of wealth, who has been induced not to hold his wealth in the shape of hoarded money, still has two alternatives between which to choose. He can lend his money at the current rate of money interest or he can purchase some kind of capital asset. Clearly in equilibrium these two alternatives must offer an equal advantage to the marginal investor in each of them. This is brought about by shifts in the money prices of capital assets relative to the prices of money loans. The prices of capital assets move until, having regard to their prospective yields and account being taken of all those elements of doubt and uncertainty, interested and disinterested advice, fashion, convention and what else you will which affect the mind of the investor, they offer an equal apparent advantage to the marginal investor who is wavering between one kind of investment and another.

This, then, is the first repercussion of the rate of interest, as fixed by the quantity of money and the propensity to hoard, namely, on the prices of capital assets. This does not mean, of course, that the rate of interest is the only fluctuating influence on these prices. Opinions as to their prospective yield are themselves subject to sharp fluctuations, precisely for the reason already given, namely, the flimsiness of the basis of knowledge on which they depend. It is these opinions taken in conjunction with the rate of interest which fix their price.

Now for stage three. Capital assets are capable, in general, of being newly produced. The scale on which they are produced depends, of course, on the relation between their costs of production and the prices which they are expected to realise in the market. Thus if the level of the rate of interest taken in conjunction with opinions about their prospective yield raise the prices of capital assets, the volume of current investment (meaning by this the value of the output of newly produced capital assets) will be increased; while if, on the other hand, these

[117]

influences reduce the prices of capital assets, the volume of current investment will be diminished.

It is not surprising that the volume of investment, thus determined, should fluctuate widely from time to time. For it depends on two sets of judgments about the future, neither of which rests on an adequate or secure foundation – on the propensity to hoard and on opinions of the future yield of capital assets. Nor is there any reason to suppose that the fluctuations in one of these factors will tend to offset the fluctuations in the other. When a more pessimistic view is taken about future yields, that is no reason why there should be a diminished propensity to hoard. Indeed, the conditions which aggravate the one factor tend, as a rule, to aggravate the other. For the same circumstances which lead to pessimistic views about future yields are apt to increase the propensity to hoard. The only element of self-righting in the system arises at a much later stage and in an uncertain degree. If a decline in investment leads to a decline in output as a whole, this may result (for more reasons than one) in a reduction of the amount of money required for the active circulation, which will release a larger quantity of money for the inactive circulation, which will satisfy the propensity to hoard at a lower level of the rate of interest, which will raise the prices of capital assets, which will increase the scale of investment, which will restore in some measure the level of output as a whole.

This completes the first chapter of the argument, namely, the liability of the scale of investment to fluctuate for reasons quite distinct (a) from those which determine the propensity of the individual to *save* out of a given income and (b) from those physical conditions of technical capacity to aid production which have usually been supposed hitherto to be the chief influence governing the marginal efficiency of capital.   [118]

If, on the other hand, our knowledge of the future was calculable and not subject to sudden changes, it might be justifiable to assume that the liquidity-preference curve was both stable and very inelastic. In this case a small decline in money income would lead to a large fall in the rate of interest, probably sufficient to raise output and employment to the full. In these conditions we might reasonably suppose that the whole of the available resources would normally be employed; and the conditions required by the orthodox theory would be satisfied.

III

My next difference from the traditional theory concerns its apparent conviction that there is no necessity to work out a theory of the demand and supply of output *as a whole*. Will a fluctuation in investment, arising for the reasons just described, have any effect on the demand for output as a whole, and consequently on the scale of output and employment? What answer can the traditional theory make to this question? I believe that it makes no answer at all, never having given the matter a single thought; the theory of effective demand, that is the demand for output as a whole, having been entirely neglected for more than a hundred years.

My own answer to this question involves fresh considerations. I say that effective demand is made up of two items – investment expenditure determined in the manner just explained and consumption expenditure. Now what governs the amount of consumption expenditure? It depends mainly on the level of income. People's propensity to spend (as I call it) is influenced by many factors such as the distribution of income, their normal attitude to the future and – though probably in a minor degree – [119] by the rate of interest. But in the main the prevailing psychological law seems to be that when aggregate income increases, consumption expenditure will also increase but to a somewhat lesser extent. This is a very obvious conclusion. It simply amounts to saying that an increase in income will be divided in some proportion or another between spending and saving, and that when our income is increased it is extremely unlikely that this will have the effect of making us either spend less or save less than before. This psychological law was of the utmost importance in the development of my own thought, and it is, I think, absolutely fundamental to the theory of effective demand as set forth in my book. But few critics or commentators so far have paid particular attention to it.

There follows from this extremely obvious principle an important, yet unfamiliar, conclusion. Incomes are created partly by entrepreneurs producing for investment and partly by their producing for consumption. The amount that is consumed depends on the amount of income thus made up. Hence the amount of consumption goods which it will pay entrepreneurs to produce depends on the amount of investment goods which they are producing. If, for example, the public are in the habit of spending nine-tenths of their income on consumption goods, it follows that if entrepreneurs were to produce consumption goods at a cost more than nine times the cost of the investment goods they are producing, some part of their output could not be sold at a price which would cover its cost of production. For the consumption goods on the market would have cost more than nine-tenths of the aggregate income of the public and would therefore be in excess of the demand for consumption goods, which by hypothesis is only the nine-tenths. Thus entrepreneurs will make a loss until they contract their output of consumption goods down to an amount at which it no longer exceeds nine times their current output of investment goods.

The formula is not, of course, quite so simple as in this illustration. The proportion of their incomes which the public will choose to consume will not be a constant one, and in the most general case other factors are also relevant. But there is always a formula, more or less of this kind, relating the output of consumption goods which it pays to produce to the output of investment goods; and I have given attention to it in my book under the name of the *multiplier*. The fact that an increase in consumption is apt in itself to stimulate this further investment merely fortifies the argument. [120]

That the level of output of consumption goods, which is profitable to the entrepreneur, should be related by a formula of this kind to the output of investment goods depends on assumptions of a simple and obvious character. The conclusion appears to me to be quite beyond dispute. Yet the consequences which follow from it are at the same time unfamiliar and of the greatest possible importance.

The theory can be summed up by saying that, given the psychology of the public, the level of output and employment as a whole depends on the amount of investment. I put it in this way, not because this is the only factor on which aggregate output depends, but because it is usual in a complex system to regard as the *causa causans* that factor which is most prone to sudden and wide fluctuation. More comprehensively, aggregate output depends on the propensity to hoard, on the policy of the monetary authority as it affects the quantity of money, on the state of confidence concerning the prospective yield of capital assets, on the propensity to spend and on the social factors which influence the level of the money wage. But of these several factors it is those which determine the rate of investment which are most unreliable, since it is they which are influenced by our views of the future about which we know so little.

This that I offer is, therefore, a theory of why output and employment are so liable to fluctuation. It does not offer a ready-made remedy as to how to avoid these fluctuations and to maintain output at a steady optimum level. But it is, properly [121] speaking, a theory of employment because it explains *why,* in any given circumstances, employment is what it is. Naturally I am interested not only in the diagnosis, but also in the cure; and many pages of my book are devoted to the latter. But I consider that my suggestions for a cure, which, avowedly, are not worked out completely, are on a different plane from the diagnosis. They are not meant to be definitive; they are subject to all sorts of special assumptions and are necessarily related to the particular conditions of the time. But my main reasons for departing from the traditional theory go much deeper than this. They are of a highly general character and are meant to be definitive.

I sum up, therefore, the main grounds of my departure as follows:

(i) The orthodox theory assumes that we have a knowledge of the future of a kind quite different from that which we actually possess. This false rationalisation follows the lines of the Benthamite calculus. The hypothesis of a calculable future leads to a wrong interpretation of the principles of behaviour which the need for action compels us to adopt, and to an underestimation of the concealed factors of utter doubt, precariousness, hope and fear. The result has been a mistaken theory of the rate of interest. It is true that the necessity of equalising the advantages of the choice between owning loans and assets requires that the rate of interest should be *equal* to the marginal efficiency of capital. But this does not tell us at what *level* the equality will be effective. The orthodox theory regards the marginal efficiency of capital as setting the pace. But the marginal efficiency of capital depends on the price of capital assets; and since this price determines the rate of new investment, it is consistent in equilibrium with only one given level of money income. Thus the marginal efficiency of capital is not determined, unless the level of money income is given. In a system in which the level of money income is capable of fluctuating, the orthodox theory is one equation short of what is required to give a solution. Undoubtedly the reason why the orthodox system has failed to discover this discrepancy is because it has always tacitly assumed that income [122] *is* given, namely, at the level corresponding to the employment of all the available resources. In other words it is tacitly assuming that the monetary policy is such as to maintain the rate of interest at that level which is compatible with full employment. It is, therefore, incapable of dealing with the general case where employment is liable to fluctuate. Thus, instead of the marginal efficiency of capital determining the rate of interest, it is truer (though not a full statement of the case) to say that it is the rate of interest which determines the marginal efficiency of capital.

(2) The orthodox theory would by now have discovered the above defect, if it had not ignored the need for a theory of the supply and demand of output as a whole. I doubt if many modern economists really accept Say's Law that supply creates its own demand. But they have not been aware that they were tacitly assuming it. Thus the psychological law underlying the multiplier has escaped notice. It has not been observed that the amount of consumption goods which it pays entrepreneurs to produce is a function of the amount of investment goods which it pays them to produce. The explanation is to be found, I suppose, in the tacit assumption that every individual spends the whole of his income either on consumption or on buying, directly or indirectly, newly produced capital goods. But, here again, whilst the older economists expressly believed this, I doubt if many contemporary economists really do believe it. They have discarded these older ideas without becoming aware of the consequences. [123]

22

CW 14, 'Alternative Theories of the Rate of Interest' (1937)

[*This excerpt is taken from the* Economic Journal, *June 1937, in which Keynes suggested a 'finance' demand for money as an addition to the transactions demand of GT.*]

Planned investment – i.e. investment *ex ante* – may have to secure its 'financial provision' *before* the investment takes place; that is to say, before the corresponding saving has taken place ... There has, therefore, to be a technique to bridge the gap between the time when the *decision* to invest is taken, and the time when the correlative investment and saving actually occur.

[207]

This service may be provided either by the new issue market or by the banks; – which it is makes no difference.

[208] ...

If investment is proceeding at a steady rate, the finance (or the commitments to finance) required can be supplied from a revolving fund of a more or less constant amount, one entrepreneur having his finance replenished for the purpose of a projected investment as another exhausts his on paying for his completed investment. But if decisions to invest are (e.g.) increasing, the extra finance involved will constitute an additional demand for money.

Now, a pressure to secure more finance than usual may easily affect the rate of interest through its influence on the demand for money; and unless the banking system is prepared to augment the supply of money, lack of finance may prove an important obstacle to more than a certain amount of investment decisions being on the tapis at the same time. But 'finance' has nothing to do with saving. At the 'financial' stage of the proceedings no net saving has taken place on anyone's part, just as there has been no net investment. 'Finance' and 'commitments to finance' are mere credit and debit book entries, which allow entrepreneurs to go ahead with assurance.

...

If by 'credit' we mean 'finance', I have no objection at all to admitting the demand for finance as one of the factors influencing the rate of interest. For 'finance' constitutes, as we have seen, an additional demand for liquid cash in exchange for [209] a deferred claim. It is, in the literal sense, a demand for money ... Thus it is precisely the liquidity premium on cash ruling in the market which determines the rate of interest at which finance is obtainable.

The above analysis is useful in exhibiting in what sense a heavy demand for investment can exhaust the market and be held up by a lack of financial facilities on reasonable terms. It is, to an important extent, the 'financial facilities' which regulate the *pace* of new investment ... It is the supply of available finance which, in practice, holds up from time to time the onrush of 'new issues'. But if the banking system chooses to make the finance available and the investment projected by the new issues actually takes place, the appropriate level of incomes will be generated out of which there will necessarily remain over an amount of saving exactly sufficient to take care of the new investment. The control of finance is, indeed, a potent, though sometimes dangerous, method for regulating the rate of investment (though much more potent when used as a curb [210] than as a stimulus). Yet this is only another way of expressing the power of the banks through their control over the supply of money – i.e. of liquidity.   [211]

23

CW 14, Methodological Issues:
Tinbergen, Harrod (1938)

[*Keynes had attacked the philosophic basis of induction in Section V of his* Treatise on Probability. *His criticism of J. Tinbergen's books* Statistical Testing of Business-Cycle Theories: I. A Method and its Application to Investment Activity *and* Business Cycles in the United States, *sent to him by the*

League of Nations, which had commissioned them, largely recapitulated the criticisms of the inductive method he had made in his earlier book.[49] *He concluded a caustic review of the first of these in the* Economic Journal, *September 1939: 'It is a strange reflection that this book looks likely, as far as 1939 is concerned, to be the principal activity and* raison d'être *of the League of Nations'.*[50] *This review, entitled 'Professor Tinbergen's Method', is reprinted in CW 14, pp. 306–18. The excerpt below comes from an earlier, more accessible, letter to R. Tyler, 23 August 1938 (CW 14, pp. 285–9).]*

Dear Mr Tyler,

You sent me a severe holiday task by forwarding Tinbergen's two books and asking for a comment! I confess that I have the utmost difficulty in making head or tail of them. No doubt this is partly due to my lack of familiarity with the matter, but partly also, I think, to the author's cryptic method of exposition. With a method so unfamiliar and untested, the author would have done well, I think, to have given the reader at least one example set forth in a very detailed manner with every initial assumption and every subsequent step fully explained. As it is, I can only answer your enquiry by cataloguing a few of the questions which the work leads me to ask, which I cannot answer myself.

There is first of all the central question of methodology, – [285] the logic of applying the method of multiple correlation to unanalysed economic material, which we know to be non-homogeneous through time. If we were dealing with the action of numerically measurable, independent forces, adequately analysed so that we knew we were dealing with independent atomic factors and between them completely comprehensive, acting with fluctuating relative strength on material constant and homogeneous through time, we might be able to use the method of multiple correlation with some confidence for disentangling the laws of their action; though, even so, our results might be only very approximate so long as we were limited by our technique to linear relations.

In fact we know that every one of these conditions is far from being satisfied by the economic material under investigation. How far does this impair the validity of the method? That seems to me to deserve a most careful preliminary enquiry. The volume which purports to be 'a note on the method' in fact faces none of these difficulties and is in fact mainly occupied, just like the other volume, with elaborate half-explained numerical examples, the method employed in which already begs the question.

To proceed to some more detailed comments. The coefficients arrived at are apparently assumed to be constant for 10 years or for a larger period. Yet, surely we know that they are not constant. There is no reason at all why they should not be different every year.

How are these coefficients arrived at? Is it by laborious trial-and-error guessing, or by a method? How are the time lags arrived at? Is it by common-sense guessing or by a method? I should add to these questions that I am not at all clear how far the method of multiple correlation is in fact employed. It seems to disappear from the surface as the work proceeds. One gets the impression that it is a process of fitting a linear equation through trial and error.

Is it assumed that the factors investigated are comprehensive [286] and that they are not merely a partial selection out of all the factors at work? How much difference does it make to the method if they are not comprehensive?

Is it claimed that there is a likelihood that the equations will work approximately *next time*. With a free hand to choose coefficients and time lag, one can, with enough industry, always cook a formula to fit moderately well a limited range of past facts. But what does this prove? Are not further and different tests required before it is properly available for inductive argument?

Is it assumed that the future is a determinate function of *past statistics*? What place is left for expectation and the state of confidence relating to the future?

What place is allowed for non-numerical factors, such as inventions, politics, labour troubles, wars, earthquakes, financial crises?

One feels a suspicion that the choice of factors is influenced (as is indeed only natural) by what statistics are available, and that many vital factors are ignored because they are statistically intractable or unprocurable. But, even so, one doubts whether the statistics actually employed are sufficiently detailed and accurate to support one-tenth of the burden which is placed on them.

Is the method such that, if a factor has in fact not varied much during the period in question, it therefore necessarily emerges as unimportant?

Is the method such as to produce a unique result? Would someone else, that is to say, faced with the same problem and using the same method and the same statistics, but without having seen these calculations, necessarily bring out the same result? Has any experiment been made to test how far the results are, so to speak, subjective and how far objective? This is important because the results are presented in such a way that it is very difficult for the reader to apply his own judgment to the material. If you have a fair number of variables and can [287] play about at will with the coefficients and time lags, is it or is it not the case that more than one equally plausible result can be obtained? In short, how far are the results mechanically and uniquely obtainable from the data, and how far do they depend on the way the cook chooses to go to work?

Let me take one particular example, which I select because it is the simplest considered in the book, namely, the demand for investment in new rolling stock. Now it is fairly evident, without these enquiries, that the demand for new rolling stock will mainly depend on the growth of traffic. Moreover, profits, which is the only other factor taken account of, is largely growth of traffic over again. In order to get a separate factor one has to segregate that part of profits which is due to growth of traffic from that part of profits which is due to better freight rates relatively to wages and other costs. Now, what one really wants to know is, not the obvious point that the demand for rolling stock is considerably affected by the growth of traffic, but how far this dominates the situation as compared with rather more subtle factors such as (1) the age of the existing rolling stock, (2) the price of new rolling stock, (3) the surplus capacity of the existing shops to produce more rolling stock, (4) the financial condition of the railways and their borrowing powers as affecting their ability to finance new rolling stock, (5) the state of confidence as to the maintenance of traffic and as to the effect of competition of other forms of transport. Now I quite agree that it would not be easy to apply the method to these factors. But that seems to me a justification for not using the method in this case rather than for ignoring these matters and telling us what we know already with the trimmings of figures which really have no significance.

Thus you will see that I am not satisfied with the logic of the method and that the book has not enabled me to understand thoroughly either its detailed operation or what is assumed or what is claimed for it or, except in the haziest way, what results are in fact obtained. I feel, therefore, that it would be dangerous to approve [288] or condemn any theory on the results so far obtained.

The notion of testing the quantitative influence of factors suggested by a theory as being important is very useful and to the point. The question to be answered, however, is whether the complicated method here employed does not result in a false precision beyond what either the method or the statistics actually available can support. It may be that a more rough and ready method which preserves the original data in a more recognisable form may be safer.

For these reasons I doubt if Tinbergen's conclusions, though well worth presenting by him personally, should receive authoritative publication, unless they have first obtained the confident and responsible imprimatur of someone more competent in these matters than I am. And, granted that this is obtained, I would still urge that the method of exposition adopted should be such as to make it easier for the reader to appreciate exactly what is being assumed, what is being done, and what the outcome is.

Yours sincerely,

[Copy initialled] J.M.K.   [289]

[Keynes took advantage of the discussion with colleagues of 'Tinbergen's method' to write the following two letters to Roy Harrod, which summed up his views on how to do economics. The first is CW 14, Letter to R. F. Harrod, 4 July 1938.]
Economics is a science of thinking in terms of models joined to the art of choosing models which are relevant to the contemporary world. It is compelled to be this, because, unlike the typical natural science, the material to which it is applied is, in

too many respects, not homogeneous through time. The object
[296] of a model is to segregate the semi-permanent or relatively constant factors from those which are transitory or fluctuating so
as to develop a logical way of thinking about the latter, and of
understanding the time sequences to which they give rise in
particular cases.

Good economists are scarce because the gift for using 'vigi-
lant observation' to choose good models, although it does not
require a highly specialised intellectual technique, appears to
be a very rare one.

In the second place, as against Robbins, economics is essentially a moral science and not a natural science. That is to say,
[297] it employs introspection and judgments of value.

[*The next letter is* CW *14, Letter to R. F. Harrod, 16 July* 1938.]
My point against Tinbergen is a different one. In chemistry and
physics and other natural sciences the object of experiment is
to fill in the actual values of the various quantities and factors
appearing in an equation or a formula; and the work when
done is once and for all. In economics that is not the case, and
to convert a model into a quantitative formula is to destroy its
usefulness as an instrument of thought. Tinbergen endeavours
to work out the variable quantities in a particular case, or perhaps in the average of several particular cases, and he then
suggests that the quantitative formula so obtained has general
validity. Yet in fact, by filling in figures, which one can be quite
sure will not apply next time, so far from increasing the value
of his instrument, he has destroyed it. All the statisticians tend
that way. Colin [*Clark*], for example, has recently persuaded
himself that the propensity to consume in terms of money is
constant at all phases of the credit cycle. He works out a figure
[299] for it and proposes to predict by using the result, regardless of
the fact that his own investigations clearly show that it is not
constant, in addition to the strong *a priori* reasons for regarding it as most unlikely that it can be so.

The point needs emphasising because the art of thinking
in terms of models is a difficult – largely because it is an
unaccustomed – practice. The pseudo-analogy with the physical

sciences leads directly counter to the habit of mind which is most important for an economist proper to acquire.

I also want to emphasise strongly the point about economics being a moral science. I mentioned before that it deals with introspection and with values. I might have added that it deals with motives, expectations, psychological uncertainties. One has to be constantly on guard against treating the material as constant and homogeneous. It is as though the fall of the apple to the ground depended on the apple's motives, on whether it is worth while falling to the ground, and whether the ground wanted the apple to fall, and on mistaken calculations on the part of the apple as to how far it was from the centre of the earth.   [300]

[*For an excellent discussion of Keynes's views on mathematics and econometrics, see* R. M. *O'Donnell,* Keynes: Philosophy, Economics and Politics *(1989), chapter 9.*]

FOUR

The Policy-maker

Before reading this section, the reader is advised to turn to excerpt 2 above, which reveals the Burkean source of JMK's philosophy of action and his notable lack of ideological extremism.

No problem with which Keynes was intimately concerned failed to produce a 'Keynes plan' for its solution. His genius was pre-eminently constructive, with theory being produced to underpin policies which he thought the situation required. Keynes's plans had the characteristic of being administratively 'shovel-ready' and taking the existing facts of the situation as their starting point. Only in the case of the International Clearing Union did they involve institution-building. Keynes was quick to adapt his remedies to changes in the situation, including the political chances of the policy being adopted. This led to the charge of inconsistency, to which he is said, by Joan Robinson, to have replied, 'When someone persuades me I am wrong, I change my mind. What do you do?'[1] However, what is striking over the whole period of Keynes's policy-building is the consistency of his approach and preoccupations.

His policy proposals fall into two areas, domestic and international; and into two main periods, before and after 1931. Since Britain was still at the centre of the world's trading and financial system, the two areas were necessarily interlinked. Keynes's aim throughout can be summed up as endeavouring to secure the right international monetary conditions for the pursuit of domestic stability of business and prices, while avoiding currency and trade wars. In short, he tried to adapt his liberal heritage to new conditions.

In the first half of the 1920s, his purpose was to secure for the Bank of England the monetary freedom to pursue a policy of domestic price stabilization. He advocated a flexible replacement for the gold standard (excerpt 26) and attacked the government's decision to put Britain back on to the gold standard in a famous polemic, 'The Economic Consequences of Mr Churchill' (excerpt 27).

In the period 1925–31, Keynes sought to mitigate the deflationary impact of the restored gold standard by means of fiscal policy and a 'revenue tariff' ('Can Lloyd George Do It?' (excerpt 28) and Policies for the Slump (excerpt 29)). He vehemently opposed the policy of cutting public expenditure in the economic crisis of 1931 (excerpt 29).

Before 1931 Keynes's plans involved the creative application of existing theory to short-run conditions, not a break with it. Thus, in his attack on the gold standard, he was a 'monetary reformer', drawing on the work of Fisher and Wicksell, as well as the Cambridge monetary school. Public works in the late 1920s were avowedly second-best policies, were widely supported as such and involved no breach with established doctrines. But after 1931 Keynes's theoretical perspective changed.

The collapse of the gold standard in 1931 had liberated monetary policy from its 'golden fetters'. But the continuance of the Depression changed Keynes's theory in three related ways which found expression in GT. First, Keynes came to doubt that economies were naturally self-correcting after a deep shock: this was his theory of 'under-employment equilibrium'. Second, he replaced the goal of price stability with the goal of full employment: this was the main consequence of his switch from the monetary theory of TM to the monetary theory of production of GT. Third, his liquidity-preference theory of the rate of interest led him to doubt the ability of monetary policy on its own either to produce recovery from a severe slump or to maintain full employment on a permanent basis.

With the change of theory came a change in policy outlook. While he welcomed 'cheap money' after 1931, he did not look to it bring about full recovery. His policy advocacy shifted to fiscal measures. To justify these, he used a new analytic tool,

'The Multiplier', invented by his student Richard Kahn, which sought to refute the standard view that fiscal policy could make no significant contribution to recovery (excerpt 30). Keynes admired Roosevelt's New Deal for its spirit, but criticized it for the meagreness of its fiscal stimulus, and for mixing up recovery with reform (excerpt 31). Fiscal policy also became Keynes's favoured instrument for maintaining full employment. The opportunity to demonstrate its power came with the war. The Keynes plan for wartime finance (excerpt 34) demonstrated how fiscal policy could be used to counter inflation as well as deflation. Thereafter, Keynes expected fiscal policy (though not permanent budget deficits!) to be the main peacetime instrument to balance aggregate demand and supply at full employment (excerpt 35).

Interest in international monetary reform had faded in the more autarkic world of the 1930s. But wartime US pressure on Britain to liquidate its imperial preference system and the sterling area, Britain's dependence on America for Lend-Lease and Keynes's own liberal heritage stimulated him to produce the last of his great plans, for an International Clearing Union (1941). This brought him round full circle to his original quest for an international monetary system able to support domestic full employment. In his last article, published posthumously (excerpt 38), he predicted that 'natural forces' would eventually restore equilibrium in the US balance of payments.

These are the main threads, but I have included an excerpt from ECP as indicating Keynes's critical attitude to debt bondage, and his consistent advocacy of debt forgiveness. It should be read in conjunction with his attack on usury, his anticipation of the 'euthanasia of the rentier' chapters 23 and 24 of excerpt 20), his insistence on creditor adjustment in his ICU plan (excerpt 36) and more generally his strong and persistent bias against deflation.][2]

24

CW 2, *The Economic Consequences of the Peace* (1919)

[*Keynes proposed that Britain should waive her claims on Germany in favour of France, Belgium and Serbia (p. 171); that all inter-Allied debts be cancelled (pp. 171–2); that the US provide Europe with a reconstruction loan (pp. 180f.) and that Germany be encouraged to reconstruct Russia (pp. 186–7). Keynes's preference for debt restructuring and forgiveness over debt collection is clear.*]

The final consideration influencing the reader's attitude to this proposal [*cancellation of debts*] must, however, depend on his view as to the future place in the world's progress of the vast paper entanglements which are our legacy from war finance both at home and abroad. The war has ended with everyone [177] owing everyone else immense sums of money. Germany owes a large sum to the Allies; the Allies owe a large sum to Great Britain; and Great Britain owes a large sum to the United States. The holders of war loan in every country are owed a large sum by the state; and the state in turn is owed a large sum by those and other taxpayers. The whole position is in the highest degree artificial, misleading, and vexatious. We shall never be able to move again, unless we can free our limbs from these paper shackles. A general bonfire is so great a necessity that unless we can make of it an orderly and good-tempered affair in which no serious injustice is done to anyone, it will, when it comes at last, grow into a conflagration which may destroy much else as well.
. . .

Before the middle of the nineteenth century no nation owed payments to a foreign nation on any considerable scale, except such tributes as were exacted under the compulsion of actual occupation in force and, at one time, by absentee princes under the sanction of feudalism. It is true that the need for European capitalism to find an outlet in the New World has led during the last fifty years, though even now on a relatively modest scale, to such countries as Argentina owing an annual sum to such countries as England. But the system is fragile; and it has only survived because this burden is represented by real assets and is bound up with the property system generally, and because the sums already lent are not unduly large in relation to those which it is still hoped to borrow. Bankers are used to this system, and believe it to be a necessary part of the permanent order of society. They are disposed to believe, therefore, by analogy with it, that a comparable system between governments, on a vaster and definitely oppressive scale, represented by no real assets and less closely associated with the property [178] system, is natural and reasonable and in conformity with human nature.

I doubt this view of the world. Even capitalism at home, which engages many local sympathies, which plays a real part in the daily process of production, and upon the security of which the present order of society largely depends, is not very safe. But however this may be, will the discontented peoples of Europe be willing for a generation to come so to order their lives that an appreciable part of their daily produce may be available to meet a foreign payment . . . ?

In short, I do not believe that any of these tributes will continue to be paid, at the best, for more than a very few years. They do not square with human nature or agree with the spirit of the age.

[179]

25

CW 17, 'A Plan for a Russian Settlement' (1922)

[*Keynes saw the Genoa Conference of April 1922 as an opportunity for giving practical expression to the ideas above, especially as concerned Germany helping to reconstruct Russia.*]

If we practise on Russia what we have already practised on Germany, and compel her under force of economic pressure to recite a promise which she cannot keep and which we know

she does not mean to keep, we shall have disgraced ourselves. Our proposal must be sensible and practical, and one which both sides will think it advantageous to carry out completely.
. . .

If the Soviet power in Russia is recognised as the *de jure* government of the country, but not otherwise, holders of Russian pre-war debt can properly claim that this debt be recognised. But many governments which recognise their debt are in arrears with its interest, and the history of the past fifty years is full of precedents of countries which have suffered war, misgovernment, or revolutions compounding with their creditors.

Private investors who lend money to a foreign government take a risk, and there is no principle of international law which guarantees them. Those who lent money to the tsar's government took a big risk, and they will be lucky to get anything back. Russia, having recognised her debt, must be allowed, therefore, to compound with her creditors. I suggest that the new bonds should, after a five years' moratorium, carry interest at 2½ per cent, which, at an outside estimate of the pre-war debt, would cost eventually 20 million a year.

[391]

The Confiscated Property Claims

There remains the question of compensation to individual foreigners whose property has been confiscated. They have the best claims, on grounds both of equity and of expedience, to an integral reimbursement, in spite of the terms of Russia's agreement with Germany. Much detail is involved, and different cases must be treated on their merits.

Wherever possible the properties should be restored to their original owners on the basis of the partnership or profit-sharing arrangement between the owners and the Bolshevik government which the latter are prepared to offer. These offers excite great indignation. Yet they open a way by which foreign capital can re-enter Russia with the much-needed extra security of a common interest between the foreign industrialist and the Soviet power. But it should be part of the settlement that where an arrangement of this kind cannot be mutually agreed, then the dispossessed owner should be entitled to receive bonds to the full value of his property as determined by an arbitral commission, such bonds to carry 5 per cent interest after a five years' moratorium. I feel confident that the amount of such bonds to be issued would fall short of 200 million sterling and might not exceed half that figure.

Such a scheme is modest compared with our present demands ... But looked at coolly it offers a degree of satisfaction to Russia's creditors which a short time ago would have seemed almost incredible. Indeed, there is not much reason to hope even now that Russia will grant anything as good.

But if we offer her something on these lines we shall at least be talking sensibly, and will be asking nothing incapable of [392] sincere acceptance. If Russia's creditors stand out for more, very well; they will certainly get nothing.

A Credit for Russia

But in addition, I suggest, though with doubt and hesitation, that a credit to Russia can be justified not merely to induce a settlement but for the sake of European reconstruction.

Russia will not be able to borrow from bankers or private investors for some time to come. The political risk is too great. Business, therefore, will not get started without a government credit. The United States being isolated, Great Britain is probably the only power now able to grant it, although her financial position is a good ground for refusing. I am generally opposed to the Treasury opening its purse-strings, and I am not guilty of underestimating the need for parsimony. But here is an opportunity for an expenditure which may have consequences altogether out of proportion to its magnitude.

If Russia exports food again one year earlier than she otherwise would, this may lower the price of wheat enough to save us a huge sum on our food bill alone. An increase of 10 per cent in the supply available on the world market may make a quite disproportionate difference to the price. It will take a long time to bring Russia back as a food exporter. But our interest in doing so is enormous, and the sooner we begin the sooner we shall reap the advantage.

In addition, a definite act which leads to tangible results may jolt the whole machine into motion. We must get a start on by artificial assistance on a fairly substantial scale and then trust
[393] that business will run itself afterwards.

I propose therefore that Great Britain grant to the Soviet power as part of a general settlement a credit of 50 million sterling to be spread over two years, the money to be expended on British goods to promote agricultural production, whether tools and machinery or for the improvement of communications, with the purpose of ameliorating the Russian famine in the first instance and encouraging export thereafter. Possibly a part of the goods might be furnished from Germany, their value to be credited to her against sums due to Great Britain on reparation account. If any other government desired to join in the credit, so much the better.

It is not essential that every power need come into this settlement. The terms outlined would be offered to the nationals of those powers which in return accorded *de jure* recognition. If any country preferred to continue in the present situation it would be entitled to do so.

I can understand the policy of repudiating the Bolshevik government altogether. But Genoa meets on a different presupposition. The whole thing may be futile, but if we are to treat with them at all we must treat on realistic lines. It is with a sort of despair that one finds oneself back again in the dreadful atmosphere of Versailles discussing a bondage of debt and insisting that as a first preliminary the other party shall make a
[394] public recital of what both parties know to be false.

26

CW 4, *A Tract on Monetary Reform* (1923)

[*Most of Keynes's policy thinking in the 1920s was overshadowed by the existence of the gold standard, and the need to achieve the best results possible in terms of domestic prosperity from this position. The following excerpts from chapter 4,*

'Alternative Aims in Monetary Policy', and chapter 5, 'Positive Suggestions for the Future Regulation of Money', touch closely on issues which are still the subject of debate. Keynes argues that the goal of monetary policy should be price stability not exchange-rate stability; that the gold standard could not achieve the former, and was, therefore, a 'barbarous relic'; and that the best international monetary system for the future was a managed 'float' between the dollar and sterling currency blocs to which other currencies should attach themselves. Notice Keynes's contention that his proposals represented not a break from the past, but the deliberate and 'scientific' development of a system already in unconscious evolution because it fitted social and business needs.]

Chapter 4
Alternative Aims in Monetary Policy

II Stability of Prices Versus Stability of Exchange

The right choice [between stability of prices and stability of exchange rates] is not necessarily the same for all countries. It must partly depend on the relative importance of foreign trade in the economic life of the country. Nevertheless, there does seem to be in almost every case a presumption in favour of the stability of prices, if only it can be achieved. Stability of exchange is in the nature of a convenience which adds to the efficiency and prosperity of those who engage in foreign trade.[3] Stability of prices, on the other hand, is profoundly important for the avoidance of the various evils described in chapter 1. [See chapter 2 of this selection, pp. 35–6] Contracts and business expectations, which presume a stable exchange, must be far fewer, even in a trading country such as England, than those which presume a stable level of internal prices.   [126]

. . .

III The Restoration of a Gold Standard

[Keynes argued that the relative success of the nineteenth-century gold standard in providing a stable standard of value and a barrier to the political manipulation of money rested on a *number of fortuitous factors, which could no longer be relied on. By chance the pace of discovery of new gold mines, the decentralization of central bank reserves and the steadiness of the private demand for gold prevented large fluctuations in the gold price. But after the war, gold had become a 'managed' currency, its value managed by three or four central banks in the interests of domestic price stability. The only way to 'strap down' finance ministers was to improve the scientific principles of central bank managment (pp. 132–8).]*

. . .

Those who advocate the return to a gold standard do not always appreciate along what different lines our actual practice has been drifting. If we restore the gold standard, are we to return also to the pre-war conceptions of bank rate, allowing the tides of gold to play what tricks they like with the internal price level, and abandoning the attempt to moderate the disas-

[137]   trous influence of the credit cycle on the stability of prices and employment? Or are we to continue and develop the experimental innovations of our present policy, ignoring the 'bank ratio' and, if necessary, allowing unmoved a piling up of gold reserves far beyond our requirements or their depletion far below them?

In truth, the gold standard is already a barbarous relic. All of us, from the Governor of the Bank of England downwards, are now primarily interested in preserving the stability of business, prices, and employment, and are not likely, when the choice is forced on us, deliberately to sacrifice these to the outworn dogma, which had its value once, of £3.17s 10½d per ounce. Advocates of the ancient standard do not observe how remote it now is from the spirit and the requirements of the age. A regulated non-metallic standard has slipped in unnoticed. *It exists.* Whilst the economists dozed, the academic dream of a hundred years, doffing its cap and gown, clad in paper rags, has crept into the real world by means of the bad fairies – always so much more potent than the good – the wicked

[138]   ministers of finance.

. . .

Chapter 5
Positive Suggestions for the Future
Regulation of Money

1 *Great Britain*

Accordingly my first requirement in a good constructive scheme can be supplied merely by a development of our existing arrangements on more deliberate and self-conscious lines. Hitherto the Treasury and the Bank of England have looked forward to the stability of the dollar exchange (preferably at the pre-war parity) as their objective. It is not clear whether they intend to stick to this irrespective of fluctuations in the value of the dollar (or of gold); whether, that is to say, they would sacrifice the stability of sterling prices to the stability of the dollar exchange in the event of the two proving to be incompatible. At any rate, my scheme would require that they should adopt the stability of sterling prices as their *primary* objective – though this would not prevent their aiming at exchange stability also as a secondary objective by co-operating with the Federal Reserve Board in a common policy. So long as the Federal Reserve Board was successful in keeping dollar prices steady the objective of keeping sterling prices steady would be identical with the objective of keeping the dollar–sterling exchange steady. My recommendation does not involve more than a determination that, in the event of the Federal Reserve Board failing to keep dollar prices steady, sterling prices should not, if it could be helped, plunge with them merely for the sake of maintaining a fixed parity of exchange.

If the Bank of England, the Treasury, and the Big Five were to adopt this policy, to what criteria should they look respectively in regulating bank rate, government borrowing, and trade advances? The first question is whether the criterion should be a precise, arithmetical formula or whether it should be sought in a general judgment of the situation based on all the available data. The pioneer of price stability as against exchange stability, Professor Irving Fisher, advocated the former in the shape of his 'compensated dollar', which was to be automatically adjusted by reference to an index number of prices without any play of judgment or discretion. He may have been influenced, however, by the advantage of propounding a method which [147] could be grafted as easily as possible on to the pre-war system of gold reserves and gold ratios. In any case, I doubt the wisdom and the practicability of a system so cut and dried. If we wait until a price movement is actually afoot before applying remedial measures, we may be too late. 'It is not the *past* rise in prices but the *future* rise that has to be counteracted.' [*Keynes cites Hawtrey,* Monetary Reconstruction, *p. 105.*] It is characteristic of the impetuosity of the credit cycle that price movements tend to be cumulative, each movement promoting, up to a certain point, a further movement in the same direction. Professor Fisher's method may be adapted to deal with long-period trends in the value of gold but not with the, often more injurious, short-period oscillations of the credit cycle. Nevertheless, whilst it would not be advisable to postpone action until it was called for by an actual movement of prices, it would promote confidence and furnish an objective standard of value, if, an official index number having been compiled of such a character as to register the price of a standard composite commodity, the authorities were to adopt this composite commodity as their standard of value in the sense that they would employ all their resources to prevent a movement of its price by more than a certain percentage in either direction away from the normal, just as before the war they employed all their resources to prevent a movement in the price of gold by more than a certain percentage. The precise composition of the standard composite commodity could be modified from time to time in accordance with changes in the relative economic importance of its various components.

As regards the criteria, other than the actual trend of prices, which should determine the action of the controlling authority, it is beyond the scope of this volume to deal adequately with the diagnosis and analysis of the credit cycle. The more deeply that our researches penetrate into this subject, the more accurately shall we understand the right time and method for controlling credit expansion by bank rate or otherwise. But in the meantime we have a considerable and growing body of general experience upon which those in authority can base [148] their judgments. Actual price movements must of course provide the most important datum; but the state of employment, the volume of production, the effective demand for credit as felt by the banks, the rate of interest on investments of various types, the volume of new issues, the flow of cash into circulation, the statistics of foreign trade and the level of the exchanges must all be taken into account. The main point is that the *objective* of the authorities, pursued with such means as are at their command, should be the stability of prices.

It would at least be possible to avoid, for example, such action as has been taken lately (in Great Britain) whereby the supply of 'cash' has been deflated at a time when real balances were becoming inflated – action which has materially aggravated the severity of the late depression. We might be able to moderate very greatly the amplitude of the fluctuations if it was understood that the time to deflate the supply of cash is when real balances are falling, i.e. when prices are rising out of proportion to the increase, if any, in the volume of cash, and that the time to inflate the supply of cash is when real balances are rising, and not, as seems to be our present practice, the other way round.

How can we best combine this primary object with a maximum stability of the exchanges? Can we get the best of both worlds – stability of prices over long periods and stability of exchanges over short periods? It is the great advantage of the gold standard that it overcomes the excessive sensitiveness of the exchanges to temporary influences, which we analysed in chapter 3. Our object must be to secure this advantage, if we can, without committing ourselves to follow big movements in the value of gold itself.

I believe that we can go a long way in this direction if the Bank of England will take over the duty of regulating the price of gold, just as it already regulates the rate of discount. 'Regulate', but not 'peg'. The Bank of England should have a buying and a selling price for gold, just as it did before the war, and this price might remain unchanged for considerable periods, [149] just as bank rate does. But it would not be fixed or 'pegged' once and for all, any more than bank rate is fixed. The Bank's rate for gold would be announced every Thursday morning at the same time as its rate for discounting bills, with a difference between its buying and selling rates corresponding to the pre-war margin between £3. 17s 10½d per oz. and £3. 17s 9d per oz.; except that, in order to obviate too frequent changes in the rate, the difference might be wider than 1½d per oz. – say, ½ to 1 per cent. A willingness on the part of the Bank both to buy and to sell gold at rates fixed for the time being would keep the dollar–sterling exchange steady within corresponding limits, so that the exchange rate would not move with every breath of wind but only when the Bank had come to a considered judgment that a change was required for the sake of the stability of sterling prices.

If the bank rate and the gold rate in conjunction were leading to an excessive influx or an excessive efflux of gold, the Bank of England would have to decide whether the flow was due to an internal or to an external movement away from stability. To fix our ideas, let us suppose that gold is flowing outwards. If this seemed to be due to a tendency of sterling to depreciate in terms of commodities, the correct remedy would be to raise the bank rate. If, on the other hand, it was due to a tendency of gold to appreciate in terms of commodities, the correct remedy would be to raise the gold rate (i.e. the buying price for gold). If, however, the flow could be explained by seasonal, or other passing influences, then it should be allowed to continue (assuming, of course, that the Bank's gold reserves were equal to any probable calls on them) unchecked, to be [150] redressed later on by the corresponding reaction.

. . .

11 *The United States*

In the United States, as in Great Britain, the methods which are being actually pursued at the present time, half consciously and half unconsciously, are mainly on the lines I advocate. In practice the Federal Reserve Board often ignores the proportion of [154] its gold reserve to its liabilities and is influenced, in determining its discount policy, by the object of maintaining stability in prices, trade, and employment. Out of convention and conservatism it accepts gold. Out of prudence and understanding it buries it. Indeed the theory and investigation of the credit cycle have been taken up so much more enthusiastically and pushed so much further by the economists of the United States than by those of Great Britain, that it would be even more difficult for the Federal Reserve Board than for the Bank of England to ignore such ideas or to avoid being, half-consciously at least, influenced by them.

The theory on which the Federal Reserve Board is supposed to govern its discount policy, by reference to the influx and efflux of gold and the proportion of gold to liabilities, is as dead as mutton. It perished, and perished justly, as soon as the Federal Reserve Board began to ignore its ratio and to accept gold without allowing it to exercise its full influence, merely because an expansion of credit and prices seemed at that moment undesirable. From that day gold was demonetised by almost the last country which still continued to do it lip-service, and a dollar standard was set up on the pedestal of the Golden Calf. For the past two years the United States has *pretended* to maintain a gold standard. *In fact* it has established a dollar standard; and, instead of ensuring that the value of the dollar shall conform to that of gold, it makes provision, at great expense, that the value of gold shall conform to that of the dollar. This is the way by which a rich country is able to combine new wisdom with old prejudice. It can enjoy the latest scientific improvements, devised in the economic laboratory of Harvard, whilst leaving Congress to believe that no rash departure will be permitted from the hard money consecrated by the wisdom and experience of Dungi, Darius, Constantine, Lord Liverpool, and Senator Aldrich.   [155]

No doubt it is worth the expense – for those that can afford it. The cost of the fiction to the United States is not more than £100 million per annum and should not average in the long run above £50 million per annum. But there is in all such fictions a certain instability. When the accumulations of gold heap up beyond a certain point the suspicions of Congressmen may be aroused. One cannot be quite certain that some Senator might

not read and understand this book. Sooner or later the fiction
[156] will lose its value.

. . .

The notion, that America can get rid of her gold by showing a
greater readiness to make loans to foreign countries, is incomplete. This result will only follow if the loans are inflationary
loans, not provided for by the reduction of expenditure and
investment in other directions. Foreign investments formed out
of real savings will no more denude the United States of her
gold than they denude Great Britain of hers. But if the United
States places a large amount of dollar purchasing power in the
hands of foreigners, as a pure addition to the purchasing power
previously in the hands of her own nationals, then no doubt
prices will rise and we shall be back on the method of depreciating the dollar, just discussed, by a normal inflationary process.
Thus the invitation to the United States to deal with the problem of her gold by increasing her foreign investments will not
be effective unless it is intended as an invitation to inflate.

I argue, therefore, that the same policy which is wise for
Great Britain is wise for the United States, namely to aim at the
stability of the commodity value of the dollar rather than at
stability of the gold value of the dollar, and to effect the former
if necessary by varying the gold value of the dollar.

If Great Britain and the United States were both embarked
on this policy and if both were successful, our secondary desid-
eratum, namely the stability of the dollar–exchange standard,
would follow as a consequence. I agree with Mr Hawtrey that
the ideal state of affairs is an intimate co-operation between the
Federal Reserve Board and the Bank of England, as a result of
which stability of prices and of exchange would be achieved at
[158] the same time. But I suggest that it is wiser and more practical
that this should be allowed to develop out of experience and
mutual advantage, without either side binding itself to the
other. If the Bank of England aims primarily at the stability of
sterling, and the Federal Reserve Board at the stability of dollars, each authority letting the other into its confidence so far as
may be, better results will be obtained than if sterling is unalter-
ably fixed by law in terms of dollars and the Bank of England

is limited to using its influence on the Federal Reserve Board to keep dollars steady. A collaboration which is not free on both sides is likely to lead to dissensions, especially if the business of keeping dollars steady involves a heavy expenditure in burying unwanted gold.

We have reached a stage in the evolution of money when a 'managed' currency is inevitable, but we have not yet reached the point when the management can be entrusted to a single authority. The best we can do, therefore, is to have *two* managed currencies, sterling and dollars, with as close a collaboration as possible between the aims and methods of the managements.   [159]

27

CW 9, 'The Economic Consequences of Mr Churchill' (1925)

[*The gold standard had been suspended in 1919. Between 1919 and 1925 the pound floated against other currencies. Keynes was deeply opposed to the official policy – recommended by the influential Cunliffe Report of 1918 – of forcing up the exchange value of the pound against the dollar in order to re-link sterling to gold at the pre-war 'parity' of £1 = $4.80 dollars.[4] On 28 April 1925, the chancellor of the exchequer, Winston Churchill, announced Britain's return to the gold standard at the pre-war parity. Keynes's attack on the policy, published by the Hogarth Press, was reproduced in* Essays in Persuasion. *Keynes's prediction that employers would be driven to reducing wages and this would encounter widespread social resistance was spectacularly vindicated a year later when the TUC (Trade Union Congress) called Britain's first and only General Strike. This excerpt is taken from the CW version.*]

1 Why Unemployment Is Worse

World trade and home consumption are both moderately good – running on a level keel, midway between slump and boom. The United States has had a year of abundant prosperity; India and the Dominions are doing fairly well; in France and Italy unemployment is non-existent or negligible; and in Germany during the last six months the numbers receiving the dole have decreased rapidly, by more than half, to 4–5 per cent against our 10 per cent. The aggregate of world production is probably greater than at any time since 1914. Therefore our troubles are not due either to world-wide depression or to reduced consumption at home. And it is obvious what does cause them. It is a question of *relative price* here and abroad. The prices of our exports in the international market are too high. About this there is no difference of opinion.

Why are they too high? The orthodox answer is to blame it on the working man for working too little and getting too much. In some industries and some grades of labour, particularly the unskilled, this is true; and other industries, for example the railways, are over-staffed. But there is no more truth in it than there was a year ago. Moreover, it is not true in those [207] export industries where unemployment is greatest.

On the contrary, the explanation can be found for certain in another direction. For we know as a fact that the value of sterling money abroad has been raised by 10 per cent, whilst its purchasing power over British labour is unchanged. This alteration in the external value of sterling money has been the deliberate act of the government and the Chancellor of the Exchequer, and the present troubles of our export industries are the inevitable and predictable consequence of it.

The policy of improving the foreign-exchange value of sterling up to its pre-war value in gold from being about 10 per cent below it, means that, whenever we sell anything abroad, either the foreign buyer has to pay 10 per cent *more in his money* or we have to accept 10 per cent *less in our money*. That is to say, we have to reduce our sterling prices, for coal or iron or shipping freights or whatever it may be, by 10 per cent in order to be on a competitive level, unless prices rise elsewhere. Thus the policy of improving the exchange by 10 per cent involves a reduction of 10 per cent in the sterling receipts of our export industries.

Now, if these industries found that their expenses for wages and for transport and for rates and for everything else were falling 10 per cent at the same time, they could afford to cut their prices and would be no worse off than before. But of course, this does not happen. Since they use, and their employees consume, all kinds of articles produced at home, it is impossible for them to cut their prices 10 per cent, unless wages and expenses in home industries generally have fallen 10 per cent. Meanwhile, the weaker export industries are reduced to a bankrupt condition. Failing a fall in the value of gold itself, nothing can retrieve their position except a general fall of all internal prices and wages. Thus Mr Churchill's policy of improving the exchange by 10 per cent was, sooner or later, a policy of reducing everyone's wages by 2s in the £. He who [208] wills the end wills the means. What now faces the Government is the ticklish task of carrying out their own dangerous and unnecessary decision.

This table [*omitted*] shows that a year ago the cost of living and the level of wages in this country, expressed in terms of gold (i.e. reduced from their sterling value in proportion to the depreciation of the sterling exchange), were in conformity with the dollar cost of living in the United States. Since then the sterling exchange has been raised by 10 per cent, whilst there has been no appreciable change in the sterling cost of living and the sterling level of wages in this country compared with the dollar cost of living in the United States. It follows, of necessity, that our money wages and cost of living are now about 10 per cent too high. The government's policy has secured that we receive 10 per cent less sterling for our exports; yet our industrialists have to pay out in wages just as much as before, and their employees have to expend just as much as before to maintain their standard of life. The movement away from equilibrium began in October last and has proceeded, step by step, with the [209] improvement of the exchange – brought about first by the anticipation, and then by the fact, of the restoration of gold, and not by an improvement in the intrinsic value of sterling. The President of the Board of Trade has asserted in the House of Commons that the effect of the restoration of the gold standard upon our export trade has been 'all to the good'. The Chancellor of the Exchequer has expressed the opinion that the return to the gold standard is no more responsible for the condition of affairs in the coal industry than is the Gulf Stream. These statements are of the feather-brained order. It is open to ministers to argue that the restoration of gold is worth the sacrifice and that the sacrifice is temporary. They can also say, with truth, that the industries which are feeling the wind most have private troubles of their own. When a *general* cause operates, those which are weak for other reasons are toppled over. But because an epidemic of influenza carries off only those who have weak hearts, it is not permissible to say that the influenza is 'all to the good', or that it has no more to do with the mortality than the Gulf Stream has.

The effect has been the more severe because we were not free from trouble a year ago. Whilst, at that date, sterling wages and sterling cost of living were in conformity with values in the United States, they were already too high compared with those in some European countries. It was also probable that certain of our export industries were over-stocked both with plant and with labour, and that some transference of capital and of men into home industries was desirable and, in the long run, even inevitable. Thus we already had an awkward problem; and one of the arguments against raising the international value of sterling was the fact that it greatly aggravated, instead of mitigating, an existing disparity between internal and external values, and that, by committing us to a period of deflation, it necessarily postponed active measures of capital expansion at home, such as might facilitate the transference of labour into the home trades. British wages, measured in gold, are now 15 per cent higher than they were a year ago. The gold cost of living in England is now so high compared with what it is in Belgium, France, Italy, and Germany that the workers in those countries can accept a gold wage 30 per cent lower than what our

[210]

workers receive without suffering at all in the amount of their real wages. What wonder that our export trades are in trouble!

Our export industries are suffering because they are the *first* to be asked to accept the 10 per cent reduction. If *every one* was accepting a similar reduction at the same time, the cost of living would fall, so that the lower money wage would represent nearly the same real wage as before. But, in fact, there is no machinery for effecting a simultaneous reduction. Deliberately to raise the value of sterling money in England means, therefore, engaging in a struggle with each separate group in turn, with no prospect that the final result will be fair, and no guarantee that the stronger groups will not gain at the expense of the weaker.

The working classes cannot be expected to understand, better than Cabinet Ministers, what is happening. Those who are attacked first are faced with a depression of their standard of life, because the cost of living will not fall until all the others have been successfully attacked too; and, therefore, they are justified in defending themselves. Nor can the classes, which are first subjected to a reduction of money wages, be guaranteed that this will be compensated later by a corresponding fall in the cost of living, and will not accrue to the benefit of some other class. Therefore they are bound to resist so long as they can; and it must be war, until those who are economically weakest are beaten to the ground.

This state of affairs is not an inevitable consequence of a [211] decreased capacity to produce wealth. I see no reason why, with good management, real wages need be reduced on the average. It is the consequence of a misguided monetary policy.

11 *What Misled Mr Churchill*

The arguments [*above*] are not arguments against the gold standard as such. That is a separate discussion which I shall not touch here. They are arguments against having restored gold in conditions which required a substantial readjustment of all our money values. If Mr Churchill had restored gold by fixing the parity lower than the pre-war figure, or if he had waited until our money values were adjusted to the pre-war parity, then these particular arguments would have no force. But in doing what he did in the actual circumstances of last spring, he was just asking for trouble. For he was committing himself to force down money wages and all money values, without any idea how it was to be done. Why did he do such a silly thing?

Partly, perhaps, because he has no instinctive judgement to prevent him from making mistakes; partly because, lacking this instinctive judgement, he was deafened by the clamorous voices of conventional finance; and, most of all, because he was gravely misled by his experts.

His experts made, I think, two serious mistakes. In the first place I suspect that they miscalculated the degree of the maladjustment of money values, which would result from restoring sterling to its pre-war gold parity, because they attended to index numbers of prices which were irrelevant or inappropriate to the matter in hand. If you want to know whether sterling values are adjusting themselves to an improvement in the exchange, it is useless to consider, for example, the price of raw cotton in Liv-[212] erpool. This *must* adjust itself to a movement of the exchange, because, in the case of an imported raw material, the parity of international values is necessarily maintained almost hour by hour. But it is not sensible to argue from this that the money wages of dockers or of charwomen and the cost of postage or of travelling by train also adjust themselves hour by hour in accordance with the foreign exchanges. Yet this, I fancy, is what the Treasury did. They compared the usual wholesale index numbers here and in America, and – since these are made up to the extent of at least two-thirds from the raw materials of international commerce, the prices of which necessarily adjust themselves to the exchanges – the true disparity of internal prices was watered down to a fraction of its true value. This led them to think that the gap to be bridged was perhaps 2 or 3 per cent, instead of the true figure of 10 or 12 per cent, which was the indication given by the index numbers of the cost of living, of the level of wages, and of the prices of our manufactured exports – which indexes are a much better rough-and-ready guide for this purpose, particularly if they agree with one another, than are the index numbers of wholesale prices.

But I think that Mr Churchill's experts also misunderstood and underrated the technical difficulty of bringing about a general reduction of internal money values. When we raise the value of sterling by 10 per cent, we transfer about £1,000 million into the pockets of the rentiers out of the pockets of the rest of us, and we increase the real burden of the national debt by some £750 million (thus wiping out the benefit of all our laborious contributions to the Sinking Fund since the war). This, which is bad enough, is inevitable. But there would be no other bad consequences, if only there was some way of bringing about a simultaneous reduction of 10 per cent in all other money payments; when the process was complete, we should each of us have nearly the same real income as before. I think that the minds of his advisers still dwelt in the imaginary academic world, peopled by City editors, members of Cunliffe and [213] Currency Committees *et hoc genus omne*, where the necessary adjustments follow 'automatically' from a 'sound' policy by the Bank of England.

The theory is that depression in the export industries, which are admittedly hit first, coupled if necessary with dear money and credit restriction, *diffuse* themselves evenly and fairly rapidly throughout the whole community. But the professors of this theory do not tell us in plain language how the diffusion takes place.

Mr Churchill asked the Treasury Committee on the Currency to advise him on these matters. He declared in his budget speech that their report 'contains a reasoned marshalling of the arguments which have convinced His Majesty's Government'. Their arguments – if their vague and jejune meditations can be called such – are there for anyone to read. What they ought to have said, but did not say, can be expressed as follows:

Money wages, the cost of living, and the prices which we are asking for our exports have not adjusted themselves to the improvement in the exchange, which the expectation of your restoring the gold standard, in accordance with your repeated declarations, has already brought about. They are about 10 per cent too high. If, therefore, you fix the exchange at this gold parity, you must either gamble on a rise in gold prices abroad, which will induce foreigners to pay a higher gold price for our exports, or you are committing yourself to a policy of forcing down money wages and the cost of living to the necessary extent.

We must warn you that this latter policy is not easy. It is certain to involve unemployment and industrial disputes. If, as some people think, real wages were already too high a year ago, that is all the worse, because the amount of the necessary wage reductions in terms of money will be all the greater.

The gamble on a rise in gold prices abroad may quite likely succeed. But it is by no means certain, and you must be prepared for the other contingency. If you think that the advantages of the gold standard are so significant and so urgent that you are prepared to risk great unpopularity and to take stern administrative action in order to secure them, the course of events will probably be as follows.

To begin with, there will be great depression in the export industries. This, in itself, will be helpful, since it will produce an atmosphere favourable to the reduction of wages. The cost of living will fall somewhat. This will be helpful too, because it will give you a good argument in favour of reducing wages. Nevertheless, the cost of living will not fall sufficiently and, consequently, the export industries will not be able to reduce their prices sufficiently, until wages have fallen in the sheltered industries. Now, wages will not fall in the sheltered industries, merely because there is unemployment in the unsheltered industries. Therefore, you will have to see to it that there is unemployment in the sheltered industries also. The way to do this will be by credit restriction. By means of the restriction of credit by the Bank of England, you can deliberately intensify unemployment to any required degree, until wages *do* fall. When the process is complete the cost of living will have fallen too; and we shall then be, with luck, just where we were before we started.

We ought to warn you, though perhaps this is going a little outside our proper sphere, that it will not be safe politically to admit that you are intensifying unemployment deliberately in order to reduce wages. Thus you will have to ascribe what is happening to every conceivable cause except the true one. We

[214]

estimate that about two years may elapse before it will be safe
for you to utter in public one single word of truth. By that time
you will either be out of office, or the adjustment, somehow or
other, will have been carried through.

III *The Policy of the Bank of England*

The effect of a high exchange is to diminish the sterling prices
both of imports and of exports. The fall in the price of imported
food tends to reduce the cost of living. It is surprising, perhaps,
that it has not had more influence in this direction. Probably
the explanation is to be found partly in the world-wide rise of
food prices, partly in a time-lag (in which case we may look
forward to some further fall in the cost of living in the near
future), and partly in the fact that by the time a commodity,
even an imported commodity, reaches the consumer, its cost
has been considerably affected by the various home services
performed on it. Nevertheless, the table printed in the first
chapter shows that some reduction of money wages on this
score is, in fact, already justifiable – though not, for that reason, much the easier to accomplish. Since the higher exchange [215]
does not help us to *afford* a higher real wage, it only grants this
boon to the workers in order that it may be snatched away
again as soon as possible. Meanwhile, the apparent cheapness
of foreign products causes us to buy more of them. At the same
time, the fall in the sterling price of exports reduces the business of the export industries.

The result is both to encourage imports and to discourage
exports, thus turning the balance of trade against us. It is at this
stage that the Bank of England becomes interested; for if nothing was done we should have to pay the adverse balance in
gold. The Bank of England has applied, accordingly, two effective remedies. The first remedy is to put obstacles in the way of
our usual lending abroad by means of an embargo on foreign
loans and, recently, on colonial loans also; and the second
remedy is to encourage the United States to lend us money
by maintaining the unprecedented situation of a bill rate 1 per
cent higher in London than in New York.

The efficacy of these two methods for balancing our account is beyond doubt – I believe that they might remain efficacious for a considerable length of time. For we start with a wide margin of strength. Before the war our capacity to lend abroad was, according to the Board of Trade, about £181 million, equivalent to £280 million at the present price level; and even in 1923 the Board of Trade estimated our net surplus at £102 million. Since new foreign investments bring in no immediate return, it follows that we can reduce our exports by £100 million a year, without any risk of insolvency, provided we reduce our foreign investments by the same amount. So far as the maintenance of the gold standard is concerned, it is a matter of indifference whether we have £100 million worth of foreign investment or £100 million worth of unemployment. If those who used to produce exports lose their job, nevertheless, our financial equilibrium remains perfect, and the Governor of the Bank of England runs no risk of losing gold, provided that [216] the loans, which were formerly paid over in the shape of those exports, are curtailed to an equal extent. Moreover, our credit as a borrower is still very good. By paying a sufficiently high rate of interest, we can not only meet any deficit but the governor can borrow, in addition, whatever quantity of gold it may amuse him to publish in his weekly return.

The President of the Board of Trade calculates that, during the year ended last May, it is probable that there was no actual deficit on our trade account, which was about square. If this is correct, there must be a substantial deficit now. In addition, the embargo on foreign investment is only partially successful. It cannot hold back all types of foreign issues and it cannot prevent British investors from purchasing securities direct from New York. It is here, therefore, that the Bank of England's other remedy comes in. By maintaining discount rates in London at a sufficient margin above discount rates in New York, it can induce the New York money market to lend a sufficient sum to the London money market to balance both our trade deficit and the foreign investments which British investors are still buying in spite of the embargo. Besides, when once we have offered high rates of interest to attract funds from the

New York short-loan market, we have to continue them, even though we have no need to increase our borrowings, in order to retain what we have already borrowed.

. . .   [217]

To pay for unemployment by changing over from being a lending country to being a borrowing country is admittedly a disastrous course, and I do not doubt that the authorities of the Bank of England share this view. They dislike the embargo on foreign issues, and they dislike having to attract short-loan money from New York. They may do these things to gain a breathing space; but, if they are to live up to their own principles, they must use the breathing space to effect what are euphemistically called 'the fundamental adjustments'. With this object in view there is only one step which lies within their power – namely, to restrict credit. This, in the circumstances, is the orthodox policy of the gold party; the adverse trade balance indicates that our prices are too high, and the way to bring them down is by dear money and the restriction of credit. When this medicine has done its work, there will no longer be any need to restrict foreign loans or to borrow abroad.

Now what does this mean in plain language? Our problem is to reduce money wages and, through them, the cost of living, with the idea that, when the circle is complete, real wages will be as high, or nearly as high, as before. By what *modus operandi* does credit restriction attain this result?

In no other way than by the deliberate intensification of unemployment. The object of credit restriction, in such a case, is to withdraw from employers the financial means to employ labour at the existing level of prices and wages. The policy can only attain its end by intensifying unemployment without limit, until the workers are ready to accept the necessary reduction of money wages under the pressure of hard facts.

This is the so-called 'sound' policy, which is demanded as a result of the rash act of pegging sterling at a gold value, which it did not – measured in its purchasing power over British labour – possess as yet. It is a policy, nevertheless, from which any humane or judicious person must shrink. So far as I can judge, the Governor of the Bank of England shrinks from it.

[218] But what is he to do, swimming, with his boat burnt, between the devil and the deep sea? At present, it appears, he compromises. He applies the 'sound' policy half-heartedly; he avoids calling things by their right names; and he hopes – this is his best chance – that something will turn up.

The Bank of England works with so much secrecy and so much concealment of important statistics that it is never easy to state with precision what it is doing. The credit restriction already in force has been effected in several ways which are partly interdependent. First, there is the embargo on new issues which probably retards the normal rate of the circulation of money; then in March the bank rate was raised; more recently market rate was worked up nearer to bank rate; lastly – and far the most important of all – the Bank has manoeuvred its assets and liabilities in such a way as to reduce the amount of cash available to the clearing banks as a basis for credit. This last is the essential instrument of credit restriction. Failing direct information, the best reflection of the amount of this restriction is to be found in the deposits of the clearing banks. The tendency of these to fall indicates some significant degree of restriction. Owing, however, to seasonal fluctuations and to the artificial character of the end-June returns, it is not yet possible to estimate with accuracy how much restriction has taken place in the last three months. So far as one can judge, the amount of direct restriction is not yet considerable. But no one can say how much more restriction may become necessary if we continue on our present lines.

Nevertheless, even these limited measures are responsible, in my opinion, for an important part of the recent intensification of unemployment. Credit restriction is an incredibly powerful instrument, and even a little of it goes a long way – especially in circumstances where the opposite course is called for. The policy of deliberately intensifying unemployment with a view to forcing wage reductions is already partly in force, and the tragedy of our situation lies in the fact that, from the misguided standpoint which has been officially adopted, this course is theoretically justifiable. No section of labour will readily accept lower wages merely in response to sentimental speeches,

[219]

however genuine, by Mr Baldwin. We are depending for the reduction of wages on the pressure of unemployment and of strikes and lockouts; and in order to make sure of this result we are deliberately intensifying the unemployment.

The Bank of England is *compelled* to curtail credit by all the rules of the gold standard game. It is acting conscientiously and 'soundly' in doing so. But this does not alter the fact that to keep a tight hold on credit – and no one will deny that the Bank is doing that – necessarily involves intensifying unemployment in the present circumstances of this country. What we need to restore prosperity today is an easy credit policy. We want to encourage business men to enter on new enterprises, not, as we are doing, to discourage them. Deflation does not reduce wages 'automatically'. It reduces them by causing unemployment. The proper object of dear money is to check an incipient boom. Woe to those whose faith leads them to use it to aggravate a depression!

IV *The Case of the Coal Industry* [220]

. . .

I should pick out coal as being above all others a victim of our monetary policy. On the other hand, it is certainly true that the reason why the coal industry presents so dismal a picture to the eye is because it has other troubles which have weakened its power of resistance and have left it no margin of strength with which to support a new misfortune.

In these circumstances the colliery owners propose that the gap should be bridged by a reduction of wages, irrespective of a reduction in the cost of living – that is to say, by a lowering in the standard of life of the miners. They are to make this sacrifice to meet circumstances for which they are in no way responsible and over which they have no control.

It is a grave criticism of our way of managing our economic affairs, that this should seem to anyone to be a reasonable proposal; though it is equally unreasonable that the colliery owner [222] should suffer the loss, except on the principle that it is the capitalist who bears the risk. If miners were free to transfer themselves to other industries, if a collier out of work or underpaid could offer himself as a baker, a bricklayer, or a railway porter at a lower wage than is now current in these industries, it would be another matter. But notoriously they are not so free. Like other victims of economic transition in past times, the miners are to be offered the choice between starvation and submission, the fruits of their submission to accrue to the benefit of other classes. But in view of the disappearance of an effective mobility of labour and of a competitive wage level between different industries, I am not sure that they are not worse placed in some ways than their grandfathers were.

Why should coal miners suffer a lower standard of life than other classes of labour? They may be lazy, good-for-nothing fellows who do not work so hard or so long as they should. But is there any evidence that they are more lazy or more good-for-nothing than other people?

On grounds of social justice no case can be made out for reducing the wages of the miners. They are the victims of the economic juggernaut. They represent in the flesh the 'fundamental adjustments' engineered by the Treasury and the Bank of England to satisfy the impatience of the City fathers to bridge the 'moderate gap' between $4.40 and $4.86. *They* (and others to follow) are the 'moderate sacrifice' still necessary to ensure the stability of the gold standard. The plight of the coal miners is the first, but not – unless we are very lucky – the last, of the economic consequences of Mr Churchill.

The truth is that we stand midway between two theories of economic society. The one theory maintains that wages should be fixed by reference to what is 'fair' and 'reasonable' as between classes. The other theory – the theory of the economic juggernaut – is that wages should be settled by economic pressure, otherwise called 'hard facts', and that our vast machine should crash along, with regard only to its equilibrium as a [223] whole, and without attention to the chance consequences of the journey to individual groups.

The gold standard, with its dependence on pure chance, its faith in 'automatic adjustments', and its general regardlessness of social detail, is an essential emblem and idol of those who sit in the top tier of the machine. I think that they are immensely

rash in their regardlessness, in their vague optimism and comfortable belief that nothing really serious ever happens. Nine
times out of ten, nothing really serious does happen – merely a
little distress to individuals or to groups. But we run a risk of
the tenth time (and are stupid into the bargain), if we continue
to apply the principles of an economics, which was worked out
on the hypotheses of *laissez-faire* and free competition, to a
society which is rapidly abandoning these hypotheses.

v *Is There a Remedy?*

The monetary policy, announced in the budget, being the real
source of our industrial troubles, it is impossible to recommend
any truly satisfactory course except its reversal. Nevertheless,
amongst the alternatives still open to this government, some
courses are better than others.

One course is to pursue the so-called 'sound' policy vigorously, with the object of bringing about 'the fundamental
adjustments' in the orthodox way by further restricting credit
and raising the bank rate in the autumn if necessary, thus intensifying unemployment and using every other weapon in our
hands to force down money wages, trusting in the belief that
when the process is finally complete the cost of living will have
fallen also, thus restoring average real wages to their former
level. If this policy can be carried through it will be, in a sense,
successful, though it will leave much injustice behind it on account
of the inequality of the changes it will effect, the stronger
groups gaining at the expense of the weaker. For the method
of economic pressure, since it bears most hardly on the weaker
industries where wages are already relatively low, tends to [224]
increase the existing disparities between the wages of different
industrial groups.

The question is how far public opinion will allow such a
policy to go. It would be politically impossible for the Government to admit that it was deliberately intensifying unemployment,
even though the members of the Currency Committee were to
supply them with an argument for it. On the other hand, it is
possible for deflation to produce its effects without being recognised. Deflation, once started ever so little, is cumulative in

its progress. If pessimism becomes generally prevalent in the business world, the slower circulation of money resulting from this can carry deflation a long way further, without the Bank having either to raise the bank rate or to reduce its deposits. And since the public always understands particular causes better than general causes, the depression will be attributed to the industrial disputes which will accompany it, to the Dawes Scheme, to China, to the inevitable consequences of the Great War, to tariffs, to high taxation, to anything in the world except the general monetary policy which has set the whole thing going.

Moreover, this course need not be pursued in a clear-cut way. A furtive restriction of credit by the Bank of England can be coupled with vague cogitations on the part of Mr Baldwin (who has succeeded to the position in our affections formerly occupied by Queen Victoria) as to whether social benevolence does not require him to neutralise the effects of this by a series of illogical subsidies. Queen Baldwin's good heart will enable us to keep our tempers, whilst the serious work goes on behind the scenes. The budgetary position will render it impossible for the subsidies to be big enough to make any real difference. And in the end, unless there is a social upheaval, 'the fundamental adjustments' will duly take place.

Some people may contemplate this forecast with equanimity. I do not. It involves a great loss of social income, whilst it is going on, and will leave behind much social injustice when it is finished. The best, indeed the only, hope lies in the possibility that in this world, where so little can be foreseen, something may turn up – which leads me to my alternative suggestions. Could we not *help* something to turn up?

There are just two features of the situation which are capable of being turned to our advantage. The first is financial – if the value of gold would fall in the outside world, that would render unnecessary any important change in the level of wages here. The second is industrial – if the cost of living would fall *first*, our consciences would be clear in asking labour to accept a lower money wage, since it would then be evident that the reduction was not part of a plot to reduce real wages.

When the return to the gold standard was first announced, many authorities agreed that we were gambling on rising prices in the United States. The rise has not taken place, so far. Moreover, the policy of the Bank of England has been calculated to steady prices in the United States rather than to raise them. The fact that American banks can lend their funds in London at a high rate of interest tends to keep money rates in New York higher than they would be otherwise, and to draw to London, instead of to New York, the oddments of surplus gold in the world markets. Thus our policy has been to relieve New York of the pressure of cheap money and additional gold which would tend otherwise to force their prices upwards. The abnormal difference between money rates in London and New York is preventing the gold standard from working even according to its own principles. According to orthodox doctrine, when prices are too high in *A* as compared with *B*, gold flows out from *A* and into *B*, thus lowering prices in *A* and *raising them in B*, so that an upward movement in *B*'s prices meets halfway the downward movement in *A*'s.

At present the policy of the Bank of England prevents this from happening. I suggest, therefore, that they should reverse [226] this policy. Let them reduce the bank rate, and cease to restrict credit. If, as a result of this, the 'bad' American money, which is now a menace to the London money market, begins to flow back again, let us pay it off in gold or, if necessary, by using the dollar credits which the Treasury and the Bank of England have arranged in New York. It would be better to pay in gold, because it would be cheaper and because the flow of actual gold would have more effect on the American price level. If we modified the rules, which now render useless three-quarters of our stock of gold, we could see with equanimity a loss of £60 million or £70 million in gold – which would make a great difference to conditions elsewhere. There is no object in paying 4½ per cent interest on floating American balances which can leave us at any moment, in order to use these balances to buy and hold idle and immobilised gold.

Gold could not flow out on this scale, unless at the same time the Bank of England was abandoning the restriction of credit and was replacing the gold by some other asset, e.g. Treasury bills. That is to say, the Bank would have to abandon the attempt to bring about the fundamental adjustments by the methods of economic pressure and the deliberate intensification of unemployment. Therefore, taken by itself, this policy might be open to the criticism that it was staking too much on the expectation of higher prices in America. To meet this, I suggest that Mr Baldwin should face the facts frankly and sincerely . . . [say to labour]:

. . .

> This is not an attack on real wages. We have raised the value of sterling 10 per cent. This means that money wages must fall 10 per cent. But it also means, when the adjustment is complete, that the cost of living will fall about 10 per cent. In this case there will have been no serious fall in real wages. Now there are two alternative ways of bringing about the reduction of money wages. One way is to apply economic pressure and to intensify unemployment by credit restriction, until wages are *forced down*. This is a hateful and disastrous way, because of its unequal effects on the stronger and on the weaker groups, and because of the economic and social waste whilst it is in progress. The other way is to effect a *uniform* reduction of wages by *agreement*, on the understanding that this shall not mean in the long run any fall in average real wages below what they were in the first quarter of this year. The practical difficulty is that money wages and the cost of living are interlocked. The cost of living cannot fall until *after* money wages have fallen. Money wages must fall *first*, in order to allow the cost of living to fall. Can we not agree, therefore, to have a uniform initial reduction of money wages throughout the whole range of employment, including government and municipal employment, of (say) 5 per cent, which reduction shall not hold good unless after an interval it has been compensated by a fall in the cost of living?

If Mr Baldwin were to make this proposal, the trade union leaders would probably ask him at once what he intended to do about money payments other than wages – rents, profits, and interest. As regards rents and profits he can reply that these are not fixed in terms of money and will therefore fall, when measured in money, step by step with prices. The worst of this reply is that rents and profits, like wages, are sticky and may not fall quick enough to help the transition as much as they should. As regards the interest on bonds, however, and particularly the interest on the national debt, he has no answer at all. For it is of [228] the essence of any policy to lower prices that it benefits the receivers of interest at the expense of the rest of the community; this consequence of deflation is deeply embedded in our system of money contract. On the whole, I do not see how labour's objection can be met except by the rough-and-ready expedient of levying an additional income tax of 1s in the £ on all income other than from employments, which should continue until real wages had recovered to their previous level.

If the proposal to effect a voluntary all-round reduction of wages, whilst sound in principle, is felt to be too difficult to achieve in practice, then, for my part, I should be inclined to stake everything on an attempt to raise prices in the outside world – that is on a reversal of the present policy of the Bank of England. This, I understand from their July *Monthly Review*, is also the recommendation of the high authorities of the Midland Bank.

That there should be grave difficulties in all these suggestions is inevitable. Any plan, such as the government has adopted, for deliberately altering the value of money, must, in modern economic conditions, come up against objections of justice and expediency. They are suggestions to mitigate the harsh consequences of a mistake; but they cannot undo the mistake. They will not commend themselves to those pessimists who believe that it is the level of real wages, and not merely of money wages, which is the proper object of attack. I mention them because our present policy of deliberately intensifying unemployment by keeping a tight hold on credit, just when on other grounds it ought to be relaxed, so as to force adjustments by using the weapon of economic necessity against individuals and against particular industries, is a policy which the country would never permit if it knew what was being done.   [229]

28

CW 9, 'Can Lloyd George Do It?' (1929)

[*In the run-up to the General Election of 1929, the Liberal leader Lloyd George had pledged a Liberal government to 'reduce the terrible figures of the workless in the course of a single year to normal proportions' by means of a large infrastructure programme. Very roughly, this meant reducing unemployment of the insured workforce from 10 per cent, where it had stuck since 1923, to 5 per cent. Keynes endorsed the policy, and this essay, co-written with Hubert Henderson, is an attempt to demonstrate its feasibility. It contains an early (non-numerical) statement of the multiplier. It is the most political, and linguistically striking, of Keynes's policy essays, and is the most succinct statement in all his writings of what a 'Keynesian' approach to the problem of slump would have been. It was in the debates surrounding the issue of this pamphlet that Keynes remarked: 'Mr Baldwin has invented the formidable argument that you must not do anything because it will mean that you will not be able to do anything else.'*]

I Mr Lloyd George's Pledge

Mr Lloyd George's pledge to reduce unemployment has been received by the great public with remarkable sympathy and enthusiasm. Some people have a suspicion that it must, surely, be a little exaggerated. But almost everyone, including the other political parties, have a much stronger suspicion that [88] there is probably something in it after all.

. . .

In this pamphlet we propose to examine the various reasons for doubt and hesitation and the criticisms which have been offered in recent weeks; and we shall try to answer the questions which reasonable men are asking. We shall not shirk any of the difficulties, even when it is not easy to express the answer in popular language.

We hope to show that the Liberal policy is not only common sense, but follows, as the appropriate remedy, from a far-reaching analysis of the fundamentals of our position.

Is the pledge too optimistic? Can Lloyd George do it?

No one can safely say beforehand what delays ingenious obstruction can interpose in getting on with business which will require a certain amount of legislation. But provided Mr Lloyd George is able to get going without delay and without obstruction – and that is what the fulfilment of his pledge within his limit of time assumes – our conclusion will be that his optimism is reasonable.

We believe that the cumulative effect of renewed prosperity will surpass expectations. It may well turn out in practice that a smaller programme than that outlined in *We Can Conquer Unemployment* will be sufficient to set the ball rolling, and to shift the whole outlook of the country from depression to prosperity. The patient looks sick. But once he turns the corner, the rapidity of his convalescence may astonish even the doctors who have cured him.

Indeed, the most solid reason for hesitation as to the fulfilment of the pledge within the stated period of time we find, not in the difficulty of finding work to do or in the difficulty of financing it, but in the 'transfer' problem – in the task of shifting men from industries where they are permanently redundant and settling them in their new work.

But this difficulty, if it proves such, is a reason not for delay, [89] for holding back, or for timidity, but for pushing on with redoubled efforts. For the longer we delay, the more difficult will the task become and the harder will it be to employ those who have been forced into long-continued habits of unemployment.

. . .

ii *The Common Sense of the Problem*

The Liberal policy is one of plain common sense. The Conservative belief that there is some law of nature which prevents men from being employed, that it is 'rash' to employ men, and [90] that it is financially 'sound' to maintain a tenth of the population in idleness for an indefinite period, is crazily improbable – the sort of thing which no man could believe who had not had his head fuddled with nonsense for years and years.

The objections which are raised are mostly not the objections of experience or of practical men. They are based on highly abstract theories – venerable, academic inventions, half misunderstood by those who are applying them today, and based on assumptions which are contrary to the facts.

When Mr Baldwin discourses on this subject, it not only *is* nonsense that he talks, but it looks like nonsense to any simple-minded person who considers it with a fresh, unprejudiced mind. There is work to do; there are men to do it. Why not bring them together? No, says Mr Baldwin. There are mysterious, unintelligible reasons of high finance and economic theory why this is impossible. It would be most rash. It would probably ruin the country. Abra would rise, cadabra would fall. Your food would cost you more. If everyone were to be employed, it would be just like the war over again. And even if everyone was employed, how can you be perfectly sure that they would still be employed three years hence? If we build houses to cover our heads, construct transport systems to carry our goods, drain our lands, protect our coasts, what will there be left for our children to do? No, cries Mr Baldwin, it would be most unjust. The more work we do now the less there will be left to do hereafter. Unemployment is the lot of man. This generation must take its fair share of it without grousing. For the more the fewer, and the higher the less.

Yet, in truth, Mr Baldwin and his colleagues are not more capable of expounding the true economic science of the matter than they would be of explaining to you the latest propositions of Einstein. They would be much safer on the ground floor of common sense where Mr Lloyd George – fortified, as it happens, by a certain amount of economic science as well – has [91] encamped his battalions.

Our main task, therefore, will be to confirm the reader's instinct that what *seems* sensible *is* sensible, and what *seems* nonsense *is* nonsense. We shall try to show him that the conclusion, that if new forms of employment are offered more men will be employed, is as obvious as it sounds and contains no hidden snags; that to set unemployed men to work on useful tasks does what it appears to do, namely, increases the national wealth; and that the notion, that we shall, for intricate reasons, ruin ourselves financially if we use this means to increase our well-being, is what it looks like – a bogy.

III *The Facts of Unemployment*

Except for a brief recovery in 1924 before the return to the gold standard, one-tenth or more of the working population of this country have been unemployed for eight years – a fact unprecedented in our history. The number of insured persons counted by the Ministry of Labour as out of work has never been less than one million since the initiation of their statistics in 1923. Today (April 1929) 1,140,000 workpeople are unemployed.

This level of unemployment is costing us out of the Unemployment Fund a cash disbursement of about £50 million a year. This does not include poor relief. Since 1921 we have paid out to the unemployed in cash a sum of about £500 million – and have got literally nothing for it. This sum would have built a million houses; it is nearly double the whole of the accumulated savings of the Post Office Savings Bank; it would build a third of all the roads in the country; it far exceeds the total value of all the mines, of every description, which we possess; it would be enough to revolutionise the industrial equipment of the country; or to proceed from what is heavy to what is lighter, it would provide every third family in the country with a motor-car or would furnish a fund enough to allow the whole population to attend cinemas for nothing to the end of time.   [92]

But this is not nearly all the waste. There is the far greater loss to the unemployed themselves, represented by the difference between the dole and a full working wage, and by the loss of strength and morale. There is the loss in profits to employers and in taxation to the Chancellor of the Exchequer. There is the incalculable loss of retarding for a decade the economic progress of the whole country.

The Census of Production of 1924 calculated that the average value of the net annual output of a British working man when employed is about £220. On this basis the waste through unemployment since 1921 has mounted up to approximately £2,000 million, a sum which would be nearly sufficient to build all the railways in the country twice over. It would pay off our debt to America twice over. It is more than the total sum that the Allies are asking from Germany for reparations.

It is important to know and appreciate these figures because they put the possible cost of Mr Lloyd George's schemes into its true perspective. He calculates that a development programme of £100 million a year will bring back 500,000 men into employment. *This expenditure is not large in proportion to the waste and loss accruing year by year* through unemployment, as can be seen by comparing it with the figures quoted above. It only represents 5 per cent of the loss already accumulated on account of unemployment since 1921. It is equal to about 2½ per cent of the national income. If the experiment were to be continued at the rate of £100 million per annum for three years, and if the whole of it were to be entirely wasted, the annual interest payable on it hereafter would increase the budget by less than 2 per cent. In short, it is a *very modest programme*. The idea that it represents a desperate risk to cure a moderate evil is the reverse of the truth. It is a negligible risk to cure a monstrous anomaly.

Nothing has been included in the programme which cannot be justified as worth doing for its own sake. Yet even if half of it were to be wasted, *we should still be better off*. Was there ever a stronger case for a little boldness, for taking a risk if there be one?

[93]

It may seem very wise to sit back and wag the head. But while we wait, the unused labour of the workless is not piling up to our credit in a bank, ready to be used at some later date. It is running irrevocably to waste; it is irretrievably lost. Every puff of Mr Baldwin's pipe costs us thousands of pounds.

IV *The Liberal Programme*

The Liberal policy of dealing with unemployment by a vigorous policy of national development aims, on the one hand, at providing immediate jobs for a large number of men, and, on the other, at lifting business and industry out of the rut into which they have fallen and setting them again on the high road of progress along which they should then be able to move forward under their own steam.

Such large arrears of national development have been allowed to accumulate, that there is enough work waiting to keep the programme going for a considerable time; more than enough to bridge the period during which men are being transferred from old industries to new and the country's industrial methods are being rationalised. The government themselves take the view that the difficulties facing us are not of a permanent character, but look like covering a two- to five-year period. In particular, the Minister of Labour has pointed out that in the course of the next five years the pressure of new entrants into industry from the growing generation will be falling very materially. Thus it is no argument against the policy that it will be on a larger scale than could be maintained *permanently.*

. . .

It is difficult to say with certainty, in advance, which of the [94] projects are the most urgent, the most practical and the more capable of being put into execution with the least delay. In order to minimise the amount of 'transfer' of labour required, it will be of great importance to select a *well-balanced* programme.

. . .

[*The pamphlet summarized the proposals as follows: transport modernization, housing, telephone development, electrical development and land drainage (pp. 95–9).*]

VI *How Much Employment Will the Liberal Plan Provide?*

In examining the Liberal claim, two distinct points arise, namely, (1) the amount of employment which a given expenditure would provide, and (2) the suitability of the employment to those who are now out of work.   [102]

On the first point, the calculations of *We Can Conquer Unemployment* have been the subject of a controversy which has resulted in their vindication. It will be convenient, therefore, to take this point first.

The amount of employment for each 1 million
The Liberal pamphlet claims that each million pounds spent annually on road improvements would employ, directly or indirectly, 5,000 workpeople. The passage in which this claim is made runs as follows:

> Expert opinion is that some 80 per cent of total expenditure represents the amounts paid directly or indirectly in wages. This would mean some 5,500 men per £1 million of total expenditure. Of these, from 2,000 to 2,500 would be employed directly, and the remainder in production of materials and their transport. A very safe total figure is 5,000 men per annum for every £1 million.

[103]   . . . .

The importance of indirect employment
There is nothing fanciful or fine-spun about the proposition that the construction of roads entails a demand for road materials, which entails a demand for labour and also for other commodities, which, in their turn, entail a demand for labour. Such reactions are of the very essence of the industrial process. Why, the first step towards a right understanding of the economic world is to realise how far-reaching such reactions are, to appreciate how vast is the range of trades and occupations which contribute to the production of the commonest commodities. That a demand for a suit of clothes implies a demand for cloth; that a demand for cloth implies [105]   a demand for yarns and tops, and so for wool; that the services of farmers, merchants, engineers, miners, transport workers, clerks, are all involved – this is the ABC of economic science. Yet our ministers and our Industrial Transference Boards argue as though the making of a suit of clothes employed none outside the tailors' shops. Such are the elementary fallacies by which our policy has been dominated in recent years.

. . .

The cumulative force of trade activity
But this is not the whole of the story. In addition to the indirect employment with which we have been dealing, a policy of development would promote employment in other ways. The

fact that many workpeople who are now unemployed would be receiving wages instead of unemployment pay would mean an increase in effective purchasing power which would give a general stimulus to trade. Moreover, the greater trade activity would make for further trade activity; for the forces of prosperity, like those of trade depression, work with a cumulative effect. When trade is slack there is a tendency to postpone placing orders, a reluctance to lay in stocks, a general hesitation to go forward or take risks. When, on the other hand, the wheels of trade begin to move briskly the opposite set of forces comes into play, a mood favourable to enterprise and capital extensions [106] spreads through the business community, and the expansion of trade gains accordingly a gathering momentum.

It is not possible to measure effects of this character with any sort of precision, and little or no account of them is, therefore, taken in *We Can Conquer Unemployment.*[5] But, in our opinion, these effects are of immense importance. For this reason we believe that the effects on employment of a given capital expenditure would be far larger than the Liberal pamphlet assumes. These considerations have a bearing, it should be observed, on the time factor in Mr Lloyd George's pledge. It is a mistake to suppose that a long interval would elapse after, let us say, the work of road construction had been commenced before the full effect on employment would be produced. In the economic world, 'coming events cast their shadows before', and the knowledge that large schemes of work were being undertaken would give an immediate fillip to the whole trade and industry of the country.

The suitability of the employment

One of the commonest objections brought against the policy of development is that the majority of the unemployed are not fitted for the kind of work which would be offered.

This objection is only plausible if the whole factor of indirect employment is ignored. To argue as though it were proposed to put the great mass of the unemployed on outdoor work like road construction is a mere caricature of the Liberal scheme. As Mr Lloyd George has shown, no fewer than forty-seven different industries play their part in the building of roads, and the greater part of the employment which road building would provide would be in these forty-seven industries, and not on the roads themselves. It is irrelevant, therefore, to point out that only a proportion of the unemployed are fitted for heavy labouring work.

[107]   It is equally irrelevant to point out that only a small part of the unemployment figures represents workpeople who can be said to be permanently unemployed, and that the majority are either on short time or have been out of work for a short period only, and have reason to hope that they may again obtain employment in their own trades. This fact makes the task simpler and not more difficult. Development expenditure will give a wide and far-reaching stimulus to industry, and will enable many industries to re-absorb the unemployed or short-time surplus which now attaches to them. This will mean fully as genuine a reduction of unemployment as the absorption of people in new occupations.

For example, the development scheme will involve a large demand for iron and steel. To meet this demand it will not be necessary for the iron and steel industry to draw in labour unfamiliar with the trade. There is a sufficient margin of workpeople unemployed or on short-time attached to it. But the absorption of this margin will mean a genuine reduction of unemployment. It is untrue, therefore, to say that men unemployed for short periods only are not 'available' for development schemes. Those on short time in the iron and steel industry are certainly available. Moreover, the substitution of full-time for short-time will mean both in reality and statistically, a reduction of unemployment.

The comparative constancy of the aggregate unemployment figures for the past eight years conceals the most significant changes in their distribution among industries. In 1924 there were nearly 1,200,000 men on the books of the colliery companies; in August 1928 there were less than 900,000. The number of miners unemployed was only 26,000 at the former date, and nearly 300,000 at the latter. It has since fallen to 145,000, partly owing to increased work at the mines, but mainly owing to transference to other occupations. In building, on the other hand, unemployment increased from 64,000 in March 1926 to 104,000 in March 1929; in works of construction such as road-making the change in the same period is from 26,000 to 37,000.

The existing unemployment is not of such a character that [108] a general fillip to trade, concentrated in the first instance on the building and contracting industries, is an inappropriate remedy. The unemployment is somewhat widely spread, and transference is duly proceeding out of the industries where the curtailment of opportunity looks like lasting. It is the general failure of industry as a whole to show absorptive power which is keeping the aggregate of unemployment at so high a figure. [109]
. . .

VII *What Will It Cost?*

Mr Lloyd George has given a pledge that the execution of his programme will not mean an addition to taxation. He has added that, of course, this does not mean that it will cost nothing, but that the cost will be less than the money which it will save in other directions *plus* the buoyancy of the revenue attributable to it *plus* economies on such things as armaments.

Perhaps this part of his pledge has attracted the most criticism from the cold-footed. But this must mean that his critics have not tried to work out the sum. We think he could safely have promised that it will cost *much less*.

Let us begin by weighting the scales against him as much as we can. Let us assume (1) that his programme costs £300 million before it is finished; (2) that not a single item in it brings in one penny of return; and (3) that we are thinking of the gain or loss, not to the national income or well-being, but to the budget in the narrowest sense of the term. Let us assume, further, that the necessary loans cost 6% per annum for interest and sinking fund.

On these assumptions, which include the fantastic hypothesis that you can spend £300 million in the course of three years on the best schemes of developing this country which can be thought of, without any of them bringing in a penny of revenue, the cost to the budget will be £18 million a year.

This sum is about 2 per cent of the existing revenue. If [110] increasing the employed population by 5 per cent were to raise the yield of the present taxes by 1½ per cent, and if expenditure on armaments were to be reduced by 7½ per cent, the bill would be met.

But this is, of course, far beyond what Mr Lloyd George is pledging himself to accomplish. For he is relying on the actual character of his programme to cost much less than £18 million.

In the first place, the road developments will be financed entirely out of 'betterment' and by pledging the existing assigned revenues of the Road Fund; so that they will cost the budget nothing.

In the second place, housing schemes, which are much the most expensive part of the programme, will, though they need a subsidy, bring in in the shape of rents an appreciable return on the money spent.

. . .

In the third place, many of the miscellaneous items in the programme, as, for example, telephones and Trade Facilities loans, will pay for themselves.

To sum up, a Ministry of Unemployment, which had at its disposal, say, £2,500,000 a year to meet the additional recurrent obligations it was incurring, chargeable on the budget, making altogether £7,500,000 (recurrent) for a three-years' programme, would be amply provided for.

On the other side of the balance sheet, the task of improving the budget by £2,500,000 each year, through improved revenue and economies on armaments, is literally a trifle. We [111] should hope that a Liberal government would do much better than that. It represents 0.33 per cent of the revenue and less than 3 per cent of the expenditure on armaments.

But this is not the end of the calculation. We have made no allowance so far for the gain to the Unemployment Fund through the reduction in the numbers of the unemployed. For, strictly speaking, the Unemployment Fund is outside the budget; so that its gains do not directly relieve the budget. Indirectly, nevertheless, they will relieve the budget; since the existing deficit on the Fund will surely fall on the budget sooner or later.

If the unemployed are reduced by 500,000, this will improve the position of the Fund by nearly £25 million a year. Let the reader note the magnitude of this figure relatively to the annual costs of each year's programme which we have estimated above, namely, *ten* times greater. This includes no allowance for the saving to the Poor Law and, therefore, to the rates.

A *quarter* of the *capital* cost of each year's programme will be balanced by the gain to the Unemployment Fund *within that year*. Probably an *eighth* would be recovered in that, or the subsequent year, through the gain to the revenue corresponding to the increased national income.

Thus, nearly a *half* of the *capital* cost would be recovered *at the time*. Accordingly there would be no appreciable national loss on the programme, even if it cost on the average 5 per cent per annum and only brought in on the average 2½ per cent.

So far our calculations have related to the limited field of the national finances, and not to the national welfare in its totality. If we are allowed to reckon in the benefits to the unemployed themselves and the national advantage, accruing otherwise than in direct cash receipts, from such things as efficient transport and healthy national housing, surely the case is overwhelming.

Take as gloomy a view as you like – the maximum cost and the maximum risk is of the mildest description, disproportionately small to the possible benefits which may ensue.   [112]

. . .

IX *Will it Merely Divert Employment from Other Enterprises?*

The objection which is raised more frequently perhaps, than any other, is that money raised by the state for financing productive schemes must diminish *pro tanto* the supply of capital available for ordinary industry. If this is true, a policy of national development will not really increase employment. It will merely substitute employment on State schemes for ordinary employment. Either that, or (so the argument often runs) it must mean inflation. There is, therefore, little or nothing that the government can usefully do. The case is hopeless, and we must just drift along.

This was the contention of the Chancellor of the Exchequer in his budget speech.

'It is the orthodox Treasury dogma, steadfastly held', he told the House of Commons, 'that whatever might be the political or social advantages, very little additional employment and no permanent additional employment, can, in fact, and as a general rule, be created by State borrowing and State expenditure.' Some State expenditure, he concluded, is inevitable, and even wise and right for its own sake, *but not as a cure for unemployment*.

In relation to the actual facts of today, this argument is, we believe, quite without foundation.

In the first place, there is nothing in the argument which limits its applicability to State-promoted undertakings. If it is valid at all, it must apply equally to a new works started by Morris, or Courtaulds, to any new business enterprise entailing capital expenditure. If it were announced that some of our leading captains of industry had decided to launch out boldly, and were about to sink capital in new industrial plant to the tune, between them, of £100 millions, we should all expect to see a great improvement in employment. And, of course, we [115] should be right. But, if the argument we are dealing with were sound, we should be wrong. We should have to conclude that these enterprising business men were merely diverting capital from other uses, and that no real gain to employment could result. Indeed, we should be driven to a still more remarkable conclusion. We should have to conclude that it was virtually out of the question to absorb our unemployed workpeople by any means whatsoever (other than the unthinkable inflation), and that the obstacle which barred the path was no other than an insufficiency of capital. This, if you please, in Great Britain, who has surplus savings which she is accustomed to lend abroad on the scale of more than a hundred millions a year.

The argument is certainly not derived from common sense. No ordinary man, left to himself, is able to believe that, if there had been no housing schemes in recent years, there would, nevertheless, have been just as much employment. And, accordingly, most ordinary men are easily persuaded by Mr Lloyd

George that, if his schemes for employment are adopted, more men will be employed.

But the argument is not only unplausible. It is also untrue. There are three resources which can enable new investment to provide a net addition to the amount of employment.

The first source of supply comes out of the savings which we are now disbursing to pay the unemployed.

The second source of supply comes from the savings which now run to waste through lack of adequate credit.

The third source of supply comes from a reduction in the *net* amount of foreign lending.

Let us consider these in turn, beginning with the first source. Individual saving means that some individuals are *producing* more than they are *consuming*. This surplus may, and should be, used to increase capital equipment. But, unfortunately, this is not the only way in which it can be used. It can also be used to enable other individuals to *consume* more than they *produce*.   [116]

This is what happens when there is unemployment. We are using our savings to pay for unemployment, instead of using them to equip the country. The savings which Mr Lloyd George's schemes will employ will be diverted not from financing other capital equipment, but partly from financing unemployment. From the Unemployment Fund alone we are now paying out £50 million a year; and this is not the whole of the cost of supporting the unemployed.

In the second place, the savings of individuals do not necessarily materialise in investments. The amount of investment in capital improvements depends, on the one hand, on the amount of credit created by the Bank of England; and, on the other hand, on the eagerness of entrepreneurs to invest, of whom the government itself – as we have already seen – is nowadays the most important. So far from the total of investment, as determined by these factors, being necessarily equal to the total of saving, dis-equilibrium between the two is at the root of many of our troubles.

When investment runs ahead of saving we have a boom, intense employment, and a tendency to inflation. When investment lags

behind, we have a slump and abnormal unemployment, as at
present.

It is commonly objected to this that an expansion of credit
necessarily means inflation. But not *all* credit-creation means
inflation. Inflation only results when we endeavour, as we did
in the war and afterwards, to expand our activities still further
after everyone is already employed and our savings are being
used up to the hilt.

The suggestion that a policy of capital expenditure, if it does
not take capital away from ordinary industry, will spell inflation, would be true enough if we were dealing with boom
conditions. And it would become true if the policy of capital
expenditure were pushed unduly far, so that the demand for
savings began to exceed the supply. But we are far, indeed, from
such a position at the present time. A large amount of defla-
[117] tionary slack has first to be taken up before there can be the
smallest danger of a development policy leading to inflation. To
bring up the bogy of inflation as an objection to capital expenditure at the present time is like warning a patient who is wasting
away from emaciation of the dangers of excessive corpulence.

The real difficulty hitherto in the way of an easier credit policy by the Bank of England has been the fear that an expansion
of credit might lead to a loss of gold which the Bank could not
afford.

Now if the Bank were to try to increase the volume of credit
at a time when, on account of the depression of home enterprise, no reliance could be placed on the additional credit being
absorbed at home at the existing rate of interest, this might
quite well be true. Since market rates of interest would fall, a
considerable part of the new credit might find its way to *foreign* borrowers, with the result of a drain of gold out of the
Bank. Thus it is not safe for the Bank to expand credit unless it
is certain beforehand that there are *home* borrowers standing
ready to absorb it at the existing rates of interest.

This is the reason why the Liberal plan is exactly suited to
the fundamentals of the present position. It provides the necessary condition for an expansion of credit to be safe.

It is, of course, essential that the Bank of England should

loyally co-operate with the government's programme of capital development, and do its best to make it a success. For, unfortunately, it would lie within the power of the Bank, provided it were to pursue a deflationary policy aimed at preventing any expansion in bank credit, to defeat the best-laid plans and to ensure that the expenditure financed by the Treasury *was* at the expense of other business enterprise.

. . .

We conclude, therefore, that, whilst an increased volume of [118] bank credit is probably a *sine qua non* of increased employment, a programme of home investment which will absorb this increase is a *sine qua non* of the safe expansion of credit.

The third source of the funds required for the Liberal policy will be found by a net reduction of foreign lending.

An important part of our savings is now finding its outlet in foreign issues. Granted that a big policy of national development could not be financed wholly out of the existing expenditure on unemployment and out of the savings which are at present running to waste, granted that, to meet the borrowing demands of the State other borrowers must go without, why should we assume that these other borrowers must be British business men? The technique of the capital market makes it far more probable that they would be some of the overseas governments or municipalities which London at present finances on so large a scale. It is the bond market that would be principally affected by a British government loan.

Now anything which served to diminish the volume of foreign issues would be welcomed by the Bank of England at the present time for its own sake. The exchange position is uncomfortable and precarious; the recent rise in bank rate is proof of that. A diminution of foreign investment would ease the strain on the exchanges. Why, it is only a year or two since the Bank of England, with this end in view, was maintaining a semi-official embargo on foreign issues. The embargo was a crude instrument, suitable only for temporary use, and we do not suggest its renewal. But the need which that embargo was designed to supply still remains, if in a less acute degree. In relation to our less favourable balance of foreign trade, we are investing abroad dangerously much; and we are investing abroad to this dangerous extent partly because there are insufficient outlets for our savings at home.

It follows, therefore, that a policy of capital expenditure, in so far as it might go beyond the mere absorption of deflation[119] ary slack, would serve mainly to divert to home development savings which now find their way abroad, and that this would be a welcome result in the interests of the Bank of England.

It has been objected that if we lend less abroad, our exports will fall off. We see no reason to anticipate this. Immediately, as we have said, the reduction in *net* foreign lending will relieve the pressure on the Bank of England's stock of gold. But, ultimately, its main effect will be realised, not in a reduction of exports, but in an increase of imports. For the new schemes will require a certain amount of imported raw materials, whilst those who are now unemployed will consume more imported food when they are once again earning decent wages.

Here, then, is our answer. The savings which Mr Lloyd George's schemes will employ will be diverted, not from financing other capital equipment, but partly from financing unemployment. A further part will come from the savings which now run to waste through lack of adequate credit. Something will be provided by the very prosperity which the new policy will foster. And the balance will be found by a reduction of foreign lending.

The whole of the labour of the unemployed is available to increase the national wealth. It is crazy to believe that we shall ruin ourselves financially by trying to find means for using it and that 'safety first' lies in continuing to maintain men in idleness.

It is precisely *with* our unemployed productive resources that we shall make the new investments.

We are left with a broad, simple, and surely incontestable proposition. Whatever real difficulties there may be in the way of absorbing our unemployed labour in productive work, an inevitable diversion of resources from other forms of employment is not one of them.

This conclusion is not peculiar to ourselves or to Mr Lloyd

George and his advisers. The theoretical question involved is not a new one. The general problem whether capital developments financed by the government are capable of increasing [120] employment has been carefully debated by economists in recent years. The result has been to establish the conclusion of this chapter as sound and orthodox and the Treasury's dogma as fallacious.

. . .

x *The Policy of Negation*

Our whole economic policy during recent years has been dominated by the preoccupation of the Treasury with their departmental problem of debt conversion. The less the government borrows, the better, they argue, are the chances of converting the national [121] debt into loans carrying a lower rate of interest. In the interests of conversion, therefore, they have exerted themselves to curtail, as far as they can, all public borrowing, all capital expenditure by the State, no matter how productive and desirable in itself. We doubt if the general public has any idea how powerful, persistent, and far-reaching this influence has been.

To all well-laid schemes of progress and enterprise, they have (whenever they could) barred the door with, No! Now it is quite true that curtailing capital expenditure exerts some tendency towards lower interest rates for government loans. But it is no less true that it makes for increased unemployment and that it leaves the country with a pre-war outfit.

Even from the budget point of view, it is a question whether the game is worth the candle. It is difficult to believe that, if this question were considered squarely on its merits, any intelligent person could return an affirmative answer. The capital market is an international market. All sorts of influences which are outside our control go to determine the gilt-edged rate of interest; and the effect which the British government can exert on it by curtailing or expanding its capital programme is limited. Suppose, which is putting the case extremely high, that the effect might be as much as ¼ per cent. This, applied to the £2,000 million of War Loan, which are ripe for conversion, would represent a difference in the annual debt charge of £5 million annually.

Compare this with the expenditure of the Unemployment Fund – over £50 million last year.

Moreover, in the course of (say) ten years it is not unlikely that a situation will arise – as used to happen from time to time before the war – when for world reasons the rate of interest will be abnormally low, much lower than we could possibly hope for by Treasury contrivances in the exceptionally unfavourable environment of abnormally high world rates. This will be the moment for a successful conversion scheme. Even, therefore, if [122] the Treasury could convert today at a saving of ¼ or ½ per cent, it might be extremely improvident to do so. A premature conversion for an inconsiderable saving would be a grave blunder. We must have the patience to wait for the ideal conjuncture of conditions, and then the Chancellor of the Exchequer of the day will be able to pull off something big.[6]

But apart from budgetary advantages and disadvantages, there is a deep-seated confusion of thought in hindering on these grounds the capital development of the country. The rate of interest can fall for either of two opposite reasons. It may fall on account of an abundant supply of savings, i.e. of money available to be spent on investments; or it may fall on account of a deficient supply of investments, i.e. on desirable purposes on which to spend the savings. Now a fall in the rate of interest for the first reason is, obviously, very much in the national interest. But a fall for the second reason, if it follows from a deliberate restriction of outlets for investment, is simply a disastrous method of impoverishing ourselves.

A country is enriched not by the mere negative act of an individual not spending all his income on current consumption. It is enriched by the positive act of using these savings to augment the capital equipment of the country.

It is not the miser who gets rich; but he who lays out his money in fruitful investment.

The object of urging people to save is *in order* to be able to build houses and roads and the like. Therefore a policy of trying to lower the rate of interest by suspending new capital improvements and so stopping up the outlets and purposes of our savings is simply suicidal. No one, perhaps, would uphold such a policy expressed in so many words. But this, in fact, is what the Treasury has been doing for several years. In some cases, the pressure of public opinion or of other government departments or local authorities has been too much for them. But whenever it has been within their power to choke something off, they have done so.

The futility of their policy and the want of sound reasoning [123] behind it have been finally demonstrated by its failure even to secure a fall in the rate of interest. For, as we have seen above, if outlets for investment at home are stopped up, savings flow abroad on a scale disproportionate to our favourable balance of trade, with the result that the Bank of England tends to lose gold. To counteract this position, the bank rate has to be raised.

So in the end we have the worst of all worlds. The country is backward in its equipment, instead of being thoroughly up to date. Business profits are poor, with the result that the yield of the income tax disappoints the Chancellor of the Exchequer and he is unable either to relieve the taxpayer or to push forward with schemes of social reform. Unemployment is rampant. This want of prosperity actually diminishes the rate of saving and thus defeats even the original object of a lower rate of interest. So rates of interest are, after all, high. And there is only one little compensation to set against all this – that the Conservative Party will be driven out of office.

XI *The Breath of Life*

It is not an accident that the Conservative government have landed us in the mess where we find ourselves. It is the natural outcome of their philosophy:

You must not press on with telephones or electricity, because this will raise the rate of interest.

You must not hasten with roads or housing, because this will use up opportunities for employment which we may need in later years.

You must not try to employ everyone, because this will cause inflation.

You must not invest, because how can you know that it will pay?

You must not do anything, because this will only mean that you can't do something else.

Safety first! The policy of maintaining a million unemployed has now been pursued for eight years without disaster. Why risk a change?

We will not promise more than we can perform. We, therefore, promise nothing.

[124]   This is what we are being fed with.

They are slogans of depression and decay – the timidities and obstructions and stupidities of a sinking administrative vitality.

Negation, restriction, inactivity – these are the government's watchwords. Under their leadership we have been forced to button up our waistcoats and compress our lungs. Fears and doubts and hypochondriac precautions are keeping us muffled up indoors. But we are not tottering to our graves. We are healthy children. We need the breath of life. There is nothing to be afraid of. On the contrary. The future holds in store for us far more wealth and economic freedom and possibilities of personal life than the past has ever offered.

There is no reason why we should not feel ourselves free to be bold, to be open, to experiment, to take action, to try the possibilities of things. And over against us, standing in the path, there is nothing but a few old gentlemen tightly buttoned-up in their frock coats, who only need to be treated with a little friendly disrespect and bowled over like ninepins.

Quite likely they will enjoy it themselves, when once they
[125]   have got over the shock.

29

Policies for the Slump

[*The sequence of short articles below is taken from Keynes's* Essays in Persuasion, *published in 1931, which he described as the 'croakings of a Cassandra, who could never influence the course of events in time'.*]

CW 9, 'Proposals for a Revenue Tariff' (1931)

[*This article, published in the* New Statesman *on 7 March 1931, made public Keynes's breach with free trade. The rise in unemployment from 1.25 million in 1929 to over 2 million at start of 1931 (the average for 1931 was 2.7 million) widened the budget deficit and raised a predictable clamour for fiscal consolidation. Keynes sought a way of raising extra taxes to relieve the budget that would at the same time increase business confidence: the revenue tariff was his ingenious solution.*]

Do you think it a paradox that we can continue to increase our capital wealth by adding both to our foreign investments and to our equipment at home, that we can continue to live (most of us) much as usual or better, and support at the same time a vast body of persons in idleness with a dole greater than the income of a man in full employment in most parts of the world – and yet do all this with one-quarter of our industrial plant closed down and one-quarter of our industrial workers unemployed? It would be not merely a paradox, but an impossibility, if our potential capacity for the creation of wealth were not much greater than it used to be. But this greater capacity does exist. It is to be attributed mainly to three factors – the ever-increasing technical efficiency of our industry (I believe that output per head is 10 per cent greater than it was even so recently as 1924), the greater economic output of women, and the larger proportion of the population which is at the working period of life. The fall in the price of our imports compared with that of our exports also helps. The result is that with three-fourths of our industrial capacity we can now produce as much wealth as we could produce with the whole of it a few [231] years ago. But how rich we could be if only we could find some way of employing *four*-fourths of our capacity today!

Our trouble is, then, not that we lack the physical means to support a high standard of life, but that we are suffering a breakdown in organisation and in the machinery by which we buy and sell to one another.

There are two reactions to this breakdown. We experience

the one or the other according to our temperaments. The one is inspired by a determination to maintain our standards of life by bringing into use our wasted capacity – that is to say, to expand, casting fear and even prudence away. The other, the instinct to contract, is based on the psychology of fear. How reasonable is it to be afraid?

We live in a society organised in such a way that the activity of production depends on the individual business man hoping for a reasonable profit, or at least, to avoid an actual loss. The margin which he requires as his necessary incentive to produce may be a very small proportion of the total value of the product. But take this away from him and the whole process stops. This, unluckily, is just what has happened. The fall of prices relatively to costs, together with the psychological effect of high taxation, has destroyed the necessary incentive to production. This is at the root of our disorganisation. It may be unwise, therefore, to frighten the business man or torment him further. A forward policy is liable to do this. For reasoning by a false analogy from what is prudent for an individual who finds himself in danger of living beyond his means, he is usually, when his nerves are frayed, a supporter, though to his own ultimate disadvantage, of national contraction.

And there is a further reason for nervousness. We are suffering from *international* instability. Notoriously the competitive power of our export trades is diminished by our high standard of life. At the same time the lack of profits in home business inclines the investor to place his money abroad, whilst high taxation exercises a sinister influence in the same direction. [232] Above all, the reluctance of other creditor countries to lend (which is the root-cause of this slump) places too heavy a financial burden on London. These, again, are apparent arguments against a forward policy; for greater activity at home due to increased employment will increase our excess of imports, and government borrowing may (in their present mood) frighten investors.

Thus the *direct* effect of an expansionist policy must be to cause government borrowing, to throw some burden on the budget, and to increase our excess of imports. In every way, therefore – the opponents of such a policy point out – it will aggravate the want of confidence, the burden of taxation, and the international instability which, they believe, are at the bottom of our present troubles.

At this point the opponents of expansion divide into two groups – those who think that we must not only postpone all ideas of expansion, but must positively contract, by which they mean reduce wages and make large economies in the existing expenditure of the budget, and those who are entirely negative and, like Mr Snowden, dislike the idea of contraction (interpreted in the above sense) almost as much as they dislike the idea of expansion.

The policy of negation, however, is really the most dangerous of all. For, as time goes by, it becomes increasingly doubtful whether we *can* support our standard of life. With 1 million unemployed we certainly can; with 2 million unemployed we probably can; with 3 million unemployed we probably cannot. Thus the negative policy, by allowing unemployment steadily to increase, must lead in the end to an unanswerable demand for a reduction in our standard of life. If we do nothing long enough, there will in the end be nothing else that we can do.

Unemployment, I must repeat, exists because employers have been deprived of profit. The loss of profit may be due to all sorts of causes. But, short of going over to Communism, there is no possible means of curing unemployment except by restoring to employers a proper margin of profit. There are two ways of doing this – by increasing the *demand* for output, [234] which is the expansionist cure, or by decreasing the *cost* of output, which is the contractionist cure. Both of these try to touch the spot. Which of them is to be preferred?

To decrease the cost of output by reducing wages and curtailing budget services may indeed increase foreign demand for our goods (unless, which is quite likely, it encourages a similar policy of contraction abroad), but it will probably diminish the domestic demand. The advantages to employers of a *general* reduction of wages are, therefore, not so great as they look. Each employer sees the advantage to himself of a reduction of the wages which he himself pays, and overlooks both the consequences of the reduction of the incomes of his customers and of the reduction of wages which his competitors will enjoy. Anyway, it would certainly lead to social injustice and violent resistance, since it would greatly benefit some classes of income at the expense of others. For these reasons a policy of contraction sufficiently drastic to do any real good may be quite impracticable.

Yet the objections to the expansionist remedy – the instability of our international position, the state of the budget, and the want of confidence – cannot be thus disposed of. Two years ago there was no need to be frightened. Today it is a different matter. It would not be wise to frighten the penguins and arouse these frigid creatures to flap away from our shores with their golden eggs inside them. A policy of expansion sufficiently drastic to be useful might drive us off the gold standard. Moreover, two years ago the problem was mainly a British problem; today it is mainly international. No domestic cure today can be adequate by itself. An international cure is essential; and I see the best hope of remedying the international slump in the leadership of Great Britain. But if Great Britain is to resume leadership, she must be strong and believed to be strong. It is of paramount importance, therefore, to restore full confidence in London. I do not believe that this is difficult; for the real strength [235] of London is being under-estimated today by foreign opinion, and the position is ripe for a sudden reversal of sentiment. For these reasons I, who opposed our return to the gold standard and can claim, unfortunately, that my Cassandra utterances have been partly fulfilled, believe that our exchange position should be relentlessly defended today, in order, above all, that we may resume the vacant financial leadership of the world, which no one else has the experience or the public spirit to occupy, speaking out of acknowledged strength and not out of weakness.

An advocate of expansion in the interests of domestic employment has cause, therefore, to think twice. I have thought twice, and the following are my conclusions.

I am of the opinion that a policy of expansion, though desirable, is not safe or practicable today, unless it is accompanied by other measures which would neutralise its dangers. Let me remind the reader what these dangers are. There is the burden on the trade balance, the burden on the budget, and the effect on confidence. If the policy of expansion were to justify itself eventually by increasing materially the level of profits and the volume of employment, the net effect on the budget and on confidence would in the end be favourable and perhaps very favourable. But this might not be the initial effect.

What measures are available to neutralise these dangers? A decision to reform the grave abuses of the dole, and a decision to postpone for the present all new charges on the budget for social services in order to conserve its resources to meet schemes for the expansion of employment, are advisable and should be taken. But the main decision which seems to me today to be absolutely forced on any wise Chancellor of the Exchequer, whatever his beliefs about protection, is the introduction of a substantial revenue tariff. It is certain that there is no other measure all the immediate consequences of which will be favourable and appropriate. The tariff which I have in mind would include no discriminating protective taxes, but would cover as wide a field as possible at a flat rate or perhaps two flat [236] rates, each applicable to wide categories of goods. Rebates would be allowed in respect of imported material entering into exports, but raw materials, which make up an important proportion of the value of exports, such as wool and cotton, would be exempt. The amount of revenue to be aimed at should be substantial, not less than £50 million and, if possible, £75 million. Thus, for example, there might be import duties of 15 per cent on all manufactured and semi-manufactured goods without exception, and of 5 per cent on all foodstuffs and certain raw materials, whilst other raw materials would be exempt. I am prepared to maintain that the effect of such duties on the cost of living would be insignificant – no greater than the existing fluctuation between one month and another. Moreover, any conceivable remedy for unemployment will have the effect, and, indeed, will be intended, to raise prices. Equally, the effect on the cost of our exports, after allowing for the rebates which should be calculated on broad and simple lines, would be very small. It should be the declared intention of the free trade parties acquiescing in this decision to remove the duties in the event of world prices recovering to the level of 1929.

Compared with any alternative which is open to us, this measure is unique in that it would at the same time relieve the pressing problems of the budget and restore business confidence. I do not believe that a wise and prudent budget can be framed today without recourse to a revenue tariff. But this is not its only advantage. In so far as it leads to the substitution of home-produced goods for goods previously imported, it will increase employment in this country. At the same time, by relieving the pressure on the balance of trade it will provide a much-needed margin to pay for the additional imports which a policy of expansion will require and to finance loans by London to necessitous debtor countries. In these ways, the buying power which we take away from the rest of the world by restricting certain imports we shall restore to it with the other hand. Some fanatical free traders might allege that the adverse effect of import duties on our exports would neutralise all this; but it would not be true.

Free traders may, consistently with their faith, regard a revenue tariff as our iron ration, which can be used once only in emergency. The emergency has arrived. Under cover of the breathing space and the margin of financial strength thus afforded us, we could frame a policy and a plan, both domestic and international, for marching to the assault against the spirit of contractionism and fear.

If, on the other hand, free traders reject these counsels of expediency, the certain result will be to break the present government and to substitute for it, in the confusion of a crisis of confidence, a Cabinet pledged to a full protectionist programme.[7] I am not unaccustomed to being in a minority. But on this occasion I believe that 90 per cent of my countrymen will agree with me.

[*The sequence of events in the British financial crisis of 1931 was as follows. The May Report was the report of the Committee on Economy, set up on 17 March, under the chairmanship of Sir George May, secretary of the Prudential Assurance*

*Company, to recommend 'all possible reductions in National
Expenditure'. It reported, on 1 August, that the government
faced a prospective budget deficit for 1931-2 of £120 million.
This should be plugged by raising £23 million in additional
taxes, and £97 million in 'economies', chiefly on unemployment
benefits. The minority Labour government resigned on 24 August
and a national or coalition government was formed to 'save the
pound' under the Labour Prime Minister Ramsay MacDonald
supported by the Conservative and Liberal parties, and a small
rump of Labour MPs. The government introduced an Economy
Bill on 8 September designed to eliminate the prospective deficit
by the year 1932-3. On 21 September Britain was forced to
suspend the gold standard. It was never restored. These articles
should be read in conjunction with Keynes's commentary on the
world depression in chapter 3. Keynes's commentary on the British crisis starts with an article in the* New Statesman, *15 August
1931.*]

CW 9, 'The Economy Report' (1931)

The report of the Economy Committee ... is an exceedingly
valuable document because it is a challenge to us to make up
our minds one way or the other on certain vital matters of policy. In particular it invites us to decide whether it is our intention
to make the deflation effective by transmitting the reduction of
international prices to British salaries and wages; though if this
is our intention, it would be absurd to pretend that the process
can stop with schoolteachers and policemen. The Committee's
report goes too far or not far enough. But this is not the question which I wish to discuss here. I would like to confine myself
to what has been so far, as it seems to me, a neglected aspect
of the report.

The Committee show no evidence of having given a moment's   [141]
thought to the possible repercussions of their programme,
either on the volume of unemployment or on the receipts
of taxation. They recommend a reduction of the purchasing
power of British citizens partly by the reduction of incomes and

partly by throwing out of work persons now employed. They give no reason for supposing that this reduction of purchasing power will be offset by increases in other directions; for their idea is that the government should take advantage of the economies proposed, not to tax less, but to borrow less. Perhaps at the back of their heads they have some crude idea that there is a fixed loan fund, the whole of which is always lent, so that, if the government borrows less, private enterprise necessarily borrows more. But they could not believe this on reflection, if they were to try to translate it into definite, concrete terms.

Their proposals do not even offer the possible advantages to our trade balance which might ensue on a reduction of industrial wages. For there is nothing in what they propose calculated to reduce the costs of production; indeed, on the contrary, they propose to increase them by raising the employers' insurance contribution.

Let us try, therefore, to write the missing paragraphs of the report and to make some guesses as to the probable consequences of reducing purchasing power in the manner proposed.

Some part of this reduction of purchasing power may be expected to lead to a reduced buying of foreign goods, e.g. if the dole is cut down, the unemployed will have to tighten their belts and eat less imported food. To this extent the situation will be helped. Some part will be economised by saving less; e.g. if teachers' salaries are cut down, teachers will probably save less or even draw on their past savings, to maintain the standard of life to which they have become accustomed. But for the rest British producers will find the receipts reaching them from the expenditure of consumers (policemen, schoolteachers, men on the dole, etc.) reduced by the balance of, say, £70 million. They cannot meet this loss without reducing their own expend-[142] iture or discharging some of their men, or both, i.e. they will have to follow the example of the government, and this will again set moving the same series of consequences, and so on.

The net result would necessarily be a substantial increase in the number of unemployed drawing the dole and a decrease in the receipts of taxation as a result of the diminished incomes and profits. Indeed the immediate consequences of the government's reducing its deficit are the exact inverse of the consequences of its financing additional capital works out of loans. One cannot predict with accuracy the exact quantitative consequences of either, but they are broadly the same. Several of the Committee's recommendations, e.g. those relating to roads, to housing, and to afforestation, do indeed expressly imply that the whole theory underlying the principle of public works as a remedy for unemployment is mistaken, and they ask, in effect, for a reversal of the policies based on this principle. Yet they do not trouble to argue the case. I suppose that they are such very plain men that the advantages of not spending money seem obvious to them. They may even be so plain as to be unaware of the existence of the problem which I am now discussing. But they are flying in the face of a considerable weight of opinion. For the main opposition to the public works remedy is based on the practical difficulties of devising a reasonable programme, not on the principle. But a proposal to reverse measures already in force involves a denial of the principle as well as of the feasibility.

I should like, though it is rash, to make, if only for purposes of illustration, a very rough guess as to the magnitudes of the more immediate consequences of the adoption of economies of £100 million, carried out on the lines of the Committee's recommendations. I should expect something like the following:

(1) An increase of 250,000–400,000 in the number of the unemployed;

(2) A decrease of, say, £20 million in the excess of our imports over our exports; [143]

(3) A decrease of £10 million to £15 million in the savings of the general public;

(4) A decrease of £20 million to £30 million in business profits;

(5) A decrease of £10 million to £15 million in the personal expenditure of business men and others, who depend on business profits, as a result of these profits being less;

(6) A decrease of £5 million to £10 million in the aggregate of capital construction and working capital and other investment at home entered upon by private enterprise, as a result of

the lower level of business profits, after allowing for any favourable psychological effects on business 'confidence' of the adoption of the Committee's recommendations;

(7) A *net* reduction in the government deficit not exceeding £50 million, as a result of the budget economies of £100 million being partly offset by the diminished yield of taxation and the cost of the increased unemployment.

The actual figures I have used are, of course, guesswork. But (2) + (3) + (4) − (5) − (6) = (7), where (7) is the net reduction in the government deficit, is a necessary truth − as necessary as 2 + 2 = 4. There is nothing rational to dispute about except the size of the various items entering into this equation. It might be held by some, for example, that there would be an *increase* under (6), instead of a decrease; and if there were a large increase of this item − which, however, could not, in my judgement, be maintained with good reason − this would make all the difference in the world to the expediency of the policy proposed.

At the present time, all governments have large deficits. For government borrowing of one kind or another is nature's remedy, so to speak, for preventing business losses from being, in so severe a slump as the present one, so great as to bring production altogether to a standstill. It is much better in every way that the borrowing should be for the purpose of financing capital works, if these works are any use at all, than for the purpose of paying doles (or veterans' bonuses). But so long as the slump [144] lasts on the present scale this is the only effective choice which we possess, and government borrowing for the one purpose or the other (or a diminished Sinking Fund, which has the same effect) is practically inevitable. For this is a case, fortunately perhaps, where the weakness of human nature will, we can be sure, come to the rescue of human wrong-headedness.

This is not to say that there are not other ways in which we can help ourselves. I am not concerned here with the possible advantages − for example − of a tariff or of devaluation or of a national treaty for the reduction of all money incomes. I am simply analysing the results to be expected from the recommendations of the Economy Committee adopted as a means of reducing the uncovered deficit of the budget. And I should add, to prevent misunderstanding, that I should prefer some of their recommendations – for they have done their work in detail with ability and fair-mindedness – to most kinds of additional taxation other than a tariff.

My own policy for the budget, so long as the slump lasts, would be to suspend the Sinking Fund, to continue to borrow for the Unemployment Fund, and to impose a revenue tariff. To get us out of the slump we must look to quite other expedients. When the slump is over, when the demands of private enterprise for new capital have recovered to normal and employment is good and the yield of taxation is increasing, then is the time to restore the Sinking Fund and to look critically at the less productive state enterprises. [145]

CW 9, 'On the Eve of Gold Suspension' (1931)

[*First printed in the* Evening Standard, *10 September 1931.*]

The moral energies of the nation are being directed into wrong channels, and serious troubles are ahead of us unless we apply our minds with more effect than hitherto to the analysis of the real character of our problems.

The exclusive concentration on the idea of 'economy', national, municipal, and personal – meaning by this the negative act of withholding expenditure which is now stimulating the forces of production into action – may, if under the spur of a sense of supposed duty it is carried far, produce social effects so shocking as to shake the whole system of our national life. [238]

There is scarcely an item in the economy programme of the May Report – whether or not it is advisable on general grounds – which is not certain to increase unemployment, to lower the profits of business, and to diminish the yield of the revenue; so much so that I have calculated that economies of £100 million may quite likely reduce the net budget deficit by not more than £50 million, and we are just hoodwinking ourselves (unless our real object is to *pretend* to balance the budget for the benefit of foreign financiers) if we suppose that we can make the economies under discussion without any repercussions on the number of the unemployed to be supported or on the yield of the existing taxes. Yet if we carry 'economy' of every kind to its logical conclusion, we shall find that we have balanced the budget at nought on both sides, with all of us flat on our backs starving to death from a refusal, for reasons of economy, to buy one another's services.

The Prime Minister has said that it is like the war over again, and many people believe him. But this is exactly the opposite of the truth. During the war it was useful to refrain from any avoidable expenditure because this would release resources for the insatiable demands of military operations. What are we releasing resources for today? To stand at street corners and draw the dole.

When we already have a great amount of unemployment and unused resources of every description, economy is only useful from the national point of view *in so far as it diminishes our consumption of imported goods*. For the rest, its fruits are entirely wasted in unemployment, business losses, and reduced savings. But it is an extraordinarily indirect and wasteful way of reducing imports.

If we throw men out of work and reduce the incomes of government employees so that those directly and indirectly affected cannot afford to buy so much imported food, to this extent the country's financial position is eased. But this is not likely to [239] amount to more than 20 per cent of the total economies enforced. The remaining 80 per cent is wasted, and represents either a mere transference of loss or unemployment due to a refusal of British citizens to purchase one another's services.

What I am saying is absolutely certain, yet I doubt if one in a million of those who are crying out for economy have the slightest idea of the real consequences of what they demand.

This is not to deny that there is a budget problem. Quite the contrary. The point is that the state of the budget is mainly a symptom and a consequence of other causes, that economy is in itself liable to aggravate rather than to remove these other causes, and that consequently the budget problem, attacked merely along the lines of economy, is probably insoluble.

What are our troubles fundamentally due to? Very largely to

the world depression, immediately to the unbelievable rashness of high finance in the City, and originally to the policy of returning to the gold standard without the slightest appreciation of the nature of the difficulties which this involved. To say that our problem is a budget problem is like saying that the German problem is a budget problem, forgetting all about reparations.

Now as regards the world depression, there is at the moment absolutely nothing that we can do, for we have now lost the power of international initiative which we seemed to be regaining last May. The results of unsound international banking by the City are also, for the time being, irreparable. The choice left to us was whether or not to adhere to the present gold parity of the exchanges.

This was decided in the affirmative for reasons which I understand but with which I do not agree. The decision was taken in a spirit of hysteria and without a calm consideration of the alternative before us. Ministers have given forecasts of what might have been expected if we had taken a different course which could not survive ten minutes' rational discussion.

I believe that we shall come to regret this decision, just as we already regret most of the critical decisions taken during the last ten years by the persons who form the present Cabinet. [240]

But that is not the point at this moment. The decision to maintain the gold standard at all costs has been taken. The point is that the Cabinet and the public seem to have no clear idea as to what has to be done to implement its own decision, apart from the obvious necessity of raising a foreign loan for immediate requirements; which simply has the effect of replacing money which we had previously borrowed in terms of sterling, by money borrowed in terms of francs and dollars. But they cannot suppose that we can depend permanently on foreign loans. The rest of the problem is primarily concerned with improving our current balance of trade on income account. This is what the Cabinet ought to be thinking about.

There are only two possible lines of attack on this. The one (which is the milder measure open to us) consists in direct measures to restrict imports (and, if possible, subsidise exports); the other is a reduction of all money wages within the country. We may have to attempt both in the end, if we refuse to devaluate.

But the immediate question is which to try first. Now the latter course, if it were to be adequate, would involve so drastic a reduction of wages and such appallingly difficult, probably insoluble, problems, both of social justice and practical method, that it would be crazy not to try first the effects of the alternative, and much milder, measure of restricting imports.

It happens that this course also has other important advantages. It will not only relieve the strain on the foreign exchanges. It would also do more than any other single measure to balance the budget; and it is the only form of taxation open to us which will actually increase profits, improve employment, and raise the spirits and the confidence of the business community.

Finally, it is the only measure for which there is (sensibly enough) an overwhelming support from public opinion. It is credibly reported that the late Cabinet were in favour of a tariff in the proportion of three to one. It looks as if the present Cabinet may favour it in the proportion of four to one. The only third alternative Cabinet is unanimously for it. But sacrifice being the order of the day, we have in the spirit of self-immolation conceived the brilliant contrivance of a 'national' government, the basis of which is that every member of it agrees, so long as it lasts, to sacrifice what he himself believes to be the only sound solution for our misfortunes.

For if we rule out devaluation, which I personally now believe to be the right remedy, but which is not yet the policy of any organised party in the state, there are three possible lines of procedure.

The first is to take the risks of brisk home development, as being preferable to enforced idleness.

The second is to organise a general reduction of wages and, in the interests of social justice, of other money incomes as well, so far as this is feasible.

The third is a drastic restriction of imports.

The 'national' government is pledged, if I understand the position rightly, to avoid all three. Their policy is to reduce the standard of life of as many people as are within their reach in the hope that some small portion of the reductions of standard will be at the expense of imports.

Deliberately to prefer this to a direct restriction of imports is to be *non compos mentis*. Or is it their hope to bring down wages both by worsening the lot of the unemployed and ensuring at the same time that their numbers shall exceed 3 million?

Here, again, if the end is desired, any sane man would prefer more direct and less wasteful measures for attaining it. By now even members of the Cabinet must surely be becoming uneasy about the course which they have set for themselves.   [242]

CW 9, 'The Economy Bill' (1931)

[*First printed in the* New Statesman, *19 September 1931.*]
The budget and the Economy Bill are replete with folly and injustice. It is a tragedy that the moral energies and enthusiasm of many truly self-sacrificing and well-wishing people should be so misdirected.

The objects of national policy, so as to meet the emergency, [145] should be primarily to improve our balance of trade, and secondarily to equalise the yield of taxation with the normal recurrent expenditure of the budget by methods which would increase, rather than diminish, output, and hence increase the national income and the yield of the revenue, whilst respecting the principles of social justice. The actual policy of the government fails on each of these tests. It will have comparatively little effect on the balance of trade. It will largely increase unemployment and diminish the yield of the revenue. And it outrages the principles of justice to a degree which I should have thought inconceivable.

To begin with the last. The incomes of well-to-do people have been cut by 2½ to 3½ per cent. The schoolteachers are cut 15 per cent, in addition to the extra taxes which they have to pay. It is a monstrous thing to single out this class and discriminate against them, merely because they happen to be employees of the government. It is particularly outrageous, because efforts have been made in recent years to attract into the profession teachers of higher qualifications by holding out to them certain expectations. It is even proposed to take powers to dissolve existing contracts. That the schoolteachers should have been singled out for sacrifice as an offering to the Moloch of finance is a sufficient proof of the state of hysteria and irresponsibility into which cabinet ministers have worked themselves. For it is impossible to represent this cut as one of unavoidable necessity. The money saved is £6 million. At the same time £32 million is going to the Sinking Fund, whilst tea, sugar, and a tariff as sources of revenue are left untapped. The Prime Minister has offered no defence, except that some of his former colleagues, who have since recovered their heads, were temporarily frightened into considering something of the same kind.

The schoolteachers are the most outstanding case of injustice. But the same considerations apply in varying degrees to all the attacks on the standards of government employees. The [146] principle of discriminating against persons in the service of the State, because they can be reached most easily, is not right. At least it would have been more decent in the circumstances if the phrase 'equality of sacrifice' had not been used.

Moreover, the government's programme is as foolish as it is wrong. Its direct effect on employment must be disastrous. It is safe to predict that it will increase the volume of unemployment by more than the 10 per cent by which the dole is to be cut. It represents a reckless reversal of all the partial attempts which have been made hitherto to mitigate the consequences of the collapse of private investment; and it is a triumph for the so-called 'Treasury view' in its most extreme form. Not only is purchasing power to be curtailed, but road building, housing, and the like are to be retrenched. Local authorities are to follow suit. If the theory which underlies all this is to be accepted, the end will be that no one can be employed, except those happy few who grow their own potatoes, as a result of each of us refusing, for reasons of economy, to buy the services of anyone else. To raid the Road Fund in order to maintain the Sinking Fund is, in present circumstances, a policy of Bedlam.

Finally there is the problem of the balance of trade, which, after all, is the main point so far as concerns the emergency.

Broadly speaking, the cost of production is left unchanged. Cutting the schoolteachers' salaries will not help us to recapture the markets of the world. Those wages and the like which are within the government's direct control happen to be just those which it is most useless to cut in the interests of the export trade. We are told that it is a wicked misrepresentation to say that all this is a preliminary to a general assault on wages. Yet it has less than no sense unless it is. But meanwhile the government have noticed that there is just one point where their activities raise the cost of production, namely, the employers' insurance contribution, which is, in effect, a poll tax on employment. So, in order to prove for certain that they are quite mad, the government have decided to *increase* it.   [147]

CW 9, 'The End of the Gold Standard' (1931)

[*First printed in the* Sunday Express, *27 September 1931.*]
There are few Englishmen who do not rejoice at the breaking of our gold fetters. We feel that we have at last a free hand to do what is sensible. The romantic phase is over, and we can begin to discuss realistically what policy is for the best.

It may seem surprising that a move which had been represented as a disastrous catastrophe should have been received with so much enthusiasm. But the great advantages to British trade and industry of our ceasing artificial efforts to maintain our currency above its real value were quickly realised.

The division of inside opinion was largely on a different point. The difficult question to decide was one of honour. The City of London considered that it was under an obligation of *honour* to make every possible effort to maintain the value of money in terms of which it had accepted large deposits from foreigners, even though the result of this was to place an intolerable strain on British industry. At what point – that was the difficult problem – were we justified in putting our own interests first?

As events have turned out, we have got the relief we needed and, at the same time, the claims of honour have been, in the judgement of the whole world, satisfied to the utmost. For the step was not taken until it was unavoidable. In the course of a few weeks the Bank of England paid out £200 million in gold or its equivalent, which was about half the total claims of foreigners on London, and did this at a time when the sums which London had re-lent abroad were largely frozen. No banker [245] could do more. Out of the ashes the City of London will rise with undiminished honour. For she has played the game up to the limits of quixotry, even at the risk of driving British trade almost to a standstill.

No wonder, then, that we feel some exuberance at the release, that stock exchange prices soar, and that the dry bones of industry are stirred. For if the sterling exchange is depreciated by, say, 25 per cent, this does as much to restrict our imports as a tariff of that amount; but whereas a tariff could not help our exports, and might hurt them, the depreciation of sterling affords them a bounty of the same 25 per cent by which it aids the home producer against imports.

In many lines of trade the British manufacturer today must be the cheapest producer in the world in terms of gold. We gain these advantages without a cut of wages and without industrial strife. We gain them in a way which is strictly fair to every section of the community, without any serious effects on the cost of living. For less than a quarter of our total consumption is represented by imports; so that sterling would have to depreciate by much more than 25 per cent before I should expect the cost of living to rise by as much as 10 per cent. This would cause serious hardship to no one, for it would only put things back where they were two years ago. Meanwhile there will be a great stimulus to employment.

I make no forecast as to the figure to which sterling may fall in the next few days, except that it will have to fall for a time appreciably below the figure which cool calculators believe to represent the equilibrium. There will then be speculation and profit-taking in favour of sterling to balance speculation and panic selling on the other side. Our authorities made a great mistake in allowing sterling to open so high, because the inevitable gradual fall towards a truer level must sap confidence and produce on the ignorant the impression of a slide which cannot be stayed. Those who were guilty of undue optimism will quite likely succumb to undue pessimism. But the pessimism will be as unfounded as the optimism was. The equilibrium [246] value of sterling is the same as it was a month ago. There are tremendous forces to support sterling when it begins to fall too far. There is no risk, in my judgement, of a catastrophic fall.

These, in brief, are the consequences in Great Britain. How will the rest of the world be influenced? Not in a uniform way. Let us take first the debtor countries to whom Great Britain has in the past lent large sums in sterling, and from whom interest is due in sterling, such as Australia, Argentina, and India. To these countries the depreciation of sterling represents a great concession. A smaller quantity of their goods will be sufficient to meet their sterling liabilities. The interest due to Great Britain from abroad, which is fixed in sterling, amounts to about £100 million a year. In respect of this sum Great Britain now plays the part of a reasonable creditor who moderates his claim in view of so great a change in the situation as the recent catastrophic fall in commodity prices.

When we try to calculate the effect on other manufacturing countries, whose competition we are now in a better position to meet, the effect is more complex. A large part of the world will, I expect, follow Great Britain in reducing the former gold value of their money. There are already signs in many countries that no great effort will be made to maintain the gold parity. In the last few days Canada, Italy, Scandinavia have moved in our direction. India and the Crown Colonies, including the Straits Settlements, have automatically followed sterling. Australia and the whole of South America had already abandoned the effort to maintain exchange parity. I shall be astonished if Germany delays long before following our example. Will Holland deal final ruin to the rubber and sugar industries of the Dutch Indies by keeping them tied to gold? There will be strong motives driving a large part of the world our way. After all, Great Britain's plight, as the result of the deflation of prices, is far less serious than that of most countries.

Now, in so far as this is the case, we and all the countries [247] following our example will gain the benefits of higher prices. But none of us will secure a competitive advantage at the expense of the others. Thus the competitive disadvantage will be concentrated on those few countries which remain on the gold standard. On these will fall the curse of Midas. As a result of their unwillingness to exchange their exports except for gold their export trade will dry up and disappear until they no longer have either a favourable trade balance or foreign deposits to repatriate. This means in the main France and the United States. Their loss of export trade will be an inevitable, a predictable, outcome of their own action. These countries largely for reasons resulting from the war and the war settlements, are owed much money by the rest of the world. They erect tariff barriers which prevent the payment of these sums in goods. They are unwilling to lend it. They have already taken nearly all the available surplus gold in the whole world. There remained, in logic, only one way by which the rest of the world could maintain its solvency and self-respect; namely, to cease purchasing these countries' exports. So long as the gold standard is preserved – which means that the prices of international commodities must be much the same everywhere – this involved a competitive campaign of deflation, each of us trying to get our prices down faster than the others, a campaign which had intensified unemployment and business losses to an unendurable pitch.

But as soon as the gold exchange is ruptured the problem is solved. For the appreciation of French and American money in terms of the money of other countries makes it impossible for French and American exporters to sell their goods. The recent policy of these countries could not, if it was persistently pursued, end in any other way. They have willed the destruction of their own export industries, and only they can take the steps necessary to restore them. The appreciation of their currencies must also embarrass gravely their banking systems. The United States had, in effect, set the rest of us the problem of finding [248] some way to do without her wheat, her copper, her cotton, and her motor-cars. She set the problem and, as it had only one solution, that solution we have been compelled to find.

Yet this is quite the opposite of the note on which I wish to end. The solution to which we have been driven, though it gives immediate relief to us and transfers the strain to others, is in truth a solution unsatisfactory for everyone. The world will never be prosperous without a trade recovery in the United States. Peace and confidence and a harmonious economic equilibrium for all the closely interrelated countries of the globe is the only goal worth aiming at.

I believe that the great events of the last week may open a new chapter in the world's monetary history. I have a hope that they may break down barriers which have seemed impassable. We need now to take intimate and candid conference together as to the better ordering of our affairs for the future. The President of the United States turned in his sleep last June. Great issues deserve his attention. Yet the magic spell of immobility which has been cast over the White House seems still unbroken. Are the solutions offered us always to be too late? Shall we in Great Britain invite three-quarters of the world, including the whole of our Empire, to join with us in evolving a new currency system which shall be stable in terms of commodities? Or would the gold standard countries be interested to learn the terms, which must needs be strict, on which we should be prepared to re-enter the system of a drastically reformed gold standard?

[249]

30

CW 9, 'The Means to Prosperity' (1933)

[*This essay was first published as four articles in* The Times *on 13, 14, 15, 16 March 1933. They were written to influence the World Economic Conference, held in the South Kensington Geological Museum from 12 June to 27 July 1933. The essay is in two parts. The first deploys Keynes case for government loan-expenditure, using for the first time the 'multiplier theory' developed by his 'favourite pupil', Richard Kahn. This remedied the lack of a calculable multiplier in his 1929 essay 'Can Lloyd George Do It?' (excerpt 28). The second argues the case for increasing the reserves of central banks through the issue of gold certificates. Aimed at restoring stable exchange rates, the conference was scuppered by President Roosevelt's rejection of international currency stabilization. In an article in the* Daily Mail, *4 July 1933, Keynes called Roosevelt's action 'magnificently right'.[8]*]

Internal Expansion

The reluctance to support schemes of capital development at home as a means to restore prosperity is generally based on two grounds – the meagreness of the employment created by the expenditure of a given sum, and the strain on national and local budgets of the subsidies which such schemes usually require. These are quantitative questions not easily answered with precision. But I will endeavour to give reasons for the belief that the answers to both of them are much more favourable than is commonly supposed. It is often said that in Great Britain it costs £500 capital expenditure on public works to give one man employment for a year. This is based on the amount of labour directly employed on the spot. But it is easy to see that the materials used and the transport required also give employment. If we allow for this as we should, the capital expenditure per man-year of additional employment is usually estimated, in the case of building for example, at £200.

But if the new expenditure is additional and not merely in substitution for other expenditure, the increase of employment does not stop there. The additional wages and other incomes paid out are spent on additional purchases, which in turn lead to further employment. If the resources of the country were already fully employed, these additional purchases would be mainly reflected in higher prices and increased imports. But in present circumstances this would be true of only a small proportion of the additional consumption, since the greater part of it could be provided without much change of price by home resources which are at present unemployed. Moreover, in so far as the increased demand for food, resulting from the increased purchasing power of the working classes, served either to raise the prices or to increase the sales of the output of primary [339] producers at home and abroad, we should today positively welcome it. It would be much better to raise the price of farm products by increasing the demand for them than by artificially restricting their supply.

Nor have we yet reached the end. The newly employed who supply the increased purchases of those employed on the new capital works will, in their turn, spend more, thus adding to the employment of others; and so on. Some enthusiasts, perceiving the fact of these repercussions, have greatly exaggerated the total result, and have even supposed that the amount of new employment thus created is only limited by the necessary intervals between the receipt of expenditure of income, in other words by the velocity of circulation of money. Unfortunately it is not quite as good as that. For at each stage there is, so to speak, a certain proportion of leakage. At each stage a certain proportion of the increased income is not passed on in increased employment. Some part will be saved by the recipient; some part raises prices and so diminishes consumption elsewhere, except in so far as producers spend their increased profits; some part will be spent on imports; some part is merely a substitution for expenditure previously made out of the dole or private charity or personal savings; and some part may reach the Exchequer without relieving the taxpayer to an equal extent. Thus in order to sum the net effect on employment of the series of repercussions, it is necessary to make reasonable assumptions as to the proportion lost in each of these ways. I would refer those who are interested in the technique of such summations to an article by Mr R. F. Kahn published in *The Economic Journal*, June 1931.

It is obvious that the appropriate assumptions vary greatly according to circumstances. If there were little or no margin of unemployed resources, then, as I have said above, the increased expenditure would largely waste itself in higher prices and increased imports (which is, indeed, a regular feature of the later stages of a boom in new construction). If the dole was as [340] great as a man's earnings when in work and was paid for by borrowing, there would be scarcely any repercussions at all. On the other hand, now that the dole is paid for by taxes and not by borrowing (so that a reduction in the dole may be expected to increase the spending power of the taxpayer), we no longer have to make so large a deduction on this head. Let me consider in some detail what the net result is likely to be in present conditions.

Let us call the gross amount of expenditure, provided out of additional borrowing, the *primary expenditure* and the employment directly created by this expenditure the *primary employment*. I have estimated above on the authority of others – and no grounds have been given for questioning the reasonable accuracy of the estimate as a rough guide to the magnitudes involved – that £200 of primary expenditure will provide one man-year of primary employment. It will make no difference to the following argument whether the object of the borrowing is to finance public works or private enterprise or to relieve the taxpayer. This primary expenditure will, in any of these cases, set up a series of repercussions leading to what it is convenient to call *secondary employment*. Our problem is to ascertain the total employment, primary and secondary together, created by a given amount of additional loan-expenditure, i.e. to ascertain the multi-
[341]   plier relating the total employment to the primary employment.

The primary expenditure of an additional £100, provided by borrowing, can be divided into two parts. The first part is the money which, for one reason or another, does not become additional income in the hands of an Englishman (or, if we apply the argument to the United States, of an American). This is mainly made up of (i) the cost of imported materials, (ii) the cost of goods, which are not newly produced but merely transferred, such as land or goods taken out of stocks which are not replenished, (iii) the cost of productive resources of men and plant which are not additionally employed but are merely drawn away from other jobs, (iv) the cost of wages which take the place of income previously provided out of funds borrowed for the dole. The second part, which is the money which does become additional income in the hands of an Englishman, has again to be divided into two portions, according as it is saved or spent (spending in this context including all the direct additional expenditure of the recipient, including expenditure on the production of durable objects).

To obtain the multiplier we simply have to estimate these two proportions, namely, what proportion of typical expenditure becomes someone's income and what proportion of this income is spent. For these two proportions, multiplied together, give us the ratio of the first repercussion to the primary effect, since they give us the ratio of the second flow of expenditure to the initial flow of expenditure. We can then sum the whole series of repercussions, since the second repercussion can be expected to bear the same ratio to the first repercussion, as the first bore to the primary effect; and so on.

The abstract argument can be illustrated as follows. Two years ago, when the dole was being financed in Great Britain out of borrowed money, this fact required a substantial deduction, which is no longer necessary, in calculating the proportion of expenditure which becomes additional income. Two years hence, if employment is much better than it is now, it may be necessary to make a substantial deduction in respect of resources [342] which are merely drawn away from other jobs; for the smaller the pool of unemployed resources, the more likely is this result from increased expenditure. I am not disposed to make much deduction at any time for goods taken out of stock, since stocks are seldom really large and the sight of depletion soon stimulates replenishment. *In existing conditions*, therefore, I should say that a deduction of 30 per cent for expenditure which for one reason or another does not increase incomes, leaving 70 per cent accruing to one person or another as current income, would be a reasonable supposition.

What proportion of this additional income will be disbursed as additional expenditure? In so far as it accrues to the wage-earning classes, one can safely assume that most of it will be spent; in so far as it increases profits and salaries and professional earnings, the proportion saved will be larger. We have to strike a rough average. In present circumstances, for example, we might assume that at least 70 per cent of the increased income will be spent and not more than 30 per cent saved.

On these assumptions the first repercussion will be 49 per cent (since $7 \times 7 = 49$) of the primary effect, or (say) one-half; the second repercussion will be one-half of the first repercussion, i.e. one-quarter of the primary effect, and so on. Thus the multiplier is 2, since, if I may take the reader back to his school-days, he will remember that $1 + \frac{1}{2} + \frac{1}{4} +$ etc. $= 2$. The amount of time which it takes for current income to be spent will separate each repercussion from the next one. But it will be seen that seven-eighths of the total effects come from the primary expenditure and the first two repercussions, so that the time-lags involved are not unduly serious.

It is to be noticed that no additional allowance has to be made for any rise of prices which the increased demand may bring with it. The effect of higher prices will be gradually to diminish the proportion which becomes new income, since it will probably be a symptom that the surplus resources are no [343] longer so adequate in certain directions, with the result that a larger proportion of the new expenditure is merely diverted from other jobs. It is also probable that higher prices will mean higher profits, with the result that, more of the increased income being profit and less of it being wages, more of it will be saved. Thus, as men are gradually brought back into employment and as prices gradually rise, the multiplier will gradually diminish. Moreover, in so far as wages rise it is obvious that the amount of employment corresponding to a given expenditure on wages will also gradually diminish. These modifications, however, would only become relevant as and when our remedy was becoming very successful. A given dose of expenditure at the present stage will, for several reasons, produce a much larger effect on employment than it will be prudent to expect later on when the margin of unused resources is reduced.

To illustrate the range of reasonable estimates for the multiplier, let us consider the effect on it of certain other assumptions. If we were to assume that each of the proportions is 60 per cent, the multiplier works out at about $1\frac{1}{2}$, which might be considered to set a minimum limit to its value, since it would seem very improbable that either proportion can be so low as this today. If, on the contrary, we were to expect that the proportion of the primary expenditure which becomes income and the proportion of the income which is spent are each 80 per cent, the multiplier becomes nearly 3 (as those readers who can still do arithmetic will easily verify). I believe myself that it is chiefly in estimating the proportion of expenditure which becomes additional income that we have to be cautious; and the estimates, which I should feel happiest in making, would be based on some such assumption as that not less than 66 per cent of additional expenditure (whether on new capital works or on additional consumption) would become additional income in the hands of an Englishman, and that not less than 75 per cent of this additional income would be spent; whilst I would more readily increase the latter proportion to 80 than the former proportion to 70. In what follows I will base my estimates on these figures, which also lead to a multiplier of 2. [344] It may interest American readers to consider what assumptions would be most appropriate to present conditions in the United States. Personally I should expect the American multiple to be greater than 2, rather than less.

The Relief to the Budget

On the assumptions which I have endeavoured to justify in the previous chapter, a primary expenditure of £100 will directly increase British incomes by two thirds of this amount, i.e. by £66. But the total increase of incomes, including the secondary effects, will be £66 $(1 + \frac{2}{3} + \frac{4}{9} + \ldots)$, i.e. £200. In order to ascertain the total relief to the budget resulting from the effects thus set up, we have to estimate, first the saving in respect of the cost of unemployment relief, and secondly the increased yield of the revenue from taxes levied on the increased income.

Not the whole of the additional income falls to men previously supported by the dole. Some part goes to profits, some part to the salaried and professional classes, and some part in wages for the increased employment of workers, who were not drawing the dole, either because they were already partly employed or for some other reason.

I consider, however, that it would be fairly safe to assume that two-thirds of the increased income, i.e. £44, will accrue to men previously supported by the dole, which means about one-third of a man-year of increased employment taking the average wage at 50s a week.

Since, on the assumptions which we have adopted, 75 per cent of the increased incomes of £66, caused by the primary expenditure of £100, will be spent, and 66 per cent of this secondary expenditure again serves to increase incomes, and so on, it follows that our primary expenditure of £100 will, sooner or later, bring about two-thirds of a man-year of employment for workers previously supported by the dole. At the same time, as we have seen, the total increase of incomes which it will bring about will be £200. If, however, the reader considers [345] some other set of figures more probable, I have here provided him with an apparatus which will enable him to work out the answer on his own assumptions.

We are now ready to estimate the total relief to the budget. For purposes of broad calculation the average cost of a man on the dole is usually taken at £50 a year. Hence a loan expenditure of £100, by affording two-thirds of a man-year of employment for workers previously supported by the dole, reduces the cost of unemployment relief by £33.

But there is a further benefit to the budget, due to the fact that our loan expenditure of £100 will increase the national income by £200. For the yield of the taxes rises and falls more or less in proportion to the national income. Our budgetary difficulties today are mainly due to the decline in the national income. Now for the nation as a whole, leaving on one side transactions with foreigners, its income is exactly equal to its expenditure (including in expenditure both consumption-expenditure and new capital-expenditure, but excluding intermediate exchanges from one hand to another); – the two being simply different names for the same thing, my expenditure being your income.

Now on the average about 20 per cent of the national income is paid to the Exchequer in taxes. The exact proportion depends on how the new income is distributed between the higher [346] ranges of income subject to direct taxation, and the lower ranges which are touched by indirect taxes; also the yield of some taxes is not closely correlated with changes in national income. To allow for these doubts, let us take the proportion of the new income accruing to the Exchequer at 10 per cent, i.e. £20 of new revenue from £200 increase of income. There will, it is true, be some time-lag in the collection of this, but we need not trouble about that; though it is a powerful argument in favour of proposals for modifying the rigidity of our annual budget and for making our estimates, on this occasion, cover a longer period than one year. Owing to the time-lag in the effect of increased taxation in reducing the national income our existing budgetary procedure is open to the serious objection that the measures which will balance this budget are calculated to unbalance the next one; and vice versa.

Thus the total benefit to the Exchequer of an additional loan-expenditure of £100 is at least £33 *plus* £20, or £53 altogether, i.e. a little more than a half of the loan-expenditure. We need see nothing paradoxical in this. We have reached a point where a considerable proportion of every further decline in the national income is visited on the Exchequer through the agency of the dole and the decline in the yield of the taxes. It is natural, therefore, that the benefit of measures to increase the national income should largely accrue to the Exchequer.

If we apply this reasoning to the projects for loan-expenditure which are receiving support today in responsible quarters, we see that it is a complete mistake to believe that there is a dilemma between schemes for increasing employment and schemes for balancing the budget – that we must go slowly and cautiously with the former for fear of injuring the latter. Quite the contrary. There is no possibility of balancing the budget except by increasing the national income, which is much the same thing as increasing employment.   [347]

Take, for example, the proposal to spend £7 million on the new Cunarder. I say that this will benefit the Exchequer by at least a half of this sum, i.e. by £3,500,000, which vastly exceeds the maximum aid which is being asked from the Exchequer.

Or take the expenditure of £100 million on housing whether for rebuilding slums or under the auspices of a National Housing Board, this would benefit the budget by the vast total of some £50 million – a sum far exceeding any needful subsidy. If the mind of the reader boggles at this and he feels that it must be too good to be true, let him recur carefully to the argument which has led up to it. And if he distrusts his own judgement, let me point out that no serious attempt has yet been made to confound the bases of the argument, where I first offered it *coram publico* in the forum of *The Times*.

Substantially the same argument also applies to a relief of taxation by suspending the Sinking Fund and by returning to the practice of financing by loans those services which can properly be so financed, such as the cost of new roads charged on the Road Fund and that part of the cost of the dole which can be averaged out against the better days for which we must hope. For the increased spending power of the taxpayer will have precisely the same favourable repercussions as increased spending power due to loan-expenditure; and in some ways this method of increasing expenditure is healthier and better spread throughout the community. If the Chancellor of the Exchequer will reduce taxation by £50 million through suspending the Sinking Fund and borrowing in those cases where formerly we thought it reasonable to borrow, the half of what he remits will in fact return to him from the saving on the dole and the higher yield of a given level of taxation – though, as I have pointed out [348] above, it will not necessarily return to him in the same budget.*

I should add that this particular argument does not apply to a relief of taxation balanced by an equal reduction of government expenditure (by reducing schoolteachers' salaries, for example); for this represents a redistribution, not a net increase, of national spending power. It is applicable to all *additional* expenditure made, not in substitution for other expenditure, but out of savings or out of borrowed money, either by private persons or by public authorities, whether for capital purposes or for consumption made possible by a relief of taxation or in some other way.

---

* I strongly support, therefore, the suggestion which has been made that the next budget should be divided into two parts, one of which shall include those items of expenditure which it would be proper to treat as loan-expenditure in present circumstances.

If these conclusions cannot be refuted, is it not advisable to act upon them? The contrary policy of endeavouring to balance the budget by impositions, restrictions, and precautions will surely fail, because it must have the effect of diminishing the national spending power, and hence the national income.

The argument applies, of course, both ways equally. Just as the effect of increased primary expenditure on employment, on the national income and on the budget is multiplied in the manner described, so also is the effect of decreased primary expenditure. Indeed, if it were not so it would be difficult to explain the violence of the recession both here and, even more, in the United States. Just as an initial impulse of modest dimensions has been capable of producing such devastating repercussions, so also a moderate impulse in the opposite direction will effect a surprising recovery. There is no magic here, no mystery; but a reliable scientific prediction.

Why should this method of approach appear to so many people to be novel and odd and paradoxical? I can only find [349] the answer in the fact that all our ideas about economics, instilled into us by education and atmosphere and tradition are, whether we are conscious of it or not, soaked with theoretical presuppositions which are only properly applicable to a society which is in equilibrium, with all its productive resources already employed. Many people are trying to solve the problem of unemployment with a theory which is based on the assumption that there is no unemployment. Obviously if the productive resources of the nation were already fully occupied, none of the advantages could be expected which, in present circumstances, I predict from an increase of loan-expenditure. For in that case increased loan-expenditure would merely exhaust itself in raising prices and wages and diverting resources from other jobs. In other words, it would be purely inflationary. But these ideas, perfectly valid in their proper setting, are inapplicable to present circumstances, which can only be handled by the less familiar method which I have endeavoured to explain.

. . .   [350]

A Proposal for the World Economic Conference

. . .

We are now advanced a stage further in our argument. We have reached the point where combined international action is of the essence of policy. We have reached, that is to say, the field and scope of the World Economic Conference. The task of this Conference, as I see it, is to devise some sort of joint action of a kind to allay the anxieties of central banks and to relieve the [356] tension on their reserves, or the fear and expectation of tension. This would enable many more countries to reach the first of the stages which I distinguished in chapter IV – the stage at which bank credit is cheap and abundant. We cannot, by international action, make the horses drink. That is their domestic affair. But we can provide them with water. To revive the parched world by releasing a million rivulets of spending power is the primary task of the World Conference.

. . .

No remedies can be quickly efficacious which do not allay the anxieties of treasuries and central banks throughout the world by supplying them with more adequate reserves of international money. There is a considerable variety of schemes which can be devised with this end in view, having a close family resemblance to one another. After much private discussion and borrowing the ideas of others, I am convinced that the following scheme is the best one. If other variants command more support, that would be a reason for preferring them.

[357]   There are certain conditions which any scheme for increasing the reserves of international money should satisfy. In the first place, the additional reserves should be based on gold. For whilst gold is rapidly ceasing to be national money, it is becoming, even more exclusively than before, the international money most commonly held in reserve and used to meet a foreign drain. In the second place, it should not be of an eleemosynary character, but should be available, not only to the exceptionally needy, but to all participating countries in accordance with a general formula. Indeed there are few, if any, countries left today which are so entirely without anxiety that they would not

welcome some strengthening of their position. In the third place, there should be an elasticity in the quantity of the additional reserves outstanding, so that they would operate, not as a net permanent addition to the world's monetary supply, but as a balancing factor to be released when prices are abnormally low as at present, and to be withdrawn again if prices were to be rising too much. These conditions can be satisfied as follows:

(i) There should be set up an international authority for the issue of gold-notes, of which the face value would be expressed in terms of the gold content of the U.S. dollar.

(ii) These notes would be issuable up to a maximum of $5,000 million and would be obtainable by the participating countries against an equal face value of the gold-bonds of their governments, up to a maximum quota for each country.

(iii) The proportionate quota of each country would be based on some such formula as the amount of gold which it held in reserve at some recent normal date, e.g. at the end of 1928, provided that no individual quota should exceed $450 million and with power to the governing board to modify the rigidity of this formula where special reasons could be given for not adhering to it strictly. (Some provision, for example, would be required for silver-using countries.) The effect of this formula would be that the quota of each country would add to its reserves an amount approximately equal to the gold which it held in 1928, subject to the above maximum proviso. The detailed allocation [358] for each country is given in an appendix to this chapter.

(iv) Each participating government would undertake to pass legislation providing that these gold-notes would be acceptable as the equivalent of gold, except that they should not enter into the active circulation but would be held only by treasuries, central banks, or in the reserves against domestic note issues.

(v) The governing board of the institution would be elected by the participating governments, who would be free to delegate their powers to their central banks, each having a voting power in proportion to its quota.

(vi) The gold-bonds would carry a rate of interest, nominal or very low in the first instance, which could be changed from time to time by the governing board subject to (viii) below.

They would be repayable at any time by the government responsible for them, or on notice given by the governing board subject to (viii) below.

(vii) The interest, after meeting expenses, would be retained in gold as a guarantee fund. In addition, each participating government would guarantee any ultimate loss, arising through a default, in proportion to the amount of its maximum quota.

(viii) The governing board would be directed to use their discretion to modify the volume of the note issue or the rate of interest on the bonds, solely with a view to avoiding, so far as possible, a rise in the gold price level of primary products entering into international trade above some agreed norm between [359] the present level and that of 1928 – perhaps the level of 1930.

31
The New Deal

[*Keynes had a huge admiration for President Roosevelt and the New Deal, which he contrasted favourably with the torpor of government in his own country. But he was not an unqualified admirer. The following excerpts from CW 21 give the gist of his attitude.*]

CW 21, 'Dear Mr President'

[*Keynes to Roosevelt, 31 December 1933.*]
Dear Mr President,

You have made yourself the trustee for those in every country who seek to mend the evils of our condition by reasoned experiment within the framework of the existing social system.

If you fail, rational change will be gravely prejudiced throughout the world, leaving orthodoxy and revolution to fight it out.

But if you succeed, new and bolder methods will be tried

everywhere, and we may date the first chapter of a new economic era from your accession to office.

This is a sufficient reason why I should venture to lay my reflections before you, though under the disadvantages of distance and partial knowledge.

Opinion in England

At the moment your sympathisers in England are nervous and sometimes despondent. We wonder whether the order of different urgencies is rightly understood, whether there is a [289] confusion of aims, and whether some of the advice you get is not crack-brained and queer.

If we are disconcerted when we defend you, this is partly due to the influence of our environment in London. For almost every one here has a wildly distorted view of what is happening in the United States.

The average City man believes you are engaged on a hare-brained expedition in face of competent advice, that the best hope lies in your ridding yourself of your present advisers to return to the old ways, and that otherwise the United States is heading for some ghastly breakdown. This is what they say they smell.

There is a recrudescence of wise head-wagging by those who believe the nose is a nobler organ than the brain. London is convinced that we only have to sit back and wait to see what we shall see. May I crave your attention, while I put my own view?

The Present Task

You are engaged on a double task, recovery and reform – recovery from the slump, and the passage of those business and social reforms which are long overdue. For the first, speed and quick results are essential. The second may be urgent, too; but haste will be injurious, and wisdom of long-range purpose is more necessary than immediate achievement. It will be through raising high the prestige of your Administration by success in short-range recovery that you will have the driving force to accomplish long-range reform.

On the other hand, even wise and necessary reform may, in some respects, impede and complicate recovery. For it will upset the confidence of the business world and weaken its existing motives to action before you have had time to put other motives in their place. It may overtask your bureaucratic machine, which the traditional individualism of the United States and the [290] old 'spoils system' have left none too strong. And it will confuse the thought and aim of yourself and your Administration by giving you too much to think about all at once.

N.R.A. Aims and Results

Now I am not clear, looking back over the last nine months, that the order of urgency between measures of recovery and measures of reform has been duly observed, or that the latter has not sometimes been mistaken for the former. In particular, though its social gains are considerable, I cannot detect any material aid to recovery in the N[ational] [Industrial] R[ecovery] A[ct]. The driving force which has been put behind the vast administrative task set by this act has seemed to represent a wrong choice in the order of urgencies. The Act is on the statute book; a considerable amount has been done toward implementing it; but it might be better for the present to allow experience to accumulate before trying to force through all its details.

That is my first reflection – that N.R.A., which is essentially reform and probably impedes recovery, has been put across too hastily, in the false guise of being part of the technique of recovery.

My second reflection relates to the technique of recovery itself. The object of recovery is to increase the national output and put more men to work. In the economic system of the modern world, output is primarily produced for sale; and the volume of output depends on the amount of purchasing power, compared with the prime cost of production, which is expected to come on the market.

Broadly speaking, therefore, an increase of output cannot occur unless by the operation of one or other of three factors. Individuals must be induced to spend more out of their existing incomes, or the business world must be induced, either by increased confidence in the prospects or by a lower rate of interest, to create additional current incomes in the hands of their employees, which is what happens when either the working or the fixed capital of the country is being increased; or [291] public authority must be called in aid to create additional current incomes through the expenditure of borrowed or printed money.

In bad times the first factor cannot be expected to work on a sufficient scale. The second factor will only come in as the second wave of attack on the slump, after the tide has been turned by the expenditures of public authority. It is, therefore, only from the third factor that we can expect the initial major impulse.

Now there are indications that two technical fallacies may have affected the policy of your Administration. The first relates to the part played in recovery by rising prices. Rising prices are to be welcomed because they are usually a symptom of rising output and employment. When more purchasing power is spent, one expects rising output at rising prices. Since there cannot be rising output without rising prices, it is essential to insure that the recovery shall not be held back by the insufficiency of the supply of money to support the increased monetary turnover.

The Problem of Rising Prices

But there is much less to be said in favour of rising prices if they are brought about at the expense of rising output. Some debtors may be helped, but the national recovery as a whole will be retarded. Thus rising prices caused by deliberately increasing prime costs or by restricting output have a vastly inferior value to rising prices which are the natural results of an increase in the nation's purchasing power.

I do not mean to impugn the social justice and social expediency of the redistribution of incomes aimed at by the N.R.A. and by the various schemes for agricultural restriction. The latter, in particular, I should strongly support in principle. But too much emphasis on the remedial value of a higher price level as an object in itself may lead to serious misapprehension of the

[292]   part prices can play in the technique to recovery. The stimulation of output by increasing aggregate purchasing power is the right way to get prices up; and not the other way around.

Thus, as the prime mover in the first stage of the technique of recovery, I lay overwhelming emphasis on the increase of national purchasing power resulting from governmental expenditure which is financed by loans and is not merely a transfer through taxation, from existing incomes. Nothing else counts in comparison with this.

Boom, Slump and War

In a boom, inflation can be caused by allowing unlimited credit to support the excited enthusiasm of business speculators. But in a slump governmental loan expenditure is the only sure means of obtaining quickly a rising output at rising prices. That is why a war has always caused intense industrial activity. In the past, orthodox finance has regarded a war as the only legitimate excuse for creating employment by government expenditure. You, Mr President, having cast off such fetters, are free to engage in the interests of peace and prosperity the technique which hitherto has only been allowed to serve the purposes of war and destruction.

The set-back American recovery experienced this past Autumn was the predictable consequence of the failure of your Administration to organize any material increase in new loan expenditure during your first six months of office. The position six months hence will depend entirely on whether you have been laying the foundations for larger expenditures in the near future.

I am not surprised that so little has been spent to date. Our own experience has shown how difficult it is to improvise useful loan expenditures at short notice. There are many obstacles to be patiently overcome, if waste, inefficiency and corruption are to be avoided. There are many factors I need not stop to [293]   enumerate which render especially difficult in the United States the rapid improvisation of a vast programme of public works. I do not blame Secretary Ickes for being cautious and careful. But the risks of less speed must be weighed against those of more haste. He must get across the crevasses before it is dark.

The other set of fallacies, of which I fear the influence, arises out of a crude economic doctrine commonly known as the quantity theory of money. Rising output and rising incomes will suffer a setback sooner or later if the quantity of money is rigidly fixed. Some people seem to infer from this that output and income can be raised by increasing the quantity of money. But this is like trying to get fat by buying a larger belt. In the United States today your belt is plenty big enough for your belly. It is a most misleading thing to stress the quantity of money, which is only a limiting factor, rather than the volume of expenditure, which is the operative factor.[9]

It is an even more foolish application of the same ideas to believe that there is a mathematical relation between the price of gold and the prices of other things. It is true that the value of the dollar in terms of foreign currencies will affect the prices of those goods which enter into international trade. In so far as an overvaluation of the dollar was impeding the freedom of domestic price-raising policies or disturbing the balance of payments with foreign countries, it was advisable to depreciate it. But exchange depreciation should follow the success of your domestic price-raising policy as its natural consequence, and should not be allowed to disturb the whole world by preceding its justification at an entirely arbitrary pace. This is another example of trying to put on flesh by letting out the belt.

Currency and Exchange

These criticisms do not mean that I have weakened in my advocacy of a managed currency or in preferring stable prices to stable exchanges. The currency and exchange policy of a country should be entirely subservient to the aim of raising output [294] and employment to the right level. But the recent gyrations of the dollar have looked to me more like a gold standard on the booze than the ideal managed currency of my dreams.

You may be feeling by now, Mr President, that my criticism is more obvious than my sympathy. Yet truly that is not so. You remain for me the ruler whose general outlook and attitude to the tasks of government are the most sympathetic in the world. You are the only one who sees the necessity of a profound change of methods and is attempting it without intolerance, tyranny or destruction. You are feeling your way by trial and error, and are felt to be, as you should be, entirely uncommitted in your own person to the details of a particular technique. In my country, as in your own, your position remains singularly untouched by criticism of this or the other detail. Our hope and our faith are based on broader considerations.

If you were to ask me what I would suggest in concrete terms of the immediate future, I would reply thus:

Constructive Criticism

In the field of gold devaluation and exchange policy the time has come when uncertainty should be ended. This game of blind man's buff with exchange speculators serves no useful purpose and is extremely undignified. It upsets confidence, hinders business decisions, occupies the public attention in a measure far exceeding its real importance, and is responsible both for the irritation and for a certain lack of respect which exist abroad.

You have three alternatives. You can devalue the dollar in terms of gold, returning to the gold standard at a new fixed ratio. This would be inconsistent with your declarations in favour of a long-range policy of stable prices, and I hope you will reject it.

[295]   You can seek some common policy of exchange stabilisation with Great Britain aimed at stable price levels. This would be the best ultimate solution; but it is not practical politics at the moment, unless you are prepared to talk in terms of an initial value of sterling well below $5 pending the realisation of a marked rise in your domestic price level.

Lastly, you can announce that you will control the dollar exchange by buying and selling gold and foreign currencies at a definite figure so as to avoid wide or meaningless fluctuations, with a right to shift the parities at any time, but with a declared intention only so to do either to correct a serious want of balance in America's international receipts and payments or to meet a shift in your domestic price level relative to price levels abroad.

The Favoured Policy

This appears to me your best policy during the transitional
period. You would be waiving your right to make future arbitrary changes which did not correspond to any relevant change
in the facts, but in other respects you would retain your liberty
to make your exchange policy subservient to the needs of your
domestic policy – free to let out your belt in proportion as you
put on flesh.

In the field of domestic policy, I put in the forefront, for the
reasons given above, a large volume of loan expenditure under
government auspices. It is beyond my province to choose particular objects of expenditure. But preference should be given
to those which can be made to mature quickly on a large scale,
as, for example, the rehabilitation of the physical condition of
the railroads. The object is to start the ball rolling.

The United States is ready to roll toward prosperity, if a
good hard shove can be given in the next six months. Could
not the energy and enthusiasm which launched the N.R.A. in
its early days be put behind a campaign for accelerating capital
expenditures, as wisely chosen as the pressure of circumstances
permits? You can at least feel sure that the country will be better enriched by such projects than by the involuntary idleness
of millions.   [296]

Plenty of Cheap Credit

I put in the second place the maintenance of cheap and abundant credit, in particular the reduction of the long-term rate of
interest. The turn of the tide in Great Britain is largely attributable to the reduction in the long-term rate of interest which
ensued on the success of the conversion of the War Loan. This
was deliberately engineered by the open-market policy of the
Bank of England.

I see no reason why you should not reduce the rate of interest on your long-term government bonds to 2½ per cent or less,
with favourable repercussions on the whole bond market, if
only the Federal Reserve System would replace its present holdings of short-dated Treasury issues by purchasing long-dated

issues in exchange. Such a policy might become effective in a few months, and I attach great importance to it.

With these adaptations or enlargements of your existing policies, I should expect a successful outcome with great confidence. How much that would mean, not only to the material prosperity of the United States and the whole world, but in comfort to men's minds through a restoration of their faith in the wisdom and the power of government!

With great respect,

Your obedient servant,

[297]   J. M. KEYNES[10]

CW 21, 'Agenda for the President'

[*This was printed in* The Times *on 11 June 1934. Keynes had visited the United States from 15 May to 8 June 1934.*]

These are a few notes on the New Deal by one who has lately visited the United States on a brief visit of pure inquisitiveness – made under the limitations of imperfect knowledge but gaining, perhaps, from the detachment of a bird's-eye view. My purpose is to consider the prospects rather than the past – taking the legislation of this Congress for granted and examining what might be done on the basis thus given. I am in sympathy with most of the social and reforming aims of this legislation; and the principal subject of these notes is the problem of consolidating economic and business recovery.

For this reason I have not much to say about N.R.A. I doubt if this is either such an advantage to recovery or such a handicap
[322]   as its advocates and its critics suppose. It embodies some important improvements in labour conditions and for securing fair trade practices. But I agree with the widespread opinion that much of it is objectionable because of its restrictionist philosophy (which has a proper place in agricultural adjustment today but not in American industry) and because of its excessive complexity and regimentation. In particular it would be advisable to discard most of the provisions to fix prices and to forbid sales below an alleged but undefinable cost basis. Nevertheless, its

net effect on recovery can easily be overestimated either way. I find most Americans divided between those who believe that higher wages are good because they increase purchasing power and those who believe that they are bad because they raise costs. But both are right, and the net result of the two opposing influences is to cancel out. The important question is the proper adjustment of relative wage rates. Absolute wage rates are not of primary importance in a country where their effect on foreign trade has been offset by exchange devaluation.

The case of A.A.A. (Agricultural Adjustment [Administration]), on the other hand, is much stronger. For the farmer has had to shoulder more than his share of the trouble and also has more lasting difficulties ahead of him than industry has. A.A.A. is organising for the farmer the advisable measure of restriction which industry long ago organised for itself. Thus, the task which A.A.A. is attempting is necessary though difficult; whereas some part of what N.R.A. seems to be aiming at is not only impracticable but unnecessary.

Problem of Recovery

I see the problem of recovery, accordingly, in the following light. How soon will normal business enterprise come to the rescue? What measures can be taken to hasten the return of normal enterprise? On what scale, by which expedients and for how long is abnormal Government expenditure advisable in the meantime? For this, I think, is how the Administration should view its task. I see no likelihood that business of its own [323] initiative will invest in durable goods of a sufficient scale for many months to come, for the following reasons.

In the first place, the important but intangible state of mind, which we call business confidence, is signally lacking. It would be easy to mention specific causes of this, for some of which the Administration may be to blame. Probably the most important is the menace of possible labour troubles. But the real explanation, in my judgement, lies deeper than the specific causes. It is to be found in the perplexity and discomfort which the business world feels from being driven so far from its accustomed moorings into unknown and uncharted waters. The business man, who may be adaptable and quick on his feet in his own particular field, is usually conservative and conventional in the larger aspects of social and economic policy. At the start he was carried away, like other people, by the prevailing enthusiasm – without being converted at bottom or suffering a sea-change. Thus he has easily reverted to where he was. He is sulky and bothered; and, with the short memory characteristic of contemporary man, even begins to look back with longing to the good old days of 1932. This atmosphere of disappointment, disillusion, and perplexity is not incurable. The mere passage of time for business to work out its new bearings and recover its equanimity should do much. If the President could convince business men that they know the worst, so to speak, that might hasten matters. Above all, experience of improving conditions might work wonders.

Serious Obstacles

In the second place there are still serious obstacles in the way of reopening the capital market to large-scale borrowing for new investment; particularly the attitude of the finance houses to the Securities Act and the high cost of borrowing to those who need loans most. Moreover, many types of durable goods are [324] already in sufficient supply and businesses will not be inclined to repair or modernise plant until they are experiencing a stronger demand than they can meet with their existing plant; to which should be added the excessively high cost of building relatively to rents and incomes.

None of these obstacles can be overcome in a day or by a stroke of the pen. The notion that if the Government would retire altogether from the economic field business left to itself would soon work out its own salvation is foolish; and even if it were not, it is certain that public opinion would allow no such thing. This does not mean that the Administration should not be assiduously preparing the way for the return of normal investment enterprise. But this will unavoidably take time. When it comes it will intensify and maintain a recovery initiated by other means. But it belongs to the second chapter of the story.

I conclude, therefore, that for six months at least, and probably for a year, the measure of recovery to be achieved will mainly depend on the degree of the direct stimulus to production deliberately applied by the Administration. Since I have no belief in the efficacy for this purpose of the price and wage raising activities of N.R.A., this must chiefly mean the pace and volume of the Government's emergency expenditure.

Up to last November such expenditure, excluding refinancing and advances to banks, was relatively small – about $90,000,000 a month. From November onwards the figure rose sharply and for the first four months of this year the monthly average exceeded $300,000,000. The effect on business was excellent. But then came what seems to me to have been an unfortunate decision. The expenditure of the Civil Works Administration was checked before the expenditure of the Public Works Administration was ready to take its place. Thus the aggregate emergency expenditure is now declining. If it is going to decline to $200,000,000 monthly, much of the ground already gained will probably be lost. If it were to rise to $400,000,000 monthly I should be quite confident that a strong [325] business revival would set in by the autumn. So little divides a retreat from an advance. Most people greatly underestimate the effect of a given emergency expenditure because they overlook the multiplier – the cumulative effect of increased additional individual incomes (volume of income rather than merely of money) because the expenditure of these incomes improves the incomes of a further set of recipients and so on. $400,000,000 monthly is not much more than 11 per cent of the national income; yet it may, directly and indirectly, increase the national income by at least three or four times this amount. Thus the difference between a monthly emergency expenditure of $400,000,000 (financed out of loans, and not out of taxation, which would represent a mere redistribution of incomes) and a $100,000,000 expenditure may be (other things being equal) to increase the national money income by 25 to 30 per cent.

But the full benefit of a given rate of emergency expenditure may not be obtained until it has been continued for a full year. For there are two dead-points to reach and pass. After a long depression, a man will spend a large proportion of this first increment of income in getting financially straight – in paying back taxes, back rents, back interest, back debts. But eventually he will raise the level of his own standard of life. As he does so, demand will revive to a scale which business cannot easily satisfy without spending money on repairs and renewals of plant – which again will put increased incomes into circulation. Thus it is essential for the scale of the emergency expenditure to be large enough to pass by these two dead-points. The best calculation I can make suggests that a monthly figure of $400,000,000, exclusive of re-financing, should be sufficient. This could be attained without reaching the maximum figure which the President has promised not to exceed. But it will not be attained unless the object is pursued more whole-heartedly [326] than in the past three months.

. . .

Continuous pressure should be exerted by the Treasury and the Federal Reserve System to bring down the long-term rate of interest. For it assuredly lies in their power, and it is a mistake to suppose that because the Government will be a large borrower interest rates will rise; inasmuch as the Treasury's resources in gold and the Reserve System's excess reserves put the market wholly in their hands. If a year hence the Administration cannot borrow for 20 years below 2½ per cent, the Treasury will have muddled its task, which their performance [327] up to date gives one no reason to expect. Meanwhile, it would seem advisable to reduce the maximum rate which Member Banks are allowed to pay on savings deposits to 2½ per cent immediately, then to 2 per cent, and ultimately to 1 per cent.

To an Englishman the high level of building costs in America appears to be scandalous, both of building materials and of direct labour. They must be nearly double what they are in England. So long as the volume of work remains as low as it is now, these high costs do not mean high incomes to producers. Thus no one benefits. It is of the first importance for the Administration to take whatever steps are in its power to reduce unit costs in these industries against an undertaking to increase the volume of business sufficiently to maintain and probably to increase actual earnings. This might involve a national programme of building working-class houses to rent, in itself beneficial.

Either by skill or by good fortune the United States seems to me to have arrived at an excellent currency policy. It was right to devalue. It is right to have a value for the dollar currently fixed in terms of gold. It is prudent to keep a discretionary margin to allow future changes in the gold value of the dollar, if a change in circumstances makes this advisable. But all these measures have been carried fully far enough. Thus there would be no risk, in my judgement, if the President were to make it plain that he has now successfully attained his objects so far as they can be attained by monetary policy, and that henceforth a wise spending policy and a gradual but obstinate attack on high interest rates through the agency of the Federal Reserve System and otherwise will occupy the foreground of the economic programme. [328]

CW 21, 'Can America Spend Its Way into Recovery?'

[*First printed in* Redbook, *December 1934. A good example of Keynes's populist style.*]

Why, obviously! – is my first reflection when I am faced by this question. No one of common sense could doubt it, unless his mind had first been muddled by a 'sound' financier or an 'orthodox' economist. We produce in order to sell. In other words, we produce in response to spending. It is impossible to suppose that we can stimulate production and employment by refraining from spending. So, as I have said, the answer is obvious.

But at a second glance, I can see that the question has been so worded as to inspire an insidious doubt. For spending means extravagance. A man who is extravagant soon makes himself poor. How, then, can a nation become rich by doing what must impoverish an individual? By this thought the public is bewildered. Yet a course of behaviour which might make a single individual poor can make a nation wealthy.

For when an individual spends, he affects not only himself

but others. Spending is a two-sided transaction. If I spend my income on buying something which you can make for me, I have not increased my own income, but I have increased yours. If you respond by buying something which I can make for you, then my income also is increased. Thus, when we are thinking of the nation as a whole, we must take account of the results as a whole. The rest of the community is enriched by an individual's expenditure – for his expenditure is simply an addition to [334] everyone else's income. If everybody spends more freely, everybody is richer and nobody is poorer. Each man benefits from the expenditure of his neighbour, and incomes are increased by just the amount required to provide the wherewithal for the additional expenditure. There is only one limit to the extent to which a nation's income can be increased in this manner, and that is the limit set by the physical capacity to produce. To refrain from spending at a time of depression, not only fails, from the national point of view, to add to wealth – it is profligate: it means waste of available man-power, and waste of available machine power, quite apart from the human misery for which it is responsible.

The nation is simply a collection of individuals. If for any reason the individuals who comprise the nation are unwilling, each in his private capacity, to spend sufficient to employ the resources with which the nation is endowed, then it is for the government, the collective representative of all the individuals in the nation, to fill the gap. For the effects of government expenditure are precisely the same as the effects of individuals' expenditure, and it is the increase in the income of the public which provides the source of the extra government expenditure.

It may sometimes be advantageous for a government to resort for part of its borrowing to the banking system rather than to the public. That makes no difference of principle to the effects of the expenditure. There are many who will raise the horror-struck cry of 'Inflation!' when borrowing from the banks is suggested. I doubt if any of those who speak in this way have a clear idea what they mean by inflation. Expenditure is either beneficial or it is harmful. I say it is beneficial, but whether I am right or wrong, it is hard to see how the effect can be altered if the money spent by the government comes from the banks rather than from the public.

When the government borrows in order to spend, it undoubtedly gets the nation into debt. But the debt of a nation to its own citizens is a very different thing from the debt of a private individual. The nation is the citizens who comprise it – no more [335] and no less – and to owe money to them is not very different from owing money to one's self. Insofar as taxes are necessary to shift the interest payments out of one pocket and into the other, this is certainly a disadvantage; but it is a small matter compared with the importance of restoring normal conditions of prosperity. If private individuals refuse to spend, then the government must do it for them. It might be better if they did it for themselves, but that is no argument for not having it done at all.

It is easy, however, to exaggerate the extent to which the government need get into unproductive debt. Let us take, for purposes of illustration, a government hydro-electric power scheme. The government pays out money, which it borrows, to the men employed on the scheme. But the benefit does not stop there. These men who, previously unemployed, are now drawing wages from the government, spend these wages in providing themselves with the necessaries and comforts of existence – shirts, boots and the like. The makers of these shirts and boots, who were hitherto unemployed, spend their wages in their turn, and so set up a fresh wave of additional employment, of additional production, of additional wages, and of additional purchasing power. And so it goes on, until we find that for each man actually employed on the government scheme, three, or perhaps four, additional men are employed in providing for his needs and for the needs of one another. In this way a given rate of government expenditure will give rise to four or five times as much employment as a crude calculation would suggest. Thus there would be some advantage even if the scheme itself were to yield but little revenue hereafter. If, however, it is even a moderately sound scheme capable of yielding (say) three per cent on its cost, the case for it is overwhelmingly established.

That is not all. Unemployment involves a serious financial

strain to the municipal, state, and federal governments. The
alleviation of unemployment, as a result of government
[336] expenditure, means a considerable reduction in outgoings on
the support of the unemployed. At the same time the receipts
from taxation mount up as the nation's taxable income increases,
and as real property values are re-established. These important
factors must be allowed for before it is possible to say how far
government expenditure involves additional unproductive government debt. The residue cannot be very large. Depression is
itself the cause of government deficits, resulting from increased
expenditure on the support of the unemployed and the falling-
off in the yield of taxation. Public debt is inevitable at a time
when private expenditure is inadequate: it is better to incur it
actively in providing employment and promoting industrial
activity than to suffer it passively as a consequence of poverty
and inactivity.

So far I have been advocating government expenditure without much reference to the purpose to which the money is
devoted. The predominant issue, as I look at the matter, is to
get the money spent. But productive and socially useful expenditure is naturally to be preferred to unproductive expenditure.
The arguments for expenditure are very much strengthened if
the government, by spending a small sum of money, can induce
private individuals and corporations to spend a much larger
sum. Thus a government guarantee to facilitate the building of
houses is, perhaps, the best measure of all. The government is
here operating under the advantage of very considerable lever-
age; every dollar which there is any risk of the government
having to find under its guarantee means a vastly greater number of dollars spent by private persons. There is no better way
by which America can spend itself into prosperity than by
spending money on building houses. The need is there waiting
to be satisfied; the labour and materials are there waiting to
be utilised. It will spread employment through every locality.
There is no greater social and economic benefit than good
houses. There is probably no greater material contribution to
[337] civilisation and a sound and healthy life which it lies within our
power to make. The man who regards all this as a senseless

extravagance which will impoverish the nation, as compared with doing nothing and leaving millions unemployed, should be recognised for a lunatic.

I stress housing, for this seems to me the happiest of the Administration's schemes. But it is difficult to organise quickly any one type of scheme on a sufficient scale. Meanwhile other forms of government expenditure, not so desirable in themselves, are not to be despised. Even pure relief expenditure is much better than nothing. The object must be to raise the total expenditure to a figure which is high enough to push the vast machine of American industry into renewed motion. If demand can be raised sufficiently by emergency measures, business men will find that they cannot meet it without repairs and renewals to their plant, and they will then once again take heart of grace to recover the care-free optimism without which none of us ever has the courage to live our lives as they should be lived.   [338]

CW 21, 'Letter to the President'

[*Dated 1 February 1938. The US economy had collapsed for the second time in nine years in October 1937.*]

Dear Mr President,

You received me so kindly when I visited you some three years ago that I make bold to send you some bird's eye impressions which I have formed as to the business position in the United States. You will appreciate that I write from a distance, that I have not re-visited the United States since you saw me, and that I have access to few more sources of information than those publicly available. But sometimes in some respects there may be advantages in these limitations! At any rate, those things which I think I see, I see very clearly.

1. I should agree that the present recession is partly due to an 'error of optimism' which led to an overestimation of future demand, when orders were being placed in the first half of this year. If this were all, there would not be too much to worry about. It would only need time to effect a readjustment; – though, even so, the recovery would only be up to the point

required to take care of the *revised* estimate of current demand, which might fall appreciably short of the prosperity reached [434] last spring.

2. But I am quite sure that this is not all. There is a much more troublesome underlying influence. The recovery was mainly due to the following factors:–

(i) the solution of the credit and insolvency problems, and the establishment of easy short-term money;

(ii) the creation of an adequate system of relief for the unemployed;

(iii) public works and other investments aided by Government funds or guarantees;

(iv) investment in the instrumental goods required to supply the increased demand for consumption goods;

(v) the momentum of the recovery thus initiated.

Now of these (i) was a prior condition of recovery, since it is no use creating a demand for credit, if there is no supply. But an increased supply will not by itself generate an adequate demand. The influence of (ii) evaporates as employment improves, so that there is a dead point beyond which this factor cannot carry the economic system. Recourse to (iii) has been greatly curtailed in the past year, (iv) and (v) are functions of the forward movement and cease – indeed (v) is reversed – as soon as the position fails to improve further. The benefit from the momentum of recovery as such is at the same time the most important and the most dangerous factor in the upward movement. It requires for its continuance, not merely the maintenance of recovery, but always *further* recovery. Thus it always flatters the early stages and steps from under just when support is most needed. It was largely, I think, a failure to allow for this which caused the 'error of optimism' last year.

Unless, therefore, the above factors were supplemented by others in due course, the present slump could have been predicted with absolute certainty. It is true that the existing policies will prevent the slump from proceeding to such a disastrous degree as last time. But they will not by themselves – at any rate, not without a large-scale recourse to (iii) – maintain pros- [435] perity at a reasonable level.

3. Now one had hoped that the needed supplementary factors would be organised in time. It was obvious what these were – namely increased investment in durable goods such as housing, public utilities and transport. One was optimistic about this because in the United States at the present time the opportunities, indeed the necessity, for such developments were unexampled. Can your Administration escape criticism for the failure of these factors to mature?

Take housing. When I was with you three and a half years ago the necessity for effective new measures was evident ... But what happened? Next to nothing. The handling of the housing problem has been really wicked. I hope that the new measures recently taken will be more successful. I have not the knowledge to say. But they will take time, and I would urge the great importance of expediting and yet further aiding them. Housing is by far the best aid to recovery because of the large and continuing scale of potential demand; because of the wide geographical distribution of this demand; and because the sources of its finance are largely independent of the stock exchanges. I should advise putting most of your eggs in this basket, *caring* about this more than about anything, and making absolutely sure that they are being hatched without delay. In this country we partly depended for many years on direct subsidies. There are few more proper objects for such than working-class houses. If a direct subsidy is required to get a move on (we gave our subsidies *through* the local authorities), it should be given without delay or hesitation.

Next utilities. There seems to be a deadlock. Neither your policy nor anyone else's is able to take effect. I think that the litigation by the utilities is senseless and ill-advised. But a great deal of what is alleged against the wickedness of holding companies as such is surely wide of the mark. It does not draw the right line of division between what should be kept and what discarded. It arises too much out of what is dead and gone. The [436] real criminals have cleared out long ago. I should doubt if the controls existing today are of much *personal* value to anyone. No one has suggested a procedure by which the eggs can be unscrambled. Why not tackle the problem by insisting that the *voting power* should belong to the real owners of the equity, and leave the existing *organisations* undisturbed, so long as the voting power is so rearranged (e.g. by bringing in preferred stockholders) that it cannot be controlled by the holders of a minority of the equity?[11]

Is it not for you to decide either to make real peace or to be much more drastic the other way? Personally I think there is a great deal to be said for the ownership of all the utilities by publicly owned boards. But if public opinion is not yet ripe for this, what is the object of chasing the utilities round the lot every other week? If I was in your place, I should buy out the utilities at fair prices in every district where the situation was ripe for doing so, and announce that the ultimate ideal was to make this policy nation-wide. But elsewhere I would make peace on liberal terms, guaranteeing fair earnings on new investments and a fair basis of valuation in the event of the public taking them over hereafter. The process of evolution will take at least a generation. Meanwhile a policy of *competing* plants with losses all round is a ramshackle notion.

Finally the railroads. The position there seems to be exactly what it was three or four years ago. They remain, as they were then, potential sources of substantial demand for new capital expenditure. Whether hereafter they are publicly owned or remain in private hands, it is a matter of national importance that they should be made solvent. Nationalise them if the time is ripe. If not, take pity on the overwhelming problems of the present managements. And here too let the dead bury their dead. (To an Englishman, you Americans, like the Irish, are so terribly historically minded!)

I am afraid I am going beyond my province. But the upshot [437] is this. A convincing policy, whatever its details may be, for promoting large-scale investment under the above heads is an urgent necessity. Those things take time. Far too much precious time has passed.

4. I must not encumber this letter with technical suggestions for reviving the capital market. This is important. But not so important as the revival of sources of demand. If demand and confidence reappear, the problems of the capital market will

not seem so difficult as they do today. Moreover it is a highly technical problem.

5. Businessmen have a different set of delusions from politicians; and need, therefore, different handling. They are, however, much milder than politicians, at the same time allured and terrified by the glare of publicity, easily persuaded to be 'patriots', perplexed, bemused, indeed terrified, yet only too anxious to take a cheerful view, vain perhaps but very unsure of themselves, pathetically responsive to a kind word. You could do anything you liked with them, if you would treat them (even the big ones), not as wolves and tigers, but as domestic animals by nature, even though they have been badly brought up and not trained as you would wish. It is a mistake to think that they are more *immoral* than politicians. If you work them into the surly, obstinate, terrified mood, of which domestic animals, wrongly handled, are so capable, the nation's burdens will not get carried to market; and in the end public opinion will veer their way. Perhaps you will rejoin that I have got quite a wrong idea of what all the back-chat amounts to. Nevertheless I record accurately how it strikes observers here.

6. Forgive the candour of these remarks. They come from an enthusiastic well-wisher of you and your policies. I accept the view that durable investment must come increasingly under state direction. I sympathise with Mr Wallace's agricultural policies. I believe that the Securities [and] E[xchange] C[ommission] is doing splendid work. I regard the growth of collective bargaining as essential. I approve minimum wage and hours regulation. I was altogether on your side the other day, when you deprecated [438] a policy of general wage reductions as useless in present circumstances. But I am terrified lest progressive causes in all the democratic countries should suffer injury, because you have taken too lightly the risk to their prestige which would result from a failure measured in terms of immediate prosperity. There *need* be no failure. But the maintenance of prosperity in the modern world is extremely *difficult*; and it is so easy to lose precious time.

I am, Mr President
Yours with great respect and faithfulness,
J. M. KEYNES   [439]

32

CW 28, 'British Foreign Policy' (1937)

[*This comment on the Spanish Civil War was published in the*
New Statesman, *10 July 1937. It is an example of Keynes's*
application of Burke's principle of prudence.]

W. H. Auden's poem, Spain, is fit to stand beside great predecessors in its moving, yet serene expression of contemporary
feeling towards the heart-rending events of the political world.
The theme of the poem lies in the comparison between the
secular achievements of the past and the hope which is possible
for the future with the horrors of the present and the sacrifices
which perhaps it demands from those of this generation who
think and feel rightly. Yesterday, all the past. To-morrow, perhaps the future. 'But to-day the struggle,' his refrain runs.
Auden conceives of 'the struggle' in terms of immediate war
and force, of death and killing:

> To-day the deliberate increase in the chances of death,
> The conscious acceptance of guilt in the necessary murder.

In this he is speaking for many chivalrous hearts. Yet, whilst he
teaches us, as a poet should, how we should feel, the object of
this article is to question whether he rightly directs how, at this
moment at least, we should act.

I view with revulsion the growing tendency to make of the
struggle between the two ideologies (or would it be conceded
that there are three?) another War of Religion, to believe that
the issue can or will be settled by force of arms, and to feel that
it is our duty to hasten to any quarter of the world where those
of our faith are oppressed. It is only too easy for men to feel
like this. The Crusades and the Thirty Years' War actually
occurred. But does it seem, looking back, that it was a duty to
join in them, or that they settled anything? Assume that the
war occurs, and let us suppose, for the sake of argument, that
we win. What then? Shall we ourselves be the better for it and

for what it will have brought with it? What are we going to do with the defeated? Are we to impose our favourite ideology on them (whatever, by then, it may be) in an up-to-date peace treaty, or do we assume that they will adopt it with spontan- [61] eous enthusiasm? At best we should be back, it seems to me, exactly where we were. Defeat is complete disaster. Victory, as usual, would be useless, and probably pernicious. It is an illusion to believe that conscious acceptance of guilt in the necessary murder can settle what is mainly a moral issue.

Therefore, and furthermore, I maintain that the claims of peace are paramount; though this seems to be an out-of-date view in what used to be pacifist circles. It is our duty to prolong peace, hour by hour, day by day, for as long as we can. We do not know what the future will bring, except that it will be quite different from anything we could predict. I have said in another context that it is a disadvantage of 'the long run' that in the long run we are all dead. But I could have said equally well that it is a great advantage of 'the short run' that in the short run we are still alive. Life and history are made up of short runs. If we are at peace in the short run, that is something. The best we can do is put off disaster, if only in the hope, which is not necessar- ily a remote one, that something will turn up. While there is peace, there is peace. It is silly and presumptuous to say that war is inevitable; for no one can possibly know. The only con- clusion which is certain is that we cannot avoid war by bringing it on. If, thinking of Spain, someone urges that self-interest does not entitle us to abandon others, I answer that for Spain peace – and to-day, I think, I would add peace on any terms – is her greatest interest. Spain will work out her future in due course. It is not the outcome of the civil war which will settle it. It would be much more plausible to argue that British imperial interests or French security require the defeat of Franco than that the interests of Spaniards require it. Those who believe in the efficacy of war are misunderstanding the kind of power we have to influence the future.

But I do not, therefore, claim that war can always be avoided. I do not need to answer the question whether war is even defensible. The question does not arise, inasmuch as our [62] knowledge of human nature tells us that in practice there are circumstances when war on our part, whether defensible or not, is unavoidable. We are brought, therefore, to the second aspect of foreign policy. The first duty of foreign policy is to avoid war. Its second duty is to ensure that, if it occurs, the circumstances shall be the most favourable possible for our cause. Let us consider the immediate position from this point of view.

By postponement we gain peace to-day. Have we anything to lose by it? Our capacity for cunctation is one of our most powerful and characteristic national weapons. It has been our age-long instrument against dictators. Since Fabius Maximus there has scarcely been a stronger case for cunctation than there is to-day. It is maddening and humiliating to have to take so much lip. We may, conceivably, have to submit to greater humiliations and worse betrayals than any yet. Those who applaud war and believe they have something to gain from it have an inevitable advantage, which cannot possibly be taken from them, in a game of bluff and in the preliminary manoeuvres; though all the time they may be running unperceived risks, which one day will catch them out. But we have to look farther ahead; believing that time and chance are with us, and taking precautions that, if we are forced to act, we can make quite sure. This seems cold and shifty to the poet. Yet I claim the benefit of the first part of one of Auden's stanzas:

> What's your proposal? To build the just city? I will.
> I agree.

leaving to him the second part:

> Or is it the suicide pact, the romantic
> Death? Very well, I accept.

For consider the immediate political factors staring us in the face. At the moment Russia is disorganised and France at a disadvantage. Each is at a low ebb but each needs mainly time. [63] Before long we ourselves will possess the most predominant sea-power in European waters that we have every enjoyed in our history. Meanwhile what is happening to the brigand powers? One of them is busily engaged in outraging every creed in turn. If they could find another institution or another community to insult or injure, they would do so. Both of them are spending a lot of money on an intensive propaganda to persuade the rest of the world that they are the enemies of the human race. It is having the desired result, not least in the United States. No one trusts or respects their word. They have not a single friend or sympathiser in the whole world, for I doubt if even Japan thrills greatly to their croonings. Yet even so, all this needs time to sink in, here at home as well as elsewhere. The full abomination is understood to-day in a degree and over an area much greater than a year ago. These tactics are not characteristic of great statesmen and conquerors. They appear to be morbid, pathological, diseased. I gravely doubt their technical efficiency and expect that every sort of idiocy is going on behind the scenes. It is unlikely that those who talk so much nonsense will act quite differently; or that they, who persecute the mind and all its works, will be employing it to the best advantage. It is very probable that, given time, they will over-play their hands, overreach themselves and make a major blunder. It is in the nature of their type of behaviour that this should happen. And if, indeed, the thieves were to have a little more success, nothing is likelier than that they would fall out amongst themselves.

Near the beginning of the Abyssinian affair our Foreign Office was guilty of the gravest and most disastrous error of policy in recent history. It is natural, therefore, to distrust them. But though it has been hateful in its immediate consequences and cruel in some of its details, I am not inclined to criticise the broad outline of Mr Eden's Spanish policy. I should have been afraid if his critics had had a chance to take over from him. The task of a cunctator is always a thankless one. To be for ever allowing the brigands yet a little more rope, to be holding up the cup for them to fill yet fuller is not a distinguished office. It is never possible, unfortunately, to estimate a statesman by his [64] results, since we never have for comparison the consequences of the alternative course. But I do not judge his policy to have been inconsistent as yet with the two prime objects stated above.

I bid Auden, therefore, to pass by on the other side. If he will be patient and unheroic, in due course, perhaps, he will be shown (in his own words):

> History the operator, the
> Organiser, Time the refreshing river.

33

CW 21, 'How to Avoid a Slump' (1937)

[Although Keynes came to believe that fiscal policy was more important than monetary policy for maintaining full employment, there never was a comprehensive Keynes Fiscal Plan. The shadow of war, or actual wartime conditions, hangs heavy over the following excerpts, in which Keynes did discuss the issue.

The problem which Keynes addresses in the excerpt below is 'how to maintain a fairly steady level of sustained prosperity'. The material of this excerpt originally appeared in three articles in The Times, *12–14 January 1937. Interestingly, he felt the sectoral flow analysis of TM more useful for the argument below than the aggregative analysis of GT.]*

Why is it that good times have been so intermittent? The explanation is not difficult. The public, especially when they are prosperous, do not spend the whole of their incomes on current consumption. It follows that the productive activities, from which their incomes are derived, must not be devoted to [385] preparing for consumption in any greater proportion than that in which the corresponding incomes will be spent on consumption; since, if they are, the resulting goods cannot be sold at a profit and production will have to be curtailed. If when incomes are at a given level the public consume, let us say, nine-tenths of their incomes, the productive efforts devoted to consumption goods cannot be more than nine times the efforts devoted to investment, if the results are to be sold without loss. Thus it is an indispensable condition of a stable increase in incomes that the production of investment goods (which must be interpreted in a wide sense so as to include working capital; and also relief works and armaments if they are paid for by borrowing) should advance *pari passu* and in the right proportion. Otherwise the proportion of income spent on consumption will be less than the proportion of income earned by producing consumption goods, which means that the receipts of the producers of consumption goods will be less than their costs, so that business losses and a curtailment of output will ensue.

Difficulty of 'Planning'

Now there are several reasons why the production of investment goods tends to fluctuate widely, and it is these fluctuations which cause the fluctuations, first of profits, then of general business activity, and hence of national and world prosperity. The sustained enjoyment of prosperity requires as its condition that as near as possible the right proportion of the national resources, neither too much nor too little, should be devoted to active investment (interpreted, as I have indicated, in a wide sense). The proportion will be just right if it is the same as the proportion of their incomes which the community is disposed to save when the national resources of equipment and labour are being fully employed.

There is no reason to suppose that there is 'an invisible hand', an automatic control in the economic system which ensures of itself that the amount of active investment shall be continuously of the right proportion. Yet it is also very difficult [386] to ensure it by our own design, by what is now called 'planning'. The best we can hope to achieve is to use those kinds of investment which it is relatively easy to plan as a make-weight, bringing them in so as to preserve as much stability of aggregate investment as we can manage at the right and appropriate level. Three years ago it was important to use public policy to increase investment. It may soon be equally important to retard certain types of investment, so as to keep our most easily available ammunition in hand for when it is more required.

The longer the recovery has lasted, the more difficult does it become to maintain the stability of new investment. Some of the investment which properly occurs during a recovery is, in the nature of things, non-recurrent; for example, the increase in working capital as output increases and the provision of additional equipment to keep pace with the improvement in consumption. Another part becomes less easy to sustain, not because saturation point has been reached, but because with each increase in our stock of wealth the profit to be expected from a further increase declines. And, thirdly, the abnormal profits obtainable, during a too rapid recovery of demand, from equipment which is temporarily in short supply is likely to lead to exaggerated expectations from certain types of new investment, the disappointment of which will bring a subsequent reaction. Experience shows that this is sure to occur if aggregate investment is allowed to rise for a time above the normal proper proportion. We can also add that the rise in stock exchange values consequent on the recovery usually leads to a certain amount of expenditure paid for, not out of current income, but out of stock exchange profits, which will cease when values cease to rise further. It is evident, therefore, what a ticklish business it is to maintain stability. We have to be preparing the way for an increase in sound investments of the second type which have not yet reached saturation point, to take the place in due [387] course of the investment of the first type which is necessarily non-current, while at the same time avoiding a temporary overlap of investments of the first and second types liable to increase aggregate investment to an excessive figure, which by inflating profits will induce unsound investment of the third type based [388] on mistaken expectations.

. . .

Unquestionably in past experience dear money has accompanied recovery; and has also heralded a slump. If we play with dear money on the ground that it is 'healthy' or 'natural', then, I have no doubt, the inevitable slump will ensue. We must avoid it, therefore, as we would hell-fire. It is true that there is a phase in every recovery when we need to go slow with postponable investment of the recurrent type, lest, in conjunction with the non-recurrent investment which necessarily attends a recovery, it raises aggregate investment too high. But we must find other means of achieving this than a higher rate of interest. For if we allow the rate of interest to be affected, we cannot easily reverse the trend. A low enough long-term rate of interest cannot be achieved if we allow it to be believed that better terms will be obtainable from time to time by those who keep their resources liquid. The long-term rate of interest must be kept *continuously* as near as possible to what we believe to be the long-term optimum. It is not suitable to be used as a short-period weapon.

Moreover, when the recovery is reaching its peak of activity, the phase of non-recurrent investment in increased working capital and the like will be almost over; and we can be practically certain that within a few weeks or months we shall require a lower rate of interest to stimulate increased investment of the recurrent type to fill the gap. Thus it is a fatal mistake to use a high rate of interest as a means of damping down the boom. It has been the occurrence of dear money hitherto which has joined with other forces to make a slump inevitable.

If the stock exchange is unduly excited or if new issues of a doubtful type are becoming too abundant, a higher rate of interest will be useless except in so far as it affects adversely the whole structure of confidence and credit. Moreover, alternative methods are available. A hint to the banks to be cautious in allowing their names to appear on prospectuses, and to the Committee of the Stock Exchange to exercise discrimination in [389] granting permissions to deal would be more efficacious. And if necessary a temporary increase of a substantial amount in the stamp on contract-notes (as distinguished from transfers) in respect of transactions in ordinary shares would help to check an undue speculative activity.

Nevertheless a phase of the recovery may be at hand when it will be desirable to find other methods temporarily to damp down aggregate demand, with a view to stabilising subsequent activity at as high a level as possible. There are three important methods open to our authorities, all of which deserve to be considered in the immediate future.

Boom Control

Just as it was advisable for the Government to incur debt during the slump, so for the same reasons it is now advisable that they should incline to the opposite policy. Aggregate demand is increased by loan expenditure and decreased when loans are discharged out of taxation. In view of the high cost of the armaments, which we cannot postpone, it would put too much strain on our fiscal system actually to discharge debt, but the Chancellor of the Exchequer should, I suggest, meet the main part of the cost of armaments out of taxation, raising taxes and withholding all reliefs for the present as something in hand for 1938 or 1939, or whenever there are signs of recession. The boom, not the slump, is the right time for austerity at the Treasury.

Just as it was advisable for local authorities to press on with capital expenditure during the slump, so it is now advisable that they should postpone whatever new enterprises can reasonably be held back. I do not mean that they should abandon their plans of improvement. On the contrary, they should have them fully matured, available for quick release at the right moment. But the boom, not the slump, is the right time for [390] procrastination at the Ministry of Health.

Just as it was advisable (from our own point of view) to check imports and to take measures to improve the balance of trade during the slump, so it is now advisable to shift in the opposite direction and to welcome imports even though they result in an adverse balance of trade. I should like to see a temporary rebate on tariffs wherever this could be done without throwing British resources out of employment. But, above all, it is desirable that we should view with equanimity and without anxiety the prospective worsening of our trade balance which is likely to result from higher prices for raw materials and from our armament expenditure and general trade activity, even though this may put a temporary strain on the Exchange Equalisation Fund.[12] The recent decrease in the Bank of England's fiduciary issue indicates that we have today a plethora of gold. It is desirable, therefore, that the raw material countries should be allowed to replenish their gold and sterling resources by sending their goods to us; especially so in view of the difficulties which would remain in the way of foreign lending on the old scale even if the existing artificial obstacles were to be removed. This policy is doubly desirable. First, because it will help to relieve a temporarily inflated demand in the home market. But, secondly, because a policy of allowing these countries to increase their resources in 1937 provides the best prospect of their using these resources to buy our goods and help our export industries at a later date when an increased demand in our home market is just what we shall be wanting.

These, I urge, are the methods which will best serve to protect us from the excesses of the boom and, at the same time, put us in good trim to ward off the cumulative dangers of the slump when the reaction comes, as come it surely will. But we also need more positive measures to maintain a decent level of continuous prosperity . . .   [391]

. . .

The menace of the next slump, and what that would mean to our institutions and traditions, if it comes, should be at our elbow, urging us to new policies and boldness of mind.

Perhaps it is absurd to expect Englishmen to think things out beforehand. But if it is not, there are various thoughts to think. So far I have stressed the importance of investment. But the maintenance of prosperity and of a stable economic life only depends on increased investment if we take as unalterable the existing distribution of purchasing power and the willingness of those who enjoy purchasing power to use it for consumption. The wealthier we get and the smaller, therefore, the profit to be gained from adding to our capital goods, the more it is incumbent on us to see that those who would benefit from increasing their consumption – which is, after all, the sole ultimate object of economic effort – have the power and the opportunity to do so. Up to a point individual saving can allow an advantageous way of postponing consumption. But beyond that point it is for the community as a whole both an absurdity and a disaster. The natural evolution should be towards a decent level of consumption for every one; and, when that is high enough, towards the occupation of our energies in the non-economic interests of our lives. Thus we need to be slowly reconstructing our social system with these ends in view. This [393] is a large matter, not to be embarked upon here. But, in particular and in detail, the relief of taxation, when the time comes for that, will do most for the general welfare if it is so directed as to increase the purchasing power of those who have most need to consume more.

Planning Investment

The capital requirements of home industry and manufacture cannot possibly absorb more than a fraction of what this country, with its present social structure and distribution of wealth, chooses to save in years of general prosperity; while the amount of our net foreign investment is limited by our exports and our trade balance. Building and transport and public utilities, which can use large amounts of capital, lie half way between private and public control. They need, therefore, the combined stimulus of public policy and a low rate of interest. But a wise public policy to promote investment needs, as I have said, long preparation. Now is the time to appoint a board of public investment to prepare sound schemes against the time that they are needed. If we wait until the crisis is upon us we shall, of course, be too late. We ought to set up immediately an authority whose business it is not to launch anything at present, but to make sure that detailed plans are prepared. The railway companies, the port and river authorities, the water, gas, and electricity undertakings, the building contractors, the local authorities, above all, perhaps, the London County Council and the other great Corporations with congested population, should be asked to investigate what projects could be usefully undertaken if capital were available at certain rates of interest – 3½ per cent, 3 per cent, 2½ per cent, 2 per cent. The question of the general advisability of the schemes and their order of preference should be examined next. What is required at once are acts of constructive imagination by our administrators, engineers, and architects, to be followed by financial criticism, sifting, and more detailed designing; so that

some large and useful projects, at least, can be launched at a
few months' notice.   [394]

There can be no justification for a rate of interest which
impedes an adequate flow of new projects at a time when the
national resources for production are not fully employed. The
rate of interest must be reduced to the figure that the new projects can afford. In special cases subsidies may be justified; but
in general it is the long-term rate of interest which should come
down to the figure which the marginal project can earn. We
have the power to achieve this. The Bank of England and the
Treasury had a great success at the time of the conversion of the
War Loan. But it is possible that they still underrate the extent
of their powers. With the existing control over the exchanges
which has revolutionised the technical position, and with the
vast resources at the disposal of the authorities through the
Bank of England, the Exchange Equalisation Fund, and other
funds under the control of the Treasury, it lies within their
power, by the exercise of the moderation, the gradualness, and
the discreet handling of the market of which they have shown
themselves to be masters, to make the long-term rate of interest
what they choose within reason. If we know what rate of interest is required to make profitable a flow of new projects at the
proper pace, we have the power to make that rate prevail in the
market. A low rate of interest can only be harmful and liable to
cause an inflation if it is so low as to stimulate a flow of new
projects more than enough to absorb our available resources.

Is there the slightest chance of a constructive or a forethought-
ful policy in contemporary England? Is it conceivable that the
Government should do anything in time? Why shouldn't they?   [395]
. . .

[*In February 1937, the Chancellor of the Exchequer, Neville
Chamberlain, announced a Defence Loan of £400 million over
five years. The* Economist *had suggested that the only way of
avoiding inflation in the event of a large loan was by a rise in
interest rates. Keynes replied in a letter to* The Economist *dated
2 February.*]

But, if you will let me, I should like to explore a little further
the technical aspects of the position.

In the first place, it does not follow that the Defence Loan cannot be gradually taken up by the public. With increased activity incomes rise and increased savings become available corresponding to the expenditure paid for out of borrowed funds; or if defence replaces other activities, then the savings which would have financed these activities are available to take up the loan. Similarly, if it is convenient for business to finance itself through bank advances rather than through public issues, the savings which would otherwise have taken up the public issues are available to relieve the banks of part of their gilt-edged securities. Thus the need for increased deposits is not measured either by the size of the Defence Loan or by the increase in [398] bank advances. It depends on two other factors; first of all, on activity as measured, roughly speaking, by the national income in money, which governs the demand for active deposits; and secondly on the psychological atmosphere towards gilt-edged and other securities which governs the degree of the desire to hold liquid balances. Unfortunately, though very naturally, the readiness to put savings into gilt-edged securities is largely influenced by the ideas which get about as to whether the gilt-edged market is likely to rise or to fall in the future.

It is the latter factor which needs careful handling. If the public is deprived of its normal supply of idle balances by the demand for active balances, or if it gets nervous about the prospects of the gilt-edged market, then I feel strongly that, unless we deliberately desire to raise the rate of interest, this demand for idle balances should be satisfied for the time being, the extra idle balances being subsequently withdrawn as a change in the atmosphere or in the circumstances permits.

Thus it is not a shortage of savings which will impair the position of gilt-edged securities, but a change in psychological expectations as to their future prospects. I believe that it is most important to prevent such a change by maintaining stability in the gilt-edged market. For, if the change occurs, it will [399] make the task of avoiding the slump more difficult.

34

CW 22, 'Paying for the War' (1939)

[*Keynes's pamphlet* How to Pay for the War *was published by Macmillan on 27 February 1940. It is reproduced on pp. 367–439 of CW 9 and is too long to print here. It was developed from two articles Keynes wrote in* The Times *(14, 15 November 1939), reproduced below, in which he puts forward a plan for 'compulsory savings', or what he later called 'deferred pay', as a way of diminishing the inflationary pressure of hugely increased military spending. 'Deferred pay' was adopted in Sir Kingsley Woods's budget of 1941, as a minor adjunct to increased taxation, borrowing and rationing. The structure of Wood's budget as a whole, though, reflected the impact of the national accounts framework*[13] *which followed from GT.*]

The Control of Consumption

Nothing is more certain than that the wages bill of this country will increase. More men will be employed, and sometimes, as a result of 'dilution', at a higher grade of work than that to which they are accustomed; they will work longer hours and at overtime rates; and it is to be expected that a demand for labour in excess of the supply will result in sporadic, and perhaps widespread, increases in wage rates themselves by at least some figure such as 5 or 10 per cent. Already in October coalminers, textile workers, agricultural labourers, and (in prospect) railway workers were given a rise. An increase in the purchasing power of wage earners by at least £500 million a year is to be expected; and by the time we have reached our maximum effort [41] a much larger increase than this would be inevitable. Failing special measures to the contrary, a substantial proportion of this sum will be spent in the shops and elsewhere.

It is the declared policy of the Government to keep the prices of consumption goods as near as they can to the pre-war level. If they succeed, it follows that the purchasing power of the working classes will command in the aggregate substantially more goods than before, even if a general rise of wages is avoided. And if a further rise of wages is allowed, to compensate for any higher cost of living resulting from this expansion of demand, the situation will be correspondingly aggravated. For all that the outside observer can observe, the problem thus created – the central problem of the home economic front, a problem which requires for its solution the coordination of price policy, budget policy, and wages policy – has not yet been faced.

It is arguable that the present rate of Government expenditure of (say) £2,500 million a year is compatible with the maintenance of something not much worse than the pre-war standard of working-class consumption. At least it will be so arguable when we are no longer reducing our productive capacity by an extravagant A.R.P. [*Air Raid Precautions*] policy out of proportion to the protection gained. But no one can suppose that we can afford an appreciable improvement over the pre-war standard. And any further increase towards our maximum war effort must be at the expense of pre-war standards of consumption.

Thus the working classes will have a substantially larger money income than before, but they must not, at the best, consume any more than they did. For the wise and just solution of this problem the leaders of the working class must be taken into earnest and sincere consultation. An economist may be able to help by indicating the alternatives which are open to us. [42] But the choice between them must depend on political and human considerations about which every one is entitled to his opinion.

There are three genuine ways of reaching equilibrium, and two pseudo-remedies. The first pseudo-remedy is by rationing. If there is so great a relative lack of an essential article of consumption that a reasonable rise in price cannot restore equilibrium between supply and demand, we must have recourse to rationing. But against a general increase of purchasing power rationing is useless. It merely serves to divert demand from the rationed to the unrationed article. Rationing is always a bad method of control because it has to go on the assumption that everyone normally spends the same amount on a given article;

and, even apart from the intolerable bureaucratic burden which is involved, this characteristic puts out of court a system of universal rationing applied to all articles. The second pseudo-remedy is an anti-profiteering measure, which exalts into undue prominence the least significant cause of rising prices. Therefore those whose first thoughts run to rationing and anti-profiteering have not begun to discern the real nature of the problem – namely, that the aggregate of purchasing power is increasing faster than the available supply of goods.

Let us turn to the three genuine remedies. All of them will have to be applied in some measure, but the degree to which we depend on each it is more difficult to decide. The first is to allow prices to rise. Some rise in prices is inevitable. Indeed, in spite of all efforts to the contrary, the cost of living has risen by 6½ per cent in the first month of the war. But some rise is also desirable. For otherwise, as a result of the depreciation of the exchange, the increased cost of transport and insurance, and the rise of prices abroad, the goods would have to be sold at a loss, quite apart from higher costs at home. There is an important distinction between a higher price corresponding to the higher world prices and a still higher price which is out of relation to the rest of the world. It is unlikely that we can avoid some further rise up to (say) 20 per cent above pre-war, due to both causes. But if we were to depend on this remedy alone, the rise in prices sufficient to restore equilibrium would be beyond all reason and endurance. The yield of the excess profits tax would gain, but most of the other consequences would be bad. We cannot avoid the 'vicious spiral' of rising prices and wages merely by attending to the cost of living; for the first step of the spiral's ascent can begin just as well at the wages end, and this, perhaps, is what happens more often. But an excessive rise of prices will assuredly set such a process in motion. Apart from this, there are grave disadvantages in this method, except in strict moderation. A rising cost of living puts an equal proportionate burden on every one, irrespective of his level of income, from the old-age pensioner upwards, and is a cause, therefore, of great social injustice. Moreover it is largely futile unless we recast our wages system. The rise in prices helps only to the [43] extent that it is greater than the rise in wages. But there are today many wage rates linked by agreement with the cost of living, so that the two move together.

The second genuine remedy is taxation. But to help solve our present problem it must involve taxation of the working classes. Three-fifths of the net expenditure on consumption (after deducting normal saving and taxation) is by those whose incomes are less than £250 a year, and it is this class whose incomes are likely to rise by upwards of 15 per cent.

Not much more can be expected from the existing indirect taxes. A general turnover tax seems to be the only unexplored source of substantial revenue from working-class incomes. A turnover tax on non-essentials deserves closer examination than it has yet received. But not too much must be hoped from it. It would be a heavy administrative task to introduce it for the first time in a war when the bureaucratic machine already [44] creaks and groans. Like a rise in prices, a general turnover tax falls with equal proportionate weight on all levels of income, and must, if it is to yield enough, fall with intolerable severity on the lower levels. So far as revenue from staple goods is concerned, the best and easiest plan is for the Government to resell at prices which yield a profit some at least of those articles of which it is monopolising the distribution. Whether this be regarded as remedy by price-raising or remedy by taxation, the benefit will accrue to the Treasury with the least possible addition to the existing machinery and without leakage.

The price remedy and the taxation remedy are alike in depriving the working class of any benefit from their increased earnings. Yet a large portion of the earnings now in question represents increased effort on their part. The third remedy is free from this objection.

It is conventional nowadays to talk about the justice and wisdom of paying for a war almost entirely out of current taxation without borrowing. We all know that such a thing is impossible; but many people seem to think that it would be just and wise to do it if we could. The argument is that the major part of the expenditure has to be met out of increased current effort and diminished current consumption, so that for the community as a whole it makes no real difference how it is financed, while the method of taxation avoids future complications. But a little reflection will show that the reason why it is impossible entirely to refrain from borrowing is also a reason why it would not be just and wise to do so. It makes all the difference in the world to each individual personally whether the excess of his income over his consumption is taken from him by tax or by loan. To him personally Government stock is an addition to his wealth, to his security, and to his comfort in facing the future. It gives him a claim over the future resources of the community. Someone will have to meet this claim. But this someone is not necessarily himself, and, even if it were, it may suit him better and involve less sacrifice to part by instal- [45] ments with his personal resources and to possess meanwhile a title to wealth which he can realise in case of need. Moreover, even in war we cannot afford to dispense altogether with the economic incentive to effort – which a too exclusive financing by taxation would involve. We have already got dangerously near to this in the case of the entrepreneurs and we must not make the same mistake with the working classes. There is a fatal family resemblance between bureaucracies in Moscow, Berlin and Whitehall; and we must be careful.

The community at war cannot allow the individuals of the working class to make a greater immediate demand on the national resources than hitherto; and it may have to ask of them a reduction. But that is no reason why they should not be rewarded by a claim on future resources. For the individual that is what wealth is. If it is physically impossible to reward the labour of the working class by immediate consumption, we should welcome and not reject the opportunity thus given to make its members individually wealthier.

The third remedy, therefore, is to distinguish two kinds of money-rewards for present effort – money which can be used, if desired, to provide immediate consumption, and money the use of which must be deferred until the emergency is over and we again enjoy a surplus of productive resources – that is to say, current cash on the one hand and on the other a blocked deposit in the Post Office Savings Bank. This is the

general idea behind the third remedy. Part payment by the second kind of money is, during the emergency, the only way by which the real earnings of the working class can be increased. Can their leaders be made to see clearly this elementary fact? To the details of a proposal on these lines I will proceed in a
[46] second article.

Compulsory Savings

At the end of our first article we were left with the conclusion that the working class, taken as a whole, can only enjoy an increase in real earnings if they are prepared to accept deferred payment. Each individual may dislike postponing his own consumption, but he will gain from a similar postponement by his fellows. If every one spends, prices will rise until no one is better off. The increased earnings of the working class will not have benefited them one penny, but will have escaped through higher prices and higher profits, partly into taxation and partly into the savings of the entrepreneur class. Here, therefore is the perfect case for compulsion; for general compulsion will benefit all its victims alike. A chance is given us to use the opportunity of war finance – an opportunity always missed hitherto – to increase the individual resources of the working class and not merely of the entrepreneur class.

The following are the details of my proposal:–

1. A percentage of all incomes in excess of a stipulated minimum income will be paid over to the Government, partly as compulsory savings and partly as direct taxes. The percentage taken will rise steeply as the level of income increases.

2. The following table illustrates the kind of scale which might be proposed, though it would have to be more complicated so as to avoid sudden jumps:– [*table omitted*]

The stipulated income, which would be free of the levy, might be 35s a week for an unmarried man, 45s for a married man, with an addition of 7s 6d a week for each child. Thus an unmarried man with 40s a week would contribute 1s a week, while a married man with two children would pay nothing until his income was above 60s a week. There might also be a provision similar to that in the most recent Finance Act to

provide mitigation or exemption where a man's income had
fallen substantially below its pre-war level. [*Table omitted.*]   [47]

3. A part of this amount will be credited to the individual as
a deposit in the Post Office Savings Bank. The balance will be
used to discharge his income tax and surtax, if any. The percentage of the levy credited as a savings deposit will fall, and
the percentage taken as taxes will obviously rise, as the level of
income increases. For example, if we take the level of income
tax and surtax which will be in force in 1940–41 for a married
man with two children, whose income is earned, with £300 a
year or less, the whole of what he pays will be credited to him
in the Post Office Savings Bank and will remain his property.
At £500 the total levy will be £105, of which £77 10s will be
credited to him and £27 10s retained to pay his income tax.
Thereafter the percentage of the levy which is credited to him
falls steadily, until at an income level just over £20,000, out of
a levy of £16,000 only £3,000 (in round figures) is credited to
him and £13,000 is taken in taxes.

The following are further illustrations. An unmarried man
with 50s a week will have to save 3s a week; a married man
with two children and £5 a week must save 10s and pays no
income tax, and with £1,000 a year he must save £107 10s a
year and pays £180 income tax. These do not seem to be
extravagant demands in time of war and may be not altogether   [48]
to his disadvantage. If his life is insured or if he owes instalments to a building society the above demands will be reduced
correspondingly, as is explained below.

4. The sums credited in the Savings Bank, which will carry
2½ per cent interest, will be blocked for the time being, and
will not be available, generally speaking, for current expenditure or as security against loans. But the holder will be allowed
to use them to meet pre-war commitments of a capital nature,
such as instalments to a building society, or for hire-purchase,
or to meet insurance premiums. He can also use them, with
the approval of a local committee, to meet exceptional and
unavoidable expenses, arising, for example, out of illness or
unemployment. They would be available to meet death duties.

5. The deposits will be unblocked and made freely available

to the holder, probably by a series of instalments, at some date after the war. The appropriate date for release would have arrived when the resources of the community were no longer fully engaged. Such releases would help us through the first post-war slump, and would give us time to concert more permanent plans. There would be perfect efficiency in this. The people could enjoy the consumption to which their war efforts had entitled them at a time when this would cost the community nothing, since the resources required would otherwise be running to waste.

6. The machinery for collection would be the same as for National Insurance in the case of wage earners, with employers stamping Post Office Savings books at a rate appropriate to the week's earnings, subject to quarterly adjustment by the Post Office should the earnings have fluctuated; and the same as for income tax in the case of others, the total lump sum due under the above scale for both purposes being deducted at source at the standard rate of income tax (i.e. 7s 6d in the £), subject to [49] subsequent adjustment by the Revenue in the individual case exactly as at present for the purposes of allowances and surtax. Thus no new machinery would be required.

7. I am not able to estimate accurately the amount of the compulsory savings which would result. The figures given above, which are only for illustration, might bring in a yield of at least £400 million over and above income tax and surtax, a yield which may seem less than one would have supposed at first sight. This is because so large a part of working-class incomes is exempt even under this proposal. A stiffer scale would bring in a correspondingly large return. But it is not suggested that the problem of purchasing power can be solved by this means alone. It is a proposal supplementary to the other remedies – more efficacious than any conceivable increase in taxation, and nearly as good as a 10 per cent fall in real wages, while doing no lasting injury to working-class consumption. Above all, it is a new fiscal resource capable of further extension if our exigencies increase.

8. This scheme would not obviate a programme of normal borrowing out of voluntary savings additional to the above.

For resources will accrue in the hands of banks, insurance offices, and the like; and Government loans can be subscribed out of company reserves, out of unexpended depreciation moneys, out of sinking funds and sundry repayments, and out of capital released by the sale of foreign investments, and the reduction of stocks, none of which will be subject to the levy. To some extent the levy will obviously come out of income which would be saved in any case. No more can be claimed for it than that it would appreciably ease the Treasury's task.

9. It might be thought fair that those serving with the Forces should be credited with additional pay by the same method. We cannot afford to pay them more now, but we can afford them the reward of deferred consumption. I see much social justice and social efficiency in this system.   [50]

At present our resources of production fall short of our needs; the time will come when the position will be reversed; and it is therefore only sensible to reward current effort out of future surplus capacity. Meanwhile we retain a reasonable incentive to present effort, and the commitments of the community among its own members are spread a little more equally.

In judging this scheme critics must compare it with the alternatives. The income group between £3 and £10 a week is scarcely touched by direct taxation and cannot be relied on to restrict its consumption when its incomes are increasing. Some method must therefore be found for restricting the use of purchasing power on present consumption, which covers this group. Are there any alternatives except those which we have considered? The method of compulsory saving is incomparably better for the class with incomes below £500 than to deprive them of their reward by high prices or taxing, while for the higher incomes the practicable limit of direct taxation is already reached. Moreover there will be great social advantages in spreading the inevitable increase in the National Debt widely among every class in the community.

All methods of war finance are open to objections. But this new one offers some positive advantages on the other side which will not go unnoticed, I hope, by the leaders of the Labour Party. If the Chancellor of the Exchequer does not

deliberately choose a positive method he will inevitably slip
[51] into inflation merely by hesitating.

...

[*Following the publication of* How to Pay for the War, *Keynes wrote to* The Times, *on 18 April 1940.*]

I am not proposing an expedient, undesirable for its own sake, just for the purpose of financing the war. I am seizing an opportunity, where the need is obvious and overwhelming, to introduce a principle of policy which may come to be thought of as marking the line of division between the totalitarian and the free economy. For if the community's aggregate rate of spending can be regulated, the way in which personal incomes are spent and the means by which demand is satisfied can be safely left free and individual. Just as in the war the regulation of aggregate spending is the only way to avoid the destruction of choice and initiative, whether by consumers or by producers, through the complex tyranny of all-round rationing, so in peace it is only the application of this principle which will provide the environment in which the choice and initiative of the individual can be safely left free. This is the one kind of compulsion of which the effect is to enlarge liberty. Those who,
[123] entangled in old unserviceable maxims, fail to see this further far-reaching objective have not grasped, to speak American,
[124] the big idea.

[*And in a further note of 21 September 1940 (CW 22, p. 218):*
'*The importance of a war Budget is not because it will "finance" the war. The goods ordered by the supply department will be financed anyway. Its importance is social: to prevent the social evils of inflation now and later; to do this in a way which satisfies the popular sense of social justice; whilst maintaining adequate incentives to work and economy.*']

35

Full Employment Policy

*[The Beveridge Report on Social Security was published on
1 December 1942. It proposed a system of national insurance
for all citizens against retirement, unemployment and disabil-
ity, centrally administered and financed by equal contributions
from employers, employees and the state to a social security
fund, with equal benefits paid at a physical subsistence level.
Discussions at the Treasury before the Report was published
gave Keynes a chance to discuss the merits of compulsory contribution versus taxation, and expound some of his principles
of fiscal policy.]*

CW 27, Keynes to Sir Richard Hopkins[14] (1942)

[A letter dated 20 July 1942.]

II

The 'fund' also is, admittedly, to some extent a 'fiction'! Certainly it is not a fund in any actuarial sense. Nevertheless, it has,
surely, most important advantages. We need to extend, rather
than curtail, the theory and practice of extra-budgetary funds
for state operated or supported functions. Whether it is the
transport system, the Electricity Board, War Damage or Social
Security. The more socialised we become, the more important it
is to associate as closely as possible the cost of particular services with the sources out of which they are provided, even
when a grant-in-aid is also required from general taxes. This is [224]
the only way by which to preserve sound accounting, to measure efficiency, to maintain economy and to keep the public
properly aware of what things cost.

The social security budget should be one section of the capital or long-term Budget. It is important that there should be a
level charge on the ordinary Budget revised at longish intervals;

and if Mr Meade's proposals are adopted [*see below, p. 419*] it will be doubly important to keep it out of the ordinary Budget. For the ordinary Budget should be balanced at all times. It is the capital Budget which should fluctuate with the demand for employment.

But there are secondary reasons why the fund is in present circumstances a valuable fiction – to put it at the lowest. Firstly, we can hope to start with good employment and relatively low pension charges in the first quinquennium and accumulate a surplus. Extra-budgetary funds accumulating surpluses are exactly what we shall pray for in the early period. Secondly, the existing Funds will end the war with a large surplus which can be appropriately transferred to the new fund, but not so easily paid into the Exchequer.

No, I am all for an extra-budgetary social security fund. The suggestion that to express the full consequences of the Beveridge proposals in terms of additional taxation as such is the best way of bringing their cost home to the public, involves sacrificing administration and long-term efficiency to what is essentially a political and short-term argument (which would, very likely, not prove sufficiently convincing).

I suggest below that the right solution is to make not a step back, but another step forward.

III

The objection to the contributory system and the Fund is not really, I suggest, to the *principle* of contribution to a Fund, but partly to the particular method of a poll tax and partly to the [225] inevitable inadequacy of the contribution so long as it is a poll tax. For everyone knows the objection to a poll tax of significant amount, which is unrelated either to profits or to earnings. But to have a better and more adequate contributory system leads us straight to a far-reaching reform of the income tax – which we all know is needed anyhow.

I venture a highly preliminary sketch below, without stopping to calculate whether or not the actual figures given (on a post-war basis) for the purpose of illustration, are anywhere near right. If we are not yet ready for something on these lines, then we had better keep to old-fashioned contributions on Beveridge lines, until we are. [226]

[*For Hopkins's benefit Keynes sketched out a reform of the tax system, with compulsory contributions to a social security fund replacing income tax. On receiving this missive, Sir Richard Hopkins wrote wearily on 21 July 1942: 'I do not feel equal to settling between now and the 15th August Lord Keynes' suggestions for a complete remodelling of the system of direct taxation in this country . . .'*[15]]

CW 27, Keynes to J. E. Meade (1943)

[*James Meade had suggested contra-cyclical variations in national insurance contributions to smooth out the business cycle. This letter, dated 25 April 1943, and the Memorandum after (see p. 421 below) throw further light on Keynes's fiscal philosophy.*]

My dear James,

The Maintenance of Full Employment

I am not quite happy about the line of argument you set forth in your letter of April 19th. I doubt if it is wise to put too much stress on devices for causing the volume of consumption to fluctuate in preference to devices for varying the volume of investment.

In the first place, one has not enough experience to say that short-term variations in consumption are in fact practicable. People have established standards of life. Nothing will upset them more than to be subject to pressure constantly to vary them up and down. A remission of taxation on which people could only rely for an indefinitely short period might have very limited effects in stimulating their consumption. And, if it was successful, it would be extraordinarily difficult from the political angle to reimpose the taxation again when employment improved. On this particular tack your proposal about varying the insurance contribution seems to me much the most practicable, partly because it could be associated with a formula, and partly because it would be pumping purchasing power into the hands of the class which can most easily vary its expenditure on consumption without radically altering its general standards. This seems to me quite enough as a beginning. I should much deprecate trying to superimpose on this proposals to reduce taxation on drink and tobacco with a view to making people drink and smoke more when they were tending to be out of work, or to dealing with income-tax, where there is a huge time lag and short-run changes [are] most inconvenient.

In the second place, it is not nearly so easy politically and to the common man to put across the encouragement of consumption in bad times as it is to induce the encouragement of capital expenditure. The former is a much more violent version of deficit budgeting. Capital expenditure would, at least partially, if not wholly, pay for itself. Assuredly it is much the easier of the two to put across. These ideas are too young and tender to be put to the strain which your present line of thought would require.

[319]

Moreover, the very reason that capital expenditure is capable of paying for itself makes it much better budget-wise and does not involve the progressive increase of budgetary difficulties, which deficit budgeting for the sake of consumption may bring about or, at any rate, would be accused of bringing about. Besides which, it is better for all of us that periods of deficiency expenditure should be made the occasion of capital development until our economy is much more saturated with capital goods than it is at present.

I recently read an interesting article by Lerner on deficit budgeting, in which he shows that, in fact, this does not mean an infinite increase in the national debt, since in course of time the interest on the previous debt takes the place of the new debt which would otherwise be required. (He, of course, is thinking of a chronic deficiency of purchasing power rather than an intermittent one.) His argument is impeccable. But, heaven help anyone who tries to put it across to the plain man at this stage of the evolution of our ideas.

Yours sincerely,

[320]   [copy initialled] K

CW 27, The Long-Term Problem of
Full Employment (1943)

[Memorandum dated 25 May 1943.]
1. It seems to be agreed to-day that the maintenance of a satisfactory level of employment depends on keeping total expenditure (consumption *plus* investment) at the optimum figure, namely [320] that which generates a volume of incomes corresponding to what is earned by all sections of the community when employment is at the desired level.

2. At any given level and distribution of incomes the social habits and opportunities of the community, influenced ([as] it may be) by the form and weight of taxation and other deliberate policies and propaganda, lead them to spend a certain proportion of these incomes and to save the balance.

3. The problem of maintaining full employment is, therefore, the problem of ensuring that the scale of investment should be equal to the savings which may be expected to emerge under the above various influences when employment, and therefore incomes, are at the desired level. Let us call this the *indicated* level of savings.

4. After the war there are likely to ensue three phases –

(i) when the inducement to invest is likely to lead, if unchecked, to a volume of investment greater than the indicated level of savings in the absence of rationing and other controls;

(ii) when the urgently necessary investment is no longer greater than the indicated level of savings in conditions of freedom, but it still capable of being adjusted to the indicated level by deliberately encouraging or expediting less urgent, but nevertheless useful, investment;

(iii) when investment demand is so far saturated that it cannot be brought up to the indicated level of savings without embarking upon wasteful and unnecessary enterprises.

5. It is impossible to predict with any pretence to accuracy what the indicated level of savings after the war is likely to be in the absence of rationing. We have no experience of a

community such as ours in the conditions assumed, with incomes and employment steadily at or near the optimum level over a period and with the distribution of incomes such as it is likely to be after the war. It is, however, safe to say that in the earliest years investment urgently necessary will be in excess of [321] the indicated level of savings. To be a little more precise the former (at the present level of prices) is likely to exceed £m1000 in these years and the indicated level of savings to fall short of this.

6. In the first phase, therefore, equilibrium will have to be brought about by limiting on the one hand the volume of investment by suitable controls, and on the other hand the volume of consumption by rationing and the like. Otherwise a tendency to inflation will set in. It will probably be desirable to allow consumption priority over investment except to the extent that the latter is exceptionally urgent, and, therefore, to ease off rationing and other restrictions on consumption before easing off controls and licences for investment. It will be a ticklish business to maintain the two sets of controls at precisely the right tension and will require a sensitive touch and the method of trial and error operating through small changes.

7. Perhaps this first phase might last five years, – but it is anybody's guess. Sooner or later it should be possible to abandon both types of control entirely (apart from controls on foreign lending). We then enter the second phase which is the main point of emphasis in the paper of the Economic Section. If two-thirds or three-quarters of total investment is carried out or can be influenced by public or semi-public bodies, a long-term programme of a stable character should be capable of reducing the potential range of fluctuation to much narrower limits than formerly, when a smaller volume of investment was under public control and when even this part tended to follow, rather than correct, fluctuations of investment in the strictly private sector of the economy. Moreover the proportion of investment represented by the balance of trade, which is not easily brought under short-term control, may be smaller than before. The main task should be to *prevent* large fluctuations by a stable long-term programme. If this is successful it should not be too

difficult to offset small fluctuations by expediting or retarding some items in this long-term programme.

8. I do not believe that it is useful to try to predict the scale [322] of this long-term programme. It will depend on the social habits and propensities of a community with a distribution of taxed income significantly different from any of which we have experience, on the nature of the tax system and on the practices and conventions of business. But perhaps one can say that it is unlikely to be less than 7½ per cent or more than 20 per cent of the net national income, except under new influences, deliberate or accidental, which are not yet in sight.

9. It is still more difficult to predict the length of the second, than of the first, phase. But one might expect it to last another five or ten years, and to pass insensibly into the third phase.

10. As the third phase comes into sight, the problem stressed by Sir H. Henderson begins to be pressing. It becomes necessary to encourage wise consumption and discourage saving, – and to absorb some part of the unwanted surplus by increased leisure, more holidays (which are a wonderfully good way of getting rid of money) and shorter hours.

11. Various means will be open to us with the onset of this golden age. The object will be slowly to change social practices and habits so as to reduce the indicated level of saving. Eventually depreciation funds should be almost sufficient to provide all the gross investment that is required.

12. Emphasis should be placed primarily on measures to maintain a steady level of employment and thus to prevent fluctuations. If a large fluctuation is allowed to occur, it will be difficult to find adequate offsetting measures of sufficiently quick action. This can only be done through flexible methods by means of trial and error on the basis of experience which has still to be gained. If the authorities know quite clearly what they are trying to do and are given sufficient powers, reasonable success in the performance of the task should not be too difficult.

13. I doubt if much is to be hoped from proposals to offset unforeseen short-period fluctuations in investment by stimulating short-period changes in consumption. But I see very great

[323] attractions and practical advantage in Mr Meade's proposal
for varying social security contributions according to the state
of employment.

14. The second and third phases are still academic. Is it
necessary at the present time for Ministers to go beyond the
first phase in preparing administrative measures? The main
problems of the first phase appear to be covered by various
memoranda already in course of preparation. Insofar as it is
useful to look ahead, I agree with Sir H. Henderson that we
should be aiming at a steady long-period trend towards a
reduction in the scale of net investment and an increase in the
scale of consumption (or, alternatively, of leisure). But the
saturation of investment is far from being in sight to-day. The
immediate task is the establishment and the adjustment of a
double system of control and of sensitive, flexible means for
gradually relaxing these controls in the light of day-by-day
experience.

15. I would conclude by two quotations from Sir H. Henderson's paper which seem to me to embody much wisdom.

Opponents of Socialism are on strong ground when they argue
that the State would be unlikely in practice to run complicated
industries more efficiently than they are run at present. Socialists
are on strong ground when they argue that reliance on supply
and demand, and the forces of market competition, as the main-
spring of our economic system, produces most unsatisfactory
results. Might we not conceivably find a *modus vivendi* for the
next decade or so in an arrangement under which the State would
fill the vacant post of entrepreneur-in-chief, while not interfering
with the ownership or management of particular businesses, or
rather only doing so on the merits of the case and not at the
behests of dogma?

We are more likely to succeed in maintaining employment if we
do not make this our sole, or even our first, aim. Perhaps employment, like happiness, will come most readily when it is not sought
for its own sake. The real problem is to use our productive powers to secure the greatest human welfare. Let us start then with

the human welfare, and consider what is most needed to increase it. The needs will change from time to time; they may shift, for example, from capital goods to consumers' goods and to services. Let us think in terms of organising and directing our productive [324] resources, so as to meet these changing needs; and we shall be less likely to waste them.

KEYNES [325]

[*On reading this paper, Sir Wilfrid Eady, Hopkins's successor as the Treasury's Permanent Secretary, commented 'It is a voyage in the stratosphere for most of us.'*

The Government's White Paper on Employment Policy (Cmd 6527) was published on 26 May 1944. Its opening sentence pledged the government after the war to maintain a 'high and stable level of employment'. An illness and negotiations with the US on the future of the international monetary system prevented Keynes from having much hand in its drafting. In a letter to Austin Robinson, 5 June 1944, he wrote: 'My own feeling is that the first sentence is more valuable than the whole of the rest' (quoted in D. E. Moggridge, Maynard Keynes: An Economist's Biography *(1992), p. 709).*]

CW 27, Letter to T. S. Eliot (1945)

[*Letter dated 5 April 1945.*]
... the full employment policy by means of investment is only one particular application of an intellectual theorem. You can produce the result just as well by consuming more or working less. Personally I regard the investment policy as first aid. In U.S., it almost certainly will not do the trick. Less work is the ultimate solution (a 35 hour week in the U.S., would do the trick now). How you mix up the three ingredients of a cure is a matter of taste and experience, i.e. of morals and knowledge.

36

CW 25, 'The Clearing Union' (1941)

[Dated 8 September 1941, this was Keynes's last attempt to construct an international monetary system compatible with the stability of domestic prices and business activity – a preoccupation going all the way back to Indian Currency and Finance, 1913. The occasion was the American demand, as part of the Lend-Lease Agreement, that Britain dismantle its imperial preference system, which discriminated against American goods.]

Post-War Currency Policy
1 The Secular International Problem

The problem of maintaining equilibrium in the balance of payments between countries has never been solved, since methods of barter gave way to the use of money and bills of exchange. During most of the period in which the modern world has been evolved and the autarky of the middle ages was gradually giving way to the international division of labour and the exploitation of new sources of supply by overseas enterprise, the failure to solve this problem has been a major cause of impoverishment and social discontent and even of wars and revolutions. In the past five hundred years there have been only two periods of about fifty years each (the ages of Elizabeth and Victoria in English chronology) when the use of money for the conduct of international trade can be said to have 'worked', – first whilst the prodigious augmentation of the supply of silver from the new world was substituting the features of inflation for those of deflation (bringing a different sort of evil with it), and again in the second half of the nineteenth century when (for reasons to be developed below) the system of international investment pivoting on London transferred the onus of adjustment from the debtor to the creditor position.

To suppose that there exists some smoothly functioning automatic mechanism of adjustment which preserves equilib- [21] rium if only we trust to methods of *laissez-faire* is a doctrinaire delusion which disregards the lessons of historical experience without having behind it the support of sound theory. So far from currency *laissez-faire* having promoted the international division of labour, which is the avowed goal of *laissez-faire*, it has been a fruitful source of all those clumsy hindrances to trade which suffering communities have devised in their perplexity as being better than nothing in protecting them from the intolerable burdens flowing from currency disorders. Until quite recently, nearly all departures from international *laissez-faire* have tackled the symptoms instead of the cause.

International currency *laissez-faire* was breaking down rapidly before the war. During the war it has disappeared completely. This complete break with the past offers us an opportunity. Things are possible to-day which would have been impossible if they involved the prior disestablishment of a settled system.

Moreover in the interval between the wars the world explored in rapid succession almost, as it were, in an intensive laboratory experiment all the alternative false approaches to the solution –

(i) the idea that a freely fluctuating exchange would discover for itself a position of equilibrium;

(ii) liberal credit and loan arrangements between the creditor and the debtor countries flowing from the mere fact of an unbalanced creditor–debtor position, on the false analogy of superficially similar nineteenth-century transactions between old-established and newly-developing countries where the loans were self-liquidating because they themselves created new sources of payment;

(iii) the theory that the unlimited free flow of gold would automatically bring about adjustments of price-levels and activity in the recipient country which would reverse the pressure;

(iv) the use of deflation, and still worse of *competitive* deflations, to force an adjustment of wage- and price-levels [22] which would force or attract trade into new channels;

(v) the use of deliberate exchange depreciation, and still worse of *competitive* exchange depreciations, to attain the same object;

(vi) the erection of tariffs, preferences, subsidies *et hoc genus omne* to restore the balance of international commerce by restriction and discrimination.

It was only in the last years, almost in the last months, before the crash, that after the above trials and errors Dr Schacht stumbled in desperation on something new which had in it the germs of a good technical idea. This idea was to cut the knot by discarding the use of a currency having international validity and substitute for it what amounted to barter, not indeed between individuals, but between different economic units. In this way he was able to return to the essential character and original purpose of trade whilst discarding the apparatus which had been supposed to facilitate, but was in fact strangling it. This innovation worked well, indeed brilliantly, for those responsible for introducing it, and allowed impoverished Germany to build up reserves without which she could scarcely have embarked on war. But as Mr Henderson remarks, the fact that this method was used in the service of evil must not blind us to its possible technical advantage in the service of a good cause. 'If Germany', he points out, 'had wished for butter instead of guns or aeroplanes, there is no reason to doubt that Dr Schacht's expedients would have enabled her to obtain the butter instead of the metal from overseas.' Moreover the use of this method with reckless disregard to the legitimate interests of the other party concerned is characteristic of the German handling of it and is not inherent, as we ourselves have shown in the variants of the method which we have devised and with the aid of which we are successfully maintaining our financial [23] front even during the war.

I expound in a separate paper a possible means of still retaining a currency having an unrestricted international validity. But the alternative to this is surely not a return to the currency disorders of the epoch between the wars, mitigated and temporarily postponed by some liberal Red Cross work by the United States, but a refinement and improvement of the Schachtian device.

II *Our Contemporary British Problem*

Unfortunately the technical task of devising a system, by which a state of international balance can be maintained once it has been reached, is made vastly more difficult by the circumstance that we start out from an existing state of extreme disequilibrium. Drastic changes in the channels along which trade is likely to run after the war if left to itself are a prior condition of the initial attainment of equilibrium, which is not quite the same problem as that of maintaining equilibrium after it has been reached. The United States never succeeded in effecting the re-orientation of her domestic economy required by the changed circumstances in which she found herself after the last war. Her necessary task after this war will be still more severe. The solution involves a serious disturbance to the vested interests both of industry and of agriculture of a kind which it would be contrary to the political traditions and national customs of the country to carry through. Her first contribution in this field is not encouraging; for she proposes the enforcement of an agreement to restrict Europe's freedom to feed herself by compelling even the poorest Eastern European states, however impoverished by war, to eat pure white bread, the admixture of any rye or potato flour being made illegal by international convention, and to buy from overseas, instead of growing it, an amount of wheat costing an additional sum as large as the German indemnity ultimately fixed after the last war which we [24] failed to collect, and, if the present price clauses were to remain, a much larger sum than this, – all this for the purpose of maintaining on a profitable basis an export of wheat from the United States which, in the interests of the restoration of international equilibrium, ought to disappear altogether.

It will be better, however, that I should discuss this phase of the problem in terms of the British prospective situation when the war is over.

Mr Henderson has summed up the position thus:–

We must expect to emerge from the war with our balance of payments very seriously deranged. A substantial portion of our export trade was permanently lost as a consequence of the last war; a further substantial portion is likely to be permanently lost as a consequence of the present one. A further substantial portion of our 'invisible exports' in respect both of interest, dividends, and of shipping receipts, is also likely to be lost. On the other hand, our need for imports, both of food and materials, will be abnormally large for some time after the war, and will always remain large if we succeed in maintaining a high standard of life.

The Lord President's economists are, I believe, engaged in preparing a reasoned estimate of the possible magnitude of the gap. Meanwhile it would be a waste of time for me to attempt a close estimate. But, remembering that the gross increase in our exports will have to exceed the net improvement required in the balance of trade by the amount of imported raw materials incorporated in the exports, I shall be surprised if the needed increase does not exceed the pre-war figure in real terms by somewhere between 50 and 100 per cent. What valid reason have we for supposing that an increment of this order will automatically accrue to us under conditions of *laissez-faire* and without the stimulus of special measures on our part?

Of the special measures which it is open to us to employ by far the most potent is to use the importance of the British market to producers of food and raw materials overseas as an [25] inducement to them to make equivalent purchases of manufactured articles from us. The Argentine, for example, cannot hope to market her wheat and maize and meat, none of which are required by the U.S., unless she can sell substantial quantities to Britain. We may have to tell her that we are not in a financial position to purchase these substantial quantities unless she is prepared to expend the proceeds on taking textiles and engineering products from us.

This is a legitimate arrangement greatly in the interests of both parties. Without it trade on the appropriate scale might be impossible and both countries would be condemned to unemployment and impoverishment. It may be the only feasible means of maximising the volume of international exchange. But the technical means for thus arranging to match imports with exports would involve a far-reaching departure from the pre-war system.

A further obstacle to the restoration of *laissez-faire* methods at any rate during the transitional period (say the first five

years) after the war is the accumulation in London of very large
overseas balances, representing what we have borrowed abroad
for war purposes over and above what we have discharged by
the liquidation of our pre-war overseas investments. This by
itself will render it essential for the maintenance of the war
controls for a considerable time afterwards, unless we can
replace them by a far-reaching constructive scheme which will
offer us the necessary protection.

It is far from certain as yet that there are no other, and better,
alternatives. I can imagine more than one fortunate turn of
affairs which would greatly mitigate the difficulties which lie
ahead. I attempt in a separate paper to sketch an ideal system
which would solve the problem of multilateral lines by international agreement. This is an ambitious scheme. But the
post-war world must not be content with patchwork. If it can
be accepted, several vital purposes will be served. But we have
yet to discover whether those in authority in the world mean [26]
seriously their brave words about radical post-war innovation.

Meanwhile it would be madness on our part to deprive ourselves of the possibility of action along the above lines until we
have a firm assurance of an equally satisfactory solution of a
different kind. Anyone who at this stage would agree to sign
away our future liberty of action would be as great a traitor to
his country as if he were to sign away the British navy before he
had a firm assurance of an alternative means of protection. For
this is the key problem of our post-war prosperity. If we can
solve it, the rest will follow without insuperable difficulty. If we
fail, our best hopes of finally abolishing economic want and of
providing continuous good employment at a high standard of
life will be lost to us. A vast disappointment, social disorders
and finally a repudiation of our ill-judged commitments will be
the result.

III The Analysis of the Problem

I believe that the main cause of failure (except in special, transient conditions) of the freely convertible international metallic
standard (first silver and then gold) can be traced to a single
characteristic. I ask close attention to this, because I should

argue that this provides the clue to the nature of any alternative which is to be successful.

It is characteristic of a freely convertible international standard that it throws the main burden of adjustment on the country which is in the debtor position on the international balance of payments, – that is on the country which is (in this context) by hypothesis the weaker and above all the smaller in comparison with the other side of the scales which (for this purpose) is the rest of the world.

[27]   Take the classical theory that the unlimited free flow of gold automatically brings about adjustments of price-levels and activity between the debtor country and the recipient creditor, which will eventually reverse the pressure. It is usual to-day to object to this theory that it is too dependent on a crude and now abandoned quantity theory of money and that it ignores the lack of elasticity in the social structure of wages and prices. But even to the extent that it holds good in spite of these grave objections, if a country is in economic importance even a fifth of the world as a whole, a given loss of gold will presumably exercise four times as much pressure at home as abroad, with a still greater disparity if it is only a tenth or a twentieth of the world, so that the contribution in terms of the resulting social strains which the debtor country has to make to the restoration of equilibrium by changing its prices and wages is altogether out of proportion to the contribution asked of its creditors. Nor is this all. To begin with, the social strain of an adjustment downwards is much greater than that of an adjustment upwards. And besides this, the process of adjustment is *compulsory* for the debtor and *voluntary* for the creditor. If the creditor does not choose to make, or allow, his share of the adjustment, he suffers no inconvenience. For whilst a country's reserve cannot fall below zero, there is no ceiling which sets an upper limit. The same is true if international loans are to be the means of adjustment. The debtor *must* borrow; the creditor is under no such compulsion.

There is a further consequence, having very great importance, of the main burden of adjustment being on the debtor country which is *small* compared with the world at large;

namely, that most of the means of adjustment open to the
debtor country are liable to have an adverse effect on its terms
of trade. (The best argument in favour of the expedient of tariffs is that it is free from this objection.) The effect on the terms
of trade is not usually understood by outside opinion; but it has
a long history in economic theory and came into particular
prominence in the controversy whether Germany would be
able to manage the comparatively moderate indemnity which [28]
was eventually fixed. The point is, however, easily explained.
Domestic deflation, exchange depreciation and the like aim at
stimulating exports by reducing their international *price* in
terms of imports. The amount of price reduction which will
prove necessary to stimulate a sufficient expansion in the *quantity* of exports relatively to imports depends on the elasticity of
demand in the world at large for the characteristic products
of the country which seeks to increase its sales. If, on account of
the nature of the products or of the reluctance of foreign competitors to relinquish their share of the trade, a large reduction
in price is necessary to stimulate a sufficient increase in quantity, the country which is forcing its products on the world
suffers a severe loss in the proceeds obtained from its *previous*
volume of trade. To take the limiting case, if it is necessary to
reduce the price in at least the same proportion as that in which
the volume is increased, the debtor country is involved in a
Sisyphus task and gets no nearer a position of equilibrium
however great its efforts. Brazilian coffee may offer an example
which approaches the limiting case. But for many agricultural
products, quite a reasonable percentage reduction in the price
paid by the ultimate consumer may, after deduction of costs of
transport and distribution overseas at a fixed rate, present
conditions to the ultimate producer which approximate to the
limiting case.

Thus it has been an inherent characteristic of the automatic
international metallic currency (apart from special circumstances) to force adjustments in the direction most disruptive of
social order, and to throw the burden on the countries least
able to support it, making the poor poorer.

It may be some confirmation of the importance to be

attached to this characteristic of the traditional system that, in the two periods in which the system 'worked', special influences were present which largely removed the burden of [29] pressure, or reversed its direction, as between the debtor country and the creditor or the world at large. In the period of inflation caused by the flow of silver from the new world, the strong, creditor countries, which first received the silver, had to take the initiative in price adjustment. (The same easing factor may have been at work in the vast development of trade and prosperity throughout the Mediterranean countries and beyond which followed the dispersal of the temple hoards of Persia by Alexander the Great.) Again, in the Victorian age the peculiar organisation in London and to a less extent in Paris, the two main creditor centres, by which a flow of gold immediately translated itself, not in the first instance into a change in prices and wages, but into a change in the volume of foreign investment by the creditors, caused the burden to be carried by the stronger shoulders.

I conclude, therefore, that the architects of a successful international system must be guided by these lessons. The object of the new system must be to require the chief initiative from the creditor countries, whilst maintaining enough discipline in the debtor countries to prevent them from exploiting the new ease allowed them in living profligately beyond their means.

There was a further defect in the pre-war system not to be overlooked. It allowed *laissez-faire* in the remittance and acceptance overseas of capital funds for refugee, speculative or investment purposes. During the nineteenth century and up to 1914 the flow of capital funds had been directed from the creditor to the debtor countries, which broadly corresponded to the older and the newer countries, and served at the same time to keep the balance of international payments in equilibrium and to develop resources in undeveloped lands. In the first phase after the last war, the flow of funds continued to be directed from the creditor to the debtor countries, but a large part of the flow, namely from the United States (and also from Great Britain) into Europe ceased to correspond to the development of [30] new resources. In the second phase preceding the present war, complete degeneration set in and capital funds flowed from countries of which the balance of trade was adverse into countries where it was favourable.

This became, in the end, the major cause of instability. If the favourable trade balance of the United States had been the only problem, the newly produced gold in the rest of the world would have been more than sufficient to discharge it. The flow of refugee and speculative funds superimposed on this brought the whole system to ruin.

We have no security against a repetition of this after the present war though not perhaps on the same scale or necessarily in the same direction. (It is easy to conceive conditions in which the American capitalists would be the refugees; and if that were to happen, it would be on a scale to swamp all previous experience.) Social changes affecting the position of the wealth-owning class are likely to occur or (what is worse in the present condition) to be threatened in many countries. The whereabouts of 'the better 'ole' will shift with the speed of the magic carpet. Loose funds may sweep round the world disorganising all steady business.

Nothing is more certain than that the movement of capital funds must be regulated; – which in itself will involve far-reaching departures from *laissez-faire* arrangements.

IV *The Alternative Before Us*

1. The United States do not at present favour any radical remedy. The suggestions current fall under three heads:–

(i) liberal relief to Europe during the reconstruction period, possibly even extending to a redistribution of a part of her redundant stocks of gold;

(ii) some reduction of tariffs and some restriction in the output of agricultural produce for export;

(iii) a general stimulus to demand by the maintenance of a high level of domestic employment as the result of adopting various New Deal expedients. [31]

(i) provides no lasting solution; and for ourselves not even a temporary solution unless we are to be beneficiaries on a scale more generous than seems likely. (We shall have been helped

during the war; it is the others who will be helped afterwards.)
There is little prospect of (ii) on an adequate scale, (iii) would
offer great, and perhaps adequate, relief if and when it happens. I should accept the view that (capital movements apart)
the more or less continuous maintenance of a high level of
employment in U.S.A. would go a long way towards redressing
the international balance of payments. But this is a happy outcome on which we cannot yet rely.

2. We shall end the war with a well developed system of payments and clearings agreements in actual operation. This might
be evolved into a permanent peace-time scheme which would
try to mitigate so far as possible the objectionable features of
bilateralism. Much will be possible which would have been
impossible if we had to start in peace-time *de novo* with the old
system of *laissez-faire* as a going concern. If, in addition, we
were to continue bulk purchasing of foodstuffs and raw materials through official bodies under instructions to direct their
contracts to countries which were prepared to reciprocate with
purchases of our exports, we might succeed in stabilising and
balancing our trade at a high level of volume.

This policy is not free from difficulties. I have given enough
consideration to the details to be fully conscious of them. But I
believe that a serviceable scheme could be worked out.

3. I should prefer, however, to sketch out, first of all, an ideal
scheme which would preserve the advantages of an international
means of payment universally acceptable, whilst avoiding those
features of the old system which did the damage.

I doubt if this plan would prove as helpful to British interests
as the second alternative mentioned above during the transi-
[32] tional period whilst we were expanding our exports to the level
we shall require in future. Against this we may set the advantages of a better system in the long run.

It is also open to the objection, as the reader will soon discover, that it is complicated and novel and perhaps Utopian in
the sense, not that it is impracticable, but that it assumes a
higher degree of understanding, of the spirit of bold innovation, and of international co-operation and trust than it is safe
or reasonable to assume.

Nevertheless, it is with this scheme that I should approach the United States. For it is an attempt to satisfy their fundamental requirements; it would allow us to subscribe to the blessed word 'discrimination'; and it is, therefore, a system in which they might be more willing to co-operate with enthusiasm. Moreover it is a good schematism by means of which the essence of the problem can be analysed and the essential elements of any satisfactory solution brought into full view. If not this, we can ask, what then? Now that you are fully seized of the essential elements of the problem, what alternative solution do you offer us?

J. M. KEYNES

8.9.41

Proposals for an International Currency Union

A.1. Within any member-country or currency unit the provision of foreign exchange to be concentrated in the hands of its central bank* which would deal with the public through the usual banks. That is to say, a member of the public here desiring to obtain dollars for a specified purpose would instruct his bank to make application to the Bank of England – much as at present.† [33]

---

* The 'national' unit for the purpose of this Currency Union would comprise the whole of any area having a common currency and banking system. It would be for those concerned in each case to decide to what central bank to adhere. Perhaps we could not expect the new sterling area to be as large as what we now call the sterling area, but we should try to make it as large as possible. Could we persuade Australia, New Zealand and India, and even South Africa, to remain within it? I should have a good try. There would be great practical advantages to them as well as to us and increased financial stability by remaining within it, against which must be set some loss of prestige and independence. In any case, most of the Crown Colonies, especially Malaya and Hong Kong, would presumably remain in the British sterling area, though Ceylon might go in with India (as also Burma) if India stayed out.

† The question how far this would interfere with the traditional international exchange and acceptance business of London would largely depend on the nature of the regulations in other countries. So far as the U.K. is concerned, there would be no greater interference than is inevitable on the assumption that exchange transactions must be examined individually at some stage, perhaps by the banks themselves if they can be fully trusted, in order to exclude unlicensed capital transactions, and that after the war we shall not have

2. Internationally all transactions to be cleared between central banks, operating on their accounts with an International Clearing Bank. Central banks would buy and sell their own currencies amongst themselves only against debits and credits to their accounts at the Clearing Bank, designated *Clearing Accounts*, and would not themselves hold any foreign currency as distinct from the permitted foreign accounts of their nationals, except as agents for their Governments where the latter required foreign trading accounts for current purposes.

3. Each central bank to have unqualified control over the *outward* transactions of its nationals, i.e. over the purchase of foreign exchange by them (including, in particular, a control of remittances on capital account), but it must always be prepared to *sell* its own currency to another central bank against a credit to its Clearing Account.

4. Each national currency to have a fixed value (subject to what follows about provisions for change) determined when the Currency Union is set up in terms of the bank money of the Clearing Bank, which would be itself expressed in terms of a [34] unit of gold.

5. A central bank to be entitled to replenish its Clearing Account by paying in gold to the Clearing Bank, but the balance on its Account only to be employed for the purpose of making a transfer to another Clearing Account; so that it could not withdraw gold.

6. Any gold held by the Clearing Bank at the end of each year in excess of the amount of its Reserve Fund may be distributed to those central banks whose Clearing Accounts are in

---

adequate liquid resources to allow us to keep outstanding with London finance a volume between £100 million and £200 million of non-domestic bills of exchange (already much diminished from their former figure). We could retain and develop the existing system of authorised dealers who would be permitted to retain floating balances abroad. In this connection also it would be most important that the newly defined sterling area should be as large as possible. It should be noticed that the restrictive conditions are merely permissive to the central bank concerned. The Bank of England could issue an open general licence for any such business as the above, should it feel itself strong enough to do so.

credit in proportion to the amounts of their credit balances, their Clearing Accounts being debited accordingly; no Clearing Bank to be entitled to acquire gold otherwise except from its own nationals (including those of its own commonwealth or dependencies) or for industrial purposes.

B.1. Each central bank to be allotted an index-quota equal to half the sum of its imports and exports (both reckoned exclusive of re-exports) on the average of the previous five years (starting with the five pre-war years, the most remote pre-war year in the average being replaced each year by the latest available post-war year), and to be allowed to overdraw its Clearing Account up to a maximum amount equal to its index-quota, provided that it shall not increase its overdraft by more than a quarter of its index-quota in any year.

2. A central bank whose Clearing Account has been in debit for more than a year by an amount exceeding a *quarter* of its index-quota shall be designated a Deficiency Bank. A Deficiency Bank shall be allowed to reduce the exchange value of its national currency by an amount not exceeding 5 per cent within any year. A Deficiency Bank may borrow from the Clearing Account of a Surplus Bank (see below) on any terms which may be mutually agreed.

3. A central bank whose Clearing Account has been in debit for more than a year by an amount exceeding a *half* of its index-quota shall be designated a Supervised Bank. A Supervised Bank may be *required* by the Governors of the Clearing [35] Bank to reduce the exchange value of its national currency by amounts not exceeding 5 per cent in any year; to hand over in reduction of its deficiency any free gold in the possession of itself or its Government; and to prohibit outward capital transactions except with the permission of the Governors, who may also disallow at their discretion any other requirement from it for foreign exchange. A Supervised Bank may be requested by the Governors to withdraw from the system in which event its debit balance shall be transferred to the Reserve Fund (see below) of the Clearing Bank.

4. A central bank whose Clearing Account has been in credit for more than a year by an amount exceeding a *quarter* of its

index-quota shall be designated a Surplus Bank. A Surplus
Bank may increase the exchange value of its national currency
by an amount not exceeding 5 per cent within any year. A Surplus Bank *shall* grant a general licence for the withdrawal of
foreign-owned balances and investments within its jurisdiction.
A Surplus Bank may make advances to the Clearing Account of
a Deficiency Bank.

5. A central bank whose Clearing Account has been in credit
for more than a year by an amount exceeding a half of its
index-quota shall be *required* by the Governors of the Clearing
Bank to increase the exchange value of its national currency by
5 per cent, and the requirement shall be repeated after any subsequent year in which the average credit balance has increased
by a further 10 per cent of its index-quota since the previous
upward adjustment.

6. If at the end of any year the credit balance on the Clearing
Account of any central bank exceeds the full amount of its
index-quota, the excess shall be transferred to the Reserve
Fund of the Clearing Bank.

7. A central bank having a credit balance on its Clearing
Account may withdraw from the system on a year's notice, but
shall surrender its credit balance to the Reserve Fund of the
[36] Clearing Bank.

8. At the request of the central bank of the borrower the International Clearing Bank may act as trustee for any foreign loan,
including loans between central banks, in which case it shall debit
the service of the loan without further specific instruction to the
Clearing Account of the central bank of the lender, so long as the
debtor is not a Supervised Bank, in which case further transfers
shall be at the discretion of the Governors of the Clearing Bank.

C.1. The International Clearing Bank shall establish a
Reserve Fund.

2. The Reserve Fund shall be employed as already provided
in B.3, 6 and 7.

3. 5 per cent of the average annual excess of the Clearing
Account of a Surplus Bank above a quarter of its index-quota
and 10 per cent of the excess above a half of its index-quota
shall be transferred to the Reserve Fund of the Clearing Bank.

4. No interest shall be allowed by the Clearing Bank on credit balances. But interest shall be charged on debit balances at rates fixed by the Governors which shall be increased as the size of the central bank's debit is increased in proportion to its index-quota. The excess of the interest earnings of the Clearing Bank over its expenses shall be transferred to the Reserve Fund.

5. The Reserve Fund may be applied at the discretion of the Board of Governors for the relief of any central bank in difficulty for special causes beyond its own control or for any other purpose.

D.1. Foreign-owned balances and investments held within the jurisdiction of a central bank at the date of the establishment of the International Clearing Bank shall be frozen in the sense that they shall not be withdrawn thereafter except by permission of the central bank concerned or under the general licence to be granted under B.4 above. The same shall apply to [37] subsequent remittances on capital account but the title to such balances and investments may be freely transferred as between foreign nationals.

2. A central bank shall be entitled at the initiation of the scheme to discharge foreign-owned assets within its jurisdiction held in the form of cash or bank deposits or the securities of its Government by paying an equivalent sum in gold to the central bank of the foreign nationals concerned; and the latter central bank shall be entitled to require such a discharge if the former central bank and its Government possess a gold reserve in excess of its index-quota.

3. If the U.S. is prepared to approve an initial redistribution of its gold reserves, it is suggested that if any country, after the adjustments provided in D.2, has a gold reserve of an amount in excess of its index-quota, a proportion of this excess should be transferred to the Clearing Bank at the outset for the credit of the post-war Relief and Reconstruction Council (see below). This would facilitate post-war reconstruction without throwing any real burden on the U.S. as compared with other creditor countries; for it would involve no charge on the budget and the real burden would be carried not by the U.S. in particular, but by all those creditor countries who as a result of this

arrangement might come to possess hereafter larger credit balances with the Clearing Bank than they would have possessed otherwise.

E.1. Clearing Accounts with the International Clearing Bank to be set up only in favour of the central banks of countries adhering to the Currency Union and of certain international bodies such as those specified below.

2. The Clearing Bank to set up an account in favour of the supra-national policing body charged with the duty of preserving the peace and maintaining international order. If any country shall have infringed its properly authorised orders, the [38] policing body shall be entitled to request the Governors of the Clearing Bank to hold the Clearing Account of the central bank of the delinquent country to its order and permit no further transactions on the account except by its authority.

3. The Clearing Bank to set up an account in favour of the international body charged with post-war relief and reconstruction. It is suggested that this body should pay the proper price for all supplies and services which it may administer, financing the excess of these costs over any sums recovered from the beneficiaries and also the cost of furnishing to certain countries by way of gift an initial credit balance in their Clearing Accounts (should this course of action commend itself) partly by funds received under D.3 above (should this come about) and partly by being allowed an overdraft on its Clearing Account up to an agreed maximum amount, the overdraft to be discharged in subsequent years at the discretion of the Governors of the Clearing Bank either out of their Reserve Fund or out of a special levy (in addition to the regular contributions under C.3) on the surplus credit balances of Surplus Banks not exceeding 5 per cent of such surplus in any year, any undischarged balance being in the nature of a fiduciary issue of the Currency Union. By this means all risk is avoided of any country being required to assume a burdensome commitment for relief and reconstruction, since the resources will be provided in the first instance by those countries having credit balances on their Clearing Accounts for which they have no immediate use and are voluntarily leaving idle, and in the long run by

those countries which have a chronic international surplus for which they have no beneficial employment.

4. The Clearing Bank to set up Clearing Accounts in favour of international bodies charged with the management of a Commodity Control, and to finance stocks of commodities held by such bodies by allowing them overdraft facilities on their accounts up to an agreed maximum. By this means the financial [39] problem of holding pools would be satisfactorily solved.

F.1. The International Clearing Bank shall be managed by a Board of eight Governors and a Chairman. They shall draw up their own rules of procedure and shall settle all matters by a bare majority except that an alteration of an article of the constitution of the Clearing Bank, which may include a change in the gold value of the Clearing Bank's money of account, shall require a two-thirds majority.

2. Any of the articles of the constitution may be modified in its application to a particular central bank by agreement between that bank and a majority of the Board of the Clearing Bank.

3. An independent Chairman of the Board shall be elected annually by the Governors and his election shall cause a vacancy in his place as a Governor if he was previously one of them. He shall have no vote except a casting vote.

4. The eight Governors shall be chosen as follows:– one by the United Kingdom, one by the British Commonwealth outside the United Kingdom, one by the United States, one by Russia, two by the European central banks, one by the South American central banks, and one by the remaining central banks. In choosing the four last-mentioned representatives the central banks concerned shall have a voting power in proportion to their index-quota.

J. M. KEYNES

8.9.41   [40]

37

CW 24, 'Overseas Financial Policy in Stage III'
(1945)

[*This is the memorandum Keynes first drafted in March 1945, setting out the options facing Britain after the termination of Lend-Lease from the United States, on the assumption that it would face a prospective post-war deficit on its balance of payments of $5 billion over three years. It was aimed at imperialists on the right and socialists on the left of politics who, for different reasons, were arguing that Britain should refuse American help after the war. Keynes's 'middle' position outlined the three options as Starvation Corner, Temptation and Justice. The memorandum became the basis of the British government's negotiating position for American financial support, and Keynes was himself entrusted with the negotiations, in Washington, for an American loan, October–December 1945. The version printed here is the CW one, dated 15 May. The memorandum starts by listing the failures and successes of British wartime finance, of which the following paragraph is typical Keynes.*]*

8. (v) . . . The hourly wage today in this country is (broadly) 2s per hour; in the United States it is 5s per hour (reckoned at an exchange of $4). Even the celebrated inefficiency of British manufacturers can scarcely (one hopes) be capable of offsetting over wide ranges of industry the whole of this initial cost-difference in their favour, though, admittedly, they have managed it in some important cases. Perhaps the chief danger at any rate in the mass-production industries, is a cut-throat competition in export prices by the Americans loading them with less than their fair share of overhead costs (a practice which the much-abused international cartel is designed to prevent). The available statistics suggest that, provided we have never made the product before, we have the rest of the world licked on cost. For a Mosquito, a Lancaster, Radar, we should have the business at our feet in conditions of free and fair competition. It is when it comes to making a shirt or a steel billet that we have to admit ourselves beaten

both by the dear labour of America and by the cheap labour of Asia or Europe. Ship- building seems to be the only traditional industry where we fully hold our own. If by some sad geographical slip the American Air Force (it is too late now to hope for much from the enemy) were to destroy every factory on the North-East coast and in Lancashire (at an hour when the directors were sitting there and no one else), we should have nothing to fear. How else we are to regain the exuberant inexperience which is necessary, it seems, for success, I cannot surmise.　　　[262]

. . .

III

24. What is the upshot? If matters go on substantially as at present, we shall be running an overseas deficit on the day of cease-fire in Asia at the rate of about £1,400 million per annum, assuming that lend lease and mutual aid for food and raw materials are then terminated, but that we have no further liability for any dollar expenditure in respect of munitions and war-stores, whether to be delivered or to be cancelled or as salvage in the sterling area. With our best efforts, current expenditure (which will have to include the clearing up of arrears) will only decline gradually. Assuming some improvement meanwhile in the unsatisfactory features just dealt with, an intensive economy drive to reduce overseas war expenditure, and a not less intensive export drive, we might get through the first year of Stage III with an adverse balance not exceeding £1,000 million. But we cannot prudently assume much less. Nor is this the end. Three to five years are likely to elapse before we reach equilibrium. There is no present warrant for putting the cumulative deficit before we reach equilibrium at less than £2,000 million. The bulk of this, and perhaps more than this, will have to be borrowed from outside the sterling area . . .　　　[270]

25. Let us hope that this will have proved to err on the pessimistic side. It may. Such estimates generally do; although other good judges fear that the above may err on the optimistic side. However that may be, if our most extravagant hopes were to come true, a deficit over the period as a whole in excess of £1,000 million seems a certainty. Thus this is not a well-chosen

moment for a declaration of our financial independence of
North America. Our necessities in the transition after the
war will put a quantitative burden on the financial machine
described earlier in this paper far greater than it can carry without further financial aid from the United States and Canada. At
the very best, even assuming a fabulous improvement in the
above weak spots, we should do well to assume that complete
financial independence of the United States would require:–

(*a*) the continuance of war rationing and war controls *more*
stringent than at present for (say) three to five years after
the war;

(*b*) the national planning and direction of foreign trade both
imports and exports, somewhat on the Russian model; and

(*c*) an indefinite postponement of colonial development and
Far Eastern rehabilitation and a virtual abandonment of all
overseas activities, whether military or diplomatic or by way of
developing our trade, wealth and influence, which involved any
considerable expenditure.

26. There remains a further, and in my judgment an overrid-
ing, consideration which, so far, has only been touched upon in
passing. A policy of economic isolationism means acceptance –
[271]   indeed, not merely the acceptance but the advocacy – of a
system of international economy after the war of a kind to
which all sections of opinion, not only in the United States but
also in Canada, are bitterly opposed. It is foolish to suppose if
we take this line that the North Americans will remain passive.
They will regard us as having deliberately rejected a helping
hand for reasons of envy and ambition, and as recklessly disrupting the common Anglo-American front which is the best
hope of the world. We must also expect strong opposition on
the part of many of the sterling area countries to gang up with
us like this against the United States and we might end up with
a greatly curtailed sterling area. Outside the sterling area the
United States would use its lending power to persuade many
countries, especially in Western Europe and South America, to
refuse to fall in with our ideas. In short, the moment at which
we have for the time being lost our financial strength and owe
vast sums all round the world is scarcely the bright and brilliant

occasion for asking all our creditors to join up with us against where financial power now rests, not for the purpose of getting paid, but for the purpose of obliging us with a little more.

27. All this is, of course, on the assumption that the Americans are in fact prepared to make us a fair offer, not so much generous as just, using their financial strength not as an instrument to force us to their will, but as a means of making it possible for us to participate in arrangements which we ourselves prefer on their merits if only they can be made practicable for us. It would be a grave misdeed to prepare for isolationism if any reasonable terms are open to us on which we can walk with the Americans and the Canadians along the path which surely, if we can keep to it, offers much the best hope both for ourselves and for others. If, on the other hand, no such terms are obtainable, if the hostile forces in the United States overwhelm the forces of light and friendship (which is possible but not probable), then the whole situation is changed. By reason [272] of this possibility, but also (much more to the point) as a matter of tactics it is necessary to keep alive the disagreeable, indeed the disastrous, alternative, without, however, disguising from ourselves its true character. Perhaps I run the risk of enlarging on the obvious. But a position of complete independence within our own family is so naturally attractive to those who are not in a position to see so clearly the other side of the medal that it might be a mistake to scamp the argument.

28. It is not merely in order to oblige the Americans (and the Canadians) and as the price of their assistance that it is in our interest to embrace the international, as opposed to the isolationist or etatist, scheme of foreign trade. The international system is, on its merits, in our interests, for two reasons. The nature of our trade does not lend itself to bilateral arrangements; what suits our exporters is to have the whole world as their playground without reference to the question what and where it suits quite another set of persons, namely, our importers, to buy. Moreover, the terms of trade under forced barter conditions are bound to be to our disadvantage. We could, I suppose, maintain a certain level of subsistence on a barter basis, but we could not expect to get fat. Nor should this

system be advocated by those who in other contexts extol the advantages of free enterprise. For barter trade is the very antithesis to individual enterprise. Every bargain would have to be undertaken by a Government Department, and exporters, unless they were subjected (as they would have to be) to compulsion, would soon find that the game was not worth the candle. Indeed, planned bilateral trade, with a view to making sure that exports balance imports, is a feeble version of the Russian method of a state monopoly of exports and imports, and likely to be much less efficient. Indeed, if the free enterprise alternative breaks down (as it may), it is probably to the Russian model, in my opinion, that we shall have to look; and we [273] may even have to make some experiments in this direction in the near future. Indeed, planned bilateralism is being chiefly advocated in this country to-day (with a few notable exceptions) by the near-Communists.

29. The second reason is our position as the financial centre of the greater part of the British Commonwealth and also of a number of countries outside it. We built up the pre-war sterling area because we were bankers amiable to treat with and having a long record of honouring our cheques. It is a great mistake to believe that we can regain or retain this position except on the basis that sterling is a freely convertible currency. Bilateral proposals are sometimes advocated on the ground that they are the best means to preserve the sterling area. Nothing could be further from the truth. They are a sure means of disrupting it. There would be very little left, if anything, of the sterling area on the basis of making sterling a permanently inconvertible currency which could only be used to purchase goods over a limited field. Each member in turn would walk out on us. The proposals of this paper are, and are intended to be, the means to recover for London its ancient prestige and its hegemony.

30. The foregoing observations do not imply a lack of sympathy with the anxiety about our future balance of payments which underlies the bilateral approach in the minds of those of its advocates who are far from desiring on its merits a State monopoly of foreign trade. They ask themselves what hope is there of reaching equilibrium on any other basis. Is not the use

of our position as a great consumer, to force our goods out on to the world in return for what the world wishes to sell to us, the only new weapon in our armoury and one we cannot do without? I do not claim that there is a conclusive answer to this. I am far from certain that we shall reach trade equilibrium in the post-war world by the methods of free enterprise. It is very possible, indeed, that the system will break down and that nothing short of a state monopoly of foreign trade (for that is [274] what planned bilateralism comes to in practice) will serve our needs.

31. No. The future is to be viewed with anxiety. The present argument does not flow from a blind faith in the blessings of free enterprise. The argument stands firm on four fixed points of conviction: First, in the actual position of this small island as the centre of an independent world system (so different in every respect from the position of Russia or of the United States) the freedom of trade is, on its merits, to our great advantage if it can be made to work. Second, at this stage of the evolution of thought and politics it is the only path along which we can walk as partners in a better hope with the United States and Canada. Third, the future is altogether unclear and unpredictable – there can be no sufficient evidence at this date of time for choosing the worse before trying the better. Fourth, if international trade on these principles breaks down (as well it may), we shall be in a vastly better position to justify a change and to ask others to join with us on new lines than if we were to go our own way now alone, and very much alone, without giving a trial to the alternative. Even if I were convinced that those will certainly prove right who believe that we can only live in the post-war world by a state planning of foreign trade, I should nevertheless think it wise statesmanship to act today on the other hypothesis.

32. I do not seek to conclude that the policy of isolation is, even in the last resort, utterly impracticable. On the contrary, as I have mentioned, we want to be able to pretend with sufficient plausibility that it offers a just possible alternative. But it might be expected to lead to serious political and social disruption at home and our withdrawal, for the time being, from the

position of a first-class Power in the outside world. We should
have to retire, as Russia did between the wars, to starve and
reconstruct. We might, like Russia, emerge in good health half
[275] a generation later, but nothing much less than Russian methods would have served our turn meanwhile. Indeed, the danger
is that our dismay at the character of this alternative will make
us weak negotiators and too willing to accept under pressure
the other extreme, which is certainly the line of least resistance.
For we shall need a robust spirit in negotiation and a willingness to face a breakdown, if necessary, in the first round. If
the alternative just described is Starvation Corner, the other
extreme, to which I now turn, should be called Temptation.

IV

33. What, then, is the amount of American aid which we are
likely to need? It is impossible to quantify this with any degree
of accuracy on the basis of what is now known. I put it at a
probable minimum of $5 billion (£1,250 million) with up to
(say) $8 billion possibly required to give us real liberty of action
and to allow us to offer from the start the full multilateralism of
trade and exchange which will be the best inducement to the
Americans to fall in with our proposals. A larger sum might
demoralise us and prevent us from ever reaching equilibrium
again except after further crisis and some humiliation. We
should certainly aim at getting through with $5 billion, but a
call on a further $3 billion is very advisable if we are to have the
full confidence and resources to develop our trade on far-sighted
lines and to play our proper part in the world after the war.

34. Let us now turn to a closer inspection of Temptation.
There is not much doubt that the Americans would be ready,
and even eager, to lend us large sums *on their own terms* –
$5 billion without doubt and perhaps the full $8 billion spread
over a period. Nor will the terms they propose be, from their
own point of view (whatever we may think), particularly unreasonable. I guess that the conditions which it would be easy
[276] to negotiate might be somewhat as follows:–

(a) A low rate of interest, certainly not higher than 2½ per
cent, and perhaps as low as 2 per cent.

(*b*) Easy terms of repayment of capital, spread over (say) thirty years and not beginning for ten years, with provisions for postponement if, when the time comes, the burden appears too great for us.

(*c*) Free multilateral clearing within the sterling area from the beginning, i.e., the unfettered conversion into dollars of the current earnings of the sterling area countries even during the provisional period.

(*d*) Perhaps the same condition in respect of the pre-zero hour sterling balances.

(*e*) A pretty full implementation of the ideals of Article VII as understood by the Americans, with substantial concessions on our part to their point of view in the matters of preferences, cartels, bulk purchasing, etc.

(*f*) The wiping out of any remaining lend lease liability, but the inclusion in the above loan of various obligations arising out of the winding-up of lend lease.

35. A good many of those whom we reckon the more friendly will start out along some such lines as the above, and will consider in their own minds, that they are offering us a square, and even a generous, deal. I am afraid that, if we could do no better, most of us would, when we were right up against it, prefer this Temptation to Starvation Corner, which is not far from politically impossible, both at home and abroad, if Temptation is offering round the corner.

36. What then, without overstating them, are the objections to this version of Temptation? –

(i) Some part, perhaps a considerable part, of what we should otherwise owe to the sterling area and other countries, which are our natural customers, we should come to owe to the United States instead. Perhaps $2 billion might get thus transferred, as compared with the result of deferring free convertibility until the end of the provisional period. [277]

(ii) We should owe the United States an annual sum of, say, $200 million in interest (assuming 2½ per cent on $8 billion), and, after an interval, say, a further $300 million for capital repayment, that is an annual service of $500 million a year, tapering away in the course of time. This would be in addition to a large outstanding debt of some $12 billion to other countries. It would be rash to say that this is impossible. Time and progress diminish the significance of what begin by seeming large figures. Moreover, we might find $5 billion sufficient. But we cannot be sure of shouldering such a burden with success, and we might find ourselves in a chronic condition of having to make humiliating and embarrassing pleas for mercy and postponement. It is interesting to note that the total war burden we should be carrying under the above assumptions adds up to exactly the same figure, namely, $20 billion, that the Russians think appropriate in the case of Germany (though they will not get it or anything like).

(iii) It would be wrong to expect us to make concessions in the field of economic policy under financial pressure.

37. But the main objection surely lies, not in these details, but in the whole proposed set-up being an outrageous crown and conclusion of all that has happened. The war would end by placing on Germany an external burden of $20 billion or less; it would end by placing on us a burden of $20 billion or more. It would end in Germany being forced into conformity with an economic policy designed from without; and the same here. She would plead to Russia from time to time for mercy and deferment; and so should we to the United States. It is not as the result of some statistical calculation about what we might be able to manage, that the mind revolts from accepting the counsels of Temptation. The fundamental reasons for rejection are incommensurable in terms of cash.

[278] 38. Nevertheless, before turning to the third line of approach, which I shall venture to call Justice, it is necessary to examine the possible mitigations of a policy on the above broad lines which one might be able to secure in negotiation. It may be that a point comes when Temptation is sufficiently transformed to approach Justice. We must be clear in our heads about the best version of what we can perhaps fall back upon.

39. I have made bold to say that the above terms would be easy to negotiate. I think there are improvements on these terms which it might not be impossible to obtain, compatibly with accepting this general line of approach. For example, the

annual service of the loan might be greatly lightened either by reducing the interest to a token figure or by deferring the final date of discharge or by both expedients. An annual service of 1 per cent would cost only $80 million a year even on a loan of $8 billion. It might be allowed that we need not release any part of the pre-zero hour sterling balances, but only their current earnings. It might be tacitly agreed that no element of financial pressure should enter into the conversations on commercial policy and other extraneous subjects.

40. Such a settlement would not be unduly onerous, financially or economically, on ourselves in relation to the United States, though it would leave us with the problem of the old sterling balances unmitigated. But it still fails to measure up to the criterion of Justice. The financial benefit to the United States would be next door to nothing, and worth less than nothing to the American economy. The sweet breath of Justice between partners, in what had been a great and magnanimous enterprise carried to overwhelming success, would have been sacrificed to some false analogy of 'business'. And even then Uncle Sam might quite likely remain under the conviction that he was Uncle Sap, a conviction which can only be removed by making him enter into the meeting-place by a different door.   [279]

41. What is this different door? It is not through the approach of relief such as is appropriate to Greece or Jugoslavia or aid in the finance of rehabilitation such as France or Czechoslovakia can properly ask; but through the approach of a general re-consideration of the proper burden of the costs of the war.

42. For a hundred good reasons we have had to accept during the war a post-war financial burden entirely disproportionate to what is fair. The theme is familiar. We did it in the interests of getting on with the war without a waste of time or loss of war-like efficiency. As a result, we, and we only, end up owing vast sums, not to neutrals and bystanders, but to our own Allies, Dominions and Associates, who ought to figure in the eyes of history as our mercenaries, unless the balance is redressed. This does not apply particularly to the United States; indeed, to them (and to Canada) proportionately least of all. It applies all round. Nevertheless, it is only through appropriate

action by the United States and Canada that there is a prospect of an agreed general re-settlement. To which it should be added that the reward to the North Americans will not merely be that their action is contributory to the establishment of Justice, but also that, at very small cost to their economies, perhaps at less than no true cost at all, we shall be made able to be their partners and coadjutors in setting up a post-war international economy of the character on which they have set their hearts.

43. The President has often used words implying that he accepted in some sense the principle of equal sacrifice. We must ask him to let us take him at his word – at least to some extent. This does not mean that there is a clear logical conclusion to which we can press matters. Sacrifices are incommensurable. Apart from which we must be practical and work with a broad [280] brush. There is a big gap between equality of sacrifice and our being left with a heavier overseas financial burden than Germany, a burden which we shall owe to our *Allies*. Let us, therefore, consider a version of what we might accept as doing at the same time substantial justice and as allowing us to fall in whole-heartedly and sincerely with the American ideal of the post-war international economy.

44. The United States would be asked to play a part in this, but, as it will be seen, by no means an exclusive part. The method of redistribution of the burden and the rubric under which it is effected, which seem to me to be the best, after considering alternatives, both technically and politically and psychologically, is the following:–

(i) During the period before lend lease came into full operations we spent some \$3 billion on purchases in the United States for what afterwards became a common war. Moreover, it was this expenditure which built up the munitions industries in the United States before they entered the war to their immense advantage after they entered it. This sum the United States would agree to refund to us as a sort of retrospective lend lease.

(ii) This payment, supplemented by the credit arrangements proposed below, would make it possible for us to undertake that we would accept *de facto* convertibility of sterling within a year after the end of the war (without necessarily waiving the other relaxations contemplated during the transitional period).

(iii) With this support behind us we would approach the various members of the sterling area with proposals for dealing with their sterling balances. These would not necessarily follow a uniform pattern, but might be, in general, except where there is good reason to the contrary, on the following lines:–

(*a*) Each member of the area would contribute a proportion of the final total of its sterling balances to the costs of the common victory. [281]

(*b*) A proportion would be left liquid and would become fully convertible over the exchanges for the purpose of meeting current transactions in any part of the world.

(*c*) The remainder would be funded on terms to be explained below.

(*d*) Alternatively, if any member of the area would not accept such proposals, no part of their sterling balances would be made available except on the terms explained below.

(*e*) The figure of the sterling balances to be handled in one or other of these ways would include an appropriate allowance for the cost of our post-war demobilisation and terminal liabilities as well as the accumulations during the war.

(iv) In addition to the relief under (i) above, the United States to give us a call on dollars exercisable over (say) ten years up to a further $5 billion if required at a token rate of interest and on easy terms of repayment. [282]

. . .

59. How can such proposals be presented with the best hope of conviction to the people of the United States and to the countries of the sterling area? This is a political, that is a psychological, question, and the best shape will only emerge, I expect, in the course of prolonged discussion. But the broad lines must be somewhat as follows:–

(i) We shall have been in the war and in the area of operations for longer than anyone else. In the interests of victory we freely abandoned financial prudence for the future. We and we alone supplemented our own resources by mortgaging the future through overseas loans. We and we alone did this.

(ii) It is precisely that expenditure which we incurred in the United States itself whilst we were holding the fort alone for which retrospective repayment would be made.

[290]   (iii) If, in the light of the final outcome and the full story, nothing is done to redress the position, we shall end by shouldering burdens incurred for the common cause, such as cannot be placed even on the defeated enemy. Our Allies will be seeking to obtain post-war reparations from this small country on a scale greater than it will be practicable to put on the enemy.

(iv) With such burdens upon us we cannot for several years to come participate in the free international economy upon which the Americans have set their hearts and which we also, no less than they, vastly prefer if it is made practicable for us.

(v) Some of our American friends are at present a little too much inclined to suggest to us that we should free ourselves from these burdens by a straight unilateral repudiation or what would amount to such, if it were to be enforced without the offer of a reasonable alternative (e.g. something like what is suggested above, for those countries which decline the option without, however, having first offered them the option). In our view we cannot do this –

(*a*) for reasons of honour;

(*b*) for reasons of justice, since the above would certainly not lead to a *fair* redistribution of the costs of the war;

(*c*) for reasons of practice, since it would not be practicable, for example, to deprive all the sterling countries of the liquid use of the whole of their currency reserves held with us.

So far from this course contributing to the solution of a free international economy, it would widen the field within which the strictest controls over foreign trade would continue to be necessary.

(vi) It is only by a more comprehensive settlement, which attempts to offer everyone what is reasonable, and so far as we can make it, fair, that the financial consequences of the war can be liquidated. This is the aim, namely, that as between the partners to the war, its financial consequences, in so far as they

[291]   affect future economic intercourse between them, should be so far as possible liquidated. These words sum up the final purpose.

Strict fairness will not be possible. On our own proposals we shall continue to carry burdens from which others will be freed. But the alternative mentioned in (v) above goes altogether too far and would shift unfairness at least as much as it diminished it.

(vii) The outcome of the war should not be such that the financial weakness of certain of the partners tempts other partners to use their financial strength to put on pressure to secure their own way.

(viii) Thus no fair solution can be reached without the participation of the Americans. The help asked from them is on relatively so small a scale that it costs them almost literally nothing. It enables them to dispose over a period of a foreign surplus far below what they are likely in any case to develop, a surplus of which in any case they will have to find means of riddance. The amount of the contribution proposed ($3 billion) is the cost of the war to the United States for a fortnight; to forgo good prospects for the sake of this saving would be surely to spoil the ship of Victory and Peace for a coat of paint. Is there any alternative way in which they can get better value? Under these proposals they can wind up the financial side of the war leaving behind a sense of justice between the partners; and all of us become free forthwith to participate in the free international economy which is one of the prime objects of American policy. They will never have a better chance of a wise act at so modest a cost.

(ix) It is essential that the settlement should not take the form of a unilateral decision on our part. It must be the result of a joint discussion and one which commends itself as fair to the general judgment of the Allied Nations. For only so can recrimination be avoided and only so can we, with a good conscience, make an enforced settlement on any, if there be any such at the last, who, being offered an arrangement which has [292] commended itself as fair to the general judgment of the Nations, decide to stand out.

(x) It is not the money that the Americans will grudge. They will spill much more for worse causes. If, in spite of the confused vapours and incorrigible ignorance which surround and condition all public discussion in the United States, the people of the United States can be brought to see the thing in its true light, looking back to what has happened and forward to what should happen, we need not doubt their approval.

60. We could, I suppose, fall back on to a variant of the above by which the $3 billion from the United States was not freely contributed as retrospective lend lease, but was provided on the same terms as the proposed credit of $5 billion, which would then become $8 billion, all the rest of the settlement remaining the same. I do not think that the financial consequences of this would be insupportable. It will be noticed that this proposal approximates to the least dangerous version of Temptation outlined in paragraph 39 above. But politically and psychologically it would be greatly inferior. It would prejudice our approach to the sterling area countries for their contributions, which could no longer be represented as part of a general, agreed re-distribution of the financial burden of the war. I should expect that the grander version would be carried more easily with the general opinion of the world than the meaner version. The Americans would have lost the sense of magnanimity for a financial benefit which is useless to them and even perhaps injurious. This variant would only appeal to those who believe that their duty to God and to mankind requires that
[293] every action must be at least dressed up to look like 'business'.

[*Keynes went to Washington in October 1945, hoping to get a grant or interest-free loan of $5 billion. Instead the loan agreement was for $3.75 billion, repayable over fifty years at 2 per cent interest: i.e., Temptation. Keynes's paean to Justice failed to move the US negotiators.*]

38

CW 27, 'The Balance of Payments of the United States' (1946)

[*Published posthumously in the* Economic Journal *in June 1946, it caused some consternation among Keynes's disciples by paying tribute to the 'invisible hand'. The context is Keynes's prediction that the 'dollar shortage' would eventually disappear.*]

Putting one thing together with another . . . may not the reader feel himself justified in concluding that the chances of the dollar becoming danerously scarce in the course of the next five to ten years are not very high? I found some American authorities thinking it at least as likely that America will lose gold in the early future as that she will gain a significant quantity . . .

In the long run more fundamental forces may be at work, if all goes well, tending towards equilibrium [*in the balance of payments*], the significance of which may ultimately transcend ephemeral statistics. I find myself moved, not the first time, to remind contemporary economists that the classical teaching embodied some permanent truths of great significance, which we are liable to-day to overlook because we associate them with other doctrines which we cannot accept without much qualification. There are in these matters deep undercurrents at work, natural forces, one might call them, or even the invisible hand, which are operating towards equilibrium . . . The United States is becoming a high-living, high-cost country beyond any previous experience. Unless their internal, as well as their external, economic life is to become paralysed by the Midas touch, they will discover ways of life which, compared with the ways of the less fortunate regions of the world, must tend towards, and not away from, external equilibrium.

Admittedly, if the classical medicine is to work, it is essential that import tariffs and export subsidies should not progressively offset its influence. [*Keynes goes on to draw comfort from recent American espousal of free trade.*] . . . It shows how [444] much modernist stuff, gone wrong and turned sour and silly, is circulating in our system, also incongruously mixed, it seems, with age-old poisons, that we should have given so doubtful a welcome to this magnificent, objective approach which a few years ago we should have regarded as offering incredible promise of a better scheme of things . . .

The great virtue of the Bretton Woods and Washington proposals, taken in conjunction, is that they marry the use of the necessary expedients to the wholesome long-run doctrine. It is for this reason that, speaking in the House of Lords, I claimed that 'Here is an attempt to use what we have learnt from modern experience and modern analysis, not to defeat, but to implement the wisdom of Adam Smith.'

[445]

The Essayist

The excerpts in this section are taken from Essays in Biography, *CW* 10. *They exhibit not only Keynes's literary skills, cramped by his big treatises, but the qualities of mind, heart and character which he most admired. Like his teacher, Alfred Marshall, he had a 'divided nature'. The excerpts in this section display his 'Bloomsbury' side, insofar as that stands for the imaginative, intuitive quality of the artist, as opposed to the logical, precise method of the scientist.*

39

CW 10, 'The Council of Four, Paris' (1919), 'Lloyd George: A Fragment' (1933)

[*The Lloyd George portrait was left out of ECP (1919), on Margot Asquith's advice. Keynes published it as 'Mr Lloyd George: A Fragment' in EB (1933), after his accounts of Clemenceau and Woodrow Wilson. The original, minus Lloyd George, appears in ECP, pp. 18–34.*]
Clemenceau was by far the most eminent member of the Council of Four, and he had taken the measure of his colleagues. He alone both had an idea and had considered it in all its consequences. His age, his character, his wit, and his appearance joined to give him objectivity and a defined outline in an environment of confusion. One could not despise Clemenceau or

dislike him, but as to the nature of civilised man, only take a different view or indulge, at least, a different hope.

The figure and bearing of Clemenceau are universally familiar. At the Council of Four he wore a square-tailed coat of very good, thick black broadcloth, and on his hands, which were never uncovered, grey suede gloves; his boots were of thick black leather, very good, but of a country style, and sometimes fastened in front, curiously, by a buckle instead of laces. His seat in the room in the President's house, where the regular meetings of the Council of Four were held (as distinguished from their private and unattended conferences in a smaller chamber below), was on a square brocaded chair in the middle of the semicircle facing the fireplace, with Signor Orlando on his left, the President next by the fireplace, and the Prime Minister opposite on the other side of the fireplace on his right. He carried no papers and no portfolio, and was unattended by any personal secretary, though several French ministers and officials appropriate to the particular matter in hand would be present round him. His walk, his hand, and his voice were not lacking in vigour, but he bore, nevertheless, especially after the attempt upon him, the aspect of a very old man conserving his strength for important occasions.

[3] He spoke seldom, leaving the initial statement of the French case to his ministers or officials; he closed his eyes often and sat back in his chair with an impassive face of parchment, his grey-gloved hands clasped in front of him. A short sentence, decisive or cynical, was generally sufficient, a question, an unqualified abandonment of his ministers, whose face would not be saved, or a display of obstinacy reinforced by a few words in a piquantly delivered English. But speech and passion were not lacking when they were wanted, and the sudden outburst of words, often followed by a fit of deep coughing from the chest, produced their impression rather by force and surprise than by persuasion.

Not infrequently, Mr Lloyd George, after delivering a speech in English, would, during the period of its interpretation into French, cross the hearthrug to the President to reinforce his case by some *ad hominem* argument in private conversation, or to sound the ground for a compromise – and this would sometimes be the signal for a general upheaval and disorder. The President's advisers would press round him, a moment later the British experts would dribble across to learn the result or see that all was well, and next the French would be there, a little suspicious lest the others were arranging something behind them, until all the room were on their feet and conversation was general in both languages. My last and most vivid impression is of such a scene – the President and the Prime Minister as the centre of a surging mob and a babel of sound, a welter of eager, impromptu compromises and counter-compromises, all sound and fury signifying nothing, on what was an unreal question anyhow, the great issues of the morning's meeting forgotten and neglected; and Clemenceau, silent and aloof on the outskirts – for nothing which touched the security of France was forward – throned, in his grey gloves, on the brocade chair, dry in soul and empty of hope, very old and tired, but surveying the scene with a cynical and almost impish air; and when at last [4] silence was restored and the company had returned to their places, it was to discover that he had disappeared.

He felt about France what Pericles felt of Athens – unique value in her, nothing else mattering; but his theory of politics was Bismarck's. He had one illusion – France; and one disillusion – mankind, including Frenchmen and his colleagues not least. His principles for the Peace can be expressed simply. In the first place, he was a foremost believer in the view of German psychology that the German understands and can understand nothing but intimidation, that he is without generosity or remorse in negotiation, that there is no advantage he will not take of you, and no extent to which he will not demean himself for profit, that he is without honour, pride, or mercy. Therefore you must never negotiate with a German or conciliate him; you must dictate to him. On no other terms will he respect you, or will you prevent him from cheating you. But it is doubtful how far he thought these characteristics peculiar to Germany, or whether his candid view of some other nations was fundamentally different. His philosophy had, therefore, no place for 'sentimentality' in international relations. Nations are real things, of which you love one and feel for the rest indifference – or hatred. The glory of the nation you love is a desirable end – but generally to be obtained at your neighbour's expense. The politics of power are inevitable, and there is nothing very new to learn about this war or the end it was fought for; England had destroyed, as in each preceding century, a trade rival; a mighty chapter had been closed in the secular struggle between the glories of Germany and of France. Prudence required some measure of lip service to the 'ideals' of foolish Americans and hypocritical Englishmen; but it would be stupid to believe that there is much room in the world, as it really is, for such affairs as the League of Nations, or any sense in the principle of self-determination except as an ingenious formula for rearranging the balance of power in one's own [5] interests.

These, however, are generalities. In tracing the practical details of the Peace which he thought necessary for the power and the security of France, we must go back to the historical causes which had operated during his lifetime. Before the Franco-German war the populations of France and Germany were approximately equal; but the coal and iron and shipping of Germany were in their infancy and the wealth of France was greatly superior. Even after the loss of Alsace-Lorraine there was no great discrepancy between the real resources of the two countries. But in the intervening period the relative position had changed completely. By 1914 the population of Germany was nearly 70 per cent in excess of that of France; she had become one of the first manufacturing and trading nations of the world; her technical skill and her means for the production of future wealth were unequalled. France, on the other hand, had a stationary or declining population, and, relatively to others, had fallen seriously behind in wealth and in the power to produce it.

In spite, therefore, of France's victorious issue from the present struggle (with the aid, this time, of England and America), her future position remained precarious in the eyes of one who took the view that European civil war is to be regarded as a normal, or at least a recurrent, state of affairs for the future, and that the sort of conflicts between organised Great Powers which have occupied the past hundred years will also engage the next. According to this vision of the future, European history is to be a perpetual prize-fight, of which France has won this round, but of which this round is certainly not the last. From the belief that essentially the old order does not change, being based on human nature which is always the same, and from a consequent scepticism of all that class of doctrine which the League of Nations stands for, the policy of France and of Clemenceau followed logically. For a Peace of magnanimity or of fair and equal treatment, based on such 'ideology' as the Fourteen Points of the President, could only have the effect of shortening the interval of Germany's recovery and hastening the day when she will once again hurl at France [6] her greater numbers and her superior resources and technical skill. Hence the necessity of 'guarantees'; and each guarantee that was taken, by increasing irritation and thus the probability of a subsequent *revanche* by Germany, made necessary yet further provisions to crush. Thus, as soon as this view of the world is adopted and the other discarded, a demand for a Carthaginian Peace is inevitable, to the full extent of the momentary power to impose it. For Clemenceau made no pretence of considering himself bound by the Fourteen Points, and left chiefly to others such concoctions as were necessary from time to time to save the scruples or the face of the President.

So far as possible, therefore, it was the policy of France to set the clock back and to undo what, since 1870, the progress of Germany had accomplished. By loss of territory and other measures her population was to be curtailed; but chiefly the economic system, upon which she depended for her new strength, the vast fabric built upon iron, coal, and transport, must be destroyed. If France could seize, even in part, what Germany was compelled to drop, the inequality of strength between the two rivals for European hegemony might be remedied for many generations. Hence sprang those cumulative provisions of the Treaty for the destruction of highly organised economic life.

This is the policy of an old man, whose most vivid impressions and most lively imagination are of the past and not of the future. He sees the issue in terms of France and Germany, not of humanity and of European civilisation struggling forwards

to a new order. The war has bitten into his consciousness somewhat differently from ours, and he neither expects nor hopes
that we are at the threshold of a new age.

It happens, however, that it is not only an ideal question that
is at issue. The Carthaginian Peace is not *practically* right or
possible. Although the school of thought from which it springs
is aware of the economic factor, it overlooks, nevertheless, the
deeper economic tendencies which are to govern the future.
The clock cannot be set back. You cannot restore Central Eur-
[7] ope to 1870 without setting up such strains in the European
structure and letting loose such human and spiritual forces as,
pushing beyond frontiers and races, will overwhelm not only
you and your 'guarantees', but your institutions, and the existing order of your Society.

By what legerdemain was this policy substituted for the
Fourteen Points, and how did the President come to accept it?
The answer to these questions is difficult and depends on elements of character and psychology and on the subtle influence
of surroundings, which are hard to detect and harder still to
describe. But, if ever the action of a single individual matters,
the collapse of the President has been one of the decisive moral
events of history; and I must make an attempt to explain it.
What a place the President held in the hearts and hopes of the
world when he sailed to us in the *George Washington*! What a
great man came to Europe in those early days of our victory!

In November 1918 the armies of Foch and the words of Wilson had brought us sudden escape from what was swallowing
up all we cared for. The conditions seemed favourable beyond
any expectation. The victory was so complete that fear need
play no part in the settlement. The enemy had laid down his
arms in reliance on a solemn compact as to the general character of the Peace, the terms of which seemed to assure a settlement
of justice and magnanimity and a fair hope for a restoration of
the broken current of life. To make assurance certain the President was coming himself to set the seal on his work.

When President Wilson left Washington he enjoyed a prestige and a moral influence throughout the world unequalled in
history. His bold and measured words carried to the peoples of

Europe above and beyond the voices of their own politicians. The enemy peoples trusted him to carry out the compact he had made with them; and the allied peoples acknowledged him not as a victor only but almost as a prophet. In addition to this moral influence, the realities of power were in his hands. The American armies were at the height of their numbers, discipline, and equipment. Europe was in complete dependence on [8] the food supplies of the United States; and financially she was even more absolutely at their mercy. Europe not only already owed the United States more than she could pay; but only a large measure of further assistance could save her from starvation and bankruptcy. Never had a philosopher held such weapons wherewith to bind the princes of this world. How the crowds of the European capitals pressed about the carriage of the President! With what curiosity, anxiety, and hope we sought a glimpse of the features and bearing of the man of destiny who, coming from the West, was to bring healing to the wounds of the ancient parent of his civilisation and lay for us the foundations of the future.

The disillusion was so complete that some of those who had trusted most hardly dared speak of it. Could it be true? they asked of those who returned from Paris. Was the Treaty really as bad as it seemed? What had happened to the President? What weakness or what misfortune had led to so extraordinary, so unlooked-for a betrayal?

Yet the causes were very ordinary and human. The President was not a hero or a prophet; he was not even a philosopher; but a generously intentioned man, with many of the weaknesses of other human beings, and lacking that dominating intellectual equipment which would have been necessary to cope with the subtle and dangerous spell-binders whom a tremendous clash of forces and personalities had brought to the top as triumphant masters in the swift game of give and take, face to face in Council – a game of which he had no experience at all.

We had indeed quite a wrong idea of the President. We knew him to be solitary and aloof, and believed him very strong-willed and obstinate. We did not figure him as a man of detail, but the clearness with which he had taken hold of certain main ideas would, we thought, in combination with his tenacity, enable him to sweep through cobwebs. Besides these qualities he would have the objectivity, the cultivation, and the wide knowledge of the student. The great distinction of language which [9] had marked his famous Notes seemed to indicate a man of lofty and powerful imagination. His portraits indicated a fine presence and a commanding delivery. With all this he had attained and held with increasing authority the first position in a country where the arts of the politician are not neglected. All of which, without expecting the impossible, seemed a fine combination of qualities for the matter in hand.

The first impression of Mr Wilson at close quarters was to impair some but not all of these illusions. His head and features were finely cut and exactly like his photographs, and the muscles of his neck and the carriage of his head were distinguished. But, like Odysseus, the President looked wiser when he was seated; and his hands, though capable and fairly strong, were wanting in sensitiveness and finesse. The first glance at the President suggested not only that, whatever else he might be, his temperament was not primarily that of the student or the scholar, but that he had not much even of that culture of the world which marks M. Clemenceau and Mr Balfour as exquisitely cultivated gentlemen of their class and generation. But more serious than this, he was not only insensitive to his surroundings in the external sense, he was not sensitive to his environment at all. What chance could such a man have against Mr Lloyd George's unerring, almost medium-like, sensibility to everyone immediately round him? To see the British Prime Minister watching the company, with six or seven senses not available to ordinary men, judging character, motive, and subconscious impulse, perceiving what each was thinking and even what each was going to say next, and compounding with telepathic instinct the argument or appeal best suited to the vanity, weakness, or self-interest of his immediate auditor, was to realise that the poor President would be playing blind-man's-buff in that party. Never could a man have stepped into the parlour a more perfect and predestined victim to the finished accomplishments of the Prime Minister. The Old World was tough in wickedness, anyhow; the Old World's heart of stone might blunt the sharpest blade of the bravest knight-errant. But this [10] blind and deaf Don Quixote was entering a cavern where the swift and glittering blade was in the hands of the adversary.

But if the President was not the philosopher-king, what was he? After all, he was a man who had spent much of his life at a university. He was by no means a business man or an ordinary party politician, but a man of force, personality, and importance. What, then, was his temperament?

The clue, once found, was illuminating. The President was like a non-conformist minister, perhaps a Presbyterian. His thought and his temperament were essentially theological, not intellectual, with all the strength and the weakness of that manner of thought, feeling, and expression. It is a type of which there are not now in England and Scotland such magnificent specimens as formerly; but this description, nevertheless, will give the ordinary Englishman the distinctest impression of the President.

With this picture of him in mind we can return to the actual course of events. The President's programme for the world, as set forth in his speeches and his Notes, had displayed a spirit and a purpose so admirable that the last desire of his sympathisers was to criticise details – the details, they felt, were quite rightly not filled in at present, but would be in due course. It was commonly believed at the commencement of the Paris Conference that the President had thought out, with the aid of a large body of advisers, a comprehensive scheme not only for the League of Nations but for the embodiment of the Fourteen Points in an actual Treaty of Peace. But in fact the President had thought out nothing; when it came to practice, his ideas were nebulous and incomplete. He had no plan, no scheme, no constructive ideas whatever for clothing with the flesh of life the commandments which he had thundered from the White House. He could have preached a sermon on any of them or have addressed a stately prayer to the Almighty for their

fulfilment, but he could not frame their concrete application to
[11] the actual state of Europe.

He not only had no proposals in detail, but he was in many
respects, perhaps inevitably, ill-informed as to European conditions. And not only was he ill-informed – that was true of
Mr Lloyd George also – but his mind was slow and unadaptable.
The President's slowness amongst the Europeans was noteworthy.
He could not, all in a minute, take in what the rest were saying,
size up the situation with a glance, frame a reply, and meet the
case by a slight change of ground; and he was liable, therefore, to
defeat by the mere swiftness, apprehension, and agility of a Lloyd
George. There can seldom have been a statesman of the first rank
more incompetent than the President in the agilities of the council
chamber. A moment often arrives when substantial victory is
yours if by some slight appearance of a concession you can save
the face of the opposition or conciliate them by a restatement of
your proposal helpful to them and not injurious to anything
essential to yourself. The President was not equipped with this
simple and usual artfulness. His mind was too slow and unre-
sourceful to be ready with *any* alternatives. The President was
capable of digging his toes in and refusing to budge ... But he
had no other mode of defence, and it needed as a rule but little
manoeuvring by his opponents to prevent matters from coming
to such a head until it was too late. By pleasantness and an
appearance of conciliation the President would be manoeuvred
off his ground, would miss the moment for digging his toes in,
and, before he knew where he had been got to, it was too late.
Besides, it is impossible month after month in intimate and ostensibly friendly converse between close associates to be digging the
toes in all the time. Victory would only have been possible to one
who had always a sufficiently lively apprehension of the position
as a whole to reserve his fire and know for certain the rare exact
moments for decisive action. And for that the President was far
too slow-minded and bewildered.

He did not remedy these defects by seeking aid from the collective wisdom of his lieutenants. He had gathered round him
for the economic chapters of the Treaty a very able group of
[12] business men; but they were inexperienced in public affairs and

knew (with one or two exceptions) as little of Europe as he did, and they were only called in irregularly as he might need them for a particular purpose. Thus the aloofness which had been found effective in Washington was maintained, and the abnormal reserve of his nature did not allow near him anyone who aspired to moral equality or the continuous exercise of influence. His fellow-plenipotentiaries were dummies; and even the trusted Colonel House, with vastly more knowledge of men and of Europe than the President, from whose sensitiveness the President's dullness had gained so much, fell into the background as time went on. All this was encouraged by his colleagues on the Council of Four, who, by the break-up of the Council of Ten, completed the isolation which the President's own temperament had initiated. Thus day after day and week after week he allowed himself to be closeted, unsupported, unadvised, and alone, with men much sharper than himself, in situations of supreme difficulty, where he needed for success every description of resource, fertility, and knowledge. He allowed himself to be drugged by their atmosphere, to discuss on the basis of their plans and of their data, and to be led along their paths.

. . .

As the President had thought nothing out, the Council was generally working on the basis of a French or a British draft. He had to take up, therefore, a persistent attitude of obstruction, criticism, and negation, if the draft was to become at all in line with his own ideas and purpose. If he was met on some points with apparent generosity (for there was always a sage margin of quite preposterous suggestions which no one took seriously), it was difficult for him not to yield on others. Compromise was inevitable, and never to compromise on the essential, very difficult. Besides, he was soon made to appear to be taking the German part, and laid himself open to the suggestion (to which he was foolishly and unfortunately sensitive) of being 'pro-German'. [13]

. . . [14]

At the crisis of his fortunes the President was a lonely man. Caught up in the toils of the Old World, he stood in great need of sympathy, of moral support, of the enthusiasm of masses. But buried in the Conference, stifled in the hot and poisoned atmosphere of Paris, no echo reached him from the outer world, and no throb of passion, sympathy, or encouragement from his silent constituents in all countries. He felt that the blaze of popularity which had greeted his arrival in Europe was already dimmed; the Paris press jeered at him openly; his political opponents at home were taking advantage of his absence to create an atmosphere against him; England was cold, critical, and unresponsive. He had so formed his *entourage* that he did not receive through private channels the current of faith and enthusiasm of which the public sources seemed dammed up. He needed, but lacked, the added strength of collective faith. The German terror still overhung us, and even the sympathetic public was very cautious; the enemy must not be encouraged, our friends must be supported, this was not the time for discord or agitations, the President must be trusted to do his best. And in this drought the flower of the President's faith withered and dried up.

Thus it came to pass that the President countermanded the *George Washington*, which, in a moment of well-founded rage, he had ordered to be in readiness to carry him from the treach-
[15] erous halls of Paris back to the seat of his authority, where he could have felt himself again. But as soon, alas, as he had taken the road of compromise the defects, already indicated, of his temperament and of his equipment were fatally apparent. He could take the high line; he could practise obstinacy; he could write Notes from Sinai or Olympus; he could remain unapproachable in the White House or even in the Council of Ten and be safe. But if he once stepped down to the intimate equality of the Four, the game was evidently up.

Now it was that what I have called his theological or Presbyterian temperament became dangerous. Having decided that some concessions were unavoidable, he might have sought by firmness and address and the use of the financial power of the United States to secure as much as he could of the substance, even at some sacrifice of the letter. But the President was not capable of so clear an understanding with himself as this implied. He was too conscientious. Although compromises were now necessary, he remained a man of principle and the Fourteen Points a contract absolutely binding upon him. He would do nothing that was not honourable; he would do nothing that was not just and right; he would do nothing that was contrary to his great profession of faith. Thus, without any abatement of the verbal inspiration of the Fourteen Points, they became a document for gloss and interpretation and for all the intellectual apparatus of self-deception, by which, I dare say, the President's forefathers had persuaded themselves that the course they thought it necessary to take was consistent with every syllable of the Pentateuch.

The President's attitude to his colleagues had now become: I want to meet you so far as I can; I see your difficulties and I should like to be able to agree to what you propose, but I can do nothing that is not just and right, and you must first of all show me that what you want does really fall within the words of the pronouncements which are binding on me. Then began the weaving of that web of sophistry and Jesuitical exegesis that was finally to clothe with insincerity the language and sub- [16] stance of the whole Treaty. The word was issued to the witches of all Paris:

> Fair is foul, and foul is fair,
> Hover through the fog and filthy air.

The subtlest sophisters and most hypocritical draftsmen were set to work, and produced many ingenious exercises which might have deceived for more than an hour a cleverer man than the President.

Thus instead of saying that German Austria is prohibited from uniting with Germany except by leave of France (which would be inconsistent with the principle of self-determination), the Treaty, with delicate draftsmanship, states that 'Germany acknowledges and will respect strictly the independence of Austria, within the frontiers which may be fixed in a Treaty between that State and the Principal Allied and Associated Powers; she agrees that this independence shall be inalienable, except with the consent of the Council of the League of Nations', which sounds, but is not, quite different. And who knows but that the President forgot that another part of the

Treaty provides that for this purpose the Council of the League must be *unanimous*.

Instead of giving Danzig to Poland, the Treaty establishes Danzig as a 'Free' City, but includes this 'Free' City within the Polish Customs frontier, entrusts to Poland the control of the river and railway system, and provides that 'the Polish Government shall undertake the conduct of the foreign relations of the Free City of Danzig as well as the diplomatic protection of citizens of that city when abroad'.

In placing the river system of Germany under foreign control, the Treaty speaks of declaring international those 'river systems which naturally provide more than one State with access to the sea, with or without transhipment from one vessel to another'.

Such instances could be multiplied. The honest and intelligible purpose of French policy, to limit the population of Germany and weaken her economic system, is clothed, for the [17] President's sake, in the august language of freedom and international equality.

But perhaps the most decisive moment, in the disintegration of the President's moral position and the clouding of his mind, was when at last, to the dismay of his advisers, he allowed himself to be persuaded that the expenditure of the Allied Governments on pensions and separation allowances could be fairly regarded as 'damage done to the civilian population of the Allied and Associated Powers by German aggression by land, by sea, and from the air', in a sense in which the other expenses of the war could not be so regarded. It was a long theological struggle in which, after the rejection of many different arguments, the President finally capitulated before a masterpiece of the sophist's art.

At last the work was finished, and the President's conscience was still intact. In spite of everything, I believe that his temperament allowed him to leave Paris a really sincere man; and it is probable that to his death he was genuinely convinced that the Treaty contained practically nothing inconsistent with his former professions.

But the work was too complete, and to this was due the last

tragic episode of the drama. The reply of Brockdorff-Rantzau naturally took the line that Germany had laid down her arms on the basis of certain assurances, and that the Treaty in many particulars was not consistent with these assurances. But this was exactly what the President could not admit; in the sweat of solitary contemplation and with prayers to God he had done *nothing* that was not just and right; for the President to admit that the German reply had force in it was to destroy his self-respect and to disrupt the inner equipoise of his soul, and every instinct of his stubborn nature rose in self-protection. In the language of medical psychology, to suggest to the President that the Treaty was an abandonment of his professions was to touch on the raw a Freudian complex. It was a subject intolerable to discuss, and every subconscious instinct plotted to [18] defeat its further exploration.

Thus it was that Clemenceau brought to success what had seemed to be, a few months before, the extraordinary and impossible proposal that the Germans should not be heard. If only the President had not been so conscientious, if only he had not concealed from himself what he had been doing, even at the last moment he was in a position to have recovered lost ground and to have achieved some very considerable successes. But the President was set. His arms and legs had been spliced by the surgeons to a certain posture, and they must be broken again before they could be altered. To his horror, Mr Lloyd George, desiring at the last moment all the moderation he dared, discovered that he could not in five days persuade the President of error in what it had taken five months to prove to him to be just and right. After all, it was harder to de-bamboozle this old Presbyterian than it had been to bamboozle him, for the former involved his belief in and respect for himself.

Thus in the last act the President stood for stubbornness and a refusal of conciliations. [19]

Mr Lloyd George: A Fragment

I should prefer to end this chapter here. But the reader may ask, what part in the result did the British Prime Minister play? What share had England in the final responsibility? The answer to the second question is not clear-cut. And as to the first, who shall paint the chameleon, who can tether a broomstick? The character of Lloyd George is not yet rendered, and I do not aspire to the task.

[20–21] The selfish, or, if you like, the legitimate interests of England did not, as it happened, conflict with the Fourteen Points as vitally as did those of France.

. . .

The co-operation, which was thus rendered possible, was largely realised in practice. The individual members of the British and American delegations were united by bonds of fraternal feeling and mutual respect, and constantly worked together and stood together for a policy of honest dealing and broad-minded humanity. And the Prime Minister, too, soon established himself as the President's friend and powerful ally against the Latins' alleged rapacity or lack of international idealism. Why then did not the joint forces of these two powerful and enlightened autocrats give us the Good Peace?

The answer is to be sought more in those intimate workings of the heart and character which make the tragedies and comedies of the domestic hearthrug than in the supposed ambitions of empires or philosophies of statesmen. The President, the Tiger, and the Welsh witch were shut up in a room together for six months and the Treaty was what came out. Yes, the Welsh *witch* – for the British Prime Minister contributed the female element to this triangular intrigue. I have called Mr Wilson a non-conformist clergyman. Let the reader figure Mr Lloyd George as a *femme fatale*. An old man of the world, a *femme fatale*, and a non-conformist clergyman – these are the characters of our drama. Even though the lady was very religious at times, the Fourteen Commandments could hardly expect to emerge perfectly intact.

I must try to silhouette the broomstick as it sped through the twilit air of Paris.

Mr Lloyd George's devotion to duty at the Paris Conference was an example to all servants of the public. He took no relaxation, enjoyed no pleasures, had no life and no occupation save that of Prime Minister and England's spokesman. His labours were immense and he spent his vast stores of spirit and of energy without stint on the formidable task he had put his hand to. His advocacy of the League of Nations was sincere; his support of [22] a fair application of the principle of self-determination to Germany's eastern frontiers was disinterested. He had no wish to impose a Carthaginian Peace; the crushing of Germany was no part of his purpose. His hatred of war is real, and the strain of pacifism and radical idealism, which governed him during the Boer War, is a genuine part of his composition. He would have defended a Good Peace before the House of Commons with more heart than he did that which he actually brought back to them.

But in such a test of character and method as Paris provided, the Prime Minister's naturally good instincts, his industry, his inexhaustible nervous vitality were not serviceable. In that furnace other qualities were called for – a policy deeply grounded in permanent principle, tenacity, fierce indignation, honesty, loyal leadership. If Mr Lloyd George had no good qualities, no charms, no fascinations, he would not be dangerous. If he were not a syren, we need not fear the whirlpools.

But it is not appropriate to apply to him the ordinary standards. How can I convey to the reader, who does not know him, any just impression of this extraordinary figure of our time, this syren, this goat-footed bard, this half-human visitor to our age from the hag-ridden magic and enchanted woods of Celtic antiquity? One catches in his company that flavour of final purposelessness, inner irresponsibility, existence outside or away from our Saxon good and evil, mixed with cunning, remorselessness, love of power, that lend fascination, enthralment, and terror to the fair-seeming magicians of North European folklore. Prince Wilson sailing out from the West in his barque *George Washington* sets foot in the enchanted castle of Paris to free from chains and oppression and an ancient curse the maid Europe, of eternal youth and beauty, his mother and his bride in one. There in the castle is the King with yellow parchment face, a million years old, and with him an enchantress with a harp singing the Prince's own words to a magical tune. If only the Prince could cast off the paralysis which creeps on him and,

[23] crying to heaven, could make the Sign of the Cross, with a sound of thunder and crashing glass the castle would dissolve, the magicians vanish, and Europe leap to his arms. But in this fairy-tale the forces of the half-world win and the soul of Man is subordinated to the spirits of the earth.

Lloyd George is rooted in nothing; he is void and without content; he lives and feeds on his immediate surroundings; he is an instrument and a player at the same time which plays on the company and is played on by them too; he is a prism, as I have heard him described, which collects light and distorts it and is most brilliant if the light comes from many quarters at once; a [24] vampire and a medium in one.

. . .

The reader will thus apprehend how Mr Lloyd George came to occupy an ostensibly middle position, and how it became his role to explain the President to Clemenceau and Clemenceau to the President and to seduce everybody all round. He was only too well fitted for the task, but much better fitted for dealing with the President than with Clemenceau. Clemenceau was much too cynical, much too experienced, and much too well educated to be taken in, at his age, by the fascinations of the lady from Wales. But for the President it was a wonderful, almost delightful, experience to be taken in hand by such an expert. Mr Lloyd George had soon established himself as the President's only real friend. The President's very masculine characteristics fell a complete victim to the feminine entice-ments, sharpness, quickness, sympathy of the Prime Minister.

We have Mr Lloyd George, therefore, in his middle position, but exercising more sway over the President than over Clem-enceau. Now let the reader's mind recur to the metaphors. Let [25] him remember the Prime Minister's incurable love of a deal; his readiness to surrender the substance for the shadow; his intense desire, as the months dragged on, to get a conclusion and be back to England again. What wonder that in the eventual settlement the real victor was Clemenceau.

Even so, close observers never regarded it as impossible right up to the conclusion of the affair that the Prime Minister's bet-ter instincts and truer judgment might yet prevail – he knew in his heart that this Peace would disgrace him and that it might ruin Europe. But he had dug a pit for himself deeper than even he could leap out of; he was caught in his own toils, defeated by his own methods. Besides, it is a characteristic of his inner being, of his kinship with the trolls and soulless simulacra of the earth, that at the great crises of his fortunes it is the lower instincts of the hour that conquer.

These were the personalities of Paris – I forbear to mention other nations or lesser men: Clemenceau, aesthetically the noblest; the President, morally the most admirable; Lloyd George, intellectually the subtlest. Out of their disparities and weaknesses the Treaty was born, child of the least worthy attributes of each of its parents, without nobility, without morality, without intellect.   [26]

40

CW 10, 'Dr Melchior: A Defeated Enemy' (1920)

[*First read to Bloomsbury's Memoir Club in February 1920, where it greatly impressed Virginia Woolf with its 'method character drawing', the essay tells the story of Keynes's emotional negotiation, as Treasury representative at the Paris peace conference, with Carl Melchior, a German banker, over German means of payment for Allied relief supplies, after the armistice which ended the First World War. They first met on Marshall Foch's train at Trèves (Trier) on 15 January 1919. For the essay's bibliographical history see David Garnett's Introduction to* Two Memoirs, *published posthumously in 1949.*]

A sad lot they [*the Germans*] were in those early days, with drawn dejected faces and tired staring eyes, like men who had been hammered on the Stock Exchange. But from amongst them stepped forward into the middle place a very small man, exquisitely clean, very well and neatly dressed, with a high stiff collar which seemed cleaner and whiter than an ordinary collar, his round head covered with grizzled hair shaved so close as to be

like in substance to the pile of a close-made carpet, the line where his hair ended bounding his face and forehead in a very sharply defined and rather noble curve, his eyes gleaming straight at us, with extraordinary sorrow in them, yet like an honest animal at bay. This was he with whom in the ensuing months I was to have one of the most curious intimacies in the world, and some very [395]   strange passages of experience – Dr Melchior.
   . . .
We bowed stiffly and sat down very crowded at opposite ends of the railway carriage with a small folding bridge-table between us, nine of us and six of them. We agreed to speak in English which had the advantage of cutting out the French. For the Comte de C [*in fact Charles de Lasteyrie*], being able to speak English perfectly, could never bring himself to admit that he couldn't understand a word of it. So he was reduced to looking down his long nose, placing a long finger against it, and saying at inappropriate moments: 'For my one self I protest', 'For my one self I cannot be in *accord*'. A foolish creature! I wonder what has become of him. [*He became French Minister of Finance in 1922!*] I don't believe that I have ever in the aggregate been so rude to anyone. I first met him at lunch in the Cafe Royal when he and I were manipulating the Spanish exchange, and we got on well enough. In fact, in a sort of way we always did. He was a genteel Catholic, who in peacetime eked out a small estate with slightly shady finance. But he had lately become Foch's spy in the French Treasury and played his game in the agreeable, sly, half-blundering mode of the Jesuit trained. I lunched with him once in his little flat in Paris. It was a small banquet. Three hired waiters of immense distinction in immaculate shirts and white cotton gloves; a new glass of new wine with each course; exquisite food produced abundantly from nowhere, but every dish and the dressings of every dish conventionalised and stereotyped [402]   down to the shapes of the potatoes, the whole thing an exact replica of an official luncheon I once attended at the Elysee . . . The graceless and confined discomfort of the apartment's exactitudes, which I still feel though I could describe none, impressed on me deeply the grasping sterility of France . . .
   Dr Melchior was their spokesman in moving, persuasive,

almost perfect English. Of the others I now visualise two only –
Dr Kaufmann, the representative of the Reichsbank, elderly,
broken, with hungry, nervous eyes, deeply middle class, looking somehow like an old, broken umbrella, who lost the thread
of the conference at the outset and never recovered it, but was
eager to affirm whatever Melchior indicated; the other a representative of the Foreign Office, his face cut to pieces with
duelling, a sort of Corps student type, sly and rather merry,
over-anxious to catch the eyes of one or other of us with a cheerful grin. Melchior spoke always deliberately without pause, in a
way which gave one an extraordinary impression that he was
truthful. His hardest task now, as on later occasions, was to
keep his companions in check, eager to jump in with little undignified misplaced appeals, or foolish *ad hominem* insincerities
which couldn't have deceived the stupidest American. This Jew,
for such, though not by appearance, I afterwards learnt him to
be, and he only, upheld the dignity of defeat.   [403]

[*After a further inconclusive meeting at Trèves, the conference
resumed at Spa in Belgium on 4 March. The Allies had agreed
to food shipments but attached to it conditions, including the
surrender of the German merchant marine.*]

We were plainly wasting our time, getting to grips neither with
one another nor with the situation. Their instructions were
incompatible with ours; ours there was no means of modifying
except by returning to Paris . . .

I looked across the table at Melchior. He seemed to feel as I
did. Staring, heavy-lidded, helpless, looking, as I had seen him
before, like an honest animal in pain. Couldn't we break down
the empty formalities of this Conference, the three-barred gate
of triple interpretations, and talk about the truth and the reality like sane and sensible persons? The Conference adjourned.
We drifted out towards the urinals. I pulled [Admiral] Hope on
one side. 'May I speak to Melchior privately?' He glanced at
me with his odd irises, startled but not shocked. 'Do what you
like', he answered. I hung about in the hall until the French
were out of sight; then stood uneasily a few steps up the central
staircase; persons I did not know were hurrying or drifting about.
I saw someone coming down the stairs whom I recognised as a   [413]

German secretary, 'I want to speak to Dr Melchior for a moment', I said to him, 'about this afternoon's arrangements.' 'If you'll come upstairs', he replied, 'I'll try to find him.' I waited for some minutes on the landing and then saw Melchior approaching. 'May I speak to you privately?' I asked him. He led me along the passage and entered one of the rooms. At the farther end of it were three young Germans; one of them was strumming loudly on the piano, one a fat ungainly creature in his short sleeves bellowed a raucous tenor, the third sprawled on a table. 'Excuse me', said Melchior, 'but I'd be much obliged if for a few minutes I could have this room for a private conference.' They roared at him vulgarly. Did he not know that this was the hour of the day when music was permitted in that place? And had he not forgotten – pointing to his cigarette – that smoking was prohibited there before five o'clock. We went farther down the passage. With a shrug of his shoulders, 'Here', he said, 'you have a picture of Germany in revolution. These are my clerks.'

At last we were by ourselves in a small room. I was quivering with excitement, terrified out of my wits at what I was doing, for the barriers of permitted intercourse had not then begun to crumble, and somewhat emotional. Melchior wondered what I wanted. My memory of the interview is blurred. I tried to convey to him what I was feeling, how we were impressed, not less than he, with the urgency of starting food supplies, how personally I believed that my Government and the American Government were really determined that food should come, but that in the giving of formal undertakings our hands were tied; that if they, the Germans, adhered in their attitude of the morning a fatal delay was inevitable; that they must make up their minds to the handing over of the ships; and that, if only he could secure a little latitude from Weimar, we could between us concoct a formula which would allow the food supplies to move in practice and would evade the obstructions of [414] the French. It was so greatly to our own interest that the German Government should survive, that we did really intend to furnish the food. I allowed that our recent actions had not been such as to lead him to trust in our sincerity; but I begged him to

believe that I, at least, at that moment, was sincere and truthful. He was as much moved as I was, and I think he believed
me. We both stood all through the interview. In a sort of way I
was in love with him. He would do his best, he said, but had
little hope of success . . . He spoke with the passionate pessimism of a Jew. German honour and organisation and morality
were crumbling; he saw no light anywhere; he expected Germany to collapse and civilisation to grow dim; we must do
what we could; but dark forces were passing over us. We
pressed hands, and I hurried quickly into the street . . .[1]   [415]

41
CW 10, 'Alfred Marshall' (1924)

[*In* Ten Great Economists *(1952), pp. 271–2, J. A. Schumpeter
called it 'the most brilliant life of a man of science I have ever
read'.*]

Like his two colleagues, Henry Sidgwick and James Ward, in
the Chairs of the Moral Sciences at Cambridge during the last
decades of the nineteenth century, Alfred Marshall belonged to
the tribe of sages and pastors; yet, like them also, endowed with
a double nature, he was a scientist too. As a preacher and pastor
of men he was not particularly superior to other similar natures.
As a scientist he was, within his own field, the greatest in the
world for a hundred years. Nevertheless, it was to the first side
of his nature that he himself preferred to give the pre-eminence.
This self should be master, he thought; the second self, servant.
The second self sought knowledge for its own sake; the first self
subordinated abstract aims to the need for practical advancement. The piercing eyes and ranging wings of an eagle were
often called back to earth to do the bidding of a moraliser.

This double nature was the clue to Marshall's mingled
strength and weakness; to his own conflicting purposes and
waste of strength; to the two views which could always be
taken about him; to the sympathies and antipathies he inspired.

In another respect the diversity of his nature was pure advantage. The study of economics does not seem to require any specialised gifts of an unusually high order. Is it not, intellectually regarded, a very easy subject compared with the higher branches of philosophy and pure science? Yet good, or even competent, economists are the rarest of birds. An easy subject, at which very few excel! The paradox finds its explanation, perhaps, in that the master-economist must possess a rare *combination* of gifts. He must reach a high standard in several different directions and must combine talents not often found together. He must be mathematician, historian, statesman, philosopher – in some degree. He must understand symbols and speak in words. He must contemplate the particular in terms of the general, and touch abstract and concrete in the same flight of thought. He must study the present in the light of the past [173] for the purposes of the future. No part of man's nature or his institutions must lie entirely outside his regard. He must be purposeful and disinterested in a simultaneous mood; as aloof and incorruptible as an artist, yet sometimes as near the earth as a politician. Much, but not all, of this ideal many-sidedness Marshall possessed. But chiefly his mixed training and divided nature furnished him with the most essential and fundamental of the economist's necessary gifts – he was conspicuously historian and mathematician, a dealer in the particular and the [174] general, the temporal and the eternal, at the same time.

. . .

Marshall, as already pointed out above, arrived very early at the point of view that the bare bones of economic theory are not worth much in themselves and do not carry one far in the direction of useful, practical conclusions. The whole point lies in applying them to the interpretation of current economic life. This requires a profound knowledge of the actual facts of industry and trade. But these, and the relation of individual men to them, are constantly and rapidly changing. Some extracts from his Inaugural Lecture at Cambridge will indicate his position:

> The change that has been made in the point of view of Economics
> by the present generation is due to the discovery that man himself

is in a great measure a creature of circumstances and changes with them. The chief fault in English economists at the beginning of the century was not that they ignored history and statistics, but that they regarded man as so to speak a constant quantity, and gave themselves little trouble to study his variations. They therefore attributed to the forces of supply and demand a much more mechanical and regular action than they actually have. Their most vital fault was that they did not see how liable to change are the habits and institutions of industry. But the Socialists were men who had felt intensely, and who knew something about the hidden springs of human action of which the economists took no account. Buried among their wild rhapsodies there were shrewd observations and pregnant suggestions from which philosophers and economists had much to learn. Among the bad results of the narrowness of the work of English economists early in the century, perhaps the most unfortunate was the opportunity which it gave to sciolists to quote and misapply economic dogmas. Ricardo and his chief followers did not make clear to others, it was not even quite clear to themselves, that what they were building up was not universal truth, but machinery of universal application in the discovery of a certain class of truths. While attributing high and transcendent universality to the central scheme of economic reasoning, I do not assign any universality to economic dogmas. It is not a body of concrete truth, but an engine for the discovery of concrete truth.

Holding these views and living at a time of reaction against economists when the faults of his predecessors, to which he [196] draws attention above, were doing their maximum amount of harm, he was naturally reluctant to publish the isolated apparatus of economics, divorced from its appropriate applications. Diagrams and pure theory by themselves might do more harm than good, by increasing the confusion between the objects and methods of the mathematical sciences and those of the social sciences, and would give what he regarded as just the wrong emphasis. In publishing his intellectual exercises without facing the grind of discovering their points of contact with the real world he would be following and giving bad example. On the other hand, the relevant facts were extremely hard to come by – much harder than now. The progress of events in the 'seventies and 'eighties, particularly in America, was extraordinarily rapid, and organised sources of information, of which there are now so many, scarcely existed. In the twenty years from 1875 to 1895 he was, in fact, greatly increasing his command over real facts and his power of economic judgment, and the work which he could have published between 1875 and 1885 would have been much inferior to what he was capable of between 1885 and 1895.

. . .

[197] Given his views as to the impossibility of any sort of finality in economics and as to the rapidity with which events change, given the limitations of his own literary aptitudes and of his leisure for book-making, was it not a fatal decision to abandon his first intention of separate independent monographs in favour of a great treatise? I think that it was, and that certain weaknesses contributed to it.

Marshall was conscious of the great superiority of his powers over those of his surviving contemporaries. In his Inaugural Lecture of 1885 he said: 'Twelve years ago England possessed perhaps the ablest set of economists that there have ever been in a country at one time. But one after another there have been taken from us Mill, Cairnes, Bagehot, Cliffe Leslie, Jevons, Newmarch, and Fawcett.' There was no one left who could claim at that date to approach Marshall in stature. To his own pupils, who were to carry on the economics of the future, Marshall was ready to devote time and strength. But he was too little willing to cast his half-baked bread on the waters, to trust in the efficacy of the co-operation of many minds, and to let the big world draw from him what sustenance it could. Was he not attempting, contrary to his own principles, to achieve an impossible finality? An economic treatise may have great educational value. Perhaps we require one treatise, as a *pièce de résistance*, for each generation. But in view of the transitory character of economic facts, and the bareness of economic principles in isolation, does not the progress and the daily usefulness of economic science require that pioneers and innovators should eschew the treatise and prefer the pamphlet or the monograph? I depreciated Jevons's *Political Economy* above on the ground that it was no more than a brilliant brochure. Yet it was Jevons's willingness to spill his ideas, to flick them at the world, that won him his great personal position and his unrivalled power of stimulating other minds. Every one of Jevons's contributions to economics was in the nature of a pamphlet. Malthus spoilt the *Essay on Population* when, after the first edition, he converted it into a treatise. Ricardo's greatest works were written as ephemeral pamphlets. Did not Mill, in achieving by his peculiar gifts a successful treatise, do more [198] for pedagogics than for science, and end by sitting like an Old Man of the Sea on the voyaging Sinbads of the next generation? Economists must leave to Adam Smith alone the glory of the quarto, must pluck the day, fling pamphlets into the wind, write always *sub specie temporis*, and achieve immortality by accident, if at all.

Moreover, did not Marshall, by keeping his wisdom at home until he could produce it fully clothed, mistake, perhaps, the true nature of his own special gift? 'Economics', he said, in the passage quoted above, 'is not a body of concrete truth, but an engine for the discovery of concrete truth.' This engine, as we employ it to-day, is largely Marshall's creation. He put it in the hands of his pupils long before he offered it to the world. The building of this engine was the essential achievement of Marshall's peculiar genius. Yet he hankered greatly after the 'concrete truth' which he had disclaimed and for the discovery of which he was not specially qualified. I have very early memories, almost before I knew what economics meant, of the sad complaints of my father, who had been able to observe as pupil and as colleague the progress of Marshall's thought almost from the beginning, of Marshall's obstinate refusal to understand where his special strength and weakness really lay, and of how his unrealisable ambitions stood in the way of his giving to the world the true treasures of his mind and genius. Economics all over the world might have progressed much faster, and Marshall's authority and influence would have been far greater, if his temperament had been a little different.

Two other characteristics must be mentioned. First, Marshall was too much afraid of being wrong, too thin-skinned towards criticism, too easily upset by controversy even on matters of minor importance. An extreme sensitiveness deprived him of magnanimity towards the critic or the adversary. This fear of being open to correction by speaking too soon aggravated other tendencies. Yet, after all, there is no harm in being sometimes wrong – especially if one is promptly found out. Nevertheless, this quality was but the defect of the high standard he never relaxed – which touched his pupils with awe – of scientific accuracy and truth.

[199]

Second, Marshall was too anxious to do good. He had an inclination to undervalue those intellectual parts of the subject which were not *directly* connected with human well-being or the condition of the working classes or the like, although *indirectly* they might be of the utmost importance, and to feel that when he was pursuing them he was not occupying himself with the Highest. It came out of the conflict, already remarked, between an intellect, which was hard, dry, critical, as unsentimental as you could find, with emotions and, generally unspoken, aspirations of quite a different type. When his intellect chased diagrams and foreign trade and money there was an evangelical moraliser of an imp somewhat inside him that was so ill-advised as to disapprove. Near the end of his life, when the intellect grew dimmer and the preaching imp could rise nearer to the surface to protest against its lifelong servitude, he once said: 'If I had to live my life over again I should have devoted it to psychology. Economics has too little to do with ideals. If I said much about them I should not be read by business men.' But these notions had always been with him. He used to tell the following story of his early life: 'About the time that I first resolved to make as thorough a study as I could of political economy (the word economics was not then invented) I saw in a shop-window a small oil painting [of a man's face with a strikingly gaunt and wistful expression, as of one "down and out"] and bought it for a few shillings. I set it up above the chimney-piece in my room in college and thenceforward called it my patron saint, and devoted myself to trying how to fit men like that for heaven. Meanwhile, I got a good deal interested in the semi-mathematical side of pure economics, and was afraid of becoming a mere thinker. But a glance at my patron saint seemed to call me back to the right path. That was particularly [200] useful after I had been diverted from the study of ultimate aims to the questions about Bimetallism, etc., which at one time were dominant. I despised them, but the "instinct of the chase" tempted me towards them.' This was the defect of that other greater quality of his which always touched his pupils – his immense disinterestedness and public spirit.   [201]

. . .

By 1890 Marshall's fame stood high, and the *Principles of Economics*, vol. I, was delivered into an expectant world. Its success was immediate and complete. The book was the subject of leading articles and full-dress reviews throughout the Press. The journalists could not distinguish the precise contributions and innovations which it contributed to science; but they discerned with remarkable quickness that it ushered in a new age of economic thought. 'It is a great thing', said the *Pall Mall Gazette*, 'to have a Professor at one of our old Universities devoting the work of his life to recasting the science of Political Economy as the Science of Social Perfectibility.'   [204]

42

CW 10, 'Thomas Robert Malthus' (1933)

[*For the history of this essay, see the editor's introduction in CW 10, p. 71. First prepared as a lecture in 1922, it was amended and extended over the years till published by Keynes in his* Essays in Biography *in 1933. Over the years his view of Malthus – 'the first Cambridge economist', as he called him – changed in line with his own theories. By 1933 he had come to appreciate him not as the theorist of population but as the grandfather of his own theory of 'effective demand' and wrote (p. 100) 'If only Malthus, instead of Ricardo, had been the*

*parent stem from which nineteenth-century economics pro-
ceeded, what a much wiser and richer place the world would be
to-day!' Keynes may well have got the phrase 'effective demand'
from Malthus; to what extent he also got the idea behind it
is disputed. See Steven Kates, 'The Malthusian Origins of the
General Theory',* History of Economics Review, *21 (1994).*]

Bacchus – when an Englishman is called Bacchus – derives
from Bakehouse. Similarly the original form of the rare and
curious name of Malthus was Malthouse. The pronunciation
of English proper names has been more constant one century
[71] with another than their spelling, which fluctuates between
phonetic and etymological influences, and can generally be
inferred with some confidence from an examination of the
written variations. On this test (Malthus, Mawtus, Malthous,
Malthouse, Mauthus, Maltus, Maultous) there can be little
doubt that *Maultus*, with the first vowel as in brewer's malt
and the *h* doubtfully sounded, is what we ought to say.

We need not trace the heredity of Robert Malthus further
back than to the Reverend Robert Malthus who became Vicar
of Northolt under Cromwell and was evicted at the Restoration. Calamy calls him 'an ancient divine, a man of strong
reason, and mighty in the Scriptures, of great eloquence and
fervour, though defective in elocution'. But his parishioners
thought him 'a very unprofitable and fruitless minister', perhaps because he was strict in the exaction of tithes, and in a
petition for his removal complained of him as having 'uttered
invective expressions against our army while they were in Scotland', and also that 'Mr Malthus is one who hath not only a
low voice but a very great impediment in his utterance'; from
which it seems probable that he shared with his great-great-
grandson not only the appellation of the Reverend Robert
Malthus, but also the defect of a cleft palate. His son Daniel
was appointed apothecary to King William by favour of the
celebrated Dr Sydenham and afterwards to Queen Anne, and
became a man of sufficient substance for his widow to own a
[72] coach and horses. Daniel's son Sydenham further improved the
family fortunes, being a clerk in Chancery, a director of the
South Sea Company, rich enough to give his daughter a dowry

of £5000, and the proprietor of several landed properties in the Home Counties and Cambridgeshire.

The golden mediocrity of a successful English middle-class family being now attained, Sydenham's son Daniel, our hero's father, found himself in a position of what is known in England as 'independence' and decided to take advantage of it. He was educated at Queen's College, Oxford, but took no degree, 'travelled much in Europe and in every part of this island', settled down in a pleasant neighbourhood, led the life of a small English country gentleman, cultivated intellectual tastes and friendships, wrote a few anonymous pieces, and allowed diffidence to overmaster ambition. It is recorded that he 'possessed the most pleasing manner with the most benevolent heart, which was experienced by all the poor wherever he lived'. When he died the *Gentleman's Magazine* (February 1800, p. 177) was able to record that he was 'an eccentric character in the strictest sense of the term'.

In 1759 Daniel Malthus had purchased a 'small elegant mansion' near Dorking 'known by the name of Chert-gate Farm, and taking advantage of its beauties, hill and dale, wood and water, displaying them in their naked simplicity, converted it into a gentleman's seat, giving it the name of The Rookery'. [73] Here on 13 February 1766 was born Thomas Robert Malthus, [*Daniel Malthus's*] second son, the author of the *Essay on the Principle of Population*. When the babe was three weeks old, on 9 March 1766, two fairy godmothers, Jean-Jacques Rousseau and David Hume, called together at The Rookery, and may be presumed to have assigned to the infant with a kiss diverse intellectual gifts. [74]

. . .

In 1798, when Malthus was thirty-two years old, there was published anonymously *An Essay on the Principle of Population, as it affects the future improvement of Society: with remarks on the speculations of Mr Godwin, M. Condorcet, and other writers.*

It was in conversation with Daniel Malthus that there occurred to Robert Malthus the generalisation which has made him famous. The story is well known on the authority of Bishop

Otter, who had it from Malthus himself. In 1793 Godwin's
Political Justice had appeared. In frequent discussion the father
defended, and the son attacked, the doctrine of a future age of
perfect equality and happiness.

> And when the question had been often the subject of animated
> discussion between them, and the son had rested his cause, prin-
> cipally upon the obstacles which the tendency of population, to
> increase faster than the means of subsistence, would always
> throw in the way; he was desired to put down in writing, for
> maturer consideration, the substance of his argument, the conse-
> quence of which was the Essay on Population. Whether the father
> was converted or not we do not know, but certain it is that he
> was strongly impressed with the importance of the views and the
> ingenuity of the argument contained in the MS., and recom-
> mended his son to submit his labours to the public.

The first edition, an octavo volume of about 50,000 words, is
an almost completely different, and for posterity a superior
book, to the second edition of five years later in quarto, which
by the fifth edition had swollen to some 250,000 words in three
volumes. The first edition, written, as Malthus explains in the
second edition, 'on the impulse of the occasion, and from the
few materials which were then within my reach in a country
situation,' is mainly an *a priori* work, concerned on the one
hand with the refutation of the perfectibilists and on the other
with the justification of the methods of the Creator, in spite of
appearance to the contrary.

The first essay is not only *a priori* and philosophical in
method, but it is bold and rhetorical in style with much *bra-
vura* of language and sentiment; whereas in the latter editions
political philosophy gives way to political economy, general
[84] principles are overlaid by the inductive verifications of a pioneer in sociological history, and the brilliance and high spirits
of a young man writing in the last years of the Directory
disappear. 'Verbiage and senseless repetition' is Coleridge's
marginal comment in his copy of the second edition: 'Are we
now to have a quarto to teach us that great misery and great

vice arise from poverty, and that there must be poverty in its worst shape wherever there are more mouths than loaves and more Heads than Brains?'   [85]

...

Malthus's *Essay* is a work of youthful genius. The author was fully conscious of the significance of the ideas he was expressing. He believed that he had found the clue to human misery. The importance of the *Essay* consisted not in the novelty of his facts but in the smashing emphasis he placed on a simple generalisation arising out of them. Indeed his leading idea had been largely anticipated in a clumsier way by other eighteenth-century writers without attracting attention.

The book can claim a place amongst those which have had great influence on the progress of thought. It is profoundly in the English tradition of humane science – in that tradition of Scotch and English thought, in which there has been, I think, an extraordinary continuity of *feeling*, if I may so express it, from the eighteenth century to the present time – the tradition which is suggested by the names of Locke, Hume, Adam Smith, Paley, Bentham, Darwin, and Mill, a tradition marked by a love of truth and a most noble lucidity, by a prosaic sanity free from sentiment or metaphysic, and by an immense disinterestedness and public spirit. There is a continuity in these writings, not only of feeling, but of actual matter. It is in this company that Malthus belongs.

Malthus's transition from the *a priori* methods of Cambridge – whether Paley, the Mathematical Tripos, or the Unitarians – to the inductive argument of the later editions was assisted by a tour which he undertook in search of materials in 1799 'through Sweden, Norway, Finland, and a part of Russia, these being the only countries at the time open to English travellers,' and another in France and Switzerland during the short peace of [86] 1802. Meanwhile Malthus had continued his economic studies with a pamphlet, published anonymously (like the first edition of the *Essay*) in 1800, entitled *An Investigation of the Cause of the Present High Price of Provisions*. This pamphlet has importance both in itself and as showing that Malthus was already disposed to a certain line of approach in handling practical economic problems which he was to develop later on in his correspondence with Ricardo, – a method which to me is most sympathetic, and, as I think, more likely to lead to right conclusions than the alternative approach of Ricardo. But it was Ricardo's more fascinating intellectual construction which was victorious, and Ricardo who, by turning his back so completely on Malthus's ideas, constrained the subject for a full hundred [87] years in an artificial groove.

According to Malthus's good common-sense notion prices and profits are primarily determined by something which he described, though none too clearly, as 'effective demand'. Ricardo favoured a much more rigid approach, went behind 'effective demand' to the underlying conditions of money on the one hand and real costs and the real division of the product on the other hand, conceived these fundamental factors as automatically working themselves out in a unique and unequivocal way, and looked on Malthus's method as very superficial. But Ricardo, in the course of simplifying the many successive stages of his highly abstract argument, departed, necessarily and more than he himself was aware, away from the actual facts; whereas Malthus, by taking up the tale much nearer its conclusion, had a firmer hold on what may be expected to happen in the real world. Ricardo is the father of such things as the quantity theory of money and the purchasing power parity of the exchanges. When one has painfully escaped from the intellectual domination of these pseudo-arithmetical doctrines, one is able, perhaps for the first time for a hundred years, to comprehend the real significance of the vaguer intuitions of Malthus.

Malthus's conception of 'effective demand' is brilliantly illustrated in this early pamphlet by 'an idea which struck him so strongly as he rode on horseback from Hastings to Town' that he stopped two days in his 'garret in town', 'sitting up till two o'clock to finish it that it might come out before the meeting of parliament'. He was pondering why the price of provisions should have risen by so much more than could be accounted for by any deficiency in the harvest. He did not, like Ricardo a few years later, invoke the quantity of money. He [88] found the cause in the increase in working-class *incomes* as a

consequence of parish allowances being raised in proportion to
the cost of living.   [89]
. . .

This *Investigation* is one of the best things Malthus ever wrote,
though there are great passages in the *Essay*; and . . . I cannot
forbear to [quote] that famous passage from the second edition
[of the *Essay*] (p. 571) . . . :

> A man who is born into a world already possessed, if he cannot
> get subsistence from his parents on whom he has a just demand,
> and if the society do not want his labour, has no claim of *right* to
> the smallest portion of food, and, in fact, has no business to be
> where he is. At nature's mighty feast there is no vacant corner for
> him. She tells him to be gone, and will quickly execute her own
> orders, if he do not work upon the compassion of some of her
> guests. If these guests get up and make room for him, other
> intruders immediately appear demanding the same favour. The
> report of a provision for all that come, fills the hall with numer-
> ous claimants. The order and harmony of the feast is disturbed,
> the plenty that before reigned is changed into scarcity; and the
> happiness of the guests is destroyed by the spectacle of misery
> and dependence in every part of the hall, and by the clamorous
> importunity of those, who are justly enraged at not finding the
> provision which they had been taught to expect. The guests learn
> too late their error, in counteracting those strict orders to all
> intruders, issued by the great mistress of the feast, who, wishing
> that all her guests should have plenty, and knowing that she could
> not provide for unlimited numbers, humanely refused to admit
> fresh comers when her table was already full.

Malthus's next pamphlet, *A Letter to Samuel Whitbread,
Esq., M.P., on his Proposed Bill for the Amendment of the
Poor Laws*, published in 1807, is not so happy. It is an extreme
application of the principle of the *Essay on Population*.
Mr Whitbread had proposed 'to empower parishes to build
cottages', in short, a housing scheme, partly to remedy the
appalling shortage, partly to create employment. But Malthus
eagerly points out that 'the difficulty of procuring habitations'

must on no account be alleviated, since this is the cause why 'the poor laws do not encourage early marriages so much as might naturally be expected'. The poor laws raise the rates, the [90] high level of rates prevents the building of cottages, and the deficiency of cottages mitigates the otherwise disastrous effect of the poor laws in increasing population.

> Such is the tendency to form early connections, that with the encouragement of a sufficient number of tenements, I have very little doubt that the population might be so pushed and such a quantity of labour in time thrown into the market, as to render the condition of the independent labourer absolutely hopeless.

[91] Economics is a very dangerous science.

. . .

The most important influence of his later years was his intimacy with Ricardo, of whom he said:

> I never loved anybody out of my own family so much. Our interchange of opinions was so unreserved, and the object after which we were both enquiring was so entirely the truth, and nothing else, that I cannot but think we sooner or later must have agreed.

As Maria Edgeworth, who knew both well, wrote of them:

> They hunted together in search of Truth, and huzzaed when they found her, without caring who found her first; and indeed I have seen them both put their able hand to the windlass to drag her up from the bottom of that well in which she so strangely loves to dwell.

The friendship between Malthus and David Ricardo began in [94] June 1811, when Malthus 'took the liberty of introducing Himself' in the hope 'that as we are *mainly* on the same side of the question, we might supersede the necessity of a long controversy in print respecting the points in which we differ, by an amicable discussion in private'. It led to a long intimacy which was never broken. Ricardo paid repeated week-end visits to

Haileybury; Malthus seldom came to London without staying, or at least breakfasting, with Ricardo, and in later years was accustomed to stay with his family at Gatcomb Park. It is evident that they had the deepest affection and respect for one another. The contrasts between the intellectual gifts of the two were obvious and delightful. In economic discussions Ricardo was the abstract and *a priori* theorist, Malthus the inductive and intuitive investigator who hated to stray too far from what he could test by reference to the facts and his own intuitions. But when it came to practical finance, the roles of the Jewish stockbroker and the aristocratic clergyman were, as they should be, reversed, as is illustrated by a trifling incident which it is amusing to record. During the Napoleonic War, Ricardo was, as is well known, a principal member of a Syndicate which took part in operations in Government stocks corresponding to what is now effected by 'underwriting'. His Syndicate would take up by tender from the Treasury a mixed bag of stocks of varying terms known as the *Omnium*, which they would gradually dispose of to the public as favourable opportunities offer. On these occasions Ricardo was in the habit of doing Malthus a friendly turn by putting him down for a small participation without requiring him to put up any money, which meant the certainty of a modest profit if Malthus did not hold on too long, since initially the Syndicate terms would always be comfortably below the current market price. Thus, as it happened, Malthus found himself a small 'bull' of Government stock a few days before the battle of Waterloo. This was, unfortunately, too much for his nerves, and he instructed Ricardo, unless 'it is either wrong or inconvenient to you', 'to take an early opportunity of realising a small profit on the share you [95] have been so good as to promise me'. Ricardo carried out the instructions, though he himself by no means shared that view, since it appears that he carried over the week of Waterloo the maximum bull position of which his resources were capable. In a letter to Malthus of 27 June 1815, he modestly reports: 'This is as great an advantage as ever I expect or wish to make by a rise. I have been a considerable gainer by the loan.' 'Now for a little of our old subject,' he continues, and plunges back into the theory of the possible causes of a rise in the price of commodities. Poor Malthus could not help being a little annoyed.

> I confess [he writes on 16 July 1815] I thought that the chances of the first battle were in favour of Buonaparte, who had the choice of attack; and it appears indeed from the Duke of Wellington's despatches that he was at one time very near succeeding. From what has happened since, however, it seems certain that the French were not so well prepared as they ought to have been. If there had been the energy and enthusiasm which might have been expected in the defence of their independence, one battle, however sanguinary and complete, could not have decided the fate of France.

This friendship will live in history on account of its having given rise to the most important literary correspondence in the whole development of Political Economy. In 1887 Dr Bonar discovered Ricardo's side of the correspondence in the possession of Colonel Malthus, and published his well-known edition. But the search for Malthus's letters, which should have been in the possession of the Ricardo family, was made in vain. In 1907 Professor Foxwell published in the *Economic Journal* a single letter from the series, which David Ricardo happened to have given to Mrs Smith of Easton Grey for her collection of autographs, and declared – with great prescience as it has turned out – that 'the loss of Malthus's share in this correspondence may be ranked by economists next to that other literary disaster, the destruction of David Hume's comments [96] on *The Wealth of Nations*'. But Mr Piero Sraffa from whom nothing is hid, has discovered the missing letters in his researches for the forthcoming complete and definitive edition of the Works of David Ricardo, which he is preparing for the Royal Economic Society (to be published in the course of the present year).[2] It will be found that the publication of both sides of the correspondence enhances its interest very greatly. Here, indeed, are to be found the seeds of economic theory, and also the divergent lines – so divergent at the outset that the destination can scarcely be recognised as the same until it is reached – along which the subject can be developed. Ricardo is investigating the theory of the *distribution* of the product in conditions of equilibrium and Malthus is concerned with what determines the *volume* of output day by day in the real world. Malthus is dealing with the monetary economy in which we happen to live; Ricardo with the abstraction of a neutral money economy. They largely recognised the real source of their differences. In a letter of 24 January 1817, Ricardo wrote:

> It appears to me that one great cause of our difference in opinion on the subjects which we have so often discussed is that you have always in your mind the immediate and temporary effects of particular changes, whereas I put these immediate and temporary effects quite aside, and fix my whole attention on the permanent state of things which will result from them. Perhaps you estimate these temporary effects too highly, whilst I am too much disposed to undervalue them. To manage the subject quite right, they should be carefully distinguished and mentioned, and the due effects ascribed to each.

To which Malthus replied with considerable effect on 26 January 1817:

> I agree with you that one cause of our difference in opinion is that which you mention. I certainly am disposed to refer frequently to things as they are, as the only way of making one's writings practically useful to society, and I think also the only way of being secure from falling into the errors of the taylors of Laputa, and by a slight mistake at the outset arrive at conclusions the most distant from the truth. Besides I really think that the progress of society consists of irregular movements, and that to omit the consideration of causes which for eight or ten years will give a great *stimulus* to production and population, or a great *check* to them, is to omit the causes of the wealth and poverty of nations – the grand object of all enquiries in Political Economy. A writer may, to be sure, make any hypothesis he pleases; but if he supposes what is not at all true practically, he precludes himself from drawing any practical inferences from his hypotheses. In your essay on

[97]

profits you suppose the real wages of labour constant; but as they vary with every alteration in the prices of commodities (while they remain nominally the same) and are in reality as variable as profits, there is no chance of your inferences being just as applied to the actual state of things. We see in all the countries around us, and in our own particularly, periods of greater and less prosperity and sometimes of adversity, but never the uniform progress which you seem alone to contemplate.

But to come to a still more specific and fundamental cause of our difference, I think it is this. You seem to think that the wants and tastes of mankind are always ready for the supply; while I am most decidedly of opinion that few things are more difficult than to inspire new tastes and wants, particularly out of old materials; that one of the great elements of demand is the value that people set upon commodities, and that the more completely the supply is suited to the demand the higher will this value be, and the more days' labour will it exchange for, or give the power of commanding . . . I am quite of opinion that *practically* the actual check to produce and population arises more from want of stimulus than want of power to produce.

One cannot rise from a perusal of this correspondence without a feeling that the almost total obliteration of Malthus's line of approach and the complete domination of Ricardo's for a period of a hundred years has been a disaster to the progress of economics. Time after time in these letters Malthus is talking plain sense, the force of which Ricardo with his head in the clouds wholly fails to comprehend. Time after time a crushing refutation by Malthus is met by a mind so completely closed [98] that Ricardo does not even see what Malthus is saying . . .

As early as 9 October 1814, in the letter printed by Prof. Foxwell in the *Economic Journal* (1907, p. 274), Malthus was writing:

I cannot by any means agree with you in your observation that 'the desire of accumulation will occasion demand just as *effectually* as a desire to consume' and that 'consumption and accumulation equally promote demand'. I confess indeed that I know no other cause for the fall of profits which I believe you will allow generally takes place from accumulation than that the price of produce falls compared with the expense of production, or in other words that the *effective* demand is diminished.

But the following extracts from two letters written by Malthus in July 1821 show that by that date the matter was still clearer in his mind and foggier still in Ricardo's:

[7 July 1821]

We see in almost every part of the world vast powers of production which are not put into action, and I explain this phenomenon by saying that from the want of a proper distribution of the actual produce adequate motives are not furnished to continued production. By inquiring into the immediate causes of the progress of wealth, I clearly mean to inquire mainly into motives. I don't at all wish to deny that some persons or others are entitled to consume all that is produced; but the grand question is whether it is distributed in such a manner between the different parties concerned as to occasion the most effective demand for future produce: and I distinctly maintain that an attempt to accumulate very rapidly which necessarily implies a considerable diminution of unproductive consumption, by greatly impairing the usual motives to production must prematurely check the progress of wealth. This surely is the great *practical* question, and not whether we ought to call the sort of stagnation which would be thus occasioned a glut. That I hold to be a matter of very subordinate importance. But if it be true that an attempt to accumulate very rapidly will occasion such a division between labour and profits as almost to destroy both the motive and the power of future accumulation and consequently the power of maintaining and employing an increasing population, must it not be acknowledged that such an attempt to accumulate, or that saving too much, may be really prejudicial to a country.   [99]

[16 July 1821]

With regard to our present subject of discussion, it seems as if we should never thoroughly understand each other, and I almost despair of being ever able to explain myself, if you could read the two first paragraphs of the first section of my last chapter, and yet 'understand me to say that vast powers of production are put into action, and the result is unfavourable to the interests of mankind'. I expressly say that it is my object to show what are the causes which call forth the powers of production; and if I recommend a certain proportion of unproductive consumption, it is obviously and expressly with the sole view of furnishing the necessary motive to the greatest continued production. And I think still that this certain proportion of unproductive consumption varying according to the fertility of the soil, etc., is absolutely and indispensably necessary to call forth the resources of a country ... Now among the motives to produce, one of the most essential certainly is that an adequate share of what is produced should belong to those who set all industry in motion. But you yourself allow that a great temporary saving, commencing when profits were sufficient to encourage it, might occasion such a division of the produce as would leave no motive to a further increase of production. And if a state of things in which for a time there is no motive to a further increase of production be not properly denominated a stagnation, I do not know what can be so called; particularly as this stagnation must inevitably throw the rising generation out of employment. We know from repeated experience that the money price of labour never falls till many workmen have been for some time out of work. And the question is, whether this stagnation of capital, and subsequent stagnation in the demand for labour arising from increased production without an adequate proportion of unproductive consumption on the part of the landlords and capitalists, could take place without prejudice to the country, without occasioning a less degree both of happiness and wealth than would have occurred if the unproductive consumption of the landlords and capitalists had been so proportioned to the natural surplus of the society as to have continued uninterrupted the motives to production, and prevented first an unnatural demand for labour, and then a necessary and sudden diminution of such demand. But if this be so, how can it be said with truth that parsimony, though it may be prejudicial to the producers cannot be prejudicial to the state; or that an increase of unproductive consumption among landlords and capitalists may not sometimes be the proper remedy for a state of things in which the motives to production fail.

If only Malthus, instead of Ricardo, had been the parent stem from which nineteenth-century economics proceeded, what a [100] much wiser and richer place the world would be to-day! We have laboriously to re-discover and force through the obscuring envelopes of our misguided education what should never have ceased to be obvious. I have long claimed Robert Malthus as the first of the Cambridge economists; and can do so, after the publication of these letters, with increased sympathy and admiration.   [101]

43

CW 10, 'Newton the Man' (1946)

[*Keynes loved fine books. In July 1936 he bought forty lots of a sale of Isaac Newton's papers at Sotheby's auction house and started preparing notes for a biographical study. Written in the late 1930s, this essay was read only after his death. Keynes saw Newton, not as the first of the scientists, but as the last of the magicians.*]

It is with some diffidence that I try to speak to you in his own home of Newton *as he was himself*. I have long been a student of the records and had the intention to put my impressions into writing to be ready for Christmas Day 1942, the tercentenary of his birth. The war has deprived me both of leisure to treat adequately so great a theme and of opportunity to consult my library and my papers and to verify my impressions. So if the brief study which I shall lay before you to-day is more perfunctory than it should be, I hope you will excuse me.

One other preliminary matter. I believe that Newton was different from the conventional picture of him. But I do not believe he was less great. He was less ordinary, more extraordinary, than the nineteenth century cared to make him out. Geniuses *are* very peculiar. Let no one here suppose that my object to-day is to lessen, by describing, Cambridge's greatest son. I am trying rather to see him as his own friends and contemporaries saw him. And they without exception regarded him as one of the greatest of men.

In the eighteenth century and since, Newton came to be thought of as the first and greatest of the modern age of scientists, a rationalist, one who taught us to think on the lines of cold and untinctured reason.

I do not see him in this light. I do not think that any one who has pored over the contents of that box which he packed up when he finally left Cambridge in 1696 and which, though partly dispersed, have come down to us, can see him like that. Newton was not the first of the age of reason. He was the last [363] of the magicians, the last of the Babylonians and Sumerians, the last great mind which looked out on the visible and intellectual world with the same eyes as those who began to build our intellectual inheritance rather less than 10,000 years ago. Isaac Newton, a posthumous child born with no father on Christmas Day, 1642, was the last wonder-child to whom the Magi could do sincere and appropriate homage.

Had there been time, I should have liked to read to you the contemporary record of the child Newton. For, though it is well known to his biographers, it has never been published *in extenso*, without comment, just as it stands. Here, indeed, is the makings of a legend of the young magician, a most joyous picture of the opening mind of genius free from the uneasiness, the melancholy and nervous agitation of the young man and student.

For in vulgar modern terms Newton was profoundly neurotic of a not unfamiliar type, but – I should say from the records – a most extreme example. His deepest instincts were occult, esoteric, semantic – with profound shrinking from the world, a paralysing fear of exposing his thoughts, his beliefs, his discoveries in all nakedness to the inspection and criticism of the world. 'Of the most fearful, cautious and suspicious temper that I ever knew', said Whiston, his successor in the Lucasian

Chair. The too well-known conflicts and ignoble quarrels with Hooke, Flamsteed, Leibnitz are only too clear an evidence of this. Like all his type he was wholly aloof from women. He parted with and published nothing except under the extreme pressure of friends. Until the second phase of his life, he was a wrapt, consecrated solitary, pursuing his studies by intense introspection with a mental endurance perhaps never equalled.

I believe that the clue to his mind is to be found in his unusual powers of continuous concentrated introspection. A case can be made out, as it also can with Descartes, for regarding him as an accomplished experimentalist. Nothing can be more charming than the tales of his mechanical contrivances when he was a boy. There are his telescopes and his optical experiments. [364] These were essential accomplishments, part of his unequalled all-round technique, but not, I am sure, his *peculiar* gift, especially amongst his contemporaries. His peculiar gift was the power of holding continuously in his mind a purely mental problem until he had seen straight through it. I fancy his pre-eminence is due to his muscles of intuition being the strongest and most enduring with which a man has ever been gifted. Anyone who has ever attempted pure scientific or philosophical thought knows how one can hold a problem momentarily in one's mind and apply all one's powers of concentration to piercing through it, and how it will dissolve and escape and you find that what you are surveying is a blank. I believe that Newton could hold a problem in his mind for hours and days and weeks until it surrendered to him its secret. Then being a supreme mathematical technician he could dress it up, how you will, for purposes of exposition, but it was his intuition which was pre-eminently extraordinary – 'so happy in his conjectures', said de Morgan, 'as to seem to know more than he could possibly have any means of proving'. The proofs, for what they are worth, were, as I have said, dressed up afterwards – they were not the instrument of discovery.

There is the story of how he informed Halley of one of his most fundamental discoveries of planetary motion. 'Yes,' replied Halley, 'but how do you know that? Have you proved it?' Newton was taken aback – 'Why, I've known it for years,' he replied. 'If you'll give me a few days, I'll certainly find you a proof of it' – as in due course he did.

Again, there is some evidence that Newton in preparing the *Principia* was held up almost to the last moment by lack of proof that you could treat a solid sphere as though all its mass was concentrated at the centre, and only hit on the proof a year before publication. But this was a truth which he had known for certain and had always assumed for many years.

Certainly there can be no doubt that the peculiar geometrical form in which the exposition of the *Principia* is dressed up [365] bears no resemblance at all to the mental processes by which Newton actually arrived at his conclusions.

His experiments were always, I suspect, a means, not of discovery, but always of verifying what he knew already.

Why do I call him a magician? Because he looked on the whole universe and all that is in it *as a riddle*, as a secret which could be read by applying pure thought to certain evidence, certain mystic clues which God had laid about the world to allow a sort of philosopher's treasure hunt to the esoteric brotherhood. He believed that these clues were to be found partly in the evidence of the heavens and in the constitution of elements (and that is what gives the false suggestion of his being an experimental natural philosopher), but also partly in certain papers and traditions handed down by the brethren in an unbroken chain back to the original cryptic revelation in Babylonia. He regarded the universe as a cryptogram set by the Almighty – just as he himself wrapt the discovery of the calculus in a cryptogram when he communicated with Leibnitz. By pure thought, by concentration of mind, the riddle, he believed, would be revealed to the initiate.

He *did* read the riddle of the heavens. And he believed that by the same powers of his introspective imagination he would read the riddle of the Godhead, the riddle of past and future events divinely fore-ordained, the riddle of the elements and their constitution from an original undifferentiated first matter, the riddle of health and of immortality. All would be revealed to him if only he could persevere to the end, uninterrupted, by himself, no one coming into the room, reading, copying, testing – all by himself, no interruption for God's sake, no disclosure, no discordant breakings in or criticism, with fear and shrinking as he assailed these half-ordained, half-forbidden things, creeping back into the bosom of the Godhead as into his mother's womb. 'Voyaging through strange seas of thought *alone*', not as Charles Lamb 'a fellow who believed nothing unless it was as clear as the three sides of a triangle'.

And so he continued for some twenty-five years.   [366]

. . .

Let me not exaggerate through reaction against the other Newton myth which has been so sedulously created for the last two hundred years. There was extreme method in his madness. All his unpublished works on esoteric and theological matters are marked by careful learning, accurate method and extreme sobriety of statement. They are just as *sane* as the *Principia*, if their whole matter and purpose were not magical. They were nearly all composed during the same twenty-five years of his mathematical studies.   [368]

. . .

A large section, judging by the handwriting amongst the earliest, relates to alchemy – transmutation, the philosopher's stone, the elixir of life. The scope and character of these papers have been hushed up, or at least minimised, by nearly all those who have inspected them. About 1650 there was a considerable group in London, round the publisher Cooper, who during [369] the next twenty years revived interest not only in the English alchemists of the fifteenth century, but also in translations of the medieval and post-medieval alchemists.

There is an unusual number of manuscripts of the early English alchemists in the libraries of Cambridge. It may be that there was some continuous esoteric tradition within the University which sprang into activity again in the twenty years from 1650 to 1670. At any rate, Newton was clearly an unbridled addict. It is this with which he was occupied 'about 6 weeks at spring and 6 at the fall when the fire in the elaboratory scarcely went out' at the very years when he was composing the *Principia* – and about this he told Humphrey Newton not a word. Moreover, he was almost entirely concerned, not in serious experiment, but in trying to read the riddle of tradition, to find meaning in cryptic verses, to imitate the alleged but largely imaginary experiments of the initiates of past centuries. Newton has left behind him a vast mass of records of these studies. I believe that the greater part are translations and copies made by him of existing books and manuscripts. But there are also extensive records of experiments. I have glanced through a great quantity of this – at least 100,000 words, I should say. It is utterly impossible to deny that it is wholly magical and wholly devoid of scientific value; and also impossible not to admit that Newton devoted years of work to it. Some time it might be interesting, but not useful, for some student better equipped and more idle than I to work out Newton's exact relationship to the tradition and MSS. of his time.

In these mixed and extraordinary studies, with one foot in the Middle Ages and one foot treading a path for modern science, Newton spent the first phase of his life, the period of life in Trinity when he did all his real work. Now let me pass to the second phase.

After the publication of the *Principia* there is a complete change in his habit and way of life. I believe that his friends, above all Halifax, came to the conclusion that he must be [370] rooted out of the life he was leading at Trinity which must soon lead to decay of mind and health. Broadly speaking, of his own motion or under persuasion, he abandons his studies. He takes up University business, represents the University in Parliament; his friends are busy trying to get a dignified and remunerative job for him – the Provostship of King's, the Mastership of Charterhouse, the Controllership of the Mint.

Newton could not be Master of Trinity because he was a Unitarian and so not in Holy Orders. He was rejected as Provost of King's for the more prosaic reason that he was not an Etonian. Newton took this rejection very ill and prepared a long legalistic brief, which I possess, giving reasons why it was not unlawful for him to be accepted as Provost. But, as ill-luck had it, Newton's nomination for the Provostship came at the moment when King's had decided to fight against the right of Crown nomination, a struggle in which the College was successful.

Newton was well qualified for any of these offices. It must not be inferred from his introspection, his absent mindedness, his secrecy and his solitude that he lacked aptitude for affairs when he chose to exercise it. There are many records to prove his very great capacity. Read, for example, his correspondence with Dr Covell, the Vice-Chancellor, when, as the University's representative in Parliament, he had to deal with the delicate question of the oaths after the revolution of 1688. With Pepys and Lowndes he became one of the greatest and most efficient of our civil servants. He was a very successful investor of funds, surmounting the crisis of the South Sea Bubble, and died a rich man. He possessed in exceptional degree almost every kind of intellectual aptitude – lawyer, historian, theologian, not less than mathematician, physicist, astronomer.

And when the turn of his life came and he put his books of magic back into the box, it was easy for him to drop the seventeenth century behind him and to evolve into the eighteenth-century figure which is the traditional Newton.

Nevertheless, the move on the part of his friends to change his life came almost too late. In 1689 his mother, to whom he [371] was deeply attached, died. Somewhere about his fiftieth birthday on Christmas Day 1692, he suffered what we should now term a severe nervous breakdown. Melancholia, sleeplessness, fears of persecution – he writes to Pepys and to Locke and no doubt to others letters which lead them to think that his mind is deranged. He lost, in his own words, the 'former consistency of his mind'. He never again concentrated after the old fashion or did any fresh work. The breakdown probably lasted nearly two years, and from it emerged, slightly 'gaga', but still, no doubt, with one of the most powerful minds of England, the Sir Isaac Newton of tradition.

In 1696 his friends were finally successful in digging him out of Cambridge, and for more than another twenty years he reigned in London as the most famous man of his age, of Europe, and – as his powers gradually waned and his affability increased – perhaps of all time, so it seemed to his contemporaries.

He set up house with his niece Catharine Barton, who was beyond reasonable doubt the mistress of his old and loyal

friend Charles Montague, Earl of Halifax and Chancellor of
the Exchequer, who had been one of Newton's intimate friends
when he was an undergraduate at Trinity. Catharine was
reputed to be one of the most brilliant and charming women in
the London of Congreve, Swift and Pope. She is celebrated not
least for the broadness of her stories, in Swift's *Journal to Stella*.
Newton puts on rather too much weight for his moderate
height. 'When he rode in his coach one arm would be out of his
coach on one side and the other on the other.' His pink face,
beneath a mass of snow-white hair, which 'when his peruke
was off was a venerable sight', is increasingly both benevolent
and majestic. One night in Trinity after Hall he is knighted by
Queen Anne. For nearly twenty-four years he reigns as President of the Royal Society. He becomes one of the principal
sights of London for all visiting intellectual foreigners, whom
[372] he entertains handsomely. He liked to have clever young men
about him to edit new editions of the *Principia* – and sometimes merely plausible ones as in the case of Fatio de Duillier.

Magic was quite forgotten. He has become the Sage and Monarch of the Age of Reason. The Sir Isaac Newton of orthodox
tradition – the eighteenth-century Sir Isaac, so remote from the
child magician born in the first half of the seventeenth century –
was being built up. Voltaire returning from his trip to London
was able to report of Sir Isaac – "twas his peculiar felicity, not
only to be born in a country of liberty, but in an Age when all
scholastic impertinences were banished from the World. Reason
alone was cultivated and Mankind cou'd only be his Pupil, not
his Enemy.' Newton, whose secret heresies and scholastic super-
stitions it had been the study of a lifetime to conceal!

But he never concentrated, never recovered 'the former consistency of his mind'. 'He spoke very little in company.' 'He had
something rather languid in his look and manner.'

And he looked very seldom, I expect, into the chest where,
when he left Cambridge, he had packed all the evidences of
what had occupied and so absorbed his intense and flaming
spirit in his rooms and his garden and his elaboratory between
the Great Gate and Chapel.

But he did not destroy them. They remained in the box to

shock profoundly any eighteenth- or nineteenth-century prying eyes. They became the possession of Catharine Barton and then of her daughter, Lady Lymington. So Newton's chest, with many hundreds and thousands of words of his unpublished writings, came to contain the 'Portsmouth Papers'.

In 1888 the mathematical portion was given to the University Library at Cambridge. They have been indexed, but they have never been edited. The rest, a very large collection, were dispersed in the auction room in 1936 by Catharine Barton's descendant, the present Lord Lymington. Disturbed by this impiety, I managed gradually to reassemble about half of them, including nearly the whole of the biographical portion, that is, the 'Conduitt Papers', in order to bring them to Cambridge [373] which I hope they will never leave. The greater part of the rest were snatched out of my reach by a syndicate which hoped to sell them at a high price, probably in America, on the occasion of the recent tercentenary.

As one broods over these queer collections, it seems easier to understand – with an understanding which is not, I hope, distorted in the other direction – this strange spirit, who was tempted by the Devil to believe, at the time when within these walls he was solving so much, that he could reach all the secrets of God and Nature by the pure power of mind – Copernicus and Faustus in one.   [374]

Quotable Quotes

General

'I do not know which makes a man more conservative – to know nothing but the present, or nothing but the past' (1926, 'The End of *Laissez-faire*', CW 9, p. 277).

'The fact that all things are *possible* is no excuse for talking foolishly' (1919, ECP, CW 2, p. 128).

'Lenin was certainly right. There is no subtler, no surer means of overturning the existing basis of society than to debauch the currency' (1919, ECP, CW 2, p. 149).

'Thus inflation is unjust and deflation is inexpedient. Of the two perhaps deflation is, if we rule out exaggerated inflations such as that of Germany, the worse; because it is worse, in an impoverished world, to provoke unemployment than to disappoint the *rentier*' (1923, TMR, CW 4, p. 36).

'The ideas of economists and philosophers, both when they are right and when they are wrong, are more powerful than is commonly understood. Indeed the world is ruled by little else. Practical men, who believe themselves to be quite exempt from any intellectual influences, are usually the slaves of some defunct economist. Madmen in authority, who hear voices in the air, are distilling their frenzy from some academic scribbler of a few years back. I am sure that the power of vested interests is vastly exaggerated compared with the gradual encroachment of ideas' (1936, GT, CW 7, p. 383).

'The theory of output as a whole . . . is much more easily adapted to the conditions of a totalitarian state, than is the theory of the production and distribution of a given output produced under conditions of free competition and a large measure of *laissez-faire*' (1936, Preface to the German edition of GT, CW 7, p. xxvi).

'Hitler [will] meet his Waterloo a long way East of Berlin and . . . we should be there' (1940, JMK to Soviet ambassador, 12 June, quoted in Robert Skidelsky, *John Maynard Keynes*, vol. 3 (2000), p. 73).

On Economics

'On grounds of social justice no case can be made out for reducing the wages of the miners' (1925, EP, CW 9, p. 223).

'Many of the greatest economic evils of our time are the fruits of risk, uncertainty, and ignorance' (1926, EP, CW 9, p. 291).

'Unemployment . . . exists because employers have been deprived of profit' (1931, EP, CW 9, p. 334).

'There are few Englishmen who do not rejoice at the breaking of our golden fetters' (1931, 27 September, on suspension of the gold standard, CW 9, p. 245).

'Let goods be homespun whenever it is reasonably and conveniently possible; and, above all, let finance be primarily national' (1933, 'National Self-Sufficiency', CW 21, p. 236).

'Words ought to be a little wild, for they are the assault of thoughts upon the unthinking. But when the seats of power and authority have been attained there should be no more poetic licence' (1933, 'National Self-Sufficiency', CW 21, p. 244).

'If the Treasury were to fill old bottles with banknotes, bury them at suitable depths in disused coal-mines which are then filled up to the surface with town rubbish, and leave it to private enterprise on well-tried principles of *laissez-faire* to dig the notes up again . . . there need be no more unemployment' (1936, GT, CW 7, p. 129).

'The right remedy for the trade cycle is not to be found in abolishing booms and thus keeping us permanently in a semi-slump; but in abolishing slumps and thus keeping us permanently in a quasi-boom' (1936, GT, CW 7, p. 322).

'A boom is a situation in which over-optimism triumphs over a rate of interest which, in a cooler light, would be seen to be excessive' (1936, GT, CW 7, p. 322).

'The policy of fixed prices plus having nothing in the shops to buy – an expedient pursued for many years by the Russian authorities – is undoubtedly one of the very best ways of preventing inflation!' (1939, 27 November, quoted in Skidelsky, *John Maynard Keynes*, vol. 3, p. 57).

On Economic Method

'In economics you can't convict your opponent of error, you can only hope to convince him of it' (attributed).

'But this *long run* is a misleading guide to current affairs. *In the long run* we are all dead. Economists set themselves too easy, too useless a task if in tempestuous seasons they can only tell us that when the storm is long past the ocean is flat again' (1923, TMR, CW 4, p. 65).

'Perhaps the chief task of economists at this hour is to distinguish afresh the *Agenda* of government from the *Non-Agenda*; and the companion task of politics is to devise forms of government within a democracy which shall be capable of accomplishing the *Agenda*' (1926, EP, CW 9, p. 288).

'If economists could manage to get themselves thought of as humble, competent people, on a level with dentists, that would be splendid!' (1930, EP, CW 9, p. 332).

'When you adopt perfectly precise language you are trying to express yourself for the benefit of those who are incapable of thought' (1933, lecture, 6 November, from Thomas K. Rymes, *Keynes's Lectures, 1932–35: Notes of a Representative Student* (1989), p. 102).

'The classical theorists resemble Euclidean geometers in a non-Euclidean world who, discovering that in experience straight lines apparently parallel often meet, rebuke the lines for not keeping straight – as the only remedy for the unfortunate collisions which are occurring. Yet, in truth, there is no remedy except to throw over the axiom of parallels and to work out a non-Euclidean geometry. Something similar is required to-day in economics' (1936, GT, CW 7, p. 16).

'Too large a proportion of recent "mathematical" economics are merely concoctions, as imprecise as the initial assumptions they rest on, which allow the author to lose sight of the complexities and interdependencies of the real world in a maze of pretentious and unhelpful symbols' (1936, GT, CW 7, pp. 298.

'When statistics do not make sense, I find it generally wiser to prefer sense to statistics' (1940, JMK to E. Rothbarth, 21 January, quoted in Skidelsky, *John Maynard Keynes*, vol. 3, p. 70).

On Bankers

'A "sound" banker, alas! is not one who foresees danger and avoids it, but one who, when he is ruined, is ruined in a conventional and orthodox way along with his fellows, so that no one can really blame him' (1932, *Vanity Fair*, January CW 9, p. 156).

'Worldly wisdom teaches that it is better for reputation to fail conventionally than to succeed unconventionally' (1936, GT, CW 7, p. 158).

On the Budget

'The budget and the Economy Bill are replete with folly and injustice. It is a tragedy that the moral energies and enthusiasm of many truly self-sacrificing and well-wishing people should be so misdirected' (1931, on Philip Snowden's Economy Bill of 8 September, CW 9, p. 145).

'The boom, not the slump, is the right time for austerity at the Treasury' (1937, *The Times*, 12–14 January CW 21, p. 390).

On Capitalism

'If irreligious capitalism is ultimately to defeat religious Communism it is not enough that it should be economically more efficient – it must be many times as efficient' (1925, EP, CW 9, pp. 267–8).

'But whatever the sociological value of [*Das Kapital*] I am sure that its contemporary *economic* value (apart from occasional but inconstructive [*sic*] and discontinuous flashes of insight) is *nil*' (1934, JMK to George Bernard Shaw, 2 December, quoted in Robert Skidelsky, *John Maynard Keynes*, vol. 2 (1992), p. 520).

'To understand my state of mind . . . you have to know that I believe myself to be writing a book on economic theory, which will largely revolutionise . . . the way the world thinks about economic problems. When my new theory has been duly assimilated and mixed with politics and feelings and passions, I can't predict what the upshot will be in its effects on actions and affairs. But there will be a great change, and, in particular, the Ricardian foundations of Marxism will be knocked away' (1935, JMK to George Bernard Shaw, 1 January, quoted in Skidelsky, *John Maynard Keynes*, vol. 2, pp. 520–21).

On Debt, Wartime and Other

'If we aim deliberately at the impoverishment of Central Europe, vengeance, I dare predict, will not limp' (1919, ECP, CW 2, p. 170).

'We shall never be able to move again, unless we can free our limbs from these paper shackles' (1919, ECP, CW 2, p. 178).

'I do not believe that any of these tributes will continue to be paid, at the best, for more than a very few years. They do not square with human nature or agree with the spirit of the age' (1919, ECP, CW 2, p. 179).

'The absolutists of contract ... are the real parents of revolution' (1923, TMR, CW 4, p. 57).

'The process of adjustment is *compulsory* for the debtor and *voluntary* for the creditor ... The debtor *must* borrow; the creditor is under no such compulsion' (1941, 'The Clearing Union', CW 25, p. 28).

On Saving

'The duty of "saving" became nine-tenths of virtue' (1919, ECP, CW 2, p. 12).

'It is not the miser who gets rich; but he who lays out his money in fruitful investment' (1929, EP, CW 9, p. 123).

'If enterprise is afoot, wealth accumulates whatever may be happening to thrift; and if enterprise is asleep, wealth decays whatever thrift may be doing' (1930, TM, CW 6, p. 132).

'The more virtuous we are, the more determinedly thrifty, the more obstinately orthodox in our national and personal finance, the more our incomes will have to fall when interest rises relatively to the marginal efficiency of capital. Obstinacy can bring only a penalty and no reward. For the result is inevitable' (1936, GT, CW 7, p. 111).

On Investment

'The social object of skilled investment should be to defeat the dark forces of time and ignorance which envelop our future. The actual, private object of the most skilled investment today is "to beat the gun"' (1936, GT, CW 7, p. 155).

'Professional investment may be likened to those newspaper competitions in which the competitors have to pick out the six prettiest faces from a hundred photographs, the prize being awarded to the competitor whose choice most nearly corresponds to the average preferences of those competitors as a whole; so that each competitor has to pick, not those faces which he himself finds prettiest, but those which he thinks likeliest to catch the fancy of other competitors, all of whom are looking at the problem from the same point of view' (1936, GT, CW 7, p. 156).

'Speculators may do no harm as bubbles on a steady stream of enterprise. But the position is serious when enterprise becomes the bubble on a whirlpool of speculation. When the capital development of a country becomes a by-product of the activities of a casino, the job is likely to be ill-done' (1936, GT, CW 7, p. 159).

'To make the purchase of an investment permanent and indissoluble, like marriage, except by reason of death or grave cause, might be a useful remedy for our contemporary evils' (1936, GT, CW 7, p. 160).

'Most, probably, of our decisions to do something positive, the full consequences of which will be drawn out over many days to come, can only be taken as a result of animal spirits – of a spontaneous urge to action rather than inaction, and not as the outcome of a weighted average of quantitative benefits multiplied by quantitative probabilities' (1936, GT, CW 7, p. 161).

On Money

'Money is that which one accepts only to get rid of it' (1909, lecture, quoted in Robert Skidelsky, *John Maynard Keynes*, vol. 1 (1983), p. 214).

'India ... is in the forefront of monetary progress' (1913, *Indian Currency and Finance*, CW 1, p. 182).

'Some people seem to infer ... that output and income can be raised by increasing the quantity of money. But this is like trying to get fat by buying a larger belt' (1933, JMK to Roosevelt, 31 December, commenting on his gold-buying policy CW 21, p. 294).

'A monetary economy ... is ... one in which changing views about the future are capable of influencing the quantity of employment and not merely its direction' (GT, CW 7, p. xxii).

'For the importance of money essentially flows from its being a link between the present and the future' (1936, GT, CW 7, p. 293).

'If . . . we are tempted to assert that money is the drink which stimulates the system to activity, we must remind ourselves that there may be several slips between the cup and the lip' (1936, GT, CW 7, p. 173).

'Why should anyone outside a lunatic asylum wish to use money as a store of wealth? Because, partly on reasonable and partly on instinctive grounds, our desire to hold money as a store of wealth is a barometer of the degree of our distrust of our own calculations and conventions concerning the future . . . The possession of actual money lulls our disquietude; and the premium which we require to make us part with money is the measure of the degree of our disquietude' (1937, 'The General Theory of Employment' CW 14, pp. 115–16).

'We must avoid [dear money] as we would hell-fire' (1937, *The Times*, 12–14 January CW 21, p. 389).

On Stockbrokers

'After all, one would expect brokers to be wrong. If, in addition to their other inside advantages, they were capable of good advice, clearly they would have retired long ago with a large fortune . . . If only one could find out for certain what brokers are recommending to their clients and do the opposite, the way to a fortune would be safe and secure' (1944, Keynes to his nephew David Hill, quoted in Skidelsky, *John Maynard Keynes*, vol. 3, pp. 163–4).

On Lawyers

'[Lawyers should] devise means by which it will be lawful for me to go on being sensible in unforeseen conditions' (1944, quoted in Skidelsky, *John Maynard Keynes*, vol. 3, p. 118).

'Isn't our scheme intended to get things done, whereas yours will merely provide a living for a large number of lawyers?' (1945, to American negotiators, quoted in Skidelsky, *John Maynard Keynes*, vol. 3, p. 416).

'At one time I had come to believe that the Mayflower came over to this country filled with lawyers. I am now inclined to go back to my original belief that it was filled with theologians' (1945, quoted in Skidelsky, *John Maynard Keynes*, vol. 3, p. 432).

'This seems to be even more stuffed with lawyers' bunk than usual. If only it could be made illegal to employ the services of a solicitor, what a lot of trouble it would save!' (1946, JMK to David Webster, quoted in Skidelsky, *John Maynard Keynes*, vol. 3, p. 299).

On Politics

'I work for a Government I despise for ends I think criminal' (1917, quoted in Skidelsky, *John Maynard Keynes*, vol. 1, p. 345).

'Politicians have ears, but not eyes' (attributed).

'It is the method of modern statesmen to talk as much folly as the public demand and to practise no more of it than is compatible with what they have said' (1922, RT, CW 3, p. 1).

'The important thing for government is not to do things which individuals are doing already, and to do them a little better or a little worse; but to do those things which at present are not done at all' (1926, EP, CW 9, p. 291).

On the Labour Party: 'But . . . it is a class party, and the class is not my class. I can be influenced by what seems to me to be justice and good sense; but the *class* war will find me on the side of the educated bourgeoisie' (1925, EP, CW 9, p. 297).

'The Conservative Party ought to be concerning itself with evolving a version of individualistic capitalism adapted to the progressive change of circumstances. The difficulty is that the capitalist leaders in the City and in Parliament are incapable of distinguishing novel measures for safeguarding capitalism from what they call Bolshevism' (1925, EP, CW 9, p. 299).

'Nothing will cause a social institution to decay with more certainty than its attachment to the hereditary principle . . . [B]y far the oldest of our institutions, the Church, is the one which has always kept itself free from the hereditary taint' (1925, EP, CW 9, p. 299).

'Possibly the Liberal Party cannot serve the State in any better way than by supplying Conservative governments with Cabinets, and Labour governments with ideas' (1926, EP, CW 9, p. 310).

On the House of Lords: 'Of course the standard is so fearfully low that any human utterance provokes special attention' (1943, JMK to his mother, May, quoted in Skidelsky, *John Maynard Keynes*, vol. 3, p. 256).

On a House of Commons debate: 'It was like a loonies' picnic or an idiots' day out, where lunatic Members who on other occasions would be doomed to decent restraint have a chance, for once, of catching the Speaker's eye' (1944, quoted in Skidelsky, *John Maynard Keynes*, vol. 3, pp. 334–5).

On Soviet Russia: 'How can I adopt a creed which, preferring the mud to the fish, exalts the boorish proletariat above the bourgeois and the intelligentsia who, with whatever faults, are the quality in life and surely carry the seeds of all human advancement? Even if we need a religion, how can we find it in the turbid rubbish of the Red bookshops?' (1925, EP, CW 9, p. 258).

On Politicians

On Clemenceau: 'He felt about France what Pericles felt of Athens – unique value in her, nothing else mattering' (1919, ECP, CW 10, p. 5).

On Woodrow Wilson: 'this blind and deaf Don Quixote' (1919, ECP, CW 10, p. 11).

On Lloyd George: 'rooted in nothing ... void and without content ... a vampire and a medium in one' (1919, ECP/EB CW 10, p. 24).

On Bonar Law: 'too pessimistic to snatch present profits and too short-sighted to avoid future catastrophe' (1923, EB, CW 10, p. 35).

On Stanley Baldwin: 'Mr. Baldwin has invented the formidable argument that you must not do anything because it will mean that you will not be able to do anything else' (1929, *The Times*, 29 May).

On the Chancellor of the Exchequer, Sir Kingsley Wood: 'No matter how ... apparently incomprehensible an economic proposition seemed to him to be, he ... had the gift of converting it ... into a platitude intelligible to the merest child. This is a great political gift, not to be despised' (1943, quoted in Skidelsky, *John Maynard Keynes*, vol. 3, p. 144).

On Sir Frederick Phillips, 2nd Secretary of the Treasury: 'he could be silent in several languages' (1943, quoted in Skidelsky, *John Maynard Keynes*, vol. 3, p. 146).

On Francis Galton, founder of eugenics: 'His original genius was superior to his intellect, but his intellect was always just sufficient to keep him on the right side of eccentricity' (1937, KP, P/6).

On Leo Crowley, US Lend-Lease Administrator: 'a Tammany Polonius [whose] ear [was] so close to the ground that he was out of range of persons speaking from an erect position' (1944, JMK to Sir John Anderson, 12 December, quoted in Skidelsky, *John Maynard Keynes*, vol. 3, p. 370).

On Marriner Eccles, US negotiator of the American loan: 'No wonder that man is a Mormon. No single woman could stand him' (1944, quoted in Skidelsky, *John Maynard Keynes*, vol. 3, p. 435).

On the USA

'I always regard a visit [to the USA] as in the nature of a serious illness to be followed by convalescence' (1941, quoted in Skidelsky, *John Maynard Keynes*, vol. 3, p. 114).

'Indeed in Washington the Ancient Mariner would have found it necessary to use a telephone to detain the wedding guest. For it is only on the telephone that one can obtain undivided attention' (1943, quoted in Skidelsky, *John Maynard Keynes*, vol. 3, p. 118).

On the Future

'The love of money as a possession . . . will be recognised for what it is, a somewhat disgusting morbidity, one of those semi-criminal, semi-pathological propensities which one hands over with a shudder to the specialists in mental disease' (1930, EPG, CW 9, p. 329).

'I am bold to predict . . . that to the economic historians of the future the slump of 1930 may present itself as the death struggle of the war-rates of interest and the re-emergence of the pre-war rates' (1930, TM, CW 6, p. 345).

'Interest to-day rewards no genuine sacrifice, any more than does the rent of land' (1936, GT, CW 7, p. 37).

'Provided we have never made the product before, we have the rest of the world licked on cost . . . If by some sad geographical slip the American Air Force (it is too late now to hope for much from the enemy) were to destroy every factory on the North-East coast and in Lancashire (at an hour when the directors were sitting there and no one else), we should have nothing to fear. How else we are to regain the exuberant inexperience which is necessary . . . for success, I cannot surmise' (1945, 'Overseas Financial Policy in stage III', CW 24, p. 262).

'Let every part of Merry England be merry in its own way. Death to Hollywood' (1946, 'The Arts Council of Great Britain', CW 28, p. 371).

Notes

1: The Philosopher

1. G .E. Moore, *Principia Ethica* (1903), pp. 188–9.
2. This is akin to Hayek's doctrine of 'unintended consequences'. But Hayek confined this to the well-meaning actions of government, whereas for Keynes they were an aspect of all rational decision-making.
3. For reactions to TP see Robert Skidelsky, *John Maynard Keynes*, vol. 2 (1992) pp. 67–73; R. M. O'Donnell, *Keynes: Philosophy, Economics and Politics* (1989), pp. 25–7. In a paper of 1926, 'Truth and Probability' read to the Cambridge Moral Science Club, the young Cambridge mathematician and philosopher Frank Ramsey argued that rational people with the same evidence can hold divergent probabilities. An internal consistency rule is all that is required to make the belief rational; the important matter is whether it turns out to be true or false. Successful beliefs are those validated by results. On this view, all probabilities can be numerically measured (they start off as bets) and are validated or falsified by frequencies. They are pragmatic, not logical. Keynes's review of a posthumous collection of Ramsey's essays, *The Foundations of Mathematics*, entitled 'Ramsey as a Philosopher', partially conceded Ramsey's critique (CW 10, pp. 336–9).

2: The Social Philosopher

1. For the pre-history of the publication see Robert Skidelsky, *John Maynard Keynes*, vol. 2 (1992), p. 664, fn. 53. See also Robert and Edward Skidelsky, *How Much Is Enough?* (2012), pp. 4–5, 15–17; Lorenzo Pecchi and Gustavo Piga (eds.), *Revisiting Keynes: Economic Possibilities for Our Grandchildren* (2008).
2. See note 17 to chapter 3 below.

3. See Skidelsky, *John Maynard Keynes*, vol. 2, p. 476. Mark Nolan, *Keynes in Dublin* (2013), supplies further context, and reproduces the original version of the lecture from Keynes's handwritten notes, which differs a little from the CW version.

3: The Economist

1. The view of Don Patinkin, *Keynes' Monetary Thought* (1976).
2. J. A. Schumpeter, *History of Economic Analysis* (1954), p. 42.
3. This is the approach of Rod O'Donnell, in his *Keynes: Philosophy, Economics and Politics* (1989).
4. It is quite true that, following the marginalist revolution, more emphasis was placed on the opportunity cost to the individual of holding money as against other assets. But the transactions view of money – the view that one acquired money only to spend it on buying goods and services 'sooner or later' – remained in the ascendant. The demand or store of value function for money was undeveloped. This meant a bias in monetary theory towards treating the quantity of money as exogenously determined – as resulting from movements of gold or issues of notes by the central bank – unrelated to individual decisions concerning the desired size of 'real' balances.
5. CW 2, p. 101, fn. 3.
6. See Robert Skidelsky, *John Maynard Keynes*, vol. 2 (1992), pp. 309–12; Donald Moggridge, *Maynard Keynes: An Economist's Biography* (1992), pp. 341–6.
7. See Irving Fisher, *The Purchasing Power of Money* (1911).
8. For an excellent discussion on the theoretical status of the quantity theory of money at this time, particularly the common confusion between the quantity theory and the 'Equation of Exchange', see Schumpeter, *History of Economic Analysis*, pp. 1095–110. For a later discussion, see David Laidler, *The Golden Age of the Quantity Theory* (1991).
9. In this formulation, Keynes ignores the marginal utility theory of money, which he ought to have got from his teacher Alfred Marshall (see J. K. Whittaker (ed.), *The Early Economic Writings of Alfred Marshall, 1867–1890*, vol. 1 (1975), p. 167). He introduces it on p. 64 of TMR (below) but makes no analytic use of it.
10. See Skidelsky, *John Maynard Keynes*, vol. 2, pp. 162–4; also Mark Blaug et al., *The Quantity Theory of Money: From Locke to Keynes and Friedman* (1995), pp. 86–9.
11. Though Axel Leijonhufvud thinks that 'handled with circumspection', the Fundamental Equations 'can still be used to

heuristic advantage' in *On Keynesian Economics and the Economics of Keynes* (1968), p. 23, n. 15.

12. As was pointed out by the young economist members of JMK's 'Cambridge Circus', Richard Kahn, James Meade, Austin and Joan Robinson and Piero Sraffa, who in 1930–31 met to 'argue out' TM.

13. Schumpeter, *History of Economic Analysis*, pp. 1103n, 1105.

14. On the tautological nature of the fundamental equations, see the subtle discussion in Don Patinkin, *Keynes' Monetary Thought* (1976), chapter 6. Keynes defines saving as the non-consumption of 'normal' (equilibrium) income, and profit as net of normal income. Therefore, the appearance of profit (positive or negative) *means* that investment is 'running ahead' or 'falling behind' saving.

15. Cf. the discussion of liquidity preference in GT, CW 7, pp. 166, 210.

16. Keynes talks here of 'inaccurate forecasting' rather than uncertainty, but on p. 133 below he anticipates GT's discussion of 'uncertainty'.

17. Keynes was influenced by Earl J. Hamilton's monetary explanation of the commercial revolution of the sixteenth and seventeenth centuries, 'American Treasure and the Rise of Capitalism (1500–1700)', *Economica*, (November 1929).

18. Cf. JMK on the transfer problem, p. 101 above.

19. CW 13, p. 345.

20. Charles P. Kindleberger, *The World in Depression 1929–1939* (1977), p. 125.

21. Milton Friedman and Anna Jacobson Schwartz, in *The Great Contraction 1929–1933* (1965), attribute its severity to the failure of the Fed to use 'open market operations' to offset the collapse in the money supply.

22. Alvin S. Johnson, 'The Farmers' Indemnity', in Jacob Hollander (ed.), *Economic Essays: Contributed in Honor of John Bates Clark* (1927), pp. 215–28.

23. JMK's *General Theory* is not quite an unread classic. It has been continuously in print, in numerous editions and translations, by different publishers, since its first publication in 1936. The latest is by Palgrave Macmillan (2007), with an introduction by Paul Krugman.

24. *Keynesian Economics: The Search for First Principles* (1983).

25. Alvin Hansen, *A Guide to Keynes* (1953), p. 28.

26. Readers can form their own judgement as to when JMK 'came' to the theory of GT, from Thomas K. Rymes, *Keynes's Lectures,*

1932–35 (1989). Rymes has synthesized lecture notes taken by students at JMK's lectures in the three years leading to GT.

27. Coddington's phrase, *Keynesian Economics*, p. 14.

28. Ibid., p. 51.

29. CW 7, p. 316.

30. CW 7, pp. 12–13.

31. Samuelson in R. Leckachman (ed.), *Keynes's General Theory: Reports of Three Decades* (1964), p. 332.

32. Axel Leijonhufvud, *Keynes and the Classics* (1969), p. 18.

33. J. R. Hicks, 'Mr. Keynes and the "Classics": A Suggested Interpretation', *Econometrica* 5(2)(April 1937), pp. 152, 155.

34. Lionel Robbins, *An Essay on the Nature and Significance of Economic Science* (1932), p. 15.

35. Cf. CW 14, p. 364 from an earlier draft of GT defining 'involuntary unemployment'. 'This does not imply that labour, which is suffering involuntary unemployment is idle. It may be employed as a *pis aller* in some occupation where it earns a real wage less than the wage potentially available. And, of course, a man who is not "out of work" might prefer to be occupied for a longer working week even at a lower hourly real wage than he is actually earning.'

36. Testimony to the Macmillan Committee, CW 20, p. 127.

37. Leijonhufvud has pointed out that the paradox of thrift is inherent in the quantity theory of money: in the aggregate, attempts to hoard must be self-defeating: see *On Keynesian Economics and the Economics of Keynes*, p. 29n.

38. Keynes had got rid of the discrepancy between saving and investment by defining income as inclusive of profits and losses. His consumption function ensures the equality of S and I at all levels of income. But see the note below.

39. In GT, saving and investment are simply different names for the same thing – unconsumed output – in which case the idea that changes in output 'equilibrate' them makes no sense. Keynes could have got round this problem by interpreting their relationship in terms of *ex ante* and *ex post*. Decisions to save and invest might diverge *ex ante* but are equalized by changes in income *ex post*. But Keynes chose not to take this route. As in TM, he seems to have endowed his identities with magical properties.

40. See Patinkin's essay 'John Maynard Keynes' in John Eatwell and Peter Newman (eds.), *The New Palgrave: A Dictionary of Economics* (1987), vol. 3, p. 25.

41. This may be interpreted in terms of the standard IS-LM diagram, showing both its ability to illuminate Keynes's theory, but also its limitations. As Donald Moggridge points out (in his *Keynes* (1976), p. 166), 'Every IS-LM diagram is in effect drawn for a given state of expectations.'

42. Hence John Eatwell and Murray Milgate (eds.), *Keynes's Economics and the Theory of Value and Distribution* (1983), and Pierangelo Garegnani, 'Notes on Consumption, Investment and Effective Demand', *Cambridge Journal of Economics* 2 and 3 (1978), interpret the *General Theory* as a long-period theory.

43. In an article in the *Economic Journal*, March 1939, Keynes, reviewing findings on wage movements by J. G. Dunlop and L. Tarshis, conceded that increasing returns to scale might outweigh the increase in marginal cost as employment improved. This would enable real wages to increase with employment and policy 'to advance farther on the road towards full employment than I had previously supposed' without running into inflationary wage pressure (CW 7, pp. 401, 405–7).

44. Bernard Mandeville (1670–1733), English doctor and writer. He was author of the satire *The Fable of the Bees, or Private Vices, Publick Benefits,* which praises luxury and attacks thrift. Adam Smith considered it so subversive he devoted several pages of his *Theory of Moral Sentiments* to refuting its pernicious teachings.

45. Cf. JMK's Galton Lecture, 16 February 1937 (CW 14, pp. 124–33): 'with a stationary population we shall . . . be absolutely dependent for the maintenance of prosperity and civil peace on policies of increasing consumption by a more equal distribution of incomes and of facing down the rate of interest so as to make profitable a substantial [shortening] of the period of production.

46. See CW 14, pp. 47, 133–4. G. C. Harcourt and P. A. Riach, editors of *A 'Second Edition' of The General Theory*, 2 vols. (1997), and their contributors speculated on what this 'Second Edition' might have contained.

47. See especially Paul Davidson's *Financial Markets, Money and the Real World* (2002). Davidson has called 'ergodic' all those economic theories, including those of the hydraulic Keynesians, which deny the existence of irreducible uncertainty.

48. An equivalent rejection of the 'Berthamite calculus', dating from this time, is in JMK's Galton Lecture, 'Some Economic Consequences of a Declining Population', delivered on 16 February 1937 (CW 14, pp. 124–33).

49. See O'Donnell, *Keynes: Philosophy, Economics and Politics*, p. 203.
50. CW 14, p. 318.

4: The Policy-maker

1. G. L. Harcourt, personal knowledge. This is more plausible than the vulgarized 'When the facts change, I change my mind. What do you do, sir?'
2. The first of the 'Keynes plans' (omitted here) was his proposal, as a member of the Royal Commission on Indian Currency and Finance (1914), to establish an Indian Central Bank. This followed from his analysis of India's monetary system in his first book, *Indian Currency and Finance* (1913). Keynes's first and only economics teacher, Alfred Marshall, described the Bank proposal as a 'prodigy of constructive work'. See Robert Skidelsky, *John Maynard Keynes*, vol. 1 (1983), p. 283.
3. In chapter 3, 'The Forward Market in Foreign Exchanges', pp. 94–115, Keynes explains how traders can hedge themselves against foreign exchange risk.
4. See Donald Moggridge, *Maynard Keynes: An Economist's Biography* (1992), chapter 17; Robert Skidelsky, *John Maynard Keynes*, vol. 2 (1992), chapter 6.
5. It was to enable more 'precise' calculation that R. F. Kahn developed his theory of the 'multiplier', which was incorporated into GT. See excerpt 30 below.
6. In June 1932, the Treasury was able to convert the 5 per cent war loan to 3½ per cent.
7. This is exactly what happened. The National Government, formed in August 1932, introduced the Import Duties Act in February 1932.
8. CW 21, pp. 273–5.
9. This comment was prompted by President Roosevelt's gold-buying policy, a 1930s version of quantitative easing and a variant of Irving Fisher's plan for a compensated dollar. From autumn 1933 to January 1934, the US Treasury bought gold at steadily increasing prices, forcing it up from $20.67 an ounce when the policy started to $35.00 an ounce when it terminated. The idea behind it was to give the gold sellers more money to spend; this would raise prices. When the domestic price effect proved negligible, Roosevelt abandoned the policy. It may have improved the dollar price of American exports.

10. Herbert Stein complained that the letter 'sounded like a letter from a school teacher to the very rich father of a very dull pupil'. But the columnist Walter Lippmann wrote to Keynes on 17 April 1934, 'I don't know whether you realise how great an effect that letter had, but I am told that it was chiefly responsible for the policy which the Treasury is now quietly but effectively pursuing of purchasing long-term Government bonds with a view to making a strong bond market and to reducing the long-term rate of interest' (see Skidelsky, *John Maynard Keynes*, vol. 2, p. 507).

11. The Wheeler–Rayburn Act of 1935 was a foundation stone of the New Deal. It gave the government power to regulate, and if necessary abolish, the holding company structure of American utility companies, whose pyramid features enabled a tiny minority of owners in the top tier to receive nearly all the revenues of the operating companies. The Act was vigorously contested in the courts, after a monumental battle in Congress itself. Regulation, together with the threat of the 'death sentence' for holding companies, is widely credited with having brought the abuses of the system to an end. The Wheeler–Rayburn Act was repealed under President George W. Bush in 2005.

12. The Exchange Equalization Fund was set up in 1932 to manage the sterling–dollar exchange rate, i.e., to prevent any undue appreciation of sterling.

13. This was worked out by James Meade and Richard Kahn.

14. Permanent Secretary, Treasury, 1942–5.

15. CW 27, fn. 228.

5: The Essayist

1. For the outcome see Robert Skidelsky, *John Maynard Keynes*, vol. 1 (1983), pp. 361–2.

2. Far from being published the following year, Sraffa's eleven-volume edition of Ricardo's works appeared almost thirty years later.

Index

Abelard, Peter xvii
abundance
  the coming age of 83
  end of capital scarcity 255
  the era of 64
Abyssinian affair 397
accountants' logic 89–90
Adding-Up Problem,
  The (Keynes) 7
Agenda/Non-Agenda (Bentham)
  55–6, 58
aggregate supply and demand
  xxiv–xxv
  need for rightly distributed
    demand 398
  neglect of aggregate demand in
    classical theory 190
  principle of effective demand
    177, 187
  used to work out spending
    withdrawal xxiv–xxv
Agricultural Adjustment
  Administration (AAA) 381
Air Raid Precautions policy
  (ARP) 408
Alexander the Great 434
'Alternative Theories of the Rate
  of Interest' (Keynes) 274–5
'Am I a Liberal?' (Keynes)
  61–4
American index of
  production 144

ancient currencies 76
Ancient Egypt 199–200
Anne, Queen 510
Argentina 287, 357, 430
Arts Council
  broadcast 91–5
  commended by Keynes 28
  'death to Hollywood' 94
  Keynes chairman-designate xvii
Auden, W. H. 394, 396, 398
'auri sacra fames' 126–7
Australia 149, 155, 357
Austria 167, 473

'Babylonian madness' 76
balance of payments
  adjustment through
    unemployment 309
  Britain's prospective
    post-WW2 deficit 444
  constraint on domestic
    policy under gold standard
    108, 129
  Germany's pre-WW1 100–101
  long-run invisible hand 459–60
  no 'automatic' adjustment
    mechanism 261
  see also gold standard; interest
    rates
'Balance of Payments of the
  United States' (Keynes)
  459–60

Baldwin, Stanley 311, 314, 316,
    318, 320, 322
Balfour, Arthur 468
Ball, Sidney 29
bananas example 113–15
bank deposits 110–111
Bank of England
    as 'conductor of the
        orchestra' 10
    control is indirect 132
    decrease in fiduciary issue 402
    easier credit policy 332–3
    and foreign lending 334
    future regulation of money 293
    and gold 295–9, 356
    and ICU proposals 437–9
    international banking
        cooperation 131, 152,
        298, 370–72
    methods of control of
        credit 120
    mistake in going back to
        gold at pre-war parity in
        1925 307–11
    monetary freedom for domestic
        price stabilization 284
    open-market operations to the
        point of saturation 132–8
    'open-market' policy of 125–6
    policy of 307–17
    reducing the rate of
        interest 152
    restoring confidence to
        international loan market
        157–8
    as social institution 56–7
    unrestricted property of private
        persons 57
    and War Loan 405
Bank of France 157
bank loans 136
bank rate
    and control of member
        banks 125

control of short-term rate 132
    as controlling rate of
        investment 124–6
    description of 111
    difficulty of controlling
        long-term rate 133–6
    exercising a stabilising
        influence 106
    and gold 129–31, 296
    'modus operandi' of 116
banking collapse 142–3
banking margins 169–73
Barton, Catharine 509–11
Bastiat, Frédéric 48–9
Bayes' Theorem 10
B.B.C. 92–4
'bear' markets 117–20, 122,
    137, 221
Bentham, Jeremy
    accepted utilitarian
        hedonism 41–2
    and Agenda/Non-Agenda 55
    calculus of pains and pleasures
        264–5
    escaping the Benthamite
        tradition 20–22
    and false knowledge of the
        future 272
    and laissez-nous faire 46–7
    responsible for nineteenth-
        century state socialism 58
Beveridge Report on Social
    Security 417–19
birth control 62–3
Bloomsbury group xvi–xvii
board of public investment (plan)
    404–5
Bolshevism 28, 64
bonds 133–4, 138–40, 152, 165,
    171, 223–4, 289, 333
booms
    connection with policy of
        capital expenditure 332
    control of 402–4

due to inadequate action by banking system 138
due to marginal efficiency of capital/rate of interest 202
and high interest rates 401
and inflation 376
purely monetary problem 176
risks 204
and the trade cycle 247–50
borrowing 135, 146–7, 150, 156–7, 163, 309
Brazil 149
Bretton Woods Agreement (1944) xxii, xxvi, 460
Brockdorff-Rantzau, Ulrich von 475
budget
  capital xxv
  ordinary xxv
'bull' markets 117–20, 137, 147, 221
Burke, Edmund xvii, 5–6, 55, 394
business class
  favours *laissez-faire* 53–4
  needs confidence to invest 158, 216
  timidity of 34, 393
business profits 159, 162

Cairnes, John Elliott 49
Cambridge Conversazione Society 3
'Can America Spend Its Way into Recovery?' (Keynes) 385–9
'Can Lloyd George Do It?' (Keynes) 318–38, 360
Canada 446–7, 453–4
capital
  assets 268–9
  controls on free movement of 89, 435
  demand for limited 255
  development 360–61
  fixed 149

funds 434
goods 109, 111–12, 121, 155–6, 218, 273
levy 38
liquid 148
marginal efficiency of 178, 200–204, 221–3, 234, 239, 255, 269
and the modern age 78, 80–81
observations on the nature of 228–31
scarcity of 255
state 71
working 148, 400
capital expenditure policy 332, 420
capital market 333, 335, 382, 392–3
capitalism
  at home 287
  Christian 67
  concerns of Keynes 27
  decadent international 87
  improving modern 59–60
  individualistic 36
  inefficiency of 60–61
  irreligious 73
  justification of 30–34, 35
  laissez-faire 50, 88
  'love of money' 65
  profiteers 33
  prospect of widespread insolvencies 173
  rentier aspect of 256
  system of 134
  unregulated markets 183
CEMA *see* Arts Council
central banks 137–41, 158, 437–9
Chamberlain, Neville 405
Chicago lecture (1931) 158
Churchill, Winston xix, 299, 301, 303–5, 312
Civil Works Administration 383

Clark, Colin 280
Clearing Accounts 438–43
Clearing Bank 438–43
'Clearing Union, The' (Keynes)
    426–43
Clemenceau, Georges 461–3,
    465, 468, 475, 478–9
coal industry 311–13
Coddington, Alan 178, 180
Coleridge, Samuel Taylor 492–3
commodities 143, 170–72
Commons, Professor 63–4
Communism 27, 65–71, 74
'compensated dollar' 294
competitive disadvantage 358
confidence, state of 162–3,
    205, 216
Congdon, Tim xxiv
'Consequences to the Banks of
    the Collapse of Money
    Values' (Keynes) 166–74
Conservative Party 62
constructive criticism 378–9
consumption
    and an increase/decrease in rate
        of investment 237
    attaining ideal distribution of
        what is available 50–52
    control of 407–12
    encouraging 423
    function 181
    as function of amount of
        investment goods
        produced 273
    goods 109, 122, 271, 398
    and the menace of the next
        slump 403
    and propensity to consume
        193–5
    and saving 228–9
    standard 131
'consumption units' 103
contract-notes 401
conventional judgments 266

Conversations on Political
    Economy (Marcet) 47
corporations 56
cost of living 409
Council of Four 461–2, 471
Council of Ten 471–2
Covell, Dr 509
credit
    cheap 379–80
    cycle 105, 109, 120–23, 294
    'easy' policy 311
    restrictions 310, 316
Credit Anstalt trouble
    (Austria) 167
'credit' theory of money 108
creditors and debtors
    debts as 'parents of
        revolution' 39
    deflation increases real burden
        of 155, 161, 168
    National Debt 387–8
    restructuring and cancellation
        of 286–8
    Tsarist debts 288
    war debts 99
Crystal Palace, the 95
Currency Committee 313
currency depreciation 38–9

Danzig 474
d'Argenson, Marquis 45
Darmstadter Bank (Berlin) 167
Darwin, Charles 43, 51
Dawes Scheme 155, 314
death duties 252–3
debt
    bondage 285
    restructuring 286
debt-deflation theory (Fisher) 166
defence loan 405–6
'deferred pay' 407
deflation
    in 1929 143
    commodity 109

cumulative in its progress 313–15
does not reduce wages 'automatically' 311
infliction of great injuries 35
Keynes's bias against 285
to force adjustment of wage/price-levels 427
use of term 105–6
demand deficiency 180
demand and supply theory 177
depressions *see* slumps
devaluation 38, 352
development expenditure 326
disequilibrium
between saving and investment 113–15
international 140–42
divine right of monarchs 40
Douglas, Hugh xxxvii, 190, 251
'Dr Melchior: A Defeated Enemy' (Keynes) 479–83
Drake, Sir Francis 79
drug and sex offences 62

Eady, Sir Wilfrid 425
earnings
changes in 113
standard 131
East India Company 79
Easy Lessons for the Use of Young People (Whately) 48
econometrics, limitations of 275–9
'Economic Analysis of Unemployment, An' (Keynes) 158–66
'Economic Consequences of Mr Churchill, The' (Keynes) 299–317
Economic Consequences of the Peace, The (Keynes)
debt cancellation 286–7

Europe before and after the war 28–34
Germany's 'capacity to pay' 99–101
publication of xviii
Versailles Conference portraits 461–79
economic internationalism 89
'Economic Possibilities for Our Grandchildren' (Keynes) 75–86
economic problems, resolution to 81
economic transition 63–4
economics
as Darwinism 51
unreal assumptions of 52, 279–81
Economy Committee report 345–9
Eden, Anthony 397
Edgeworth, Maria 263, 496
effective demand, principle of 187–91, 270, 494
Eliot, T. S. 425
Elizabeth I, Queen 79
employment
and aggregate consumption 195–6
classical theory of 184–5
full 183, 235, 253, 255–8, 284–5, 421–5
full policy 417–20
indirect 324
primary 362
secondary 362
theory of 188
and the volume of investment 223, 271
Employment Policy White Paper (1944) 425
'End of Laissez-faire' 39–61
England *see* Great Britain
enterprise 123–4, 140, 156, 213–16

entrepreneurs 112, 115, 203
equilibrium
   anti-profiteering measure 409
   in balance of payments
      between countries 426,
      432, 434
   between savings and new
      investment 120
   conditions of 111–13
   and the General Theory 179
   and investment 422
   level of employment 188–9
   long-period 263, 268
   and prices 409–10
   rate of interest fixed by outside
      circumstances 129
   and rationing 408–9, 416
   and supernational
      management 141
   and taxation 410–13
   theory of shifting 244–5
   theory of stationary 244
   in trade 449
   under-employment 182–4
equities 138
Essay on Population
   (Malthus) 487
'Essays in Persuasion' (Keynes)
   338–59
'Ethics in Relation to Conduct'
   (Keynes) 3–5, 7
Europe
   after WW1 32–4
   average standard of life in 79
   before WW1 28–32
   borrowing from the US 147
   in complete dependence
      on US 467
   impositions from US 429
   and Leninism 66
   and material poverty 61
   obstacles to output 80
   vanished world of pre-war
      28–30

evil 18, 24, 36
exchange depreciation 427
Exchange Equalisation Fund
   402, 405
exchange rates
   fixed 108, 129
   high 307
expansion policy 342–3

'fallacy of composition' xxix,
   7, 155, 185–6, 228–31,
   242–3, 385–6
'farmers' indemnity' 161
Fascism 64
Federal Reserve Board 140, 152,
   157, 293, 296–9, 384
finance, control of 275
financial accounting 90
financial circulation 116–17,
   120
First World War xxx, 72, 98–9,
   466
fiscal stimulus 143–4, 285
Fisher, Irving 166, 284, 293–4
Foch, Marshall 479–80
foreign investment 333, 339
foreign lending 333
foreign trade 291
Fourteen Points 472–3
Foxwell, Professor Herbert
   Somerton 498, 500
France 156–8, 171, 358, 396,
   463–5, 474
Franklin, Benjamin 46
free competition 44
free trade 46–7, 344
Freud, Sigmund 19, 126–7
Friedman, Milton xxxi
'frozen' mortgages 171

Garnett, David 25
General Strike (1926) 299
'General Theory of Employment'
   262–73

General Theory of Employment, Interest and Money, The (Keynes)
and the banana parable 115
consumption demand 193–8
cracking the riddle of unused resources xx–xxi
effect of cutting money wages on employment 240–43
'euthanasia of the rentier' 255
fallacy of composition 192–3
genesis of 176–87
on 'heretics' 250–51
Hicks' reconciliation 182
hydraulic and fundamentalist interpretations contrasted 178–82
ideas and interests 262
inflation defined 246
interest rate and wage adjustment 'out of action' 180–81
investment demand 200–218
link between GT and EPG 183
and the 'Manchester System' 258
money's 'own rate of interest' 231–5
most important book xxiv–xxv, xxvii
'output adjusts not prices' 178
'paradox of thrift' 228–31
policy v. theory Keynesians 181
the rate of interest 218–23
socialisation of investment 257
summary of GT 188–9, 236–40
and the task of overturning orthodox theory xv
the trade cycle in 250
on usury 252
General Theory summary 235–8
General Will 41

Genoa Conference (1922) 287, 290
Germany
and Austria 473
and barter 428
Britain should waive her claims on 286
capacity to pay reparations 99–101
characteristics peculiar to 463–4
confiscated property claims 288–9
crisis of July 1931 167
helping to reconstruct Russia 286–8
inflation in 35–6
and Lloyd George 477
millions of workers idle in the slump 153
moderate indemnity controversy 433
new modes of political economy 88
and President Wilson 475
recovery of 465
river system under foreign control 474
weight of reparation payments 161
Young/Dawes plans 155
Gesell, Silvio 250, 258
'Gibson paradox' 151
gilt-edged securities 406
global monetary order 99
gold
Bank of England regulation of 295–6, 332, 337
consequences of unlimited free flow of 432
and devaluation uncertainty 378
enormous change in value of 167

gold – *cont.*
  and foreign-exchange value of
    sterling 300
  gold-bonds proposal 371–2
  gold-notes proposal 371
  and international money 370
  international
    movements of 152
  mines 198–9
  movement in the price of 294
  and open-market
    operations 141
  proportion banks are required
    to hold 126–8
  and the raw material countries
    402–3
  unlimited free flow of 427
  and US policy towards 297–8
  for use as the standard of value
    235
  using to control the dollar
    378–9
gold standard
  arguments against having
    restored 303–4, 308–14
  a 'barbarous relic' 290–92
  burden of indebtedness 167
  decision to maintain at all costs
    351
  and the general return to
    145–6
  Great Britain restoration of
    284, 305, 315, 321
  Great Britain suspension of
    167, 173, 345, 349, 355–9
  international 260
  Keynes opposed Britain's
    return to xxx, 106–7
  understanding 127–8
golden rule xxv
good 19, 21
government employees 354
Grant, Duncan xviii
Great Britain

bank deposits in 168
banking system of 136
and bond ownership 171
capital expenditure on public
  works 360
control of money 222
and corporations 56–7
credit to Russia problem
  289–90
debt to the United States 286
and the debtor countries 357
decline in prosperity 77
discrimination in terms of
  lending 119
and economic
  internationalism 89
exchange stabilisation with US
  possibility 378
exports 130
and external value of sterling
  299–303
and financial aid from US
  446–7, 450–58
financial remedies for in
  1929–30 142
firmness in real estate
  values 171
flow of capital funds 434
foreign policy of 394–8
and full employment 108
future regulation of
  money in 293
and the gold standard 127,
  146, 298
government construction
  programmes 163–4
impossible to cut wages 160
and investment
  resources 150
and limited/oscillatory
  inflations 36
millions of workers idle in the
  slump 153
money supply 106–7

national debt in the slump
    155, 161
and the New Deal 373
'open-market' policy 125–6
and prolongation of near-full
    employment 250
reduction in long-term rate of
    interest 379
refusal of American help
    proposal 444
remedying the international
    slump 342
return to the gold standard
    101, 299
should waive her claims on
    Germany 286
special problem of 1920s 115
standard of life 90–91
starting the machine
    again 158
strength of banks 173
striving for a new
    economic plan 88
suspension of the gold standard
    167, 173
US pressure to liquidate 285
value of foreign investments
    78–9
view of high level of building
    costs in US 384
Great Depression
    collapse of commodity prices
        144
    collapse of employment, profits
        and prices etc. 154–5
    collapse of investment
        throughout the world 158
    collapse of prices of assets 173
    comparisons with the Great
        Recession of 2008–9 142–4
    cumulative effect of falling
        prices 148
    'death struggle of the war-rates
        of interest' 150

gap between market and
    natural rate of interest 145
JMK's analyses of 142–74
Keynes's view of 77, 86
'one of the greatest economic
    catastrophes of modern
    history' 152
partial recovery to be
    expected 149
and prevailing view of
    monetary disturbances 98
previous boom not a
    delusion 153
proposals to fight it xxx
public investment
    programmes 163
remedies, coordinated
    measures by central
    banks 152
widening gap between
    ideas of lenders and
    borrowers 157

Halley, Edmund 505–6
Harmonies Economiques
    (Bastiat) 48
Harrod, Roy xx, xxiv, 176–7,
    251, 279–81
Hawtrey, Ralph xx, 298
Hayek, Friedrich xxi, xxiv, 247
Henderson, Hubert xix, 318,
    423–5, 428–30
Hicks, John xxiv, 182
hoarding 267–9
Hobson, John Atkinson 251
Hopkins, Sir Richard 417,
    419, 425
House, Colonel 471
housing 328–30, 391
'How to Avoid a Slump' (Keynes)
    398–407
Hume, David 40–42, 491, 498
hydraulic Keynesianism
    179–82, 184

imports 142, 339, 341, 351–3
income 191–5, 253–4, 270–71
India 357
individualism 40, 42, 53, 259–60
industrial circulation 116–18,
    120–21, 137
industry 117
inflation
    allows governments to confiscate
        wealth of citizens 33–4
    in booms 376
    and credit-creation 332
    inflicts great injuries 35
    as a method of taxation 36–8
    oscillatory 36
    use of term 105–6
inter-Allied debts 286
interest
    compound 217
    essential properties of 231–5
interest rates
    an over-valued currency 108
    and the banking system 165
    for capital projects 164–5
    dependency and desire to hold
        wealth 231
    general 107
    general theory of 218–23
    high, as a means of damping
        down boom 401
    Keynes' theory of 267–8
    'liquidity trap' 180–81
    and liquidity-preference 223–6,
        284
    long-term 132, 140, 144,
        147–9, 166
    low short-term 151–2
    market 112, 144,
        147–8, 332
    and monetary policy 218
    natural 112, 121–2, 145
    and natural forces 88–9
    not self-adjusting 251
    pure 203

raising to check a boom xxv
reducing present output below
    optimum 119
and Russian breakdown in 228
and savings 197
short-term 132–3, 136
theory of 254
internal expansion 360–65
International Bank for
    Reconstruction and
    Development xxii
International Clearing Union
    creditor hoarding as cause of
        global deflation 433
    creditor/debtor
        adjustment 432
    destabilising nature of
        speculative capital flows
        434–5
    global imbalances problem
        426–8
    last great constructive effort
        xxi–xxii, xxvi, 285
    prospective British trade deficit
        429–30
    sketch of ideal system 437–43
    tax on persistent surpluses 440
international long-term loan
    market 158
International Monetary
    Fund xxii
international monetary systems
    129–31, 285
international trade 261
Investigation of the Cause of the
    Present High Price of
    Provisions, An (Malthus)
    493–5
investment
    banking system control 136
    breakdown of 158
    control of prices 124
    control of the rate of 125,
        132–42

distinction between savings and
113–15
economies 183
fall in spending 178
foreign 130, 142
and full employment 421–2
goods 109, 399
importance of 403
and income/saving 191–2,
331–2
increase relative to saving
necessary 162
increasing attractions of 121
inducement to 256
planned 274–5
planning 404–7
present organisation of
investment market 59
price level of new investment
goods 110
private sector 180
professional 206–15
prospective yield of 200
rate of 136
running ahead of savings 118
stability of new 400
stopping home outlets 337
and 'theory of monetary
production' 98
two types of risk 203
in US in 1928-9 249
Ireland 88
IS-LM diagram 182
Italy 88

Japan 397
Jevons, William 487
Jews 69, 84, 481
Johnson, Professor Alvin 161
joint stock institutions 56–7, 91

Kahn, Richard F. xx–xxi, xxiv,
xxviii, 285, 361
Kaldor, Nicholas xxi

Kaufmann, Dr, Reichsbank
president 481
Keynes, John Maynard
birth of/early life xvii–xviii
death of xxii
and the Economic Advisory
Council xix–xx
the economist 97–281
the essayist 461–503
legacy xxiii–xxx
marriage xviii–xix
the philosopher 3–25
the policy-maker 286–459
return to the Treasury xxi–xxii
the social philosopher 27–95
Kindleberger, Charles 143
Klotz, Louis-Lucien 99
knowledge 16–17
direct 10

labour
demand for 178, 324
no US shortages in 1928–9 249
for public works 360–61
unemployment of 59
Labour Party 62
labouring classes 31–2
laissez-faire policy
capital funds for refugee/
speculative/investment
purposes 434–5
capitalism 88
domestic 260
end of 39–61
and gold policy 313
international 426–7, 430
orthodox theories of 63–4,
181
towards foreign loans 130
and Wall Street 214
laissez-nous faire 45
Lasteyrie, Charles de 480
Law, Andrew Bonar 523
Lawrence, D. H. 13, 20, 23–5

League of Nations 464–5, 469,
    473–4, 477
Leijonhufvud, Professor
    Axel 182
Lend-Lease xxi–xxii, 285, 426,
    444–5, 451
lenders 156–7
Lenin, Vladimir 32, 34, 71
Leninism 66–9, 71
Leslie, Cliff 46
Levant Company 79
Liberal Party xx, 62, 64, 318,
    322–34
liberty 48, 63
Lloyd George, David 318–22,
    325–7, 330–31, 334–5, 462,
    468, 470, 475–9
Locke, John 40–41
London 90, 94–5, 214, 342, 355,
    431, 448
Lopokova, Lydia xviii–xix, 65
love 14–16
    rational self 40
Lucas, Robert Lucas xv
Lymington, Lady 511

MacDonald, Ramsay 345
macro-economics 98
Malthus, Daniel 491
Malthus, Thomas Robert xx,
    46–7, 190–91, 250, 487,
    489–503
'Manchester System' 258
Mandeville, Bernard 250
Manual of Political Economy, A
    (Bentham) 47
manufacturers 154
Marcet, Caroline 47
marginal propensity to consume
    198–200
market economies
    normally operate below full
        capacity 182–3
    self-adjusting 179–80

Marshall, Alfred xxvii, 49–50,
    53–4, 175, 263, 483–9
Marx, Karl 19, 21, 52–3, 64,
    190, 251
May, Sir George 344–5, 349
Meade, J. E. 418–19, 424
'Means to Prosperity, The'
    (Keynes) 359–72
Medieval Church 251
Melchior, Carl 479–83
methodological individualism 7
'Methodological Issues:
    Tinbergen, Harrod' (Keynes)
    275–81
Middle Ages 200
Mill, John Stuart 49, 487
monetary economics 175
'Monetary Theory of Production,
    A' (Keynes) 174–6
money
    art of management of 125
    and bonds 138
    change in attitude towards 70
    change in the quantity of 224
    changes in money-wages
        240–43
    changes in value of 118
    'cheap' xxv, 284, 315
    circulation of 310
    conditions required for
        'neutrality' of 176
    as convenient means of
        effecting exchanges 174–5
    'dear' 311, 400
    decline in values threatens
        financial structure 172
    deliberately altering the value
        of 317
    discarded for all purposes 38
    disorganization of
        after WWI 98
    easy short-term 390
    effect of change in
        value of 168

essential properties of 231–5
fiat 113
flexible wages and demand
    deficiency 181
and liquidity-preference
    219–27, 233, 275
'love of' 51, 65, 69, 74–5
natural alternative to
    holding 193
old-fashioned advocates of
    sound 107
payments 316–17
printing paper 36
proposal for 'stamped' 250
proposals to increase reserves
    of international 370
purchasing power of 131
quantity theory of 186–7, 377
social dangers of
    hoarding 215
spending on durable
    objects 37
as store of wealth 266–8
supply by the banking system
    122, 137
and the economic system 223
theory of 98
true value of 84
veil of, between real asset and
    wealth owner 168
monopolies 52
Moore, G. E. xvii, 3, 13–21
moral risk 12
'Mr. Keynes and the
    "Classics"'(Hicks) 182
'Mr. Keynes' special theory' 182
'multiplier' theory of the 181,
    198–9, 271, 318, 359,
    363–9, 383
'My Early Beliefs' (Keynes) 13–25

national debts 161, 414
National Industrial Recovery Act
    (NRA) 374–5, 379–80, 383

'National Self-Sufficiency'
    (Keynes) 86–91
National Theatre 95
natural liberty 40, 55
New Deal
    attacks on gold-buying
        policy 377
    business confidence lacking
        381–2, 393
    criticism of NRA 374, 380
    criticized for meagreness of its
        fiscal stimulus 285
    managed currency 379, 385
    need for government loan
        expenditure 376, 383
    need for housing policy 391–2
    purchase of long dated stock
        378–80, 384
    recovery versus reform 373
    restriction of output 375
    US 'the economic laboratory of
        the world' xx
new issue market 274
new rolling stock,
    investment in 278
Newton, Isaac 503–11

'open market' operations 124–6,
    137, 141, 143, 224
organic unity doctrine
    (Moore) 7
Origin of Species (Darwin) 54
original sin 22
Orlando, Signor 462
output changes 177, 271–2
'Overseas Financial Policy in
    Stage III' (Keynes) 444–59

Paley, William 41–3, 493
'paradox of thrift' xxix, 7, 184
Paris Peace Conference (1919)
    xviii, 479–81
'Paying for the War' (Keynes)
    407–16

Pigou, Professor 175, 185, 243, 263

'Plan for a Russian Settlement, A' (Keynes) 287–90

Plato 19–20, 23

Plesch, Janos xxi

Poland 474

'Political Doctrines of Edmund Burke, The' (Keynes) 5–6

Political Economy (Jevons) 487

'Political Economy and *Laissez-faire*' (Cairnes) 49

Political Justice (Godwin) 492

poll tax 418

poor laws 496

population control 85

Post Office Savings Bank 413–14

precautionary-motive 224

price stability 35, 284

price-elasticity xxvi

prices
of commodities 172
control of 124–5, 162
disorganization of after WWI 98
falling 168
price level 106, 109, 113
rising 160, 375–6
theory of 243–6

primary expenditure 362–5

Principia Ethica (Moore) 3–4, 13–14, 16, 18–20

Principia (Newton) 506–8

principle of prudence (Burke) 394

Principles of Economics (Marshall) 489

Principles of Mathematics (Russell) 16, 20

'Principles of Probability, The' (Keynes) 8–9

private enterprise 43, 56, 88

probability theory 4–5, 9–12, 99, 263–4

production 52, 131, 149

propensity to consume 188, 193–8, 238–9, 256, 259

protectionism 87

Protestantism 73

public utility enterprises 57

Public Works Administration 383

purchasing power 103, 409

Puritanism 73

'purposive' man 84

Quantity Theory of Money (QTM) xix, 102–7, 107–9, 178

Queen's Hall 95

quotable quotes
on bankers 516
on the budget 516–17
on capitalism 517
on debt, wartime and other 517–18
on economic method 515–16
on economics 514–15
on the future 525
general 513–14
on investment 518–19
on lawyers 520–21
on money 519–20
on politicians 522–3
on politics 521–2
on saving 518
on stockbrokers 520
on the USA 524

railroads 392

real-exchange economy 174–5

recovery 158–9, 401

religion 14–15, 66–8, 73–4

replacement cost 200

Reserve Fund 438–42

revenue tariff proposal 339, 343

Ricardo, David 46, 190, 263, 487, 494, 496–503

risk 58, 203–4

Robbins, Lionel 183, 280

Robertson, Dennis Holme xx

Robinson Crusoe economy 186
Robinson, Joan xxi, xxviii,
181, 283
Roosevelt, Franklin D. 285, 360,
372, 389
Rousseau, Jean-Jacques 41–2, 491
Royal Opera House 95
Russell, Bertrand 16, 20, 24
Russia
alone in her particular
experiment 87
between the wars 450
Bolshevik Revolution in 28
confiscated property claims
288–9
'credit to' argument 290
disorganised 396
example of breakdown in
stability of interest rate 228
Germany helping to
reconstruct 286–8
Keynes view of 65–75
printing paper money 36
state monopolies of exports 448
theatres/concert-halls 94

Samuelson, Paul 181
savings
behind investment 118
communal 59, 256
compulsory 412–16
and consumption 229–30
difficult to find an
outlet for 166
and income 191–3
for old age or for your children
31–2
in relation to investment
162, 197
sanctification of 75
stimulated by a high rate of
interest 112–13
to augment capital equipment
of the country 336

Say's Law 178, 273
scarcity 64–5
Schacht, Dr Hjalmar 428
schoolteachers 353–5
Schumpeter, Joseph xxiv, 108, 483
Second World War xxx
securities
and 'bears' 117–20
deision to hold cash in 110–11
and liquidity-preference 223
long-term 133
remedy for slumps 138
Securities and Exchange
Commission (SEC) 393
sex questions 62
'Short View of Russia, A'
(Keynes) 65–75
Sidgwick, Henry 46, 483
Sidney Ball Lecture 39
Sinking Fund 305, 327, 348–9,
354, 368
slump of 1921 169
slump of 1930 144, 148,
150, 152–8
slumps
avoidance of over-investment
247–8
the cause of government
deficits 388
and 'dear' money 400
incurring debt during 402
and marginal efficiency of
capital/rate of interest 202–3
menace of the next 403
not a purely monetary problem
176
policies for 338–59
remedy for the persistence
138–40
remedying the
international 342
and short-/long-term
expectations 204
when investment lags 331–2

Smith, Adam 42, 46, 184, 460, 487
Snowden, Philip 341
Social Contract 41
social security budget 417–18
socialism
  and *laissez-faire* economics 42, 44–5
  Marxian 52–3
  offers no middle course 64
  and the State 57–8
  utilitarian 42
  views of Professor Edwin Cannan 49
Socrates 18
South America 155
'South Sea Bubble' crisis 509
Spain 78, 395, 397
Spanish Civil War 394–8
speculation 213
speculative-motive 224
Spencer, Herbert 51
spending power 115, 385–9, 416
Sprague, Oliver 159, 161
Sraffa, Piero 498
stabilisation period 64
stabilization policy xxv, 27
Starvation Corner 450–51
state of confidence 205–6
state of long-term expectation 204–18
State, the
  borrowing 38–9
  common will 256
  communal saving 256
  death duties 253
  and propensity to consume 257
  recognition of semi-autonomous bodies 56
  and socialism 57–8
Statistical Testing of Business-Cycle Theories (Tinbergen) 275–9
sterling area 285, 448

Stock Exchange 207, 214, 401
Strachey, Giles Lytton xvii–xviii, 14
Supervised Banks 439
supply price 200
Surplus Banks 440, 442
Sydenham, Dr Thomas 490–91

theatres/concert-halls 93–4
'theory of monetary production' (Keynes) 98
Theory of Moral Sentiments (Smith) 46
Theory of Unemployment (Pigou) 243
thrift 123–4
Tinbergen, Jan 275–6, 279–80
'Tinbergen's method' 279
Tract on Monetary Reform, A (Keynes) xix, xx, xxiii, xxix, 35–9, 102–7, 290–99
trade cycle 247–50
transactions-motive 224
Treatise on Money, A (Keynes)
  and the 1930 slump 144–52
  aim of monetary policy 118–20
  banana parable 113–15
  control of short and long rates of interest 131–3
  credit cycle 120–23
  determinants of investment 110–11
  earnings behaviour 113
  enterprise not thrift creates wealth 123–4
  fixed or floating exchange rates 129–31
  industrial and financial circulation 116–17
  methods of monetary control 124–6
  a model of an ideal equilibrium 107–9
  natural and market rate of interest 112

open-market operations
  136–41
origins of xix, xxiii, xxv
psychology of gold 125–8
psychology of investors 134–6
speculation, bulls and bears
  117–18
theory of an open economy 108
Treatise on Probability, A
  (Keynes) xxii, 4, 9–12
Treaty of Versailles 28, 99

'under-employment equilibrium'
  theory 178–9, 235–6, 284
unemployment
  abnormal 332
  classical theory of 186–7
  cure of 162
  facts of 321–3
  Lloyd George's pledge to
    reduce 318–38
  mass 98, 154, 181, 350
  a moral problem 97
  negative policy on 341
  paying for 309
  and reduction of wages 311
  serious financial strain of
    387–8
  a statistical artefact 184
  technological 80
  toleration of 260
Unemployment Fund 328–9, 336,
  349
Union of Soviet Socialist
  Republics *see* Russia
United Kingdom *see* Great Britain
United States
  and addicts 63
  arrived at an excellent currency
    policy 385
  average standard of life in 79
  and bank deposits in 168
  becoming a high-living/
    high-cost country 459
  collapse of new investment
    inside 157
  control of money 222
  crisis of liquidation in 1932
    228
  discrimination in terms of
    lending 119
  economy heavily leveraged in
    the 2000s 142
  employment satisfactory in
    1928–9 249
  Europe in complete dependence
    on 467
  exchange stabilisation with GB
    possibility 378
  factory output per head 80
  farm value decline 171
  Federal Reserve System of
    140, 157
  flow of capital funds 434–5
  and the gold standard 296–8,
    315–16, 358
  gold-notes proposal 371
  and Great Britain's debt 286
  high-level building costs in 384
  indebtedness of her associates
    in WWI 155
  and investment resources 150
  isolated 289
  lack of economic rigidity 160
  and Lend-Lease xxi–xxii
  as a lending country 145
  lending on long term 146–7
  lending to Britain 307, 446–7,
    450–58
  maintenance of high level of
    employment in 436
  and material poverty 61
  millions of workers idle in the
    slump 153
  mortgages of the farmers 161
  and the 'multiplier' 365
  need for a trade recovery 359
  and the New Deal 285, 372–85

United States – *cont.*

no re-orientation of domestic economy 429

oscillatory inflations of 36

pressure on Britain to liquidate 285

and prolongation of near-full employment 250

protecting money-motives 60

redistribution of gold reserves proposal 441

securities of 130

should provide Europe with a reconstruction loan 286

sinking funds and depreciation allowances 196

small bank failures in 1929 143

starting the machine again 158

and the stock market 213–14

striving for a new economic plan 88

supplies from 28

weakness of banks 173

withdrawal from long-term loans 156

usury 85, 251, 285

utilitarianism

act 4

calculations of 40

and *laissez-faire* economics 45

rule 4

value, theory of 98, 244

virtue 41

Voltaire 510

Wall Street 214

Wall Street crash (1929) 118

Walrasian system of general equilibrium 107

war debts 161, 163

War Loan 286, 335–6, 379, 405

Ward, James 483

wealth

capacity for the creation of 339

and death duties 253

social and psychological justification for inequalities 254

whole object of 264–8

Wealth of Nations, The (Smith) 498

'weight' of evidence 12

Whately, Archbishop Richard 48

Whitbread, Samuel 495

Wicksell, Knut 109, 112, 284

Wilson, Woodrow 466–75, 476, 478–9

Wittgenstein, Ludwig 23

women

greater economic output of 339

liberties of 63

wonder-cities 89

Wood, Kingsley xxi, 407, 523

Woolf, Virginia 479

World Economic Conference (1933) 359, 370

Young Plan 155